Annual Editions:
American Government, 46e

Bruce Stinebrickner

http://create.mheducation.com

ISBN-10: 1259665283   ISBN-13: 9781259665288

Contents

Unit 3   167

Unit 4   227

Detailed Table of Contents

Preface

In publishing ANNUAL EDITIONS we recognize the important role played by magazines, newspapers, and journals in providing current, first-rate, educational information on a variety of subjects. Many of these articles are appropriate for students, researchers, and professionals seeking accurate, up-to-date material to help bridge the gap between principles and theories and the real world. These articles, however, become more useful for study when those of lasting value are carefully collected, organized, indexed, and reproduced in a low-cost format that provides convenient access when the material is needed. That is the role played by ANNUAL EDITIONS.

This edition of *American Government* is the forty-sixth in an *Annual Editions* series that has long been a mainstay in many introductory courses on American government. The educational goal is to provide a readable collection of up-to-date articles that are informative and interesting to students and that shed light on the workings of the contemporary American political system.

A year ago as I wrote the preface for the 45th edition of this book, I identified "four particularly significant and instructive sets of events" of the preceding twelve months. Now, as I write this preface a year later—in late October 2015—we can see that, in one way or another, these same issues or related ones continue to be prominent in the American political system.

Here is my listing of the four events that loomed large a year ago: "(1) the resolution—for at least a year or so—of the fiscal and debt ceiling crises that had beset the American political system for several years; (2) the implementation of the Affordable Care Act of 2010 (also known as "Obamacare"); (3) two troubling developments in the national security realm: (i) Russia's annexation of Crimea over Ukraine's objections and the associated tensions in other Ukrainian territory bordering on Russia, and (ii) the rise of ISIS, an Islamic extremist organization based in Syria that became a threat not only to the governments of Syria and Iraq but to United States interests as well; and (4) the anticipation of the November 2014 mid-term elections." In the following paragraphs, I shall present updates relating to each of these four matters.

The first issue from a year ago, fiscal and debt ceiling crises, has continued to beset the American political system. On the last day of September, 2015, the U.S. national government averted a "government shutdown"

one day before government funding would have expired. On September 30, 2015, Congress passed and President Obama signed a "continuing resolution" that would keep the government running through December 11, 2015. As has become the pattern in recent years, once again Congress had failed to follow its own "regular order" and pass the twelve annual appropriations bills to fund the government for the fiscal year beginning on the first day of October. Observers were quick to say that Congress "had kicked the can down the road" yet again and they anticipated another "shutdown" crisis in December. In addition to the December 11, 2015 deadline, the government also faced an early November deadline to raise the national debt ceiling. Prominent economists said that a failure of the U.S. government to avoid a first-ever default would likely plunge the world economy into a depression that would rival—or even exceed—the Great Depression of the 1930s.

Most observers' explanations for the congressional brinkmanship on fiscal and debt matters centered on the House Freedom Caucus, forty or so Republican members of the U.S. House of Representatives who adopt strong positions on funding and other policy matters (e.g., Planned Parenthood) and are willing to risk shutdowns and default in pursuit of their policy goals. In the last week of September 2015, Republican House Speaker John Boehner, tired of dealing with the House Freedom Caucus inside his own Republican Conference (the group of all Republican members of the House of Representatives) announced his intention to resign once a successor was named. That surprising announcement contributed to Boehner's ability to push through the short-term continuing resolution that averted a government shutdown on October 1.

Boehner's pending departure set off a few tumultuous weeks as the House Republican Conference wrestled with the selection of Boehner's successor. By late October the House elected Republican Congressman Paul D. Ryan of Wisconsin to succeed Boehner. Meanwhile, during his last weeks as Speaker, Boehner, other congressional leaders, and the White House reached a compromise agreement on spending limits for the next two fiscal years and also averted a U.S. government default. The House and the Senate each passed the measure in the last few days of October, with more Democrats than Republicans supporting the bill in each chamber.

The second issue from a year ago involved the Affordable Care Act of 2010, which is also, of course, known as Obamacare. In June 2015 the U.S. Supreme Court voted 6-3 in a case upholding one important element in the administration of the Act by the Obama administration. This much-awaited decision afforded Obamacare supporters cause for relief because the opposite decision would likely have created serious problems for the signature domestic policy initiative of the Obama presidency. (The Supreme Court issued another much-anticipated decision in June 2015. In that 5-4 ruling, the Court declared that prohibition of same-sex marriage is unconstitutional. This legitimation of same-sex marriage in *Obergefell v. Hodges* was a civil rights/civil liberties landmark.)

Let us now move to the third set of issues about which I wrote a year ago and which involved national security: (i) unwelcome moves by Russian President Vladimir Putin with respect to Ukraine and Crimea and (ii) the rise of ISIS. Twelve months later, U.S.-Russian tensions and ISIS both remain as prominent agenda items for the United States. President Putin has moved aggressively to support Syrian President Bashad al-Assad, while ISIS remains a serious threat to U.S. national security interests in the Middle East and elsewhere.

The fourth issue a year ago was the coming November 2014 congressional elections, which resulted in Republicans winning majority control of the Senate and keeping their majority control of the House of Representatives. In late October 2015, the competition to succeed Barack Obama as president in 2017 is already looming large. And nothing has been more surprising—and unsettling to some—than the front-running candidacies of "outsiders" Donald Trump and Ben Carson on the Republican side. Another "outsider" candidate, Carly Fiorina, has also gained more supporters than almost anyone anticipated. Relatively speaking, the more conventional candidacies of experienced government office-holders such as Jeb Bush, Marco Rubio, John Kasich, Chris Christie, and Scott Walker (who has dropped out of the race) have been foundering. On the Democratic side, front-runner Hillary Clinton has weathered sustained criticism of her email arrangements while serving as Secretary of State and survived a full day of nationally televised questioning by the House Select Committee on Benghazi in late October 2015.

At this writing, Republicans seem highly likely to maintain their majority in the House of Representatives in the 2016 elections, and Hillary Clinton seems virtually assured of becoming the 2016 Democratic presidential nominee. Far more difficult to predict are the outcomes of the 2016 Republican presidential nomination contest and the 2016 presidential general election, as well as the party composition of the U.S. Senate after the November 2016 elections.

A year ago I wrote that "a year in American politics can indeed be a *very* long time." That certainly remains true. Yet, as shown by this re-visiting of the four prominent matters that I identified a year ago, there can be considerable continuity in challenges and issues in the contemporary American political system.

The systems approach provides the rough organizational framework for this book. The first unit focuses on ideological and constitutional underpinnings of American politics from both historical and contemporary perspectives. The second unit treats the major institutions of U.S. national government. The third addresses the "input" or "linkage" mechanisms of the system—political parties, elections, interest groups, and media. The fourth and concluding unit shifts the focus to policy choices that confront the government in Washington and the resulting "outputs" of the political system.

Every year as I prepare a preface for the new edition of this book, I suggest that readers can look forward to another interesting year in American politics. The events of the past year certainly confirmed my prediction of a year ago. As I write this preface in October 2015, I am once again confident in predicting that the next twelve months will be another interesting year for observers of the American political system. I hope that the selections in this book will help the reader understand and sometimes even anticipate political events as they unfold.

Each year thousands of articles about the American political system appear, and deciding which to reprint in a collection of readings such as this can be difficult. Articles are chosen with an eye toward providing viewpoints from left, right, and center. Nearly a third of the selections are new to this year's edition, a reflection of my continuing efforts to help keep those who read this book abreast of contemporary developments in the American political system.

Next year will bring another opportunity for change, and you, the reader, are invited to participate in the revision process by providing your reaction to the contents of the 46th edition of this book.

Bruce Stinebrickner
Editor

EDITOR

Bruce Stinebrickner *DePauw University* Bruce Stinebrickner is Professor of Political Science at DePauw University in Greencastle, Indiana, and has taught American politics at DePauw since 1987. He has also taught at Herbert H. Lehman College of the City University of New York (1974–1976), at the University of Queensland in Brisbane, Australia (1976–1987), and in DePauw programs in Argentina (1990) and Germany (1993). He served 14 years as chair of his department at DePauw after heading his department at the University of Queensland for two years. He earned his BA *magna cum laude* from Georgetown University in 1968, his MPhil from Yale University in 1972, and his PhD from Yale in 1974.

Professor Stinebrickner is the co-author (with Robert A. Dahl) of *Modern Political Analysis,* sixth edition (Prentice Hall, 2003), and has published articles on the U.S. presidential selection process, American local governments, the career patterns of Australian politicians, freedom of the press, and public policies relating to children. He has served as editor of 38 earlier editions of this book as well as 16 editions of its *State and Local Government* counterpart in the McGraw-Hill Contemporary Learning Series. His current research interests focus on government policies involving children (e.g., schooling, child custody, adoption, foster care, youth curfews, and juvenile justice systems).

In his teaching and writing, Professor Stinebrickner uses insights on politics gained from living, teaching, and lecturing abroad, as well as from his four years (2008–2012) serving on the Greencastle, Indiana, school board and Greencastle Redevelopment Commission.

Academic Advisory Board

Members of the Academic Advisory Board are instrumental in the final selection of articles for Annual Editions books. Their review of the articles for content, level, and appropriateness provides critical direction to the editor(s) and staff. We think that you will find their careful consideration reflected here.

Oladimeji Adeoye
University of Illinois, Chicago

Alton Alade-Chester
San Bernardino Valley College

Brent Andersen
University of Maine at Presque Isle

Kwame Antwi-Boasiako
Stephen F. Austin State University

Joseph Avitable
Northwestern Connecticut Community College

Ryan J. Barilleaux
Miami University of Ohio, Oxford

Larry Berman
University of California, Davis

Steven J. Campbell
University of South Carolina, Lancaster

Michael Coulter
Grove City College

Elsa Dias
Pikes Peak Community College

Gary Donato
Bentley University

John Errigo
Chestnut Hill College

Dean A. Frantsvog
Minot State University

Joe Gaziano
Lewis University

Mitchel Gerber
Southeast Missouri State University

Beth Ginsberg
University of Connecticut

Gregory Granger
Northwestern State University

Christopher Grill
Empire State College, Northeast Center

James Guyot
Baruch College CUNY

Michael Harkins
William Rainey Harper College

Suzan Harkness
University of the District of Columbia

Meg Heubeck
University of Virginia

Jean-Gabriel Jolivet
Ashford University

John L. Kaczynski
Saginaw Valley State University

William E. Kelly
Auburn University

Roger Kemp
University of New Haven

Jeff Key
Hardin-Simmons University

Lisa Krasner
Truckmee Meadows Community College

Jeffrey Kraus
Wagner College

Michael G. Krukones
St. Xavier University

Anne Thrower Leonard
Embry-Riddle Aeronautical University

Tal Levy
Marygrove College

Eloise F. Malone
U.S. Naval Academy

Maurice Mangum
Texas Southern University

Will Miller
Southeast Missouri State University

Marjorie Nanian
Schoolcraft College

Carol L. Palermo
Rowan University

Teresa Pijoan
University of New Mexico at Valencia

Andreas W. Reif
Manchester Community College

Mark E. Rush
Washington and Lee University

Carlos Scalisi
San Bernardino Valley College

Cammy Shay
HCC Southeast College

Karl Smith
Delaware Technical Community College – Owens Campus

Howard W. Starks Jr.
Wayne State University

Karen Stewart
Collin College

David Tabb
San Francisco State University

Pak W. Tang
Chaffey College

Andrew J. Taylor
North Carolina State University - Raleigh

Carole Taylor
Limestone College

Lowell F. Wolf
Dowling College

Unit 1

UNIT

Prepared by: Bruce Stinebrickner, *DePauw University*

Foundations of American Politics

This unit treats some of the less concrete elements of the U.S. political system—historic ideals, contemporary ideas and values, and constitutional and legal issues. These dimensions of the system are not immune to change. Instead, they interact with the wider political environment in which they exist and are modified accordingly. Usually this interaction is a gradual process, but sometimes events foster more rapid change.

Human beings can be distinguished from other species by their ability to think and reason at relatively high levels of abstraction. In turn, ideas, ideals, values, and principles can and do play important roles in politics. Most Americans value ideals such as democracy, freedom, equal opportunity, and justice. Yet the precise meanings of these terms and the best ways of implementing them are the subject of much dispute in the political arena. Such ideas and ideals, as well as disputes about their "real" meanings, play important roles in the practice of American politics. Although selections in this unit were written over a span of more than 200 years, they are related to one another in fundamental ways. Understanding contemporary political and legal viewpoints is easier if the ideals and principles of the past are also taken into account. In addition, we can better appreciate the significance of historic documents such as the Declaration of Independence and the Constitution if we are familiar with contemporary ideas and perspectives. The interaction of different ideas and values plays an important part in the continuing development of the foundations of the U.S. political system.

Historic documents from decades or even centuries ago can still have political relevance and impact today. As one example, consider the Declaration of Independence, which was written in 1776. It proclaims the Founders' views of why independence from England was justified and, in doing so, identifies certain "unalienable" rights that "all men" are said to possess. Also consider the Constitution of 1787, which remains in effect to this day. It provides an organizational blueprint for the structure of American national government, outlines the federal relationship between the national government and the states, and expresses limitations on what government can do. Twenty-seven amendments have been added to the original Constitution in two centuries. Another example of historic writings that continue to

facilitate understanding of the contemporary U.S. political system is *The Federalist Papers,* a series of newspaper articles written in support of the proposed new constitution. Appearing in 1787 and 1788, *The Federalist Papers* addressed various provisions of the new constitution and argued that putting that constitution into effect would help produce good government.

Articles on contemporary political ideas and viewpoints can also help explain the operation of the U.S. political system. Such selections contain interesting commentary and debate as they relate political beliefs to contemporary circumstances and events. "Liberal" and "conservative" are two labels often used in American political discussions, but political views and values have far more complexity than these two terms can capture by themselves. Today's commentaries on the U.S. political system generally reflect current preoccupations of Americans, which include, in no set order, the overall health of the economy; the uneven distribution of wealth and income in contemporary American society; the national government's mounting deficits and debt; growing government secrecy, surveillance, and intrusion into individuals' lives; the cost and delivery of health-care; homeland security against terrorist attacks; the country's military and diplomatic roles in world affairs; climate change; and the difficulties of sustaining current Social Security and Medicare entitlements as the baby boomer generation reaches retirement age.

Constitutional and legal issues and interpretations are tied to historic principles as well as to contemporary ideas and values. Observers have suggested that throughout American history almost every important political or policy question has, at one time or another, appeared as a constitutional or legal issue. This unit's commentaries on contemporary constitutional and legal matters illustrate these points.

Some selections in this unit may be more difficult to understand than typical articles in other units of the book. Some of them may have to be read and reread carefully to be fully appreciated. But to grapple with the important material treated here is to come to grips with a variety of conceptual foundations—both historic and contemporary—of the U.S. political system. To ignore the theoretical issues raised would be to overlook an important element of American politics today.

Article

Prepared by: Bruce Stinebrickner, *DePauw University*

The Declaration of Independence

Thomas Jefferson

Learning Outcomes

After reading this article, you will be able to:

- Identify beliefs and attitudes about politics and related matters that underlie the Declaration of Independence and still resonate in the United States today.

- Evaluate the persuasiveness of the main arguments for independence made in the Declaration of Independence.

When in the Course of human events, it becomes necessary for one people to dissolve the political bands which have connected them with another, and to assume among the powers of the earth, the separate and equal station to which the Laws of Nature and of Nature's God entitle them, a decent respect to the opinions of mankind requires that they should declare the causes which impel them to the separation. We hold these truths to be self-evident, that all men are created equal, that they are endowed by their Creator with certain unalienable Rights, that among these are Life, Liberty and the pursuit of Happiness. That to secure these rights, Governments are instituted among Men, deriving their just powers from the consent of the governed. That whenever any Form of Government becomes destructive of these ends, it is the Right of the People to alter or to abolish it, and to institute new Government, laying its foundation on such principles and organizing its powers in such form, as to them shall seem most likely to effect their Safety and Happiness. Prudence, indeed, will dictate that Governments long established should not be changed for light and transient causes; and accordingly all experience hath shewn, that mankind are more disposed to suffer, while evils are sufferable, than to right themselves by abolishing the forms to which they are accustomed. But when a long train of abuses and usurpations, pursuing invariably the same Object evinces a design to reduce them under absolute Despotism, it is their right, it is their duty, to throw off such Government, and to provide new Guards for their future security. Such has been the patient sufferance of these Colonies; and such is now the necessity which constrains them to alter their former Systems of Government. The history of the present King of Great Britain is a history of repeated injuries and usurpations, all having in direct object the establishment of an absolute Tyranny over these States. To prove this, let Facts be submitted to a candid world.

He has refused his Assent to Laws, the most wholesome and necessary for the public good. He has forbidden his Governors to pass Laws of immediate and pressing importance, unless suspended in their operation till his Assent should be obtained; and when so suspended, he has utterly neglected to attend to them. He has refused to pass other Laws for the accommodation of large districts of people, unless those people would relinquish the right of Representation in the Legislature, a right inestimable to them and formidable to tyrants only. He has called together legislative bodies at places unusual, uncomfortable, and distant from the depository of their public Records, for the sole purpose of fatiguing them into compliance with his measures. He has dissolved Representative Houses repeatedly, for opposing with manly firmness his invasions on the rights of the people. He has refused for a long time, after such dissolutions, to cause others to be elected; whereby the Legislative powers, incapable of Annihilation, have returned to the People at large for their exercise; the State remaining in the meantime exposed to all the dan-gers of invasion from without, and convulsions within. He has endeavoured to prevent the population of these States; for that purpose obstructing the Laws for Naturalization of Foreigners; refusing to pass others to encourage their migrations hither, and raising the conditions of new Appropriations of Lands. He has obstructed the Administration of Justice, by refusing his Assent to Laws for establishing Judiciary powers. He has made Judges dependent on his Will alone, for the tenure of their offices, and the amount and payment of their salaries. He has erected a multitude of New Offices, and sent hither swarms of Officers to harass our people, and eat out their substance. He has kept among us, in times of peace, Standing Armies without the Consent of our legislatures. He has affected to render the Military independent of and superior to the Civil power. He has combined with others to subject us to a jurisdiction foreign to our constitution, and unacknowledged by our laws; giving his Assent to their Acts of pretended Legislation: For quartering large bodies of armed troops among us: For protecting them, by a mock Trial, from punishment for any Murders which they should commit on the Inhabitants of these States: For cutting off our Trade with all parts of the world: For imposing Taxes on us without our Consent: For depriving us in many cases, of the benefits of Trial by Jury: For transporting us beyond Seas to be tried for pretended offences: For abolishing the free System of English Laws in a neighboring Province, establishing therein an Arbitrary government, and enlarging its Boundaries so as to render it at once an example and fit instrument for introducing the same absolute rule into these Colonies: For taking away our Charters, abolishing our most valuable Laws and altering fundamentally the Forms of our Governments: For suspending our own Legislatures, and declaring themselves invested with power to legislate for us in all cases whatsoever. He has abdicated Government here, by declaring us out of his Protection and waging War against us. He has plundered our seas, ravaged our Coasts, burnt our towns, and destroyed the lives of our people. He is at this time transporting large Armies of foreign Mercenaries to compleat the works of death, desolation and tyranny, already begun with circumstances of Cruelty & perfidy scarcely paralled in the most barbarous ages, and totally unworthy the Head of a civilized nation. He has constrained our fellow Citizens taken Captive on the high Seas to bear Arms against their Country, to become the executioners of their friends and Brethren, or to fall themselves by their Hands. He has excited domestic insurrections amongst us, and has endeavoured to bring on the inhabitants of our frontiers, the merciless Indian Savages, whose known rule of warfare, is an undistinguished destruction of all ages, sexes and conditions. In every stage of these Oppressions We have Petitioned for Redress in the most humble terms: Our repeated Petitions have been answered only by repeated injury. A Prince, whose character is thus marked by every act which may define a Tyrant, is unfit to be the ruler of a free people. Nor have We been wanting in attentions to our British brethren. We have warned them from time to time of attempts by their legislature to extend an unwarrantable jurisdiction over us. We have reminded them of the circumstances of our emigration and settlement here. We have appealed to their native justice and magnanimity, and we have conjured them by the ties of our common kindred to disavow these usurpations, which would inevitably interrupt our connections and correspondence. They too have been deaf to the voice of justice and of consanguinity. We must, therefore, acquiesce in the necessity, which denounces our Separation, and hold them, as we hold the rest of mankind, Enemies in War, in Peace Friends.

WE, THEREFORE, the Representatives of the UNITED STATES OF AMERICA, in General Congress, Assembled, appealing to the Supreme Judge of the world for the rectitude of our intentions, do, in the Name, and by Authority of the good People of these Colonies, solemnly publish and declare, That these United Colonies are, and of Right ought to be FREE AND INDEPENDENT STATES; that they are Absolved from all Allegiance to the British Crown, and that all political connection between them and the State of Great Britain, is and ought to be totally dissolved; and that as Free and Independent States, they have full Power to levy War, conclude Peace, contract Alliances, establish Commerce, and to do all other Acts and Things which Independent States may of right do. And for the support of this Declaration, with a firm reliance on the protection of divine Providence, we mutually pledge to each other our Lives, our Fortunes and our sacred Honor.

Critical Thinking

1. What are the three inalienable rights outlined in the Declaration of Independence?
2. Break down the main arguments for independence as outlined in the document.
3. From where do governments draw their power, according to the Declaration of Independence?

Create Central

www.mhhe.com/createcentral

Internet References

U.S. History.org
   www.ushistory.org/declaration
Smithsonian.com: The Dark Side of Thomas Jefferson
   www.smithsonianmag.com/history-archaeology/The-Little-Known-Dark-Side-of-Thomas-Jefferson-169780996.html
National Park Service: Independence Hall
   www.nps.gov/inde/historyculture/index.htm

The Declaration of Independence, 1776.

Article   Prepared by: Bruce Stinebrickner, *DePauw University*

The Constitution of the United States, 1787

Learning Outcomes

After reading this article, you will be able to:

- Identify provisions of the U.S. Constitution that have not stood the test of time well and which seem, in retrospect, foolish, unwise, or even immoral.

- Understand the different subjects that the provisions of the Constitution address: structure of the proposed new national government; procedures and powers of various elements in the proposed new national government; how various government officials are to be selected; relationships between the proposed new national government and the constituent states; citizens' rights; etc. In addition, divide provisions of the Constitution into these different categories.

Constitution of the United States. The Articles of Confederation did not provide the centralizing force necessary for unity among the new states and were soon found to be so fundamentally weak that a different political structure was vital. Conflicts about money and credit, trade, and suspicions about regional domination were among the concerns when Congress, on February 21, 1787, authorized a Constitutional Convention to revise the Articles. The delegates were selected and assembled in Philadelphia about three months after the call. They concluded their work by September.

The delegates agreed and abided to secrecy. Years afterward James Madison supported the secrecy decision writing that "no man felt himself obliged to retain his opinions any longer than he was satisfied of their propriety and truth, and was open to the force of argument." Secrecy was not for all time. Madison, a delegate from Virginia, was a self-appointed but recognized recorder and took notes in the clear view of the members. Published long afterward, Madison's Journal gives a good record of the convention.

The delegates began to assemble on May 14, 1787, but a majority did not arrive until May 25. George Washington was elected President of the Convention without opposition. The lag of those few days gave some of the early arrivals, especially Madison, time to make preparations on substantive matters, and Gov. Edmund Jennings Randolph presented a plan early in the proceedings that formed the basis for much of the convention deliberations. The essentials were that there should be a government adequate to prevent foreign invasion, prevent dissension among the states, and provide for general national development, and give the national government power enough to make it superior in its realm. The decision was made not merely to revise the articles but to create a new government and a new constitution.

One of the most crucial decisions was the arrangement for representation, a compromise providing that one house would represent the states equally, the other house to be based on popular representation (with some modification due to the slavery question). This arrangement recognized political facts and concessions among men with both theoretical and practical political knowledge.

Basic Features. Oliver Wendell Holmes, Jr., once wrote that the provisions of the Constitution were not mathematical formulas, but "organic living institutions *[sic]* and its origins and growth were vital to understanding it." The constitution's basic features provide for a supreme law—notwithstanding any other legal document or practice, the Constitution is supreme, as are the laws made in pursuance of it and treaties made under the authority of the United States.

The organizational plan for government is widely known. Foremost is the separation of powers. If the new government were to be limited in its powers, one way to keep it limited would have been executive, legislative, and judicial power [given] to three distinct and non-overlapping branches. A government could not actually function, however, if the separation meant the independence of one branch from the others. The answer was a design to insure cooperation and the sharing of some functions. Among these are the executive veto and the power of Congress to have its way if it musters a super-majority to override that veto. The direction of foreign affairs and the war power are both dispersed and shared. The appointing power is shared by the Senate and the president; impeaching of officers and financial controls are powers shared by the Senate and the House.

A second major contribution by the convention is the provision for the judiciary, which gave rise to the doctrine of judicial review. There is some doubt that the delegates comprehended this prospect but Alexander Hamilton considered it in *Federalist* No. 78: "The interpretation of the laws is a proper and peculiar province of the Courts. . . . Wherever a particular statute contravenes the Constitution, it will be the duty of the judicial tribunals to adhere to the latter and disregard the former."

Another contribution is the federal system, an evolution from colonial practice and the relations between the colonies and the mother country. This division of authority between the new national government and the states recognized the doctrine of delegated and reserved powers. Only certain authority was to go to the new government; the states were not to be done away with and much of the Constitution is devoted to insuring that they were to be maintained even with the stripping of some of their powers.

It is not surprising, therefore, that the convention has been called a great political reform caucus composed of both revolutionaries and men dedicated to democracy. By eighteenth-century standards the Constitution was a democratic document, but standards change and the Constitution has changed since its adoption.

Change and Adaptation. The authors of the Constitution knew that provision for change was essential and provided for it in Article V, insuring that a majority could amend, but being restrictive enough that changes were not likely for the "light and transient" causes Jefferson warned about in the Declaration of Independence.

During the period immediately following the presentation of the Constitution for ratification, requiring assent of nine states to be effective, some alarm was expressed that there was a major defect: there was no bill of rights. So, many leaders committed themselves to the presentation of constitutional amendments for the purpose. Hamilton argued that the absence of a bill of rights was not a defect; indeed, a bill was not necessary. "Why," he wrote, in the last of *The Federalist Papers,* "declare things that shall not be done which there is no power to do?" Nonetheless, the Bill of Rights was presented in the form of amendments and adopted by the states in 1791.

Since 1791 many proposals have been suggested to amend the Constitution. By 1972 sixteen additional amendments had been adopted. Only one, the Twenty-first, which repealed the Eighteenth, was ratified by state conventions. All the others were ratified by state legislatures.

Even a cursory reading of the later amendments shows they do not alter the fundamentals of limited government, the separation of powers, the federal system, or the political process set in motion originally. The Thirteenth, Fourteenth, Fifteenth, and Nineteenth amendments attempt to insure equality to all and are an extension of the Bill of Rights. The others reaffirm some existing constitutional arrangements, alter some procedures, and at least one, the Sixteenth, states national policy.

Substantial change and adaptation of the Constitution beyond the formal amendments have come from national experience, growth, and development. It has been from the Supreme Court that much of the gradual significant shaping of the Constitution has been done.

Government has remained neither static nor tranquil. Some conflict prevails continually. It may be about the activities of some phase of government or the extent of operations, and whether the arrangement for government can be made responsive to current and prospective needs of society. Conflict is inevitable in a democratic society. Sometimes the conflict is spirited and rises to challenge the continuation of the system. Questions arise whether a fair trial may be possible here or there; legislators are alleged to be indifferent to human problems and pursue distorted public priorities. Presidents are charged with secret actions designed for self-aggrandizement or actions based on half-truths. Voices are heard urging revolution again as the only means of righting alleged wrongs.

The responses continue to demonstrate, however, that the constitutional arrangement for government, the allocation of powers, and the restraints on government all provide the needed flexibility. The Constitution endures.

Adam C. Breckenridge, University of Nebraska-Lincoln

The Constitution of the United States

We the People of the United States, in Order to form a more perfect Union, establish Justice, insure domestic Tranquility, provide for the common defence, promote the general Welfare, and secure the Blessings of Liberty to ourselves and our Posterity, do ordain and establish this Constitution for the United States of America.

Article. I.

SECTION. 1. All legislative Powers herein granted shall be vested in a Congress of the United States, which shall consist of a Senate and House of Representatives.

SECTION. 2. The House of Representatives shall be composed of Members chosen every second Year by the People of the several States, and the Electors in each State shall have the Qualifications requisite for Electors of the most numerous Branch of the State Legislature.

No Person shall be a Representative who shall not have attained to the age of twenty five Years, and been seven Years a Citizen of the United States, and who shall not, when elected, be an Inhabitant of that State in which he shall be chosen.

Representatives and direct Taxes shall be apportioned among the several States which may be included within this Union, according to their respective Numbers, which shall be determined by adding to the whole Number of free Persons, including those bound to Service for a Term of Years, and excluding Indians not taxed, three fifths of all other Persons. The actual Enumeration shall be made within three Years after the first Meeting of the Congress of the United States, and within every subsequent Term of ten Years, in such Manner as they shall by Law direct. The Number of Representatives shall not exceed one for every thirty Thousand, but each State shall have at Least one Representative; and until such enumeration shall be made, the State of New Hampshire shall be entitled to chuse three, Massachusetts eight, Rhode-Island and Providence Plantations one, Connecticut five, New York six, New Jersey four, Pennsylvania eight, Delaware one, Maryland six, Virginia ten, North Carolina five, South Carolina five, and Georgia three.

When vacancies happen in the Representation from any State, the Executive Authority thereof shall issue Writs of Election to fill such Vacancies.

The House of Representatives shall chuse their Speaker and other Officers; and shall have the sole Power of Impeachment.

SECTION. 3. The Senate of the United States shall be composed of two Senators from each State, chosen by the Legislature thereof, for six years; and each Senator shall have one Vote.

Immediately after they shall be assembled in Consequence of the first Election, they shall be divided as equally as may be into three Classes. The Seats of the Senators of the first Class shall be vacated at the Expiration of the second Year, of the second Class at the Expiration of the fourth Year, and of the third Class at the Expiration of the sixth Year, so that one third may be chosen every second year; and if Vacancies happen by Resignation, or otherwise, during the Recess of the Legislature of any State, the Executive thereof may make temporary Appointments until the next Meeting of the Legislature, which shall then fill such Vacancies.

No Person shall be a Senator who shall not have attained to the Age of thirty Years, and been nine Years a Citizen of the United States, and who shall not, when elected, be an Inhabitant of that State for which he shall be chosen.

The Vice President of the United States shall be President of the Senate, but shall have no Vote, unless they be equally divided.

The Senate shall chuse their other Officers, and also a President pro tempore, in the Absence of the Vice President, or when he shall exercise the Office of President of the United States.

The Senate shall have the sole Power to try all Impeachments. When sitting for that Purpose, they shall be on Oath or Affirmation. When the President of the United States is tried the Chief Justice shall preside: And no Person shall be convicted without the Concurrence of two thirds of the Members present.

Judgment in Cases of Impeachment shall not extend further than to removal from Office, and disqualification to hold and enjoy any Office of honor, Trust or Profit under the United States: but the Party convicted shall nevertheless be liable and subject to Indictment, Trial, Judgment and Punishment, according to Law.

SECTION. 4. The Times, Places and Manner of holding Elections for Senators and Representatives, shall be prescribed in each State by the Legislature thereof; but the Congress may at any time by Law make or alter such Regulations, except as to the Places of chusing Senators.

The Congress shall assemble at least once in every Year, and such Meeting shall be on the first Monday in December, unless they shall by Law appoint a different Day.

SECTION. 5. Each House shall be the Judge of the Elections, Returns and Qualifications of its own Members, and a Majority of each shall constitute a Quorum to do Business; but a smaller Number may adjourn from day to day, and may be authorized to compel the Attendance of absent Members, in such Manner, and under such Penalties as each House may provide.

Each House may determine the Rules of its Proceedings, punish its Members for disorderly Behaviour, and, with the Concurrence of two thirds, expel a Member.

Each House shall keep a Journal of its Proceedings, and from time to time publish the same, excepting such Parts as may in their Judgment require Secrecy; and the Yeas and Nays of the Members of either House on any question shall, at the Desire of one fifth of those Present, be entered on the Journal.

Neither House, during the Session of Congress, shall, without the Consent of the other, adjourn for more than three days, nor to any other Place than that in which the two Houses shall be sitting.

SECTION. 6. The Senators and Representatives shall receive a Compensation for their Services, to be ascertained by Law, and paid out of the Treasury of the United States. They shall in all Cases, except Treason, Felony and Breach of the Peace, be privileged from Arrest during their Attendance at the Session of their respective Houses, and in going to and returning from the same; and for any Speech or Debate in either House, they shall not be questioned in any other Place.

No Senator or Representative shall, during the Time for which he was elected, be appointed to any civil Office under the Authority of the United States, which shall have been created, or the Emoluments whereof shall have been encreased during such time; and no Person holding any Office under the United States, shall be a Member of either House during his Continuance in Office.

SECTION. 7. All Bills for raising Revenue shall originate in the House of Representatives; but the Senate may propose or concur with amendments as on other Bills.

Every Bill which shall have passed the House of Representatives and the Senate, shall, before it become a Law, be presented to the President of the United States; If he approve he shall sign it, but if not he shall return it, with his Objections to that House in which it shall have originated, who shall enter the Objections at large on their Journal, and proceed to reconsider it. If after such Reconsideration two thirds of that House shall agree to pass the Bill, it shall be sent, together with the Objections, to the other House, by which it shall likewise be reconsidered, and if approved by two thirds of that House, it shall become a Law. But in all such Cases the Votes of both Houses shall be determined by Yeas and Nays, and the Names of the Persons voting for and against the Bill shall be entered on the Journal of each House respectively. If any Bill shall not be returned by the President within ten Days (Sundays excepted) after it shall have been presented to him, the Same shall be a Law, in like Manner as if he had signed it, unless the Congress by their Adjournment prevent its Return, in which Case it shall not be a Law.

Every Order, Resolution, or Vote to which the Concurrence of the Senate and House of Representatives may be necessary (except on a question of Adjournment) shall be presented to the President of the United States; and before the Same shall take Effect, shall be approved by him, or being disapproved by him, shall be repassed by two thirds of the Senate and House of Representatives, according to the Rules and Limitations prescribed in the Case of a Bill.

SECTION. 8. The Congress shall have Power To lay and collect Taxes, Duties, Imposts and Excises, to pay the Debts and provide for the common Defence and general Welfare of the United States; but all Duties, Imposts and Excises shall be uniform throughout the United States;

To borrow Money on the credit of the United States;

To regulate Commerce with foreign Nations, and among the several States, and with the Indian Tribes;

To establish an uniform Rule of Naturalization, and uniform Laws on the subject of Bankruptcies throughout the United States;

To coin Money, regulate the Value thereof, and of foreign Coin, and fix the Standard of Weights and Measures;

To provide for the Punishment of counterfeiting the Securities and current Coin of the United States;

To establish Post Offices and post Roads;

To promote the Progress of Science and useful Arts, by securing for limited Times to Authors and Inventors the exclusive Right to their respective Writings and Discoveries;

To constitute Tribunals inferior to the supreme Court;

To define and punish Piracies and Felonies committed on the high Seas, and Offences against the Law of Nations;

To declare War, grant Letters of Marque and Reprisal, and make Rules concerning Captures on Land and Water;

To raise and support Armies, but no Appropriation of Money to that Use shall be for a longer Term than two Years;

To provide and maintain a Navy;

To make Rules for the Government and Regulation of the land and naval Forces;

To provide for calling forth the Militia to execute the Laws of the Union, suppress Insurrections and repel Invasions;

To provide for organizing, arming, and disciplining, the Militia, and for governing such Part of them as may be employed in the Service of the United States, reserving to the States respectively, the Appointment of the Officers, and the Authority of training the Militia according to the discipline prescribed by Congress;

To exercise exclusive Legislation in all Cases whatsoever, over such District (not exceeding ten Miles square) as may, by Cession of Particular States, and the Acceptance of Congress, become the Seat of the Government of the United States, and to exercise like Authority over all Places purchased by the Consent of the Legislature of the State in which the Same shall be, for the Erection of Forts, Magazines, Arsenals, dock-Yards, and other needful Buildings;—And

To make all Laws which shall be necessary and proper for carrying into Execution the foregoing Powers, and all other Powers vested by this Constitution in the Government of the United States, or in any Department or Officer thereof.

SECTION. 9. The Migration or Importation of such Persons as any of the States now existing shall think proper to admit, shall not be prohibited by the Congress prior to the Year one thousand eight hundred and eight, but a Tax or duty may be imposed on such Importation, not exceeding ten dollars for each Person.

The Privilege of the Writ of Habeas Corpus shall not be suspended, unless when in Cases of Rebellion or Invasion the public Safety may require it.

No Bill of Attainder or ex post facto Law shall be passed.

No Capitation, or other direct, Tax shall be laid, unless in Proportion to the Census or Enumeration herein before directed to be taken.

No Tax or Duty shall be laid on Articles exported from any State.

No Preference shall be given by any Regulation or Commerce or Revenue to the Ports of one State over those of another; nor shall Vessels bound to, or from, one State, be obliged to enter, clear or pay Duties in another.

No Money shall be drawn from the Treasury, but in Consequence of Appropriations made by Law; and a regular Statement and Account of the Receipts and Expenditures of all public Money shall be published from time to time.

No Title of Nobility shall be granted by the United States: And no Person holding any Office of Profit or Trust under them, shall, without the Consent of the Congress, accept of any present Emolument, Office, or Title, of any kind whatever, from any King, Prince, or foreign State.

SECTION. 10. No State shall enter into any Treaty, Alliance, or Confederation; grant Letters of Marque and Reprisal; coin Money; emit Bills of Credit; make any Thing but gold and silver Coin a Tender in Payment of Debts; pass any Bill of Attainder, ex post facto Law, or Law impairing the Obligation of Contracts, or grant any Title of Nobility.

No State shall, without the Consent of the Congress, lay any Imposts or Duties on Imports or Exports, except what may be absolutely necessary for executing its inspection Laws: and the net Produce of all Duties and Imposts, laid by any State on Imports or Exports, shall be for the Use of the Treasury of the United States; and all such Laws shall be subject to the Revision and Controul of the Congress.

No state shall, without the Consent of Congress, lay any Duty of Tonnage, keep Troops, or Ships of War in time of Peace, enter into any Agreement or Compact with another State, or with a foreign Power, or engage in War, unless actually invaded, or in such imminent Danger as will not admit of delay.

Article. II.

SECTION. 1. The executive Power shall be vested in a President of the United States of America. He shall hold his Office during the Term of four Years, and, together with the Vice President, chosen for the same Term, be elected as follows.

Each State shall appoint, in such Manner as the Legislature thereof may direct, a Number of Electors, equal to the whole Number of Senators and Representatives to which the State may be entitled in the Congress: but no Senator or Representative, or Person holding an Office of Trust or Profit under the United States, shall be appointed an Elector.

The Electors shall meet in their respective States, and vote by Ballot for two Persons, of whom one at least shall not be an Inhabitant of the same State with themselves. And they shall make a List of all the persons voted for, and of the Number of Votes for each; which List they shall sign and certify, and transmit sealed to the Seat of Government of the United States, directed to the President of the Senate. The President of the Senate shall, in the Presence of the Senate and House of Representatives, open all the Certificates, and the Votes shall then be counted. The Person having the greatest Number of Votes shall be the President, if such Number be a Majority of the whole Number of Electors appointed; and if there be more than one who have such Majority, and have an equal Number of Votes, then the House of Representatives shall immediately chuse by Ballot one of them for President; and if no Person have a Majority, then from the five highest on the List the said House shall in like Manner chuse the President. But in chusing the President, the Votes shall be taken by States, the Representation from each State having one Vote; a quorum for this Purpose shall consist of a Member or Members from two thirds of the States, and a Majority of all the States shall be necessary to a Choice. In every Case, after the Choice of the President, the Person having the greatest Number of Votes of the Electors shall be the Vice President. But if there should remain two or more who have equal Votes, the Senate shall chuse from them by Ballot the Vice President.

The Congress may determine the Time of chusing the Electors, and the Day on which they shall give their Votes; which Day shall be the same throughout the United States.

No Person except a natural born Citizen, or a Citizen of the United States, at the time of the Adoption of this Constitution, shall be eligible to the Office of President; neither shall any person be eligible to that Office who shall not have attained to the Age of thirty five Years, and been fourteen Years a Resident within the United States.

In Case of the Removal of the President from Office, or of his Death, Resignation, or Inability to discharge the Powers and Duties of the said Office, the Same shall devolve on the Vice President, and the Congress may by Law provide for the Case of Removal, Death, Resignation or Inability, both of the President and Vice President, declaring what Officer shall then act as President, and such Officer shall act accordingly, until the Disability be removed, or a President shall be elected.

The President shall, at stated Times, receive for his Services, a Compensation, which shall neither be encreased nor diminished during the Period for which he shall have been elected, and he shall not receive within that period any other Emolument from the United States, or any of them.

Before he enter on the Execution of his Office, he shall take the following Oath or Affirmation:—"I do solemnly swear (or affirm) that I will faithfully execute the Office of President of the United States, and will to the best of my Ability, preserve, protect and defend the Constitution of the United States."

SECTION. 2. The President shall be Commander in Chief of the Army and Navy of the United States, and of the Militia of the several States, when called into the actual Service of the United States; he may require the Opinion, in writing, of the principal Officer in each of the executive Departments, upon any Subject relating to the Duties of their respective Offices, and he shall have Power to grant Reprieves and Pardons for Offences against the United States, except in Cases of Impeachment.

He shall have Power, by and with the Advice and Consent of the Senate, to make Treaties, provided two thirds of the Senators present concur; and he shall nominate, and by and with the Advice and Consent of the Senate, shall appoint Ambassadors, other public Ministers and Consuls, Judges of the supreme Court, and all other Officers of the United States, whose Appointments are not herein otherwise provided for, and which shall be established by Law: but the Congress may by Law vest the Appointment of such inferior Officers, as they think proper, in the President alone, in the Courts of Law, or in the Heads of Departments.

The President shall have Power to fill up all Vacancies that may happen during the Recess of the Senate, by granting

Commissions which shall expire at the End of their next Session.

SECTION. 3. He shall from time to time give to the Congress Information of the State of the Union, and recommend to their Consideration such Measures as he shall judge necessary and expedient; he may, on extraordinary Occasions, convene both Houses, or either of them, and in Case of Disagreement between them, with Respect to the Time of Adjournment, he may adjourn them to such Time as he shall think proper; he shall receive Ambassadors and other public Ministers; he shall take Care that the Laws be faithfully executed, and shall Commission all the Officers of the United States.

SECTION. 4. The President, Vice President and all civil Officers of the United States, shall be removed from Office on Impeachment for, and Conviction of, Treason, Bribery, or other high Crimes and Misdemeanors.

Article. III.

SECTION. 1. The judicial Power of the United States, shall be vested in one supreme Court, and in such inferior Courts as the Congress may from time to time ordain and establish. The Judges, both of the supreme and inferior Courts, shall hold their Offices during good Behaviour, and shall, at stated Times, receive for their Services, a Compensation, which shall not be diminished during their Continuance in Office.

SECTION. 2. The judicial Power shall extend to all Cases, in Law and Equity, arising under this Constitution, the Laws of the United States, and Treaties made, or which shall be made, under their Authority;—to all Cases affecting Ambassadors, other public Ministers and Consuls;—to all Cases of admiralty and maritime Jurisdiction;—to Controversies to which the United States shall be a Party;—to Controversies between two or more States;—between a State and Citizens of another State;—between Citizens of different States;—between Citizens of the same State claiming Lands under Grants of different States, and between a State, or the Citizens thereof, and foreign States, Citizens or Subjects.

In all Cases affecting Ambassadors, other public Ministers and Consuls, and those in which a State shall be Party, the supreme Court shall have original Jurisdiction. In all the other Cases before mentioned, the supreme Court shall have appellate Jurisdiction, both as to Law and Fact, with such Exceptions, and under such Regulations as the Congress shall make.

The Trial of all Crimes, except in Cases of Impeachment, shall be by Jury; and such Trial shall be held in the State where the said Crimes shall have been committed; but when not committed within any State, the Trial shall be at such Place or Places as the Congress may by Law have directed.

SECTION. 3. Treason against the United States, shall consist only in levying War against them, or in adhering to their Enemies, giving them Aid and Comfort. No Person shall be convicted of Treason unless on the Testimony of two Witnesses to the same overt Act, or on Confession in open Court.

The Congress shall have Power to declare the Punishment of Treason, but no Attainder of Treason shall work Corruption

of Blood, or Forfeiture except during the Life of the Person attained.

Article. IV.

SECTION. 1. Full Faith and Credit shall be given in each State to the public Acts, Records, and judicial Proceedings of every other State. And the Congress may by general Laws prescribe the Manner in which such Acts, Record and Proceedings shall be proved, and the Effect thereof.

SECTION. 2. The Citizens of each State shall be entitled to all Privileges and Immunities of Citizens in the several States.

A Person charged in any State with Treason, Felony, or other Crime, who shall flee from Justice, and be found in another State, shall on Demand of the executive Authority of the State from which he fled, be delivered up, to be removed to the State having Jurisdiction of the Crime.

No Person held to Service or Labour in one State, under the Laws thereof, escaping into another, shall, in Consequence of any Law or Regulation therein, be discharged from such Service or Labour, but shall be delivered up on Claim of the Party to whom such Service or Labour may be due.

SECTION. 3. New States may be admitted by the Congress into this Union; but no new State shall be formed or erected within the Jurisdiction of any other State; nor any State be formed by the Junction of two or more States, or Parts of States, without the Consent of the Legislatures of the States concerned as well as of the Congress.

The Congress shall have Power to dispose of and make all needful Rules and Regulations respecting the Territory or other Property belonging to the United States; and nothing in this Constitution shall be so construed as to Prejudice any Claims of the United States, or of any particular State.

SECTION. 4. The United States shall guarantee to every State in this Union a Republican Form of Government, and shall protect each of them against Invasion; and on Application of the Legislature, or of the Executive (when the Legislature cannot be convened) against domestic Violence.

Article. V.

The Congress, whenever two thirds of both Houses shall deem it necessary, shall propose Amendments to this Constitution, or, on the Application of the Legislature of two thirds of the several States, shall call a Convention for proposing Amendments, which, in either Case, shall be valid to all Intents and Purposes, as Part of this Constitution, when ratified by the Legislatures of three fourths of the several States, or by Conventions in three fourths thereof, as the one or the other Mode of Ratification may be proposed by the Congress; Provided that no Amendment which may be made prior to the Year One thousand eight hundred and eight shall in any Manner affect the first and fourth Clauses in the Ninth Section of the first Article; and that no State, without its Consent, shall be deprived of its equal Suffrage in the Senate.

Article. VI.

All Debts contracted and Engagements entered into, before the Adoption of this Constitution, shall be as valid against the United States under this Constitution, as under the Confederation.

This Constitution, and the Laws of the United States which shall be made in Pursuance thereof; and all Treaties made, or which shall be made, under the Authority of the United States, shall be the supreme Law of the Land; and the Judges in every State shall be bound thereby, any Thing in the Constitution or Laws of any State to the Contrary notwithstanding.

The Senators and Representatives before mentioned, and the Members of the several State Legislatures, and all executive and judicial Officers, both of the United States and of the several States, shall be bound by Oath or Affirmation, to support this Constitution; but no religious Test shall ever be required as a Qualification to any Office or public Trust under the United States.

New Hampshire	JOHN LANGDON
	NICHOLAS GILMAN
Massachusetts	NATHANIEL GORHAM
	RUFUS KING
Connecticut	Wm. SAML JOHNSON
	ROGER SHERMAN
New York . . .	ALEXANDER HAMILTON
New Jersey	WIL: LIVINGSTON
	DAVID BREARLEY
	Wm. PATERSON
	JONA: DAYTON
Pennsylvania	B FRANKLIN
	THOMAS MIFFLIN
	ROBt MORRIS
	GEO. CLYMER
	THOs. FITZSIMONS
	JARED INGERSOLL
	JAMES WILSON
	GOUV MORRIS
Delaware	GEO: READ
	GUNNING BEDFORD jun
	JOHN DICKINSON
	RICHARD BASSETT
	JACO: BROOM
Maryland	JAMES McHENRY
	DAN OF St THOs. JENIFER
	DANL CARROLL
Virginia	JOHN BLAIR
	JAMES MADISON Jr.
North Carolina	Wm. BLOUNT
	RICHd. DOBBS SPAIGHT
	HU WILLIAMSON
South Carolina	J. RUTLEDGE
	CHARLES COTESWORTH PINCKNEY
	CHARLES PINCKNEY
	PIERCE BUTLER
Georgia	WILLIAM FEW
	ABR BALDWIN

Article. VII.

The Ratification of the Conventions of nine States, shall be sufficient for the Establishment of this Constitution between the States so ratifying the Same.

Done in Convention by the Unanimous Consent of the States present the Seventeenth Day of September in the Year of our Lord one thousand seven hundred and Eighty seven and of the Independence of the United States of America the Twelfth In witness whereof We have hereunto subscribed our Names,

Go. WASHINGTON—Presidt. and deputy from Virginia
In Convention Monday, September 17th 1787.

Present The States of

New Hampshire, Massachusetts, Connecticut, Mr. Hamilton from New York, New Jersey, Pennsylvania, Delaware, Maryland, Virginia, North Carolina and Georgia.

Resolved,

That the preceeding Constitution be laid before the United States in Congress assembled, and that it is the Opinion of this Convention, that it should afterwards be submitted to a Convention of Delegates, chosen in each State by the People thereof, under the Recommendation of its Legislature, for their Assent and Ratification; and that each Convention assenting to, and ratifying the Same, should give Notice thereof to the United States in Congress assembled. Resolved, That it is the Opinion of this Convention, that as soon as the Conventions of nine States shall have ratified this Constitution, the United States in Congress assembled should fix a Day on which Electors should be appointed by the States which shall have ratified the same, and a Day on which the Electors should assemble to vote for the President, and the Time and Place for commencing Proceedings under this Constitution. That after such Publication the Electors should be appointed, and the Senators and Representatives elected: That the Electors should meet on the Day fixed for the Election of the President, and should transmit their Votes certified, signed, sealed and directed, as the Constitution requires, to the Secretary of the United States in Congress assembled,

Ratification of the Constitution

State	Date of Ratification
Delaware	Dec 7, 1787
Pennsylvania	Dec 12, 1787
New Jersey	Dec 19, 1787
Georgia	Jan 2, 1788
Connecticut	Jan 9, 1788
Massachusetts	Feb 6, 1788
Maryland	Apr 28, 1788
South Carolina	May 23, 1788
New Hampshire	June 21, 1788
Virginia	Jun 25, 1788
New York	Jun 26, 1788
North Carolina	Nov 21, 1789
Rhode Island	May 29, 1790

that the Senators and Representatives should convene at the Time and Place assigned; that the Senators should appoint a President of the Senate, for the sole Purpose of receiving, opening and counting the Votes for President; and, that after he shall be chosen, the Congress, together with the President, should, without Delay, proceed to execute this Constitution.

By the Unanimous Order of the Convention

Go. WASHINGTON—Presidt.

W. JACKSON Secretary.

ARTICLES IN ADDITION TO, AND AMENDMENT OF, THE CONSTITUTION OF THE UNITED STATES OF AMERICA, PROPOSED BY CONGRESS, AND RATIFIED BY THE SEVERAL STATES, PURSUANT TO THE FIFTH ARTICLE OF THE ORIGINAL CONSTITUTION.

Amendment I.

Congress shall make no law respecting an establishment of religion, or prohibiting the free exercise thereof; or abridging the freedom of speech, or of the press; or the right of the people peaceably to assemble, and to petition the Government for a redress of grievances.

Amendment II.

A well regulated Militia, being necessary to the security of a free State, the right of the people to keep and bear Arms, shall not be infringed.

Amendment III.

No Soldier shall, in time of peace be quartered in any house, without the consent of the Owner, nor in time of war, but in a manner to be prescribed by law.

Amendment IV.

The right of the people to be secure in their persons, houses, papers, and effects, against unreasonable searches and seizures, shall not be violated, and no Warrants shall issue, but upon probable cause, supported by Oath or affirmation, and particularly describing the place to be searched, and the persons or things to be seized.

Amendment V.

No person shall be held to answer for a capital, or otherwise infamous crime, unless on a presentment or indictment of a Grand Jury, except in cases arising in the land or naval forces, or in the Militia, when in actual service in time of War or public danger; nor shall any person be subject for the same offence to be twice put in jeopardy of life or limb; nor shall be compelled in any criminal case to be a witness against himself, nor

be deprived of life, liberty, or property, without due process of law; nor shall private property be taken for public use, without just compensation.

Amendment VI.

In all criminal prosecutions, the accused shall enjoy the right to a speedy and public trial, by an impartial jury of the State and district wherein the crime shall have been committed, which district shall have been previously ascertained by law, and to be informed of the nature and cause of the accusation; to be confronted with the witnesses against him; to have compulsory process for obtaining witnesses in his favor, and to have the Assistance of Counsel for his defence.

Amendment VII.

In Suits at common law, where the value in controversy shall exceed twenty dollars, the right of trial by jury shall be preserved, and no fact tried by a jury, shall be otherwise re-examined in any Court of the United States, than according to the rules of the common law.

Amendment VIII.

Excessive bail shall not be required, nor excessive fines imposed, nor cruel and unusual punishments inflicted.

Amendment IX.

The enumeration in the Constitution, of certain rights, shall not be construed to deny or disparage others retained by the people.

Amendment X.

The powers not delegated to the United States by the Constitution, nor prohibited by it to the States, are reserved to the States respectively, or to the people.

Amendment XI.

(Adopted Jan. 8, 1798)

The Judicial power of the United States shall not be construed to extend to any suit in law or equity, commenced or prosecuted against one of the United States by Citizens of another State, or by Citizens or Subjects of any Foreign State.

Amendment XII.

(Adopted Sept. 25, 1804)

The Electors shall meet in their respective states and vote by ballot for President and Vice-President, one of whom, at least, shall not be an inhabitant of the same state with themselves; they shall name in their ballots the person voted for as President, and in distinct ballots the person voted for as Vice-President, and they shall make distinct lists of all persons voted for as President, and of all persons voted for as Vice-President, and of the number of votes for each, which lists they shall sign and certify, and transmit sealed to the seat of the government of the United States, directed to the President of the Senate;—The President of the Senate shall, in the presence of the Senate and House of Representatives, open all the certificates and the votes shall then be counted;—The person having the greatest number of votes for President, shall be the President, if such number be a majority of the whole number of Electors appointed; and if no person have such majority, then from the persons having the highest numbers not exceeding three on the list of those voted for as President, the House of Representatives shall choose immediately, by ballot, the President. But in choosing the President, the votes shall be taken by states, the representation from each state having one vote; a quorum for this purpose shall consist of a member or members from two-thirds of the states, and a majority of all the states shall be necessary to a choice. And if the House of Representatives shall not choose a President whenever the right of choice shall devolve upon them, before the fourth day of March next following, then the Vice-President shall act as President, as in the case of the death or other constitutional disability of the President.—The person having the greatest number of votes as Vice-President, shall be the Vice-President, if such number be a majority of the whole number of Electors appointed, and if no person have a majority, then from the two highest numbers on the list, the Senate shall choose the Vice-President; a quorum for the purpose shall consist of two-thirds of the whole number of Senators, and a majority of the whole number shall be necessary to a choice. But no person constitutionally ineligible to the office of President shall be eligible to that of Vice-President of the United States.

Amendment XIII.

(Adopted Dec. 18, 1865)

SECTION 1. Neither slavery nor involuntary servitude, except as a punishment for crime whereof the party shall have been duly convicted, shall exist within the United States, or any place subject to their jurisdiction.

SECTION 2. Congress shall have power to enforce this article by appropriate legislation.

Amendment XIV.

(Adopted July 28, 1868)

SECTION 1. All persons born or naturalized in the United States and subject to the jurisdiction thereof, are citizens of the United States and of the State wherein they reside. No State shall make or enforce any law which shall abridge the privileges or immunities of citizens of the United States; nor shall any State deprive any person of life, liberty, or property,

without due process of law; nor deny to any person within its jurisdiction the equal protection of the laws.

SECTION 2. Representatives shall be apportioned among the several States according to their respective numbers, counting the whole number of persons in each State, excluding Indians not taxed. But when the right to vote at any election for the choice of electors for President and Vice President of the United States, Representatives in Congress, the Executive and Judicial officers of a State, or the members of the Legislature thereof, is denied to any of the male inhabitants of such State, being twenty-one years of age, and citizens of the United States, or in any way abridged, except for participation in rebellion, or other crime, the basis of representation therein shall be reduced in the proportion which the number of such male citizens shall bear to the whole number of male citizens twenty-one years of age in such State.

SECTION 3. No person shall be a Senator or Representative in Congress, or elector of President and Vice President, or hold any office, civil or military, under the United States, or under any State, who, having previously taken an oath, as a member of Congress, or as an officer of the United States, or as a member of any State legislature, or as an executive or judicial officer of any State, to support the Constitution of the United States, shall have engaged in insurrection or rebellion against the same, or given aid or comfort to the enemies thereof. But Congress may by a vote of two-thirds of each House, remove such disability.

SECTION 4. The validity of the public debt of the United States, authorized by law, including debts incurred for payment of pensions and bounties for services in suppressing insurrection or rebellion, shall not be questioned. But neither the United States nor any State shall assume or pay any debt or obligation incurred in aid of insurrection or rebellion against the United States, or any claim for the loss or emancipation of any slave; but all such debts, obligations and claims shall be held illegal and void.

SECTION 5. The Congress shall have power to enforce, by appropriate legislation, the provisions of this article.

Amendment XV.

(Adopted March 30, 1870)

SECTION 1. The right of citizens of the United States to vote shall not be denied or abridged by the United States or by any State on account of race, color, or previous condition of servitude.

SECTION 2. The Congress shall have power to enforce this article by appropriate legislation.

Amendment XVI.

(Adopted Feb. 25, 1913)

The Congress shall have power to lay and collect taxes on incomes, from whatever source derived, without apportionment among the several States, and without regard to any census or enumeration.

Amendment XVII.

(Adopted May 31, 1913)

The Senate of the United States shall be composed of two Senators from each State, elected by the people thereof, for six years; and each Senator shall have one vote. The electors in each State shall have the qualifications requisite for electors of the most numerous branch of the State legislatures.

When vacancies happen in the representation of any State in the Senate, the executive authority of such State shall issue writs of election to fill such vacancies: Provided, That the legislature of any State may empower the executive thereof to make temporary appointments until the people fill the vacancies by election as the legislature may direct.

This amendment shall not be so construed as to affect the election or term of any Senator chosen before it becomes valid as part of the Constitution.

Amendment XVIII.

(Adopted Jan. 29, 1919)

SECTION 1. After one year from the ratification of this article the manufacture, sale or transportation of intoxicating liquors within, the importation thereof into, or the exportation thereof from the United States and all territory subject to the jurisdiction thereof for beverage purposes is hereby prohibited.

SECTION 2. The Congress and the several States shall have concurrent power to enforce this article by appropriate legislation.

SECTION 3. This article shall be inoperative unless it shall have been ratified as an amendment to the Constitution by the legislatures of the several States, as provided in the Constitution, within seven years from the date of the submission hereof to the States by the Congress.

Amendment XIX.

(Adopted Aug. 26, 1920)

The right of citizens of the United States to vote shall not be denied or abridged by the United States or by any State on account of sex.

Congress shall have power to enforce this article by appropriate legislation.

Amendment XX.

(Adopted Feb. 6, 1933)

SECTION 1. The terms of the President and Vice President shall end at noon on the 20th day of January, and the terms of Senators and Representatives at noon on the 3d day of January, of the years in which such terms would have ended if this article had not been ratified; and the terms of their successors shall then begin.

SECTION 2. The Congress shall assemble at least once in every year, and such meeting shall begin at noon on the 3d day of January, unless they shall by law appoint a different day.

SECTION 3. If, at the time fixed for the beginning of the term of the President, the President elect shall have died, the Vice President elect shall become President. If a President shall not have been chosen before the time fixed for the beginning of his term, or if the President elect shall have failed to qualify, then the Vice President elect shall act as President until a President shall have qualified; and the Congress may by law provide for the case wherein neither a President elect nor a Vice President elect shall have qualified, declaring who shall then act as President, or the manner in which one who is to act shall be selected, and such person shall act accordingly until a President or Vice President shall have qualified.

SECTION 4. The Congress may by law provide for the case of the death of any of the persons from whom the House of Representatives may choose a President whenever the right of choice shall have devolved upon them, and for the case of the death of any of the persons from whom the Senate may choose a Vice President whenever the right of choice shall have devolved upon them.

SECTION 5. Sections 1 and 2 shall take effect on the 15th day of October following the ratification of this article.

SECTION 6. This article shall be inoperative unless it shall have been ratified as an amendment to the Constitution by the legislatures of three-fourths of the several States within seven years from the date of its submission.

Amendment XXI.

(Adopted Dec. 5, 1933)

SECTION 1. The eighteenth article of amendment to the Constitution of the United States is hereby repealed.

SECTION 2. The transportation or importation into any State, Territory, or possession of the United States for delivery or use therein of intoxicating liquors, in violation of the laws thereof, is hereby prohibited.

SECTION 3. This article shall be inoperative unless it shall have been ratified as an amendment to the Constitution by conventions in the several States, as provided in the Constitution, within seven years from the date of the submission hereof to the States by the Congress.

Amendment XXII.

(Adopted Feb. 27, 1951)

SECTION 1. No person shall be elected to the office of the President more than twice, and no person who has held the office of President, or acted as President, for more than two years of a term to which some other person was elected President shall be elected to the office of the President more than once. But this Article shall not apply to any person holding the office of President when this Article was proposed by the Congress, and shall not prevent any person who may be holding the office of President, or acting as President, during the term within which this Article becomes operative from holding the office of President or acting as President during the remainder of such term.

SECTION 2. This Article shall be inoperative unless it shall have been ratified as an amendment to the Constitution by the legislatures of three-fourths of the several States within seven years from the date of its submission to the States by the Congress.

Amendment XXIII.

(Adopted Mar. 29, 1961)

SECTION 1. The District constituting the seat of Government of the United States shall appoint in such manner as the Congress may direct:

A number of electors of President and Vice President equal to the whole number of Senators and Representatives in Congress to which the District would be entitled if it were a State, but in no event more than the least populous State; they shall be in addition to those appointed by the States, but they shall be considered, for the purposes of the election of President and Vice President, to be electors appointed by a State; and they shall meet in the District and perform such duties as provided by the twelfth article of amendment.

SECTION 2. The Congress shall have power to enforce this article by appropriate legislation.

Amendment XXIV.

(Adopted Jan. 23, 1964)

SECTION 1. The right of citizens of the United States to vote in any primary or other election for President or Vice President, for electors for President or Vice President, or for Senator or Representative in Congress, shall not be denied or abridged by the United States or any State by reason of failure to pay any poll tax or other tax.

SECTION 2. The Congress shall have the power to enforce this article by appropriate legislation.

Amendment XXV.

(Adopted Feb. 10, 1967)

SECTION 1. In case of the removal of the President from office or of his death or resignation, the Vice President shall become President.

SECTION 2. Whenever there is a vacancy in the office of the Vice President, the President shall nominate a Vice President who shall take the office upon confirmation by a majority vote of both houses of Congress.

SECTION 3. Whenever the President transmits to the President pro tempore of the Senate and the Speaker of the House of Representatives his written declaration that he is unable to discharge the powers and duties of his office, and until he transmits to them a written declaration to the contrary, such powers and duties shall be discharged by the Vice President as Acting President.

SECTION 4. Whenever the Vice President and a majority of either the principal officers of the executive departments or of such other body as Congress may by law provide, transmit to the President pro tempore of the Senate and the Speaker of the House of Representatives their written declaration that the President is unable to discharge the powers and duties of his office, the Vice President shall immediately assume the powers and duties of the office as Acting President.

Thereafter, when the President transmits to the President pro tempore of the Senate and the Speaker of the House of Representatives his written declaration that no inability exists, he shall resume the powers and duties of his office unless the Vice President and a majority of either the principal officers of the executive department or of such other body as Congress may by law provide, transmit within four days to the President pro tempore of the Senate and the Speaker of the House of Representatives their written declaration that the President is unable to discharge the powers and duties of his office. Thereupon Congress shall decide the issue, assembling within forty-eight hours for that purpose if not in session. If the Congress within twenty-one days after receipt of the latter written declaration, or, if Congress is not in session, within twenty-one days after Congress is required to assemble, determines by two-thirds vote of both Houses that the President is unable to discharge the powers and duties of his office, the Vice President shall continue to discharge the same as Acting President; otherwise, the President shall resume the powers and duties of his office.

Amendment XXVI.

(Adopted June 30, 1971)

SECTION 1. The right of citizens of the United States, who are 18 years of age or older, to vote shall not be denied or abridged by the United States or by any state on account of age.

SECTION 2. The Congress shall have the power to enforce this article by appropriate legislation.

Amendment XXVII.

(Adopted May 7, 1992)

No law, varying the compensation for the services of the Senators and Representatives, shall take effect, until an election of Representatives shall have intervened.

Critical Thinking

1. In light of the procedures for ratifying the Constitution that appear in Article VII, consider the Preamble and its claim that "We the People" did "ordain and establish" the Constitution.

2. Name the three main branches of government as outlined in the Constitution and identify a half-dozen or so of the powers shared between two or more branches.

3. What is a federal system? What powers do individual states retain in the U.S. federal system? What powers does the national government have? What is the Bill of Rights? What are some of the key protections it specifies?

Create Central

www.mhhe.com/createcentral

Internet References

National Constitution Center
http://constitutioncenter.org

The New York Times: 'We the People' Loses Appeal with People around the World
www.nytimes.com/2012/02/07/us/we-the-people-loses-appeal-with-people-around-the-world.html?pagewanted=all

The New Yorker—The Commandments: The Constitution and Its Worshippers
www.newyorker.com/arts/critics/atlarge/2011/01/17/110117crat_atlarge_lepore

The Constitution of the United States, 1787.

Article   Prepared by: Bruce Stinebrickner, *DePauw University*

Federalist No. 10

JAMES MADISON

Learning Outcomes

After reading this article, you will be able to:

- Identify the main arguments of James Madison in *Federalist* 10 and evaluate their persuasiveness.

- Consider whether the "mischiefs of faction" seem as dangerous to the American political system as Madison seems to think.

To the People of the State of New York

Among the numerous advantages promised by a well-constructed Union, none deserves to be more accurately developed than its tendency to break and control the violence of faction. The friend of popular governments never finds himself so much alarmed for their character and fate, as when he contemplates their propensity to this dangerous vice. He will not fail, therefore, to set a due value on any plan which, without violating the principles to which he is attached, provides a proper cure for it. The instability, injustice, and confusion introduced into the public councils, have, in truth, been the mortal diseases under which popular governments have everywhere perished; as they continue to be the favorite and fruitful topics from which the adversaries to liberty derive their most specious declamations. The valuable improvements made by the American constitutions on the popular models, both ancient and modern, cannot certainly be too much admired; but it would be an unwarrantable partiality, to contend that they have as effectually obviated the danger on this side, as was wished and expected. Complaints are everywhere heard from our most considerate and virtuous citizens, equally the friends of public and private faith, and of public and personal liberty, that our governments are too unstable, that the public good is disregarded in the conflicts of rival parties, and that measures are too often decided, not according to the rules of justice and the rights of the minor party, but by the superior force of an interested and overbearing majority. However anxiously we may wish that these complaints had no foundation, the evidence of known facts will not permit us to deny that they are in some degree true. It will be found, indeed, on a candid review of our situation, that some of the distresses under which we labor have been erroneously charged on the operation of our governments; but it will be found, at the same time, that other causes will not alone account for many of our heaviest misfortunes; and, particularly, for that prevailing and increasing distrust of public engagements, and alarm for private rights, which are echoed from one end of the continent to the other. These must be chiefly, if not wholly, effects of the unsteadiness and injustice with which a factious spirit has tainted our public administrations.

By a faction, I understand a number of citizens, whether amounting to a majority or minority of the whole, who are united and actuated by some common impulse of passion, or of interest, adverse to the rights of other citizens, or to the permanent and aggregate interests of the community.

There are two methods of curing the mischiefs of faction: the one, by removing its causes; the other, by controlling its effects.

There are again two methods of removing the causes of faction: the one, by destroying the liberty which is essential to its existence; the other, by giving to every citizen the same opinions, the same passions, and the same interests.

It could never be more truly said than of the first remedy, that it was worse than the disease. Liberty is to faction what air is to fire, an aliment without which it instantly expires. But it could not be less folly to abolish liberty, which is essential to political life, because it nourishes faction, than it would be to wish the annihilation of air, which is essential to animal life, because it imparts to fire its destructive agency.

The second expedient is as impracticable as the first would be unwise. As long as the reason of man continues fallible, and he is at liberty to exercise it, different opinions will be formed. As long as the connection subsists between his reason and his self-love, his opinions and his passions will have a reciprocal influence on each other; and the former will be objects to which the latter will attach themselves. The diversity in the faculties of men, from which the rights of property originate, is not less an insuperable obstacle to a uniformity of interests. The protection of these faculties is the first object of government. From the protection of different and unequal faculties of acquiring property, the possession of different degrees and kinds of property immediately results; and from the influence of these on the sentiments and views of the respective proprietors, ensues a division of the society into different interests and parties.

The latent causes of faction are thus sown in the nature of man; and we see them everywhere brought into different degrees of activity, according to the different circumstances of civil society. A zeal for different opinions concerning religion, concerning government, and many other points, as well of speculation as of practice; an attachment to different leaders ambitiously contending for pre-eminence and power; or to persons of other descriptions whose fortunes have been interesting to the human passions, have, in turn, divided mankind into parties, inflamed them with mutual animosity, and rendered them much more disposed to vex and oppress each other than to co-operate for their common good. So strong is this propensity of mankind to fall into mutual animosities, that where no substantial occasion presents itself, the most frivolous and fanciful distinctions have been sufficient to kindle their unfriendly passions and excite their most violent conflicts. But the most common and durable source of factions has been the various and unequal distribution of property. Those who hold and those who are without property have ever formed distinct interests in society.

Those who are creditors, and those who are debtors, fall under a like discrimination. A landed interest, a manufacturing interest, a mercantile interest, a moneyed interest, with many lesser interests, grow up of necessity in civilized nations, and divide them into different classes, actuated by different sentiments and views. The regulation of these various and interfering interests forms the principal task of modern legislation, and involves the spirit of party and faction in the necessary and ordinary operations of the government.

No man is allowed to be a judge in his own cause, because his interest would certainly bias his judgment, and, not improbably, corrupt his integrity. With equal, nay with greater reason, a body of men are unfit to be both judges and parties at the same time; yet what are many of the most important acts of legislation, but so many judicial determinations, not indeed concerning the rights of single persons, but concerning the rights of large bodies of citizens? And what are the different classes of legislators but advocates and parties to the causes which they determine? Is a law proposed concerning private debts? It is a question to which the creditors are parties on one side and the debtors on the other. Justice ought to hold the balance between them. Yet the parties are, and must be, themselves the judges; and the most numerous party, or, in other words, the most powerful faction must be expected to prevail. Shall domestic manufactures be encouraged, and in what degree, by restrictions on foreign manufactures? are questions which would be differently decided by the landed and the manufacturing classes, and probably by neither with a sole regard to justice and the public good. The apportionment of taxes on the various descriptions of property is an act which seems to require the most exact impartiality; yet there is, perhaps, no legislative act in which greater opportunity and temptation are given to a predominant party to trample on the rules of justice. Every shilling with which they overburden the inferior number, is a shilling saved to their own pockets.

It is in vain to say that enlightened statesmen will be able to adjust these clashing interests, and render them all subservient to the public good. Enlightened statesmen will not always be at the helm. Nor, in many cases, can such an adjustment be made at all without taking into view indirect and remote considerations, which will rarely prevail over the immediate interest which one party may find in disregarding the rights of another or the good of the whole.

The inference to which we are brought is, that the *causes* of faction cannot be removed, and that relief is only to be sought in the means of controlling its *effects*.

If a faction consists of less than a majority, relief is supplied by the republican principle, which enables the majority to defeat its sinister views by regular vote. It may clog the administration, it may convulse the society; but it will be unable to execute and mask its violence under the forms of the Constitution. When a majority is included in a faction, the form of popular government, on the other hand, enables it to sacrifice to its ruling passion or interest both the public good and the rights of other citizens. To secure the public good and private rights against the danger of such a faction, and at the same time to preserve the spirit and the form of popular government, is then the great object to which our inquiries are directed. Let me add that it is the great desideratum by which this form of government can be rescued from the opprobrium under which it has so long labored, and be recommended to the esteem and adoption of mankind.

By what means is this object attainable? Evidently by one of two only. Either the existence of the same passion or interest in a majority at the same time must be prevented, or the majority, having such coexistent passion or interest, must be rendered, by their number and local situation, unable to concert and carry into effect schemes of oppression. If the impulse and the opportunity be suffered to coincide, we well know that neither moral nor religious motives can be relied on as an adequate control. They are not found to be such on the injustice and violence of individuals, and lose their efficacy in proportion to the number combined together, that is, in proportion as their efficacy becomes needful.

From this view of the subject it may be concluded that a pure democracy, by which I mean a society consisting of a small number of citizens, who assemble and administer the government in person, can admit of no cure for the mischiefs of faction. A common passion or interest will, in almost every case, be felt by a majority of the whole; a communication and concert result from the form of government itself; and there is nothing to check the inducements to sacrifice the weaker party or an obnoxious individual. Hence it is that such democracies have ever been spectacles of turbulence and contention; have ever been found incompatible with personal security or the rights of property; and have in general been as short in their lives as they have been violent in their deaths. Theoretic politicians, who have patronized this species of government, have erroneously supposed that by reducing mankind to a perfect equality in their political rights, they would, at the same time, be perfectly equalized and assimilated in their possessions, their opinions, and their passions.

A republic, by which I mean a government in which the scheme of representation takes place, opens a different prospect, and promises the cure for which we are seeking. Let us examine the points in which it varies from pure democracy, and we shall comprehend both the nature of the cure and the efficacy which it must derive from the Union.

The two great points of difference between a democracy and a republic are: first, the delegation of the government, in the latter, to a small number of citizens elected by the rest; secondly, the greater number of citizens, and greater sphere of country, over which the latter may be extended.

The effect of the first difference is, on the one hand, to refine and enlarge the public views, by passing them through the medium of a chosen body of citizens, whose wisdom may best discern the true interest of their country, and whose patriotism and love of justice will be least likely to sacrifice it to temporary or partial considerations. Under such a regulation, it may well happen that the public voice, pronounced by the representatives of the people, will be more consonant to the public good than if pronounced by the people themselves, convened for the purpose. On the other hand, the effect may be inverted. Men of factious tempers, of local prejudices, or of sinister designs, may, by intrigue, by corruption, or by other means, first obtain the suffrages, and then betray the interests, of the people. The question resulting is, whether small or extensive republics are more favorable to the election of proper guardians of the public weal; and it is clearly decided in favor of the latter by two obvious considerations.

In the first place, it is to be remarked that, however small the republic may be, the representatives must be raised to a certain number, in order to guard against the cabals of a few; and that, however large it may be, they must be limited to a certain number, in order to guard against the confusion of a multitude. Hence, the number of representatives in the two cases not being in proportion to that of the two constituents, and being proportionally greater in the small republic, it follows that, if the proportion of fit characters be not less in the large than in the small republic, the former will present a greater option, and consequently a greater probability of a fit choice.

In the next place, as each representative will be chosen by a greater number of citizens in the large than in the small republic, it will be more difficult for unworthy candidates to practise with success the vicious arts by which elections are too often carried; and the suffrages of the people being more free, will be more likely to centre in men who possess the most attractive merit and the most diffusive and established characters.

It must be confessed that in this, as in most other cases, there is a mean, on both sides of which inconveniences will be found to lie. By enlarging too much the number of electors, you render the representative too little acquainted with all their local circumstances and lesser interests; as by reducing it too much, you render him unduly attached to these, and too little fit to comprehend and pursue great and national objects. The federal Constitution forms a happy combination in this respect; the great and aggregate interests being referred to the national, the local and particular to the State legislatures.

The other point of difference is, the greater number of citizens and extent of territory which may be brought within the compass of republican than of democratic government; and it is this circumstance principally which renders factious combinations less to be dreaded in the former than in the latter. The smaller the society, the fewer probably will be the distinct parties and interests composing it; the fewer the distinct parties and interests, the more frequently will a majority be found of the same party; and the smaller the number of individuals composing a majority, and the smaller the compass within which they are placed, the more easily will they concert and execute their plans of oppression. Extend the sphere and you take in a greater variety of parties and interests; you will make it less probable that a majority of the whole will have a common motive to invade the rights of other citizens; or if such a common motive exists, it will be more difficult for all who feel it to discover their own strength, and to act in unison with each other. Besides other impediments, it may be remarked that, where there is a consciousness of unjust or dishonorable purposes, communication is always checked by distrust in proportion to the number whose concurrence is necessary.

Hence, it clearly appears, that the same advantage which a republic has over a democracy, in controlling the effects of faction, is enjoyed by a large over a small republic,—is enjoyed by the Union over the States composing it. Does the advantage consist in the substitution of representatives whose enlightened views and virtuous sentiments render them superior to local prejudices and to schemes of injustice? It will not be denied that the representation of the Union will be most likely to possess these requisite endowments. Does it consist in the greater security afforded by a greater variety of parties, against the event of any one party being able to outnumber and oppress the rest? In an equal degree does the increased variety of parties comprised within the Union, increase this security. Does it, in fine, consist in the greater obstacles opposed to the concert and accomplishment of the secret wishes of an unjust and interested majority? Here, again, the extent of the Union gives it the most palpable advantage.

The influence of factious leaders may kindle a flame within their particular States, but will be unable to spread a general conflagration through the other States. A religious sect may degenerate into a political faction in a part of the Confederacy; but the variety of sects dispersed over the entire face of it must secure the national councils against any danger from that source. A rage for paper money, for an abolition of debts, for an equal division of property, or for any other improper or wicked project, will be less apt to pervade the whole body of the Union than a particular member of it; in the same proportion as such a malady is more likely to taint a particular county or district, than an entire State.

In the extent and proper structure of the Union, therefore, we behold a republican remedy for the diseases most incident to republican government. And according to the degree of pleasure and pride we feel in being republicans, ought to be our zeal in cherishing the spirit and supporting the character of Federalists.

PUBLIUS

Critical Thinking

1. According to Madison, can the causes of faction be eliminated? Can its effects be controlled?

2. What, according to Madison, are the two key differences between a democracy and a republic?

3. What are the advantages of a republican form of government? Does Madison advocate a democratic or a republican government? Why?

4. "Extend the sphere and you take in a greater variety of parties and interests." So begins several sentences that present one of the most central claims in *Federalist 10*. Do you find that claim persuasive?

Create Central

www.mhhe.com/createcentral

Internet References

The Federalist Papers.org
www.thefederalistpapers.org

Teaching American History.org: Introduction to the Antifederalists
http://teachingamericanhistory.org/fed-antifed/antifederalist

James Madison's Montpelier
www.montpelier.org

From The Federalist No. 10, 1787.

Article   Prepared by: Bruce Stinebrickner, *DePauw University*

Federalist No. 51

JAMES MADISON

Learning Outcomes

After reading this article, you will be able to:

- Identify the main arguments of James Madison in *Federalist* 51 and evaluate their persuasiveness.

- Consider whether the first half of this article by James Madison is primarily about democracy or primarily about the so-called separation of powers structure of the proposed new constitution.

- Consider whether the advantages of a "compound republic" that Madison notes outweigh possible disadvantages.

To the People of the State of New York

To what expedient, then, shall we finally resort, for maintaining in practice the necessary partition of power among the several departments, as laid down in the Constitution? The only answer that can be given is, that as all these exterior provisions are found to be inadequate, the defect must be supplied, by so contriving the interior structure of the government as that its several constituent parts may, by their mutual relations, be the means of keeping each other in their proper places. Without presuming to undertake a full development of this important idea, I will hazard a few general observations, which may perhaps place it in a clearer light, and enable us to form a more correct judgment of the principles and structure of the government planned by the convention.

In order to lay a due foundation for that separate and distinct exercise of the different powers of government, which to a certain extent is admitted on all hands to be essential to the preservation of liberty, it is evident that each department should have a will of its own; and consequently should be so constituted that the members of each should have as little agency as possible in the appointment of the members of the others. Were this principle rigorously adhered to, it would require that all the appointments for the supreme executive, legislative, and judiciary magistracies should be drawn from the same fountain of authority, the people, through channels having no communication whatever with one another. Perhaps such a plan of constructing the several departments would be less difficult in

practice than it may in contemplation appear. Some difficulties, however, and some additional expense would attend the execution of it. Some deviations, therefore, from the principle must be admitted. In the constitution of the judiciary department in particular, it might be inexpedient to insist rigorously on the principle: first, because peculiar qualifications being essential in the members, the primary consideration ought to be to select that mode of choice which best secures these qualifications; secondly, because the permanent tenure by which the appointments are held in that department, must soon destroy all sense of dependence on the authority conferring them.

It is equally evident, that the members of each department should be as little dependent as possible on those of the others, for the emoluments annexed to their offices. Were the executive magistrate, or the judges, not independent of the legislature in this particular, their independence in every other would be merely nominal.

But the great security against a gradual concentration of the several powers in the same department, consists in giving to those who administer each department the necessary constitutional means and personal motives to resist encroachments of the others. The provision for defence must in this, as in all other cases, be made commensurate to the danger of attack. Ambition must be made to counteract ambition. The interest of the man must be connected with the constitutional rights of the place. It may be a reflection on human nature, that such devices should be necessary to control the abuses of government. But what is government itself, but the greatest of all reflections on human nature? If men were angels, no government would be necessary. If angels were to govern men, neither external nor internal controls on government would be necessary. In framing a government which is to be administered by men over men, the great difficulty lies in this: you must first enable the government to control the governed; and in the next place oblige it to control itself. A dependence on the people is, no doubt, the primary control on the government; but experience has taught mankind the necessity of auxiliary precautions.

This policy of supplying, by opposite and rival interests, the defect of better motives, might be traced through the whole system of human affairs, private as well as public. We see it particularly displayed in all the subordinate distributions of power, where the constant aim is to divide and arrange the several offices in such a manner as that each may be a check on the other—that the private interest of every individual may be a sentinel over the public rights. These inventions of prudence cannot be less requisite in the distribution of the supreme powers of the State.

But it is not possible to give to each department an equal power of self-defence. In republican government, the legislative authority necessarily predominates. The remedy for this inconveniency is to divide the legislature into different branches; and to render them, by different modes of election and different principles of action, as little connected with each other as the nature of their common functions and their common depen-dence on the society will admit. It may even be necessary to guard against dangerous encroachments by still further precautions. As the weight of the legislative authority requires that it should be thus divided, the weakness of the executive may require, on the other hand, that it should be fortified. An absolute negative on the legislature appears, at first view, to be the natural defence with which the executive magistrate should be armed. But perhaps it would be neither altogether safe nor alone sufficient. On ordinary occasions it might not be exerted with the requisite firmness, and on extraordinary occasions it might be perfidiously abused. May not this defect of an absolute negative be supplied by some qualified connection between this weaker department and the weaker branch of the stronger department, by which the latter may be led to support the constitutional rights of the former, without being too much detached from the rights of its own department?

If the principles on which these observations are founded be just, as I persuade myself they are, and they be applied as a criterion to the several State constitutions, and to the federal Constitution, it will be found that if the latter does not perfectly correspond with them, the former are infinitely less able to bear such a test.

There are, moreover, two considerations particularly applicable to the federal system of America, which place that system in a very interesting point of view.

First. In a single republic, all the power surrendered by the people is submitted to the administration of a single government; and the usurpations are guarded against by a division of the government into distinct and separate departments. In the compound republic of America, the power surrendered by the people is first divided between two distinct governments, and then the portion allotted to each subdivided among distinct and separate departments. Hence a double security arises to the rights of the people. The different governments will control each other, at the same time that each will be controlled by itself.

Second. It is of great importance in a republic not only to guard the society against the oppression of its rulers, but to guard one part of the society against the injustice of the other part. Different interests necessarily exist in different classes of citizens. If a majority be united by a common interest, the rights of the minority will be insecure. There are but two methods of providing against this evil: the one by creating a will in the community independent of the majority—that is, of the society itself; the other, by comprehending in the society so many separate descriptions of citizens as will render an unjust

combination of a majority of the whole very improbable, if not impracticable. The first method prevails in all governments possessing an hereditary or self-appointed authority. This, at best, is but a precarious security; because a power independent of the society may as well espouse the unjust views of the major, as the rightful interests of the minor party, and may possibly be turned against both parties. The second method will be exemplified in the federal republic of the United States. Whilst all authority in it will be derived from and dependent on the society, the society itself will be broken into so many parts, interests and classes of citizens, that the rights of individuals, or of the minority, will be in little danger from interested combinations of the majority. In a free government the security for civil rights must be the same as that for religious rights. It consists in the one case in the multiplicity of interests, and in the other in the multiplicity of sects. The degree of security in both cases will depend on the number of interests and sects; and this may be presumed to depend on the extent of country and number of people comprehended under the same government. This view of the subject must particularly recommend a proper federal system to all the sincere and considerate friends of republican government, since it shows that in exact proportion as the territory of the Union may be formed into more circumscribed Confederacies, or States, oppressive combinations of a majority will be facilitated; the best security, under the republican forms, for the rights of every class of citizens, will be diminished; and consequently the stability and independence of some member of the government, the only other security, must be proportionally increased. Justice is the end of government. It is the end of civil society. It ever has been and ever will be pursued until it be obtained, or until liberty be lost in the pursuit. In a society under the forms of which the stronger faction can readily unite and oppress the weaker, anarchy may as truly be said to reign as in a state of nature, where the weaker individual is not secured against the violence of the stronger; and as, in the latter state, even the stronger individuals are prompted, by the uncertainty of their condition, to submit to a government which may protect the weak as well as themselves; so, in the former state, will the more powerful factions or parties be gradually induced, by a like motive, to wish for a government which will protect all parties, the weaker as well as the more powerful. It can be little doubted that if the State of Rhode Island was separated from the Confederacy and left to itself, the insecurity of rights under the popular form of government within such narrow limits would be displayed by such reiterated oppressions of factious majorities that some power altogether independent of the people would soon be called for by the voice of the very factions whose misrule had proved the necessity of it. In the extended republic of the United States, and among the great variety of interests, parties, and sects which it embraces, a coalition of a majority of the whole society could seldom take place on any other principles than those of justice and the general good; whilst there being thus less danger to a minor from the will of a major party, there must be less pretext, also, to provide for the security of the former, by introducing into the government a will not dependent on the latter, or, in other words, a will independent of the society itself. It is no less certain than it is important, notwithstanding the contrary opinions which have been entertained, that the larger the society, provided it lie within a particular sphere, the more duly capable it will be of self-government. And happily for the *republican cause,* the practicable sphere may be carried to a very great extent, by a judicious modification and mixture of the *federal principle.*

                                                          PUBLIUS

Critical Thinking

1. Explain the rationale for what has come to be called the "separation of powers."

2. *Federalist 51* argues that members of one branch should not be involved in the selection of members of another branch. Why, according to *Federalist 51*, is a "deviation" from this principle warranted in the case of the judiciary?

3. According to Madison, why is a system of independent "departments" (that is, branches) of government with separate powers necessary?

4. Which branch does Madison believe will be predominant? How does the structure of government outlined in the proposed constitution minimize or remedy the problem of that one branch being too powerful?

5. Explain what is meant by calling the United States a "compound republic" and summarize the advantages of being a "compound republic."

Create Central

www.mhhe.com/createcentral

Internet References

The Federalist Papers.org
www.thefederalistpapers.org

Teaching American History.org: Introduction to the Antifederalists
http://teachingamericanhistory.org/fed-antifed/antifederalist

James Madison's Montpelier
www.montpelier.org

From The Federalist No. 51, 1787.

Article Prepared by: Bruce Stinebrickner, *DePauw University*

The End of American Exceptionalism

Why the United States is less religious, less patriotic, and more class-conscious than we think it is.

PETER BEINART

Learning Outcomes

After reading this article, you will be able to:

- Identify three basic attributes that are said to make the United States different from European countries.

- Cite the evidence that suggests that each of these basic attributes is eroding.

- Explain how "backlash" might be a source of hope for those who lament the erosion of American exceptionalism in the three areas on which the article focuses.

From the moment Barack Obama appeared on the national stage, conservatives have been searching for the best way to describe the danger he poses to America's traditional way of life. Secularism? Check. Socialism? Sure. A tendency to apologize for America's greatness overseas? That, too. But how to tie them all together?

Gradually, a unifying theme took hold. "At the heart of the debate over Obama's program," declared Rich Lowry and Ramesh Ponnuru in an influential 2010 *National Review* cover story, is "the survival of American exceptionalism." Finally, a term broad and historically resonant enough to capture the magnitude of the threat. A year later, Newt Gingrich published *A Nation Like No Other: Why American Exceptionalism Matters,* in which he warned that "our government has strayed alarmingly" from the principles that made America special. Mitt Romney deployed the phrase frequently in his 2012 campaign, asserting that President Obama "doesn't have the same feelings about American exceptionalism that we do." The term, which according to *Factiva* appeared in global English-language publications fewer than 3,000 times during the Bush administration, has already appeared more than 10,000 times since Obama became president.

To liberals, the charge that Obama threatens American exceptionalism is daft. He is, after all, fond of declaring, "In no other country on Earth is my story even possible." For some progressive pundits, things hit rock bottom when conservative *Washington Post* columnist Kathleen Parker flayed Obama for not using the words "American exceptionalism" in his 2011 State of the Union speech, even though he had called America a "light to the world" and "the greatest nation on Earth." The entire discussion, declared liberal *Post* blogger Greg Sargent, had become "absurd," "self-parodic," and an exercise in "nonstop idiocy."

But that's not quite right. When conservatives say American exceptionalism is imperiled, they're onto something. In fundamental ways, America *is* becoming less exceptional. Where Gingrich and company go wrong is in claiming that the Obama presidency is the cause of this decline. It's actually the result. Ironically, the people most responsible for eroding American exceptionalism are the very conservatives who most fear its demise.

To understand what's threatening American exceptionalism, one must first understand what its contemporary champions mean by the term. American exceptionalism does not simply mean that America is different from other countries. (After all, every country is different from every other one.) It means that America departs from the established way of doing things, that it's an *exception* to the global rule. And from Alexis de Tocqueville, who chronicled America's uniqueness in the 1830s, to Joseph Stalin, who bemoaned it in the 1920s, to social scientists like Louis Hartz, who celebrated it during the Cold War, the established way of doing things has always been defined by Europe. What makes America exceptional, in other words, is our refusal to behave like the Old World. "Exceptionalism," wrote historian Joyce Appleby, "is America's peculiar form of Eurocentrism."

As America and Europe have changed over time, so have the attributes that exceptionalists claim distinguish us from them. But for the contemporary Right, there are basically three: our belief in organized religion; our belief that America has a special mission to spread freedom in the world; and our belief that we are a classless society where, through limited government and free enterprise, anyone can get ahead. Unfortunately for conservatives, each of these beliefs is declining fast.

The Rise of Anticlericalism

For centuries, observers have seen America as an exception to the European assumption that modernity brings secularism. "There is no country in the world where the Christian religion retains a greater influence over the souls of men than in America," de Tocqueville wrote. In his 1996 book, *American Exceptionalism: A Double-Edged Sword*, Seymour Martin Lipset quoted Karl Marx as calling America "preeminently the country of religiosity," and then argued that Marx was still correct. America, wrote Lipset, remained "the most religious country in Christendom."

Today's conservatives often cast themselves as defenders of this religious exceptionalism against Obama's allegedly secularizing impulses. "Despite the fact that our current president has managed to avoid explaining on at least four occasions that we are endowed by our creator," declared Gingrich at a 2011 candidates forum, "the fact is that what makes American exceptionalism different is that we are the only people I know of in history to say power comes directly from God."

But in important ways, the exceptional American religiosity that Gingrich wants to defend is an artifact of the past. The share of Americans who refuse any religious affiliation has risen from one in 20 in 1972 to one in 5 today. Among Americans under 30, it's one in 3. According to the Pew Research Center, millennials—Americans born after 1980—are more than 30 percentage points less likely than seniors to say that "religious faith and values are very important to America's success." And young Americans don't merely attend church far less frequently than their elders. They also attend far less than young people did in the past. "Americans," Pew notes, "do not generally become more [religiously] affiliated as they move through the life cycle"—which means it's unlikely that America's decline in religious affiliation will reverse itself simply as millennials age.

Americans remain far more willing than Europeans to affirm God's importance in their lives (although that gap has closed somewhat among the young). But when the subject shifts from belief in God to association with churches, America's famed

religious exceptionalism virtually disappears. In 1970, according to the *World Religion Database*, Europeans were over 16 percentage points more likely than Americans to eschew any religious identification. By 2010, the gap was less than half of 1 percentage point. According to Pew, while Americans are today more likely to affirm a religious affiliation than people in Germany or France, they are actually less likely to do so than Italians and Danes.

Even more interesting is the reason for this change. Many of the Americans who today eschew religious affiliation are neither atheists nor agnostics. Most pray. In other words, Americans aren't rejecting religion, or even Christianity. They are rejecting churches. There are various explanations for this. As Princeton's Robert Wuthnow notes in his book *After the Baby Boomers,* the single and childless historically attend church at lower rates than married parents do. And women who work outside the home attend less than women who don't. Which means that with women marrying later, having children later, and working more outside the home, it's logical that church attendance would drop.

But it's not just changes in family and work patterns that drive the growth of religious nonaffiliation. It's politics. In the mid-20th century, liberals were almost as likely to attend church as conservatives. But starting in the 1970s, when the Religious Right began agitating against abortion, feminism, and gay rights, liberals began to identify organized Christianity with conservative politics. In recent years, the Religious Right's opposition to gay marriage has proved particularly alienating to millennials. "The actions of the Religious Right," argue sociologists Michael Hout and Claude Fischer, "prompted political moderates and liberals to quit saying they had a religious preference." In their book, *American Grace: How Religion Divides and United Us,* Robert D. Putnam and David E. Campbell cite a study suggesting that many "young Americans came to view religion . . . as judgmental, homophobic, hypocritical, and too political." Today, according to Pew, the religiously unaffiliated are disproportionately liberal, pro-gay-marriage, and critical of churches for meddling too much in politics. Not coincidentally, so are America's young.

What is growing in contemporary America, in other words, is something long associated with Europe: anticlericalism. In Europe, noted the late political scientist James Q. Wilson in a 2006 essay on American exceptionalism, the existence of official state religions led secularists to see "Christians as political enemies." America, Wilson argued, lacked this political hostility to organized religion because it separated church and state. But today, even without an established church, the Religious Right plays such a prominent and partisan role in American politics that it has spurred the kind of antireligious backlash long associated with the old world. Barack Obama is the beneficiary of that backlash, because voters who say they "never" attend religious services favored him by 37 percentage points in 2008 and 28 points in 2012. But he's not the cause. The people most responsible for America's declining religious exceptionalism are the conservatives who have made organized Christianity and right-wing politics inseparable in the minds of so many of America's young.

Noninterventionism

If the champions of American exceptionalism see religion as one key dividing line between the new and old worlds, they see America's special mission overseas as another. "I believe," declared Romney in 2011, that "we are an exceptional country with a unique destiny and role in the world . . . that of a great champion of human dignity and human freedom." For many Washington conservatives, that unique world role gives America unique obligations: We cannot stand aside while evil triumphs. But it also gives America unique privileges: We need not be bound by the opinions of others. As George W. Bush declared in his 2004 State of the Union address, America does not need a "permission slip" from other nations to protect itself and fulfill its mission in the world.

But young Americans are far less likely than their elders to endorse this exceptional global role. They want the United States to do less overseas; and what America must do, they want done more consensually. Americans under 30, for instance, are 23 percentage points more likely than older Americans to say the United States should take its allies' interests into account, even if that means compromising our own. They are 24 points more favorable to the United Nations than Americans over 50, the largest age gap in the 17 countries that Pew surveyed. And as with religious affiliation, this generation gap within the United States is eroding the gap between Americans and Europeans. Among respondents over 50, Pew found in 2011, Americans were 29 percentage points more likely than Britons to deny that their country needed U.N. approval before going to war. Among respondents under 30, by contrast, the gap was only 8 points.

Were young Americans merely embracing multilateralism over unilateralism, this shift wouldn't be so fundamental. But for conservatives, America's exceptional role in the world isn't merely about what we do overseas. What we do overseas expresses our belief in ourselves. It's no coincidence that Romney's campaign manifesto was titled *No Apology: Believe in America,* a reference to Obama's supposed tendency to apologize for America's global misdeeds. In Lowry and Ponnuru's words, Obama threatens American exceptionalism because he threatens "America's civilizational self-confidence."

That's where things get interesting, because, as conservatives suspect, Americans' declining belief in our special virtue as a world power really is connected to our declining belief in our special virtue as a people. And the young are leading the way.

Empty Pews

Americans today are much more likely than Americans 20 years ago to say they have no formal religious affiliation.

Change in share of American adults with no religious affiliation

	1990	2012
Total	7.7(%)	19.7(%)
Conservative	5.0	9.1
Moderate	6.1	17.9
Liberal	14.6	39.6
Age 75+	3.8	7.1
65–74	5.2	11.9
55–64	7.1	14.7
45–54	5.9	16
35–44	8.0	18.8
25–34	10.1	28.6
18–24	9.7	32.0

Source: "More Americans Have No Religious Preference: Key Findings From the 2012 General Social Survey."

A 2013 poll by the Public Religion Research Institute found that while almost two in three Americans over 65 call themselves "extremely proud to be American," among Americans under 30 it is fewer than two in five. According to a Pew study in 2011, millennials were a whopping 40 points less likely than people 75 and older to call America "the greatest country in the world."

Young Americans, in fact, are no more "civilizationally self-confident" than their European counterparts. When Pew asked respondents in 2011 whether "our culture is superior" to others, it found that Americans over the age of 50 were, on average, 15 points more likely to answer yes than their counterparts in Britain, France, Germany, and Spain. Americans under 30, by contrast, were actually *less* likely to agree than their peers in Britain, Germany, and Spain. And as the millennials, who are still reaching adulthood, constitute an ever-growing share of America's adult population, Americans are becoming a people no more likely to assert their national supremacy than are Europeans. In 2002, according to Pew, Americans were 20 percentage points more likely than Germans to declare their culture superior to that of other nations. By 2011, the gap was down to 2 points.

One reason for this shift is demographic. According to the Public Religion Research Institute, African-Americans and Hispanics, who comprise a larger share of America's young than of its old, are less likely to call themselves "extremely proud" of the United States than whites are. In their skepticism of unilateral foreign policy and overt patriotism, young Americans are also reflecting broader national and international trends. Millennials are coming of age at a time when America's relative power overseas has declined. They're also products of an educational system that, more than in the past, emphasizes inclusion and diversity, which may breed a discomfort with claims that America is better than other nations.

But however important these long-term trends, they can't explain the abruptness of the shift away from exceptionalist attitudes about America's role in the world. For this, we must look to George W. Bush.

Ever since Karl Mannheim's writing in the 1920s, sociologists have observed that people are most influenced by events that occur in their late teens and early 20s—once they separate from their parents but before they establish stable lifestyles and attitudes of their own. For most millennials, these plastic years coincided with the Bush presidency. And it is Bush's vision

Measuring Up

Older Americans and conservatives are much more likely than liberals and young people to assert American superiority.

Which of these statements best describes your opinion about the United States?

	The United States stands above all other countries	It is one of the greatest, among some others	There are other countries that are better than the United States
Total	38(%)	53(%)	8(%)
Age 65+	50	46	3
50–64	40	52	7
30–49	38	53	7
18–29	27	59	12
Very Con.	65	33	2
Conservative	49	46	5
Moderate	29	61	9
Liberal	29	61	9
Very Lib.	26	52	17

Source: Pew Research Center (2011).

of America's aggressive, unfettered world role, especially as manifested in the Iraq War, that young Americans are rebelling against.

Young Americans actually began the Bush presidency more supportive of invading Iraq than the population at large. But their disillusionment has proved far more intense. Between 2002 and 2008, the percentage of older Americans who supported the Iraq War dropped 15 points. Among Americans under 30, by contrast, it dropped a whopping 47 points. As young Americans turned against the war, they turned against Bush's exceptionalist vision of an America with unique burdens and privileges. Even more fundamentally, they turned against the chest-thumping, "We're No. 1" brand of patriotism that often accompanied it. In 2004, Jon Stewart—whose comedy show that year regularly drew more young viewers than any other cable news show—published *America (The Book)*, in which, according to one reviewer, "no aspect of our patriotic pride is too sacred to be sacrificed on the altar of irony." The following year, Stewart's colleague, Stephen Colbert, launched *The Colbert Report,* which occasionally featured him wrapped nude in the American flag. Between 2003 and 2011, according to Pew, the percentage of Americans calling themselves "very patriotic" dropped by less than 3 points among older Americans but by 10 points among millennials.

This turn against exceptionalist foreign policy—like young America's turn against organized religion—has undoubtedly boosted Obama's political career. Had he not opposed the Iraq War, and then seen the war prove catastrophic, it's unlikely he would have won the Democratic nomination, let alone the presidency. Among antiwar voters, he beat John McCain by 54 points. But as with dwindling religious affiliation, Obama's presidency has been more the result of the decline American exceptionalism than its cause. If any president bears responsibility for the public's souring on the idea that the United States can play by its own rules on the world stage, it is Bush, assisted by many of the same conservative politicians and pundits who now bemoan American exceptionalism's demise.

Class-Consciousness

American exceptionalism's third, and most fundamental, contemporary meaning is about neither religion nor foreign policy. It's about mobility. Starting in the 19th century, foreign observers began noting that white Americans were less likely than Europeans to be prisoners of their birth. Because America's white poor could more easily rise above their parents' station, they did not constitute a static, aggrieved working class—and were less tempted by socialism. In the words of Princeton historian Daniel Rodgers, "Socialism's weakness in the United States was taken as further proof of the point: that the old rules of caste and class relations had been superseded."

For the most part, today's conservatives lustily endorse this exceptionalist narrative. "Class is not a fixed designation in this country," declared Paul Ryan in 2011. Unlike Europe, where "masses of the long-term unemployed are locked into the new lower class," America is "an upwardly mobile society." Lowry and Ponnuru add, "In America, there really hasn't been a disaffected proletariat—because the proletariat has gotten rich."

But conservatives worry that by encouraging reliance on government and discouraging individual initiative, Obama is making America more like Europe. Obama, warns former Republican presidential candidate Michele Bachmann, is hooking Americans on the "crack cocaine of [government] dependency." "It's not a traditional America anymore," Fox's Bill O'Reilly despaired on the night Obama won re-election. "People feel that they are entitled to things" from the state.

When conservatives worry that America is not as economically exceptional anymore, they're right. A raft of studies suggests that upward mobility is now rarer in the United States than in much of Europe. But if America's exceptional economic mobility is largely a myth, it's a myth in which many older Americans still believe. Among the young, by contrast, attitudes are catching up to reality. According to a 2011 Pew poll, young Americans were 14 points more likely than older Americans to say that the wealthy in America got there mainly because "they know the right people or were born into wealthy families" rather than because of their "hard work, ambition, and education." And as young Americans internalize America's lack of economic mobility, they are developing the very class consciousness the United States is supposed to lack. In 2011, when Pew asked Americans to define themselves as either a "have" or a "have-not," older Americans chose "have" by 27 points. In contrast, young Americans, by a 4-point margin, chose "have-not." According to the exceptionalist story line, Americans are all supposed to consider themselves "middle class," regardless of their actual economic fortunes. For seniors, that's largely true. According to a 2012 Pew study, they were 43 points more likely to call themselves "middle" than "lower" class. Among young Americans, by contrast, the percentage calling themselves "middle" and "lower" class was virtually the same.

And in the final undoing of the exceptionalist narrative, young Americans are expressing greater interest in "socialism," although it's unclear what they mean by it. A 2011 Pew study found that while Americans over 30 favored capitalism over socialism by 27 points, Americans under 30 narrowly favored socialism. Compared with older Americans, millennials are 36 points more likely to prefer a larger government that provides more services over a smaller one that provides fewer.

As millennials grow older, Americans as a whole—whose actual economic mobility is no longer exceptional—are becoming less exceptional in their attitudes about class. Between 1988 and 2011, the percentage of Americans who identified as "have-nots"

doubled, from fewer than one in five to more than one in three. In 1988, Americans earning under $30,000 a year were 18 points more likely to call themselves "haves." By 2011, those numbers, adjusted for inflation, had flipped: The poorest Americans were 15 points more likely to call themselves "have-nots."

Americans are also becoming less exceptional in their views of capitalism. In 2003, according to GlobeScan, Americans were more than 14 percentage points more likely than Italians, Britons, Canadians, and Germans to say the "free market economy is the best system on which to base the future of the world." By 2010, they were almost 2 points *less* likely.

When conservatives acknowledge these trends, they often chalk them up to Obama's policies, which have supposedly drained Americans of their rugged individualism and habituated them to government handouts. "Once the public is hooked on government health care," Lowry and Ponnuru note, "its political attitudes shift leftward." But Obama is less the driver of this shift in economic attitudes than the beneficiary. It's certainly true that Obama won the votes of Americans skeptical that they can rise via the unfettered market. Among the majority of 2012 voters

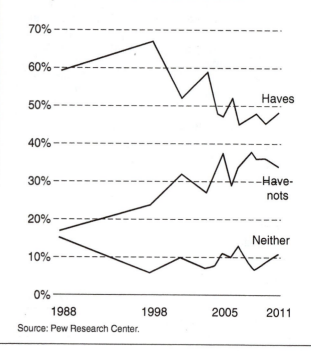

Fortunate Ones

An increasing percentage of Americans identify themselves as "have-nots."

Q: If you had to choose, which of these groups are you in, the haves or the have-nots?

Source: Pew Research Center.

who believe America's economic system favors the wealthy, Obama beat Romney by 45 points. But Obama is not the reason so many Americans believe that. For more than a century, commentators have chalked up Americans' support for capitalism and lack of economic resentment to America's exceptional upward mobility. It's unclear when exactly American upward mobility began to decline. But it's not surprising that, eventually, that decline would cause class attitudes to harden.

The question exceptionalists should be asking is why America, once vaunted for its economic mobility, now trails much of the advanced world. Single-parent families clearly play a role, since poor children born into two-parent homes are far more upwardly mobile than those who are not. Housing patterns that segregate the poor from the middle class also seem to limit poor kids' chances of getting ahead. But economic inequality is also a big part of the story. Across the world, the University of Ottawa's Miles Corak has demonstrated, countries with higher inequality suffer lower mobility. The same is true inside the United States: The flatter a city is economically, the more likely its poor will rise.

Part of the reason is "opportunity hoarding." In recent decades, the wealth gap between the richest Americans and everyone else has dramatically widened. Rich Americans have used this influx of cash to give their children special advantages that keep them from losing their spots atop the income ladder to children born with lesser means. Think about test preparation, which became a national industry only in the 1970s. Or the way wealthy parents subsidize unpaid internships or buy expensive houses to gain access to the best public schools. In the early 1970s, rich families spent four times as much on their children's education as poor ones. Today, they spend almost seven times as much. Culture plays a large role in this. If the rich didn't value education, they wouldn't spend their cash on it. But until recently, they didn't have so much cash to spend. As a paper by Stanford sociologists Pablo Mitnik, Erin Cumberworth, and David Grusky notes, "Inequality provides privileged families with more resources that can then be lavished on their children, resources that raise their chances of securing desirable class positions for themselves." Whether this lavishing has contributed to an absolute decline in upward mobility in the United States in recent decades, it has certainly contributed to America's decline relative to other advanced countries.

All of which begs another question that conservative exceptionalists should be asking: What's behind skyrocketing inequality? Why do the top 1 percent of Americans, who took in roughly 11 percent of national income in the mid-1970s, account for more than double that today? Globalization and technology are clearly part of the story. If you're an American who works with your hands, you're competing with low-paid workers across the globe, not to mention machines, to an extent scarcely imaginable a few decades ago. That competition pushes down wages for Americans without a college degree, and widens the gap between rich and poor.

What globalization and technology can't explain is why inequality is so much higher in America than in Europe, where the same tectonic forces are at play. Indeed, if you eliminate government policies on taxing and spending, America is about as unequal as Sweden, Norway, and Denmark and a bit *more* equal than Finland, Germany, and Britain. America claims its place as the most unequal major Western country only when you add in government policy. Which is to say that while globalization and technology may be increasing inequality everywhere, they are increasing it more in the United States because, compared with Europe, the United States redistributes less money from rich to poor.

Which brings us back to conservatives, because it is their champions—Ronald Reagan in the 1980s, Newt Gingrich in the 1990s, George W. Bush in the 2000s—who pushed many of the policies that have boosted inequality. In the mid-1970s, the federal government's top tax rate for regular income was 70 percent and its top rate for long-term capital gains was almost 40 percent. When Bush left office, the rate on regular income had fallen to 35 percent and the rate on long-term capital gains was down to 15 percent. (That has crept up under Obama to almost 40 percent on regular income and 20 percent on capital gains for individuals making over $400,000.) These huge shifts in tax policy have been partially offset by antipoverty spending, which has grown significantly since the 1970s, largely because skyrocketing health care costs have made Medicaid far more expensive. But even if you take that increase into account, America is still doing far less to combat inequality than other advanced democracies.

If you believe, as academics increasingly do, that economic inequality goes hand in hand with calcified class relations, then decades of conservative policy have contributed to America's relative lack of economic mobility.

This, in turn, has soured young Americans on the belief that through the free market they can rise above the circumstances of their birth. Which means that, when it comes to declining faith in the American Dream of upward mobility, as with declining faith in organized religion and declining faith in America's special mission in the world, conservatives have helped foment the very backlash against American exceptionalism that they decry.

The Turnaround

But in all three areas, this backlash may actually prove a source of hope. It may not entirely restore public belief in America's unique virtues, but it may reverse some of the trends that sapped that belief in the first place.

Start with religion. To some, the rise in religious nonaffiliation is a frightening departure from American tradition. It may turn out, however, to be just the challenge American Christianity needs.

Historically, American religion has benefited greatly from its independence from the state. In recent decades, however, that independence has been compromised. The Religious Right has become a wing of the Republican Party, led by power brokers who speak biblically but act politically. In response, many young Americans have begun voting against the GOP on Sundays by declining to attend church.

Their alienation has jolted religious leaders and contributed to a new willingness to question the corrupting entanglement between churches and partisan politics. "When I talk to neighbors or strangers and tell them that I try my best to follow Jesus," wrote David Kuo, an evangelical who worked for Ralph Reed, John Ashcroft, William Bennett, and George W. Bush, "their first thoughts about me are political ones—they figure I don't care about the environment, I support the war in Iraq, I oppose abortion. . . . That is what they associate with my faith." So disturbing was this realization that Kuo in 2006 published a book arguing, "It is time for Christians to take a temporary step back from politics, to turn away from its seductions."

That's beginning to happen. According to John S. Dickerson, an influential young evangelical pastor, "The pulse of evangelicalism is . . . shifting, in many ways for the good, from American politics to aid for the global poor." Inspired by Pope Francis, prominent Catholic Republicans such as Paul Ryan are questioning whether a Christianity that blesses the lobbying agenda of the chamber of commerce will ever truly challenge secular society or reengage America's disaffected young.

So far, there's no evidence this shift is stemming the rising tide of religious nonaffiliation. Even Francis, although widely admired by American Catholics, hasn't yet brought them back to the pews. Still, the new spirit of humility and self-criticism among America's church leaders is healthy. And it's unlikely it would be occurring had young people not shattered the stereotype of Americans as unquestioning churchgoers. Moreover, since most of these young Americans reject a partisan church—but not a loving God—they may one day create a constituency for religious institutions that spurns the temptations of state power. Which is, in a way, what American religious exceptionalism was supposed to be all about.

The backlash against America's special mission in the world may prove heartening, too. Over the last decade, that special mission has justified policies—such as the invasion, occupation, and failed reconstruction of Afghanistan and Iraq—that have cost the United States massively in money and blood. And it has justified ignoring international norms, most importantly on torture, which has sapped America's moral authority. Yet many hawkish elites remain loath to acknowledge the limits of American power, let alone American wisdom.

In desiring a more modest and consensual foreign policy, young people are recapturing the wisdom of an earlier era.

In the 1950s, after a painful and costly war in Korea, Dwight Eisenhower warned that by dispatching troops to oppose every communist advance, America would undermine its economic strength and democratic character even as it extended its military reach. Today, whether it is their support for a smaller, cheaper military or their skepticism about unchecked government surveillance, young Americans are the age group most sensitive to the financial and moral costs of continuing Bush's expansive "war on terror." Eisenhower's fear of overreach led him to resist calls for sending U.S. troops to Vietnam; young Americans are today 30 points more likely than their elders to say the United States should avoid war with Iran.

Underlying this more modest foreign policy vision is a more modest assessment of America itself, a modesty that may look to conservatives such as Lowry and Ponnuru like "lack of civilizational self-confidence." But here, too, young Americans are reclaiming the insights of an earlier time. In 1947, with politicians drawing ever brighter lines between the virtue of American democracy and the evil of Soviet totalitarianism, George Kennan told students at the National War College, "There is a little bit of totalitarian buried somewhere, way down deep, in each and every one of us." Kennan, and like-minded mid-20th-century intellectuals such as Walter Lippmann and Reinhold Niebuhr, considered America's political system superior to the Soviet Union's. But they argued that, paradoxically, what made it superior was its recognition of American fallibility. America, unlike the U.S.S.R., bound its leaders within restraining systems of law that denied them the right to unfettered action no matter how convinced they were of their own good intentions. That same spirit led the United States to help build institutions like the United Nations and NATO, which gave smaller nations some voice over America's behavior, and won the United States a measure of legitimacy among its allies that the Soviet Union never enjoyed.

As young men, Lippmann and Niebuhr had seen two epic visions—Woodrow Wilson's dream of a war to end war, and the socialist dream of a revolution to end class oppression—turn ugly. And it was their disillusionment with political crusades that woke them to the importance of building restraints against America's capacity to do evil rather than merely unleashing its supposedly innate inclination to do good. Perhaps young Americans, having in their formative years watched Bush's epic post-9/11 vision breed lies, brutality, and state collapse, and America's celebrated capitalist system descend into financial crisis, have gained their own appreciation of American fallibility. Let's hope so, because as Niebuhr and Lippmann understood, the best way to ensure that America remains an exceptional power—better than the predatory empires of the old world—is to remember that we are not inherently better at all.

The third backlash may prove most significant of all. Americans are right to cherish economic mobility. But the myth that America still enjoys exceptional mobility has become an opiate impeding efforts to make that mobility real again. When newly elected New York Mayor Bill de Blasio called for raising taxes on the wealthy to fund preschool and after-school programs, he was instantly accused of "class warfare," as if sullying the natural, classless, reality of New York City life. Critics of the inheritance tax often invoke a mythic America where the people passing on multimillion-dollar estates to their children are latter-day Horatio Algers who have gotten rich because of their gumption and hard work. They do so even though the estate tax affects just over 0.1 percent of American families, the same tiny elite that in recent decades has used its massive economic gains to insulate its children from competition from the very economic strivers that opponents of the inheritance tax celebrate.

Since the 1970s, the conservative movement has used the myth of a classless America to redistribute wealth upward, thus hardening class divisions, at least relative to other nations. It's no surprise that the young, having no memory of the more equal, more mobile America of popular legend, see this reality more clearly. And because they do, they are more eager to change it. Unlike every other age group, which opposed the Occupy movement by double digits, millennials supported it by double digits.

As millennials constitute a larger share of the electorate—rising from 29 percent of eligible voters in 2012 to a projected 36 percent in 2016 and 39 percent in 2020—they are creating a constituency for politicians willing to both acknowledge America's lack of class mobility and try to remedy it. The key to such an effort is increasing the number of poor students who graduate from college. Having a college degree quadruples someone's chances of moving from the poorest fifth of the population to the wealthiest. But educationally, many poor students fall so far behind so early that their chances of attending college are crippled by the time they leave elementary school. By eighth grade, children from wealthy families are already an astonishing four grade levels ahead of children who grow up poor.

There is evidence from France and Denmark that expanding preschool enrollment can significantly close this performance gap. A Brookings Institution study found that enrolling low-income children in high-quality preschools could boost their lifetime earnings by as much as $100,000. Building on such data, de Blasio has famously proposed making preschool universal in New York City, to be paid for with a tax on people earning over $500,000 a year. Now New York Gov. Andrew Cuomo has gone one better, promising universal preschool throughout the state. President Obama proposed something similar in his recent State of the Union address.

These efforts still face resistance, but they stand any chance at all only because of the growing recognition that America is not the highly mobile nation its cheerleaders proclaim it to be. To Mitt Romney, the public's growing alienation from this and other national myths may reflect a disturbing refusal to "believe in America." But "discontent," Thomas Edison once quipped, "is the first necessity of progress." And by challenging the comforting stories we tell about ourselves, a new American generation might just begin the long, hard work of making America exceptional again.

Critical Thinking

1. What changes are threatening American exceptionalism, at least in the terms in which Peter Beinart presents it?

2. What are the three basic attributes that conservatives believe do and should distinguish Americans from people of other nations?

3. What does it mean to say that the Obama presidency is the *result,* not the *cause,* of the decline in American exceptionalism? Do you agree?

Create Central

www.mhhe.com/createcentral

Internet References

American Enterprise Institute: American Exceptionalism
   http://www.aei.org/module/1/american-exceptionalism
The Economist
   http://www.economist.com/news/finance-and-economics/21615598-japan-no-longer-odd-one-out-rich-world-american-exceptionalism
The Guardian
   http://www.theguardian.com/commentisfree/2013/feb/18/american-exceptionalism-north-korea-nukes

---

PETER BEINART, a *National Journal* contributing editor, is a professor at the City University of New York and a senior fellow at the New America Foundation.

Article   Prepared by: Bruce Stinebrickner, *DePauw University*

Take It Down

The Confederate flag Means Treason

ALLEN C. GUELZO

Learning Outcomes

After reading this article, you will be able to:

- Put the Confederate flag into perspective by articulating and thinking about several sorts of messages that it can—and does—convey in the contemporary United States.

- Assess the author's views about what he says is the most "obnoxious" meaning of the Confederate flag and how he proposes thinking Americans should react to it and those who display it.

The Confederate States of America hasn't been in operation for a century and a half. Nevertheless, after a photograph of mass murderer Dylann Roof holding a toy-sized Confederate flag flashed onto television and computer screens, "Take it down!" became the newest meme burning through social media. The trustees of The Citadel voted to remove a Confederate battle flag from the campus chapel. Walmart emptied its shelves of items featuring the most minute images of the flag. In Gettysburg, the battlefield's on-site gift store announced that it "will no longer sell stand-alone items that solely feature the Confederate flag, including display and wearable items."

I don't have much personal investment in, or use for, the Confederate flag. I'm a Lincoln biographer and Civil War historian, from the town that gave the Confederacy its most serious defeat. The flag was the emblem of a regime based on what Confederate vice president Alexander Stephens called "the great truth that the negro is not equal to the white man; that slavery—subordination to the superior race—is his natural and normal condition." On those terms alone, the flag's defenders ought to take the advice of the Confederacy's most famous poet:

Touch it not—unfold it never;
Let it droop there, furled forever . . .
Furl it, hide it,—let it rest!

But there is also a substantial civil-liberties question at stake here, especially in the context of campaigns for trigger warnings, denunciations of micro-aggressions, prosecutions of Evangelical florists, and a claimed "right to be undisturbed by anything." Banning displays of the Confederate flag threatens to acquire an association with banning Ovid, the absurdities of carrying a mattress as simultaneous protest and performance art, and the dubious editorial judgment of *Rolling Stone*.

Dealing with the Confederate flag really involves asking two questions. The first is whether the "Southern Cross" flag actually *is* a sign of racial hate. Only the most self-deluded can tell me that white racial supremacy was not the core of what made the Confederacy; so, to the extent that the flag represented that Confederacy, it is. South Carolina's secession ordinance in 1860 stated as clearly as anyone could wish that secession was a response to the election of Abraham Lincoln, "whose opinions and purposes are hostile to slavery." Mississippi followed South Carolina into secession, declaring that "our position is thoroughly identified with the institution of slavery—the greatest material interest in the world." Jefferson Davis in his inaugural address as the Confederacy's provisional president accused Lincoln's Republicans of "surrounding [us] entirely by States in which slavery should be prohibited . . . thus rendering the property in slaves so insecure as to be comparatively worthless." This, at least, was obvious to Southerners *then*. "The South went to war on account of Slavery," admitted the famed Confederate guerrilla captain John S. Mosby. "South Carolina went to war—as she said in her Secession proclamation—because slavery wd. Not be secure under Lincoln."

After the Emancipation Proclamation, after Appomattox, and after the 13th Amendment, slavery was as dead as Marley's doornail, and so was the Confederate flag, which practically disappeared from popular view until D. W. Griffith's infamous epic, *The Birth of a Nation*. It was taken up again by the second Ku Klux Klan in the 1920s and by segregationists in the 1950s. But it also acquired a number of other meanings—libertarian resistance to centralized government, the hostility of an agrarian society to capitalism, the defiance of the loner, even a free-spirited *Duck Dynasty* goofiness. Defenders of the flag will want to argue that racial animosity is not its only message, or even its principal message, anymore, and they have a point that people who see race and only race in the flag should take it a little more seriously.

One thing that has gotten lost in this sound and fury is a meaning in the Confederate flag more obnoxious even than its racial message, and that is treason. When Union general Alex Hayes jubilantly trailed a captured Confederate flag in the dust behind his horse after the failure of Pickett's Charge at Gettysburg, he was not doing it because of any particular concerns about race but because he saw the Confederate flag as a fist shaken at the United States. "We believed then, and believe now, that we had a good government, worth fighting for, and, if need be, dying for," said Ulysses S. Grant. Which is why the old veterans angrily refused to participate in mixed "blue and gray" reunions if the Confederate flag was to be displayed, and declared that "the flag of treason should be suppressed."

This is the voice that has not been heard. Partly, that is because, in an increasingly globalized and cosmopolitan culture, of Julian Assange and Edward Snowden, the idea of treason sounds antiquated, even slightly medieval; and partly, it's because the cultural Left has never, since the Rosenbergs, been able to regard treason against the United States as a genuine crime. Neo-Confederate partisans curl the lip at this, too, as they have for 150 years, insisting that an attempt to overthrow the Constitution was actually completely consistent with the Constitution.

However strong the reasons for banning the flag as an ensign of hate, or however blurred with affection and nonconformity the flag's meaning has become, we are talking primarily about perceptions, about how people feel about the flag. But treason is a legal fact, and anything that minimizes it is an offense to all Americans.

The second question is Who should do the taking down? In places where the Confederate flag is displayed on public property, the answer is clear: The people, through their representatives, have the authority to take down whatever they wish to take down.

But that will not remove all the difficulties, because the line between public and private has become so blurred. If the Confederate flag should be removed from state-funded flagpoles, should it also be removed from state-funded museums, or from privately held museums that are open to the public? Should living-history programs with Confederate re-enactors (and their flags) be banned from National Park Service sites? One could argue that these are strictly historical displays, and aren't intended to send the same message that Dylann Roof sent—but that then begs the whole question.

So, here is my proposal. The Confederate flag was and is a symbol of many things, and in racial matters, a symbol of profound offense. But its most undeniable and constant meaning is rebellion. It is the emblem of treason, not only in 1861 but at any time someone defends the legitimacy of secession. Therefore, let every American who thinks treason is a crime take down the Confederate flag, and ask others to do likewise. And when (or if) we are refused, let us turn our backs on it, and dishonor it.

That is the response of the free citizen.

Critical Thinking

1. What is the connection between Dylan Roof and the Confederate flag?
2. What does the Confederate flag have to do with "racial hate" in the eyes of many people?
3. What messages besides "racial hate" can the Confederate flag also convey to people?

Internet References

Confederate Wave
   http://www.confederatewave.org/wave/2005/confederate-flag.php

PBS Newshour
   http://www.pbs.org/newshour/rundown/8-things-didnt-know-confederate-flag

---

MR. GUELZO is the **HENRY R. LUCE** *Professor of the Civil War Era at Gettysburg College and the author of* Gettysburg: The Last Invasion.

Article   Prepared by: Bruce Stinebrickner, *DePauw University*

Acculturation Without Assimilation

We reject American identity at our peril.

STANLEY KURTZ.

Learning Outcomes

After reading this article, you will be able to:

- Distinguish the two phenomena that the author labels "assimilation" and "acculturation."

- Critically assess the author's overall argument and determine whether you agree with it.

- Critically assess the author's views about muliticulturalism programs at schools and colleges.

The Boston Marathon terror attack has pushed the problem of assimilation to the forefront of the debate over immigration reform. The younger bomber, Dzhokhar Tsarnaev, took his oath of citizenship on September 11, 2012, of all dates. Although his older brother and the mastermind of the plot, Tamerlan Tsarnaev, had been investigated by the FBI in 2011, his citizenship application was still pending at the time of the bombing. These terrorists wanted to be Americans, yet they nursed a murderous hatred for the United States. Clearly the quest for citizenship is no guarantee of assimilation. Sad to say, the Tsarnaevs are but extreme examples of a far wider breakdown in America's system of assimilation. We ought not to be mulling amnesty for millions of illegal immigrants before putting that system back in order.

One of the architects of this country's ethos of assimilation, Teddy Roosevelt, delivered an 1894 address called "True Americanism," which seems almost to have been written with the Tsarnaevs in mind: "We freely extend the hand of welcome and of good-fellowship to every man, no matter what his creed or birthplace, who comes here honestly intent on becoming a good United States citizen like the rest of us; but we have a right, and it is our duty, to demand that he shall indeed become so and shall not confuse the issues with which we are struggling by introducing among us Old World quarrels and prejudices." It's a message today's immigrants are no longer hearing.

From the late 1960s on, a multiculturalism hostile to everything Teddy Roosevelt stood for has entrenched itself in our schools, our universities, large corporations, and the mainstream press. Pockets of traditional assimilationist thinking remain, yet the trend is clearly in the opposite direction. Federal and state governments reinforce the new multiculturalism by funding bilingual education, multilingual voting, diversity training, and the like.

The famous melting-pot metaphor notwithstanding, America has never required a total sacrifice of culture or creed from its immigrants. Instead we've called on prospective citizens to attach their personal heritage to American principles and identity. In a 1997 essay, the Manhattan Institute's Peter Salins identifies three core components of what he calls "assimilation, American style": acceptance of English as the national language, willingness to live by the Protestant work ethic (self-reliance, hard work, moral integrity), and pride in American identity and belief in our democratic principles. Knowing J. Lo from Jay-Z isn't enough, in other words. That's mere "acculturation." Genuine assimilation—true Americanism, in Roosevelt's words—is something more.

Many studies purporting to show that our assimilation system is flourishing do not adopt Roosevelt's standard—that immigrants should embrace Americanism—as their own. A 2010 research report for the Center for American Progress by Dowell Myers and John Pitkin and a 2013 study for the Manhattan Institute by Jacob Vigdor, for example, use the rate at which immigrants become citizens as an index of civic assimilation. Yet citizenship itself in no way guarantees assimilation, as the Tsarnaevs show.

A newly published Hudson Institute study by John Fonte and Althea Nagai provides a more reliable assessment. In "America's Patriotic Assimilation System Is Broken," Fonte and Nagai found wide differences between native-born and naturalized citizens on a series of questions measuring patriotic attachment to the United States. For example, native-born citizens are, by large margins, more likely than immigrant citizens to believe that schools should focus on American citizenship rather than on ethnic pride, or that the U.S. Constitution ought to be a higher legal authority for Americans than international law. Republicans who believe that amnesty for illegal immigrants will be a political boon for the GOP, whether because they view Hispanics as "natural conservatives" or because they hope to win them over in time, may be taking for granted a pattern of assimilation that no longer exists.

America's vaunted ability to forge a cohesive society out of many immigrant strands is now in doubt. The implications of this breakdown range well beyond terrorism, but the connection between terrorism and the weakening of assimilation cannot be dismissed as a side issue.

Salins, in his 1997 essay, presciently singled out several Arab-born perpetrators of the failed 1993 World Trade Center bombing as pure examples of "acculturation without assimilation." These men were quite familiar with American society. The sister of one of the ringleaders said of her brother, "We always considered him a son of America. He was always saying, 'I want to live in America forever.'" As observers on both left and right have pointed out since the Marathon bombings, post-9/11 terror attacks in Europe were likewise carried out by plotters conversant with the culture of their targets.

Many of those terrorists were children of poorly assimilated immigrants from Muslim countries. These second-generation European Muslims had an easy familiarity with the ways of their birthplace, yet they never felt quite at home in the adopted countries of their still unassimilated parents. Caught between two worlds, fully belonging to neither, these young men turned to radical Islam for certainty and identity when they felt the hard knocks of adulthood. The same thing happened to the Tsarnaevs. The collapse of cultural self-confidence in the West has left us with too little spiritual food to offer the children of Muslim immigrants, leaving some to turn to militant Islam in a search for lost roots. This suggests that opening our doors to new citizens without first paring back the excesses of multiculturalism and confidently reasserting traditional American principles of assimilation is asking for trouble.

Unlike immigration from regions wracked by violent ethnic and religious conflict, such as the Tsarnaevs' homeland, Hispanic immigration raises no specter of terrorism. Yet the abandonment of Roosevelt-style assimilation has caused problems for the immigrants themselves. In 2000, Brookings Institution scholar Peter Skerry described a process by which the children of such immigrants undergo a sort of reverse assimilation. According to Skerry, many Mexican Americans who largely assimilate into majority-Anglo environments in their K–12 years, scarcely even thinking of themselves as members of a minority group, dramatically change when they reach college. The politicized multiculturalism that dominates America's universities substantially deassimilates many of them, leading them to attribute virtually all of their discontent to race-based grievances. That process may not make for terrorism, but it won't foster civil comity either, much less a raft of Republican recruits.

The reversal of assimilation at the university is by no means a worst-case scenario. Too often, says Skerry, high-school-aged Latinos born in the United States are "prone to adopt an adversarial stance toward school and a cynical anti-achievement ethic." Even left-leaning assimilation researchers such as Marcelo and Carola Suárez-Orozco, who want more multiculturalism, not less, describe the tough urban schools that many immigrants attend as riven by racial and ethnic tensions. The Manhattan Institute's Heather Mac Donald recently called the fast-growing split between America's English-speaking and Spanish-speaking cultures "E pluribus duo."

Fixing our broken system of assimilation won't be easy, because the problem is deeply rooted. Fonte and Nagai propose doing away with the apparatus of state and federal supports for multiculturalism and bilingualism. That step would surely have positive consequences beyond the programs directly affected by the change, and Republican leaders should advocate it. They also ought to insist on guarantees of border security that far exceed those on offer in the Senate's "Gang of Eight" immigration proposal before considering a path to citizenship. Should Democrats demur, it will show they were never truly serious about comprehensive immigration reform to begin with.

Critical Thinking

1. What sentiments about immigrants and "True Americanism" did Teddy Roosevelt hold and do you agree with them?

2. What are your views about multiculturalism programs and their goals at your school or college?

Create Central

www.mhhe.com/createcentral

Internet References

Hudson Institute

www.hudson.org/index.cfm?fuseaction=publication_details&id=9569

The Newberry: Foreign Language Press Survey

http://flps.newberry.org/article/5423404_2_0244

STANLEY KURTZ is a senior fellow at the Ethics and Public Policy Center.

Article

Prepared by: Bruce Stinebrickner, *DePauw University*

Survival of the Richest

The recession left the middle class treading water. But it's been smooth sailing for the 1 percent.

DAVE GILSON

Learning Outcomes

After reading this article, you will be able to:

• Summarize the economic situations of the very wealthy and the rest of Americans, both in the present and in the past.

• Ponder whether the overall picture of income and wealth distribution in the United States should be a cause for concern. And discuss why or why not.

• Read and assess the statements of six billionaires that appear at the end of this selection.

• Discuss why you do or do not essentially agree or disagree with the sentiments the six billionaires express.

T he Great Recession officially ended five years ago, but that's news for millions of Americans: A stunning 95 percent of income growth since the recovery started has gone to the superwealthy. If an average household currently earning $71,000 had enjoyed the same gains as the 1 percent since 2000, it would now make more than $83,000. And the widening income gap is not just about the 1 percent anymore: Take a closer look, and you'll see that it's really a tiny fraction—the 1 percent of the 1 percent—that hoovers up the lion's share of the nation's wealth. With Washington paralyzed on bread-and-butter issues and the mid-terms ahead, we put together a primer on the state of America's frozen paychecks.

Illustrations By Mattias Mackler

Trickle Up

For every dollar earned by a family in the bottom 90 percent, one in the top 0.01 percent earns nearly $1,000.

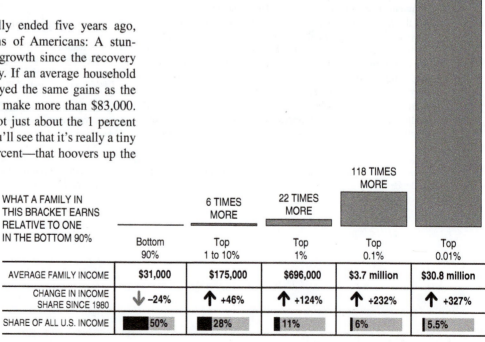

WHAT A FAMILY IN THIS BRACKET EARNS RELATIVE TO ONE IN THE BOTTOM 90%	Bottom 90%	Top 1 to 10%	Top 1%	Top 0.1%	Top 0.01%
		6 TIMES MORE	22 TIMES MORE	118 TIMES MORE	993 TIMES MORE
AVERAGE FAMILY INCOME	$31,000	$175,000	$696,000	$3.7 million	$30.8 million
CHANGE IN INCOME SHARE SINCE 1980	↓ −24%	↑ +46%	↑ +124%	↑ +232%	↑ +327%
SHARE OF ALL U.S. INCOME	50%	28%	11%	6%	5.5%

Whose Recovery?

The top 1 percent has captured almost all post-recession income growth. Compare that with how they did during these historic booms.

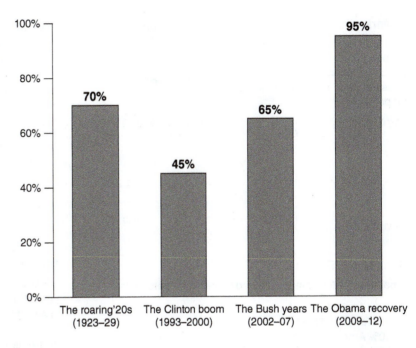

| The roaring '20s (1923–29) | The Clinton boom (1993–2000) | The Bush years (2002–07) | The Obama recovery (2009–12) |
| 70% | 45% | 65% | 95% |

The Rich and the Megarich

Since 1980, the average real income of the 1 percent has shot up more than 175 percent, while the bottom 90 percent's real income didn't budge. But the vast majority of gains have gone to the tippy-top.

Working More, Earning Less

You're working harder than ever, but you're still treading water. In 2012, the median household income had dropped to where it was in 1996 (adjusted for inflation).

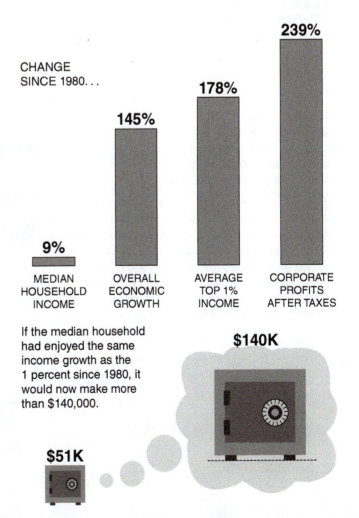

CHANGE SINCE 1980...

| MEDIAN HOUSEHOLD INCOME | OVERALL ECONOMIC GROWTH | AVERAGE TOP 1% INCOME | CORPORATE PROFITS AFTER TAXES |
| 9% | 145% | 178% | 239% |

If the median household had enjoyed the same income growth as the 1 percent since 1980, it would now make more than $140,000.

$140K

$51K

X Marks the Spot

For the first time in a century, the top 10 percent of Americans control more than half of all income. Economist Thomas Piketty foresees that their share soon will rise to 60 percent.

SHARE OF TOTAL INCOME

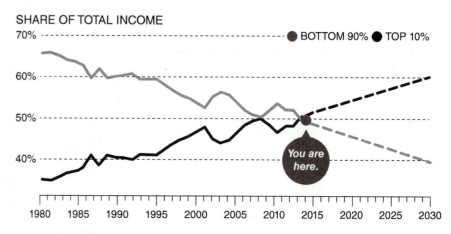

Back to the Future

Amount of total income controlled by the top 1 percent in…

16% Ancient Rome*
7% America 1774*
10% America 1860*
22% America 1929
10% America 1960
22% America 2012

*Includes slaves

Race to the Bottom

Whites' average household income is 56 percent larger than blacks' and 39 percent larger than Hispanics'. But the discrepancy is even bigger when it comes to wealth: The median white family holds nearly 20 times more assets than the median black family and 74 times more assets than the median Hispanic family.

Median assets of white families **$97,000**
Median assets of black families **$4,900**
Median assets of Hispanic families **$1,300**

The Asset Crash

Looking beyond income to assets like houses and stocks gives a broader picture of Americans' financial health. Here, too, the recovery's gains have yet to trickle down.

● Bottom 90%
○ Top 10%

Between 2007 and 2010, Americans' median real net worth hit its lowest level since the late 1960s, largely due to the collapse of the housing market. Nearly one-quarter of Americans had negative net worth in 2010.

SHARE OF TOTAL GAINS IN NET WORTH BETWEEN 1983 AND 2010

SHARE OF TOTAL NET WORHT IN 2010

SHARE OF TOTAL ASSETS AND DEBTS

● Top 1%   ○ Bottom 99%

MEDIAN NET WORTH OF ALL HOUSEHOLDS

$107,800
2007

$57,000
2010

Securities
64% | 36%

Principal Residence
9% | 91%

Debt
6% | 94%

Happy Returns

Even as the incomes of the 1 percent have risen, their taxes have plummeted.

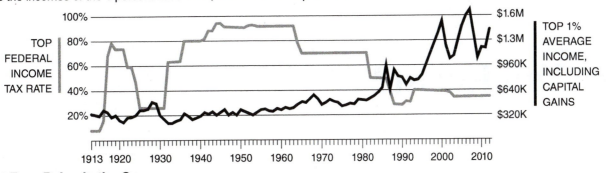

It's Not Easy Being in the Green

Billionaires weigh in on the oppression of the wealthy.

"If you go back to 1933, with different words, this is what Hitler was saying in Germany. You don't survive as a society if you encourage and thrive on envy or jealousy."

HOME DEPOT COFOUNDER KEN LANGONE

"This country should not talk about envy of the 1 percent. It should talk about emulating the 1 percent. The 1 percent work harder."

"DISTRESSED ASSET KING" SAM ZELL

"It's a war... it's like when Hitler invaded Poland in 1939."

BLACKSTONE GROUP CHAIRMAN STEPHEN SCHWARZMAN ON EFFORTS TO RAISE TAXES ON PRIVATE-EQUITY FIRMS

"President Obama is a member of a minority and as such I'm sure during his lifetime he has been prejudiced against. . .Now he's doing the exact same thing, talking about the top 1 percent as if there's something wrong with us."

CYPRESS SEMICONDUCTOR CEO TJ RODGERS

"I would call attention to the parallels of fascist Nazi Germany to its war on its '1 percent,' namely its jews, to the progressive war on the American 1 percent, namely the 'rich.'"

VENTURE CAPITALIST TOM PERKINS

"Hedge funds really need a community organizer."

AQR CAPITAL MANAGEMENT MANAGING PARTNER CLIFF ASNESS ON OBAMA'S "BULLYING" OF HEDGE FUNDS

Critical Thinking

1. What have been the trends since 1980 in the distribution of income in the United States?

2. Compare how the top one percent of income-earners fared in the 1920s, the 1990s, the George W. Bush years, and the 2009–2012 recovery.

3. Of all the graphs and charts presented in this selection, which ones seem most significant? Why?

Internet References

Encyclopedia Brittanica
   http://www.britannica.com/topic/distribution-of-wealth-and-income
Gallup Poll
   http://www.gallup.com/poll/166904/dissatisfied-income-wealth-distribution.aspxwebsite

Article   Prepared by: Bruce Stinebrickner, *DePauw University*

Are You Racist?

CHRIS MOONEY

Learning Outcomes

After reading this article, you will be able to:

- Assess what psychological research shows about racial prejudice having "innate" components well beyond a particular individual's life experiences.

- Ponder, in light of psychological research on racism, whether the solutions or "interventions" suggested in the article are likely to have much impact on racism in American society.

- Consider whether members of the American public are familiar with the psychological research reported in this selection and, if Americans were familiar with it, whether they would believe it. Do you believe it? Why or why not?

"You're not, like, a total racist bastard," David Amodio tells me. He pauses. "Today." I'm sitting in the soft-spoken cognitive neuroscientist's spotless office nestled within New York University's psychology department, but it feels like I'm at the doctor's, getting a dreaded diagnosis. On his giant monitor, Amodio shows me a big blob of data, a cluster of points depicting where people score on the Implicit Association Test. The test measures racial prejudices that we cannot consciously control. I've taken it three times now. This time around my uncontrolled prejudice, while clearly present, has come in significantly below the average for white people like me.

That certainly beats the first time I took the IAT online, on the website UnderstandingPrejudice.org. That time, my results showed a "strong automatic preference" for European Americans over African Americans. That was not a good thing to hear, but it's extremely common—51 percent of online test takers show moderate to strong bias.

Taking the IAT, one of the most popular tools among researchers trying to understand racism and prejudice, is both extremely simple and pretty traumatic. The test asks you to rapidly categorize images of faces as either "African American" or "European American" while you also categorize words (like "evil," "happy," "awful," and "peace") as either "good" or "bad." Faces and words flash on the screen, and you tap a key, as fast as you can, to indicate which category is appropriate.

Sometimes you're asked to sort African American faces and "good" words to one side of the screen. Other times, black faces are to be sorted with "bad" words. As words and faces keep flashing by, you struggle not to make too many sorting mistakes.

And then suddenly, you have a horrible realization. When black faces and "bad" words are paired together, you feel yourself becoming faster in your categorizing—an indication that the two are more easily linked in your mind. "It's like you're on a bike going downhill," Amodio says, "and you feel yourself going faster. So you can say, 'I know this is not how I want to come off,' but there's no other response option."

You think of yourself as a person who strives to be unprejudiced, but you can't control these split-second reactions. As the milliseconds are being tallied up, you know the tale they'll tell: When negative words and black faces are paired together, you're a better, faster categorizer. Which suggests that racially biased messages from the culture around you have shaped the very wiring of your brain.

I went to NYU to learn what psychologists could tell me about racial prejudice in the wake of the shooting of a black teenager, Michael Brown, by a white police officer, Darren Wilson, in Ferguson, Missouri. We may never really know the exact sequence of events and assumptions that led to the moment when Brown, unarmed and, according to witnesses, with his hands in the air, was shot multiple times. But the incident is the latest embodiment of America's racial paradox: On the one hand, overt expressions of prejudice have grown markedly less common than they were in the Archie Bunker era. We elected, and reelected, a black president. In many parts of the country, hardly anyone bats an eye at interracial relationships.

Most people do not consider racial hostility acceptable. That's why it was so shocking when Los Angeles Clippers owner Donald Sterling was caught telling his girlfriend not to bring black people to games—and why those comments led the NBA to ban Sterling for life. And yet, the killings of Michael Brown, Jordan Davis, Renisha McBride, Trayvon Martin, and so many others remind us that we are far from a prejudice-free society.

Science offers an explanation for this paradox—albeit a very uncomfortable one. An impressive body of psychological research suggests that the men who killed Brown and Martin need not have been conscious, overt racists to do what they did (though they may have been). The same goes for the crowds that flock to support the shooter each time these tragedies become public, or the birthers whose racially tinged conspiracy theories paint President Obama as a usurper. These people who voice mind-boggling opinions while swearing they're not racist at all—they make sense to science, because the paradigm for understanding prejudice has evolved. There "doesn't need to be intent, doesn't need to be desire; there could even be desire in the opposite direction," explains University of Virginia psychologist Brian Nosek, a prominent IAT researcher. "But biased results can still occur."

The IAT is the most famous demonstration of this reality, but it's just one of many similar tools. Through them, psychologists have chased prejudice back to its lair—the human brain.

We're not born with racial prejudices. We may never even have been "taught" them. Rather, explains Nosek, prejudice draws on "many of the same tools that help our minds figure out what's good and what's bad." In evolutionary terms, it's efficient to quickly classify a grizzly bear as "dangerous." The trouble comes when the brain uses similar processes to form negative views about groups of people.

But here's the good news: Research suggests that once we understand the psychological pathways that lead to prejudice, we just might be able to train our brains to go in the opposite direction.

Dog, cat. Hot, cold. Black, white. Male, female. We constantly categorize. We have to. Sorting anything from furniture to animals to concepts into different filing folders inside our brains is something that happens automatically, and it helps us function. In fact, categorization has an evolutionary purpose: Assuming that all mushrooms are poisonous, that all lions want to eat you, is a very effective way of coping with your surroundings. Forget being nuanced about nonpoisonous mushrooms and occasionally nonhungry lions—certitude keeps you safe.

But a particular way of categorizing can be inaccurate, and those false categories can lead to prejudice and stereotyping. Much psychological research into bias has focused on how people "essentialize" certain categories, which boils down to assuming that these categories have an underlying nature that is tied to inherent and immutable qualities. Like the broader sorting mechanism of categorization, an essentialist cognitive "style" emerges very early in our development and may to some extent be hardwired. Psychologist Susan Gelman of the University of Michigan [10] explains it this way: The category of "things that are white" is not essentialized. It simply contains anything that happens to share the attribute of "white": cars, paint, paper, and so on. There's nothing deep that unites the members of this category.

But now consider white and black *people*. Like other human attributes (gender, age, and sexual orientation, for example), race tends to be strongly—and inaccurately—essentialized. This means that when you think of people in that category, you rapidly or even automatically come up with assumptions about their characteristics—characteristics that your brain perceives as unchanging and often rooted in biology. Common stereotypes with the category "African Americans," for example, include "loud," "good dancers," and "good at sports." (One recent study found that white people also tend to essentialize African Americans as magical—test subjects associated black faces with words like "paranormal" and "spirit.") Of course, these assumptions are false. Indeed, essentialism about any group of people is dubious—women are not innately gentle, old people are not inherently feebleminded—and when it comes to race, the idea of deep and fundamental differences has been roundly debunked by scientists.

Even people who know that essentializing race is wrong can't help absorbing the stereotypes that are pervasive in our culture. But essentialist thinking varies greatly between individuals. It's kind of like neurosis: We all have a little bit, but in some people, it's much more pronounced. In national polls, for example, fewer and fewer Americans admit openly to holding racist views. But when told to rate various groups with questions like, "Do people in these groups tend to be unintelligent or tend to be intelligent?" more than half of those asked exhibited strong bias against African Americans [11]. Even the labels we use seem to affect our level of prejudice: Another study found that test subjects associated the term "black" with more negative attributes [12]—such as low socioeconomic status—than "African American."

One of the earliest and most insightful researchers on these varying rates of bias was Else Frenkel-Brunswik, part of a pioneering generation of post-World War II psychologists who sought to understand why some people seem to find prejudiced and fascist ideas so appealing. Born in 1908 to a Jewish family in what is now Ukraine, Frenkel-Brunswik might never have managed to do her research at all had she not twice escaped the forces of prejudice herself. When she was young, a 1914 pogrom forced her family to flee to Vienna. When Germany annexed Austria in 1938, she sought refuge in the United States.

Frenkel-Brunswik's work came long before the days of high-tech tools like eye trackers and computer games that measure bias based on millisecond differences between reactions. Instead she used something far simpler: cards.

She studied young children, some of whom she had previously documented to be highly prejudiced and ethnocentric. In one of many experiments, Frenkel-Brunswik showed the children a sequence of cards. On the first card, the animal is clearly and distinctly a cat. On the last card, it is just as clearly and distinctly a dog. But in between, the cat slowly transforms into the dog.

At each of the stages, the children were asked to identify the animal on the card. Among the more prejudiced children, Frenkel-Brunswik noted something striking: As the image became increasingly ambiguous, "there was a greater reluctance to give up the original object about which one had felt relatively certain…a tendency not to see what did not harmonize with the first set as well as a shying away from transitional solutions." In other words, for these children, it was much harder to let go of the idea that a cat was a cat.

What Frenkel-Brunswik realized back in 1949, modern research reaffirms. The Implicit Association Test, after all, boils down to how your mind automatically links certain categories. "It's really how strongly you associate your category of 'black people' with the general category of 'good things' or 'bad things,'" David Amodio told me. "The capacity to discern 'us' from 'them' is fundamental in the human brain," he wrote in a 2014 paper. "Although this computation takes just a fraction of a second, it sets the stage for social categorization, stereotypes, prejudices, intergroup conflict and inequality, and, at the extremes, war and genocide." Call it the banality of prejudice.

The process of categorizing the world obviously includes identifying the group or groups to which you belong. And that's where the next psychological factor underpinning prejudice emerges. Much research has found that humans are tribal creatures, showing strong bias against those we perceive as different from us and favoritism toward those we perceive as similar.

In fact, we humans will divide ourselves into in-groups and out-groups even when the perceived differences between the specific groups are completely arbitrary. In one classic study [20], subjects are asked to rate how much they like a large series of paintings, some of which are described as belonging to the "Red" artistic school and others to the "Green" school. Then participants are sorted into two groups, red or green—not based on their favoring one school of painting, as they are made to think, but actually at random. In subsequent tasks, people consistently show favoritism toward the arbitrary color group to which they are assigned. When asked to allocate money to other participants, the majority of "reds" more generously fund other reds—despite the fact that they have never actually met them. The same goes for "greens."

The upshot of such "minimal group" experiments is that if you give people the slightest push toward behaving tribally, they happily comply. So if race is the basis on which tribes are identified, expect serious problems.

As these experiments suggest, it is not that we are either prejudiced or unprejudiced, period. Rather, we are more and less prejudiced, based on our upbringings and experiences but also on a variety of temporary or situational prompts (like being told we're on the green team).

One simple, evolutionary explanation for our innate tendency toward tribalism is safety in numbers. You're more likely to survive an attack from a marauding tribe if you join forces with your buddies. And primal fear of those not in the in-group also seems closely tied to racial bias. Amodio's research suggests that one key area associated with prejudice is the amygdala, a small and evolutionarily ancient region in the middle of the brain that is responsible for triggering the notorious "fight or flight" response. In interracial situations, Amodio explains, amygdala firing can translate into anything from "less direct eye gaze and more social distance" to literal fear and vigilance toward those of other races.

We've seen how a variety of cognitive behaviors feed into prejudice. But you know what will really blow your mind? The way that prejudice (or rather, the cognitive styles that underlie it) can interfere with how our brains function—often for the worse.

Consider, for instance, research by Carmit Tadmor, a psychologist at the Recanati School of Business at Tel Aviv University. In one 2013 paper, Tadmor and her colleagues showed that racial prejudice can play a direct and causal role in making people less creative. We're not talking about artistic creativity here, but more like seeing beyond the constraints of traditional categories—"thinking outside the box."

Tadmor's team first uncovered a simple positive correlation between one's inclination to endorse an essentialist view of race (like associating racial differences with abilities and personality traits) and one's creativity. To measure the latter, the researchers used a simple open-ended test in which individuals are asked to list as many possible uses of a brick as they can think of. People who can think outside of traditional categories—realizing that a brick can be used for many things other than buildings (it can make a good paperweight, for starters)—score better. This study showed that people who essentialized racial categories tended to have fewer innovative ideas about a brick.

But that was just the beginning. Next, a new set of research subjects read essays that described race either as a fundamental difference between people (an essentialist position) or as a construct, not reflecting anything more than skin-deep differences (a nonessentialist position). After reading the essays, the subjects moved on to a difficult creativity test that requires you to identify the one key word that unites three seemingly unassociated words. Thus, for instance, if you are given the words "call," "pay," and "line," the correct answer is "phone."

Remarkably, subjects who'd read the nonessentialist essay about race fared considerably better on the creativity test. Their mean score was a full point—or 32 percent—higher than it was for those who read the essentialist essay.

It's not like the people in this study were selected because of their preexisting racial prejudices. They weren't. Instead, merely a temporary exposure to essentialist thinking seemed to hamper their cognitive flexibility. "Essentialism appears to exert its negative effects on creativity not through *what* people think but *how* they think," conclude Tadmor and her colleagues. That's because, they add, "stereotyping and creative stagnation are rooted in a similar tendency to overrely on existing category attributes." Those quick-judgment skills that allowed us to survive on the savanna? Not always helpful in modern life.

So, yes: Prejudice and essentialism are bad for your brain—if you value creative thinking, anyway. But they can also be downright dangerous.

At NYU, David Amodio sat me down to take another test called the Weapons Identification Task. I had no idea what I was in for.

In this test, like on the IAT, you have two buttons that you can push. Images flash rapidly on the screen, and your task is to push the left shift key if you see a tool (a wrench, or a power drill, say) and the right shift key if you see a gun. You have to go super fast—if you don't respond within half a second, the screen blares at you, in giant red letters, "TOO SLOW."

"It does that to keep you from thinking too much," Amodio would later explain.

But it's not just guns and tools flashing on the screen: Before each object you see a face, either white or black. The faces appear for a split second, the objects for a split second, and then you have to press a key. If you are faster and more accurate at identifying guns after you see a black face than after you see a white face, that would suggest your brain associates guns (and threat) more with the former. You might also be more inclined to wrongly think you see a gun, when it's actually just a tool, right after seeing a black face. (The weapons task was created by psychologist Keith Payne of the University of North Carolina-Chapel Hill in response to the tragic 1999 death of Amadou Diallo, a Guinean immigrant shot by New York City police after the officers mistook the wallet in his hand for a weapon.)

I'm sorry to ruin the suspense: I don't know what my score was on the Weapons Identification Task. The test ruffled me so much that I messed up badly. It is stressful to have to answer quickly to avoid being rebuked by the game. And it's even more upsetting to realize that you've just "seen" a gun that wasn't actually there, right after a black face flashed.

This happened to me several times, and then I suddenly found myself getting "TOO SLOW" messages whenever the object to be identified was a gun. This went on for many minutes and numerous trials. For a while, I thought the test was broken. But it wasn't: I finally realized that rather than pressing the right shift key, I had somehow started pressing the enter key whenever I thought I saw a gun. It's almost like I'd subconsciously decided to stop making "gun" choices at all. (Psychoanalyze that.)

But don't take that as a cop-out: Before I (arguably) tried to dodge responsibility by pressing the wrong key, I clearly showed implicit bias. And it was horrifying.

The upshot of all of this research is that in order to rid the world of prejudice, we can't simply snuff out overt, conscious, full-throated racism. Nor can we fundamentally remake the human brain, with its rapid-fire associations and its categorizing, essentializing, and groupish tendencies. Instead, the key lies in shifting people's behavior, even as we also make them aware of how cultural assumptions merge with natural cognitive processes to create biases they may not know they have.

And that just might be possible. Take the Implicit Association Test: In a massive study, Brian Nosek of the University of Virginia and his colleagues tested 17 different proposed ways [24] of reducing people's unconscious bias on the IAT. Many of these experimental interventions failed. But some succeeded, and there was an interesting pattern to those that did.

The single best intervention involved putting people into scenarios and mindsets in which a black person became their ally (or even saved their life) while white people were depicted as the bad guys. In this intervention, participants "read an evocative story told in second-person narrative in which a White man assaults the participant and a Black man rescues the participant." In other words, study subjects are induced to feel as if they have been personally helped or even saved by someone from a different race. Then they took the IAT—and showed 48 percent less bias than a control group. (Note: The groups in these various studies were roughly three-fourths white; no participants were black.)

Other variations on this idea were successful too: making nonblack people think about black role models, or imagine themselves playing on a dodgeball team with black teammates against a team of white people (who proceed to cheat). In other words, it appears that our tribal instincts can actually be co-opted to decrease prejudice, if we are made to see those of other races as part of our team.

When it comes to weakening racial essentialism, Carmit Tadmor and her colleagues undertook a variety of experiments to try to produce what they called "epistemic unfreezing." Subjects were exposed to one of three 20-minute multimedia presentations: one exclusively about American culture, one exclusively about Chinese culture, and one comparing American and Chinese cultures (with different aspects of each culture, such as architecture or food, presented back to back). Only in the last scenario were subjects pushed to compare and contrast the two cultures, presumably leading to a more nuanced perspective on their similarities and differences.

This experimental manipulation has been found to increase creativity. But surprisingly, it also had a big effect on reducing anti-black prejudice. In one study, Tadmor et al. found that white research subjects who had heard the multicultural presentation (but not the American-only or Chinese-only presentation) were less likely than members of the other study groups to endorse stereotypes about African Americans. That was true even though the subjects had learned about Chinese and American cultures, not African American culture.

In a variation, the same 20-minute lecture also produced fewer discriminatory hiring decisions. After hearing one of the three kinds of lectures, white study subjects were shown a series of résumés for the position of "Sales Manager" at a company. The résumés were varied so that some applicants had white-sounding names, and some had black-sounding names. It's a research paradigm that has often been shown to produce discriminatory effects, which presumably occur through the manifestation of uncontrolled or implicit prejudices—but this time around, there was a glimmer of hope in the findings.

White subjects who had heard the lecture exclusively about American culture (with topics like Disney, Coca-Cola, and the White House) picked a white candidate over an equally qualified black candidate 81 percent of the time. Subjects who had heard a lecture exclusively about Chinese culture picked a white candidate a full 86 percent of the time. But subjects who had heard the culture-comparing lecture selected the white candidate only 56 percent of the time.

These studies clearly suggest that, at least for the relatively short time span of a psychology experiment, there are cognitive ways to make people less prejudiced. That's not the same as—nor can it be a substitute for—broader cultural or institutional change. After all, there is ample evidence that culture feeds directly into the mind's process of generating prejudices and adopting stereotypical beliefs.

Nonetheless, if prejudice has both a psychological side and a cultural side, we must address both of these aspects. A good start may simply be making people aware of just how unconsciously biased they can be. That's particularly critical in law enforcement, where implicit biases can lead to tragic outcomes.

In fact, this phenomenon has been directly studied in the lab, particularly through first-person shooter tests, where subjects must rapidly decide whether to shoot individuals holding either guns or harmless objects like wallets and soda cans. Research suggests that police officers (those studied were mostly white) are much more accurate at the general task (not shooting unarmed people) than civilians, thanks to their training. But like civilians, police are considerably slower to press the "don't shoot" button for an unarmed black man than they are for an unarmed white man—and faster to shoot an armed black man than an armed white man. (Women weren't included—the extra variable of gender would have complicated the results.)

Such research has led to initiatives like the Fair and Impartial Policing program [26], which has trained officers across the United States on how implicit biases work and how to control them. Few officers look forward to these trainings, says program founder Lorie Fridell [27], a criminologist; they don't consider themselves to be racist. "Police are very defensive about this issue," she says. "That's because we have been dealing with this issue using outdated science. We treat them as if they have an explicit bias. They are offended by that."

So instead, Fridell's team focuses first on showing the officers the subtle ways in which implicit bias might influence their actions. For example: The trainers present a role-play where there are three people: a female victim of domestic violence, and a male and female comforting her. When the officers are asked to address the situation, says Fridell, most assume that the man is the perp. Then, the trainers reveal that it was actually the woman—and the officers learn that they do, in fact, act on bias. It's not because they are bad people; in fact, in their work, they may have experiences that reinforce stereotypes. Which is why it's important that police officers—who see the worst in people in their everyday duties—teach themselves not to *assume* the worst.

The program, which receives support from the US Department of Justice, has trained officers in more than 250 precincts and agencies, but it's hard to measure its success—there is no baseline comparison, since prejudiced policing isn't always rigorously documented. But the feedback is encouraging. "I have a new awareness of bias-based policing within my own agency," one participant wrote in an evaluation [28]. "The presentation of scientific data provided me with a more convincing argument that supported the existence of unintentional, but widespread racial bias, which I was typically quick to dismiss."

Staff members at the University of California-Los Angeles-based Center for Policing Equity [29] use implicit-bias research in a different way: They take unconscious prejudice as a given—and try to make changes within communities to ensure that it does as little damage as possible. A few years ago, Las Vegas was seeking to address police officers' use of force [30], especially against people of color. Most of the incidents occurred after pursuits of suspects on foot, the majority of which happened in nonwhite neighborhoods. Center president Phillip Atiba Goff [31] explains that he knew how difficult it would be to change the pursuing officers' thinking. "You're an officer, you're pumping adrenaline, you don't have time to evaluate whether your implicit bias is driving your behavior," he says. So instead, the center worked with the department to make a small but meaningful tweak to the rules: In foot chases, the pursuing officer would no longer be allowed to touch the person being chased; if use of force was necessary, a partner who wasn't involved in the pursuit would step in. "We recognized implicit bias, and we took it out of the equation," Goff says. "We decoupled the prejudice from the behavior." Sure enough, use of force in foot chases—and, as a result, overall use of force against people of color—declined significantly shortly after the policy went into effect.

Unsettling though it is, the latest research on our brains could actually have some very positive outcomes—if we use it in the right way. The link between essentialism and creativity doesn't just tell us how we might reduce prejudice. It could also help us to become a more innovative country—by prioritizing diversity, and the cognitive complexity and boost in creativity it entails. The research on rapid-fire, implicit biases, meanwhile, should restart a debate over the role of media—the news segment that depicts immigrants as hostile job snatchers, the misogynistic lyrics in a song—in subtly imparting stereotypes that literally affect brain wiring. Indeed, you could argue that not only does the culture in which we live make us subtly prejudiced, but it does so against our will. That's a disturbing thought.

Especially when you consider how biases affect government policy. Consider this: In October 2012, researchers from the University of Southern California sent emails asking legislators [32] in districts with large Latino populations what documentation was needed in order to vote. Half the emails came from people with Anglo-sounding names; the other half, Latino-sounding names. Republican politicians who had sponsored voter ID laws responded to 27 percent of emails from "Latino" constituents and 67 percent of emails from "white" constituents. For Republicans who'd voted against voter ID laws, the gap was far less dramatic—the response figures were 38 percent for Latino names and 54 percent for white names.

You can imagine how this kind of thing might create a vicious cycle: When biased legislators make it harder for certain communities to vote, they are also less likely to serve alongside lawmakers from those communities—thus making it less likely for a coalitional experience to change their biases.

So how do we break the cycle? We could require lawmakers to engage in exercises to recognize their own unconscious prejudice, like the Fair and Impartial Policing program does. Or we could even go a step further and anonymize emails they receive from constituents—thus taking implicit bias out of the equation.

Short of that, you can do something very simple to fight prejudice: Trick your brain. UNC-Chapel Hill's Payne suggests that by deliberately thinking a thought that is directly counter to widespread stereotypes, you can break normal patterns of association. What counts as counterstereotypical? Well, Payne's study found that when research subjects were instructed to think the word "safe" whenever they saw a black face—undermining the stereotypical association between black people and danger—they were 10 percent less likely than those in a control group to misidentify a gun in the Weapons Identification Task.

To be sure, it will take more than thought exercises to erase the deep tracks of prejudice America has carved through the generations. But consciousness and awareness are a start—and the psychological research is nothing if not a consciousness-raiser. Taking the IAT made me realize that we can't just draw some arbitrary line between prejudiced people and unprejudiced people, and declare ourselves to be on the side of the angels. Biases have slipped into all of our brains. And that means we all have a responsibility to recognize those biases—and work to change them.

Critical Thinking

1. What is the gist of the scientific explanation for racial prejudice? Do you find it convincing? Why or why not?
2. How is evolutionary theory thought to relate to racial prejudice in human beings today?
3. Describe several of the psychological tests that provide fundamental insights into racial prejudice.

Internet References

The Huffington Post
   http://www.huffingtonpost.com/news/racism-in-america
PBS Newshour
   http://www.pbs.org/newshour/updates/americas-racism-problem-far-complicated-think

Article   Prepared by: Bruce Stinebrickner, *DePauw University*

Our Revolution Has Just Begun

"I would be crazy if I didn't understand that this was a medal for the entire women's movement," said Gloria Steinem on receiving the Presidential Medal of Freedom, the highest civilian honor in the U.S. Steinem's recognition was for her work on behalf of women's equality and empowerment.

On the eve of the White House awards ceremony this past November, Steinem—the esteemed writer, strategist and cofounder of *Ms.*—gave a talk at the National Press Club in Washington, D.C., before an audience of journalists and feminist leaders and activists. In that speech, which she has adapted here, she looked ahead at some of the critical unfinished goals of the feminist movement—including equal valuing of women's work, ending violence against women, recognizing reproductive freedom as a basic human right, and uprooting racism and sexism together.

GLORIA STEINEM

Learning Outcomes

After reading this article, you will be able to:

- Identify and assess what are said to be two important myths about the women's movement.

- Summarize and assess a number of issues relating to women and gender equality that remain problematic for Gloria Steinem.

If I had to pick a couple of myths about the women's movement that are most wrong, I think two might be tied for worst place. One is that this movement—also known as women's liberation, feminism, womanism, mujerista, grrrls and more—is only for white, middle-class women. The second is that the need for a movement is over, and we are now in a post-feminist and post-racist age.

From the beginning, the first myth was the opposite of fact. For instance, a 1972 poll by Louis Harris and Associates—the first to survey U.S. women on issues of our own equality—showed that black women were almost *twice* as likely as white women to support these issues. It shouldn't have been a surprise. The same could be learned from listening to Shirley Chisholm, or reading Alice Walker or, later, reading *Feminism Is for Everybody* by bell hooks or blogs and websites by girls and women of color who are on the cutting edge. That "white, middle-class" claim turned out to be mostly a way of turning women off change. So was its global version: that feminism was a luxury of rich Western countries. As we now see, women's movements for equality are global and basic, from New Delhi to the Democratic Republic of the Congo, from Liberia to Liberation Square.

The second myth is that women of the 1970s did all that could or should be done, and young women can now relax; feminism was their mothers' movement. Even the abolitionist and suffragist era shows how ridiculous this is. If it took more than a century for black men and all women to gain a legal *identity* as citizens instead of chattel, it's likely to take at least a century to gain a legal and social *equality* as everything from workers to candidates to parents. Even equal pay for women who do the same jobs as white men is still in the future, and parenthood and housework aren't equal either, to put it mildly. There is also a powerful backlash to the victories won, with right-wing extremists passing misogynist, racist, immigrant-fearing laws in state legislatures, and redistricting their way into control of Congress. This country still profiteers on the underpaid or unpaid work of females, comes near the bottom of modern democracies in electing women to political office and is at the bottom when it comes to child care or family-friendly work policies.

Let's face it, such deep changes take time. That's why I'm glad that, as I travel, I see more diverse and determined young feminists than ever before in history. In fact, public opinion polls show the majority of young women voters self-identify as feminist. Yet I fear that my age—and that of all of us who started this work in the 1970s—is an excuse to focus on the past.

So I'm listing here a few of the adventures that lie ahead of us. Each is crucial, so there is no order of importance. Take up the one that's part of your life, or you care about most. These are reminders that we're not even halfway there.

- In political campaigns and the media, "women's issues" are mysteriously separated from "economic issues." This conceals solutions. In the last financial crisis, for instance, the government propped up hanks, Detroit, mortgage profiteers and other powers that are overwhelmingly white and male, and rewarded greed or error in the name of economic stimulus. However, the most effective economic stimulus would have been—and would still be—paying women equally for comparable work done by white men.

As the Institute for Women's Policy Research documents, equal pay for equal work would put $200 billion more into the economy every year. That's an average of $148 more per woman per week, more for most women of color since they are likely to be doubly discriminated against. Not only would this money be injected where it's needed most—for instance, helping the poorest kids who depend on a single mother's income, and reducing government money spent on food stamps and other parts of the safety net—but it would reward work and prevent employers from profiteering from discrimination. Also, these women are not going to put their money into a Swiss bank account or invest it in China. They'll spend it here, thus creating jobs. Yet how often do you see "economic stimulus" and "equal pay" in the same sentence?

Besides revaluing work, we also need to redefine it. Almost two-thirds of adults in the United States are caregivers, which includes those raising children and caring for the ill and the growing population of the elderly—yet caregiving is economically invisible. A woman or man who does it full time at home is still called someone who "doesn't work." But it's in the national interest to reward caregiving, which is often higher quality and far less expensive at home than in institutions. So why not value caregiving at replacement level—not the current tiny exemptions—and make that amount tax deductible? Or tax refundable for those too poor to pay taxes? This would require only a change in tax policy, not a piece of legislation. It has been championed for years by Theresa Funiciello, the brilliant economic strategist on poverty, but it will only become a reality when women, who are still the majority of fulltime home caregivers, demand it.

- A woman's ability to decide when and whether to bear a child is not a "social issue"; it is a human right. Like freedom of speech, it affects everything else in life—whether a woman is educated or not, works outside the home or not, is healthy or not, and how long she lives. Nonetheless, as I write this, Pope Francis is being praised for his stance on "economic issues," and forgiven for being no help at all on contraception and abortion. Yet for the female half of the world, reproductive freedom *is* the biggest economic issue.

In this country, we don't yet have reproductive freedom. The United States has the highest rate of unplanned pregnancies, teenage pregnancies, and medically complicated births in the developed world. It also has inadequate sex education, so pornography on the Web often attracts the curiosity that ought to go to sex education—and pornography is about sexualized violence and domination, not sex. It's even present in the words: *Porne* means female slaves; *eros* means love and mutual pleasure. Though the women's movement has shown that rape is about violence, not sex, we're a very long way from understanding that pornography is not erotica. The result is a distortion of human sexuality that endangers women's lives—and children's lives, too. Since pornography focuses on dominance and power and requires submission and helplessness, it often sexualizes children.

- Women with children are less likely to get hired and fairly paid, while men with children are more likely to get hired and *well* paid. This is just the tip of the iceberg. Nothing else is going to be equal in a deep sense until men are raising children as much as women are. Children will continue to grow up believing males *can't* be loving and nurturing, and girls will keep believing they must do that by themselves. Women will go on choosing cold and distant men because those men feel like home. Also, we voters will go on associating female authority with childhood—the main time it was experienced—and thus be uncomfortable with women who lead in public and political life. This is huge. Discomfort with a woman who is powerful has cost this country untold amounts of talent. Read *The Mermaid and the Minotaur* by Dorothy Dinnerstein to discover that men raising children—also participating in childbirth, as in many original societies—is the key to world peace. I think we're finally ready for her.

- The United States is a modern democracy, and yet we don't have some form of a national child-care system. The average cost of child care here has surpassed the average cost of college tuition. I rest my case.

- We are an advanced country that saddles its college students with debt at the exact time when they should be most free to explore. Also, women pay the same tuition as men, yet are paid an average of $1 million less over their lifetimes, making it harder to repay those loans. Which reminds me: Much has been made of the fact that women now slightly outnumber men on college campuses. However, many are just trying to get out of the pink-collar ghetto of low-wage female jobs, and into the white-collar ghetto of slightly better paid female jobs. Also, a campus is a place where women are more welcome because we're paying money to be there; we're consumers. It's when we want to get paid that the trouble starts. Meanwhile, men with only a high school education are earning more than a woman with her associate degree, on average. No wonder fewer men than women are running up a college debt.

- The Digital Divide is a pretty good proxy for world power. For instance, almost 80 percent of Internet users live in Asia, Europe, and North America. The rest of the world makes up a vast minority, and the continent with the fewest is Africa. It also tells us something here at home. Though men and women are only about 1 percent apart in computer use, 63 percent of white non-Hispanic households use the Internet while only 45 percent of black households have access. So let's hear it for public librarians who are fighting to democratize computer use for both children and adults.

- While we're celebrating victories for marriage equality, let's not forget that just 60 percent of people in the United States say that "homosexuality should be accepted by society," while 80 percent of people in Canada do, and so do 87 percent of people in Germany. On campuses, students still ask me why the same groups oppose, say, lesbians *and* birth control. This means many of us don't yet understand that the same groups oppose *all* forms of sexual expression that can't end in conception. Sometimes I fear our opposition understands our shared interests better than we do. This is crucial for females because the big reason for controlling our bodies is to control reproduction. Yet from school and the media, we learn way more about the politics of *production* than the politics of *re*production.

- Do enough people understand that racism and sexism are intertwined, and can only be uprooted together? Think about it: To maintain racial difference, you have to control female bodies. Women of the so-called superior racial group tend to be restricted to maintain "purity"—or at least visible difference—while women of the

so-called inferior group are often exploited to produce cheap labor. This is true for sex and caste in India, where high-caste women are confined and those of low caste are often exploited, just as it is for sex and race here. Yet we hear the media's surrealistic debates about which is more important: race or sex? This is ridiculous for everybody, but especially for women of color—the majority of women in the world—who live both.

- Here's a final shocker: Violence against females in the world has reached such heights that, for what may be the first time in history, females are no longer half the human race. There are now 100 women per 101.3 men on this Spaceship Earth. The causes are everything from son preference, which has produced a son surplus and a daughter deficit in China and other countries, to the lethal results of female genital cutting, domestic violence, sex trafficking, sexualized violence in war zones, honor killings, child marriage, and much more. For instance, child marriage contributes to the fact that the biggest cause of death among teenage girls worldwide is pregnancy and childbirth. Also, consider what happens to the spirit of a mother who must withhold food and medical care from her female child, the child whose body is most like hers.

Before we think these causes of violence are distant, let me remind you that, even by conservative FBI statistics, if you add up all the women in the United States who have been murdered by their husbands or boyfriends since 9/11—and then add up all the Americans killed in 9/11 plus the wars in Iraq and Afghanistan—many more women have been killed by their husbands and boyfriends. Yet we put much more thought and money into ending foreign terrorism than into ending domestic terrorism.

As for those so-called senseless crimes—mass shootings in our schools, workplaces, and movie theaters—they are almost always committed by males, and by males who are white and non-poor, exactly the group most likely to be addicted to supremacy and control. Indeed, those crimes should be called "supremacy crimes." Though we've had the courage to raise our daughters more like our sons, we've rarely had the courage to raise our sons like our daughters. Some brave members of a long-running men's movement are challenging the prison called *masculinity*, but it is not yet in the national consciousness. Even in daily life, we're far more likely to pay attention to the bullied than to address the reasons for bullying.

Thanks to a landmark book by Valerie Hudson and other scholars called *Sex and World Peace,* we now can prove that the biggest indicator of whether a country is violent within itself, or will use military violence against another country, is not poverty, or natural resources, or even degree of democracy: It's violence against females. That's what normalizes all other violence.

How different would our domestic and foreign policy be if we acted on this?

Okay, those are just a few of the adventures ahead. They require making connections—between race and sex and among all our movements that are part of a new world view; between democracy in the family and democracy in public life; between the so-called masculine acts of conquering women and conquering nature; between religions with a male God and cultures of male dominance—and much more. As Bella Abzug would say, our movement started with dependence, is now working toward independence and can envision interdependence. As she put it, we need a declaration of "interdependence."

How do we move forward? It's not rocket science. We need to worry less about doing what is most important, and more about doing whatever we can. Those of us who are used to power need to learn to listen as much as we talk, and those with less power need to learn to talk as much as we listen. The truth is that we can't know which act in the present will make the most difference in the future, but we can behave as *if* everything we do matters.

Even the presence or absence of adjectives can challenge ranking. For instance, everybody except heterosexual white men still tends to require an adjective—as in *women* writers, *black* physicians and *gay* or *lesbian* candidates. The powerful only need the noun. Though we may still need adjectives to make "out" groups visible, we can underline the politics of words by, say, using adjectives for the powerful, too. Thus, Philip Roth is not a novelist, but a *man* novelist, and Donald Trump is not a real estate developer but a *white* real estate developer. Since Hollywood belittles some movies about daily life as "chick flicks," why not call those about daily death "prick flicks."

Nothing is too small—or too big—to change consciousness.

All together, we are changing from a society whose organizing principle is the pyramid or hierarchy to one whose image is the circle. Humans are linked, not ranked. Humans and the environment are linked, not ranked.

And remember, the end doesn't justify the means; the means *are* the ends. If we want dancing and laughter and friendship and kindness in the future, we must have dancing and laughter and friendship and kindness along the way.

That is the small and the big of it.

At my age, in this still hierarchical time, people often ask me if I'm "passing the torch." I explain that I'm keeping my torch, thank you very much—and I'm using it to light the torches of others.

Because only if each of us has a torch will there be enough light.

Critical Thinking

1. What two myths about the women's movement does Gloria Steinem identify? Are you persuaded that they are indeed "myths"?

2. What, according to Gloria Steinem, is the consequence of the "mysterious" separation between "women's issues" and "economic issues" in news media reports and political campaigns? Do you agree?

3. What are the half-dozen or so issues relating to women and gender equality that Steinem identifies as still needing to be addressed? Which do you think are most important?

Create Central

www.mhhe.com/createcentral

Internet References

Feminist.com
http://feminist.com

Gloria Steinem Official Website
www.gloriasteinem.com

Ms. Magazine
www.msmagazine.com

GLORIA STEINEM is cofounder, and currently consulting editor, of Ms. magazine. She also is active with the Women's Media Center, Equality Now and Donor Direct Action.

Article   Prepared by: Bruce Stinebrickner, *DePauw University*

Return to Nixonland

How the NSA slipped its leash.

LISA GRAVES

Learning Outcomes

After reading this article, you will be able to:

- Summarize what President Nixon directed the NSA to do soon after he became president and Congress's reaction to what he had done once members of Congress knew about it.

- Draw and assess parallels between what happened under President Nixon and what happened after 9/11.

- Identify and assess the roles and relevance of courts and the Fourth Amendment in both the Nixon-initiated and post-9/11 activities reported in the article.

The documents leaked by Edward Snowden and published by the *Guardian* and other outlets confirm what privacy advocates have been saying for years: The government has secretly turned its most powerful weapons of foreign intelligence surveillance inward on millions of Americans.

How can an ordinary citizen cut through the brush—with the avalanche of complicated, classified materials released, the flurry of political finger-pointing, and the various denials and narrowly crafted dodges? Welcome to a guided tour of the National Security Agency (NSA) scandal. We'll explore how we got here and what Nixon's got to do with it.

Who? Me?

The NSA has rebuffed demands by some in Congress for an estimate of the number of Americans whose information has been gathered, stored, and searched, but the math is simple. Unless you are a child, a Luddite or a hermit who has never dialed a phone or used the Internet, records of your phone calls and online interactions have been captured by the NSA.

This includes your number and everyone you dial or text, plus how often and how long you talk, as well as your location—although the NSA has claimed it doesn't actually use the location data. In other words, the NSA has the fact of all your calls with your friends, family, lover(s), bank(s), and doctors' offices for whatever ails you, along with calls to psychic hotlines or phone sex workers, if that's your thing. The number of innocent Americans affected: at least 260 million.

That's not all. For nearly a decade, the NSA was gathering records about Americans' "Internet transactions," including "metadata" such as the "to, from, cc, and bcc lines of a standard email," when your email was sent and opened, your IP address and location, and an array of data about you as you search the Internet, and interact with friends and strangers through social media. That program is no longer *authorized* by a secret court in Washington, D.C., but whether it continues is unknown. Also unknown: whether the NSA's gathering of Americans' credit card transactions is continuing or was secretly stopped.

Even that's not all. Though the NSA has emphasized that it does not obtain the "contents" of your calls or emails through *this* program, the government has decided that the contents of *all* international phone calls and emails "to or from" Americans and others abroad are fair game for acquisition by the NSA without a warrant. At least 40 million American citizens travel internationally each year, and America is home to 40 million immigrants, who call or email their loved ones overseas about their most intimate worries and desires.

And there's more. Newly declassified documents prove that countless purely "domestic" conversations between innocent Americans here in the United States have also been acquired and searched by the NSA.

Additionally, the affidavits in lawsuits filed in 2006 by the Electronic Frontier Foundation present evidence that shortly after 9/11 the NSA installed "NARUS" devices at AT&T's

main transmission station in San Francisco and at other telecommunications hubs across the country. Those devices are designed to make a duplicate of the communications stream (content and data) as it passes through the system at the speed of light.

Accordingly, such devices can give the NSA access to all American domestic and international phone calls and Internet activity that travel through AT&T, which provides the backbone of the communications system that other phone and Internet service providers rely on. So, as a technological matter, if law were no barrier, the evidence indicates that the NSA could technically acquire, store, and analyze almost every word spoken or written on American phones and computers.

Snowden's revelations include Power Point presentations referencing an array of tools—with code names like "PRISM"—the NSA has used to target the social media activities, Internet searches and emails of specific people. But there's still a lot we don't know. And that's a problem in a democracy in which the government is supposed to govern by consent of the people.

Sen. Frank Church (D-Idaho), 1975: "The technological capacity that the intelligence community has given the government could enable it to impose total tyranny."

The Risk of "Total Tyranny"

Sen. Frank Church (D-Idaho) said after his investigation of the NSA in 1975, following leaks about President Richard M. Nixon's use of the NSA to spy on his enemies, opponents of the war in Vietnam and others:

> If this government ever became a tyrant, if a dictator ever took charge in this country, the technological capacity that the intelligence community has given the government could enable it to impose total tyranny, and there would be no way to fight back because the most careful effort to combine together in resistance to the government, no matter how privately it was done, is within the reach of the government to know. Such is the capability of this technology. . . . We must see to it that this agency and all agencies that possess this technology operate within the law and under proper supervision so that we never cross over that abyss. That is the abyss from which there is no return.

Those were the late Senator Church's fears *before* almost every American had a "smart phone" and *before* most of us heard of the Internet—which in the 1970s was merely a

computer network within the Pentagon and a few Silicon Valley companies—let alone traversed it daily.

Indeed, before Google was a word, let alone an empire; before almost all of our telephone conversations, emails, and transactions of daily life were transmuted into a searchable digital world; and before a handful of murderers crashed into the World Trade Center and the Pentagon on September 11, 2001, we needed greater protections for our privacy and liberty.

Now that need is even more urgent.

Along with the seismic transformation in the way we communicate, the legal controls on the NSA's powers have been systematically loosened, if not obliterated, by the White House, Congress and the courts at the urging of leaders of the military intelligence community.

The NSA says it has "internal controls" but once information about Americans is stored by the NSA—including in a gargantuan 1-million-square-foot data storehouse being finalized in Bluffdale, Utah—it can be accessed by numerous civilians at home and abroad. The agency claims there have been only 12 incidents of NSA staffers using its "Signals Intelligence" (SIGINT) improperly. Most of them spied on lovers, such as girlfriends suspected of infidelity. However, almost all of these were discovered only through polygraph tests of workers renewing security clearances. How many more times have lovers or enemies been "targeted" by government employees, the military and intelligence contractors with access to the trove of SIGINT data?

More importantly, how can we ever trust that the NSA's new powers won't be misused by those in power? We already know that during the Occupy Wall Street protests, federal "counterterrorism" dollars were used by the Federal Bureau of Investigation, the Department of Homeland Security and local law enforcement to monitor Americans guilty only of speaking against Wall Street's destruction of our economy and its corruption of our democracy. And the government got away with it.

So the question isn't whether the information that the NSA has been allowed to gather on Americans will be misused. The question is, when? And by whom? Perhaps our next president? Religious-Reactionary Rick (Santorum)? Tea Party Ted (Cruz)? Take-Two Rick (Perry)? You may laugh, but remember that prior to the 1980 presidential election, Trees-Cause-More-Pollution-Than-Automobiles Ronald (Reagan) was a joke.

The U.S. Supreme court, 1972: "The fourth amendment does not contemplate the executive officers of government as neutral and disinterested magistrates."

Who in the NSA's quasi-military hierarchy has the power to question a demand to provide information in its databases about specific Americans when made under the authority of the commander in chief, no matter who the president is or which power-hungry advisors aid the White House in 2016 or 2020 or beyond?

It's a state of affairs that would make Nixon smirk. It's also why foreign citizens who've lived under authoritarian regimes, in Germany and elsewhere, have expressed some of the greatest horror at the revelations over the NSA's ubiquitous monitoring.

The Past Isn't Even Past

To understand what happened to the rule of law since 9/11, it's important to understand the path of the law before the World Trade Center towers fell.

It begins with the Fourth Amendment, which makes no distinction between "intelligence gathering" and "law enforcement." The Constitution speaks instead to the rights of Americans regardless of the agent that would violate them:

> The right of the people to be secure in their persons, houses, papers and effects, against unreasonable searches and seizures, shall not be violated, and no Warrants shall issue, but upon probable cause, supported by Oath or affirmation, and particularly describing the place to be searched, and the persons or things to be seized.

Those words were born of the vanquishing of an authoritarian tyrant whose officers used "general warrants" to search colonists at will to protect the crown and its interests.

Surprisingly, it was not until 1967 that the Supreme Court ruled that the government needed a warrant to listen to Americans' phone calls. The following year, in 1968, Congress passed a crime bill to provide rules for obtaining warrants for wiretaps but—at the secret urging of the NSA—the legislature exempted surveillance in the name of national security.

In November of that year, Nixon was elected president.

In 1969, just six months after taking office, Nixon directed the NSA to search its files for information on specific Americans whom he and J. Edgar Hoover had placed on a watch list.

At that time, the existence of the NSA, formally established in 1952, was so secret that almost no one in Congress knew about it, and its funding was concealed in the Pentagon's classified "black budget." For decades, the NSA and its predecessors had acted as the government's signal corps, listening for radio communications from enemy ships, tapping into the cables of diplomats of the Soviet Union and decrypting ciphers sent by spies. Unbeknownst to Congress, the NSA and its predecessor, the Armed Forces Security Agency, had also been spying on Americans for decades, making duplicates of all of the international telegrams sent to or from Americans by "wire" or cable since 1945, as well as gathering radio transmissions from

across the globe through earth-bound satellite receivers and satellites. By the early 1970s, the NSA's analysts were reading over 150,000 telegrams to or from Americans a month under that program, called "Operation SHAMROCK."

With this vast and secret intelligence-gathering apparatus at his disposal, Nixon later expanded his watch list, directing the NSA to search for anything "subversive" or related to drug-dealing. In the meantime, in 1972, a case involving Nixon spying on Americans under the guise of national security, with no link to a foreign government, made its way to the Supreme Court. In that case, known as the *Keith* case, the Court unanimously declared:

> The Fourth Amendment freedoms cannot properly be guaranteed if domestic security surveillances may be conducted solely within the discretion of the Executive Branch. . . .
> The Fourth Amendment does not contemplate the executive officers of Government as neutral and disinterested magistrates.

In August 1974, in the wake of the Watergate scandal involving the illegal surveillance activities of the Committee to Re-Elect the President (CREEP), Nixon resigned in disgrace.

Yet the extent of electronic surveillance under the administration wasn't revealed until December 1974, when the *New York Times* published a front-page story by Seymour Hersh under the headline "Huge C.I.A. Operation Reported in U.S. Against Anti-War Forces." The article exposed part of Nixon's spying under a program code-named "Operation MINARET," which made use of the cables the NSA searched via SHAMROCK and by capturing radio transmissions.

Congress was shocked. During the investigation led by Sen. Church in 1975, Congress discovered that the NSA had access to communications involving millions of Americans and that there were about 1,200 Americans on watch lists, mostly people opposing the Vietnam War.

But the names of some Americans on the watch list were kept sealed until they were released this September. The newly declassified documents reveal that the NSA's spying targeted prominent Americans even before Nixon took office. According to the National Security Archive, the NSA "eaves-dropped on civil rights leaders Martin Luther King and Whitney Young, as well as boxing champion Muhammad Ali, *New York Times* journalist Tom Wicker, and *Washington Post* columnist [and humorist] Art Buchwald"—and Sen. Church himself.

In response to Sen. Church's investigation, Congress passed the Foreign Intelligence Surveillance Act (FISA) of 1978, over the objections of a few hard-liners in the Ford administration, including Laurence Silberman. It was intended to ensure that the NSA was focusing on foreigners and not on Americans, and "to curb the practice by which the Executive Branch may conduct warrantless electronic surveillance on its own unilateral determination that national security justifies it."

FISA barred the NSA from intentionally acquiring radio signals of the domestic communications of Americans without a warrant. It also barred the NSA from acquiring wire communications here that were to or from Americans, whether intentional or not. And it barred the NSA from intentionally targeting radio communications to or from a known U.S. person in the country. It also created rules for obtaining warrants to target Americans, requiring probable cause that a person was knowingly aiding an agent of a foreign power or someone planning "terrorism" or sabotage, as well as short-term rules for emergency or war.

Congress also created a special court, the Foreign Intelligence Surveillance Court (FISC), to hear these warrant requests. At the same time, Congress established permanent Senate and House Intelligence Committees to conduct oversight of the NSA, CIA, and more.

Project MINARET and Operation SHAMROCK were said to be terminated when FISA passed, and the public believed such activities were barred. By almost all accounts, the NSA was directing its powerful surveillance tools outside of the United States, discarding Americans' communications that were not relevant to its operations, and tuning its radio channels to foreign navies and diplomats. Meanwhile, a Soviet reformer named Mikhail Gorbachev came to power, the Cold War thawed, the Berlin Wall fell, and the need for enormous military and intelligence budgets was being questioned.

Then came 9/11.

Checks and Balances?

This much is clear: In the weeks following 9/11 a handful of men in the Executive Branch literally rewrote our rights as citizens. While Americans were sold war to secure "freedom" against al-Qaeda, our freedoms at home were deliberately undone in the name of protecting us.

That revision of our rights occurred on two fronts. One was a public debate over the Patriot Act, which obscured the second: even more dramatic changes being orchestrated by Vice President Dick Cheney's office behind the scenes.

As the Pentagon prepared for war in Afghanistan and Congress passed an "Authorization for the Use of Military Force," the George W. Bush administration sent Congress a wish list of changes to the law that were later titled "Uniting and Strengthening America by Providing Appropriate Tools Required to Intercept and Obstruct Terrorism Act of 2001," otherwise known as the "USA Patriot Act," or Patriot Act.

The Patriot Act changed some parts of FISA, but nowhere did it authorize the NSA to acquire all of Americans' phone or Internet records. Nor did it change FISA's rules to allow Operation SHAMROCK-style monitoring of the content of Americans' international communications.

While Congress was considering the Patriot Act, the White House had already secretly changed the rules for NSA surveillance on these shores. Arch-autocrat David Addington (Vice President Cheney's right-hand man) hand-picked one Justice Department official—the newly hired John Yoo—to write a legal memo justifying the NSA surveillance programs that Edward Snowden would expose 12 years later. Yoo wrote a secret memo asserting that the president is not bound by FISA's legal rules for warrants because he has plenary powers as commander in chief.

In regard to the Fourth Amendment, FISA court of review judge Laurence Silberman wrote in 2002, "the key to the reasonableness of any search is the exterior threat."

Attorney General John Ashcroft, who was busy pushing the Patriot Act, did not even know Yoo had written that memo about what became known as the "President's Surveillance Program" when he cosigned the president's first authorization document on October 5, 2001 and the NSA began asking telecommunications companies for access to their switches.

It was two years after the launch of the new NSA surveillance before the White House told even one judge on the Foreign Intelligence Surveillance Court (FISC) about the programs. That judge, the chief judge, was not asked to approve the surveillance and was not allowed to tell the other FISC judges about it.

In 2004, the Justice Department hunkered down to create a new legal memo rationalizing the program as implicitly authorized by the Authorization to Use Military Force in Afghanistan. Later that year, the FISC was asked to approve an order authorizing this surveillance for the first time, and it did.

While this battle was brewing and the presidential election was in full swing, James Risen and Eric Lichtblau of the *New York Times* were onto a story about the NSA's domestic surveillance, but the White House claimed the story would hurt national security and risk American lives, and so publisher Arthur Ochs Sulzberger, Jr. held it until more than a year after the election.

On December 16, 2005, the Risen-Lichtblau story broke: "Bush Lets U.S. Spy on Callers Without Courts." The Bush administration responded by declassifying the least controversial component of the program and rebranding it as the "Terrorist Surveillance Program," or TSP. As Bush famously quipped in trying to distract from the revelations: "If somebody from al-Qaeda is calling you, we'd like to know why."

In the midst of the uproar over the NSA spying, the Patriot Act was reauthorized in March 2006.

But in May of that year, more leaks came, with *USA Today* publishing a story that said the NSA was "amassing information about the calls of ordinary Americans—most of whom aren't suspected of any crime."

By the time these extraordinary surveillance programs had been operational for six years, nearly 3,000 unelected executive branch employees (and an unknown number in the private sector) knew of the programs, but only 60 out of the 535 members of Congress.

Nevertheless, in 2007, aided by lobbying from telecommunications companies like AT&T—which feared it would be held criminally or civilly liable for violating the Wiretap Act and FISA—Director of National Intelligence Mike McConnell began a full-court press to get FISA changed to give retroactive immunity to the companies and Congress's blessing to the programs. After a court struck down a portion of the program, McConnell demanded Congress temporarily authorize it through the Protect America Act, which was replaced a few months later in 2008 by the FISA Amendments Act.

Then-Sen. Obama, despite expressing earlier concerns about the NSA's warrantless electronic surveillance, supported those bills as he began to seek the White House. As president, he has embraced those (and other) controversial uses of power that were initiated by the Bush administration. Although he immediately sought to shut down Guantánamo, only to be thwarted by Congress, on the issue of NSA spying he has largely continued the programs and defended them. There has been little "change" or "hope" when it comes to protecting Americans' privacy from the NSA's surveillance powers. It's been mostly business as usual under for the NSA, FBI, and DHS.

Moreover, in light of the full weight of the Snowden revelations, when one looks at the statutory constraints on the NSA now, the limits in FISA that ostensibly protect Americans' rights look slippery.

For example, Section 702 of the FISA Amendments Act repeats the traditional rule that the NSA cannot acquire communications that "intentionally target any person known at the time of acquisition to be located in the United States." Given the revelations, though, does this mean the statute allows targeting of Americans in pools of information *after* international communications are seized?

Similarly, the NSA "may not intentionally acquire any communication as to which the sender and all intended recipients *are known at the time of the acquisition to be located in the United States.*" However, at the time an email is transmitted and thus acquired, the NSA could argue that it does not *know* where all the recipients are located, as a Bush rep argued "hypothetically" to privacy advocates in 2007.

Thus the protections in the FISA statute that at first appear to be shields against spying on Americans, appear upon closer inspection to operate as swords.

Where's the Fourth Amendment?

Three rulings issued by FISA judges hand-picked by the Chief Justice have narrowly construed people's Fourth Amendment rights when it comes to two core issues: the rules for content and data acquired by the NSA.

The Bush administration set the stage for its evasion of the Fourth Amendment in 2002, when it asked for a ruling from the FISA Court of Review (FISCR), which oversees FISC, in a case involving a Patriot Act provision changing the purpose of FISA surveillance. Judge Silberman (who testified against FISA in 1978) and two other judges heard government arguments—arguments originally concocted by Yoo. Silberman acted like an advocate from the bench, arguing that the Constitution does not require a warrant before the government can acquire the content of Americans' communications.

The FISCR ruling opined that the constitutional test for searches in intelligence cases was "reasonableness," not a warrant, and "the key to the reasonableness of any search is the exterior threat." In 2008, an unnamed "Internet Service Provider" (ISP) challenged "directives" issued after FISA Amendments Act as unconstitutional, but the FISCR ruled that the Constitution did not require a warrant based on probable cause to demand content of communications. In balancing whether a search order was "reasonable" under the Fourth Amendment, the court ruled that national security is of the "highest order of magnitude."

In the most recent decision issued by the FISC, a lower court judge ruled that the NSA could acquire Americans' call records en masse because Americans have "no reasonable expectation of privacy" in their phone or Internet data—a claim based on a Supreme Court decision from 1979 that most Americans have never heard of.

In that obscure case, *Smith v. Maryland*, a robbery suspect named Michael Lee Smith sued the state after police obtained his call records from his phone company without a search warrant. The Supreme Court, dominated by four new Nixon appointees, ruled that Smith had no constitutional expectation of privacy in information about himself conveyed to a third party, such as the phone company. (Justices Thurgood Marshall, Potter Stewart, and William J. Brennan, Jr. dissented, noting that using a telephone does not carry with it an assumption that this information will be released to others, let alone the government.)

The FISC embraced this precedent despite dramatic changes in technology since the original decision. In the old days, the numbers you dialed could be obtained by law enforcement through a court order, without accessing the content of the conversation. But in the digital age, if the government has access to the calls as they transit the phone company in fiber optic cables, the government can duplicate the content as it seizes data.

Despite these differences, the FISC ruled that Americans' electronic call records can be vacuumed up by the NSA.

Additionally, the court servilely stated that the NSA's computers work best when they have records of all of your calls—so all the call records they must have.

The FISC also claimed that the surveillance was consistent with the statutory rules for access to third party records, as modified by the Patriot Act, which allow courts to order businesses to turn over records "relevant to an authorized investigation." The court's order deemed all Americans' phone records to be relevant to a general investigation to prevent terrorism because any record might be a link to a potential terrorist.

If everything is relevant or potentially relevant, then relevance means nothing.

Now What?

The good news is that Americans are rejecting these rationales and are doing so in a way that transcends traditional political party divides. A growing number of Americans dissent from these policies. Most Americans know they have should have a right to privacy in their communication and Internet records. A growing number of Americans believe that the content of their emails, phone calls, and Internet searches should not be given to the NSA if they have done nothing wrong.

No government agency should be allowed to access the backbone of America's communications infrastructure inside or outside the United States.

Two of the most recent directors of national intelligence, James Clapper (USAF-ret.) and Mike McConnell (USN-ret.) have led efforts to turn the NSA inward on Americans and have misled Americans about the scope of these powers in the name of keeping us safe. Both cashed out their military service with the private-sector consulting firm of Booz Allen Hamilton (Edward Snowden's former employer) and then moved to top government "civilian."

Concerns about trusting the NSA are only underscored when the government has been deceptive in its communications with the American people and with congressional and judicial overseers. In March, Sen. Ron Wyden (D-Ore.) asked Clapper: "Does the NSA collect any type of data at all on millions or hundreds of millions of Americans?" Clapper replied stoutly, "No, sir."

This denial was exposed as a demonstrable lie four months later, when the Snowden materials surfaced.

The NSA should only be allowed to access the contents of Americans' calls or emails based on an individualized warrant predicated on probable cause of wrongdoing. As for international calls and emails to or from an American, they should be subject to the requirement of an individual warrant on one end before they can be searched.

No American's name should be queried in the NSA database of calls, emails, and Internet searches without an individualized warrant.

Americans' phone and Internet data should not be acquired at all, unless it is directly connected (in one or two hops) to a specific person who is a legitimate target of a terrorism or espionage investigation.

We also need better protections for information we have already "shared" with a company—including the data that trails you as a result of digital communications—to protect our inherent right to privacy against both the private sector and government.

As Sen. Sam Ervin (D-N.C.)—a staunch advocate of civil liberties despite his Southern segregationist roots—said in 1974 after investigating government spying on Americans, "Each time we give up a bit of information about ourselves to the Government, we give up some of our freedom. For the more the Government or any institution knows about us, the more power it has over us. When the Government knows all of our secrets, we stand naked before official power. Stripped of our privacy, we lose our rights and privileges. The Bill of Rights then becomes just so many words."

Critical Thinking

1. What are the parallels between NSA activities under President Nixon and in the post 9/11 era?

2. How effective do you think the Fourth Amendment and federal courts have been in protecting Americans' privacy from NSA intelligence-gathering efforts?

Create Central

www.mhhe.com/createcentral

Internet References

Church Committee
  http://www.intelligence.senate.gov/churchcommittee.html
National Security Agency/Central Security Service
  https://www.nsa.gov
The Patriot Act (U.S. Department of Justice)
  http://www.justice.gov/archive/ll/highlights.htm
Reform the Patriot Act (ACLU)
  https://www.aclu.org/reform-patriot-act

Article   Prepared by: Bruce Stinebrickner, *DePauw University*

The Autocrat Next Door

Ferguson has proved that the biggest threat to liberty in America isn't big government. It's the tyranny of small, local governments.

FRANKLIN FOER

Learning Outcomes

After reading this article, you will be able to:

- Explain why the article is titled "The Autocrat Next Door" and assess the central argument(s) that seem to justify that title.

- Explain why the author thinks that states increasingly being strongly Democratic *or* Republican makes it more likely that state and local governments will act like "autocrats."

The Libertarian's Jeremiads about creeping tyranny often seem the ravings of a paranoid. Then along comes Ferguson to confirm the dark warnings: Warrior cops stalk suburban streets, dressed in Desert Storm green and wielding automatic weapons aimed to fire. They detain journalists, hurl smoke bombs into unarmed crowds, and bury incriminating details.

And yet, even though libertarians were plenty prescient in warning about the militarization of the police, they still managed to get it wrong. As Rand Paul argued in an impassioned op-ed on the conflagration in Missouri: "Not surprisingly, big government has been at the heart of the problem." But what Ferguson shows is that the heart of the problem is, in fact, *small* government—the cops, prosecutors, and their bosses with an inflated sense of their powers. The great and growing threat to liberty in this country comes from states and localities run amok.

These are boom times for provincial autocrats. In many chunks of the country, state and local politics were once a competitive affair; there was an opposing political party ready to pounce on its foe's malfeasance. That sort of robust rivalry, however, hardly exists in an era in which blue and red states have become darker shades of themselves. Thirty-seven states now have unified governments, the most since the early '50s. And in many of these places, there's not even a remote chance that the ruling party will be deposed in the foreseeable future. The rise of one-party government has been accompanied by the evisceration of the local press and the near-extinction of metro-desk muckrakers (14,000 newsroom jobs have vanished in the last six years), crippling the other force most likely to call attention to official misdeeds.

The end of local media hasn't just removed a watchdog; it has helped to complete a cultural reversal. Once upon a time, Jefferson and Tocqueville could wax lyrical about local government, which they viewed as perfectly in sync with the interests of its yeoman citizenry. Whether this arcadia ever truly existed is debatable. But it certainly hasn't persisted into the age of mass media. Nowadays, most Americans care much more passionately about national politics than they do about the governments closer to their homes. They may harbor somewhat warmer feelings toward states and localities, but those sentiments are grounded in apathy. Most Americans can name their president. But according to a survey conducted by Georgetown University's Dan Hopkins, only 35 percent can identify their mayor. The nostrum that local government is actually closer to the people is now just a hollow piece of antique rhetoric.

With so many instances of unobstructed one-party rule, conditions are ripe for what the political scientist Jessica Trounstine calls "political monopoly"—officials and organizations who have so effectively defeated any potential predators that they can lazily begin to gorge. She writes: "When politicians cease to worry about reelection, they become free to pursue government policy that does not reflect constituent preferences. They acquire the ability to enrich themselves and their supporters or pursue policies that would otherwise lead to their electoral defeat."

This past year alone has provided some spectacular examples. Chris Christie rough-housing a political enemy in Fort Lee; Robert McDonnell stuffing his closet full of gifts from a dietary-supplement magnate; Ray Nagin sentenced to prison for swapping New Orleans's city contracts for several truckloads of granite for his kids' countertop company; two former attorneys general of Utah arrested for pocketing bribes and tampering with evidence to protect their pipeline of lucre. When the Center for Public Integrity commissioned a comprehensive study of state governments, 18 states received Ds, eight outright flunked, and not one got an A.

It's not just egomaniacal politicians who have amassed power and riches for themselves. At times, it seems, the whole system has followed their lead, with entire branches of government falling into the hands of oligarchs. In West Virginia, the mining boss Don Blankenship spent more than $3 million electing a state Supreme Court judge. His beneficiary then provided the decisive vote in a favorable verdict that saved him $50 million. (Photographs also later showed Blankenship vacationing with the court's chief justice on the French Riviera.) Or there was the especially grotesque example of the impoverished town of Bell, California, where nearly every public official extracted Wall Street–sized salaries for themselves. Even the city manager's assistant pulled in $375,000 a year.

If there's a signature policy of this age of unimpeded state and local government, it's civil-asset forfeiture. The program sounds benign enough: Authorities can unilaterally confiscate cash or property that it considers illegally begotten; many states then place the proceeds straight into its own coffers to fund further crime-fighting. But the reality of the policy is aggressive and arbitrary. As Sarah Stillman graphically exposed in a magisterial *New Yorker* investigation last year, in many states law enforcement can seize a person's assets without ever charging him with a crime. Her reporting chronicled one appalling story after another—cops who ran a $50 million forfeiture ring in Bal Harbour, which funded the purchase of luxe cars and first-class airplane tickets; a party at the Contemporary Art Institute of Detroit, where guests were knocked to the ground and forced to hand over their cars. Their offense: Dancing and drinking in a space that wasn't properly permitted. Even if local governments wanted to roll back this legalized Boss Hoggism, they couldn't. Police depend far too heavily on the revenue it generates. (Something similar seems to have happened in Ferguson, where police processed an average of three warrants for each household—milking millions in fines and court fees from the poorest residents to bankroll its operations.)

The greatest danger of untrammeled local power is that majorities will use their control of government to stampede the rights of minorities, both racial and political, in their midst. Since the 2010 election, more than 20 states—most of them under GOP control—have enacted new voting restrictions, thinly veiled efforts to suppress the minority vote. And Republicans have also ruthlessly redrawn the legislative map of the South, creating supermajorities that have started to roll back the gains of the civil rights era.

Immigrants, too, are especially vulnerable to the whims of local leaders. Surges of nativism in the last two decades haven't produced draconian national reforms, due to the knotty national politics of the issue. But at the state and local levels, harsh feelings translate directly into cruel laws. In 2011, Alabama briefly gave police the authority to demand that immigrants show their papers at traffic stops and ordered schools to check the status of kids and their parents. A raft of towns have passed laws forbidding landlords from renting to undocumented immigrants.

The seer who predicted much of this was, of course, James Madison. In "Federalist #10," he warned that smaller units of government were particularly susceptible to being coopted by its elites. He favored a larger republic that would draw from a greater population pool and therefore recruit a higher caliber of talent. And since successful electoral coalitions would require a substantial number of votes, a larger republic would limit the potential of a corrupt faction seizing power: "It will be more difficult for unworthy candidates to practice with success the vicious arts by which elections are too often carried."

Madison wasn't remotely opposed to empowering states, which have been at the vanguard of many movements to expand individual rights. And he worried obsessively about the potential for the federal abuse of powers. But he also helped design a central government equipped to curtail its own overreaching impulses, which are real and plentiful enough. The national government, after all, has a less than impeccable record, especially during wartime, when it produces the likes of the Patriot Act or worse. Yet its abuses, unlike those of its smaller counterparts, tend to quickly emerge into public view, as they did with the National Security Agency scandal. They are raked over by a feisty national press, interrogated by congressional committees, and reviewed by layers of courts. Federal abuses aren't always corrected, but at least they get vigorously debated, which is itself a barricade against future encroachments.

Centuries ago, in the age of monarchs, the preservation of liberty required constraining the power of the central state. In our era, protecting rights requires the opposite. Only a strong federal government can curb the autocratic tendencies burbling across the country. Libertarians worry about the threat of local tyrants, too, but only abstractly. In practice, they remain so fixated on the perils of Washington that they rigidly insist on devolving power down to states, cities, and towns—the very places where their nightmares are springing to life.

Critical Thinking

1. Explain why the author argues that libertarians, including Senator Rand Paul, are misguided in thinking that the national government in Washington poses the biggest threat to "liberty" in the United States.
2. How has the growing Red State/Blue State division of the United States led to state and local governments being greater threats to individual liberties?
3. Report the developments in state and local media outlets and the effects of those developments on the behavior of state and local governments.

Internet References

Advocates for Self-Government
   http://www.theadvocates.org

Libertarianism.org
   http://www.libertarianism.org

USA Today—Timeline: Michael Brown Shooting in Ferguson, MO
   http://www.usatoday.com/story/news/nation/2014/08/14/michael-brown-ferguson-missouri-timeline/14051827

FRANKLIN FOER is editor of *The New Republic*.

Article   Prepared by: Bruce Stinebrickner, *DePauw University*

Better Beings

MARK LEIBOVICH

Learning Outcomes

After reading this article, you will be able to:

- Put into perspective the phenomenon of "flip-flopping" or "evolution of ideas" in contemporary American politics.

- Assess how important or troubling the phenomenon of flip-flopping or changes of mind seems to be for you, for American politicians, and for the American public.

- Consider whether "flip-flopping" applies to any of *your* political views and, if you have yourself flip-flopped, explain why.

As a general rule, it is difficult for people in public life to change their minds. There is an immediate rush to portray politicians as "flip-floppers" when they shift position on anything, even if they do so following a careful consideration of an issue rather than a meeting with a pollster. The hecklers will reliably accuse them of lacking the "courage of their convictions," of being "typical politicians," even though the typical politician actually tries to change his mind as rarely as possible, to avoid the hecklers.

Luckily, politicians don't have to admit to about-faces as often as they used to, thanks to a nifty new rhetorical disguise: Now their thinking simply "evolves." Senator Rand Paul, for instance, called for the Republican Party to "evolve" on immigration, though he could have been talking about the need for his party to appeal to Hispanic voters. In January, Representative Tim Ryan, a reliably anti-abortion Democrat from Ohio, wrote an essay in *The Akron Beacon Journal* explaining that he was abandoning his opposition to abortion. "I am not afraid to say that my position has evolved as my experiences have broadened, deepened and become more personal," he wrote. As is often the case with "evolving" politicians, Ryan couched (or, if you prefer, spun) his switch in terms of a hard-fought personal

journey. Whereas "changing my mind" invites an immediate question of motive and suspicion of opportunism, "evolving" carries the tone of a solemn and thoughtful seeker, of someone striving for a better self.

More than any other issue, same-sex marriage has occasioned the most dramatic evolution of the word "evolution." "Attitudes evolve, including mine," President Obama famously said in October 2010 when he was asked by a group of liberal bloggers to clarify his position on the subject. This was not the first time Obama said he did not support same-sex marriage, though a 1996 questionnaire he reportedly completed during his campaign for the State Senate suggested he once did support it. (A White House spokesman later disavowed the questionnaire, saying someone else had filled it out.) But Obama's use of the word "evolve" became a rhetorical benchmark for how public figures talk about changing their public positions on the topic. John Kerry, Bill Clinton, the Republican senators Rob Portman and Lisa Murkowski, among others, have all spoken of their evolutions toward support of the practice. (A spokesman for Hillary Clinton declared the issue to be "in a state of evolution" as far back as 2003, though Clinton herself did not achieve that state for another decade.)

Obama and his surrogates often accompanied references to his "evolving" position with reassurance that he was "wrestling with" the subject, as if to portray his as a vigorous journey. But embedded in the word "evolving" is more than a hint of self-congratulation. "Evolve" derives from the Latin *evolvere*, which means unroll or unfold. It implies that you are headed somewhere better. The familiar diagram of humankind in its graduating stages of evolution (from monkey to Cro-Magnon to upright man) suggests a progression to a higher being and a more refined and civilized species.

As a slur rather than a form of footwear, "flip-flop" seemed to gain momentum in the 1980s, a decade in which candidates were striving to emulate the fatherly resolve associated with Ronald Reagan. *You might not agree with him, but at least you knew where he stood!* In the 1988 Democratic primaries, the candidate Richard Gephardt was subjected to merciless ridicule by opponents for his switches on several key issues—an assault capped off by a brutal ad from Michael Dukakis that depicted Gephardt as a gymnast, somersaulting back and forth. The ad became a perfect dramatization of what a supposed flip-flopper does, and a perfect lesson to politicians about the dangers of changing their minds.

Sixteen years later, John Kerry turned into a similar caricature when he was caught on video saying, "I actually did vote for the $87 billion before I voted against it," in reference to an Iraq-war funding bill. The clip not only bolstered a growing impression of Kerry as [a] politician incapable of taking a decisive stance. It also became a new construction with which to attack future flip-floppers: The candidate was for *x* before he was against it. More recently, Mitt Romney found himself vulnerable to the perception that he wanted to have it both ways. "When this is over, I will have built a brand name," the former Massachusetts governor concluded wistfully in "Mitt," the Netflix documentary about his two campaigns for president. His opponents were so adept at highlighting his wavering positions, Romney said, that he feared he had been reduced to a caricature of "the flipping Mormon."

In everyday life, of course, people change their minds all the time. I just returned from a lunch date in which I first ordered a bowl of chicken soup, flip-flopped to a turkey sandwich while my friend ordered, then changed back to the soup by the time the waiter returned with our drinks (tap water, later adjusted to sparkling). Call me a flipping Jew; I don't care. I tend to change my mind a lot, not because I am a liar but because I can be indecisive about certain things, including menus. I have a right to, especially because I am not running for anything.

The use of 'evolve' as a euphemism continues a long tradition among public figures, namely, framing uncomfortable revelations in a way that diminishes their own role in them.

The use of "evolve" as a euphemism continues a long tradition among public figures, namely, framing uncomfortable revelations in a way that diminishes their own role in them. "Mistakes were made"—the comically unsatisfying admission from the Watergate-era press secretary Ron Ziegler—is considered the gold standard of such statements. William Safire, the late Nixon White House veteran and *New York Times* wordsmith, described Zeigler's mealy-mouthed grandiloquence as a "passive-evasive way of acknowledging error while distancing the speaker from responsibility for it."

Safire actually wrote a column in 1992 about a previous incarnation of "evolve." Then, at the dawn of the Clinton era, the "evolved" person was believed to be enlightened. Safire observed that Barbra Streisand, "the political activist and singer," had recently described her friend, the tennis player Andre Agassi, as being "very evolved; more than his linear years … very in the moment." Safire sent a note to Streisand asking her to elaborate. She replied: "Thank you for the offer to respond. If you vote for Clinton, I just might." (Safire added that he did in fact wind up voting for Clinton, but Streisand never did elaborate. "This double cross augurs ill for the new administration," he concluded.)

The Safire-Streisand example offers a perfect distillation of how the word "evolve" has changed. As smug as the 1992 usage was, it at least implied a statement of intent. The speaker welcomed her association with a certain "evolved" outlook; she could even use it as a compliment to describe someone else. But in the modern, politicized version, the word is more of a defensive crouch. It might, in its best form, suggest improvement—but it also suggests a kind of helplessness, or an abdication of responsibility, someone being swept along. The world is changing, and I am changing, too; I have no choice.

As the two-year reality show that was Barack Obama's evolution on same-sex marriage unrolled to its logical conclusion, watching the process, with its various updates and teases, became akin to following the birth of a baby panda. The arrival was inevitable; it was just a question of when. "I'm still working on it," Obama said in October 2011 when ABC's George Stephanopoulos asked for an update. By that point, the outcome was so obvious that Obama was even becoming meta in his responses. "I probably won't make news right now, George," Obama said. In other words, I have news to make, and I'm just choosing to make it some other time. (Certainly, those frustrated by Obama's position on same-sex marriage spoke of his "evolution" with impatience, if not contempt. The gay activist and journalist Dan Savage wore an Evolve Already button to a White House reception he attended in 2011.)

But can an evolution be intelligently designed? Not always. Sometimes an unforeseen mutation comes along: Joe Biden, for instance. In an appearance on "Meet the Press" in May 2012, the vice president said that he was "comfortable" with the idea of gay people getting married. Damn it, Joe was not supposed to "make news" on that, not yet. The president was supposed to give birth to his panda first. The White House quickly arranged an interview for President Obama with ABC's Robin Roberts so that he, too, could announce the culminating step of his support for same-sex marriage. It was an anticlimax, to be sure, but at least the evolution would be televised.

It is worth noting, though, a couple of recent remarks that might indicate the start of an anti-evolutionary trend in political discourse. Gov. Bobby Jindal of Louisiana, a likely candidate for president, not only reiterated that he opposed same-sex marriage but also made a point of sneering at "those politicians" who have "so-called evolved" on the issue. Not long after, one of Jindal's probable opponents in the Republican primaries, Scott Walker of Wisconsin, admitted that he had, in so many words, blatantly flip-flopped on immigration policy. He did not bother finessing it. "My view has changed, I'm flat out saying it," Walker remarked in an interview with Chris Wallace on "Fox News Sunday." "Candidates can say that. Sometimes they don't."

If might, in its best form, suggest improvement—but it also suggests a kind of helplessness, or an abdication of responsibility, someone being swept along.

And Walker did. For the political species, I call it progress.

Critical Thinking

1. What is a "flip-flopper" as the term is used in contemporary political rhetoric?

2. What is the "nifty new rhetorical disguise" that American politicians are using with increasing frequency?

3. Report and discuss (i) the wording that President Obama used in 2010 to describe his changing views on same-sex marriage and (ii) presidential candidate John Kerry's well-known statement about his voting on an Iraq-war funding bill that resulted in his being called a "flip-flopper."

Internet References

National Journal (on John Kerry and Mitt Romney and flip-flops)
  http://news.yahoo.com/john-kerrys-revenge-flip-flop-214411560—politics.html;_ylt=A0LEVjkfSSpW6usABQQnnIlQ;_ylu=X3oDMTByN XM5bzY5BGNvbG8DYmYxBHBvcwMzBHZ0aWQDBHNlYwNzcg—
Washington Post (on Barack Obama and same-sex marriage)
  https://www.washingtonpost.com/news/the-fix/wp/2015/02/10/axelrod-says-obama-lied-about-opposing-gay-marriage-its-another-convenient-evolution

Article   Prepared by: Bruce Stinebrickner, *DePauw University*

Get Me Rewrite

The Constitution doesn't need tinkering. It neetds a top-to-bottom overhaul. Americans deserve a document that reflects what we've learned about governance over the past two centuries.

ALEX SEITZ-WALD

Learning Outcomes

After reading this article, you will be able to:

- Assess the legitimacy and persuasiveness of arguments in favor of writing and adopting a new constitution (and system of government) for the United States.

- Identify and assess a number of prominent criticisms of the current U.S. Constitution and the government structure it created.

- Discuss and evaluate different possibilities for resolving dysfunction and gridlock in the American political system.

America, we've got some bad news: Our Constitution isn't going to make it. It's had 224 years of commendable, often glorious service, but there's a time for everything, and the government shutdown and permanent-crisis governance signal that it's time to think about moving on. "No society can make a perpetual constitution," Thomas Jefferson wrote to James Madison in 1789, the year ours took effect. "The earth belongs always to the living generation and not to the dead. . . . Every constitution, then, and every law, naturally expires at the end of 19 years." By that calculation, we're more than two centuries behind schedule for a long, hard look at our most sacred of cows. And what it reveals isn't pretty.

If men (and, finally, women) as wise as Jefferson and Madison set about the task of writing a constitution in 2013, it would look little like the one we have now. Americans today can't agree on anything about Washington except that they want to "blow up the place," in the words of former Republican Sen. George Voinovich as he left Congress, and maybe that thought isn't so radical.

Clocking in at some 4,500 words—about the same length as the screenplay for an episode of *Two and a Half Men*—and without serious modification since 18-year-olds got the vote in 1971, the Constitution simply isn't cut out for 21st-century governance. It's full of holes, only some of which have been patched; it guarantees gridlock; and it's virtually impossible to change. "It gets close to a failing grade in terms of 21st-century notions on democratic theory," says University of Texas law professor Sanford Levinson, part of the growing cadre of legal scholars who say the time has come for a new constitutional convention.

Put simply, we've learned a lot since 1787. What was for the Founders a kind of providential revelation—designing, from scratch, a written charter and democratic system at a time when the entire history of life on this planet contained scant examples of either—has been worked into science. More than 700 constitutions have been composed since World War II alone, and other countries have solved the very problems that cripple us today. It seems un-American to look abroad for ways to change our sacred text, but the world's nations copied us, so why not learn from them?

No Longer a Model

Supreme Court Justice Ruth Bader Ginsburg was pilloried when she told Egyptian revolutionaries last year that she "would not look to the U.S. Constitution, if I were drafting a constitution in the year 2012." But her sentiment is taken for granted by anyone who has actually tried to write a constitution since politicians stopped wearing powdered wigs. "Our Constitution really has been a steady force guiding us and has been perhaps the most stable in the world," says Louis Aucoin, who has helped draft constitutions in Cambodia, East Timor, Kosovo, Rwanda, and elsewhere while working with the U.N. and other groups. "But the disadvantage to the stability is that it's old, and there are things that more-modern constitutions address more clearly."

Almost nobody uses the U.S. Constitution as a model—not even Americans. When 24 military officers and civilians were given a single week to craft a constitution for occupied Japan in 1946, they turned to England. The Westminster-style parliament they installed in Tokyo, like its British forbearer, has two houses. But unlike Congress, one is clearly more powerful than the other and can override the less powerful one during an impasse.

The story was largely the same in defeated Nazi Germany, and more recently in Iraq and Afghanistan, which all emerged from American occupation with constitutions that look little like the one Madison and the other framers wrote. They have the same democratic values, sure, but different ways of realizing them. According to researchers who analyzed all 729 constitutions adopted between 1946 and 2006, the U.S. Constitution is rarely used as a model. What's more, "the American example is being rejected to an even greater extent by America's allies than by the global community at large," write David Law of Washington University and Mila Versteeg of the University of Virginia.

That's a not a fluke. The American system was designed with plenty of checks and balances, but the Founders assumed the elites elected to Congress would sort things out. They didn't plan for the political parties that emerged almost immediately after ratification, and they certainly didn't plan for Ted Cruz. And factionalism isn't the only problem. Belgium, a country whose ethnic divisions make our partisan sparring look like a thumb war, was unable to form a governing coalition for 589 days in 2010 and 2011. Nevertheless, the government stayed open and fulfilled its duties almost without interruption, thanks to a smarter institutional arrangement.

As the famed Spanish political scientist Juan Linz wrote in an influential 1990 essay, dysfunction, trending toward constitutional breakdown, is baked into our DNA. Any system that gives equally strong claims of democratic legitimacy to both the legislature and the president, while also allowing each to be controlled by people with fundamentally different agendas, is doomed to fail. America has muddled through thus far by compromise, but what happens when the sides no longer wish to compromise? "No democratic principle exists to resolve disputes between the executive and the legislature about which of the two actually represents the will of the people," Linz wrote.

"There are about 30 countries, mostly in Latin America, that have adopted American-style systems. All of them, without exception, have succumbed to the Linzian nightmare at one time or another, often repeatedly," according to Yale constitutional law professor Bruce Ackerman, who calls for a transition to a parliamentary system. By "Linzian nightmare," Ackerman

means constitutional crisis—your full range of political violence, revolution, coup, and worse. But well short of war, you can end up in a state of "crisis governance," he writes. "President and house may merely indulge a taste for endless backbiting, mutual recrimination, and partisan deadlock. Worse yet, the contending powers may use the constitutional tools at their disposal to make life miserable for each other: The house will harass the executive, and the president will engage in unilateral action whenever he can get away with it." He wrote that almost a decade and a half ago, long before anyone had heard of Barack Obama, let alone the tea party.

You can blame today's actors all you want, but they're just the product of the system, and honestly it's a wonder we've survived this long: The presidential election of 1800, a nasty campaign of smears and hyper-partisan attacks just a decade after ratification, caused a deadlock in the House over whether John Adams or Thomas Jefferson should be president. The impasse grew so tense that state militias opposed to Adams's Federalist Party prepared to march on Washington before lawmakers finally elected Jefferson on the 36th vote in the House. It's a near miracle we haven't seen more partisan violence, but it seems like tempting fate to stick with the status quo for much longer.

How would a parliamentary system handle a shutdown? It wouldn't have one. In Canada a few years ago, around the same time Washington was gripped in yet another debt-ceiling crisis, a budget impasse in Ottawa led to new elections, where the parties fought to win over voters to their fiscal plan. One side won, then enacted its plan—problem solved. Most parliamentary systems, which unify the executive and legislative branches, have this sort of fail-safe mechanism. If a budget or other must-pass bill can't get passed, or a prime minister can't be chosen, then funding levels are placed on autopilot and new elections are called to resolve things. The people decide.

Arend Lijphart is a political scientist who has spent much of his career trying to answer the fundamental question, "What works best?" and he thinks he knows the answer. "Democracies work best if they are consensus instead of majoritarian democracies. The most important constitutional provisions that help in this direction is to have a parliamentary system and elections by [proportional representation]. The United States is the opposite system, with a presidential system and plurality single-member-district elections," he said an email, drawing on complex quantitative analysis he's done to compare economic and political outcomes across dozens of democratic countries with different systems.

If he had to pick any country whose system we might like to try on for size, he'd pick Germany. "Some aspects of it do need to change, of course," he says. Yet it's a nice bicameral federal system for a large country, like ours, but it has a proportional representation parliamentary system.

Thinking Outside the Box

Still, latter-day framers probably won't be able to start from scratch. So how might they remodel?

Take the Senate. What started as a compromise to preserve states' rights lost even that pretext with the ratification of the 17th Amendment, which gave the people, and not state legislatures, the right to elect their representatives in the upper chamber. Today, the Senate is an undemocratic relic where 41 senators, representing just 11 percent of the nation's population, can use the filibuster to block almost anything and bring government to its knees. A single voter in Wyoming, a state with a mere 600,000 people, has the equivalent representation of 66 Californians unfortunate enough to live in a place with 38 million other people. The two-senator allotment to each state also makes it essentially impossible to change the makeup of the states or admit new ones like the District of Columbia. And the House, of course, isn't a more attractive alternative.

Larry Sabato, the ubiquitous and mild-mannered political prognosticator by day, is a radical constitution-rewriter by night. In his 2008 book, *A More Perfect Constitution: Why the Constitution Must Be Revised,* Sabato offers a number of pragmatic ideas: The Senate, he says, should be expanded to give more populous states at least a bit more representation, and it should also include "national senators"—all former presidents and vice presidents, maybe others—whose job it is to guard national interests over parochial ones. Sabato's plan would also double the size of the House (to make representatives closer to the people) and enforces a nonpartisan redistricting process to end gerrymandering. Elections for president, Senate, and House, in Sabato's vision, are rescheduled to coincide more often, while presidents would serve a single, six-year term (the idea is to make their governing less political, while giving them enough time to implement change).

Regardless of how you feel about *Citizens United,* something needs to be done about campaign finance. No one thinks lawmakers should spend several hours every day raising money (some estimates say lawmakers spend 25 percent to 50 percent of their time "dialing for dollars"). No one prefers that a tiny fraction of wealthy Americans provide the vast majority of the money needed to supply our democracy with leaders. (Only about one-half of 1 percent of Americans have given more than $200 to a candidate, PAC, or party, while just under 10 percent report donating at all.)

Lawrence Lessig, the iconoclastic professor who is now at Harvard, traces the rise of hyper-partisanship to the emergence of the perpetual campaign and the constant need for money. "Since the end of earmarks, the best way to raise money is to increase partisanship. Look at the shutdown. It cost the economy billions of dollars but raised millions of dollars for both Democrats and Republicans," he says. At some point, this money chase has to take a psychological toll. How do you spend all morning attacking your opponent and then make a deal with them in the afternoon? Instead, Lessig, along with fellow Harvard law professor Laurence Tribe and many others, proposes a bottom-up form of public financing where voters get a voucher of, say, $50 off their taxes, which they can use to donate to candidates.

Then there's just basic housekeeping. Any constitutional lawyer can point out the places that need work: How much authority should presidents have in the case of a national emergency? Can they lock up Japanese-Americans, as FDR did? Do individuals have a right to privacy in an age of high-tech snooping by the National Security Agency? How is power really divided between the states and the federal government?

The list of questions goes on, but the Constitution doesn't answer them, so judges have had to fill in the blanks. Where modern constitutions in other nations get specific, we get judicial activism. Sometimes it works, but it's not an approach without serious drawbacks. Take civil rights, which the courts have done a decent job of protecting—only after reversing earlier mistakes. And there's theoretically nothing to stop judges from flip-flopping back to their pre-*Brown v. Board of Education* jurisprudence.

"A lot of people have conniptions" when you start talking about changing the Constitution, acknowledges Nick Dranias, a constitutional lawyer at the conservative Goldwater Institute in Arizona. "But the idea that the Founders thought the Constitution would be a perfect and unchanging document is simply not true." The problem is that they didn't realize how difficult they'd made it to actually change things. The U.S. Constitution is the world's hardest to amend, according to Levinson. (Yugoslavia used to hold that distinction; perhaps not coincidentally, Yugoslavia no longer exists.)

Surprisingly, considering their reverence of the Founders, conservatives have led the way in reimagining the Constitution, so they can add an amendment to create a right to life after *Roe v. Wade* or to rein in the federal government with a balanced-budget amendment. Others have called for more holistic changes, to empower states vis-à-vis Washington. But a full-on constitutional convention goes too far, says Dranias, and would inevitably descend into chaos (just imagine dealing with abortion, for instance, or gun rights).

Instead, Dranias and a diverse band of compatriots—including acerbic radio host Mark Levin, Lessig, and Harold R. DeMoss, a senior judge on the U.S. Court of Appeals for the Fifth Circuit—advocate a convention to propose amendments to the Constitution, as laid out in Article V, as opposed to starting from scratch. "The vehicle is not ideological—you put on whatever ideology you want," Dranias says. He wants a balanced-budget amendment; Lessig wants campaign finance reform; someone else might want to change the Senate. The states can call a convention to propose amendments if three-fourths (38) are in favor. Congress would still need to approve the changes, but the process puts the states, and not Washington, in charge.

They join a long line of fellow travelers from Republican Sen. Everett Dirksen, who called for a second constitutional convention throughout his long political career, to William Safire, who wrote in 1987 that he wanted to "be a delegate to the next Constitutional Convention (Con Con II)."

If Americans managed to convoke a constitutional convention, they could draw on hundreds of possible tweaks with text already written, available online thanks to the Google-funded Comparative Constitutions Project. After hundreds of tries, we (humans) have gotten so good at chartering governments that we've developed a set of best practices. Our Constitution violates many of them.

For one, the Public International Law & Policy Group, a pro-bono law firm that advises transitioning countries on the rule of law, developed a 222-page U.N.-endorsed "Post-Conflict Constitution Drafter's Handbook" that practically offers constitution-writing by the word game Mad Libs. It comes complete with sample language ("The capital city of [State] is [Capital City]"), instructions on how to write a preamble, and a veritable choose-your-own adventure story of democratic forms of governance: Would you like to be a federal state, where power flows from the regions to the capital, or a unity state, where all power derives from the seat of government? Religious or secular? Democracy is available off the shelf.

Far Out

As we've learned what works and what doesn't, constitutions have started to look and more alike. Not surprisingly, the U.S. has one of the world's least generic constitutions. (Djibouti has the most.) American exceptionalism is a fine thing, but there are still things we can learn from other places. "The Founders had only impressionistic, sometimes wrong, assumptions about human behavior," says Ryan Enos, a political scientist at Harvard. "We know a great deal more now, due to advances in psychology and other fields, about the nature of cooperation, group identities, incentives, et cetera."

Take elections, the most basic function of any democracy. We've been doing them the same way since the Progressive era, but instant-runoff voting has become increasingly popular because it allows voters to rank multiple choices instead of picking just one. Australia, India, Ireland, and dozens of other countries have adopted it, as has San Francisco and the Academy Awards. IRV, as it's known, would make room for new parties by allowing people to vote for a third-party candidate first without "wasting" it, and then for a mainstream candidate

second. This change would force politicians to compete for everyone's votes, because they would need non-first-choice votes too. Alternately, we could also eliminate party primaries, as California did recently, and replace them with a nonpartisan runoff between the top two vote-getters. These innovations would help reduce one-party monopoly and avoid the radicalizing effects of partisan primaries.

Other thinkers are even further out on the cutting-edge of democracy. Germany's Pirate Party advocates something called "liquid democracy." A cross between New England-style town meetings and Facebook, this model of delegative democracy leverages social relationships and expertise on an open-source software platform for collaborative decision-making. The process is a bit complicated, but essentially citizens can participate directly, say, by proposing legislation. They can also delegate their vote to a proxy they trust, who can then in turn delegate her vote and the original vote to a third proxy, and so on down the line until you get something that resembles a legislature.

For techno-evangelists, this is the future. Clay Shirky, a futurist at New York University, advocated for a "distributed version control democracy" in a recent TED talk. The New York state Legislature is already experimenting with this on its Open Legislation platform, while the OpenGov Foundation, a nonprofit organization cofounded by Rep. Darrell Issa, R-Calif., is doing something similar on the federal level, allowing anyone to comment on and annotate legislation pending before the House.

These tools are still in their infancy, but scaled up they could change what democracy looks like in ways we're only just beginning to imagine. At the extreme, we could theoretically have smartphone-enabled direct democracy, where the public could vote directly on legislation and where Congress would almost be irrelevant. At the same time, Lorelei Kelly of the New America Foundation and the Smart Congress project warns against "mob sourcing." One glance at what's trending on the White House's "We the People" petition platform—e.g., "Investigate Jimmy Kimmel Kid's Table Government Shutdown Show on ABC Network"—confirms this. Instead, she says, we need something more like *Rotten Tomatoes* democracy. Unlike typical crowd sourcing, the movie-reviewing site privileges expertise and aggregates reviews for smarter results.

For a glimpse of where this is headed, turn to science fiction, where writers have long experimented with radical new social orders. In *Imperial Earth,* for instance, Arthur C. Clarke proposes something sure to appeal to the "throw-the-bums-out" crowd. The society in that novel automatically disqualifies from office anyone who wants to govern and instead asks the public to choose leaders from a preselected pool of candidates who have been algorithmically chosen for leadership potential.

In Robert Anton Wilson's *Schroedinger's Cat* trilogy, scientist cum President Eve Hubbard turns her country into a utopia by promoting a scientific approach and offering incentives, such as offering X-prize-style rewards to citizens who can better improve life. Even further down the techno-utopian rabbit role, Robert Heinlein's *Starship Troopers* requires people to serve in the military if they want the full rights of citizenship.

One group that sounds like science fiction has real-world champions. The Seasteading Institute in San Francisco wants to create floating cities of thousands of people or more, at sea, beyond the reach of terrestrial governments, where residents can write whatever constitution and laws they like in any form of government they prefer. "I know that what made the United States great a few hundred years ago was that it was innovative and new and great," says Randolph Hencken, the executive director. "But it's still all wrapped up in the same system that was written 240 years ago. . . . It's old technology."

Jump-Starting a Conversation

When the original constitutional convention convened in May 1787, members were tasked, simply, with proposing amendments to the Articles of Confederation. But once they got going, they realized that the Articles were so flawed and they wanted to change so much that they would need to start from scratch.

What a convention might look like is for the public to decide. It might, as Levinson proposes, be populated by citizens selected by lottery and given two years and plenty of staff and resources to come up with something. Or it might look like what Dranias and Lessig propose, where 38 states can come together to agree on the text of an amendment and then present it to Congress and demand ratification. "The most important thing a convention would do is to simply jump-start and conduct a national conversation that we're not having," Levinson says. After all, the status quo isn't working. We badly need a more perfect union.

Critical Thinking

1. Why is the U.S. Constitution no longer viewed as a model for other countries' constitutions?

2. What are some of the often-cited weaknesses of the U.S. Constitution?

3. How have political parties contributed to rendering ineffective the U.S. Constitution and the government it created?

Create Central

www.mhhe.com/createcentral

Internet References

National Constitution Center
   Constitutioncenter.org

New York Times: "We the People" Loses Appeal with People around the World"
   http://www.nytimes.com/2012/02/07/us/we-the-people-loses-appeal-with-people-around-the-world.html?pagewanted=all&_r=0

Article   Prepared by: Bruce Stinebrickner, *DePauw University*

Debating *Citizens United*

One year ago a conservative majority of the Supreme Court opened the floodgates to unlimited independent election expenditures by corporations. This magazine decried the *Citizens United* ruling as a "dramatic assault on American democracy," and we called for the passage of a constitutional amendment stating that corporations don't have the same rights to political expression as individuals. We stand by that editorial. Tracking the role that corporate money plays in politics is an urgent priority for this magazine, as is championing electoral reform. But we're also committed to airing dissenting opinions. In this case, some First Amendment scholars and groups have supported the Court's decision as being consistent with free speech, and we've asked Floyd Abrams, a respected constitutional lawyer, to express those views. We've also invited another renowned advocate of civil liberties, Burt Neuborne, to reply. Their exchange follows.

—*The Editors*

FLOYD ABRAMS AND BURT NEUBORNE

Learning Outcomes

After reading this article, you will be able to:

- Assess the merits of the opposing positions espoused by Floyd Abrams and Burt Neuborne and decide which one you support.

- Consider whether the Supreme Court's ruling in the *Citizens United* case is as important as many observers of American politics, including Abrams and Neuborne, think it is.

Remember the First Amendment?

When the *Citizens United* decision was released, many commentators treated it as a desecration. People who would enthusiastically defend the free speech rights of Nazis, pornographers and distributors of videos of animals being tortured or killed were appalled that corporations and unions should be permitted to weigh in on who should be elected president.

That the opinion was based on the First Amendment seemed only to add to their sense of insult. Some dealt with that uncomfortable reality by simply ignoring what the opinion said. When President Obama denounced the opinion in his State of the Union address and elsewhere, he made no reference to the First Amendment. And this magazine chose to mention it only once in its four-page editorial in the February 15, 2010, issue ["Democracy Inc. [1]"] denouncing the ruling and urging the adoption of a constitutional amendment that would reverse it—an amendment that would, for the first time in American history, limit the scope of the First Amendment.

Now that almost a year has passed since the ruling, it is time to return to what the case actually does and does not say, to distinguish between myth and reality. A good deal of inaccurate press commentary, for example, has asserted that the Supreme Court in *Citizens United* declared unconstitutional requirements that contributors or other supporters of campaigns be identified, thus leading to "secret" corporate contributions. Not a word of that is true. In fact, the Court said just the opposite, affirming by an 8-1 vote (with only Justice Clarence Thomas dissenting) the constitutionality of Congressionally imposed disclosure requirements because "prompt disclosure of expenditures can provide shareholders and citizens with the information needed to hold corporations and elected officials accountable."

Citizens United had no legal impact on the nondisclosure of the identity of contributors to certain not-for-profit groups organized under Section 501(c)(4) of the Internal Revenue Code, ranging from Moveon.org Civic Action to recent Karl Rove–created conservative entities like Crossroads GPS. That is because Congress has never required such disclosure. It could still do so, but if it doesn't, don't blame *Citizens United*.

Nor can *Citizens United* be held responsible for the results of the midterm election. As the *Washington Post* pointed out on November 3, in two-thirds of the Congressional races that flipped from Democratic to Republican, more money was spent by the losing Democrat. Viewing all sixty-three races, Democrats and their supporters spent $206.4 million while the generally victorious Republicans spent $171.7 million. So in the first post–*Citizens United* election, one thing is clear: the much predicted one-sided corporate takeover of the political system did not occur.

Citizens United concluded that the First Amendment bars Congress from criminalizing independent expenditures by corporations and unions supporting or condemning candidates for federal office. Concern about the constitutionality of such a law is not new. The Taft-Hartley Act, passed by an antiunion Republican Congress in 1947, was the first law barring unions and corporations from making independent expenditures in support of or opposition to federal candidates. That law was vetoed by the not-at-all conservative President Harry Truman on the ground that it was a "dangerous intrusion on free speech."

In fact, in those days it was not the conservative jurists on the Supreme Court but the liberal ones who were most concerned about the constitutionality of such legislation. In 1948, in a case commenced against the CIO, the four most liberal justices concluded that whatever "undue influence" was obtained by making large expenditures was outweighed by "the loss for democratic processes resulting from the restrictions upon free and full public discussion." Nine years later, in a case involving the United Auto Workers, a dissenting opinion of the three liberal giants, Justices William Douglas and Hugo Black and Chief Justice Earl Warren, rejected the notion that either a corporation or a union could be limited in its speech because it was "too powerful," since that was no "justification for withholding First Amendment rights from any group—labor or corporate."

The opinion of Justice Anthony Kennedy in *Citizens United* was written in that spirit. It was rooted in two well-established legal propositions. The first was that political speech, especially political speech about whom to vote for or against, is at the core of the First Amendment. There has never been doubt that generally, as Justice Kennedy put it, "political speech must prevail against laws that would suppress it, whether by design or inadvertence."

The second prong of Justice Kennedy's opinion addressed the issue (much discussed in this magazine and elsewhere) of whether the fact that Citizens United was a corporation could deprive it of the right that individuals have long held to support or oppose candidates by making independent expenditures. In concluding that the corporate status of an entity could not negate this right, Justice Kennedy cited twenty-five cases of the Court in which corporations had received full First Amendment protection. Many of them involved powerful newspapers owned by large corporations; others involved non-press entities such as a bank, a real estate company and a public utility company. Justice John Paul Stevens's dissenting opinion (unlike most of the published criticism of *Citizens United*) took little issue with this historical record, acknowledging, "We have long since held that corporations are covered by the First Amendment."

The dangers of any statute barring speech advocating the election or defeat of candidates for office were starkly illustrated through the justices' questioning of the lawyers representing the United States. There were two arguments. In the first, the assistant solicitor general defending the constitutionality of the statute was forced to concede that the same logic that the government used to defend the statute would, as well, permit the government to criminalize the publication of a book by a corporation urging people to vote for a candidate. In the second, then–Solicitor General Elena Kagan was required to acknowledge that the government's position would provide constitutional justification for applying Taft-Hartley to criminalize the publication of a political pamphlet. As these quite accurate responses indicated, the notion that no serious First Amendment challenge was raised in *Citizens United* is itself a myth.

Consider the group that commenced the case and the film it prepared. Citizens United is a conservative organization, partially funded by corporate grants. It prepared and sought to air on video-on-demand a documentary-style movie it had made castigating then–Senator Hillary Clinton when she was viewed as the leading Democratic presidential candidate in 2008. It was an opinionated, tendentious and utterly unfair political documentary—precisely what the First Amendment most obviously protects.

For me, that's the real issue here. Were the five jurists—yes, conservative jurists—right in concluding that this is the sort of speech that must be protected under the First Amendment? Or were the four dissenting jurists correct that the airing of that documentary could be treated as a crime? I know my answer to that question.

Corporations Aren't People

We don't know exactly where the corporate money came from in the midterm elections, or where it went. We know that more than $4 billion was spent by both sides, much of it on negative and misleading advertising. We also know that about $300 million, maybe much more, came from corporate treasuries. And we know that in fifty-three of seventy-two contested Congressional districts and at least three contested Senate races in which corporations heavily backed the Republican candidate over the Democrat, the Republican won. But we don't know how much corporations actually spent, or where, because the disclosure laws broke down and the Senate Republicans blocked every attempt to repair them. And we can only guess at the size of the massive tidal wave of secret corporate money ready to wash away the 2012 presidential election.

We do know this—thanks to the Supreme Court's 5-4 decision in *Citizens United* granting corporations a First Amendment right to spend unlimited sums to win an election, we are facing a second Gilded Age where American democracy is for sale to the highest corporate bidder. Justice Kennedy's opinion, touted by some as a great victory for free speech, begins with a glaring First Amendment mistake. Kennedy claims that the case is about the constitutionality of discriminating between two categories of First Amendment speakers—corporations and human beings. But that just begs the question. The real issue in *Citizens United* was whether corporations should be viewed as First Amendment speakers in the first place. The business corporation is an artificial state-created entity with unlimited life; highly favorable techniques for acquiring, accumulating and retaining vast wealth through economic transactions having nothing to do with politics; and only one purpose—making money. Human beings, on the other hand, die, do not enjoy economic advantages like limited liability and, most important, have a conscience that sometimes transcends crude economic self-interest. Those dramatic differences raise a threshold question, ignored by Justice Kennedy, about whether corporations are even in the First Amendment ballpark.

One hundred years ago, confronted by the same question, the Supreme Court ruled that corporations, as artificial entities, are not protected by the Fifth Amendment's privilege against self-incrimination. That's still the law. In 1988 Justice Kennedy wrote that huge corporations do not deserve the self-incrimination privilege because the privilege "is an explicit right of a natural person, protecting the realm of human thought and expression." Kennedy never explains in *Citizens United* why freedom of speech is not exclusively a "right of a natural person, protecting the realm of human thought and expression." The closest he comes is the argument that voters will somehow benefit from a massive, uncontrolled flow of corporate propaganda. But he never explains how a voter is helped by being subjected to an avalanche of one-sided speech just before an election from a corporation with an unlimited budget and an economic stake in the outcome, especially when the voter often doesn't even know the speech is coming from a corporation.

We invented the business corporation for one reason—its economic potential. It makes sense, therefore, to vest it with constitutional protection for its property. It is, however, a huge and unsupported jump to vest business corporations with non-economic constitutional rights (like free speech and the privilege against self-incrimination) that flow from respect for human dignity. Robots have no souls. Neither do business corporations. Vesting either with free speech rights is legal fiction run amok.

Nor is it persuasive to argue that since newspaper corporations enjoy First Amendment protection, the electoral speech of oil companies and banks must be similarly protected. The short answer is that the First Amendment has a separate "press" clause that applies to newspapers but not to oil companies or banks. The fact that the First Amendment provides limited protection to commercial speech not only fails to support a general right of corporate free speech; it cuts strongly against it. Precisely because corporations lack human dignity, the Supreme Court has upheld bans on false, misleading and harmful advertising. A similar ban would wipe out most election ads by corporations.

Don't get me wrong. The government had no business trying to suppress the video from Citizens United, a ninety-minute right-wing hatchet job on Hillary Clinton. The video didn't fall under the campaign laws because it was necessary to take the affirmative step of downloading it, the equivalent of taking a book off a library shelf. The need for active collaboration by willing viewers should have ended the *Citizens United* case before it got started. In addition, the campaign statute applied only if 50,000 eligible voters were likely to view the video. How likely was it that 50,000 Democrats would have affirmatively downloaded a hatchet job on Hillary Clinton just before the primary? Moreover, lower court precedent had already recognized an exemption for electioneering communications with only tiny amounts of corporate funding, such as the less than 1 percent in *Citizens United*. Finally, the Supreme Court had already carved out a First Amendment safe harbor for nonprofit grassroots groups with *de minimis* corporate funding.

Justice Kennedy simply leapfrogged the numerous narrower grounds for a decision in order to overrule two precedents and grant as much power as possible to corporate America. Talk about "judicial activism." Given its inconsistent and gratuitous

nature, *Citizens United* is good law only as long as five votes support it. The decision should not be treated as binding precedent once the Court's personnel change. In 2012, anyone?

In fairness, *Citizens United* only makes an already terrible system worse. Campaign finance law rests on four mistakes made by judges. Taken together they are a democratic disaster. First, the Supreme Court insists that unlimited spending during an election campaign is pure speech, not speech mixed with conduct. Second, the Court insists that avoiding huge concentrations of electoral power is not important enough to justify limits on massive campaign spending by the superrich. Third, the Court insists that while the spending of unlimited amounts of campaign money is virtually immune from government regulation, the contribution of money to a candidate may be restricted. Finally, the Court has ruled that while preventing corruption justifies regulating campaign contributions, it does not justify limiting independent expenditures. The Court simply ignores the sense of obligation—or fear—generated by huge independent political expenditures.

In the world the Supreme Court has built, the very rich enjoy massively disproportionate political power. What's worse, the exercise of that power can now take place in secret and can tap the almost unfathomable wealth available to our newly minted corporate co-citizens. Say "hello" to Citizen Exxon. Almost fifty years ago, Felix Frankfurter warned that we would rue the day we allowed judges to shape American democracy. Maybe he was right. The first decade of this century opened with the Supreme Court's coup in *Bush v. Gore,* and closed with a putsch granting First Amendment rights to huge corporations to spend as much as they want to buy an election. At the rate the Court is going, soon we will be able to be adopted by a corporation. Maybe even marry one. Until then, I'm afraid we'll just have to settle for being fucked by them.

Protecting Speech

What is it about the *Citizens United* case that seems to drive so many of its learned critics close to the edge? What is it that now drives my friend Burt Neuborne, a most sophisticated legal observer, to wind up sounding somewhat more like Lady Chatterley's gamekeeper than the esteemed scholar he is?

It certainly shouldn't be the impact of the ruling on the 2010 midterm elections. As the Campaign Finance Institute, a nonpartisan research organization, concluded, "Party and non-party spending to help competitive Democrats and Republicans was about equal across the board. As a result, neither set of expenditures could be said to have tipped the electoral balance."

Nor should Burt be so agitated at the notion that for-profit corporations have First Amendment rights. That was not only well established in the law for many years before *Citizens United*—again, Justice Kennedy cited twenty-five prior cases in his opinion in which corporations had received full First Amendment rights—but has been essential to the protection of such rights for all.

Burt would limit such rights only to "press" entities. A free press is essential to a free society. But as Justice William Brennan, no slouch in defending First Amendment rights, repeated in an opinion he wrote twenty-five years ago, "The inherent worth of . . . speech in terms of its capacity for informing the public does not depend upon the identity of its source, whether corporation, association, union, or individual." Justice John Paul Stevens, the author years later of the dissent in *Citizens United,* joined that opinion, which also rejected out of hand the notion that "speakers other than the press deserve lesser First Amendment protection." Brennan and Stevens (then) were right; Burt isn't.

In the end, though, the issue isn't what speech Burt or I would allow. Or even what speech the Supreme Court should protect. It's what power Congress should have over speech. The McCain-Feingold law and other legislation held unconstitutional in *Citizens United* contained sweeping bans on speech. They made criminal, as Justice Kennedy pointed out, a Sierra Club ad within sixty days of an election condemning a member of Congress who favored logging in national parks. They barred unions from publishing pamphlets endorsing candidates for president. A ruling that protects such speech should be celebrated, not mocked.

The Censorship Canard

Not even Floyd Abrams, one of the best lawyers I know, can defend *Citizens United.* Floyd notes, correctly, that the case does not prevent Congress from requiring disclosure of corporate election expenditures. He fails to note, though, that Congress attempted to do just that but was blocked on a 59-39 Republican Senate filibuster vote. Thirty-nine senators representing a minority of the population are enough to prevent disclosure of corporate election spending. What are the odds that a wholly owned Congress dependent on massive corporate financial support will find sixty votes in the Senate for disclosure?

Floyd argues that First Amendment concern by liberals about corporate election speech isn't new. He cites Truman's veto of the Taft-Hartley Act and liberal justices' (unsuccessful) efforts to protect speech by the CIO and the UAW. He assumes that the First Amendment rights of unions and corporations are joined at the hip. But unions are free associations of individuals who join together to advance their economic and political interests. A union's money comes from its members' dues. If support for a union is required by law, a dissenter is entitled to a refund for any speech with which he or she disagrees. But corporations derive their funds from market transactions having nothing to do with politics. When you put gas in your car or buy a beer, do you think you are making a political contribution? If individuals associated with corporations want to form voluntary associations analogous to unions, that's fine—as long as they use their own money.

The twenty-five prior cases cited by Floyd allegedly recognizing corporate speech rights deal solely with commercial speech designed to flog a corporation's products or to the right of the press to carry on its constitutionally protected activities.

Just because we let corporations sell soap and own newspapers doesn't mean we have to turn our democracy over to them.

Finally, Floyd plays the lawyer's trump—the ad horrendum argument—warning that corporate-financed books are next on the censorship radar. He ignores the First Amendment's press clause, which protects corporate publishers. More fundamental, though, he ignores the fact that a book needs a voluntary reader. The law struck down in *Citizens United* had nothing to do with books. It targeted only those forms of speech—TV and radio ads—that blast their way into your consciousness with no help from the hearer.

In the end, *Citizens United* licenses a small group of corporate managers to use a vast trove of other people's money to buy elections in secret, using forms of speech that cannot be easily avoided. Although 80 percent of Americans don't want to be bombarded with corporate electoral propaganda, *Citizens United* insists that unrestricted, massive corporate electioneering is really good for us. Even Floyd Abrams can't make that medicine go down.

Critical Thinking

1. How and why do Abrams and Neuborne differ on how corporations should be treated in the context of freedom of speech?

2. What are the key gaps between myth and reality in connection with the *Citizens United* decision, according to Floyd Abrams?

3. Does the *Citizens United* ruling prevent corporations' election spending from being disclosed? Why, according to Neuborne, is such disclosure not required and what are the consequences?

4. On what four mistakes made by judges, according to Neuborne, does current campaign finance law rest?

Create Central

www.mhhe.com/createcentral

Internet References

Federal Election Commission
  www.fec.gov
Brennan Center for Justice
  www.brennancenter.org
OpenSecrets.org: Center for Responsive Politics
  www.opensecrets.org

FLOYD ABRAMS, a senior partner in the firm of Cahill Gordon and Reindel LLP, is the author of *Speaking Freely: Trials of the First Amendment* (2005). **BURT NEUBORNE**, the Inez Milholland Professor of Civil Liberties at New York University Law School, is the founding legal director of the Brennan Center for Justice at New York University. He served as national legal director of the ACLU during the Reagan administration, and has represented Senators John McCain and Russ Feingold in litigation over campaign finance reform.

Article   Prepared by: Bruce Stinebrickner, *DePauw University*

Bill of (Unwritten) Rights

We've been stuck on 27 amendments for a while. Here are 16 ideas that are vying to become the Twenty-Eighth.

RICHARD MORGAN

Learning Outcomes

After reading this article, you will be able to:

- Consider the frequency with which the U.S. Constitution has been amended since 1787 and ponder the implications of the current "drought" in adding new amendments.

- Assess the desirability of a wide variety of proposals for amendments to the Constitution.

America's longest drought between constitutional amendments since the Civil War was from 1870 to 1913. In that time, there were two presidential assassinations and several financial panics; the light bulb, telephone, movie theater, radio, and airplane were invented; the Supreme Court legalized segregation; fire destroyed Chicago and an earthquake flattened San Francisco; and the United States added 11 new states. Despite the frenzy, the Constitution went untouched.

The most recent amendment—the Twenty-Seventh in 1992, which prohibits changes to congressional salaries from taking effect until the next term—was an unfinished James Madison plan unearthed by University of Texas student Gregory Watson, who earned a C for finding it. The amendment before that, the Twenty-Sixth, was the last to add an original idea to the Constitution. It lowered the voting age to 18 and passed in 1971.

Measuring from the Twenty-Sixth, the country is about to tie that long drought between amendments. Even counting from the Twenty-Seventh, for the first time since 1913 (when Congress passed two amendments), it will soon be possible for someone to enter law school having lived his or her entire life under a static Constitution.

Which isn't to say Washington hasn't tried. Most ideas for new amendments fall into one of two categories: either political

amendments, which seek to settle hot-button issues like gay marriage and abortion; or procedural amendments, which seek to change how we practice politics in the United States. None has passed muster, failing either in Congress or the state legislatures, if it made it that far at all.

We got law professors to weigh in on the various proposals over the years. Here's a look at amendments that might have been, still could be, and never stood a chance of becoming the Twenty-Eighth Amendment.

Political

The Equal Rights Amendment
Passed Congress in 1972;
Fell Three States Short of Ratification by 1982 Deadline

This famous effort to enshrine women's equal rights in the Constitution failed in 1982, but since 1976, the Supreme Court has said the Fourteenth Amendment bans gender discrimination except where there is an important government purpose. "What would it accomplish?" asks NYU's Barry Friedman, who adds it could be rebooted as a gay-equality amendment.

The Adam & Eve Amendment
Defeated in the Senate in 2004 and 2006;
Reintroduced Unsuccessfully in 2008 and 2013

An amendment to restrict marriage to heterosexual couples never made it to state legislatures in 2006. Since then, 12 states and the District of Columbia have legalized gay marriage; 12 states have banned it. Public opinion has shifted strongly in favor of gay rights, making a successful revival unlikely.

The Balanced-Budget Amendment
Passed By the House in 1995; Defeated in the Senate

Forty-five states have already amended their constitutions to require legislatures to balance their budgets, but Washington has held out. If he had to bet on the Twenty-Eighth Amendment, Georgetown Law's Louis Michael Seidman's money is on this one. In 2011, Warren Buffett suggested a legislative alternative: "You just pass a law that says that, anytime there is a deficit of more than 3 percent of GDP, all sitting members of Congress are ineligible for re-election."

The Personhood Amendment
Introduced in Hundreds of Slightly Differing Forms Since 1973

This year, the North Dakota state legislature passed an amendment granting full personhood rights to human embryos—and anti-abortion activists hope the nation will one day, too. Pro-choice advocates, meanwhile, have already devised a clever rebuttal: Personhood would extend citizenship to anyone conceived in the United States, not merely born here.

The Non-Personhood Amendment
Introduced in 2011; Since Abandoned

While conservatives attempted to write fetal personhood into the Constitution, Senator Bernie Sanders, the socialist from Vermont, tried to erase corporate personhood from it. His amendment declared, once and for all, that corporations aren't people—and therefore lack free-speech protections. With that settled, Sanders's amendment would have then outlawed all corporate campaign contributions.

The Star-Spangled Amendment
Passed by the House Every Congressional Term From 1995 Until 2005; Always Stalled in the Senate

It reads in full: "The Congress shall have power to prohibit the physical desecration of the flag of the United States." It's popular in Republican Congresses, but even some conservatives chafe: "It becomes much harder to defend displays of the Confederate flag as free expression if you have an amendment banning flag-burning," says Eugene Volokh, a law professor at UCLA.

The This-Is-How-Much-We-Hate-Obamacare Amendment
Subcommittee Purgatory

After the House's 37 failed attempts to rescind Obamacare, Senator Marco Rubio, the Florida Republican with White House ambitions, proposed an amendment that "Congress shall make no law that imposes a tax on a failure to purchase goods or services." Representative Steven Palazzo, a Mississippi Republican, introduced a similar proposal in the House. Look for this to gain some fans as Obamacare rolls into effect in 2014.

The Campaign-Finance Amendment
Proposed in the House in 2012

Less radical than Bernie Sanders's proposal, this amendment would empower Congress and the states to publicly fund elections and limit private campaign contributions. Representative Adam Schiff, a California Democrat, introduced it last year, with Harvard Law Professor Laurence Tribe's assistance. The proposal came as the 2012 presidential race saw $524 million in spending from independent groups.

Procedural
The Schwarzenegger Amendment
Introduced in Congress More Than Two Dozen Times Since 1870, Most Recently in 2003 by Orrin Hatch; Never Passed

Believe it or not, the Founders actually allowed foreign-born Americans to become president—as long as they had been naturalized by 1787. That was too early for Arnold Schwarzenegger, who at the height of his popularity as California's governor sparked hopes for an amendment to allow immigrants into the highest offices.

The Gore Amendment
Unintroduced

"I had thought an election where the presidency goes to the loser of the popular vote would trigger an amendment abolishing or restructuring the electoral college, but I was wrong," says Yale Law School's Akhil Reed Amar. He has proposed a clever, non-constitutional initiative where state legislatures bind their electors to the national popular vote.

The Armageddon Amendment
Introduced 2001; Since Abandoned

After 9/11, Representative Brian Baird, a Washington Democrat, proposed a constitutional amendment spelling out the response to a disaster that wipes out huge swaths of Congress or the Cabinet. It never gathered much steam, even as intelligence officials bemoaned the Beltway's lack of imagination in the war on terror. "People don't like to write their own obituaries," says Alex Kozinski, chief judge of the Ninth Circuit's Court of Appeals.

The D.C.-Statehood Amendment
Passed Congress in 1978; Ratified by Only 16 States by 1985 Deadline

Local license plates bemoaning "TAXATION WITHOUT REPRESENTATION" have done little to change things in Washington, D.C.: The District's status is explicitly laid out in the Constitution, and Washingtonians will need to amend it if they want full representation. One recent piece of legislation decreed the District "shall be treated as though it were a state," but Republicans balked: They are not about to add more Democrats to Congress.

The No-More-Term-Limits Amendment
Last Introduced in the House in January 2013

It took the Great Depression in conjunction with World War II to enable FDR's epic, four-term presidency—and the Twenty-Second Amendment was passed to ensure no one would repeat the performance. But Congress might be persuaded to pass a new amendment to repeal the two-term limit if, say, a charismatic president were in office during a confluence of catastrophes. It's exactly what the 2008 financial crisis did to the mayorship of New York.

The Congressional-Collar Amendment
Subcommittee Purgatory

This year alone, at least eight representatives and two senators (including Rand Paul, the Kentucky Republican and White House hopeful) have proposed amendments to impose congressional term limits. Such a move would forever protect the record of Representative John Dingell, the Michigan Democrat with the longest-ever stint in Congress. He shouldn't count on it, though: His colleagues are unlikely to cut short their own careers.

The Voters' Amendment
Subcommittee Purgatory

In May, Representative Jim Cooper, a Tennessee Democrat, proposed a simple amendment: "The right of adult citizens of the United States to vote shall not be denied or abridged by the United States or any State." It was sparked by a rash of voter-ID controversies (mostly in Southern states) and exacerbated this summer when the Supreme Court gutted the historic Voting Rights Act of 1965.

The To-Hell-With-Amendments Amendment
Unintroduced

"There is such ridiculous veneration attached to the U.S. Constitution," says University of Texas Law Professor Sanford Levinson, "that almost nobody takes amendment as a serious possibility." He advocates a new constitutional convention—but Yale's Amar says you wouldn't even need a convention for an overhaul: "You could just have an amendment that says. The foregoing is repealed in favor of the following,' and then write a whole new Constitution."

Critical Thinking

1. How frequently, relatively speaking, has the U.S. Constitution been amended in recent years?
2. What are some current or recent proposals or ideas for amending the Constitution, including those that have never been introduced and those that have been introduced but not passed?

Create Central
www.mhhe.com/createcentral

Internet References

National Constitutional Center
Constitutioncenter.org
New York Times: "We the People" Loses Appeal with People around the World"
http://www.nytimes.com/2012/02/07/us/we-the-people-loses-appeal-with-people-around-the-world.html?pagewanted=all&_r=0

Unit 2

UNIT

Prepared by: Bruce Stinebrickner, *DePauw University*

Structures of American Politics

James Madison, one of the primary architects of the American system of government, observed that the three-branch structure of government created at the Constitutional Convention of 1787 pitted the ambitions of some individuals against the ambitions of others. Nearly two centuries later, political scientist Richard Neustadt wrote that the structure of American national government is one of "separated institutions sharing powers." These two eminent students of American politics suggest an important proposition: The very design of American national government contributes to the struggles that occur among government officials who have different institutional loyalties and potentially competing goals. This unit is divided into four sections. The first three treat the three traditional branches of American government and the last one treats the bureaucracy.

Building on Madison's deliberate pitting of ambition versus ambition, a second point to remember when studying the institutions of American national government is that the Constitution provides only the bare skeleton of the workings of the American political system. The flesh and blood of the presidency, Congress, judiciary, and bureaucracy are derived from decades of experience and the expectations and behavior of today's political actors. The way a particular institution functions and interacts with other institutions is partly determined by the identities of those who occupy relevant offices, even as the offices shape the persons occupying them.

The presidency operates differently with Barack Obama in the White House than it did when George W. Bush was president. Similarly, Congress and the Supreme Court function differently according to who are serving as members and especially who hold leadership positions within the institutions. There were significant changes in the House of Representatives after Republican John Boehner succeeded Democrat Nancy Pelosi as Speaker of the House in 2011 and, before that, when Pelosi took over from Republican Dennis Hastert in 2007. In the Senate, within a two-year period beginning in January 2001, Republican majority leader Trent Lott was succeeded by Democrat Tom Daschle, who in turn was succeeded by Republican Bill Frist. These rapid changes in Senate leadership brought changes in the operation of the Senate. Changes were evident again when

Democrat Harry Reid succeeded Frist in 2007 and once more when Republican Mitch McConnell became Senate majority leader in January 2015.

A third point about American national government today is that in recent decades traditional branch-versus-branch conflict has been accompanied and probably even overshadowed by increasing polarization between the two major parties. In the first six years of George W. Bush's presidency, Republican members of Congress seemed to be substantially more influenced by the party affiliation that they shared with President Bush than the branch loyalty that, in Madison's eyes, should and would pit Congress against the president.

In the November 2006 elections, Democrats regained majority control of both houses of Congress. For Democrats in the 110th Congress, party affiliation and a belief in institutional or branch prerogatives reinforced one another. Both their party differences with President Bush *and* the belief that Congress is and should be co-equal to the executive branch fueled opposition to the Iraq war and to other Bush actions. President Bush no doubt had both party loyalties and executive branch prerogatives in mind as he contended with Democratic leaders and Democratic majorities in the 110th Congress. The 2008 elections brought Democratic control to all three elected institutions of the national government (Presidency, House of Representatives, and Senate), a situation that political scientists call "unified government." In January 2009, a new period of unified government, this time under Democratic control, began. In January 2011, however, "divided government" returned after Republicans regained majority control of the House of Representatives in the November 2010 elections. The hard-fought 2012 elections resulted in continuing the same divided government arrangement as before: Democrats Obama and Biden were re-elected to the presidency and vice presidency, Republicans kept majority control of the House, and Democrats maintained their majority in the Senate. Divided government continued after the November 2014 elections, although in a different configuration: Republicans retained their control of the House but also gained majority control of the Senate.

Some observers of the American political system, Wood-row Wilson among them, have argued that unified government is likely to be more effective and efficient than its counterpart, divided government, wherein no party controls all three elected elements of American national government. Others, most notably Professor David Mayhew of Yale University, arguably the most respected contemporary political scientist specializing in the study of American politics, have concluded that "unified governments" vary very little from "divided governments" in what they accomplish. For more than 60 percent of the time since World War II, Americans have lived under divided government.

The primary focus of articles on the presidency in this unit is the presidency of Barack Obama, although other presidencies are also treated in some of the selections. In November 2008, Obama won the presidential election over Republican John McCain in the midst of the Great Recession resulting from the collapse of several key financial institutions earlier in 2008. Obama's candidacy also benefited from widespread disapproval of Republican President George W. Bush's performance in office. By the third year of Obama's presidency and amidst a still struggling economy, however, public opinion polls showed growing disapproval of Obama's performance. Many of his policy initiatives were unpopular, including the historic Affordable Care Act, Obama's signature legislative accomplishment enacted in early 2010 and known as "Obamacare." A year after his November 2012 re-election, Obama's public approval ratings hovered somewhat over 40 percent, which is where they generally remained for another year or so. As of this writing in October 2015, the president's public approval ratings are averaging about 45 percent . It is in such contexts that selections in this unit address the presidency and reflect how individuals both shape the presidency—and American government more generally—and are shaped by it.

Selections in this unit also treat Congress, which has undergone noteworthy changes in the past five decades after more than a half-century of relative stability anchored by the extremely powerful seniority system instituted in the early twentieth century. In the 1970s, reforms in the seniority system worked to decentralize power in committees on Capitol Hill, most notably in the House of Representatives. As a result of the November 1994 elections, Republicans unexpectedly took over the House after forty consecutive years of Democratic majorities and the resulting change in leadership brought more changes. Incoming Republican Speaker Newt Gingrich reduced the power of committees and the importance of the seniority system, imposed term limits on committee chairs, consolidated power in the Speaker's office, and became a prominent and powerful figure on the national scene. Republicans maintained control of the House for twelve consecutive years, but Democrats then regained a House majority for four years (2007–2011), followed by a Republican majority that will last until at least January 2017. After Speaker Gingrich resigned in late 1998, the speakership has been occupied by the somewhat lackluster Republican Dennis Hastert (1999–2007); Nancy Pelosi, the first woman speaker in history and a strong Democratic partisan (2007–2011);

and Republican John Boehner (2011–2015), who presided over a fractious House Republican party caucus that included Tea Party and other very conservative members who did not consistently support his leadership. In late October 2015 Republican Paul D. Ryan was elected to succeed Boehner, who a month earlier announced his intention to resign the speakership as well as his House seat.

Party control of the Senate was in Democratic hands from 2009 to 2015, which, as already noted, contributed to unified government during the first two years of the Obama presidency. In 2009, Democrats (joined by two independents) controlled 60 seats in the Senate, making for what sometimes operated as a "filibuster-proof" majority in support of Democratic policy initiatives. During that year, the $787-billion stimulus was enacted and the ground-work was laid for the historic Obamacare legislation (signed into law by President Obama in March 2010) and the far-reaching Dodd-Frank financial regulation act (signed into law in July 2010).

The selections on Congress address various dimensions of congressional operations and problems. Taken together, they illustrate the three points introduced at the beginning of this unit overview: the pitting of the institutional ambitions of Congress against those of the president, the impact of individual officeholders on the functioning of their institutions (and of American national government more generally), and the increased party polarization on Capitol Hill. This last phenomenon seems to make decision making and problem solving in a period of divided government all the more difficult. In turn, stalemate, brinkmanship, gridlock, and "kicking the can down the road" (that is, foregoing long-term solutions in favor of temporary fixes that do not resolve underlying problems) have increasingly seemed to characterize government operations in Washington.

The Supreme Court sits at the top of the U.S. court system and is the subject of a number of selections in this unit. The Court is not merely a legal institution; it is a policymaker whose decisions can affect the lives of millions of citizens. The Court's decisive role in determining the outcome of the 2000 presidential election illustrated its powerful role in the American political system. Membership of the nine-member Court—and, in turn, operation of the institution as a whole—was unusually stable between 1994 and 2005, one of the longest periods in American history during which no Supreme Court vacancies occurred. In July 2005, Associate Justice Sandra Day O'Connor announced her intention to resign, and a few months later Chief Justice William Rehnquist died. President Bush's nominees to fill the two vacancies, John Roberts and Samuel Alito, became chief justice and associate justice, respectively. Less than four months into Barack Obama's presidency, Associate Justice David Souter announced his retirement. President Obama nominated Sonia Sotomayor to replace Souter, and she became the first Hispanic woman to sit on the Court. In 2010, President Obama nominated Elena Kagan to succeed retiring Associate Justice John Paul Stevens, and she became the fourth woman in history to serve on the Court and brought the number of women justices currently serving to three, an all-time high. The current Supreme

Court includes six Catholics, three Jews, and *no* Protestants, a remarkable demographic array in an institution that for more than two centuries had been dominated by Protestant white males.

In June 2012 Americans awaited with great anticipation the Court's ruling on the constitutionality of Obamacare. Three years later they awaited another pivotal Court ruling on Obamacare as well as a landmark decision on the constitutionality of same-sex marriage. The 5-4 decision in *National Federation of Business v. Sebelius* (2012) and the June 2015 6-3 decision supporting Obamacare, coupled with the Court's 5-4 ruling in *Obergefell v. Hodges* on the same day upholding same-sex marriage, have led to numerous assessments of the inner workings of the Roberts Court.

Like all people in high government offices, the chief justice and the eight associate justices have policy and political views of their own, and the nine justices both shape the Court and are shaped by it. The selections on the judiciary address the ways the chief justice and the eight associate justices act on their views and how they interact with one another in shaping decisions of the Court.

The bureaucracy of the national government is responsible for carrying out policies determined by top-ranking officials. As several selections in this unit make clear, however, the bureaucracy is not simply a neutral administrative instrument and bureaucrats are often criticized for waste and inefficiency. Even so, government bureaucracies must be given credit for many of the accomplishments of American government. Regardless of whether we like it, government bureaucracies wield great power and the interactions of bureaucracies with the three traditional branches are key elements in the functioning of U.S. national government. In July 2010, Congress passed, and the president signed, the Dodd-Frank Wall Street Reform and Consumer Protection Act, which established the Bureau of Consumer Financial Protection. This new agency was to oversee and regulate financial dealings of the sort that had triggered the Great Recession of 2008–2009. According to the U.S. Chamber of Commerce, the mammoth bill directed bureaucrats to formulate 350 rules, conduct 47 studies, and write 74 reports!

Article   Prepared by: Bruce Stinebrickner, *DePauw University*

The Founders' Great Mistake

Who is responsible for the past eight years of dismal American governance? "George W. Bush" is a decent answer. But we should reserve some blame for the Founding Fathers, who created a presidential office that is ill-considered, vaguely defined, and ripe for abuse. Here's how to fix what the Founders got wrong—before the next G. W. Bush enters the Oval Office.

GARRETT EPPS

Learning Outcomes

After reading this article, you will be able to:

- Consider whether you agree with the author's contention that those who wrote the Constitution made a "great mistake" in creating the presidency that they did.

- Judge whether President George W. Bush was indeed a "runaway president."

For the past eight years, George W. Bush has treated the White House much as Kenneth Grahame's Mr. Toad treated a new automobile—like a shiny toy to be wrecked by racing the motor, spinning smoke from the tires, and smashing through farmyards until the wheels come off. Bush got to the Oval Office despite having lost the popular vote, and he governed with a fine disdain for democratic and legal norms—stonewalling congressional oversight; detaining foreigners and U.S. citizens on his "inherent authority"; using the Justice Department as a political cudgel; ordering officials to ignore statutes and treaties that he found inconvenient; and persisting in actions, such as the Iraq War, that had come to be deeply unpopular in Congress and on Main Street.

Understandably, most Americans today are primarily concerned with whether Barack Obama can clean up Bush's mess. But as Bush leaves the White House, it's worth asking why he was able to behave so badly for so long without being stopped by the Constitution's famous "checks and balances." Some of the problems with the Bush administration, in fact, have their source not in Bush's leadership style but in the constitutional design of the presidency. Unless these problems are fixed, it will only be a matter of time before another hot-rodder gets hold of the keys and damages the country further.

The historian Jack N. Rakove has written, "The creation of the presidency was [the Framers'] most creative act." That may be true, but it wasn't their best work. The Framers were designing something the modern world had never seen—a republican

chief executive who would owe his power to the people rather than to heredity or brute force. The wonder is not that they got so much wrong, but that they got anything right at all.

According to James Madison's *Notes of Debates in the Federal Convention of 1787,* the executive received surprisingly little attention at the Constitutional Convention in Philadelphia. Debate over the creation and workings of the new Congress was long and lively; the presidency, by contrast, was fashioned relatively quickly, after considerably less discussion. One important reason for the delegates' reticence was that George Washington, the most admired man in the world at that time, was the convention's president. Every delegate knew that Washington would, if he chose, be the first president of the new federal government—and that the new government itself would likely fail without Washington at the helm. To express too much fear of executive authority might have seemed disrespectful to the man for whom the office was being tailored.

Washington's force of personality terrified almost all of his contemporaries, and although he said little as presiding officer, he was not always quiet. Once, when an unknown delegate left a copy of some proposed provisions lying around, Washington scolded the delegates like a headmaster reproving careless prep-schoolers, and then left the document on a table, saying, "Let him who owns it take it." No one did.

Even when Washington remained silent, his presence shaped the debate. When, on June 1, James Wilson suggested that the executive power be lodged in a single person, no one spoke up in response. The silence went on until Benjamin Franklin finally suggested a debate; the debate itself proceeded awkwardly for a little while, and was then put off for another day.

Many of the conversations about presidential authority were similarly awkward, and tended to be indirect. Later interpreters have found the original debates on the presidency, in the words of former Supreme Court Justice Robert H. Jackson, "almost as enigmatic as the dreams Joseph was called upon to interpret for Pharaoh."

In the end, the Framers were artfully vague about the extent and limits of the president's powers. Article I, Section 8 of the Constitution, which empowers Congress, runs 429 words; Article II, Section 2, the presidential equivalent, is about half as long. The powers assigned to the president alone are few: he can require Cabinet members to give him their opinions in writing; he can convene a special session of Congress "on extraordinary occasions," and may set a date for adjournment if the two houses cannot agree on one; he receives ambassadors and is commander in chief of the armed forces; he has a veto on legislation (which Congress can override); and he has the power to pardon.

The president also *shares* two powers with the Senate—to make treaties, and to appoint federal judges and other "officers of the United States," including Cabinet members. And, finally, the president has two specific *duties*—to give regular reports on the state of the union, and to "take care that the laws be faithfully executed."

All in all, the text of Article II, while somewhat ambiguous—a flaw that would be quickly exploited—provided little warning that the office of president would become uniquely powerful. Even at the convention, Madison mused that it "would rarely if ever happen that the executive constituted as ours is proposed to be would have firmness enough to resist the legislature." In fact, when citizens considered the draft Constitution during the ratification debates in 1787 and 1788, many of their concerns centered on the possibility that the Senate would make the president its cat's-paw. Few people foresaw the modern presidency, largely because the office as we know it today bears so little relation to that prescribed by the Constitution.

The modern presidency is primarily the intellectual handiwork not of "the Framers" but of one Framer—Alexander Hamilton. Hamilton's idea of the presidency can be found in a remarkable speech he gave to the convention, on June 18, 1787. In it, Hamilton argued that the president should serve for life, name Cabinet members without Senate approval, have an absolute veto on legislation, and have "the direction of war" once "authorized or begun." The president would be a monarch, Hamilton admitted, but an "elective monarch."

Hamilton's plan was so far from the mainstream of thought at the convention that none of its provisions was ever seriously discussed. Nonetheless, Hamilton was and remains the chief theorist of the presidency, first in writing his essays for *The Federalist* and then in serving as George Washington's secretary of the Treasury. In this latter role, acting as Washington's de facto prime minister, Hamilton took full advantage of the vagueness and brevity of Article II, laying the groundwork for an outsize presidency while the war-hero Washington was still in office.

In *The Federalist,* Hamilton had famously proclaimed that "energy in the executive is a leading character in the definition of good government." Just how much energy he favored became clear during America's first foreign crisis, the Neutrality Proclamation controversy of 1793. When Britain and France went to war, many Americans wanted to aid their Revolutionary ally. But Washington and the Federalists were rightly terrified of war with the powerful British Empire. Washington unilaterally proclaimed that the United States would be neutral.

France's American supporters, covertly aided by Thomas Jefferson, fiercely attacked Washington for exceeding his

constitutional authority. The power to make treaties, they said, was jointly lodged in the president and the Senate; how could Washington unilaterally interpret or change the terms of the treaty of alliance with France?

Under the pen name "Pacificus," Hamilton wrote a defense of Washington's power to act without congressional sanction. The first Pacificus essay is the mother document of the "unitary executive" theory that Bush's apologists have pushed to its limits since 2001. Hamilton seized on the first words of Article II: "The executive power shall be vested in a President of the United States of America." He contrasted this wording with Article I, which governs Congress and which begins, "All legislative powers herein granted shall be vested in a Congress of the United States." What this meant, Hamilton argued, was that Article II was "a general grant of . . . power" to the president. Although Congress was limited to its enumerated powers, the executive could do literally anything that the Constitution did not expressly forbid. Hamilton's president existed, in effect, outside the Constitution.

That's the Bush conception, too. In 2005, John Yoo, the author of most of the administration's controversial "torture memos," drew on Hamilton's essay when he wrote, "The Constitution provides a general grant of executive. power to the president." Since Article I vests in Congress "only those legislative powers 'herein granted',," Yoo argued, the more broadly stated Article II must grant the president "an unenumerated executive authority."

Hamilton's interpretation has proved durable even though there is little in the record of constitutional framing and ratification to suggest that anyone else shared his view. In times of crisis, power flows to the executive; too rarely does it flow back. And while Washington himself used his power wisely (Jeffersonians found out in 1812 that pulling the British lion's tail was poor policy), it was during his administration that the seeds of the "national-security state" were planted.

The system that the Framers developed for electing the president was, unfortunately, as flawed as their design of the office itself. When Madison opened discussion on presidential election in Philadelphia, he opined that "the people at large" were the "fittest" electorate. But he immediately conceded that popular election would hurt the South, which had many slaves and few voters relative to the North. To get around this "difficulty" he proposed using state electors. Electoral-vote strength was based on a state's total population, not on its number of voters—and the South received representation for three-fifths of its slaves both in the House of Representatives and in the Electoral College.

Scholars still debate whether the Framers foresaw the prospect of a contested presidential election, followed by a peaceful shift of power. (Remember that, as Shakespeare pointed out in *Richard II,* kings left office feet first.) Some members of the founding generation believed that a duly elected president would simply be reelected until his death, at which point the vice president would take his place, much like the Prince of Wales ascending to the throne.

Perhaps as a result, the mechanics of presidential election laid out in the Constitution quickly showed themselves to be utterly unworkable. The text of Article II contained no provision for a presidential ticket—with one candidate for president and one for vice president. Instead, each elector was supposed to vote for any two presidential candidates; the candidate who received the largest majority of votes would be president; the runner-up would be vice president. In 1800, this ungainly system nearly brought the country to civil war. Thomas Jefferson and Aaron Burr ran as a team; their electors were expected to vote for both of them. Jefferson assumed that one or two would drop Burr's name from the ballot. That would have given Jefferson the larger majority, with Burr winning the vice presidency. But due to a still-mysterious misunderstanding, all the electors voted for both candidates, producing a tie in the electoral vote and throwing the election to a House vote.

The ensuing drama lasted six days and 36 ballots before Hamilton threw Federalist support to Jefferson (as much as he despised Jefferson, he regarded Burr as "an embryo-Caesar"). This choice began the chain of events that led to Hamilton's death at Burr's hands three years later. More important, the imbroglio exposed the fragility of the election procedure.

In 1804, the Electoral College was "repaired" by the Twelfth Amendment; now the electors would vote for one candidate for president and another for vice president. This was the first patch on Article II, but far from the last—the procedures for presidential election and succession were changed by constitutional amendment in 1933, 1951, 1961, and 1967. None of this fine-tuning has been able to fix the system. In 1824, 1876, 1888, and 2000, the Electoral College produced winners who received fewer popular votes than the losers, and it came startlingly close to doing so again in 2004; in 1824, 1876, and 2000, it also produced prolonged uncertainty and the prospect of civil unrest—or the fact of it.

Even when the election system works passably, a president-elect must endure another indefensible feature of the succession process. In England, a new prime minister takes office the day after parliamentary elections; in France, a newly elected president is inaugurated within a week or two. But when Americans choose a new leader, the victor waits weeks—nearly a quarter-year—to assume office. The presidential interregnum is a recurrent period of danger.

Originally, a new president didn't take office until March 4. This long delay nearly destroyed the nation after the 1860 election. During the disastrous "secession winter," Abraham Lincoln waited in Illinois while his feckless predecessor, James Buchanan, permitted secessionists to seize federal arsenals and forts. By March 1861, when Lincoln took office, the Civil War was nearly lost, though officially it had not even begun.

In 1932, Franklin Roosevelt crushed the incumbent, Herbert Hoover, but had to wait four months to take office. During that period, Hoover attempted to force the president-elect to abandon his proposals for economic reform. Roosevelt refused to commit himself, but the resulting uncertainty led the financial system to the brink of collapse.

The Twentieth Amendment, ratified in 1933, cut the interregnum nearly in half, but 11 weeks is still too long. After his defeat in 1992, President George H. W. Bush committed U.S. troops to a military mission in Somalia. The mission turned toxic, and Bill Clinton withdrew the troops the following year. Clinton was criticized for his military leadership, perhaps rightly—but the Constitution should not have permitted a repudiated president to commit his successor to an international conflict that neither the new president nor Congress had approved.

As the elder Bush did, an interregnum president retains the power of life or death over the nation. As Clinton did, an interregnum president may issue controversial or corrupt pardons. In either case, the voters have no means of holding their leader accountable.

The most dangerous presidential malfunction might be called the "runaway presidency." The Framers were fearful of making the president too dependent on Congress; short of impeachment—the atomic bomb of domestic politics—there are no means by which a president can be reined in politically during his term. Taking advantage of this deficiency, runaway presidents have at times committed the country to courses of action that the voters never approved—or ones they even rejected.

John Tyler, who was never elected president, was the first runaway, in 1841. William Henry Harrison had served only a few weeks; after his death, the obscure Tyler governed in open defiance of the Whig Party that had put him on the ticket, pressing unpopular proslavery policies that helped set the stage for the Civil War.

Andrew Johnson was the next unelected runaway. Politically, he had been an afterthought. But after Lincoln's assassination, Johnson adopted a pro-Southern Reconstruction policy. He treated the party that had nominated him with such scorn that many contemporaries came to believe he was preparing to use the Army to break up Congress by force. After Johnson rebuffed any attempt at compromise, the Republican House impeached him, but the Senate, by one vote, refused to remove him from office. His obduracy crippled Reconstruction; in fact, we still haven't fully recovered from that crisis.

American political commentators tend to think loosely about exertions of presidential authority. The paradigm cases are Lincoln rallying the nation after Fort Sumter, and Roosevelt, about a year before Pearl Harbor, using pure executive power to transfer American destroyers to embattled Britain in exchange for use of certain British bases. Because these great leaders used their authority broadly, the thinking goes, assertions of executive prerogative are valid and desirable.

Certainly there are times when presidential firmness is better than rapid changes in policy to suit public opinion. Executive theorists in the United States often pose the choice that way—steady, independent executive leadership or feckless, inconstant pursuit of what Hamilton called "the temporary delusion" of public opinion. But not all shifts in public opinion are delusive or temporary. An executive should have some independence, but a presidency that treats the people as irrelevant is not democratic. It is authoritarian.

Lincoln and Roosevelt asserted emergency powers while holding popular mandates. Lincoln had just won an election that also provided him with a handy majority in Congress; Roosevelt was enormously popular, and in 1940 his party outnumbered the opposition 3-to-1 in the Senate and by nearly 100 seats in the House.

But sometimes a president with little or no political mandate uses the office to further a surprising, obscure, or discredited political agenda. Under these circumstances, what poses as bold leadership is in fact usurpation. The most egregious case arises when a president's policy and leadership have been repudiated by the voters, either by a defeat for reelection or by a sweeping rejection of his congressional allies in a midterm election. When that happens, presidents too often do what George Bush did in 2006—simply persist in the conduct that has alienated the country. Intoxicated by the image of the hero-president, unencumbered by any direct political check, stubborn presidents in this situation have no incentive to change course.

When the voters turn sharply against a president mid-term, his leadership loses some or all of its legitimacy, and the result can be disastrous. Clinton was decisively repudiated in November 1994. After the election, the administration and the new Republican Congress remained so far apart on funding decisions that the government had to shut down for 26 days in 1995 and 1996. This episode is now remembered for Clinton's political mastery, but it was actually a dangerous structural failure. (Imagine that the al-Qaeda attacks of September 11, 2001, had happened instead on December 20, 1995, when the stalemate had forced the executive branch to send most of its "nonessential" employees home.)

To sum up, while George W. Bush may have been a particularly bad driver, the presidency itself is, and always has been, an unreliable vehicle—with a cranky starter, an engine too big for the chassis, erratic steering, and virtually no brakes. It needs an overhaul, a comprehensive redo of Article II.

Constitutional change is a daunting prospect. But consider how often we have already changed the presidency; it is the Constitution's most-amended feature. And this is the moment to think of reform—the public's attention is focused on the Bush disaster, and ordinary people might be willing to look at the flaws in the office that allowed Bush to do what he did.

So how should the presidency be changed?

First, voters should elect presidents directly. And once the vote is counted, the president-elect (and the new Congress) should take office within a week. Americans accustomed to the current system will object that this would not allow enough time to assemble a Cabinet—but in England and France, the new chief executive considers ministerial nominations before the election. A shorter interregnum would force the creation of something like the British shadow cabinet, in which a candidate makes public the names of his key advisers. That would give voters important information, and provide the president with a running start.

Next, Article II should include a specific and limited set of presidential powers. The "unitary executive" theorists should no longer be allowed to spin a quasi-dictatorship out of the bare phrase *executive power;* like the responsibilities of Congress, those of the president should be clearly enumerated.

It should be made clear, for example, that the president's powers as commander in chief do not crowd out the power of Congress to start—and stop—armed conflict. Likewise, the duty to "take care that the laws be faithfully executed" needs to be clarified: it is not the power to decide which laws the president wants to follow, or to rewrite new statutes in "signing statements" after Congress has passed them; it is a duty to uphold the Constitution, valid treaties, and congressional statutes (which together, according to the Constitution, form "the supreme law of the land").

After a transformative midterm election like that of 1994 or 2006, the nation should require a compromise between the rejected president and the new Congress. A president whose party has lost some minimum number of seats in Congress should be forced to form the equivalent of a national-unity government. This could be done by requiring the president to present a new Cabinet that includes members of both parties, which the new Congress would approve or disapprove as a whole—no drawn-out confirmation hearings on each nominee. If the president were unwilling to assemble such a government or unable to get congressional approval after, say, three tries, he would have to resign.

This would not give Congress control of the executive branch. A resigning president would be replaced by the vice president, who would not be subject to the new-Cabinet requirement. This new president might succeed politically where the previous one had failed (imagine Al Gore becoming president in 1995, and running in 1996—and perhaps in 2000—as an incumbent). And that possibility would discourage the new congressional majority from simply rejecting the compromise Cabinet. Resignation might be worse for them than approval.

As a final reform, we should reconsider the entire Hamiltonian concept of the "unitary executive." When George Washington became president, he left a large organization (the Mount Vernon plantation) to head a smaller one (the federal government). But today, the executive branch is a behemoth, with control over law enforcement, the military, economic policy, education, the environment, and most other aspects of national life. That behemoth is responsible to one person, and that one person, as we have seen, is only loosely accountable to the electorate.

In other areas, the Framers solved this problem neatly: they divided power in order to protect against its abuse. Congress was split into the House and the Senate to ensure that the legislative process would not be so efficient as to absorb powers properly belonging to the other branches. The problem now is not an overweening Congress but an aggrandized executive branch; still, the remedy is the same. We should divide the executive branch between two elected officials—a president, and an attorney general who would be voted in during midterm elections.

As we are learning from the ongoing scandal of the torture memos, one of the drawbacks of a single executive is that Justice Department lawyers may consider it their job to twist the law to suit the White House. But the president is not their client; the United States is. Justice Department lawyers appointed by an elected attorney general would have no motive to distort law and logic to empower the president, while the White House counsel's office, which does represent the president, would have every incentive to monitor the Justice Department to ensure that it did not tilt too strongly against the executive branch. The watchmen would watch each other.

This arrangement would hardly be unprecedented: most state governments elect an attorney general. The new Article II could make clear that the president has the responsibility for setting overall legal policy, just as governors do today.

None of these changes would erode the "separation of powers." That happens only when a change gives one branch's prerogatives to another branch. These changes refer in each instance back to the people, who are the proper source of all power. The changes would still leave plenty of room for "energy in the executive" but would afford far less opportunity for high-handedness, secrecy, and simple rigidity. They would allow presidential firmness, but not at the expense of democratic self-governance.

It's not surprising that the Framers did not understand the perils of the office they designed. They were working in the dark, and they got a lot of things right. But we should not let our admiration for the Framers deter us from fixing their mistakes.

Our government is badly out of balance. There is a difference between executive energy and autocratic license; between leadership and authoritarianism; between the democratic firmness of a Lincoln and the authoritarian rigidity of a Bush. The challenge we face today is to find some advantage in Bush's sorry legacy. Reform of the executive branch would be a good place to start.

Critical Thinking

1. What powers are assigned to the president acting alone? What powers are shared with the legislative branch? What two specific duties does the Constitution assign to the president?

2. How was the vice presidential selection process as originally outlined in the Constitution flawed? How have those challenges been addressed?

3. What are the problems associated with the relatively long time span between election results and inauguration day?

4. What four specific reforms to the presidency does the author propose? Do you favor them?

5. Do you agree that "our government is badly out of balance"? Why or why not?

Create Central

www.mhhe.com/createcentral

Internet References

White House
www.whitehouse.gov

The Atlantic Monthly, November, 1973: The Runaway Presidency
www.theatlantic.com/magazine/archive/1973/11/the-runaway-presidency/306211

Wall Street Journal, 2 September 2013: How War Powers, Congressional Action Have Intersected over Time
http://online.wsj.com/article/SB1000142412788732393260457904993334 2339844.html

Article   Prepared by: Bruce Stinebrickner, *DePauw University*

Do Presidents Matter?

Where foreign policy is concerned, the most-valuable traits are not always the ones we value most highly.

JOSEPH S. NYE, JR.

Learning Outcomes

After reading this article, you will be able to:

- Distinguish "transformational" and "transactional" presidents and determine when one sort of presidency is likely to be preferable to the other.

- Evaluate particular presidents for whether they pursued "transformational" or "transactional" presidencies and explain why.

- Project what place in the world the United States is likely to hold in comparison to other nations in the coming decades and the implications for how the United States "behaves" in international and world affairs.

The 21st century began with an extraordinary imbalance in world power. The United States was the only country able to project military force globally; it represented more than a quarter of the world economy, and had the world's leading soft-power resources in its universities and entertainment industry. America's primacy appeared well established.

Americans seemed to like this situation. In the 2012 presidential campaign, both major-party candidates insisted that American power was not in decline, and vowed that they would maintain American primacy. But how much are such promises within the ability of presidents to keep? Was presidential leadership ever essential to the establishment of American primacy, or was that primacy an accident of history that would have occurred regardless of who occupied the Oval Office?

Leadership experts and the public alike extol the virtues of transformational leaders—those who set out bold objectives and take risks to change the world. We tend to downplay "transactional" leaders, whose goals are more modest, as mere managers. But in looking closely at the leaders who presided over key periods of expanding American primacy in the past century, I found that while transformational presidents such as Woodrow Wilson and Ronald Reagan changed how Americans viewed their nation's role in the world, some transactional presidents, such as Dwight D. Eisenhower and George H. W. Bush, were more effective in executing their policies.

Transformation involves large gambles, the outcomes of which are not always immediately evident. One of history's great strategists, Otto von Bismarck, successfully bet in 1870 that a manufactured war with France would lead to Prussian unification of Germany. But he also bet that he could annex Alsace-Lorraine, a move with enormous costs that became clear only in 1914.

Franklin D. Roosevelt and Harry Truman made transformational bets on, respectively, the nation's entry into World War II and the subsequent containment of the Soviet Union, but each did so only after cautious initial approaches (and in Roosevelt's case, only after the Japanese bombed Pearl Harbor). John F. Kennedy and Lyndon Johnson mistakenly bet that Vietnam would prove to be a game of dominoes, whereas Eisenhower—who, ironically, had coined the domino metaphor—wisely avoided combat intervention. And Richard Nixon, who successfully bet on an opening to China in 1971, lost a nearly simultaneous bet in severing the dollar's tie to gold, thus contributing to rampant inflation over the subsequent decade.

Compare Woodrow Wilson, a failed transformational president, with the first George Bush, a successful transactional one. Wilson made a costly and mistaken bet on the Treaty of Versailles at the conclusion of the First World War. His noble vision of an American-led League of Nations was partially vindicated in the long term. But he lacked the leadership skills to implement this vision in his own time, and this shortcoming contributed to America's retreat into isolationism in the 1930s. In the case of Bush 41, the president's lack of what he called "the vision thing" limited his ability to sway Americans' perceptions of the nation and its role in the world. But his execution and management of policy was first-rate.

Consider, too, the contrast between the elder Bush's presidency and that of his son, George W. Bush, who has been described as having been obsessed with being a transformational president. Members of the younger Bush's administration often compared him to Ronald Reagan or Harry Truman, but the 20th-century president he most resembled was Wilson.

Both were highly religious and moralistic men who initially focused on domestic issues without an eye toward foreign policy. Both projected self-confidence, and both responded to a crisis boldly and resolutely. As Secretary of State Robert Lansing described Wilson's mind-set in 1917: "Even established facts were ignored if they did not fit in with his intuitive sense, this semi-divine power to select the right." Similarly, Tony Blair observed in 2010 that Bush "had great intuition. But his intuition was less . . . about politics and more about what he thought was right and wrong." Like Wilson, Bush placed a large, transformative bet on foreign policy—the invasion of Iraq—and, like Wilson, he lacked the skill to implement his plan successfully.

This is not an argument against transformational leaders in general. In turbulent situations, leaders such as Gandhi, Mandela, and King can play crucial roles in redefining a people's identity and aspirations. Nor is it an argument against transformational leaders in American foreign policy in particular. FDR and Truman made indelible contributions to the creation of the American era; others, such as Nixon, with his opening to China, or Carter, with his emphasis on human rights and nuclear nonproliferation, reoriented important aspects of foreign policy. But in judging leaders, we need to pay attention both to acts of commission and to acts of omission—dogs that barked and those that did not. For example, Ike refused to follow numerous recommendations by the military to use nuclear weapons during the Korean, Dien Bien Phu, and Quemoy-Matsu crises, at one point telling an adviser, "You boys must be crazy. We can't use those awful things against Asians for the second time in less than 10 years." In 1954, he explained his broader thinking to the Joint Chiefs of Staff. Suppose it would be possible to destroy Russia, he said. "Here would be a great area from the Elbe to Vladivostok . . . torn up and destroyed, without government, without its communications, just an area of starvation and disaster. I ask you, what would the civilized world do about it?" George H. W. Bush likewise largely eschewed transformational objectives, with one important exception: the reunification of Germany. But even here, he acted with caution. When the Berlin Wall was opened in November 1989, partly because of a mistake by East Germany, Bush was criticized for his low-key response. But his deliberate choice not to gloat or to humiliate the Soviets helped set the stage for the successful Malta summit with Mikhail Gorbachev a month later.

George W. Bush most resembled not Ronald Reagan or Harry Truman, but Woodrow Wilson.

Transformational leaders are important because they make choices that most other leaders would not. But a key question is how much risk a democratic public wants its leaders to take in foreign policy. The answer very much depends on the context, and that context is enormously complex, involving not only potential international effects, but the intricacies of domestic politics in multiple societies. This complexity gives special relevance to the Aristotelian virtue of prudence. We live in a world of diverse cultures, and we know very little about social engineering and how to "build nations." And when we cannot be sure how to improve the world, hubristic visions pose a grave danger. For these reasons, the virtues of transactional leaders with good contextual intelligence are also very important. Good leadership in this century may or may not be transformational, but it will almost certainly require a careful understanding of the context of change.

Decline, for example, is a misleading description of the current state of American power—one that President Obama has thankfully rejected. American influence is not in absolute decline, and in relative terms, there is a reasonable probability that the country will remain more powerful than any other single state in the coming decades. We do not live in a "post-American world," but neither do we live any longer in the American era of the late 20th century. No one has a crystal ball, but the National Intelligence Council may be correct in its 2012 projection that although the unipolar moment is over, the U.S. most likely will remain *primus inter pares* at least until 2030 because of the multifaceted nature of its power and the legacies of its leadership.

The U.S. will certainly face a rise in the power of many others—both states and nonstate actors. Presidents will increasingly need to exert power *with* others as much as *over* others; our leaders' capacity to maintain alliances and create networks will be an important dimension of our hard and soft power. The problem of America's role in the 21st century is not the country's supposed decline, but its need to develop the contextual intelligence to understand that even the most powerful nation cannot achieve the outcomes it wants without the help of others. Educating the public to both understand the global information age and operate successfully in it will be the real task for presidential leadership.

All of which suggests that President Obama and his successors should beware of thinking that transformational proclamations are the key to successful adaptation amid these rapidly changing times. American power and leadership will remain crucial to stability and prosperity at home and abroad. But presidents will be better served by remembering their transactional predecessors' observance of the credo "Above all, do no harm" than by issuing stirring calls for transformational change.

Critical Thinking

1. What is the difference between "transformational" and "transactional" presidents?

2. What are the strong similarities between Presidents George W. Bush and Woodrow Wilson?

3. What is the United States' place in the world projected to be in the next couple of decades?

Create Central

www.mhhe.com/createcentral

Internet References

U.S. Department of State
www.state.gov

The White House
www.whitehouse.gov

Joseph S. Nye, Jr.
www.hks.harvard.edu/about/faculty-staff-directory/joseph-nye

JOSEPH S. NYE, JR. is a University Distinguished Service Professor at Harvard. This article is adapted from his upcoming book, *Presidential Leadership and the Creation of the American Era*.

Article   Prepared by: Bruce Stinebrickner, *DePauw University*

Think Again: Obama's New Deal

The president's Republican critics are dead wrong. The stimulus worked.

MICHAEL GRUNWALD

Learning Outcomes

After reading this article, you will be able to:

- Understand and assess the Keynesian approach to a national economy such as that of the United States.

- Assess a number of negative and positive appraisals of the American Recovery and Reinvestment Act, a big and expensive law passed early in the Obama administration.

- Make judgments about how the huge stimulus package, enacted early in Obama's presidency, reflects on him and his presidency.

U.S. President Barack Obama's $787 billion stimulus bill was certainly a political failure. Obama signed it during his first month in office, cutting taxes for more than 95 percent of American workers, while pouring cash into health care, education, energy, infrastructure, and aid to victims of the Great Recession. It was textbook Keynesian economics, using public dollars to revive private demand, but within a year, the percentage of those who thought it had created jobs was lower than the percentage of Americans who believe Elvis is alive. Republicans mocked it as "Porkulus," a bloated encapsulation of everything wrong with the Obama regime, and it helped launch their Tea Party-fueled political revival. The media breathlessly chronicled its silly expenditures, like costumes for water-safety mascots; silly-sounding legitimate expenditures, like a brain-chemistry study of cocaine-addicted monkeys; and fictitious expenditures, like levitating trains to Disneyland. Democrats got so weary of the nonstop ridicule that they stopped using the word "stimulus."

Nearly four years later, Obama's economic recovery bill—and the tepid economic recovery that followed it—is at the heart of the debate over his campaign for a second term. To his Republican challenger, Mitt Romney, the stimulus was a big-government boondoggle that blew up the national debt without putting Americans back to work, a profligate exercise in tax-and-spend liberalism, crony capitalism, and airy-fairy

green utopianism. Obama doesn't use the s-word today, but he does argue that the bill, formally the American Recovery and Reinvestment Act, saved the country from a second Great Depression, ending an economic nightmare in the short term (the Recovery part) while laying the groundwork for a more competitive and sustainable economy in the long term (the Reinvestment part). Meanwhile, disgruntled liberals complain that the stimulus was far too small, because Obama was far too timid, and that jobless Americans are still paying the price for the president's spinelessness.

When it comes to the Recovery Act, the facts are on Obama's side.

For starters, there is voluminous evidence that the stimulus did provide real stimulus, helping to stop a terrifying free-fall, avert a second Depression, and end a brutal recession. America's top economic forecasters—Macroeconomic Advisers, Moody's Economy.com, IHS Global Insight, JPMorgan Chase, Goldman Sachs, and the Congressional Budget Office—agree that it increased GDP at least 2 percentage points, the difference between contraction and growth, and saved or created about 2.5 million jobs. The concept of "saved or created" has inspired a lot of sarcasm—Obama joked after his 2009 Thanksgiving pardon that he had just saved or created four turkeys—but it simply means 2.5 million more people would have been jobless without the Recovery Act. The unemployment rate might still be in the double digits.

Of course, as Obama's critics on the left and right correctly point out, the 8 percent U.S. jobless rate is still terribly high. And there's no way to run a double-blind study of an alternative U.S. economy without the stimulus, so there's no smoking gun to prove the stimulus launched a recovery. But the ballistics certainly match. The economy shrank at a Depression-level rate in the fourth quarter of 2008, and job losses peaked in January 2009. After the stimulus bill passed in February, however, output had its second-biggest quarterly improvement in 25 years, and employment had its biggest quarterly improvement in 30 years. The recession officially ended that June. A *Washington Post* review of Recovery Act studies found six that showed a positive economic effect versus one useful study (by prominent Republican economist John B. Taylor) that concluded the stimulus failed—and critics noted that Taylor's data just as easily support the conclusion that the stimulus was too small.

Keynesian stimulus has since become a political football, but before Obama took office, just about everyone agreed that when the economy slumps, government can boost growth and create jobs by injecting money into the economy, whether by taxing less or spending more. In early 2008, every Republican and Democratic presidential candidate proposed a stimulus plan—in fact, Romney's was the largest. And Republicans still use Keynesian pump-priming arguments to push tax cuts, military spending, and other stimulus they happen to support. Of course, the most powerful argument for aggressive stimulus has been the experience of European countries like Britain and Spain that have turned back toward austerity and stumbled back into recession.

Republicans have ripped the Recovery Act's food stamps, unemployment benefits, and other aid to the less fortunate for fostering a culture of dependency, but with a few exceptions (more generous tuition grants for low-income students and tax credits for low-income workers), the handouts were temporary. And there's no doubt that they made an extraordinarily painful time less painful, lifting at least 7 million Americans above the poverty line while making 32 million poor Americans less poor. As a result, the poverty rate increased only slightly during the worst downturn since the 1930s. Homelessness actually declined slightly, largely because an innovative Recovery Act experiment in "homelessness prevention" helped house 1.2 million Americans in crisis. If half of them had ended up on the streets instead, the country's homeless population would have doubled.

Politically, it's awkward for the president to argue that without the stimulus, the bad economy would have been much worse. It sounds lame to point out that recessions caused by financial meltdowns tend to be unusually long and nasty. But it's true.

In early January 2009, the incoming president's transition team did release a politically disastrous report warning that the jobless rate could hit 9 percent *without* the Recovery Act, while predicting it would stay below 8 percent *with* the Recovery Act, a gaffe that launched a thousand talking points after unemployment reached 10 percent *despite* the Recovery Act. The report was cluttered with caveats about "significant margins of error" and such. But nobody remembers caveats. The authors, economists Christina Romer and Jared Bernstein, even included a humdinger of a footnote about the pre-stimulus baseline: "Some private forecasters anticipate unemployment rates as high as 11% in the absence of action." But nobody remembers footnotes. We remember that unemployment still hasn't gotten below 8 percent, because Republicans have never stopped reminding us. And the media have repeatedly cited the report to dismiss the Recovery Act as a failure by the administration's own standards.

Clearly, the 8 percent prediction was a mistake—an understandable mistake, a marketing mistake, a mistake well below Obama's pay grade, but a mistake. The Romer-Bernstein report was not nearly pessimistic enough. Unemployment passed 8 percent before the stimulus money even started to flow. But that's no reflection on the stimulus. Romer and Bernstein correctly predicted that the Recovery Act would

reduce unemployment by a couple of percentage points—what they underestimated was the pre-stimulus baseline. They knew things were awful, but they had no idea just how awful. Hardly anyone did back then. The Bureau of Economic Analysis initially pegged growth for the fourth quarter of 2008 at a horrific −4 percent, but that was later revised to a beyond horrific −9 percent; at that rate, the United States would have lost more than an entire Canada's worth of output in 2009.

Even at the time, Obama and his advisors understood that the Recovery Act would not restore full employment by itself; as Vice President Joe Biden told me in his quirky way, it was never supposed to carry the whole sleigh. The White House expected the Wall Street bailout, the auto-industry bailout, and its fledgling plan to aid struggling homeowners to provide additional support for the economy. Obama's top economic aide, Larry Summers, has been savaged for keeping Romer's warnings that $1.8 trillion would be needed to close the output gap out of a key memo to the president, but even Romer agrees that's a bum rap. The memo did warn that an $850 billion stimulus would close "just under half of the output gap," insufficient to return the unemployment rate to its "normal, pre-recession level." As one aide told me, whatever you think of Obama, he knows how to multiply by two.

While Republicans have been trashing the stimulus as big government run amok, more liberal critics led by *New York Times* columnist (and Nobel-winning economist) Paul Krugman have dissed it as ludicrously small. And it's true: More stimulus would have closed more of the output gap and replaced more of the 8 million jobs lost in the Great Recession. More tax cuts would have injected more money into the economic bloodstream. More public works would have created more jobs for laid-off construction workers. More aid to states would have prevented America's governors from offsetting the Recovery Act's impact by raising taxes, laying off teachers and other public employees, and slashing Medicaid and other services. Overall, their spending cuts and tax hikes pulled almost as much money out of the economy as the stimulus pushed in, and public-sector employment has shrunk during the Obama presidency.

Even so, the common belief among liberals that pumping inadequate stimulus into the economy was Obama's original sin is ahistoric and unfair. The Recovery Act was still massive—the latest estimate is $831 billion, larger than the entire New Deal in constant dollars—and it wasn't Obama's fault it wasn't bigger.

In September 2008, a mere $56 billion stimulus package died in the Senate, with two Democrats voting no. And after the wildly unpopular bank bailout, there was even less congressional appetite for big spending. By late November, as the market's death spiral created a grudging consensus that Congress needed to act, 387 predominantly left-leaning economists—many of whom later trashed Obama for skimping on stimulus—signed a letter calling for a package of just $300 billion to $400 billion. Even by January 2009, House Speaker Nancy Pelosi, the heroine of the left, was reluctant to approve anything above $600 billion. The president was way out in front of his Democratic blockers.

Presidents do not have magic wands, and Republicans had decided to oppose the Recovery Act en masse. So unless Obama wanted to start his presidency with an epic failure during an economic emergency, he needed to round up 60 votes in the Senate. Democrat Al Franken was still embroiled in a recount in Minnesota, so Obama needed at least two Republicans to support the stimulus. The three moderate GOP senators—Olympia Snowe and Susan Collins of Maine, and Arlen Specter of Pennsylvania—along with conservative Democrat Ben Nelson of Nebraska all agreed that none of them would vote yes unless all of them were satisfied. And all insisted that the stimulus had to be less than $800 billion. Congressional sources confirm that at least half a dozen additional centrist Democratic senators also drew an unpublicized line in the sand at $800 billion. Everyone who was in the room during the congressional horse-trading agrees that Obama got as much as he could have. "There simply wasn't any room for anything bigger," then-Senator Byron Dorgan, a Democrat from North Dakota, told me. "That's representative government."

Some of Obama's progressive critics acknowledge that he couldn't have gotten more stimulus in February 2009, but they complain that he should have gotten more out of Congress once it became clear the initial jolt wouldn't restore a vibrant economy. It's true that some of Obama's advisors vastly overestimated the ease with which they could go back to Capitol Hill. Even Summers, who doesn't make admissions like this often, acknowledged to me that he had been wrong and his rival Krugman, who had warned that inadequate stimulus would give stimulus a bad name, had been right. "At the time, I didn't agree," Summers said. "That was a mistake."

Obama did end up squeezing another $700 billion of stimulus out of an extremely reluctant Congress, through a dozen separate bills. It wasn't easy. Snowe and Collins were the only Republican senators to support an extension of unemployment benefits. Republicans also filibustered a bill to save teaching jobs; Snowe and Collins finally agreed to a shrunken version. (Specter did too, but he had already switched to the Democratic Party after GOP backlash over his stimulus vote.) It took more than two months for Obama to finagle two Republican votes for a $42 billion bill to cut taxes for small businesses. "What could be more Republican than that?" asks former Sen. George Voinovich, an Ohio Republican who defied his party leaders to back the bill. "Instead of doing what was right, partisan politics always came first."

This is the biggest misconception about the American Recovery and Reinvestment Act, and it's understandable, because it was marketed as a jobs bill. But it was about reinvestment as well as recovery, long-term transformation as well as short-term stimulus.

For starters, the Recovery Act was the biggest, most transformative energy bill in history, financing unprecedented government investments in a smarter grid, cleaner coal, energy efficiency in every imaginable form, "green-collar" job training, electric vehicles and the infrastructure to support them, advanced biofuels and the refineries to brew them, renewable power from the sun, the wind, and the heat below the earth, and factories to manufacture all that green stuff in the United States. In 1999, President Bill Clinton proposed a five-year

$6.3 billion clean-energy bill that was dismissed as unrealistic and quickly shelved. A decade later, during his first month in office, Obama poured $90 billion into clean energy with a stroke of his pen, leveraging an additional $100 billion in private capital. The entire renewable-energy industry was on the brink of death after the 2008 financial crisis, but thanks to the stimulus, Obama has kept his promise to double the generation of renewable power during his first term.

The stimulus was also the biggest and most transformative education reform bill since the Great Society, shaking up public schools with a "Race to the Top" competition designed to reward innovation and punish mediocrity. It was a big and transformative health-care bill, too, laying the foundation for Obama's even bigger and more transformative reforms a year later; for example, it poured $27 billion into computerizing America's pen-and-paper medical system, which should reduce redundant tests, dangerous drug interactions, and fatal errors by doctors with chicken-scratch handwriting. It included America's biggest foray into industrial policy since FDR, the biggest expansion of anti-poverty initiatives since LBJ, the biggest middle-class tax cut since Ronald Reagan, and the biggest infusion of research money ever. It sent $8 billion into a new high-speed passenger rail network, the biggest new transportation initiative since the interstate highways, and another $7 billion to expand the country's existing high-speed Internet network to underserved communities, a modern twist on the New Deal's rural electrification.

Critics often argue that while the New Deal left behind iconic monuments—the Hoover Dam, Skyline Drive, Fort Knox—the stimulus will leave a mundane legacy of sewage plants, repaved potholes, and state employees who would have been laid off without it. But it's creating its own icons: the world's largest wind and solar plants, the country's first cellulosic ethanol refineries, zero-energy border stations, a bullet train that will connect Los Angeles to San Francisco in less than three hours. It's also restoring old icons: the Brooklyn Bridge and the Bay Bridge, the imperiled Everglades and the dammed-up Elwha River, Seattle's Pike Place Market and the Staten Island ferry terminal. It's creating an advanced-battery industry for electric vehicles almost entirely from scratch, financing factories that are supposed to boost the U.S. share of global capacity from 1 percent when Obama took office to about 40 percent in 2015. Its only new government agency, ARPA-E, an incubator for cutting-edge energy research modeled on the Pentagon's DARPA, is already producing breakthroughs that will help accelerate the transition to a low-carbon economy.

Its main legacy, like the New Deal's, will be change.

Experts had warned that 5 percent of the stimulus could be lost to fraud, but investigators have documented less than $10 million in losses—about 0.001 percent. "It's been a giant surprise," Earl Devaney, the legendary federal watchdog who oversaw the stimulus as head of the Recovery Accountability and Transparency Board, told me. "We don't get involved in politics, but whether you're a Democrat, Republican, communist, whatever, you've got to appreciate that the serious fraud just hasn't happened."

The Porkulus attacks are particularly brazen, because the usual definition of "pork" is an earmark for a specific project inserted by a specific legislator, and the Recovery Act was the first spending bill in decades with no earmarks. There were a few quasi-earmarks, most notably the $1 billion Future-Gen clean-coal project inserted by Senate Majority Whip Dick Durbin of Illinois, but they paled in comparison to the 6,376 earmarks stuffed into President George W. Bush's last transportation bill. Most of the supposedly wasteful spending singled out by Republicans was never in the stimulus (like "mob museums"), was removed from the stimulus (like "smoking cessation funds"), or wildly distorted something in the stimulus (like an alleged $248 million outlay for "government furniture," which was actually a project to build a new Department of Homeland Security headquarters that would have furniture in it).

Still . . . Solyndra! The California solar firm that went belly up after receiving a half-billion-dollar stimulus loan has become the Republican Party's one-word response to any stimulus-related achievement. It's supposedly a case study in ineptitude, cronyism, and the failure of green industrial policy. Republicans investigated for a year, held more than a dozen hearings, and subpoenaed hundreds of thousands of documents, but they uncovered no evidence of wrongdoing. "Is there a criminal activity? Perhaps not," the lead Republican investigator, Rep. Darrell Issa, told *Politico*. "Is there a political influence and connections? Perhaps not."

Solyndra was a start-up that failed. It happens. In early 2009, Solyndra and its revolutionary cylindrical solar panels were the toast of Silicon Valley, raising $1 billion from elite investors like the Walton family of WalMart fame, Oklahoma oil magnate George Kaiser, and British mogul Richard Branson. Kaiser was an Obama fundraiser, but the Waltons were Republican donors; as Issa acknowledged, there was no evidence of any improper political influence. In fact, the Bush administration fully embraced Solyndra and tried to fast-track its loan. The loan program originally had bipartisan support; the goal was to help firms like Solyndra cross the so-called Valley of Death for innovative technologies with major start-up and scale-up costs. Some loans would go bust, but that's why Congress provided loan reserves, enough to cover plenty of Solyndra-sized failures. Several independent reviews have found no danger that taxpayers will be on the hook for more losses.

Solyndra's failure is often described as a failure of the solar industry, but in fact it's just the opposite. Solyndra produced efficient but pricey panels; the company was essentially a bet that solar power would remain expensive. Instead, the price of solar has crashed by more than two-thirds since 2009, partly because of the stimulus but also because the Chinese government dumped $30 billion into its own solar manufacturers. In any case, the collapsing prices that doomed Solyndra reflect an industry on a roll; U.S. solar installations soared from 290 megawatts in 2008 to 1,855 megawatts in 2011, and 7,000 megawatts of new projects were proposed in the two months before Solyndra went bust—the equivalent of seven new nuclear reactors.

The latest bogus Republican attacks—obviously in response to accusations that Romney outsourced jobs at Bain & Co.—have accused Obama of outsourcing jobs in clean-energy

industries through the stimulus. In fact, the stimulus insourced jobs. For example, it brought the U.S. wind industry back from the dead, creating manufacturing as well as installation jobs. In 2006, the United States imported 80 percent of the components in its wind turbines; after the stimulus, that fell to 40 percent. Yes, many of those new factories are foreign-owned, but they put Americans to work; it really doesn't matter whose name is on the corporate polo shirts. The Spanish company Iberdrola delayed wind farms in Illinois and Texas after the global economy collapsed in 2008; the day after the stimulus passed, the company announced it would pour $6 billion back into U.S. wind projects.

This kind of statement is usually intended as an insult; critics on the right and the left describe the Recovery Act as the essence of Obama-ism. It is, but not in the way they mean.

To Republicans, the "failed" stimulus is a classic Obama exercise in big-government liberalism, fiscal irresponsibility, and incompetence. But those are all bum raps. The Recovery Act included $300 billion in tax cuts, just as Republicans had requested; ARPA-E was its only new government agency, and most of its spending went to priorities (from highways to electric vehicles to unemployment insurance) that had always been bipartisan until they were associated with Obama. The stimulus did increase the deficit—that's the whole point of Keynesian stimulus—but its impact on the long-term debt was negligible compared with the Bush tax cuts, the wars in Iraq and Afghanistan, and collapsing revenues during the Great Recession. And the Recovery Act really was an exercise in good government. Not only was it scandal-free and earmark-free, on time and under budget, but it also engineered a quiet bureaucratic revolution, harnessing the power of competition to award tax dollars to the worthiest applicants instead of just spreading cash around the country. The stimulus created dozens of competitive, results-oriented races to the top for everything from lead-paint removal to the smart grid to innovative transportation projects.

Yet somehow, to many liberals, the stimulus exposed the president as a spineless sellout, more interested in cutting deals than chasing dreams, happy to throw his base under the bus, and desperate to compromise with uncompromising Republicans. But progressive purity wouldn't have gotten 60 votes in the Senate. And Obama isn't a progressive purist. In reality, the Recovery Act provided early evidence that Obama is pretty much what he said he was: a left-of-center technocrat who is above all a pragmatist, comfortable with compromise, solicitous of experts, disinclined to sacrifice the good in pursuit of the ideal but determined to achieve big things. It reflected his belief in government as a driver of change, but also his desire for better rather than bigger government. And it was the first evidence that despite all his flowery talk during the campaign, he understood that bills that don't pass Congress don't produce change.

Ultimately, the stimulus was the purest distillation of what Obama meant by Change We Can Believe In. It was about saving the economy from a calamity, but also changing the economy to prepare America to compete in the 21st century. On the trail, Obama often talked about cleaner energy, better schools, health reform, and fairer taxation not only as moral imperatives, but as economic prerequisites for American renewal and leadership. He warned that the United States couldn't afford to let the green industries of the future drift abroad; or fail to prepare children for the information age; or lose control of skyrocketing health-care costs that were bankrupting families, companies, and the country. And the Recovery Act took steps—in some cases, giant steps—in all those directions. Nearly four years later, the stimulus has become a punch line, a talking point in a political battle over big government, but it's moving America toward that hopey-changey policy vision he laid out during his last campaign.

In the end, the stimulus didn't live up to the hype, but it made things better. That's the whole point of change.

Critical Thinking

1. What are the essentials of Keynesian economics? Was Obama's stimulus package an example of the Keynesian approach to the American economy?

2. What unemployment figures—some stated by the president's incoming team in January 2009 and some actual unemployment figures at relevant points in time—did

Republicans and other observers use to discredit and even belittle the American Recovery and Reinvestment Act?

3. What are some of the "lasting legacies" of Obama's stimulus package that justify, according to the author, calling it "Obama's New Deal"?

Create Central

www.mhhe.com/createcentral

Internet References

The White House
www.whitehouse.gov

Recovery.gov: Track the Money
www.recovery.gov/Pages/default.aspx

About.com: U.S. Economy
http://useconomy.about.com/od/candidatesandtheeconomy/a/Obama_Stimulus.htm

---

MICHAEL GRUNWALD, senior national correspondent at *Time* magazine, is author, most recently, of *The New New Deal: The Hidden Story of Change in the Obama Era.*

Article

Prepared by: Bruce Stinebrickner, *DePauw University*

What Went Wrong

Assessing Obama's Legacy

DAVID BROMWICH

Learning Outcomes

After reading this article, you will be able to:

- Critically assess the evaluation of the Obama presidency that the author presents.

- Consider the extent to which an observer can give an "objective" assessment of any president's performance and discuss if an objective assessment is possible, and why or why not.

A political virtuoso ... might write a manifesto suggesting a general assembly at which people should decide upon a rebellion, and it would be so carefully worded that even the censor would let it pass. At the meeting itself he would be able to create the impression that his audience had rebelled, after which they would all go quietly home—having spent a very pleasant evening.

—Kierkegaard, *The Present Age*

Any summing-up of the Obama presidency is sure to find a major obstacle in the elusiveness of the man. He has spoken more words, perhaps, than any other president; but to an unusual extent, his words and actions float free of each other. He talks with unnerving ease on both sides of an issue: about the desirability, for example, of continuing large-scale investment in fossil fuels. Anyone who voted twice for Obama and was baffled twice by what followed—there must be millions of us—will feel that this president deserves a kind of criticism he has seldom received. Yet we are held back by an admonitory intuition. His predecessor was worse, and his successor most likely will also be worse.

One of the least controversial things you can say about Barack Obama is that he campaigned better than he has governed. The same might be said about Bill Clinton and George W. Bush, but with Obama the contrast is very marked. Governing has no relish for him. Yet he works hard at his public statements, and he wishes his words to have a large effect. Even before he ascended to the presidency, Obama enjoyed the admiration of diverse audiences, especially within black communities and the media. The presidency afforded the ideal platform for creating a permanent class of listeners.

Winning has always been important to Obama: to win and be known as a winner. (Better, in fact, to withdraw from a worthwhile venture than be seen not to succeed.) Alongside this trait, he has exhibited a peculiar avoidance of the business of politics. The pattern was set by the summer of 2009. It came out in the way he shunned the company of his own party, the invitations that didn't issue from the White House, the phone calls that weren't made, the curiosity that never showed. Much of politics is a game, and a party leader must enter into the mood of the game; it is something you either do or don't have an appetite for. Of our recent presidents, only Eisenhower revealed a comparable distaste.

Obama has sometimes talked as if he imagined that, once he moved to the White House, the climb would be in the past. Indeed, some major drawbacks of his first year as president—the slowness in explaining policies and nominating persons to the federal judiciary and other important posts—may be traced to his special understanding of that year's purpose. It was intended as a time for the country to get to know him. According to a tally published by the CBS correspondent Mark Knoller, the twelve months between January 2009 and January 2010 included 411 occasions for speeches, comments, or remarks by Obama, forty-two news conferences, and 158 interviews. The theory seemed to be that once the public trust was sealed, persuasion and agreement would follow. Mastery of the levers of government was desirable, of course, but it could be postponed to another day.

Meanwhile, Obama's hesitation in assuming his practical responsibilities was unmistakable; it could be glimpsed at unguarded moments. There was his comment in response to a peevish remark by John McCain during the February 2010 health-care summit, which the president moderated. "Let me just make this point, John," he said, "because we are not campaigning anymore." He meant: there are lots of things that we shouldn't argue about anymore. McCain looked more bewildered than affronted, and his emotion was shared by others who noticed the curt finality of the reply.

Obama meant that the game was over. Now was the time for putting his policies into practice (doubtless with suitable modifications). We had heard enough about those policies during the campaign itself. Postelection, we had left discussion behind and entered the phase of implementation. In the same vein and with the same confidence, he told Republicans on Capitol Hill three days after his inauguration: "You can't just listen to Rush Limbaugh and get things done." But they could, and they did. The Republicans had an appetite for politics in its rawest form; for them, the game had barely begun.

To declare the argument over in the midst of a debate is to confess that you are lacking in resources. This defect, a failure to prepare for attacks and a corresponding timidity in self-defense, showed up in a capital instance in 2009. Obama had vowed to order the closure of the prison at Guantánamo Bay as soon as he became president. He did give the order. But as time passed and the prison didn't close of its own volition, the issue lost a good deal of attraction for him. The lawyer Obama had put in charge of the closure, Greg Craig, was sacked a few months into the job (on the advice, it is said, of Obama's chief of staff, Rahm Emanuel). Guantánamo had turned into baggage the president didn't want to carry into the midterm elections. But the change of stance was not merely politic. For Obama, it seemed, a result that failed to materialize after a command had issued from his pen was sapped of its luster.

Yet as recently as March of this year, Obama spoke as if the continued existence of the prison were an accident that bore no relation to his own default. "I thought we had enough consensus where we could do it in a more deliberate fashion," he said. "But the politics of it got tough, and people got scared by the rhetoric around it. Once that set in, then the path of least resistance was just to leave it open, even though it's not who we are as a country and it's used by terrorists around the world to help recruit jihadists." One may notice a characteristic evasion built in to the grammar of these sentences. "The politics" (abstract noun) "got tough" (nobody can say why) "and people" (all the people?) "got scared" (by whom and with what inevitability?). Adverse circumstances "set in" (impossible to avoid because impossible to define). In short, once the wrong ideas were planted, the president could scarcely have done otherwise.

The crucial phrase is "the path of least resistance." In March 2015, in the seventh year of his presidency, Barack Obama was presenting himself as a politician who followed the path of least resistance. This is a disturbing confession. It is one thing to know about yourself that in the gravest matters you follow the path of least resistance. It is another thing to say so in public. Obama was affirming that for him there could not possibly be a question of following the path of courageous resistance. He might regret it six years later, but politics set in, and he had to leave Guantánamo open—a symbol of oppression that (by his own account) tarnished the fame of America in the eyes of the world.

It is perhaps understandable that Obama felt a declaration of his intention to close Guantánamo need not be followed by the political work of closing it. For Barack Obama sets great store by words. He understands them as a relevant form of action—almost, at times, a substitute for action. He takes considerable authorial pride in the autobiography he published before becoming a politician. We may accordingly ask what impression his spoken words have made in his presidency, from the significant sample we now possess. He employs a correct and literate diction (compared with George W. Bush) and is a polite and careful talker (compared with Bill Clinton), but by the standard of our national politics Obama is uncomfortable and seldom better than competent in the absence of a script. His show of deliberation often comes across as halting. His explanations lack fluency, detail, and momentum. Take away the script and the suspicion arises that he would rather not be onstage. The exception proves the rule: Obama has a fondness for ceremonial occasions where the gracious quip or the ironic aside may be the order of the day, and he is deft at handling them. As for his mastery in delivering a rehearsed speech, the predecessor he most nearly resembles is Ronald Reagan.

This presents another puzzle. Obama said during the 2008 primaries that he admired Reagan for his ability to change the mood of the country—the ability itself, he meant, abstracted from the actual change Reagan brought. Astonishingly, Obama seems to have believed, on entering the White House, that his power as an interpreter of the American dream was on the order of Reagan's. But this ambition was less exorbitant than it looked; the differences between their certitudes are small and cosmetic. Reagan spoke of the "shining city on a hill." Obama says: "I believe in American exceptionalism with every fiber of my being."

He came into office under the pressure of the financial collapse and the public disenchantment with the conduct of the Bush–Cheney "war on terror." It has been said that this was an impossible point of departure for our first black president. Might the opposite be true? The possibilities were large because the breakthrough was unheard-of. The country was exhausted by eight years on a crooked path. The nature of the doubt, the nature of the uncertainty, it is possible to think, made the early months of 2009 one of those plastic hours of history when the door to a large transformation swings open. Obama himself evidently saw it that way. On June 3, 2008, having just won the Democratic primaries, he declared in Minnesota that people would look back and say, "This was the moment when the rise of the oceans began to slow, and our planet began to heal." The language was messianic, but the perception of a crisis and of the opportunity it offered was true.

Obama's warmest defenders have insisted, against the weight of his own words, that such hopes were absurd and unreal—often giving as evidence some such conversation stopper as "this is a center-right country" or "the American people are racist." But the same American people elected an African American whose campaign had been center-left. He inherited a majority in both houses of Congress. It takes a refined sense of impossibility to argue that Obama in his first two years actually traveled the length of what was possible.

During Obama's first year in office, the string of departures from his own stated policy showed the want of connection between his promises and his preparation to lead. The weakness was built-in to the rapid rise that carried him from his late twenties through his early forties. His appreciative, dazzled, and grateful mentors always took the word for the deed. They made the allowance because he cut a brilliant figure. Obama's ascent was achieved too easily to be answerable for the requirement of performing much. This held true in law school, where he was elected president of the *Harvard Law Review* without an article to his name, and again in his three terms as an Illinois state senator, where he logged an uncommonly high proportion of noncommittal "present" votes rather than "ayes" or "nays." Careless journalists have assumed that his time of real commitment goes further back, to his three years as a community organizer in Chicago. But even in that role, Obama was averse to conflict. He was never observed at a scene of disorder, and he had no enemies among the people of importance in the city.

He came to the presidency, then, without having made a notable sacrifice for his views. Difficulty, however—the kind of difficulty Obama steered clear of—can be a sound instructor.

Stake out a lonely position and it sharpens the outline of your beliefs. When the action that backs the words is revealed with all its imperfections, the sacrifice will tell the audience something definite and interesting about the actor himself. Barack Obama entered the presidency as an unformed actor in politics.

In responding to the opportunities of his first years in office, Obama displayed the political equivalent of dead nerve endings. When the news broke in March 2009 that executives in AIG's financial-products division would be receiving huge bonuses while the federal government paid to keep the insurance firm afloat, Obama condemned the bonuses. He also summoned to the White House the CEOs of fifteen big banks. "My administration," Obama told them, as Ron Suskind reported in *Confidence Men,* "is the only thing between you and the pitchforks." But the president went on to say that "I'm not out there to go after you. I'm protecting you." Obama was signaling that he had no intention of asking them for any dramatic sacrifice. After an embarrassed reconsideration, he announced several months later that he had no use for "fat cats." But even that safe-sounding disclaimer was turned upside down by his pride in his acquaintance with Lloyd Blankfein, of Goldman Sachs, and Jamie Dimon, of JPMorgan Chase: "I know both those guys; they are very savvy businessmen." His attempt to correct the abuses of Wall Street by bringing Wall Street into the White House might have passed for prudence if the correctives had been more radical and been explained with a surer touch. But it was Obama's choice to put Lawrence Summers at the head of his economic team.

In foreign policy, Afghanistan was the first order of business in Obama's presidency. His options must have appeared exceedingly narrow. During the campaign, he had followed a middle path on America's wars. He said that Iraq was the wrong war and that Afghanistan was the right one: Bush's error had been to take his eye off the deeper danger. By early spring of 2009, Obama knew that his judgment—though it earned him praise from the media—had simply been wrong. The U.S. effort in Afghanistan was a shambles, and nobody without a vested interest in the war was saying otherwise.

Two incidents might have been seized on by a leader with an eye for a political opening. The first arrived in the form of diplomatic cables sent to the State Department in early November 2009 by Karl W. Eikenberry, the ambassador to Afghanistan and, before that, the senior commander of U.S. forces there. Eikenberry's length of service and battlefield experience made him a more widely trusted witness on Afghanistan than General David Petraeus; his cables said that the war could not be won outside the parts of the country already held by U.S. forces. No more troops ought to be added. Eikenberry recommended, instead, the appointment of a commission to investigate the state of the country. Any reasonably adroit politician would have made use of these documents and this moment. With a more-in-sorrow explanation, such a leader could have announced that the findings, from our most reliable observer on the ground, compelled a reappraisal altogether different from the policy that had been anticipated in 2008. Though Obama had his secretary of state, Hillary Clinton; his secretary of defense, Robert Gates; and the chairman of the joint chiefs, Michael Mullen, arrayed against him, he also had opponents of escalation, including Vice President Biden and others, at the heart of his policy team. He chose to do nothing with the cables. A lifeline was tossed to him and he treated it as an embarrassment.

A plainer opportunity came with the killing of Osama bin Laden on May 2, 2011. This operation was the president's own decision, according to the available accounts, and it must be said that many things about the killing were dubious. It gambled a further erosion of trust with Pakistan, and looked to give a merely symbolic lift to the American mood, since bin Laden was no longer of much importance in the running of Al Qaeda: the terrorist organization was atomized into a hundred splinter groups in a dozen countries. The temporary boost to patriotic morale that came from this spectacular revenge may also have influenced Americans to accept more casually the legitimacy of assassinations.

That he killed the instigator of the September 11 attacks surely helped Obama to win reelection in 2012. With a larger good in view, he might also and very plausibly have used the death of bin Laden as an occasion for ending the occupation of Afghanistan. If the Eikenberry cables afforded a chance to tell the unpopular truth no politician wants to utter—"We can't win the war"—the death of bin Laden offered a prime opportunity to recite a comforting fiction to the same effect: "Al Qaeda is our enemy. It is now a greatly diminished force, and we have killed its leader. At last, after so much pain and sacrifice, we can begin to wind down the war on terror."

But Obama made no such gesture. He held on to his December 2009 plan, which had called for an immediate escalation in Afghanistan to be followed by de-escalation on a clock arbitrarily set eighteen months in advance. The days after the killing saw the White House inflating and deflating its accounts of what happened in Abbottabad, while Obama himself paid a visit to SEAL Team 6. A truth about the uses of time in politics—as Machiavelli taught indelibly—is that the occasion for turning fortune your way is unlikely to occur on schedule. The delay in withdrawing from Afghanistan was decisive and fatal, and it is now a certainty that we will have a substantial military presence in that country at the end of Obama's second term.

Much of the disarray in foreign policy was inevitable once Obama resolved that his would be a "team of rivals." The phrase comes from the title of Doris Kearns Goodwin's book

about the Civil War cabinet headed by President Lincoln. To a suggestible reader, the team-of-rivals conceit might be taken to imply that Lincoln presided in the role of moderator; that he listened without prejudice to the radical William Seward, his secretary of state, and the conservative Montgomery Blair, his postmaster general; that he heard them debate the finer points of strategy and adjudicated between them. Actually, however, Goodwin's book tells a traditional (and true) story of Lincoln as a leader, both inside the cabinet and out.

The idea of a team of rivals stuck in Obama's mind because it suited his temperament. But the cabinet he formed in 2009 involved a far more drastic accommodation than any precedent can explain. Obama hoped to disarm all criticism preemptively. He had run against Hillary Clinton—who did lasting damage by saying that he was unqualified to lead in a time of emergency—and he paid her back by putting her in charge of the emergency. For the rest, Obama selected persons of conventional views, largely opposed to his own and in some cases opposed to one another. It was an unorganized team, perhaps not a team at all, but that hardly mattered. The Cabinet met nineteen times during his first term, an average of only once every eleven weeks.

The largest issues on which Obama won the Democratic nomination were his opposition to the Iraq war and his stand against warrantless domestic spying. He had vowed to filibuster any legislation giving immunity to telecommunications companies, and withdrew that pledge (with a vow to keep his eye on the issue) only after he secured the nomination. And yet among all the names in the cabinet there was not one opponent of warrantless surveillance on his domestic team, and, on his foreign-policy team, no one except Obama himself who had spoken out or voted against the Iraq war. (Lincoln, by contrast, placed abolitionists in two critical posts: Seward at State and Salmon Chase at Treasury.) Thus, on all the relevant issues, Obama stood alone; or rather, he would have stood alone if his views had remained steady. His choice not only of cabinet members but of two chief advisers—Summers and Emanuel—could be read as a confession that he was intimidated in advance.

Obama's foreign policy also revealed a trait he shares with most other Democratic presidents: he considers domestic policy his major responsibility. Foreign policy is a necessary encumbrance; it is a burden to be transferred to other hands. What Democrats have never properly recognized is that for any powerful and expanding state, foreign entanglements set definite limits on what is possible at home. The energy and expenditure that went into wars such as Korea, Vietnam, Afghanistan, and Iraq had broad consequences for domestic benefits as various as social insurance and environmental protection.

Obama's domestic policy has, for the most part, exhibited a pattern of intimation, postponement, and retreat. The president and his handlers like to call it deliberation. A fairer word would be "dissociation." Once Obama walks out of a policy discussion, he does not coordinate and does not collaborate. This fact is attested by so many in Congress that it will take a separate history to chronicle the disconnections. He intensely dislikes the rituals of keeping company with lesser lawmakers, even in his own party. Starting with the Affordable Care Act, he has stayed aloof from negotiations, as if recusing himself afforded a certain protection against being blamed for failure. He does not cultivate political friends, or fraternize with comrades. Add to this record his episodic evacuations of causes (global warming between 2010 and 2012; nuclear proliferation between 2011 and 2015) and the activists who got him the nomination in 2008 may be pardoned for wondering what cause Obama ever espoused in earnest.

One of the surprises of reviewing the conception and execution of the Affordable Care Act is that Obama came to the subject late and almost experimentally. In the 2008 primaries, the health-care policies of Hillary Clinton and John Edwards were widely judged to be more comprehensive than Obama's, and he would later concede he had been wrong to reject the individual mandate. But in the earliest days of the new administration, he tested the popularity of two quite different investments of political capital: health care and climate change. Health care won out. He delegated the responsibility for drafting the measure to five separate committees of Congress and sent his vice president to run interference for many months. No serious speech was given to explain the policy, and how could there be a speech? There wasn't yet a policy. In the meantime, he suspended engagement with most of the other issues that might be judged important. Between January 2009 and March 2010, health care swallowed everything. Obama did it because he wanted to "do big things," to have a piece of "signature legislation."

If he was a cautious president-elect in November 2008, he seemed to be in full retreat by the end of 2010. A few days after the midterm disaster, Obama vowed to carry forward the Bush tax cuts for the richest Americans. When the Republican majority saw weakness so clearly telegraphed, their threat to close the government and their refusal to raise the debt ceiling in 2011 were foreseeable obstructions. The president for his part—as Harry Reid's chief of staff observed with genuine shock—had no Plan B. Eventually, Obama spun out an improbable compromise. He met the Republican ultimatum with an offer of sequestration of government funds, which would enforce across-the-board budget cuts in the absence of a later deal. This measure was extorted by panic. Obama apparently assumed that the drawbacks in funding for education, food inspection, highway construction, and other essential activities of government would be immediately evident to the American public. It has proved an empty hope. Sequestration will be part of the Obama legacy as much as the Affordable Care Act.

When the Tea Party sprang up in reaction to the Troubled Asset Relief Program and the A.C.A., Obama never mentioned the protest and never sought to refute the movement. Through his first term he barely recognized its existence. Only when pressed would he name the Tea Party, but even then he spoke of the threat to his policies in a vague generic way: the Tea Party represented an age-old tendency in American politics, founded on innocent misunderstanding. There was nothing to be done about it.

This strain of quietism has been a recurrent and uneasy motif of Obama's presidency. But the trait is deeply rooted. How else to explain his avoidance of meetings with Kathleen Sebelius in the run-up to the launch of the A.C.A.'s insurance exchanges? That a busy president might not ask for a weekly progress report in the year preceding the rollout is understandable. But considering how much the result mattered—not just to his legacy but also to the trust in government he had pledged to restore—what could be the excuse for conversing face-to-face with the secretary of health and human services only once in the three and a half years before the unraveling? The new law is bringing medical care to millions who never before could rely on such protection. In the long run, it is likely to be a tremendous benefit to the society at large. Yet opposition to the reform has never let up.

Given the weight of the moment, it was extraordinarily careless of the president to have allowed its effect to be diluted by a succession of avoidable delays. He also missed the opportunity to supply a single conclusive explanation of the meaning of his reform. Along with his contradictory declarations on Syria, the botched health-care rollout did more than anything else to spoil the first year of Obama's second term. It scuttled any chance the Democrats may have had for preserving their Senate majority.

Different as the issues have been, Obama's retreat from controversy in dealing with Guantánamo, his deference to the generals in Afghanistan even when circumstances took his side, and his willingness to cede health care to a complex bureaucratic machine that lacked any competent controls all shared a characteristic signature. His resort to the path of least resistance has been a consistent and almost reflexive response to friendly conditions that turn suddenly hostile. But the hostility in question may be something more than partisan suspicion and rancor.

It now seems clear that during the presidential transition, between November 2008 and January 2009, Obama was effectively drilled in the intricacies of U.S. operations abroad, the secret deployment of special forces, the expansion of domestic spying by the NSA, and the full extent of terror threats both inside and outside the United States (as determined by the high officials of the security apparatus). More than might have been expected from a principled politician, he was set back on his heels. It would be understandable if he was also frightened.

The first visible effect of his reeducation was the speech he gave at the National Archives on May 21, 2009. Whatever might become of Guantánamo itself, the policy Obama laid down at the National Archives ensured that the United States would maintain a category of enemy combatants charged with no specific crime. These prisoners would be as helpless as those whom Bush and Cheney had "rendered" or sent to Guantánamo. The speech defined a category of permanent detainees—their cases impossible to try in court, because the evidence against them had been obtained by torture; their condition now irremediable, because they posed a continuing threat to the United States.

Obama also followed Cheney's path in keeping much of the war on terror off the books by employing mercenaries—known now by the euphemism "contractors." He held on to another Cheney innovation when he invoked the state-secrets privilege to undercut legal claims by prisoners seeking redress and citizens invoking the Fourth Amendment protection against searches and seizures. Privilege of this kind is not compatible with the functional necessities of a constitutional democracy.

The right to a fair and speedy trial is guaranteed by the Constitution, as are all the conditions for a relevantly informed discussion of public affairs. In the Obama Administration, however, as in the Bush–Cheney Administration before it, the war on terror was to stand on a different footing. Matters relating to war and domestic security were closed to the scrutiny of the people. The shift in Obama's attitude between April and June 2009 could not have been more conspicuous. He delivered the National Archives speech in response to many weeks of harsh and testing attacks by the Republican right, and especially by Cheney, who denounced the decision by the new president to publish the torture memos and a second series of Abu Ghraib photographs. When Obama surrendered on these fronts, they knew they had him on the run in Guantánamo, Afghanistan, and elsewhere.

Obama's expansion of the war on terror was predictable, but at every stage he raised people's hopes before dashing them. He made waterboarding illegal, together with many other practices of "enhanced interrogation." This was a brave achievement to which no minus sign can be attached. At the same time, he brought John Brennan into the White House to organize command procedures for drone killings. In the manner of Cheney, Obama kept secret the document establishing the legal rationale for the strikes. By the end of 2014, Obama had ordered 456 drone attacks (compared with fifty-two by Bush). Unhappily, there is truth in the charge by Bush's supporters that President Obama has spared himself the illegality of torture by killing the suspects whom his predecessor would have kidnapped for "enhanced interrogation."

In foreign policy across the greater Middle East, Obama's major concern was to avoid any suggestion of a religious war against Islam. His speech in Cairo on June 4, 2009, was the first step in that direction. His plan to negotiate a State of Palestine was supposed to be the second. In the drawn-out confusion of the Arab Spring, however, he allowed himself to be trapped by the combination of neoconservative advocates of never-ending war, such as Robert Kagan, and liberal believers in humanitarian war, such as Samantha Power and Anne-Marie Slaughter, whose claim to a "responsibility to protect" licensed NATO's bombing of Libya and the overthrow of Muammar Qaddafi. Obama's decision to follow their advice has brought anarchy to Libya and made it a depot for jihadists in the region.

The scale of the Libyan disaster was already known when the same advisers and opinion makers knocked on Obama's door for intervention in Syria. Once again, he had a hard time resisting, and was almost lured into a major bombing attack and an attempt at the overthrow of Bashar al-Assad. Only much later would Obama acknowledge that it was "a fantasy" that the United States could outflank the Islamist rebels by subsidizing an American-vetted moderate force, "essentially an opposition made up of former doctors, farmers, pharmacists and so forth." The worst feature of the engagements in Libya and Syria has been the president's refusal of honest explanations to the public. In Libya, this refusal was accompanied by something approaching a denial of responsibility. He has referred most questions regarding Libya to Hillary Clinton's State Department, but Obama was the president. He approved the no-fly interdiction that shaded into the destruction of a government and wrought a civil war. If the chaos that ensued has added to the horrors of the sectarian conflict in the region, part of the fault lies with Obama. In both Syria and Iraq, a necessary ally in the fight against Sunni fanatics (including the recent incorporation that calls itself the Islamic State) has been the Shiite regime in Iran. Yet Obama has been hampered from explaining this necessity by his extreme and programmatic reticence on the subject of Iran generally.

About the time the last sentence was written, President Obama announced the framework of a nuclear deal between the P5 + 1 powers and Iran. If he can clear the treaty with Congress and end the state of all but military hostility that has prevailed for nearly four decades between the United States and Iran, the result will stand beside health care as a second major achievement. To bring it off will demand tremendous resourcefulness and a patience as unusual as the impetus that drove the Affordable Care Act. And it will require even greater strength of resolution. An uncompromising personal investment will have to be shown, and will have to persist against fierce opposition. Obama will have to recognize that his most dedicated opponents—the neoconservatives who dictate Republican foreign policy—are relentless and that they will not stop until they are stopped. Nevertheless, a lasting détente with Iran seems possible; what are the obstacles?

Until this moment, Obama has taken care not to disturb the American consensus that Iran is a uniquely dangerous country. He has said and done little to counter the right-wing Israeli propaganda that pictures Iran as the greatest exporter of terrorism in the world. His peace-bearing Ramadan messages to non-fanatical believers in Islam have eluded notice in the American press and made no impact on public opinion. The arrogance of his executive action on Libya, too, left a residual irritation that can now be exploited to throw a cloak of principle over merely partisan or expedient opposition to the nuclear deal. These obstacles can only be resisted by the constant pressure of argument that gives reasons and tirelessly repeats its reasons. A president whose main talent has seemed to be inspiration, not explanation, will have to venture now, very far and very often, into the field of lucid explanation. But Obama today has Europe backing him; and elements of the Israeli intelligence community show signs of breaking away from Netanyahu's insistence on the posture of war. The result may depend ultimately on the willingness of a few well-placed senators to part with an old enemy whose status has become familiar and almost customary.

A forgotten aspect of the current nuclear negotiations is that they had a precursor. The agreement that Obama hopes to secure was anticipated and turned down by the president himself in May 2010. At that time Turkey and Brazil had offered to receive low-enriched uranium from Iran in return for allowable nuclear fuel and the opening of trade and lifting of sanctions. Why Obama spurned the offer, as Trita Parsi related in *A Single Roll of the Dice,* remains something of a mystery. It may have been ill suited to domestic politics on the way to a midterm election; and the deal had not been properly coordinated with Russia. Perhaps, too, there was an element of pique: credit for the breakthrough would have been stolen from the American president by two upstart minor powers. Mrs. Clinton also played a significant part in deflecting the Brazil–Turkey proposal.

When such incidents add up to a critical mass, they can no longer be taken as accidents. They tell us something discouraging about the Obama White House and its relation to the State Department. The shortest description of the disorder is that President Obama does not seem to control his foreign policy. A recent and dangerous instance, still unfolding in Ukraine, began in November 2013 and reached its climax in the February 2014 coup that overturned the Yanukovych government. But the coup in Kiev was only the last stage of a decade-long policy of "democracy promotion" that looked to detach Ukraine from Russia. Victoria Nuland, the assistant secretary of state for European and Eurasian affairs, boasted in December 2013 that the United States had spent $5 billion since 1991 in the attempt to convert Ukraine into a Western asset. The later stages of the enterprise called for the defamation of Vladimir Putin, which

went into high gear with the 2014 Sochi Olympics and has not yet abated. When Nuland appeared in Kiev to hand out cookies to the anti-Russian protesters, it was as if a Russian operative had arrived to cheer a mass of anti-American protesters in Baja California.

Through the many months of assisted usurpation, no word of reprimand ever issued from President Obama. An intercepted phone call in which Nuland and Geoffrey Pyatt, the ambassador to Ukraine, could be heard picking the leaders of the government they aimed to install after the coup aroused no scandal in the American press. But what could Obama have been thinking? Was he remotely aware of the implications of the crisis—a crisis that plunged Ukraine into a civil war and splintered U.S. diplomacy with Russia in a way that nothing in Obama's history could lead one to think he wished for? His subsequent statements on the matter have all been delivered in a sedative nudge-language that speaks of measures to *change the behavior* of a greedy rival power. As in Libya, the evasion of responsibility has been hard to explain. It almost looks as if a cell of the State Department assumed the management of Ukraine policy and the president was helpless to alter their design.

Suppose something of this sort in fact occurred. How new a development would that be? Five months into Obama's first term, a coup was effected in Honduras with American approval. A lawyer for the businessmen who engineered the coup was the former Clinton special counsel Lanny Davis. Did Obama know about the Honduras coup and endorse it? The answer can only be that he should have known; and yet (as with Ukraine) it seems strange to imagine that he actually approved. It is possible that an echo of both Honduras and Ukraine may be discerned in a recent White House statement enforcing sanctions against certain citizens of Venezuela. The complaint, bizarre on the face of it, is that Venezuela has become an "unusual and extraordinary threat" to the national security of the United States. These latest sanctions look like a correction of the president's independent success at rapprochement with Cuba—a correction administered by forces inside the government itself that are hostile to the White House's change of course. Could it be that the coup in Ukraine, on the same pattern, served as a rebuke to Obama's inaction in Syria? Any progress toward peaceful relations, and away from aggrandizement and hostilities, seems to be countered by a reverse movement, often in the same region, sometimes in the same country. Yet both movements are eventually backed by the president.

The situation is obscure. Obama's diffidence in the face of actions by the State Department (of which he seems half-aware, or to learn of only after the fact) may suggest that we are seeing again the syndrome that led to the National Archives speech and the decision to escalate the Afghanistan war. Edward Snowden, in an interview published in *The Nation* in November 2014, seems to have identified the pattern. "The Obama Administration," he said, "almost appears as though it is afraid of the intelligence community. They're afraid of death by a thousand cuts . . . leaks and things like that." John Brennan gave substance to this surmise when he told Charlie Rose recently that the new president, in 2009, "did not have a good deal of experience" in national security, but now "he has gone to school and understands the complexities." This is not the tone of a public servant talking about his superior. It is the tone of a schoolmaster describing an obedient pupil.

However one reads the evidence, there can be no doubt that Obama's stance toward the NSA, the CIA, and the intelligence community at large has been the most feckless and unaccountable element of his presidency. Indeed, his gradual adoption of so much of Cheney's design for a state of permanent emergency should prompt us to reconsider the importance of the Deep State—an entity that is real but difficult to define, about which the writings of James Risen, Mike Lofgren, Dana Priest, William Arkin, Michael Glennon, and others have warned us over the past several years. There is a sense—commonly felt but rarely reflected upon by the American public—in which at critical moments a figure like John Brennan or Victoria Nuland may matter more than the president himself. There could be no surer confirmation of that fact than the frequent inconsequence of the president's words, or, to put it another way, the embarrassing frequency with which his words are contradicted by subsequent events.

Bureaucracy, by its nature, is impersonal. It lacks an easily traceable collective will. But when a bureaucracy has grown big enough, the sum of its actions may obstruct any attempt by an individual, no matter how powerful and well placed, to counteract its overall drift. The size of our security state may be roughly gauged by the 854,000 Americans who enjoy top-secret security clearances, according to the estimate published by Priest and Arkin in the *Washington Post* in 2010. The same authors reported that nearly 2,000 private companies and 1,300 government organizations were employed in the fields of counterterrorism, intelligence gathering, mass surveillance, and homeland security.

When Obama entered the White House, it was imperative for him to rid the system of the people who would work against him. Often they would be people far back in the layers of the bureaucracy; and where removal or transfer was impossible, he had to watch them carefully. But in his first six years, there was no sign of an initiative by Obama to reduce the powers that were likeliest to thwart his projects from inside the government. On the contrary, his presumption seems to have been that all the disparate forces of our political moment would flow through him, and that the most discordant tendencies would be improved and elevated by this contact as they continued on their way.

One ought to say the best one can for a presidency that has created its own obstacles but has also been beset by difficulties no one could have anticipated. Obama has governed in a manner that is moderate-minded and expedient. He has been mostly free of the vengeful and petty motives that can derail even a consummate political actor. His administration, the most secretive since that of Richard Nixon, has been the reverse of transparent, but it has also been entirely free of political scandal. There is a melancholy undercurrent to his presidency that recalls Melville's lines in "The Conflict of Convictions": "I know a wind in purpose strong—It spins *against* the way it drives."

Though Obama has hardly been a leader strong in purpose, his policies have indeed spun against the way they drove. Nobody bent on mere manipulation would so often and compulsively utter a wish for things he could not carry out. Yet Obama has done little to counteract the regression of constitutional democracy that began with the security policies and the wars of Bush and Cheney. This degeneration has been assisted under his negligent watch, sometimes with his connivance, occasionally by exertions of executive power that he has innovated. Much as one would like to admire a leader so good at showing that he means well, and so earnest in projecting the good intentions of his country as the equivalent of his own, it would be a false consolation to pretend that the years of the Obama presidency have not been a large lost chance.

Critical Thinking

1. Why does the author think that Barack Obama "campaigned better than governed"?
2. Give some examples of President Obama seemingly following the "path of least resistance."
3. For what reasons does the author think that the Obama Presidency has been a "large lost chance"?

Internet References

Organizing for Action
    https://www.barackobama.com
The White House
    https://www.whitehouse.gov

Article   Prepared by: Bruce Stinebrickner, *DePauw University*

Ten Secret Truths about Government Incompetence

Donald F. Kettl

Learning Outcomes

After reading this article, you will be able to:

- Reflect on the performance of the U.S. national government from the perspectives provided by the author's "ten secret truths."

- Assess the persuasiveness of the "ten secret truths" that political scientist Donald F. Kettl identifies and discusses.

Wednesday, November 9, 2016

To: President-elect

From: Donald F. Kettl

Subject: Ten Secret Truths About Government Incompetence: What you can learn from the management mistakes of Obama and Bush.

Congratulations! You've won the nasty 2016 election for president of these United States. It was a long slog through more bad chicken dinners and dusty halls than anyone could be expected to tolerate. You won because you listened carefully to Republican strategist Frank Luntz's take on the 2014 midterm election, that the "results were less about the size of government than about making government efficient, effective, and accountable." And that's just what you built your campaign on.

On January 20, 2017, you'll be sworn in at noon, give a great speech, sneak out of the Beast for as much of a walk down Pennsylvania Avenue as the Secret Service will allow, cheer your hometown high school band, and dance the night away.

And then you'll take over as chief executive and actually have to do what Luntz said: make government more efficient, effective, and accountable. As you settle into your new chair in the Oval Office, here are ten handy truths worth keeping in your pocket or purse.

I. Government Works Better than People Think. Most of the Time

You told us during the campaign that government programs fail often, and a September 2014 *Washington Post*/ABC News poll shows that most Americans agree. Of those surveyed, 74 percent said they were dissatisfied or angry with the way the federal government works. Another 23 percent were satisfied—but not enthusiastic. Those enthusiastic about the federal government's performance? Just 1 percent.

In fact, however, much of government actually works pretty well, most of the time. The Heritage Foundation points to "the breathtaking, long-term improvements in safety in the airline industry," with tough, smart work by the National Transportation Safety Board leading to just a single fatal accident on an American airline since 2009, when a commuter jet crashed near Buffalo. For all the (often overblown) concerns about the long-term fiscal strength of Social Security, the bureaucracy that actually administers the program, the Social Security Administration, makes monthly payments to sixty-four million Americans with an accuracy rate of more than 99 percent and administrative costs that are (at 0.7 percent) but a fraction of those of private pension plans. Harvard University researchers found that stronger government regulations for air quality have led to longer lives. Even at the troubled Veterans Health Administration, a new technology system shrank the claims backlog by 60 percent.

Government usually gets only the hard problems—the puzzles that the private sector cannot or will not tackle, or that the private sector itself creates. In 2009, the United States found itself the majority stockholder in General Motors and pumped billions into Chrysler. Government bailouts saved an insurance company (AIG) and a bank (Citigroup). With its $49.5 billion bailout, the feds saved GM and millions of jobs, lost just $11.2 billion in the turnaround, and got out of the car business by the end of 2013. The government actually made money—$22.7 billion—on the AIG bailout and another $15 billion on Citigroup, far offsetting its auto-industry loss. Six years after the government launched these bailouts, it's still staggering to imagine how bad things would have gotten if the government had left private enterprise to itself. And these weren't aberrations. Again and again over the years, Washington has bailed out companies deemed vital to the economy, like Lockheed in 1971, Chrysler in 1980, and the entire airline industry after 9/11. Each time, the actions saved the companies and Washington made a profit on its investments.

A huge part of government works pretty well most of the time, as we take for granted every time safe drinking water comes out of the tap. You start your administration with a lot of points on the board, even if not many citizens notice the score.

II. Good Management Doesn't Win Elections—But Bad Management Can Ruin Presidencies. Fast

The painful experiences of your two predecessors create a stark warning: voters don't reward good performance, but they fiercely punish bad management. For George W. Bush, the point at which his negatives exceeded his positives and never recovered was not "Mission Accomplished" or Abu Ghraib. Rather, it was the aftermath of Hurricane Katrina in September 2005. Barack Obama tumbled down the same road after the failed launch of the Obamacare website in October 2013, at almost the same point in his presidency.

It isn't an inevitable part of second-termitis. Bill Clinton fought off the impeachment barrage and Ronald Reagan was besieged by Iran-Contra, but neither took the hit in presidential approval that Bush and Obama suffered. The difference? The Clinton and Reagan battles were fundamentally political. The Bush and Obama problems were at their core managerial. The managerial failures created a negative narrative into which other problems played and on which their opponents relentlessly piled. For Team Obama, there's been Benghazi, the IRS, the Obamacare website, the VA, the Secret Service, Ebola, and a lengthening list of other managerial mishaps. The Republicans turned this into a winning play in their battle for Congress in 2014: the president didn't know what he was doing, they said, and Democrats needed to pay.

III. We Don't Distinguish Between Failures that are Truly Consequential and those that Have Lesser Impact

You've benefited from the "Obama is incompetent" narrative. It increased the public's appetite for getting you—and some fresh air—into Washington. But let's be honest: you lucked out because of the media's inability or unwillingness to notice, care about, or explain the difference between hugely consequential management screw-ups and only modestly consequential ones.

Failing to plan for the occupation of Iraq? Disbanding the Iraqi military? Putting inexperienced political cronies in charge of the Federal Emergency Management Agency and downsizing the agency prior to Hurricane Katrina? Now *those* were screw-ups—big, far-reaching, world-historic blunders that led directly to the deaths of thousands.

But Ebola? In the United States (as opposed to Africa) Ebola claimed two victims through the first few months, both travelers from West Africa who arrived at hospitals already gravely ill. In all, three health care workers, two in Dallas, one in New York, caught the disease—and then they recovered. The media's freak-out over this story was insane. True, administration officials fed the frenzy with some inaccurate early assertions and advice—for instance, that the safety protocols the Centers for Disease Control had provided hospitals were not as careful and detailed as they needed to be. But within a few days the administration had better calibrated its media presence, the CDC had issued stronger protocols, and the outbreak had died down, just as the agency predicted. Meanwhile, in Texas alone, twenty children died in the 2012–13 flu season, and annual deaths from the flu across the nation range from 3,000 to 49,000—numbers that provoke mostly yawns from reporters.

The media mis-calibrated other big stories. In the Obamacare website fiasco, no one died. It took people a few extra months to sign up for care. Early press reports that forty veterans had died because of long wait times for primary care appointments at the Phoenix and other VA hospitals turned out to be bogus. The department's acting inspector general told lawmakers that the embarrassingly long wait times in places like Phoenix "may have contributed" to patient deaths but that his investigations had turned up no conclusive proof that *any* vet had died.

Of course, these were big stories—but they were mostly big *political* stories. The stumbles embarrassed the Obama administration, hinted at an underlying management problem in the administration (more on that shortly), and helped the

Republicans weave a powerful campaign narrative. But the stories weren't about big failures with huge consequences. They were about putting torpedoes below the political waterline.

IV. We Say We Want To Run Government More Like the Private Sector—But We Expect Government To Meet Standards that the Private Sector Could Never Manage

You made the case in your campaign that government needs to learn from the best-run private companies. That's an irresistible line that Republicans invented and Democrats—especially Obama—have come to champion. But, of course, you know that the private sector isn't always a model of good management. Remember New Coke, Windows 8, the collapse of Chi-Chi's restaurants, and shrapnel-filled airbags? That's even before we get to the wholesale financial miscalculations and fraud that led to global economic collapse.

The private market has a big advantage over government: it can bury its bodies in balance sheets and deal with its failures by quietly turning out the lights and locking the doors. Government's problems, no matter how small, are fodder for news headlines (see point #3): "Report: DHS Employees Put $30,000 Worth of Starbucks on Government Credit Card." We need to insist on government transparency, but sometimes that only creates more fodder.

For instance, how do we know that some VA facilities failed to measure up to the department's fourteen-day maximum wait time for first-time primary care appointments? Because the VA *measures* such wait times and then, through its inspector general, makes its failure rates public. Private health care systems don't disclose their wait times or have an inspector general looking out for patients and the financials. The only data we have on wait times at private-sector hospitals comes from a periodic survey by a health care consulting group. Compare those survey numbers and the VA's numbers (the audited ones, not the "juked" stats), and it turns out that on average the wait time at the VA isn't much different than in the private sector.

Expectations for government are higher than for the private sector and impossible to meet. Failures, no matter how small, hit the media spotlight. Government even gets blamed for private-sector failures. When investigators from the National Highway Traffic Safety Administration discovered that Takata airbags killed and injured drivers, they recalled millions of cars. And who did members of Congress blame for the failure of private

car companies to oversee the quality of supplies they bought from another private company in Japan? The NHTSA, of course.

V. Much of Government's Work Isn't Done By Government

You might think you're the chief executive, but you don't directly manage most of the programs for which the public holds you accountable. That's because much of government isn't actually done by government. The federal government spends $1 trillion per year on Medicare, Medicaid, and related programs, but private and nonprofit medical facilities actually provide the care. The Affordable Care Act is a federal mandate that requires individuals to have health insurance, and it provides subsidies for people who can't afford it. But the government doesn't provide the health insurance under the ACA, or the health care the insurance buys: all that comes from the private-sector actors, including some who are greedy, dishonest, and incompetent. The defense budget is a similar story. The Pentagon doesn't build its own weapon system; private-sector defense contractors do. Amtrak doesn't own most of the track on which its trains run. When Amtrak trains run late—and only two of its routes meet the national on-time standard of 85.5 percent—it's most often because privately owned railroads have failed to maintain the tracks or have given priority to their own freight trains. Most of what the federal government does is outsourced to the private sector or to state and local governments. Only about one-sixth of the budget goes to work performed by government employees.

Of course, this doesn't mean citizens won't hold you accountable for fraud, waste, abuse, and mismanagement. You just don't have direct management control over many of these problems. Much of your job isn't what people think it is, or what you imagined it would be when you ran for office.

VI. The Problem Isn't Too Many Bureaucrats—It's Too Few

Out of frustration, critics—including pundits, many members of Congress, and a fair number of presidential candidates (maybe even you), play an "Off with their heads" strategy: Fire some bureaucrats, and then fire some more until they get the message. Fire more still, to starve the government's ability to intrude into citizens' lives. It makes for good press, but it's a dangerous game, for several reasons.

First, while Washington is the nerve center of the federal government, 88 percent of all feds work outside the D.C. metropolitan area, and most of them do things around the country that citizens want or that government can't do without. There are Social Security claims workers who help people get their monthly checks, air traffic controllers and Transportation Security Administration screeners who keep air travel running, rangers who tend to national parks, and FBI field agents who track down the most wanted. If you cut across the board, you'd have to eliminate seven feds around the country for each D.C.-based bureaucrat who'd lose a job. The government shutdowns have shown that people quickly notice the difference.

Second, because government workers don't do much of government's work (see point #5), cutting feds reduces government's leverage over the vast and interconnected network of private programs and contracting firms that actually work the front lines. If you want to cut defense waste, you have to figure out how Pentagon staffers can do a better job overseeing contracts. Estimates of waste and improper payments in the Medicare program range as high as $120 billion a year, but you can't reduce that without getting a handle on people outside government who don't work for you—and to them, that $120 billion isn't waste, it's a windfall they'll fight to keep.

Here's a cautionary tale. In the 1990s, thanks to the Clinton administration's military downsizing and mandates by the GOP Congress, the number of contracting officers at the Department of Defense fell by 50 percent—from 460,000 to 230,000. Many of those civil servants didn't have the skills to oversee increasingly complex weapon systems and service contracts, and they needed to be replaced. But better-skilled replacements were not hired. Then came 9/11 and the wars in Afghanistan and Iraq. Suddenly, defense spending soared by hundreds of billions of dollars. Much of that money went to contractors, but it was overseen by what a later Army report called "a skeleton contracting force" of civilian bureaucrats. One result was a horrific chain of accidents—at least twelve in all—in which soldiers serving in Iraq were electrocuted while taking showers. Congressional investigators pointed to the failure of a contractor hired by the Pentagon to perform maintenance on the facilities. Private-sector contractors committed many of the atrocities at the Abu Ghraib prison, to the point that Iraqi prisoners won a $5.8 million judgment against one company. The depleted ranks of civil service acquisitions specialists also contributed to a huge spike in weapon cost overruns, from 6 percent for the average weapon system in 2000 to 25 percent in 2009. Cost overruns for that year alone totaled $296 billion.

Since then, the Obama administration has beefed up the Pentagon contracting force and brought more work in-house, and that's helped. But Obama, too, has felt the political pain of relying on undermanned bureaucracies to carry out his signature policies.

The Centers for Medicare and Medicaid Services (CMS) manage about $1 trillion in federal spending—the two health programs plus the state Children's Health Insurance Program—with just 5,720 employees. That's 0.2 percent of all federal employees responsible for 28 percent of all federal spending;

each employee is responsible, on average, for an astounding $175 million in government spending. Every employee who is cut puts more money at risk, unless government can figure out a smarter way of overseeing the programs. And that hasn't happened—the CMS's programs were charter members of the Government Accountability Office's (GAO) "high-risk list" of the programs most prone to waste, fraud, and abuse and have been there for twenty-four years.

Meanwhile, as the CMS was overwhelmed with managing two of the government's biggest programs, it got the job of setting up the federal Obamacare website and creating the federal insurance marketplace. But it didn't have the staff or the expertise to do the job—the CMS, after all, is a payment-management agency, not a website-design operation. The GAO found that the agency launched the procurement without figuring out what it wanted to buy, which led to a system that didn't work at first and suffered from enormous cost overruns. Bad things happen when agencies are responsible for important work they don't have the capacity to do.

This only scratches the surface of the chilling stories that spill out of the GAO's reports, especially its high-risk list. The biennial report is gripping reading only for the most wonky of policy wonks, but the underlying story is scary and clear. There are thirty programs on the list, and twenty-nine of them have roots in human capital—getting the right people with the right skills in the right place to solve these problems. The thirtieth program? Human capital itself.

In an August column in the *Washington Post,* the political scientist John DiIulio asked, "Want better, smaller government?" His answer: "Hire another million federal bureaucrats." We have no hope of making government work, he wrote, if we don't hire the government we need to run it—and to rein in the proxies who do so much of the government's work on its behalf. Much of the talk you hear about how government should be run more like the private sector is nonsense—there are too many fundamental differences in mission, expectations, and accountability. But one piece of advice from successful CEOs you should heed is that the people who work for you are your most important asset. Make sure you have enough of them, in the right places, with the right skills. If you run them down, you undermine yourself.

VII. Half the Time, When it Looks Like it's the President's Fault, the Problems Really Come from Congress

Citizens, reporters, and members of Congress deeply believe that the president is responsible for problems when they pop up. But in a huge number of cases, problems in executing laws start in the way Congress writes them.

Let's go back to the VA for a moment. The ultimate reason why front-line employees at some VA centers couldn't meet the department's fourteen-day maximum wait time standard (and chose instead to falsely report their results) was that there was a shortage of primary care doctors to meet the demand from newly enrolled veterans. But the shortage of primary care docs is a nationwide challenge, and Congress contributes mightily to the problem. Every year Congress dishes out $13 billion to academic medical centers for physician training, most of which goes to producing more cardiologists, radiologists, and other specialists that fatten the hospitals' bottom lines. Congress could demand that more of those dollars go to training primary care docs. It could also increase Medicare reimbursement rates for primary care relative to specialty care. These two reforms would go a long way toward relieving the primary care doc shortage. But because of pressure from the specialist physician lobbies, Congress chooses not to.

Or consider the beleaguered U.S. Postal Service. Congress demands that the service cover all its own costs, like a for-profit business, with no help from the Treasury. Yet it still insists on micromanaging the agency. To cover its growing revenue shortfalls, USPS leaders and outside experts have proposed a long list of ideas: End Saturday delivery. Close underutilized processing facilities. Spend less on pre-funding the employee retirement system. Open revenue-producing "postal banking" services for customers. Congress has refused to approve any of these ideas.

Congested highways making your commute longer? Maybe that's because Congress can't even pass a transportation bill, let alone legislation that adequately funds transportation infrastructure, including mass-transit systems. Got food poisoning? Maybe that's because Congress has all but defunded meat inspection. Worried about where the next big storm is heading? Congress has undercut the National Weather Service's ability to collect and distribute data. Pick almost any government performance problem and at least some (often most) of it can be traced back to some congressional action or inaction: conflicting statutory mandates, poor oversight, a failure to grant agencies sufficient authority to get the job done, ridiculous loopholes for favored private interests, grossly inadequate funding, and other problems.

It's certainly not the case that Congress doesn't care about government. Sometimes it smothers bureaucracy with love: a mind-boggling collection of 108 committees and subcommittees have oversight over the Department of Homeland Security. In fact, homeland security oversight is getting even more popular. The homeland security committee menagerie was just eighty-six in 2004, when the 9/11 Commission warned about the fragmentation of congressional oversight. It's ballooned since then into one of the Capitol's biggest time sinks. The *Hill*

reports that in 2012 and 2013, 391 officials from the department testified before Congress in 257 hearings, in addition to 4,000 briefings. The department's remote location on Nebraska Avenue, six miles from the Capitol, guarantees that department officials will spend a huge amount of their time stuck in traffic to satisfy the insatiable congressional appetite for a piece of the homeland security action. But there's no evidence that this oversight is helping: the department is one of the government's most troubled, and its management has been on the GAO's high-risk list.

VIII. Critics of Your Government Will Create Self-Fulfilling Prophecies by Underfunding and Otherwise Sabotaging Programs They Don't Like

An especially cynical strategy has emerged in recent years. Antigovernment forces have consciously tried to sabotage government—by shutting it down, slashing the budget, and attacking bureaucrats—with the clear goal of undermining the president's ability to manage. If opponents can't eliminate the programs they oppose, they can starve and cripple them. Failures then inevitably crop up. The news cycle doesn't differentiate between problems that are consequential and those that aren't (see point #3). What matters is creating a drumbeat of a gang that can't shoot straight, and finding new stories to reload the ammo as the old tales fade away. Doing the public's business gets lost in the battle of driving the other guy out of town. The Constitution anticipated one way to deal with the core questions about government, of course: if you don't like a law, change or repeal it. In gridlocked Washington, however, it's too hard to do that (or much of anything else). It's much easier to sabotage government's long-term operations for short-term political purposes.

This strategy is made possible by a quirk in public opinion: most Americans don't like government, but they sure do like government programs. When sequestration loomed in early 2013, the Pew Research Center for the People and the Press surveyed citizens about what programs ought to be cut. The result: of the nineteen programs on the Pew list, none commanded a 50 percent vote for cutting.

Cutting government waste, of course, really means cutting the other guy's programs. Deep in the heart of Texas Tea Party country in 2011, there were constant cries to slash government spending. But when wildfires swept through the central part of the state, GOP Representative Michael McCaul, who represents a district stretching from Austin to Houston, complained that the U.S. Forest Service didn't have tankers at the ready. "Despite all the warnings that Texas faced with it being the driest summer in more than 100 years, there was no prepositioned aircraft to help," he said. Local residents savaged the USFS for canceling a contract with Aero Union, a California company whose ancient planes, some of which were fifty years old, didn't meet basic safety standards. They complained more when the agency went looking for help and brought in air tankers from outside the country. But the USFS is responsible only for fires in national forests, and only a tiny fraction of the Texas fires were on federal land. So the agency caught flak from antigovernment activists who complained that they weren't getting government help fast enough—and that the feds weren't there to do the state and local governments' work. By the way, Representative McCaul was reelected in 2014, winning 62 percent of the vote.

IX. Government Can Be Made Much Better Relatively Quickly— and Can Be Made Worse Even More Quickly

After the disastrous launch in 2013 of the ACA website, many Washington pundits asked whether Americans would ever trust the government again. But an equally important story, one almost no one knows, is how quickly a skilled team of feds and private contractors turned the website around. Obama put a former top Office of Management and Budget official, Jeff Zients, in charge. He hired a systems integrator to ride herd on the project and launched a "tech surge" to fix the site and its back-office operations. By December 2013, in three months of nonstop work, the team stabilized the site and ended the "Please try again" messages that bedeviled it at its launch. In November 2014, when the health marketplaces went live around the country, the headlines said "Insurance Exchanges Launch with Few Glitches," with up to nine million people expected to sign up by the end of open enrollment on February 15, 2015.

There's an important lesson here for you: government screw-ups can happen quickly, but with the right leadership and energy they can be resolved quickly, too. That is true not just of individual initiatives, like the exchanges, but of whole agencies.

No federal agency demonstrates more clearly how fast big problems can be solved—or how quickly progress can evaporate—than FEMA. The agency created its own disaster when it fumbled the response to Hurricane Andrew's devastating blow to Florida in August 1992. Pundits afterward wondered if the management failures nearly cost George H. W. Bush the state's electoral votes. When he became president, Bill

Clinton appointed a skilled administrator, James Lee Witt, to engineer a FEMA turnaround. By 1995, Daniel Franklin wrote in the *Washington Monthly* that "FEMA transformed itself from what many considered to be the worst federal agency (no small distinction) to among the best." Instead of showing up to write checks after disasters, FEMA worked with communities *before* disasters happened to reduce risk and damage. The agency discovered, for example, that it was much cheaper to retrofit homes in advance of storms to keep the roofs from blowing off than to pay afterward to put the roofs back on—and to repair or replace flooded homes—so it built partnerships with Florida local governments to make that happen.

FEMA's success didn't last long, however. The mega-consolidation that brought twenty-two agencies, including FEMA, into the new Department of Homeland Security derailed the improvements of the Clinton years. After Hurricane Katrina nearly drowned New Orleans, President George W. Bush put his arm around FEMA administrator Michael Brown and famously said, "Brownie, you're doing a heck of a job," at precisely the time it was clear that neither he nor FEMA were. David Paulson soon replaced Brown and began getting the agency back on track. Obama's appointee, Craig Fugate, continued the progress so that, when Superstorm Sandy attacked the northeastern coast, the headline that didn't appear was "FEMA Fails Again." The agency's partnerships with state and local governments, as well as with the private sector, proved a model of disaster response. Companies like Home Depot and Walmart became integral parts of FEMA's "whole community" strategy, focused on "creating active public-private partnerships to build disaster-resistant communities." That made a huge difference when the storm hit.

The bad news is that the loss of top-level attention can quickly drive well-functioning agencies to disaster. The good news is that strong top-level leadership can turn poorly performing agencies around. FEMA has gone through the down-and-up cycle twice in the last twenty years. If you pay attention to the game—see point #10—you can avoid this roller-coaster ride.

X. Presidents Can Win the Game If They Pay Attention

You won't be able to avoid the nine truths we've explored so far, and they're full of traps that can undermine your presidency when you least expect it. But you have more ways to avoid those traps than you might imagine.

There are five important, straightforward steps. First are the 3,000 appointments that you directly make in the executive branch. You need a White House personnel operation that goes beyond satisfying campaign contributors to making sure you get the right people in the right jobs with the right skills and instincts.

The second is the civil service. You badly need the best and the brightest to support the executive branch's work. If you don't get good performance, you'll pay—dearly. And the huge impending turnover in the federal workforce is a bigger challenge than you think. Almost a third of the federal workforce will be eligible to retire as you take office. Half of all air traffic controllers could move out as you're moving in. In the Department of Housing and Urban Development, that number is 42 percent, and it's 44 percent in the Small Business Administration. You might look to millennials, who want to find jobs where they can have an impact. But right now, many of them are drawn to the nonprofit sector, because the government hiring process is a mess and they worry that if they join the government they'll be caught up in too much red tape and too little entrepreneurship. More generally, the feds are getting fed up with being the punching bag for dysfunction elsewhere in government. You need to worry about this—and to recruit a leader for the Office of Personnel Management who can get the federal government's strategy right.

The third step is making sure that the President's Management Council runs well. This is the group of the departments' deputy secretaries, chaired by the OMB's deputy director for management. The PMC has had its ups and downs—but when it has been run well, it has provided a direct connection between the White House and the people who actually manage the agencies. The PMC members can be the best friends you didn't know you needed.

A fourth step is tougher. You need a chief operating officer, someone who can look after the details when you are busy with everything else and speak for you when management muscle is needed. You've got three options here.

Option 1: Make your vice president the chief operating officer. Al Gore got Clinton's blessing to run the National Performance Review from the vice president's office. Dick Cheney had a huge scope of operating responsibilities in the Bush years. Joe Biden launched and oversaw the $831 billion Recovery Act with nary a scary headline about fraud. These VPs-as-COOs provided valuable service to their presidents, but it's a potentially risky strategy, since it can create a rival political camp. Moreover, the history has been uneven—Gore barely mentioned the NPR in his presidential campaign, Cheney's power unsettled many Washington hands, and Biden's role ebbed after the Recovery Act's successes. But the vice presidency can be a lot more than a "bucket of warm spit," as one of Franklin Roosevelt's vice presidents, John Nance Garner, put it.

Option 2: Run government management through the "M" in OMB. The Office of Management and Budget has a deputy director for management, charged with overseeing the federal government's operations. You could strengthen this post and give the deputy director muscle (it needs at minimum a doubling of its staff). But this has been a troubled position for a very long time. The "B" (budget) side of OMB has always been more powerful than the much smaller "M" (management) side, and both wings have struggled with staffing reductions in recent years. You need help. This could be the place to get it.

Option 3: Create a czar of czars in the White House. A new post of deputy chief of staff of operations would pull management more clearly into the presidential orbit and give the president's voice to management issues when the czar of czars speaks (quietly and behind the scenes, of course). It would be an ugly job, pushed aside by the inner-circle power brokers (jealous of their time with you), charged with doing things that most people around you won't think are important (until it's too late), ignored by bureaucrats (unless you make it clear that they need to listen), and staffed by someone who will always struggle to stay a step ahead of what's going on out there (because the more powerful your deputy becomes, the less administrators will want to tell him or her). But the post could also help your administration become less insular. That was a growing problem for both Bush and Obama, the deeper they got into their terms.

The fifth step is dealing with Congress on the management of government. The political rule in Washington is that whatever goes wrong in the bureaucracy is the president's fault, even if so many problems flow from Capitol Hill. For your sake and the country's, this misperception needs to be shattered, and you can strike a blow for sanity right away. At your first State of the Union address, announce that you will submit a sweeping plan to fix the big problems in law that cripple the federal government's management and performance. Tell the assembled lawmakers that if they fail to act on these proposals and screw-ups arise, you know you will be held responsible, and that's part of your job. But this time, tell them, Congress will share the blame. The point here is not to duck responsibility but to create joint accountability. Fixing a federal bureaucracy as big and complex as ours is not something any president can do alone. You need Congress's help, and Congress needs political incentives to care. Create those incentives, and great things could happen.

You have more options than you think. You ignore them at your peril. And if you're like most presidents, you won't discover that peril until you're up to your knees in it trying to figure out how it happened. You can learn these ten truths the easy way now, or suffer from them the hard way later. But you can't escape them.

Critical Thinking

1. Why does the statement "we want to run government more like the private sector" not make sense to political scientist Donald F. Kettl? Do you agree with him?

2. Explain "much of government's work isn't done by government" and "the problem isn't too many bureaucrats—it's too few."

3. How, according to Kettl, can presidents overcome the management problems that they inevitably face?

Internet References

Brookings Institution: Donald F. Kettl
   http://www.brookings.edu/experts/kettld

Wisegeek: What is Public Management?
   http://www.wisegeek.org/what-is-public-management.htm

DONALD F. KETTL is a nonresident senior fellow at the Volcker Alliance and the Brookings Institution and a professor in the University of Maryland School of Public Policy, where he served as dean from 2009 to 2014.

Article
Prepared by: Bruce Stinebrickner, *DePauw University*

The Gridlock Clause

You Will Note Its Absence from the Constitution

Josh Blackman

Learning Outcomes

After reading this article, you will be able to:

- Consider the phenomenon of "gridlock" in American national government and assess whether it is good or bad (or neither?) and explain why.

- Explore the implications of the article's title in conjunction with the accompanying statement that "you will note its absence from the Constitution."

Since 2010, when the Democrats lost their majority in the House and their filibuster-proof majority in the Senate, President Obama's ability to pursue legislative changes has ground to a halt. Headline after headline blares that the "do-nothing congress" has enacted the fewest laws in decades. But that gridlock hasn't halted the president's plans to implement his policies. In fact, he claims it has strengthened his power to act alone—if congress won't act, he can, and will.

President Obama routinely cites congress's obstinacy to his agenda as a justification for engaging in a series of executive actions that suspend, waive, and even rewrite statutes. His frustration is understandable, but his response is not justifiable. Brazenly maneuvering around the lawmaking function of congress is an affront to the constitutional order.

There is nothing new about congressional gridlock. It is perhaps worse than ever today, but partisan impasses are not novel. There is also nothing new about presidents' creatively reinterpreting the law in order to justify executive policies. What is new is the relationship between these two factors—invoking gridlock as a justification for redefining executive authority. This disruptive constitutional philosophy poses a threat to our separation of powers. It establishes a precedent for this and future presidents to permanently blur the lines between the executive and legislative prerogatives.

Generally, when a president suffers a congressional setback, he has two choices: advance a more moderate compromise proposal that can get past the political roadblock or table the issue. Yet, since 2010, the president has chosen a third path: act as if congress supported him, and proceed with his agenda unilaterally. He has done this with his unconstitutional recess appointments to the national Labor Relations Board, his unilateral modifications to the Affordable care Act, his unprecedented expansion of immigration authority via Deferred Action for childhood Arrivals, and many other actions.

The president isn't just relying on congressional intransigence as a *political* reason for acting, as University of chicago law professor Eric Posner has suggested he is. It is also part of his *legal* reason. A careful study of his executive actions reveals a broader constitutional philosophy of executive power based on gridlock.

I refer to the president's purported authority in this realm as his *corrective powers*. Perceiving a breakdown in the normal political process, the president takes unilateral action to right the wrongs of congressional inaction.

In 2011, Senate republicans blocked a vote on the president's nominees to the National Labor relations Board. To prevent the Senate from going into recess and allowing the president to make recess appointments, republicans forced the chamber to hold a series of short, minute-long pro forma sessions every three days. This tactic was introduced by Democrats to prevent George W. Bush from making recess appointments.

Without new appointees, the NLRB would lose its quorum, and its ability to issue decisions—an urgent problem. The president had two legitimate options in the face of this political deadlock. First, he could have prevailed upon Senate Democrats to trigger the so-called nuclear option—that is, to eliminate the filibustering of presidential nominations. (Two years later, Senate majority leader Harry Reid did just this, paving the way for confirmations with only a majority vote in the Senate.)

Second, he could have picked more palatable nominees. (a year later, he did just this, by withdrawing the nomination of a controversial board member and substituting an alternative whom republicans were more willing to back.)

But the president chose Door No. 3. Faced with a political problem that called for a political solution, the president turned to an unconstitutional shortcut: although the Senate hadn't gone on recess—what he wanted to happen—Obama acted as if it had. During a 72-hour window between pro forma sessions on January 3 and January 6, 2012, the president deemed the Senate in recess and made three appointments to the NLRB.

In the case of *NLRB v. Noel Canning,* the Supreme Court unanimously rejected the president's legal defense of his action and found the recess appointments unconstitutional. But all nine justices went even further than that, specifically refuting the president's argument that gridlock justified his redefinition of the separation of powers. During oral arguments, Solicitor General Donald H. Verrilli, the administration's top lawyer, argued that the president's decision to disregard the pro forma sessions was justified as a "safety valve" in response to "congressional intransigence." If the president did not make the recess appointees, "the NLRB was going to go dark," Verrilli said. "It was going to lose its quorum." The solicitor general's arguments represented a crystallization of the executive philosophy of the Obama administration.

It was clear that the justices were not in the least persuaded by the solicitor general's reasoning. Justice Alito charged that the solicitor general was "making a very, very aggressive argument in favor of executive power [that] has nothing whatsoever to do with whether the Senate is in session or not." The government was asserting, alito explained, that "when the Senate acts, in [the government's view] view, irresponsibly and refuses to confirm nominations, then the president must be able to fill those positions." Chief Justice Roberts put it bluntly: "You spoke of the intransigence of the Senate. Well, they have an absolute right not to confirm nominees that the president submits." Justice Kagan said that the NLRB's going "dark" was directly "a result of congressional refusal." Justice Breyer added, "I can't find anything that says the purpose of [the recess-appointments clause] has anything at all to do with political fights between Congress and the president." Ultimately, all nine justices emphatically rejected the president's position.

Writing for the majority, Justice Breyer made clear that "political opposition in the Senate would not qualify as an unusual circumstance" to justify the president's making recess appointment during the pro forma sessions. Breyer stressed that this was a "political problem, not a constitutional problem." Justice Scalia made the point forcefully in a concurring opinion, writing that the Obama administration "asked us to view the recess-appointment power as a 'safety valve' against Senatorial 'intransigence.'" Scalia charged that this was a dangerous argument that translated a political dilemma into a constitutional crisis. The lesson from all nine justices was clear: Gridlock does not give the chief executive a license to redefine his constitutional powers.

Perhaps the boldest example of the president's corrective powers has been his response to the failure of his efforts to enact immigration reform. The DREAM Act, which the administration endorsed, would have provided work permits and a form of permanent residency for immigrants who were brought to the United States illegally as minors. Though the bill received bipartisan support in both houses, a republican-led filibuster killed it in the Senate.

The president again had two legitimate courses open to him. He could propose a compromise immigration policy that would receive enough support to overcome the Senate filibuster—perhaps by also strengthening border security and increasing enforcement action. But this was probably impossible. So his only practicable option was to accept a legislative defeat, which he could then use as a political issue as he campaigned against republicans in his upcoming reelection campaign.

Instead, the president again chose Door No. 3. He determined that he now had the power unilaterally to defer deportation of the immigrants in question and announced the imposition of this policy (called Deferred action for Childhood arrivals). Using "prosecutorial discretion," the president declared that "eligible individuals who do not present a risk to national security or public safety will be able to request temporary relief from deportation proceedings and apply for work authorization." Deferred action for Childhood arrivals (DACA) in effect accomplished the key statutory objectives of the DREAM Act, a law Congress had expressly declined to enact, without the benefit of a statute. Although the administration justified the policy as selective enforcement of the immigration laws, the scale of this "discretion" was without precedent. The administration excused over 1 million people, as a class, from the scope of Congress's naturalization power.

"In the absence of any immigration action from Congress to fix our broken immigration system," Obama said, "we're improving" immigration policy on our own. Through a novel reinterpretation of his executive discretion to deport, the president was able to maneuver around a Congress that would not agree to defer deportations. In his mind, he corrected the vote on the DREAM Act, which should have passed.

If the president initially believed that an act of Congress was needed to accomplish deferred action, what changed his mind? Why bother going to Congress in the first place? He admitted it—if Congress won't do it, then I will. He was justified in doing what Congress should have done.

Since then, the president has doubled down on this position. In June 2014, after much debate within his caucus, Speaker John Boehner announced that the house would not bring an immigration bill to a vote in 2014: The gridlock would continue. That same day, in impromptu remarks delivered in the Rose Garden, President Obama explained that in response he would take *more* unilateral executive action on immigration reform: "I take executive action only when we have a serious problem, a serious issue, and Congress chooses to do nothing." he would "fix the immigration system on my own, without Congress," he promised.

Executive action cannot be justified as a means to end gridlock when constitutionally authorized political reforms—such as eliminating the filibuster, reducing gerrymandering, or uniting American popular opinion—could do so instead. I suffer no delusions about how difficult it would be to use these legitimate means in our increasingly polarized society. But unconstitutionally redefining the president's authority so that the administration can resolve intractable political disputes should not be casually accepted. As Justice Scalia made clear in his it Canning opinion, gridlock is "not a bug to be fixed by this Court, but a calculated feature of the constitutional framework."

While many may like the results of the president's executive actions, acquiescence to his claims of authority sets a dangerous precedent for the separation of powers. Each president builds on the power of his predecessor, in a one-way ratchet of executive authority. And the threat transcends partisan interest. Imagine if a President Romney, relying on the same sort of power that President Obama has claimed, had indefinitely delayed implementation of Obamacare's mandates because he could not overcome a Senate filibuster blocking repeal of the law. Or if a President Rand Paul, unable to pass a tax reform, decided not to enforce the corporate income tax against Fortune 500 companies, citing prosecutorial discretion similar to that relied on with DACA. Or if a President Hillary Clinton, unsuccessful in convincing Congress to pass welfare reform, decided

to waive the requirement that welfare recipients participate in the work force in order to receive benefits. Or if a President Ted Cruz, in keeping with President Obama's decision not to enforce controlled-substance laws in two states, unilaterally decided not to prosecute Texas businesses for violations of environmental laws. Or if a President Elizabeth Warren decided that the government would no longer collect any interest on federally guaranteed student loans, waiving any enforcement against defaulting debtors. Or imagine if President George W. Bush, when faced with the defeat of his Social Security plan, had instructed the Treasury Department to let workers deposit payroll taxes directly into individual retirement accounts.

If the president is allowed effectively to suspend laws in the name of breaking gridlock, the executive will have power to enact policies that could never be approved through the legislative process. The solution to political gridlock is to use politics to end the gridlock—not to redefine the Constitution's separation of powers. Political compromise is hard, but disregarding the Constitution is a hazardous alternative.

Critical Thinking

1. Identify what, according to the author, are the two choices between which presidents have traditionally chosen when Congress has blocked or opposed them.

2. Identify the "third path" that, according to the author, President Obama has regularly chosen.

3. Summarize the background and the content of the Supreme Court's ruling in *NLRB v. Noel Canning* and the relation of that ruling to "gridlock."

Internet References

The Huffington Post
   http://www.huffingtonpost.com/news/political-gridlock
The Tea Party (Federalist 51)
   http://www.teaparty911.com/info/federalist-papers-summaries/no_51.htm

MR. BLACKMAN *is a constitutional-law professor at the South Texas College of Law, Houston, and the author of* Unprecedented: The Constitutional Challenge to Obamacare. *He blogs at www.JoshBlackman. com. This essay is an adaptation of Mr. Blackman's new paper "Gridlock and Executive Power."*

Article   Prepared by: Bruce Stinebrickner, *DePauw University*

When Congress Stops Wars
Partisan Politics and Presidential Power

WILLIAM G. HOWELL AND JON C. PEVEHOUSE

Learning Outcomes

After reading this article, you will be able to:

- Assess the proper balance of power between Congress and the president in decisions to use U.S. military force.

- Consider the implications of the authors' contention that the party composition of Congress and the presidency is the decisive factor in determining the reaction of Congress to "presidential calls for war."

For most of George W. Bush's tenure, political observers have lambasted Congress for failing to fulfill its basic foreign policy obligations. Typical was the recent *Foreign Affairs* article by Norman Ornstein and Thomas Mann, "When Congress Checks Out," which offered a sweeping indictment of Congress' failure to monitor the president's execution of foreign wars and antiterrorist initiatives. Over the past six years, they concluded, Congressional oversight of the White House's foreign and national security policy "has virtually collapsed." Ornstein and Mann's characterization is hardly unique. Numerous constitutional-law scholars, political scientists, bureaucrats, and even members of Congress have, over the years, lamented the lack of legislative constraints on presidential war powers. But the dearth of Congressional oversight between 2000 and 2006 is nothing new. Contrary to what many critics believe, terrorist threats, an overly aggressive White House, and an impotent Democratic Party are not the sole explanations for Congressional inactivity over the past six years. Good old-fashioned partisan politics has been, and continues to be, at play.

It is often assumed that everyday politics *stops* at the water's edge and that legislators abandon their partisan identities during times of war in order to become faithful stewards of their constitutional obligations. But this received wisdom is almost always wrong. The illusion of Congressional wartime unity misconstrues the nature of legislative oversight and fails to capture the particular conditions under which members of Congress are likely to emerge as meaningful critics of any particular military venture.

The partisan composition of Congress has historically been the decisive factor in determining whether lawmakers will oppose or acquiesce in presidential calls for war. From Harry Truman to Bill Clinton, nearly every U.S. president has learned that members of Congress, and members of the opposition party in particular, are fully capable of interjecting their opinions about proposed and ongoing military ventures. When the opposition party holds a large number of seats or controls one or both chambers of Congress, members routinely challenge the president and step up oversight of foreign conflicts; when the legislative branch is dominated by the president's party, it generally goes along with the White House. Partisan unity, not institutional laziness, explains why the Bush administration's Iraq policy received such a favorable hearing in Congress from 2000 to 2006.

The dramatic increase in Congressional oversight following the 2006 midterm elections is a case in point. Immediately after assuming control of Congress, House Democrats passed a resolution condemning a proposed "surge" of U.S. troops in Iraq and Senate Democrats debated a series of resolutions expressing varying degrees of outrage against the war in Iraq. The spring 2007 supplemental appropriations debate resulted in a House bill calling for a phased withdrawal (the president vetoed that bill, and the Senate then passed a bill accepting more war funding without withdrawal provisions). Democratic heads of committees in both chambers continue to launch hearings and investigations into the various mishaps, scandals, and tactical errors that have plagued the Iraq war. By all indications, if the government in Baghdad has not met certain benchmarks by September, the Democrats will push for binding legislation that further restricts the president's ability to sustain military operations in Iraq.

Neither Congress' prior languor nor its recent awakening should come as much of a surprise. When they choose to do so, members of Congress can exert a great deal of influence over the conduct of war. They can enact laws that dictate how long military campaigns may last, control the purse strings that determine how well they are funded, and dictate how appropriations may be spent. Moreover, they can call hearings and issue public pronouncements on foreign policy matters. These powers allow members to cut funding for ill-advised military ventures, set timetables for the withdrawal of troops, foreclose opportunities to expand a conflict into new regions, and establish reporting requirements. Through legislation, appropriations, hearings, and public appeals, members of Congress can substantially increase the political costs of military action—sometimes forcing presidents to withdraw sooner than they would like or even preventing any kind of military action whatsoever.

The Partisan Imperative

Critics have made a habit of equating legislative inactivity with Congress' abdication of its foreign policy obligations. Too often, the infrequency with which Congress enacts restrictive statutes is seen as prima facie evidence of the institution's failings. Sometimes it is. But one cannot gauge the health of the U.S. system of governance strictly on the basis of what Congress does—or does not do—in the immediate aftermath of presidential initiatives.

After all, when presidents anticipate Congressional resistance they will not be able to overcome, they often abandon the sword as their primary tool of diplomacy. More generally, when the White House knows that Congress will strike down key provisions of a policy initiative, it usually backs off. President Bush himself has relented, to varying degrees, during the struggle to create the Department of Homeland Security and during conflicts over the design of military tribunals and the prosecution of U.S. citizens as enemy combatants. Indeed, by most accounts, the administration recently forced the resignation of the chairman of the Joint Chiefs of Staff, General Peter Pace, so as to avoid a clash with Congress over his reappointment.

To assess the extent of Congressional influence on presidential war powers, it is not sufficient to count how many war authorizations are enacted or how often members deem it necessary to start the "war powers clock"—based on the War Powers Act requirement that the president obtain legislative approval within 60 days after any military deployment. Rather, one must examine the underlying partisan alignments across the branches of government and presidential efforts to anticipate and preempt Congressional recriminations.

During the past half century, partisan divisions have fundamentally defined the domestic politics of war. A variety of factors help explain why partisanship has so prominently defined the contours of interbranch struggles over foreign military deployments. To begin with, some members of Congress have electoral incentives to increase their oversight of wars when the opposing party controls the White House. If presidential approval ratings increase due to a "rally around the flag" effect in times of war, and if those high ratings only benefit the president's party in Congress, then the opposition party has an incentive to highlight any failures, missteps, or scandals that might arise in the course of a military venture.

After all, the making of U.S. foreign policy hinges on how U.S. national interests are defined and the means chosen to achieve them. This process is deeply, and unavoidably, political. Therefore, only in very particular circumstances—a direct attack on U.S. soil or on Americans abroad—have political parties temporarily united for the sake of protecting the national interest. Even then, partisan politics has flared as the toll of

war has become evident. Issues of trust and access to information further fuel these partisan fires. In environments in which information is sparse, individuals with shared ideological or partisan affiliations find it easier to communicate with one another. The president possesses unparalleled intelligence about threats to national interests, and he is far more likely to share that information with members of his own political party than with political opponents. Whereas the commander in chief has an entire set of executive-branch agencies at his beck and call, Congress has relatively few sources of reliable classified information. Consequently, when a president claims that a foreign crisis warrants military intervention, members of his own party tend to trust him more often than not, whereas members of the opposition party are predisposed to doubt and challenge such claims. In this regard, Congressional Democrats' constant interrogations of Bush administration officials represent just the latest round in an ongoing interparty struggle to control the machinery of war.

Congressional Influence and Its Limits

Historically, presidents emerging from midterm election defeats have been less likely to respond to foreign policy crises aggressively, and when they have ordered the use of force, they have taken much longer to do so. Our research shows that the White House's propensity to exercise military force steadily declines as members of the opposition party pick up seats in Congress. In fact, it is not even necessary for the control of Congress to switch parties; the loss of even a handful of seats can materially affect the probability that the nation will go to war.

The partisan composition of Congress also influences its willingness to launch formal oversight hearings. While criticizing members for their inactivity during the Bush administration, Ornstein and Mann make much of the well-established long-term decline in the number of hearings held on Capitol Hill. This steady decline, however, has not muted traditional partisan politics. According to Linda Fowler, of Dartmouth College, the presence or absence of unified government largely determines the frequency of Congressional hearings. Contrary to Ornstein and Mann's argument that "vigorous oversight was the norm until the end of the twentieth century," Fowler demonstrates that during the post–World War II era, when the same party controlled both Congress and the presidency, the number of hearings about military policy decreased, but when the opposition party controlled at least one chamber of Congress, hearings occurred with greater frequency. Likewise, Boston University's Douglas Kriner has shown that Congressional authorizations of war as well as legislative initiatives that establish timetables for the withdrawal of troops, cut funds, or otherwise curtail military operations critically depend on the partisan balance of power on Capitol Hill.

Still, it is important not to overstate the extent of Congressional influence. Even when Congress is most aggressive, the executive branch retains a tremendous amount of power when it comes to military matters. Modern presidents enjoy extraordinary advantages in times of war, not least of which the ability to act unilaterally on military matters and thereby place on Congress (and everyone else) the onus of coordinating a response. Once troops enter a region, members of Congress face the difficult choice of either cutting funds and then facing the charge of undermining the troops or keeping the public coffers open and thereby aiding a potentially ill-advised military operation.

On this score, Ornstein and Mann effectively illustrate Bush's efforts to expand his influence over the war in Iraq and the war on terrorism by refusing to disclose classified information, regularly circumventing the legislative process, and resisting even modest efforts at oversight. Similarly, they note that Republican Congressional majorities failed to take full advantage of their institution's formal powers to monitor and influence either the formulation or the implementation of foreign policy during the first six years of Bush's presidency. Ornstein and Mann, however, mistakenly attribute such lapses in Congressional oversight to a loss of an "institutional identity" that was ostensibly forged during a bygone era when "tough oversight of the executive was common, whether or not different parties controlled the White House and Congress" and when members' willingness to challenge presidents had less to do with partisan allegiances and more to do with a shared sense of institutional responsibility. In the modern era, foreign-policy making has rarely worked this way. On the contrary, partisan competition has contributed to nearly every foreign policy clash between Capitol Hill and the White House for the past six decades.

Divided We Stand

Shortly after World War II—the beginning of a period often mischaracterized as one of "Cold War consensus"—partisan wrangling over the direction of U.S. foreign policy returned to Washington, ending a brief period of wartime unity. By defining U.S. military involvement in Korea as a police action rather than a war, President Truman effectively freed himself from the constitutional requirements regarding war and established a precedent for all subsequent presidents to circumvent Congress when sending the military abroad. Although Truman's party narrowly controlled both chambers, Congress hounded him throughout the Korean War, driving his approval ratings down into the 20s and paving the way for a Republican electoral victory in 1952. Railing off a litany of complaints about the president's firing of General Douglas MacArthur and his meager progress toward ending the war, Senator Robert Taft, then a Republican presidential candidate, declared that "the greatest failure of foreign policy is an unnecessary war, and we have been involved in such a war now for more than a year. . . . As a matter of fact, every purpose of the war has now failed. We are exactly where we were three years ago, and where we could have stayed."

On the heels of the Korean War came yet another opportunity to use force in Asia, but facing a divided Congress, President Dwight Eisenhower was hesitant to get involved. French requests for assistance in Indochina initially fell on sympathetic ears in the Eisenhower administration, which listed Indochina

as an area of strategic importance in its "new look" defense policy. However, in January 1954, when the French asked for a commitment of U.S. troops, Eisenhower balked. The president stated that he "could conceive of no greater tragedy than for the United States to become involved in an all-out war in Indochina." His reluctance derived in part from the anticipated fight with Congress that he knew would arise over such a war. Even after his decision to provide modest technical assistance to France, in the form of B-26 bombers and air force technicians, Congressional leaders demanded a personal meeting with the president to voice their disapproval. Soon afterward, Eisenhower promised to withdraw the air force personnel, replacing them with civilian contractors.

Eventually, the United States did become involved in a ground war in Asia, and it was that war that brought Congressional opposition to the presidential use of force to a fever pitch. As the Vietnam War dragged on and casualties mounted, Congress and the public grew increasingly wary of the conflict and of the power delegated to the president in the 1964 Gulf of Tonkin resolution. In 1970, with upward of 350,000 U.S. troops in the field and the war spilling over into Cambodia, Congress formally repealed that resolution. And over the next several years, legislators enacted a series of appropriations bills intended to restrict the war's scope and duration. Then, in June 1973, after the Paris peace accords had been signed, Congress enacted a supplemental appropriations act that cut off all funding for additional military involvement in Southeast Asia, including in Cambodia, Laos, North Vietnam, and South Vietnam. Finally, when South Vietnam fell in 1975, Congress took the extraordinary step of formally forbidding U.S. troops from enforcing the Paris peace accords, despite the opposition of President Gerald Ford and Secretary of State Henry Kissinger.

Three years later, a Democratic Congress forbade the use of funds for a military action that was supported by the president—this time, the supply of covert aid to anticommunist forces in Angola. At the insistence of Senator Dick Clark (D-Iowa), the 1976 Defense Department appropriations act stipulated that no monies would be used "for any activities involving Angola other than intelligence gathering." Facing such staunch Congressional opposition, President Ford suspended military assistance to Angola, unhappily noting that the Democratic-controlled Congress had "lost its guts" with regard to foreign policy.

In just one instance, the case of Lebanon in 1983, did Congress formally start the 60-day clock of the 1973 War Powers Act. Most scholars who call Congress to task for failing to fulfill its constitutional responsibilities make much of the fact that in this case it ended up authorizing the use of force for a full 18 months, far longer than the 60 days automatically allowed under the act. However, critics often overlook the fact that Congress simultaneously forbade the president from unilaterally altering the scope, target, or mission of the U.S. troops participating in the multinational peacekeeping force. Furthermore, Congress asserted its right to terminate the venture at any time with a one-chamber majority vote or a joint resolution and established firm reporting requirements as the U.S. presence in Lebanon continued.

During the 1980s, no foreign policy issue dominated Congressional discussions more than aid to the contras in Nicaragua, rebel forces who sought to topple the leftist Sandinista regime. In 1984, a Democratic-controlled House enacted an appropriations bill that forbade President Ronald Reagan from supporting the contras. Reagan appeared undeterred. Rather than abandon the project, the administration instead diverted funds from Iranian arms sales to support the contras, establishing the basis for the most serious presidential scandal since Watergate. Absent Congressional opposition on this issue, Reagan may well have intervened directly, or at least directed greater, more transparent aid to the rebels fighting the Nicaraguan government.

Regardless of which party holds a majority of the seats in Congress, it is almost always the opposition party that creates the most trouble for a president intent on waging war. When, in the early 1990s, a UN humanitarian operation in Somalia devolved into urban warfare, filling nightly newscasts with scenes from Mogadishu, Congress swung into action. Despite previous declarations of public support for the president's actions, Congressional Republicans and some Democrats passed a Department of Defense appropriations act in November 1993 that simultaneously authorized the use of force to protect UN units and required that U.S. forces be withdrawn by March 31, 1994.

A few years later, a Republican-controlled Congress took similar steps to restrict the use of funds for a humanitarian crisis occurring in Kosovo. One month after the March 1999 NATO air strikes against Serbia, the House passed a bill forbidding the use of Defense Department funds to introduce U.S. ground troops into the conflict without Congressional authorization. When President Clinton requested funding for operations in the Balkans, Republicans in Congress (and some hawkish Democrats) seized on the opportunity to attach additional monies for unrelated defense programs, military personnel policies, aid to farmers, and hurricane relief and passed a supplemental appropriations bill that was considerably larger than the amount requested by the president. The mixed messages sent by the Republicans caught the attention of Clinton's Democratic allies. As House member Martin Frost (D-Tex.) noted, "I am at a loss to explain how the Republican Party can, on one hand, be so irresponsible as to abandon our troops in the midst of a military action to demonstrate its visceral hostility toward the commander in chief, and then, on the other, turn around and double his request for money for what they call 'Clinton's war.'" The 1999 debate is remarkably similar to the current wrangling over spending on Iraq.

Legislating Opinion

The voice of Congress (or lack thereof) has had a profound impact on the media coverage of the current war in Iraq, just as it has colored public perceptions of U.S. foreign policy in the past. Indeed, Congress' ability to influence executive-branch decision-making extends far beyond its legislative and budgetary powers. Cutting funds, starting the war powers clock, or forcing troop withdrawals are the most extreme options available to them. More frequently, members of Congress make appeals designed to influence both media coverage and public opinion of a president's war. For example, Congress' vehement criticism of Reagan's decision to reflag Kuwaiti tankers during the Iran-Iraq War led to reporting requirements for the administration. Similarly, the Clinton administration's threats to invade Haiti in 1994 were met with resistance by Republicans and a handful of skeptical Democrats in Congress, who took to the airwaves to force Clinton to continually justify placing U.S. troops in harm's way.

Such appeals resonate widely. Many studies have shown that the media regularly follow official debates about war in Washington, adjusting their coverage to the scope of the discussion among the nation's political elite. And among the elite, members of Congress—through their own independent initiatives and through journalists' propensity to follow them—stand out as the single most potent source of dissent against the president. The sheer number of press releases and direct feeds that members of Congress produce is nothing short of breathtaking. And through carefully staged hearings, debates, and investigations, members deliberately shape the volume and content of the media's war coverage. The public posturing, turns of praise and condemnation, rapid-fire questioning, long-winded exhortations, pithy Shakespearean references, graphs, timelines, and pie charts that fill these highly scripted affairs are intended to focus media attention and thereby sway the national conversation surrounding questions of war and peace. Whether the media scrutinize every aspect of a proposed military venture or assume a more relaxed posture depends in part on Congress' willingness to take on the president.

Indeed, in the weeks preceding the October 2002 war authorization vote, the media paid a tremendous amount of attention to debates about Iraq inside the Beltway. Following the vote, however, coverage of Iraq dropped precipitously, despite continued domestic controversies, debates at the United Nations, continued efforts by the administration to rally public support, and grass-roots opposition to the war that featured large public protests. Congress helped set the agenda for public discussion, influencing both the volume and the tone of the coverage granted to an impending war, and Congress' silence after the authorization was paralleled by that of the press.

Crucially, Congressional influence over the media extended to public opinion as well. An analysis of local television broadcast data and national public-opinion surveys from the period reveals a strong relationship between the type of media coverage and public opinion regarding the war. Even when accounting for factors such as the ideological tendencies of a media market (since liberal markets tend to have liberal voters and liberal media, while conservative districts have the opposite), we found that the airing of more critical viewpoints led to greater public disapproval of the proposed war, and more positive viewpoints buoyed support for the war. As Congress speaks, it would seem, the media report, and the public listens.

As these cases illustrate, the United States has a Congress with considerably more agenda-setting power than most analysts presume and a less independent press corps than many would like. As the National Journal columnist William Powers observed during the fall of 2006, "Journalists like to think they are reporting just the facts, straight and unaffected by circumstance." On the contrary, he recognized, news is a product of the contemporary political environment, and the way stories are framed and spun has little to do with the facts. In Washington, the party that controls Congress also determines the volume and the tone of the coverage given to a president's war. Anticipating a Democratic Congressional sweep in November 2006, Powers correctly predicted that "if Bush suffers a major political setback, the media will feel freed up to tear into this war as they have never done before."

With the nation standing at the precipice of new wars, it is vital that the American public understand the nature and extent of Congress' war powers and its members' partisan motivations for exercising or forsaking them. President Bush retains extraordinary institutional advantages over Congress, but with the Democrats now in control of both houses, the political costs of pursuing new wars (whether against Iran, North Korea, or any other country) and prosecuting ongoing ones have increased significantly.

Congress will continue to challenge the president's interpretation of the national interest. Justifications for future deployments will encounter more scrutiny and require more evidence. Questions of appropriate strategy and implementation will surface more quickly with threats of Congressional hearings and investigations looming. Oversight hearings will proceed at a furious pace. Concerning Iraq, the Democrats will press the administration on a withdrawal timetable, hoping to use their agenda-setting power with the media to persuade enough Senate Republicans to defect and thereby secure the votes they need to close floor debate on the issue.

This fall, the Democrats will likely attempt to build even more momentum to end the war in Iraq, further limiting the president's menu of choices. This is not the first instance of heavy Congressional involvement in foreign affairs and war, nor will it be the last. This fact has been lost on too many political commentators convinced that some combination of an eroding political identity, 9/11, failures of leadership, and dwindling political will have made Congress irrelevant to deliberations about foreign policy.

On the contrary, the new Democratic-controlled Congress is conforming to a tried-and-true pattern of partisan competition between the executive and legislative branches that has characterized Washington politics for the last half century and shows no signs of abating. Reports of Congress' death have been greatly exaggerated.

Critical Thinking

1. In what ways is Congress able to influence the conduct of military action?
2. What evidence suggests that partisanship lies at the center of the domestic politics of war?
3. What are some of the advantages that a president has in exerting influence during wartime?
4. What congressional reactions to the Vietnam War illustrate congressional opposition to the presidential use of force?
5. How can Congress's opposition or support of military action affect media and public perceptions of war?

Create Central

www.mhhe.com/createcentral

Internet References

Cornell University Law: Legal Information Institute—The War Powers Resolution
    www.law.cornell.edu/uscode/text/50/chapter-33
Yahoo! Voices: Is the United States Constitution an "Invitation to Struggle?"
    http://voices.yahoo.com/is-united-states-constitution-invitation-to-5562759.html

WILLIAM G. HOWELL and JON C. PEVEHOUSE are Associate Professors at the Harris School of Public Policy at the University of Chicago and the authors of *While Dangers Gather: Congressional Checks on Presidential War Powers*.

Article   Prepared by: Bruce Stinebrickner, *DePauw University*

The Case for Corruption

Why Washington needs more honest graft

JONATHAN RAUCH

Learning Outcomes

After reading this article, you will be able to:

- Describe and assess the sort of political process depicted in "Plunkitt of Tammany Hall."

- Assess Jonathan Rauch's proposition that "in most political systems, the right amount of corruption is greater than zero."

The Government shutdown last fall wasted billions of dollars, upset innumerable plans, and besmirched both political parties. But it did have one constructive effect. Surveying the wreckage, grown-ups in both parties realized that the politics of public confrontation is a lot better at closing the government than running it. So, to avoid a repeat, they decided to try something old. Something *very* old. In a healthy return to machine politics, they handed budget negotiations over to political hacks cutting deals behind closed doors.

Once upon a time, the budget process was reasonably regular. In fact, it was conducted under what was called regular order. The budget-committee chairmen would do some horse trading to build a consensus within each chamber, the House and Senate would then pass those budgets without too much ado, and the two chambers would work out their differences in a conference committee. Then the appropriations committees would do more or less the same thing, making sure to spread around enough pork-barrel goodies to get their friends paid off and the budget passed. The president and the congressional leaders would be involved throughout the process, every now and then calling a budget summit, but most of the real work would go on behind the scenes.

In the past few years, by contrast, regular order has been replaced by regular chaos. Public ultimatums supplanted private negotiations, games of chicken replaced mutual back-scratching, and bumptious Republican House members took to dictating terms to their putative leadership. Last fall, after one tantrum too many, Congress seemed exhausted. As part of a deal to reopen the government, it returned the task of setting the next fiscal year's budget to the budget and appropriations committees, sending them off to a smoke-free smoke-filled room to cut a deal. The result, a trillion-dollar spending bill loaded with incentives for each side, sailed through Congress in January.

How often backroom deal making will work in today's age of hyper-partisanship remains to be seen, but Congress's recourse to it represents a welcome rediscovery of a home truth. Politics needs good leaders, but it needs good followers even more, and they don't come cheap. Loyalty gets you only so far, and ideology is divisive. Political machines need to exist, and they need to work. No one understood this better than the street-smart political sage George Washington Plunkitt, who articulated the concept of honest graft.

Plunkitt was a factotum of New York's renowned Tammany Hall political machine during the late 19th and early 20th centuries. Among his accomplishments was holding four public offices at once, drawing salaries for three of them. It was his custom to opine on politics from the shoeshine stand at the county courthouse, where his reflections were taken down by a reporter named William L. Riordon and published in a 1905 classic called *Plunkitt of Tammany Hall*. His greatest insight was the distinction between honest and dishonest graft.

"There's the biggest kind of a difference between political looters and politicians who make a fortune out of politics by keepin' their eyes wide open," Plunkitt said. "The looter goes in for himself alone without considerin' his organization or his city. The politician looks after his own interests, the organization's interests, and the city's interests all at the same time." Dirty graft is parasitic, mere larceny, whereas honest graft helps knit together a patronage network that ensures leaders can lead and followers will follow. Reformers who failed to understand this crucial distinction, Plunkitt said, courted anarchy. "First," he reasoned, "this great and glorious country was built up by political parties; second, parties can't hold together if their workers don't get the offices when they win; third, if the parties go to pieces, the government they built up must go to pieces, too; fourth, then there'll be h—to pay."

Plunkitt's warning, however colorfully expressed, was no mere wheeze. Writing just a few months ago in *The National Interest,* the political scientist Vivek S. Sharma, sounding like Plunkitt with a PhD, made an academic version of exactly the same point, noting that in many countries, patronage "is the grease that keeps the gears of the system running." Well-intentioned Americans who try to stamp out patronage networks in places like Afghanistan and Iraq usually just make things worse, Sharma observed, because "building formal institutions can in no way substitute for the creation of incentive structures that govern actual lives."

In other words, in most political systems, the right amount of corruption is greater than zero. Leaders need to be able to reward followers and punish turncoats and free agents. Sometimes that will look sleazy, undemocratic, or both, but it is often better than the alternatives.

For decades, America did a good job of equilibrating honest graft. We called it pork-barrel spending and earmarks, and we brought it aboveboard, so that politicians were openly lining their constituents' pockets rather than secretly lining their own. We also gave party bosses the power to twist defiant arms. If a member of Congress defied the leadership on a key vote, he might see his campaign contributions dry up, or his committee assignments downgraded, or the party elders throwing their support behind someone else in the next election. Members did defy the leadership, of course. But they thought twice before they did.

Plunkitt would be dismayed to see that since his day, the gears of the party machines have been stripped, one by one. Instead of being chosen by party elders, candidates are now selected in primary elections or caucuses, which tend to be dominated by ideological extremists. Conservative Republicans are thus much more afraid of the Tea Party than of House Speaker John Boehner. Reformers, worried about corruption, also put tight limits on direct political contributions to candidates and

parties. The result has been to divert money to unaccountable private groups, many of which clobber candidates who take tough votes to support party leaders. Meanwhile, rules requiring deliberations to be public have proved a mixed blessing, because it's hard to negotiate in earnest while striking ideological postures for TV cameras.

In a final blow, Tea Partiers and other righteous types waged a successful jihad against earmarks, the appropriations made for senators' and representatives' pet projects. No longer could the speaker tell a recalcitrant House member, "If I don't get your vote for the budget compromise, you can say goodbye to that new irrigation project in your district." By the time Congress banned earmarks, they were transparent (publicly disclosed) and inexpensive (a rounding error in the federal budget). With them went probably the last remnant of honest graft. Lo and behold, Plunkitt's prediction that "there'll be h—to pay" has come to pass.

I don't disagree that the high-handed corruption of Tammany Hall was too much of a bad thing. (Tammany, efficiency-minded, centralized its bribe-collecting for convenient one-stop service.) We obviously shouldn't go back to the Tammany ways, even if that were possible. Still, one can also have too little of a bad thing, and the overshoot against honest graft is an example. The next round of political reform should make party bosses and political machines stronger, not weaker. The candidate-selection process should be tweaked to reduce the sway of grass-roots activists and return power to party grandees. To bring special interests into the open, limits on direct political contributions to parties and candidates should be raised, if not eliminated altogether (something the Supreme Court may attend to later this year, when it decides *McCutcheon v. FEC,* a challenge to certain contribution limits). Congress should do more business through back channels, off camera. And, yes, the ban on earmarks should be revoked.

More important than such specific tinkering, though, is to relearn the timeless lesson that George Washington Plunkitt taught. Earnest campaigns to take the politics out of politics can make governing more difficult, with results that serve no one very well. The next time you see some new reform scheme touted in the name of stopping corruption, pause to recall the wisdom of another old-school pol, the late Representative Jimmy Burke, of Massachusetts: "The trouble with some people is that they think this place is on the level."

Critical Thinking

1. What is the difference between "regular order" and what Jonathan Rauch calls "regular chaos" in the national government's budgeting process?

2. What was Plunkitt's distinction between "honest" and "dishonest" graft?

3. Why, according to Jonathan Rauch, is "the right amount of corruption" "greater than zero"?

Create Central

www.mhhe.com/createcentral

Internet References

George Washington Plunkitt in the Gilded Age
http://www.shmoop.com/gilded-age/george-washington-plunkitt.html

Plunkitt and Civil Service Reform
https://stonybrook.digication.com/egimenez/Plunkitt_and_Civil_Service_Reform

Plunkitt of Tammany Hall
http://www.marxists.org/reference/archive/plunkett-george/tammany-hall

Article   Prepared by: Bruce Stinebrickner, *DePauw University*

End of an Era

How one man's retirement captures Congress's transformation into a quasi-parliamentary institution.

RONALD BROWNSTEIN

Learning Outcomes

After reading this article, you will be able to:

- Summarize and assess the persuasiveness of the proposition that changes in Congress since the 1980s have made it possible or even likely that there will not be "Henry Waxmans" in Congress in the future.

- Evaluate whether the changes in Congress described in the article represent positive or negative developments for the American political system as a whole.

Henry Waxman could be the last person in Washington to acknowledge that there may never be another Henry Waxman. His departure captures a fundamental shift in Congress that has vastly reduced the ability of any individual member to shape policy as consequentially as he did.

Waxman, a Democratic representative from Los Angeles first elected in the 1974 Watergate class, announced last week he would retire after this session. No other legislator over his four-decade career—and few in any era—affected the daily lives of more Americans than Waxman, who shepherded into law landmark bills on clean air, clean water, access to health care, tobacco regulation, nutritional labeling, food safety, HIV/AIDS, and generic drugs.

Over his remarkable tenure, Waxman embodied the definition of a great legislator: He created coalitions that would not have existed without him. Most of his major accomplishments were passed with significant Republican support. Waxman demonstrated that a single legislator, with enough skill and tenacity, can leave an indelible mark.

That has been true through most of Congress's history. But since the 1980s, power has passed from individual legislators to the parties collectively. Each side has centralized more authority in the party leadership. And far fewer members are willing to buck their party's consensus to partner with legislators from the other side, no matter how skillfully they craft a compromise.

The result has been to greatly diminish the ability of even the most brilliant legislators—whether Waxman or senators like Ted Kennedy and Bob Dole—to break stalemates by creatively assembling coalitions no one else could envision. "It's hard for a guy like that to emerge now on either side," says former Rep. Tom Davis, the Republican who chaired the House Oversight and Government Reform Committee when Waxman was the ranking Democrat. Adds Steve Elmendorf, a former top House Democratic aide, "The leadership is not going to give you the space to do it."

Instead, in almost all cases, each party's leadership now decides whether to reach agreement with the opposition—or, more often, to not agree. Rather than negotiating their own compromises, legislators are expected to salute their party's collective decision. "The best way to put it," Davis says, "is we've turned into a parliamentary system."

Waxman's own career illustrates the constricting effect of this new dynamic. His reform-minded class of 1974 drove a historic decentralization of authority, passing rules that shattered the power of seniority and forced previously autocratic committee chairs to respond more to their party's rank-and-file consensus. That era's House speakers, recognizing the democratizing current, governed lightly and gave members enormous latitude. In an emblematic moment, Waxman recalls that while he and Rep. John Dingell, then-chairman of the mighty House Energy and Commerce Committee, fought their titanic duel over extending the Clean Air Act through the 1980s, Speakers Tip O'Neill and Jim Wright essentially stood aside. "Neither took that much of an active role because they didn't see that as their job," Waxman told me.

Waxman thrived in this fluid atmosphere. He attracted 159 GOP votes for his landmark AIDS bill in 1990, 154 for the Clean Air Act amendments he passed in 1989 after finally outlasting Dingell, and so much bipartisan consensus on issues like safe water and nutrition labeling that the bills passed without recorded votes. The House approved his generic-drug bill unanimously. It was sometimes reluctant, but Ronald Reagan and George H.W. Bush signed into law many of Waxman's greatest accomplishments, particularly his tenacious step-by-step Medicaid expansion across the 1980s.

But the Congress that Waxman mastered is gone. Starting with Newt Gingrich in 1995, each party's leadership has seized more control over the congressional agenda: In contrast to O'Neill's hands-off posture, Waxman recalled, then-Speaker Nancy Pelosi compelled the three relevant committee chairs to start the Affordable Care Act debate with a common legislative draft. Bipartisan support is infinitely more difficult to attract today, both because party leaders and interest groups discourage it and because polarized population patterns have culled the number of House centrists. While Waxman drew broad bipartisan backing on clean air in 1989, he attracted just eight House Republicans to his climate bill in 2010, even though he based it on a proposal from an alliance of environmentalists and business leaders. That experience still frustrates Waxman. "It was a shock that the Republicans . . . weren't interested in what the business community had to say," he says.

To observers such as Brookings Institution senior fellow Thomas Mann, these changes mean that in today's quasi-parliamentary Congress "individuals are just really diminished in what they can accomplish." One who rejects that conclusion is Waxman. Congress may be paralyzed now, he says, with many Republicans in particular believing "compromise is a dirty word," but he insists that determined legislators can cut through the polarization to forge meaningful agreements. "I still think it can be done," he says firmly. Optimism and patience have been two of Waxman's greatest legislative assets—but it will take big shifts in the way Congress operates, and probably many years, for his confidence to be rewarded.

Critical Thinking

1. Why, according to Ronald Brownstein, may there "never be another Henry Waxman" in Congress?
2. What is Ronald Brownstein's definition of a "great legislator"?
3. Who has gained more control over the congressional agenda since the 1980s, thus reducing the importance of members of Congress like Henry Waxman?

Create Central

www.mhhe.com/createcentral

Internet References

Henry Waxman: Relic of When Congress Used to Work (The Atlantic)
http://www.theatlantic.com/politics/archive/2014/02/henry-waxman-a-relic-of-the-era-when-congress-used-to-work/283630

Henry Waxman (U.S. House of Representatives website)
http://waxman.house.gov

Rep. Henry Waxman to Retire (LA Times)
http://articles.latimes.com/2014/jan/30/news/la-pn-henry-waxman-retire-congress-20140130

Article   Prepared by: Bruce Stinebrickner, *DePauw University*

The Big Lobotomy

How Republicans Made Congress Stupid.

PAUL GLASTRIS AND HALEY SWEETLAND EDWARDS

Learning Outcomes

After reading this article, you will be able to:

- Summarize and evaluate the changes in Congress since Newt Gingrich became Speaker in the 1990s.

- Assess the authors' explanation for why making Congress "dumber" has not made government smaller, notwithstanding Gingrich's intentions.

L ast September, as they scrambled to decide on one final ultimatum before shutting down the federal government, Republican House leaders came up with what seemed like an odd demand: to strip their own staff of health care benefits.

At the time, staffers reacted to the news with a mixture of despair and disbelief. "It was like getting sucker-punched by your boss," one aide told me. "Everyone was thinking, What's the point? How is screwing *us* going to help *you*?"

The dubious logic behind the House Republicans' demand can be traced back to a contested provision in the Affordable Care Act (ACA), the gutting of which was the price the Republicans were demanding for agreeing to fund the government. The provision requires employees of the U.S. Congress, including members and their staffs, to buy insurance on the new health care exchanges, while still allowing them to receive subsidies from their employer. Over the course of more than a year, ideologues at several conservative think tanks, especially the Tea Party-friendly Heritage Foundation, which was pushing for the shutdown, managed to put an imaginative spin on the provision, convincing the conservative world that members and their staff were getting a sneaky, backroom deal, a "special exemption from Obamacare."

In fact, had the Republicans' desired language passed, congressional personnel would have become the only employees in America whose employer (in their case, the federal government) was explicitly forbidden from contributing to their health care—a blow that, in all likelihood, would have caused most of the best and brightest staffers, and perhaps some lawmakers, to simply hightail it for the door. Some quite conservative members even said as much. Representative Jim Sensenbrenner, in a candid moment later, called the move "political theater" that would do nothing more than catalyze a rapid "brain drain" in Congress.

While Sensenbrenner was right, one must appreciate the irony. A debilitating brain drain has actually been under way in Congress for the past 25 years, and it is Sensenbrenner and his conservative colleagues who have engineered it.

A quick refresher: In 1995, after winning a majority in the House for the first time in 40 years, one of the first things the new Republican House leadership did was gut Congress's workforce. They cut the "professional staff" (the lawyers, economists, and investigators who work for committees rather than individual members) by a third. They reduced the "legislative support staff" (the auditors, analysts, and subject-matter experts at the Government Accountability Office [GAO], the Congressional Research Service [CRS], and so on) by a third, too, and killed off the Office of Technology Assessment (OTA) entirely. And they fundamentally dismantled the old committee structure, centralizing power in the House speaker's office and discouraging members and their staff from performing their own policy research. (The Republicans who took over the Senate in 1995 were less draconian, cutting committee staff by about 16 percent and leaving the committee system largely in place.) Today, the GAO and the CRS, which serve both House and Senate, are each operating at about 80 percent of their 1979 capacity. While Senate committee staffs have rebounded somewhat under Democratic control, every single House standing committee had fewer staffers in 2009 than in 1994. Since 2011, with a Tea Party-radicalized GOP back in control of the House, Congress has cut its budget by a whopping 20 percent, a far higher ratio than any other federal agency, leading, predictably, to staff layoffs, hiring and salary freezes, and drooping morale.

> **Every single House standing committee has fewer staffers than in 1994. Since 2011, Congress has cut its budget by a whopping 20 percent, a far higher ratio than any other federal agency, leading, predictably, to staff layoffs, hiring and salary freezes, and drooping morale.**

Why would conservative lawmakers decimate the staff and organizational capacity of an institution they themselves control? Part of it is political optics: What better way to show the conservative voters back home that you're serious about shrinking government than by cutting your own staff? But a bigger reason is strategic. The Gingrich Revolutionaries of 1995 and the Tea Partiers of 2011 share the same basic dream: to defund and dismantle the vast complex of agencies and programs that have been created by bipartisan majorities since the New Deal. The people in Congress who knew those agencies and programs best and were most invested in making them work—the professional staffers, the CRS analysts, the veteran committee chairs—were not going to consent to seeing them swept away. So *they* had to be swept away.

> **The Gingrich Revolutionaries wanted to defund and dismantle the federal government. The professional staffers and others in Congress who knew government best were not going to consent to seeing it swept away. So they had to be swept away.**

Of course, all of this slashing and cutting has done nothing to actually help shrink the federal government. Real federal spending has increased 50 percent since 1995, in line with the growth of the U.S. population and economy. Meanwhile, Washington has fought two major land wars, added two large new entitlement programs (Medicare's prescription drug benefit under George W. Bush, the ACA under Barack Obama),

and created several new federal bureaucracies, ranging from the Consumer Financial Protection Bureau to the gigantic Department of Homeland Security.

At the same time, as political scientist Lee Drutman of the Sunlight Foundation has noted, both the government and the issues it has to deal with have grown more complex. There are more contractors to manage, more stakeholders to liaison with, more technologies to adapt to, more industry-funded research studies to take account of. That, in turn, has made the jobs of congressional staffers, of keeping an eye on government and sorting through the ever-growing amount of information coming at them from lobbyists and constituents, far more difficult, even as their numbers have not remotely kept pace with the growth of government and K Street. In 2010, the House spent $1.37 billion and employed between 7,000 and 8,000 staffers. That same year, corporations and special interests spent twice as much—$2.6 billion—on lobbying (which excludes billions spent on other forms of influence) and employed 12,000 federally registered lobbyists, according to Sunlight Foundation.

Instead of helping to shrink the government, the gutting of congressional expertise and institutional capacity—what New America Foundation scholar and former congressional staffer Lorelei Kelly refers to as a "self-lobotomy"—has had two other effects, both of which have advanced conservative power, if not necessarily conservative ideals.

The first effect is an outsourcing of policy development. Much of the research, number crunching, and legislative wordsmithing that used to be done by Capitol Hill staffers working for the government is now being done by outside experts, many of them former Hill staffers, working for lobbying firms, think tanks, consultancies, trade associations, and PR outfits. This has strengthened the already-powerful hand of corporate interests in shaping legislation, and given conservative groups an added measure of influence over Congress, as the shutdown itself illustrates.

Recall that last summer and fall many establishment Republicans, having lived through Newt Gingrich's disastrous shutdown in the 1990s, argued that doing so again would be folly. So why did so many GOP House members ignore those warnings and listen instead to the Heritage Foundation? Part of the reason was that they were conditioned to do so. Over the years, as Congress's in-house capacity for independent policy thinking atrophied, the House GOP largely ceded that responsibility to Heritage, which has aligned itself with the Tea Party since former Senator Jim DeMint took the helm in 2013. The think tank became the only outside group that was allowed to brief members and their staff at the influential weekly lunches of the Republican Study Committee, the policy and messaging arm of House conservatives. So when Heritage promised, despite all the evidence to the contrary, that the Democrats would cave to

GOP demands for a delay in the individual mandate and cuts to "special" health care benefits for congressional staffers, many GOP members believed them. (Many who didn't followed Heritage's instructions anyway when its lobbying arm, Heritage Action, orchestrated a grassroots email campaign demanding that members hang tough. Subtext? Or else.)

The second effect of the brain drain is a significant decline in Congress's institutional ability to monitor and investigate a growing and ever-more-complex federal government. This decline has been going on quietly, behind the scenes, for so many years that hardly anyone even notices anymore. But like termites eating away at the joists, there's a danger of catastrophic collapse unless regular inspections are done. While Congress continues to devote what limited investigative resources it has into the fished-out waters of the Internal Revenue Service and Benghazi "scandals" (13 Benghazi hearings in the House alone, with a new select committee launched in May), just in the last year we've witnessed two appalling government fiascoes that better congressional oversight might have avoided: the botched rollout of the health insurance exchanges and the uncontrolled expansion of the National Security Agency's surveillance programs. (Fun fact: while annual federal spending on intelligence has roughly doubled since 1997, staff levels on the Senate Select Committee on Intelligence have actually *declined*.) Debacles like these, by undermining the public's faith in government, wind up perversely advancing the conservative antigovernment agenda—another reason why many Republicans don't worry much about the brain drain on the Hill. But the rest of us should.

The decline of congressional oversight has been going on quietly, behind the scenes, for so many years that hardly anyone even notices anymore. But like termites eating away at the joists, there's a danger of catastrophic collapse unless regular inspections are done.

The organizational capacity that conservatives began attacking in 1995 had been painstakingly built up by their liberal and moderate predecessors over the previous quarter century. In the late 1960s, there was a general sense in Congress that the institution needed to upgrade its ability to understand and confront the challenges of a more technologically and socially complex country. Meanwhile, with the Vietnam War heading south and the Richard Nixon administration resorting to such high-handed moves as the secret bombing of Cambodia, many liberal Democrats and moderate Republicans became convinced of the need to counter the power of the White House and of the hawkish southern Democrats, who, because of seniority and other rules, treated the major congressional committees like personal fiefdoms. The result was a series of major reforms in the early to mid-1970s that changed the institution in two fundamental ways.

First, recognizing that information is power in Washington (the first standing committees in the House were established in the 1790s as an independent source of information to counter that of George Washington's powerful but controversial treasury secretary, Alexander Hamilton), Congress enhanced its internal data-gathering and analytical capacities. It bulked up the staffs of committees and member offices. It expanded its in-house think tank, the Legislative Reference Service, renaming it the Congressional Research Service. It overhauled the rules of the budget process and created the Congressional Budget Office (CBO) to produce nonpartisan fiscal information and projections. And it formed the Office of Technology Assessment to provide timely analyses of the promises and pitfalls of cutting-edge science and technology developments. This expansion of expertise changed the very landscape of Capitol Hill. Congress built the vast Madison Building on Pennsylvania Avenue to house the expanded CRS. It bought the Congressional Hotel to accommodate the growing ranks of committee staff and appropriated an old FBI fingerprint records warehouse for the new CBO.

Fun fact: while annual federal spending on intelligence has roughly doubled since 1997, staff levels on the Senate Select Committee on Intelligence have actually declined. It is any wonder that details of the NSA's surveillance programs went largely unnoticed?

Second, congressional reformers took on the committee chairs and their ironfisted control over everything from the hiring and firing of staff to which lawmakers got to sit on which subcommittees. A series of rules changes in the House allowed chairmen to be deposed via a secret ballot of committee members; some were, and subcommittees won more control over their budgets, staff, and agendas. The minority party was guaranteed a set percentage of resources and staff. As power flowed down and out, it also flowed up, with the speaker of the House garnering the authority to, among other things, refer bills to committees, privileges once reserved for committee chairs. In the Senate, where individual members always enjoyed more freedom of action, various reforms decentralized power even further.

The result was a great spike in congressional policy development and oversight. A rough but useful measure of both is the number of committee meetings. These rose by half in the Senate and 80 percent in the House from the late 1960s through the 1970s. In the 1980s and mid-1990s, they plateaued, at about 5,000–6,000 per year. (Then, with the GOP takeover in 1995, the number of hearings plummeted by nearly 50 percent in the House and by a quarter in Senate. To put it in perspective, in 1958 congressional committees met almost *three times* more often than they did in 2010. Those numbers rose again, if only briefly, under the Democrats from 2007 through 2010, the latest years for which figures are available.)

With the GOP takeover in 1995, the number of hearings plummeted by nearly 50 percent in the House and by a quarter in senate. To put it in perspective, in 1958 congressional committees met almost three times more often than they did in 2010.

The 1960s and 1970s marked one of the great eras of congressional oversight, with the Church and Pike committees investigating intelligence abuses and the Watergate hearings exposing the crimes of the Nixon White House. The latter investigations not only made a bipartisan group of committee members household names (Sam Ervin, Howard Baker) but also employed staffers who would themselves become famous (Fred Thompson, Hillary Rodham).

It was also an important era of policymaking. In his book *The Last Great Senate,* former Senate staffer Ira Shapiro details how lawmakers of that period—George McGovern, Bob Dole, Charles Mathias, Jacob Javits, Robert Byrd, Ted Kennedy—used their mastery of subject matter and process to move complex, politically gnarly legislation, from the successful bailouts of Chrysler and New York City to the Panama Canal Treaty. He recounts, for instance, how Senator Henry "Scoop" Jackson made himself so knowledgeable on defense issues that he became a thorn in the side of Nixon and Henry Kissinger, whose policy of détente he deplored for, among other things, ignoring the Soviets' human rights abuses. Aided by brilliant and well-connected staffers who shared his hawkish views—people like Richard Perle and Dorothy Fosdick—Jackson passed the Jackson-Vanik Amendment, which denied most-favored-nation trading status to communist-bloc countries that restricted emigration. The amendment ultimately led to the emigration of millions of Soviet Jews and was used by Soviet dissidents as a vital tool in mobilizing support for the overthrow of communism.

The House, too, became a bastion of professional expertise. In the early 1970s, for instance, Representative Henry Reuss, a diligent conservation-minded Wisconsin liberal, and his staff on the Subcommittee on Conservation and Natural Resources, discovered a dusty old piece of legislation, the Refuse Act of 1899, that required anyone who pollutes a lake or stream to have a permit to do so from the Army Corps of Engineers. Reuss then got the U.S. attorney in his home state to successfully sue four major polluters—actions that, Reuss later recalled, "convinced industry to stop fighting federal antipollution legislation and instead accept the reasonable federal regulatory system created by the Clean Water Act of 1972."

Similarly, in the early days of the effort to pass tax reform in 1984, House Ways and Means Committee Chairman Dan Rostenkowski organized a retreat on an Air Force base in Florida where 20 committee members of both parties and 10 committee staffers spent 3 days, with no lobbyists or reporters around, listening to 15 experts, both liberal and conservative, lecture on how tax reform might work. A year later, when the tax reform legislation was on the ropes, Rostenkowski organized another retreat in rural Virginia between members and top Treasury officials. This kind of deep, bipartisan engagement in the complexities of the tax code (almost inconceivable in today's House) helped lead to what is still seen as one of the great legislative achievements of the decade, the Tax Reform Act of 1986.

That's not to say that the 1970s and 1980s were some golden age of evidence-based legislating. The era saw its share of ill-advised government programs, like the Synthetic Fuels Corporation, launched by a Democratic Congress during the 1979 energy crisis despite prescient warnings from the GAO that it would turn out to be a boondoggle. The bipartisan willingness to work together on substantive issues also frayed in the late 1980s and early 1990s when, among other things, a pair of hard-core conservative judicial nominees (Robert Bork, Clarence Thomas) received especially rough treatment by Senate Democrats. Meanwhile, in the House, as the ranks of confrontational antigovernment conservatives grew, Democrats responded by arrogantly exploiting their majority control. Republicans were especially incensed when Speaker Tip O'Neill orchestrated the seating of a Democratic candidate in a contested election for an Indiana House seat and his successor, Jim Wright, used parliamentary maneuvers to limit the GOP's ability to affect legislation. The leader of the Republicans' restive House conservatives, Newt Gingrich, rose to power in part by decrying the Democrats' tactics as "corrupt" in front of C-SPAN cameras. The requirement that all House floor speeches be televised was, ironically, one of the democratizing reforms liberals put in place in the early 1970s.

When Newt Gingrich became speaker of the House in the fall of 1994, he set about almost immediately creating "the most controversial majority leadership since 1910," according to longtime Congress watchers and political scientists Thomas Mann and Norman Ornstein in their 2006 book, *The Broken Branch*. Under his leadership, backed up by 73 conservative Republican freshmen who swept to power that year, the goal was not to reform, but to destroy; not to compromise, but to advance a highly conservative agenda no matter the means. The shift in culture was palpable almost immediately, with freshman lawmakers eschewing bipartisan freshman orientations in favor of partisan ones, and the vast majority joining what's known as the "Tuesday-Thursday Club," flying in on Tuesday evening and out Thursday afternoon so as to reduce the likelihood of contracting "Potomac fever." "There was a total contempt for the institution," said Scott Lilly, who served as a high-level staffer in Congress for 31 years before joining the Center for American Progress in 2004. John Dingell, who will have served in the House for 59 years when he retires this year, said it succinctly: "The place just got meaner."

Gingrich's strategy, as he explained it to Mann and Ornstein, was simple: Cultivate a seething disdain for the institution of Congress itself, while simultaneously restructuring it so as to eliminate anything—powerful chairmen, contradictory facts from legislative support agencies, more moderate Republicans—that would stand in the way of his vision.

Gingrich's first move in 1995 was to dismantle the decentralized, democratic committee system that the liberals and moderates had created in the 1970s and instead centralize that power on himself. Under his new rules, committee chairs were no longer determined by seniority or a vote by committee members, but instead appointed by the party leadership (read: by Newt himself, who often made appointees swear their loyalty to him). Subcommittees also lost their ability to set their own agendas and schedules; that too largely became the prerogative of the leadership. At the same time, Gingrich imposed six-year term limits and required chairs to be reappointed (by leadership) every two years. Finally, Gingrich protected, and in some cases bulked up, the staff leadership offices and increasingly had those offices write major pieces of legislation and hand them to the committees.

These rules, taken together, essentially stripped all congressional Republicans, especially those in previously senior positions, of power; instead, whether or not they advanced in their careers—whether they were reappointed or on which committee they were appointed—would be determined by party leaders based on their loyalty and subservience. (Two years after the Democrats took the majority in the House in 2007, they eliminated the term-limits rule; Speaker John Boehner reinstated it when the Republicans regained control in 2010.) "If you were

thinking about the next stage in your career, you did what you were told to do," observes Scott Lilly. The point of this centralization of power was to give the leadership maximum control of the legislative agenda and to jam through as many conservative bills as possible. That, it achieved: the Gingrich House passed 124 measures in 1995, more than double the 53 that Tip O'Neill's House passed in 1981. But over time it also had the effect of dumbing down the institution.

After the first round of term-limit expirations rolled around in 2001, for instance, Republican Representative Ralph Regula was termed out of his chairmanship of the Interior Subcommittee, a position he had held off and on for 26 years, during which time he had become the chamber's de facto expert on public lands and natural resources. Regula was famous in environmental circles for his relentless interest in the unglamorous issue of national park infrastructure maintenance. (At one point his committee uncovered a $330,000 outhouse complete with a slate roof, picture windows, and a twenty-nine-inch-thick earthquake-proof foundation.) His detailed understanding and thrifty instincts helped Regula win support in his caucus for increased funding to reduce the backlog of national park maintenance projects. But that knowledge and clout went with him when he was termed out.

It's worth noting, of course, that term limits do, in theory, have an upside. They sweep away lawmakers who, over the years, have been captured by the agencies they oversee and the special interests they interact with. And they bring new blood into the committee leadership. In the 1970s, many liberal reformers advocated for term limits for these reasons, and as a means of limiting the power of long-serving southern Democrats who then dominated the chairmanships of the powerful committees. But in order to work, limiting committee chairs' power and hard-won knowledge needs to be offset by enough staff who have sufficient institutional memory to educate the new members and explain, for instance, when they're being lied to by the agencies and the special interests. Gingrich, of course, cut the staff, too.

And anyway, the problem with term limits in the mid-1990s was not only a loss of experience in a given subject; it was also a decline in the motivation to learn a subject in depth in the first place. After all, members who know they will move to a new committee in a few years are sometimes hard-pressed to really dig into a subject matter. That natural inclination has been greatly exacerbated by the fact that, beginning in 1995 and continuing to the present day, the leadership often dictates to committees what it wants bills to look like or drafts them outright. So instead of learning deeply about a given subject, debating various policy options, engaging in the nitty-gritty of a topic over the course of years and sometimes decades, committee members nowadays are often asked either to reverse-engineer a piece of legislation based on party leadership's description of what kind of bill they'd like to see or to simply vote on a bill they did not write to begin with. Is it any surprise that, under those circumstances, deep policy knowledge, curiosity, and innovation have gone out the window? "What's the payoff for doing a good job? If you take your job seriously as a chairman, who gives a shit?" says Bruce Bartlett, who worked as a congressional staffer in the 1970s and 1980s for Representative Jack Kemp, Representative Ron Paul, and the Joint Economic Committee.

In the past, members angled for committee assignments in part based on their personal backgrounds and the interests of their states or constituencies—another factor that favored the accumulation of subject-area knowledge—but under the new rules, leadership made the choices based more on political calculation. Seats on the "prestigious" committees began to go most often to members who were likely to face a strong challenger in the next election, so that they could brag to constituents about their powerful role or, more to the point, position themselves for corporate campaign contributions. "There was an immediate atrophy of the professional qualifications of the committees," said Mike Lofgren, a former Republican congressional aide who has since been publicly critical of the Republican Party. "Knowing anything about the committee's jurisdiction just didn't factor in."

Of course, it's hard to learn much about the substance of the issues if you're spending four hours a day "dialing for dollars" to raise campaign funds, as both parties recently instructed their members to do, in addition to another hour or two of attending fund-raisers. Compare that to the three to four hours per day members spend on average attending hearings, voting, meeting with constituents, studying, debating, and legislating. But while both parties are equally aggressive in hunting for money, Democrats have repeatedly tried to pass public financing bills to lessen the fund-raising burdens on incumbents and challengers alike. Republicans have just as frequently (and successfully) fought those bills. That's an indication of how the parties differ philosophically on the role of private money in politics. But it's also a fair gauge of how much weight each party gives to the importance of lawmakers knowing the substance of the issues they are legislating on.

Gingrich's second move in 1995 was to go after the pooled funding that paid for the so-called professional staffers, who worked for the institution itself. Professional staff, most of whom were not explicitly partisan, were often deeply knowledgeable not only about policy issues within their expertise but also about the institution itself. They knew what had worked in the past, what members' preferences and personalities were like, and how to draft a bill that would pass. As one member described it to me, professional staffers are

"legislative lubricant," often acting as referees or liaisons during committee debates. Within months, Gingrich had laid off about 800 of them. All told, he cut the total population of professional staffers by more than a third—a wound from which Congress has never recovered. In 1993, Congress employed nearly 2,150 professional committee staff; in 2011, there were just 1,316, according to the most recent data.

The professional staff also helped to run legislative service organizations (LSOs), informal study groups where members, often of both parties, would discuss specific issues, debate, share information, build trust, and "gain expertise on 'big-picture' national issues outside the jurisdiction of committees," notes the New America Foundation's Lorelei Kelly. The LSOs vanished along with pooled funding and shared staff in 1995.

Those professional staffers who were there at the time remember the atmosphere changing. "After Newt put the kibosh on shared staff, the whole place began to work more like Politico," said one former senior staffer who worked on the Hill for two decades, referring to the website's 24/7 attention to scandal, intrigue, and political strategy over deeper policy discussions. "No one was asking, What kind of legislation will this be? How can we make it better? Where do we need to go to get a compromise? They were asking, What kind of political fallout will this have? Who will look good? Who can we make look bad?"

Gingrich also cut the number of staffers working directly for House members. While those numbers later rose, they did so in a way that further reflects the intellectual hollowing out of the institution. Nearly all of the net increase in member staff since the late 1990s has been not in Washington, where the actual legislating happens, but in district offices, where the main jobs are handling constituent complaints, shuttling members around to local events, and getting them press—in short, ensuring their re-election. Not surprisingly, in the past decade, members have moved roughly 33 percent of their staff capacity away from policymaking and toward communications roles, according to a recent Congressional Management Foundation report.

Keeping good staff, professional or otherwise, is also a struggle considering the pay scales. While it's difficult to compare salaries—the direct equivalent of a "legislative assistant" in the private sector is hotly debated—a measured 2009 report by the Sunlight Foundation concluded that Hill staffers are paid roughly a third less than they could make in the private sector. The on-the-job knowledge and connections staffers accumulate become exponentially more valuable over time to the lobbying shops on K Street, and the opportunity costs of staying become hard to ignore. According to a 2012 *Washington Times* analysis, 82 percent of Senate staffers and 70 percent of House staffers hired in 2005 had left the Hill by 2012.

The one thing that has traditionally kept at least some Hill staffers from leaving for the private sector is the heady nature of the work on Capitol Hill—the ability to fight for issues they believe in, to be in the room when the big decisions are being made, to put their personal stamp on legislation that will change history. But even that motivation has been undermined by the Tea Party-inspired gridlock that has blocked most major legislation in both houses since 2010 and squandered staff energies in pointless budget standoffs. "Those who are nourished by accomplishment are starving," observes former Senator Byron Dorgan. "People who come highly motivated, they want to feel good about their challenge, their work, what they're doing for the country. When they're not getting that, they start looking around."

The third target of Gingrich's attacks was the legislative support agencies. The Government Accountability Office, Congressional Budget Office, Congressional Research Service, and now-defunct Office of Technology Assessment operated on a bipartisan basis, offering measured reports on topics suggested by members themselves. Sometimes, these agencies act as helpful librarians, and sometimes they're more like referees, carefully adjudicating among the competing quantitative claims of various members and outside groups.

Gingrich, perhaps not surprisingly, viewed them all as potential rivals to his singular narrative. He particularly despised the OTA, as did many other conservatives, despite its evident usefulness. For instance, Congress saved hundreds of millions of dollars by incorporating OTA recommendations when the Social Security Administration moved to replace its old-school mainframe computers with a new computer network in the mid-1990s. (One wonders how things might have been different if the OTA had been around when the health care insurance exchanges were being built.) But over the years, the OTA had also cast doubt on some conservative ideas—a mortal sin as far as Gingrich and his followers were concerned. For example, an OTA report raising serious questions about the feasibility of Reagan's Star Wars project was later used by Democrats to help defund the program.

Within a few months of taking the helm in 1995, Gingrich eliminated the OTA entirely and cut roughly a third of the staff in all the other congressional service agencies. According to the Brookings Institution's Vital Statistics of Congress, those agencies have never recovered. The GAO lost more than 2,000 staffers between 1993 and 2010. CRS staff lost about 20 percent of its capacity. All told, in 1993 Congress employed 6,166 researchers; by 2011, that number was down to just over 4,000.

How has the brain drain affected Washington? To begin with, just look at all the construction cranes that dot the city's skyline. The ongoing migration of talent out of Capitol Hill has helped drive the building boom in downtown D.C. as surely as the Pentagon's contracting-out craze,

which also took off in the 1990s, gave rise to the corporate office towers of Northern Virginia.

You can see the effect in the shabby, politicized work product coming out of many committees. In May, for instance, the House Energy and Commerce Committee released a survey conducted by its GOP staff purporting to show that only 67 percent of people who signed up for health insurance on the federal exchange had paid their first premium—a number that, if true, would have embarrassed the administration. In fact, the survey gave a false impression by counting as nonpayers people who hadn't yet been billed. Insurance company executives later testified in public to the committee that their estimated payment rate was 80 percent. "Republicans were visibly exasperated," reported The Hill, "as insurers failed to confirm certain claims about ObamaCare, such as the committee's allegation that one-third of federal exchange enrollees have not paid their first premium."

You can see it in the recent string of surprise retirement announcements from House GOP committee chairman who will be term-limited out of their positions next year. That includes Ways and Means Chairman Dave Camp, whose committee (which has miraculously retained some level of bipartisan competence) labored to put together a credible tax reform plan. The GOP said the plan was one of the party's top legislative goals, but John Boehner tabled the measure in an effort not to muddy the midterm elections with substantive issues. "It used to be that the chairman would call the speaker up and say, 'I want this bill on this floor at this time,'" explains Dingell. "Now it's the opposite."

You can see it in frequent little dustups meant to undermine the legitimacy of the findings of congressional service organizations, like the one that engulfed the Congressional Research Service in 2012, when its economics division published a report surveying the effects of tax cuts going back decades and concluding that they do not generate sufficient new tax revenues from economic growth to pay for themselves—the main tenet of supply-side economics. A firestorm of anger from Senate Republicans led the CRS to pull the report.

You can also see the effects in stories like the one that appeared on the front page of the New York Times last May about a House bill that would exempt broad swaths of derivative trades from new Dodd-Frank Act regulations. The bill, which passed the House 292 to 122 before dying in the Senate, was written not only at the behest of lobbyists from Citigroup but *by* Citigroup lobbyists:

In a sign of Wall Street's resurgent influence in Washington, Citigroup's recommendations were reflected in more than 70 lines of the House committee's 85-line bill. Two crucial paragraphs, prepared by Citigroup in conjunction with other Wall Street banks, were copied nearly word for word. (Lawmakers changed two words to make them plural.)

It's true that both parties have outsourced much of their policy development over the years. Groups like the Center for American Progress to some extent do for Democrats what Heritage does for Republicans (or did prior to Jim DeMint's takeover), and plenty of lawmakers from both parties take their policy instructions from Wall Street lobbyists. But whereas for Democrats the outsourcing of policy has happened more by necessity, for Republicans it's been by design. Newt Gingrich began the process in the 1990s with his attacks on in-house congressional expertise. Leaders like Tom DeLay in the House and Rick Santorum in the Senate advanced that process in the 2000s with the "K Street Project," an organized effort to place GOP Hill staffers in key jobs in the most important D.C. law firms and trade associations.

As Nicholas Confessore explained in these pages ("Welcome to the Machine," July/August 2003), the K Street Project tried to harness the muscle and campaign cash of a fractious lobbying community behind the specific legislative agenda of the George W. Bush administration with the ultimate aim of creating a permanent GOP majority. While it failed in that larger goal, it did succeed in providing GOP congressional leaders with something they needed: an alternative to the in-house legislative expertise Gingrich had decimated. With the leadership's own former employees now in charge of D.C.'s biggest lobbying shops and all the research and other resources they commanded, K Street became, in a sense, the new permanent staff of the GOP Congress. (Democratic leaders have since attempted to place more of their former staffers on K Street, but have yet to catch up to Republicans in terms of numbers and clout.)

In addition to the outsourcing of policy development, the other big effect of the brain drain has been the atrophying of congressional oversight. Good oversight requires teams of educated, detail-oriented staffers who have the time to cull through documents, review thousands of line items in a budget, read budget justifications, and then follow up with federal agencies or local programs to determine what is really happening in government programs on the ground. Those teams have traditionally resided in the committees, buttressed by permanent staff and long-serving members, and in the legislative service agencies like the GAO. As we've seen, both were greatly downsized in the 1990s and remained profoundly understaffed and under-resourced.

Of course, good oversight has always been more the exception than the rule in Congress, in part because it has never been a particularly sexy part of a Congress member's job, and in part because voters don't generally reward members who excel at it. Rare are the headlines congratulating Congress for catching disasters before they happen. Even today, valuable oversight still happens on occasion. In the run-up to the 2010 census, for instance, the GAO identified fatal flaws in the handheld computer devices the Census Bureau was planning to use as a cost-saving measure. Thanks to the GAO's reports, major fixes to the devices were made, the officials originally in charge of the project canned, and a possible disaster with the decennial census averted.

Still, there has unquestionably been a massive falloff in congressional oversight. In the decade after the GOP takeover of Congress in 1994, the number of Senate oversight hearings dropped by a third, and House oversight hearings fell by half, according to the Brookings Institution. And even these numbers probably understate the problem. A lot of oversight hearings today are almost strictly for show, especially in the House. And even those that are meant to be serious suffer from the ignorance and poor preparation of many lawmakers. "In the old days, the member used to know more than any witness from the outside that came before the committee," Dingell said. "Today, they don't. Members don't even understand the issues. They don't even ask questions that are relevant. Sometimes they just want to give a political speech."

Congress's failure of oversight is perhaps least obvious but most critical on the appropriations committees and subcommittees. These entities control the purse strings for every government program and agency. It has traditionally been their job—and they once took it seriously—to ensure that dollars were being spent on programs that were doing what they said they were doing. That sort of line-item oversight takes time and a dedicated staff that is paying an inordinate amount of attention to detail. "It was never a thrilling process," said Scott Lilly, who served as a clerk and staff director of the House Appropriations Committee, "but it was vital."

And it has all but ceased to happen in the past decade or so, as staff numbers have dwindled and the passing of sweeping, omnibus budgets have become the norm. Even when they do try to look, appropriations subcommittees are snowed under by literally thousands of pages—"multiple tomes," as one staffer put it—of oversight reports that no one has the time to read. "Agencies just fill up these budget justifications with all sorts of meaningless metrics, which is a convenient tool to overwhelm a handful of staffers, who are stretched so thin they don't have the time to find out anything that's going on," Lilly said. The result, Republican Senator Tom Coburn pointed out in a 2012 report, is wasted money, uncontrolled government programs, and a panicky sense of "fire-alarm oversight" in which members of Congress don't ask questions until a scandal breaks and there's a mad scurry to assign blame.

This widespread, decades-long congressional brain drain could be fixed overnight. Members of Congress, after all, control the national budget. All they need to do is allocate a couple hundred million bucks—chump change in the $4.8 trillion budget—to boost staff levels, increase salaries to retain the best staff, and fill out the institutional capacity of the body. This wouldn't necessarily mean recreating precisely the infrastructure of the 1970s—hundreds of guys in white short-sleeved shirts sitting in cubicles in some building on South Capitol Street. As New America's Lorelei Kelly has observed, technology now allows for any number of ways to create distributed networks of expertise. Congress could place policy and oversight staff in district offices, for instance, where they'd be closer to the ground, or create research and advisory partnerships between Congress and universities.

> **The congressional brain drain could be fixed overnight. Congress, after all, controls the national budget. For a couple hundred million bucks—chump change in the $4.8 trillion budget—it could boost staff levels, increase salaries to retain the best staff, and rebuild its institutional capacity.**

Regardless of how it's organized or what new technologies can be brought to bear, what's clear is that members of Congress need the institutional capacity to help them make sense of it all. As the issues facing members of Congress become increasingly intertwined and technological in our complex global economy, what we need is not *fewer* people in government who understand the implications of, say, the international derivatives market; what we need is *more*. And we need them, whether they be knowledgeable committee chairs or long-serving professional staff, to be experienced, well paid, and appreciated so they want to stick around for a while.

The problem, however, is that conservatives as a rule don't see this lack of expertise as a problem. Quite the contrary: they've orchestrated the brain drain precisely as a way to advance the conservative agenda. Why, when your aim is less government, would you want to add to government's intellectual capacity?

The answer, as some conservatives are beginning to realize, is that making Congress dumber has not, in fact, made government smaller. As the conservative but independent-minded Senator Tom Coburn wrote in his 2012 report, cuts to the GAO budget and declines in Senate and House committee oversight activity have resulted in billions of dollars in unnecessary, duplicative, and wasteful government spending. In another sign of dawning awareness, last year the House leadership, having been led astray one too many times by the Heritage Foundation and its Heritage Action lobbyists, barred those lobbyists from attending the Republican Study Committee's weekly meetings.

At a press conference in the aftermath of last fall's pointless government shutdown, a dazed and incredulous Speaker Boehner squinted into the cameras and proclaimed that groups like Heritage had "lost all credibility." You'll recall, he noted, that "the day before the government reopened, one of those groups stood up and said, 'We never really thought it would work,'" Boehner said, his eyes bugging theatrically. He waited a beat or two for dramatic emphasis before his voice crackled with dismay: *"Are you kidding me?"*

It's a long way from these glimmers of recognition that outsourcing Congress's thinking ability may not be such a good idea to a willingness to do something serious to reverse the brain drain. The Republicans are nowhere near even considering that (which means the best hope for now may be a Democratic takeover of both houses). But it's a start.^{WM}

Critical Thinking

1. What changes have occurred in Congress since Newt Gingrich rose to power in the 1990s?
2. What was Speaker Gingrich's underlying rationale for making the changes in the House of Representatives that he did?
3. Why, according to the authors, has making Congress "dumber" not resulted in smaller government?

Create Central

www.mhhe.com/createcentral

Internet References

Gingrich Productions
http://www.gingrichproductions.com

U.S. House of Representatives
www.house.gov

What Does Newt Gingrich Know? (New York Times)
http://www.nytimes.com/2011/07/03/magazine/what-does-newt-gingrich-know.html?pagewanted=all

PAUL GLASTRIS is editor in chief of the *Washington Monthly*. **HALEY SWEETLAND EDWARDS** is a former editor at the *Washington Monthly*. This story was supported by the American Independent.

Article   Prepared by: Bruce Stinebrickner, *DePauw University*

We Need Both Insiders and Outsiders in Congress

LEE HAMILTON

Learning Outcomes

After reading this article, you will be able to:

- Assess whether, as Lee Hamilton suggests, Congress and the United States more generally are well-served by the presence of both "insiders" and "outsiders" in Congress.

- Reread the relevant parts of the article and consider whether Lee Hamilton is indeed "making a judgment as to which kind of member [insider or outsider] is more valuable," even while he says that he is not.

Insiders in Congress put in long, tedious hours on the minutiae of developing legislation. Outsiders mostly use Congress as a platform to build a following beyond their own constituency. Both types are needed to make the system work.

Members of Congress get categorized in all sorts of ways. They're liberal or conservative; Republican or Democrat; interested in domestic affairs or specialists in foreign policy.

There's one very important category, though, that I never hear discussed: whether a member wants to be an inside player or an outside player. Yet where members fall on the continuum helps to shape the institution of Congress.

First, I should say that the categories are not hard and fast. Some politicians are insiders part of the time and outsiders at other times. Still, most fall on one side of the line or [the] other, especially as they go on in their careers.

Insiders focus on making the institution work. They tend to give fewer speeches on the floor, issue fewer press releases, and spend less time considering how to play the public relations game or how to raise money. Instead, they put in long, tedious hours on the minutiae of developing legislation, attending

hearings, listening to experts, exploring policy options, and working on building consensus. They're dedicated to finding support for a bill or a set of proposals wherever they can, and they appreciate the necessity of bipartisanship.

They're constantly engaged in networking and so tend to be popular within the Congress—they have the respect of their colleagues because other members know these are the people who make the institution move forward. They're the ones who do the necessary work of legislating.

Outsiders pass through the institution of Congress, but many of them are using Congress—and especially the House of Representatives—as a stepping-stone to another office: the Senate, a governorship, the presidency.

On Capitol Hill, these people behave very differently from insiders. They raise money aggressively, put a lot of effort into developing a public persona, and are consumed with public relations. They travel a lot and take every opportunity they can to meet and address conferences and large organizations. They churn out press releases and speak on the floor on every topic they can find something to deliver an opinion about.

They miss votes more frequently than insiders, and often do not attend committee hearings.

They tend not to socialize with other members, and so generally are not as popular as insiders. When they do attend a committee hearing, they use it as a platform to help them build a constituency beyond their own district or state. They tend to be more partisan than insiders, because they are seeking to build a political base. They're often impatient with House and Senate traditions, and are impatient with the democratic process.

I remember late one night—actually, it was more like 3:00 or 4:00 in the morning—standing behind the rail of the House talking with a charismatic, charming congressman from the South. He'd been in the House for only a term or two, and was chagrined at the parliamentary tangle we were working our way through that night. "Lee," he said, "how can you stand this place? I'm going to go home and run for governor!" And he did.

I want to be clear that I'm not making a judgment here as to which kind of member is more valuable. I may prefer to spend my time with insiders, but both are needed to make the system work. You have to have members reaching out to the broader public, talking about the big issues and engaging Americans in the issues of the day. And you need people on the inside who are dedicated to resolving those issues by attending to the legislation that will make this possible.

The truth is, Congress wouldn't work if everyone were an outside player. The process is tedious: especially when you're trying to draft a bill, you get into arcane arguments over language; you have to go line by line over the bill and each amendment. Outsiders have little patience for this process, and often don't show up for it.

Yet if everyone were an insider, the country would be deprived of the dialogue, debate, and sheer spectacle that give Americans a sense of stake and participation in the policy-making process.

Critical Thinking

1. Distinguish what Lee Hamilton calls "insiders" and "outsiders" in Congress.
2. Explain why "outsiders often find the congressional process 'tedious.'"
3. Summarize Lee Hamilton's views about the contributions of congressional insiders and outsiders.

Internet References

The Center on Congress at Indiana University
http://centeroncongress.org
The U.S. House of Representatives
http://www.house.gov

LEE HAMILTON is Director of the Center on Congress at Indiana University; Distinguished Scholar, IU School of Global and International Studies; and Professor of Practice, IU School of Pubilc and Environmental Affairs. He was a member of the U.S. House of Representatives for 34 years.

Article Prepared by: Bruce Stinebrickner, *DePauw University*

Save the Sequester

It's the most successful program of spending cuts in modern times.

STEPHEN MOORE

Learning Outcomes

After reading this article, you will be able to:

- Put into perspective the recent changes in national government spending as a proportion of GDP and consider whether you favor the change that occurred between 2011 and 2014.

- Consider U.S. government spending on military forces, domestic discretionary spending, and the "big three" entitlement programs (Medicare, Social Security, and Medicaid) and assess whether you like the current spending patterns in these areas relative to one another.

T he most unheralded achievement of the Republican Congress over the last four years has undoubtedly been the Budget Control Act of 2011 (BCA), which has shrunk the size of government more effectively than any budget tool in a generation. A sign of how well the budget caps and across-the-board spending cuts called "sequester" have worked is how much President Obama and left-wing special-interest groups have come to despise what the president calls this "mindless" spending-reduction formula.

But for a growing number of congressional Republicans—especially the appropriators—this success has become too much of a good thing, and they are looking to undo some of the sequester-imposed cuts. President Obama is enticing members concerned about national security by offering to devote half of the extra spending to beefing up the defense budget. If Republicans get suckered into this fiscal jailbreak, it will effectively kill the sequester for good and give a green light to the Obama budget blowout, which would add nearly half a trillion dollars of spending over just three years. All the hard-fought fiscal gains would be lost. Fiscal conservatives would be smarter to force Obama to comply with the sequester and

overall caps while shifting spending within the caps from domestic to defense programs.

Let's start with the salutary impact that the sequester and caps have had by slamming the brakes on the Bush-Obama full-throttle spending from 2008 to 2011. The sequester came about as a by-product of the famous 2011 "debt ceiling" negotiations between Obama and Republican house speaker John Boehner. Before those negotiations, the federal government was spending 24.4 percent of GDP. In 2014, expenditures fell to 20.3 percent.

This 4.1-percentage-point reduction in federal spending as a share of national output is the equivalent of an annual $714 billion in resources that the government would have spent and squandered. This constitutes one of the largest fiscal retrenchments in modern times. And all of this is happening while the White House is occupied by the most liberal president since LBJ.

To understand how this fiscal miracle happened, we have to revisit the final days of the 2011 debt-limit showdown between Obama and Boehner. Boehner and then–House majority leader Eric Cantor shrewdly agreed to the cap-and-sequester mechanism proposed by Jack Lew, the lead budget negotiator for the White House—with half the cuts to come from defense and half from domestic discretionary programs. Lew thought he had set a trap, because Republicans would never go along with these tight military-spending restraints.

But Boehner played Lew like a fiddle. He rejected a phony entitlement-reform-for-tax-hike deal—an outcome that much of Washington was cheerleading for, but that would have caused a civil war within the GOP—and instead wisely embraced the binding spending controls and the automatic sequester cuts. It was his finest hour. Liberals never knew what was about to hit them.

Under the BCA, total federal outlays have fallen from $3.603 trillion in 2011 to $3.506 trillion in 2014, in nominal dollars. This is the first three-year stretch of declining federal outlays since Dwight Eisenhower's first term in office (though in 2015 federal outlays have started to rise again). Not all of this reduction is due to the BCA sequester. A fall in interest rates has reduced federal borrowing costs, and the repayment of funds to Fannie Mae and Freddie Mac and the reduction in welfare payments caused by the end of the recession have played a role as well. But the sequester's spending guardrail is also a reason the deficit has fallen by two-thirds from its towering height of $1.4 trillion. Call it the tea-party movement's revenge.

To fully appreciate this turnaround in budget policy, consider the breadth of the Washington spending frenzy in recent years. Federal expenditures from 2007 to 2011 skyrocketed by $874 billion in nominal dollars—a nearly one-third blowout during an era of modest inflation. Now, thanks to the caps and sequester, discretionary programs, after peaking in 2011 at $1.347 trillion, have been sliced and diced to $1.179 trillion—a near 13 percent three-year actual cut in agency spending (16 percent in inflation-adjusted dollars). A little more than 60 percent of these cuts has come from the defense budget, and the remaining portion from domestic programs—everything from transit grants to foreign aid to the IRS to Head Start to bridges to nowhere.

Actual discretionary spending (in nominal dollars) from 2011 to 2014 was $427 billion lower than that projected by the Congressional Budget Office in January 2011, prior to the caps' implementation. Not bad.

Republicans rightly warn that the severity of the military cuts hurts national security. But many of these cuts would have happened anyway as a result of the wind-down of military operations in Iraq and Afghanistan. At least Republicans were able to secure domestic cuts at the same time. There has been no replay of the post-Vietnam domestic-spending boom that liberals scored from 1968 to 1978, when military spending as a percentage of GDP shrank by half while entitlements grew by nearly 50 percent. To maximize national security and money for troops, spending on non-defense items in the Pentagon, including billions of dollars of green-energy programs, should be eliminated, but the Obama administration and Republican appropriators have rejected this option.

One complaint is that entitlements are still inflicting relentless fiscal destruction. The budgets for the big three programs—Medicare, Medicaid, and Social Security—plus a new fourth one, Obama care subsidies, are expected to nearly double (86 percent growth) between 2014 and 2025. These fiscal Goliaths are only minimally constrained by the BCA, because the White House has steadfastly resisted any reductions to their growth rate. Alas, the prospects of badly needed market-based entitlement restructuring, such as personal accounts for Social Security, are close to zero under this president.

Some argue that spending cuts are "austerity" and that the sequester has hurt the economy. Wrong. The economy and jobs have picked up steam as the government has shrunk. Though it's still a flimsy recovery, economic growth and government spending have been shown to move in opposite directions in recent years, refuting the Keynesian gospel of the Left. This has been the pattern for the last 50 years at least. Milton Friedman had it exactly right: Less government spending means more private-sector growth; there is no magical "multiplier effect" of government spending.

> **Though it's still a flimsy recovery, economic growth and government spending have been shown to move in opposite directions in recent years.**

All of this is to say that right now Republicans hold all the cards on the budget. If they can force President Obama to live within the overall spending caps that he has twice agreed to and that are cemented into law, then with a pickup in economic growth, federal spending could fall below 20 percent of GDP by the last year of the most statist president in modern times. There is no executive order the president could issue to stop it. Only Republicans can bail out the big spenders.

That is why liberals—who had hoped the reelection of Barack Obama would bring on a second Great Society spending binge—have learned to hate the term "sequester." And it is why conservatives should keep loving it.

Critical Thinking

1. Under what circumstances and in the context of what legislation did the "sequester" get enacted?

2. Summarize the consequences of the "sequester" for spending as a proportion of GDP between 2011 and 2014.

3. Why, according to the author, should conservatives "love" the "sequester," while liberals should "hate" it?

Internet References

Congressional Budget Office
 https://www.cbo.gov

Office of Management and Budget
 https://www.whitehouse.gov/omb

MR. MOORE is a contributor to NATIONAL REVIEW ONLINE and Fox News.

Article Prepared by: Bruce Stinebrickner, *DePauw University*

Clones on the Court

A Supreme Court that once included former senators and governors is populated today by judges with identical résumés. Here's why that's a mistake.

AKHIL REED AMAR

Learning Outcomes

After reading this article, you will be able to:

- Ponder whether, as Akhil Reed Amar argues, "portfolio diversification" on the Supreme Court is beneficial for the American political system.

- Consider what you think is the best background or experience for a Supreme Court justice and explain why.

T he path to America's highest court nowadays narrows at a remarkably early stage in life and narrows even further soon thereafter. As youngsters, all of the justices on today's Supreme Court attended elite colleges: three Ivy League schools, Stanford, Georgetown, and Holy Cross. From there, they all went on to study law at Harvard or Yale (though Ruth Bader Ginsburg defected to Columbia for her final year); most then clerked for a judge in the Northeast. And from there, they advanced to the bench. On the day Samuel Alito replaced Sandra Day O'Connor, in early 2006, not only was every justice a former judge, but each had been a (1) sitting (2) federal (3) circuit-court judge at the time of his or her Supreme Court appointment.

Since then, the basic pattern has remained in place. After graduating from Princeton and then Yale Law (like Alito before her), Sonia Sotomayor spent 17 years as a judge before being tapped to be a justice. More recently, Elena Kagan, after graduating from Princeton and Harvard Law, did two early clerkships and later served as the solicitor general of the United States. (The solicitor general, while not, strictly speaking, a judge, is very similar to one: he or she has an office in the Supreme Court building, and specializes in Supreme Court oral arguments.)

To appreciate how novel this Court-replenishment pattern is, recall the greatest case of the last century: *Brown v. Board of Education,* decided in 1954. Apart from the rather forgettable former Senator Sherman Minton, who had sat on a federal appellate court, none of the members of the *Brown* Court—not Earl Warren, not Hugo Black, not Robert Jackson, not Felix Frankfurter, not William O. Douglas—had *any* prior experience as a federal judge.

Indeed, before John Roberts became chief justice, in late 2005, the Court had always had at least one member who had arrived without judicial experience. On this point, the biographies of America's chief justices are particularly illustrative. From John Marshall, appointed in 1801, to Melville Fuller, who served until 1910, every one of the nation's chief justices came to the Court with zero judicial experience. The same was true of Earl Warren, who joined the Court in 1953. Three other twentieth-century chiefs—Charles Evans Hughes, Harlan Fiske Stone, and William Rehnquist—came to the Court as associate justices wholly lacking any experience as a judge.

None of this means that these various pre-Roberts chiefs were unqualified. Rather, their pre-Court credentials involved notable service outside the judiciary. For example, among the justices who decided *Brown* in 1954, Hugo Black, Sherman Minton, and Harold Burton all came to the Court having served in the Senate; Earl Warren had served three terms as the governor of California and in 1948 had come within a whisker of being elected vice president, as Thomas Dewey's running mate; Robert Jackson and Tom Clark had served as U.S. attorney general, and William O. Douglas had headed up the Securities and Exchange Commission.

Until the resignation of Sandra Day O'Connor—who had served as the majority leader in Arizona's state legislature—America had always had at least one justice who brought to the

Court high-level elective or ultra-high-level appointive political experience. By contrast, none of the current justices has ever served in the Cabinet or been elected to any prominent legislative or executive position—city, state, or federal.

The aversion to nominating former politicians may be new, but from a president's perspective, it's hardly irrational. For starters, presidents have more sitting federal judges than ever to pick from. In the 1790s, there were six Supreme Court justices and only 15 judges in the lower federal courts. Today, while the number of Supreme Court justices has edged up to nine, the number of judges in the lower federal courts has skyrocketed to nearly 1,000. And about 200 judges now sit on federal circuit courts, where they hear cases and write appellate opinions as members of judicial panels—a job rather analogous to that of a Supreme Court justice. Not surprisingly, presidents now look first to the wide and deep federal appellate bench.

Appointing a sitting federal appellate judge also gives a president a unique twofer opportunity, creating a lower-court vacancy that the president can fill with a second (presumably supportive) appointee. If a sitting federal appellate judge placed on the Supreme Court is in turn replaced by a sitting federal trial judge, a president can turn a single Supreme Court vacancy into *three* judicial appointments.

Now factor in today's televised Senate confirmation hearings, in which nominees are grilled on the finer points of current Supreme Court doctrine. The rules of this game advantage sitting federal judges, whose daily job involves applying the Court's intricate commands, over, say, thoughtful lawyers in other parts of the government who may be less familiar with the Court's jargon and multipart doctrinal tests.

And let's not forget the value of prior vetting and confirmation. Every sitting federal judge has already been approved once by the Senate for a job in the judiciary. By contrast, most elected officials and other plausible Supreme Court candidates have never been confirmed by the Senate for any position.

WHY, YOU MAY ASK, is any of this a problem? Why would we want ex-senators—or ex–Cabinet officials, or ex-governors, or other sorts of ex-pols, for that matter—on our highest court?

While a bench overloaded with ex-pols would be unfortunate, the Court would benefit from having at least one or two justices who know how Washington works at the highest levels, and who have seen up close how presidents actually think, how senators truly spend their days, how bills in fact move through Congress, and so on—in short, one or two justices whose résumés resemble those of former Secretary of State John Marshall, Hugo Black, and Robert Jackson. Think of it as simple portfolio diversification: The Court works best when its justices can bring different perspectives to bear on difficult legal issues. Constitutional law, done right, requires various tools and techniques of argumentation and analysis. No single technique works best across all constitutional questions that have ever arisen or will eventually arise. Some problems may be best considered through a combination of close textual analysis of a particular clause and holistic analysis of the Constitution's overall structure. On other topics, the original intent behind a provision may be especially significant. Still other issues should be approached through the prism of prior case law. Sometimes, however, text, structure, original intent, and precedent may not cast much light on the legal issue at hand. In those cases, justices would be better off focusing on the relevant nonjudicial actors' past institutional practices—say, settlements and agreements between members of different political branches that effectively glossed ambiguous constitutional text. Ex–attorneys general such as Robert Jackson and ex-senators such as Hugo Black may enrich the Court by brilliantly deploying tools and techniques of constitutional interpretation that lifelong judges may lack.

Only one of the *Brown v. Board of Education* justices had any prior experience as a federal judge.

One virtue of appointing federal appellate judges to the Court is that these highly judicialized folk are already masters at applying Supreme Court doctrine. After all, this is what circuit-court judges do every day: they study and apply what the Supreme Court has said about one legal issue or another. One problem, however, is that Supreme Court precedent can be dead wrong. Sometimes, in fact, it is baloney. And lower-court judges, who daily slice and eat this doctrinal baloney, may be ill-equipped to see it for what it is. Specifically, they may be inclined to think that judges are more right than they really are, and other branches of government, more wrong. sA lower court's job is to follow the Supreme Court's precedents, whether right or wrong. But the Supreme Court's job, in certain situations, is to correct its past mistakes—to overrule or depart from erroneous precedents. (*Brown* famously and gloriously abandoned *Plessy v. Ferguson*'s malodorous "separate but equal" doctrine.) Someone who has not spent his or her entire life reading Supreme Court cases—who has instead spent time thinking directly about the Constitution and also spent time in a nonjudicial branch of government with its own distinct constitutional perspectives and traditions—may be particularly good at knowing judicial baloney when he or she sees it.

Consider a piece of judicial analysis that is, by acclamation, one of the greatest Supreme Court performances of the last century: Robert Jackson's concurring opinion in *Youngstown Sheet*

& *Tube Co. v. Sawyer.* In that case, the Court upheld a lower court's injunction barring President Harry Truman from continuing to hold private steel mills his government had seized. Truman had argued that this action was necessary to prevent a strike that threatened the production of steel needed for the Korean War.

In his concurring opinion, Jackson—a justice appointed by a Democratic president, voting against a Democratic president in a landmark case—repeatedly called attention to his own past professional life. He began by noting that he had served "as legal adviser to a President in time of transition and public anxiety," an experience that, he confessed, probably had a greater influence on his view of the case than the Court's prior case law. From his unique vantage point, judicial precedent was not the be-all and end-all that some blinkered lifetime judicialized folk might imagine it to be. "Conventional materials of judicial decision," he wrote, "seem unduly to accentuate doctrine and legal fiction." Instead of single-mindedly focusing on judicial precedent, Jackson carefully canvassed the history of congressional and presidential actions over the centuries, paying respect to the ways that the legislative and executive branches had come to understand and implement the ambiguous constitutional clauses allocating powers between these branches.

ROBERT JACKSON skipped college and did not go to a fancy law school, nor did he work as a judicial law clerk. But once on the Court, he did hire law clerks, and one of his most notable hires was William Rehnquist, who later became chief justice. And in turn, one of William Rehnquist's law clerks was John Roberts, who eventually replaced Rehnquist as chief, in 2005.

In some ways, John Roberts is rather like his judicial grandsire, Robert Jackson, and in other ways he is quite different. Like Jackson, Roberts served as solicitor general, albeit in a temporary capacity. Like Jackson, Roberts brought to the Court years of service as a lawyer within the executive branch. But unlike Jackson, Roberts never reached the highest rung of executive-branch service. He was never in the president's innermost circle.

Now let us turn to the biggest judicial decision of John Roberts's career, in which he provided the crucial fifth vote to uphold the Affordable Care Act in the 2012 case of *National Federation of Independent Business v. Sebelius.* Most scholars believe that the law, whether or not it is good policy, is easily and obviously constitutional. But in our hyperpolarized political world, various interest groups ginned up newfangled constitutional attacks that fooled some otherwise admirable justices who had been appointed to the Court by Republican presidents.

Roberts was not entirely deceived, and ultimately voted to uphold the law as a simple exercise of the congressional power to raise revenue. The ACA is, among other things, a tax law, and the Constitution was emphatically adopted and later pointedly amended to give Congress sweeping tax power. None of the other conservative justices credited this basic point, but Roberts did, perhaps because he had spent more time than the other conservatives in executive-branch positions in which the tax power was highly relevant. The party that put him on the Court was none too pleased with his act of judicial integrity, but somewhere, Robert Jackson must have been smiling.

Whether Roberts and his Court will continue to shine in the days ahead is less certain. Consider the two biggest issues of the current Supreme Court term. In *King v. Burwell,* the ACA is back before the Court. This time, the question at hand seems hypertechnical, involving the meaning of a single phrase in the sprawling statute. But if the justices read this phrase without heeding the basic objectives of the lawmakers who enacted the statute and of the executive agency charged with administering it, insurance markets could unravel, imperiling health care for millions of families. Justices with congressional or Cabinet experience—the John Marshalls and the Robert Jacksons of Courts past—were sensitive to the concerns (and the wisdom) of nonjudicial players. Will the current Court be similarly attuned?

As for this term's same-sex marriage cases—the *Brown v. Board of Education* of our era—the justices will surely pay close attention to judicial precedent. But no one on today's Court has spent years studying the Fourteenth Amendment, with its grand principle of equality, as the great Hugo Black did prior to *Brown.* Nor does anyone on the Court have Earl Warren's track record of bipartisan achievement at the highest levels of American politics.

I hope that today's justices will nonetheless rise to the occasion.* But I would feel more confident about a bench that was not lacking a crucial advantage enjoyed by every bench prior to 2005. Supreme Court precedent is a deep source of wisdom, but so is our nation's long-standing tradition of composing a Court whose justices, and decisions, reflect a broad range of experience.

Critical Thinking

1. What is meant by "portfolio diversification" in the context of U.S. Supreme Court membership and why does Akhil Reed Amar think that the Supreme Court would profit from it?

---

*In late June 2015, after this article was published, the Supreme Court issued much-anticipated rulings in the two important cases addressed in the preceding two paragraphs. The Court's 6-3 ruling on Obamacare did indeed seem "attuned" to the "basic objectives" of those who enacted the Affordable Care Act, and its 5-4 decision declaring that the Constitution legitimated same-sex marriage was supported by a majority of Americans.

2. Compare the backgrounds of U.S. Supreme Court justices who decided the landmark *Brown v. Board of Education* case in 1954 and the 2012 case *National Federation of Independent Business v. Sebelious* on the constitutionality of Obamacare.

3. Explain how Justice Robert Jackson's concurring opinion in *Youngstown Sheet & Tube Co. v. Sawyer* (1952) reflected his experiences before becoming a judge.

Internet References

Akhil Reed Amar
   https://www.law.yale.edu/akhil-reed-amar
Supreme Court of the United States
   http://www.supremecourt.gov

Article   Prepared by: Bruce Stinebrickner, *DePauw University*

Angering Conservatives and Liberals, Chief Justice Defends Steady Restraint

Adam Liptak

Learning Outcomes

After reading this article, you will be able to:

- Ponder what the role of the Supreme Court and the chief justice should be in the American political system.

- Evaluate the consistency—or lack thereof—in Chief Justice Roberts's positions in two pivotal cases decided in June 2015: the Supreme Court ruling "saving the Affordable Care Act for the second time" and the ruling legitimizing same-sex marriage.

- Explain why someone might say that he or she favors same-sex marriage and *also* say that, if he were a U.S. Supreme Court justice, he or she would not have voted to declare a constitutional right to same-sex marriage.

Washington—On Thursday, when Chief Justice John G. Roberts Jr. helped save the Affordable Care Act for a second time, conservatives accused him of everything short of treason.

On Friday, when he dissented from a decision establishing a constitutional right to same-sex marriage, liberals not too busy celebrating charged that he had tarnished his legacy and landed on the wrong side of history.

Now completing his 10th term as the leader of a deeply divided court, Chief Justice Roberts remains more apt to surprise than any of his colleagues, and therefore more likely to disappoint.

He seemed to anticipate the dueling critiques, and used this week's opinions to cast himself as a steady practitioner of judicial modesty. Indeed, he employed very similar language to suggest that his votes were consistent and principled.

The court's job in the health care case, he wrote on Thursday, was to let the political process work and ensure that Congress's intentions were honored. "In a democracy, the power to make the law rests with those chosen by the people," he wrote.

The court's job in the marriage case was the same, he said on Friday. "It can be tempting for judges to confuse our own preferences with the requirements of the law," he wrote. "The majority today neglects that restrained conception of the judicial role. It seizes for itself a question the Constitution leaves to the people, at a time when the people are engaged in a vibrant debate on that question."

The two cases illuminate the puzzle that is Chief Justice Roberts. When President George W. Bush nominated him in 2005 to replace Justice Sandra Day O'Connor, his work as a lawyer in Republican administrations and his brief record as an appeals court judge gave every indication that his would be a reliably conservative vote.

But then Chief Justice William H. Rehnquist died, and President Bush nominated Judge Roberts to take over leadership of the court. Taking the center seat at the Supreme Court may have moved him toward the ideological center, too, if only a little.

The chief justice has, after all, institutional responsibilities along with jurisprudential ones. He is the custodian of the Supreme Court's prestige, authority and legitimacy, and he is often its voice in major cases.

His most recent predecessors each served for more than 15 years and participated in more than 1,000 decisions. But just a handful of those rulings came to define their legacies.

The court led by Chief Justice Earl Warren is remembered for its cases on desegregation, voting and the rights of criminals. The one led by Chief Justice Warren E. Burger moved right in criminal cases, but also identified a constitutional right to abortion. Under Chief Justice Rehnquist, the Supreme Court delivered the 2000 election to George W. Bush.

The Roberts court's most memorable decisions include campaign finance, health care and Second Amendment cases in which the chief justice was in the majority. But with Friday's marriage decision, a civil rights landmark, Chief Justice Roberts was on the losing side, and it seemed to sting.

His colleagues, he said, had portrayed him and other fair-minded people "as bigoted" for not sharing their understanding of the Constitution.

"In the face of all this," he wrote, "a much different view of the court's role is possible. That view is more modest and restrained. It is more skeptical that the legal abilities of judges also reflect insight into moral and philosophical issues. It is more sensitive to the fact that judges are unelected and unaccountable, and that the legitimacy of their power depends on confining it to the exercise of legal judgment."

He suggested but did not quite say that he might vote for same-sex marriage were he an elected lawmaker.

"Stripped of its shiny rhetorical gloss, the majority's argument is that the due process clause gives same-sex couples a fundamental right to marry because it will be good for them and for society," he wrote. "If I were a legislator, I would certainly consider that view as a matter of social policy. But as a judge, I find the majority's position indefensible as a matter of constitutional law."

His tone on Friday may have been understated, but he compared the reasoning of Justice Anthony M. Kennedy's majority opinion in the marriage case with some of the court's most discredited decisions. He cited *Dred Scott*, the 1857 decision that said black slaves were property and not citizens, saying that there, too, "the court relied on its own conception of liberty." The chief justice also cited *Lochner v. New York*, a 1905 decision that struck down a New York work-hours law and has become shorthand for improper interference with matters properly left to legislatures.

Chief Justice Roberts chided members of the majority for inconsistency by quoting their own words. Just last year, the chief justice wrote, Justice Kennedy had insisted on respect for voters' judgments in an affirmative action case. "It is demeaning to the democratic process," Justice Kennedy had written,

"to presume that voters are not capable of deciding an issue of this sensitivity on decent and rational grounds."

Then Chief Justice Roberts quoted another member of the majority, Justice Ruth Bader Ginsburg, from a 1985 law review article criticizing the court for moving too fast in *Roe v. Wade,* the 1973 decision identifying a constitutional right to abortion: "Heavy-handed judicial intervention was difficult to justify and appears to have provoked, not resolved, conflict."

The chief justice bristles at accusations that the court's decisions are motivated by partisan politics. He cannot have enjoyed the barrage of name calling after Thursday's health care decision from commentators on the right—"a disgrace," "Nancy Pelosi's copy editor," "a disastrous choice" for the Supreme Court. The *Wall Street Journal*'s editorial page worried that the chief justice may be "moving pointedly to the left on the bench, like former Justices David H. Souter or Harry A. Blackmun," Republican appointees who had disappointed their conservative sponsors.

But Chief Justice Roberts's opinion in the same-sex marriage case pointed in another direction, disappointing those liberals who thought he might find a way to provide a sixth vote for a constitutional right to such unions. Critics on the left expressed deep disappointment, saying, for instance, that the chief justice had "treated gay men and lesbians to a lecture."

In his dissent on Friday, Chief Justice Roberts suggested that the two opinions were entirely consistent. "Under the Constitution," he wrote, "judges have the power to say what the law is, not what it should be."

Critical Thinking

1. Summarize the "puzzle" that some observers say that Chief Justice Roberts represents.

2. Distinguish jurisprudential and institutional responsibilities that a chief justice, and indeed any Supreme Court justice, might feel.

3. Summarize Chief Justice Roberts's positions in two pivotal cases decided in June 2015: the case "saving the Affordable Care Act for the second time" and the case legitimizing same-sex marriage.

Internet References

U.S. Government Information (about John G. Roberts)
  http://usgovinfo.about.com/od/uscourtsystem/a/bioroberts.htm
U.S. Supreme Court
  http://www.supremecourt.gov

Article   Prepared by: Bruce Stinebrickner, *DePauw University*

Change Is Gonna Come

Nine judges are being asked to compensate for political stalemate. This is both troubling and essential.

Learning Outcomes

After reading this article, you will be able to:

- Consider whether the role of the U.S. Supreme Court, as described in this article, is a healthy and beneficial one for the American political system.

- Consider whether the U.S. Supreme Court acts like "an umpire who calls balls and strikes".

When big social shifts happen in America, most people outside the corridors of Capitol Hill wonder what the response of the federal institutions will be. Washington's politicos, by contrast, quickly set to thinking up a dozen reasons why fresh legislation should not be passed. Then, with surprising speed, something that hitherto looked impossible becomes the law of the land. The Supreme Court's ruling on gay marriage, on June 26, is the latest example of this.

America is a country that changes rapidly, governed by a set of national institutions with a bias towards inertia. A 50-year-old American was born into a world where some states had laws banning her from marrying a black man. Now she finds herself inhabiting one where she is allowed to marry a woman. In 2004 political consultants wondered whether John Kerry's support of same-sex civil unions damaged his chances of becoming president; 11 years later, a rainbow was projected onto the White House to celebrate the court's decision, and some pundits are wondering whether hostility to gay marriage will damage Republican chances in the next presidential election.

Views on gay marriage have shifted unusually quickly, but that is not an isolated example. In 2002 only 45% of Americans thought that having a baby outside marriage was morally acceptable, according to polling by Gallup. Now 61% do. Stem-cell research, one of the most controversial ethical questions during George W. Bush's presidency, now has the backing of 64% of Americans. On climate change, where America has long been an outlier in the rich world, the country

now looks less exceptional: 64% of adults support stricter limits on carbon emissions from power plants, according to polling by Pew, including half of all those who identify themselves as, or say they lean, Republican.

In another political system, these changes might result in new laws. In America's, which combines the most energetic conservative movement found in any rich country with a proliferation of vetoes over federal legislation, they do not. This leads to a build-up of pressure in the tubes that connect Americans to their government. Increasingly, this pressure finds an escape through the Supreme Court, as the court's most recent term shows.

In his tenth year as chief justice, John Roberts has presided over an unusually large bundle of important cases. As well as embracing gay marriage, the justices rescued Obamacare from a potentially fatal semantic glitch, rejected a challenge to a lethal-injection drug that seems to result in botched executions, scolded the Environmental Protection Agency for failing to consider costs before regulating power plants, clarified the meaning of racial discrimination under the Fair Housing Act, and allowed Arizonans to take action against partisan gerrymandering.

And that was just in the last five days of the term. Earlier the justices expanded the rights of pregnant women in the workplace, issued two rulings favourable to Muslims seeking accommodations for their religious views, told the feds to keep their hands off a Californian farmer's raisins, clarified the rules when police stop drivers on the highway and reversed the conviction of a man who had threatened to kill his wife on Facebook.

The role of a judge, Mr Roberts told senators during his confirmation hearings in 2005, is that of an umpire who calls balls and strikes. That is true, he insisted, despite the public's sense that the justices may be little more than politicians in robes. "I'm worried about people having that perception, because it's not an accurate one," Mr Roberts told an audience at the University of Nebraska last autumn. "It's not how we do our work, and it's important that we make that as clear as we can to the public. We're not Republicans or Democrats."

The Roberts court has indeed shown that the justices are willing to wander out of their ideological comfort zones. In February two liberal justices, Ruth Bader Ginsburg and Elena Kagan, found themselves on opposite sides of a dispute over John Yates, a fisherman who tossed overboard some fish he had caught which were smaller than the rules permitted. Justice Ginsburg held that because fish do not qualify as "tangible objects" under an evidence-tampering law passed in the wake of the Enron scandal, Mr Yates should not face up to 20 years in prison. Justice Kagan disagreed, writing that "a 'tangible object' is an object that's tangible".

There were other examples of unusual splits. In it *Zivotofsky v. Kerry* Clarence Thomas, the court's most conservative justice, voted with Anthony Kennedy and the four liberals to expand presidential power in international diplomacy. In it *Walker v. Sons of Confederate Veterans*, Justice Thomas again departed from his fellow conservatives in allowing Texas to refuse to print a licence-plate emblazoned with the Confederate flag. This decision, when combined with the murder of nine blacks in a church in Charleston, South Carolina on June 17th, led to the swift removal of the flag—which had lingered on sentimentally for decades—not only from public places in the South but also from Walmart and eBay.

For the second time in three years, too, Mr Roberts gravely disappointed conservatives when he voted to save the Affordable Care Act (ACA), Barack Obama's biggest legislative accomplishment and the target of more than 50 repeal attempts in the House of Representatives. The legal nub of the case, *King v. Burwell*, was a mere four words in the 900-page law involving the allocation of tax credits to low- and middle-income Americans. These subsidies, the law reads, are for people buying policies through "exchanges established by the state". But 34 states had left the job of setting up these marketplaces to the federal government. Were millions of Americans ineligible for support because their states had not set up their own exchanges?

No, Mr Roberts wrote. Though the plaintiffs' interpretation of the four words might be the "most natural" reading, dropping the subsidies would make health insurance unaffordable for as many as 8m Americans, leading to fewer enrolments and higher premiums. The result, the chief justice wrote, would be a "death spiral" that would bring the law to a "calamitous" end. "Congress," he concluded, "passed the Affordable Care Act to improve health-insurance markets, not to destroy them."

Chief Justice Roberts, a natural pragmatist, had no interest in making his court appear overtly partisan. Yet that is how the rulings of this session have been received anyway. Ted Cruz,

Warming to Obamacare

"Do you think it is the responsibility of the federal government to make sure all Americans have health-care coverage?"% replying

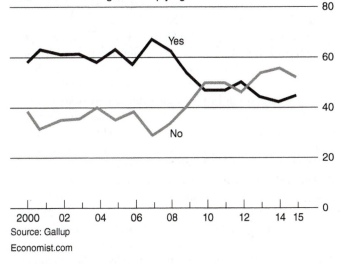

Source: Gallup
Economist.com

a former Supreme Court clerk and now a Republican presidential candidate, accused the court of lawless behaviour "that undermines [. . .] the very foundations of our representative form of government". Kevin Williamson, writing in the right-wing *National Review,* declared that the decisions marked the moment of "peak leftism". The greatest outrage, though, came from within the court in *Obergefell v. Hodges*, the landmark 5-4 ruling that opened marriage to gays and lesbians nationwide. "Allow[ing] the policy question of same-sex marriage to be considered and resolved by a select, patrician, highly unrepresentative panel of nine," wrote Antonin Scalia, the court's chief conservative scourge, "is to violate a principle even more fundamental than no taxation without representation: no social transformation without representation."

The Public Pulse

Unlike Congress, though, the Supreme Court is obliged to take a position when confronted by social change.* Even the dissenting opinions in the gay-marriage decision showed a sensitivity to public opinion which some politicians lack. In his dissent in *Obergefell*, Chief Justice Roberts spoke directly to Americans, using conciliatory tones. "If you are among the many Americans—of whatever sexual orientation—who favour expanding same-sex marriage, by all means celebrate today's decision," he wrote. "Celebrate the achievement of a desired goal. Celebrate the opportunity for a new expression

---

*This assertion seems somewhat of an overstatement. The U.S. Supreme Court can also avoid ruling on matters that it prefers to avoid, and indeed sometimes does.

of commitment to a partner. Celebrate the availability of new benefits." Were he a legislator, he went on, he "would certainly consider" the benefits of marriage equality "as a matter of social policy". As a judge, however, he had to hold that the constitution demands nothing of the sort. "I have no choice," he wrote, almost apologetically, "but to dissent."

The Supreme Court rarely likes to get very far ahead of public opinion. Before issuing rulings giving rise to a major social change like the desegregation of public schools (*Brown v. Board of Education* in 1954), the legalisation of interracial marriage (*Loving v. Virginia* in 1967), or abortion (*Roe v. Wade* in 1973) the justices seem to like at least half of Americans to be on board. In this light, the justices' tones in the *Obergefell* opinions owe much to the environment into which they were released.**

When he dissented from the pro-gay-rights holding in *United States v Windsor* in 2013, a ruling striking down the heart of the Defence of Marriage Act, Chief Justice Roberts included no words of support for the gay-rights advocates he was voting against. Same-sex marriage was legal then in only a dozen states. But the tide changed significantly over the ensuing two years. While he was writing his dissent in *Obergefell,* the number of states with gay nuptials had surged to 37 and popular support for gay marriage had reached 60%.

Next autumn, two racially charged cases await the justices. In it *Fisher v. University of Texas (II)*, the court will rehear a challenge from a white woman who says the university violated the 14th Amendment when it rejected her because of race-conscious admissions criteria. And they will consider *Evenwel v. Abbott*, a major case deciding whether Latino votes are "over-weighted" in Texan legislative districts. In either case it may become the turn of Democrats to denounce the court for judicial meddling.

The pattern of Congress leaving the court to rule on social changes that Congress cannot rouse itself to address is troubling for American democracy. But if the alternative is no change—which, given the political polarisation of the country, is highly probable—it is also hard to regret. The danger is that, relieved of responsibility for legislating on some of the most charged social questions, elected politicians are left free to posture without having to face the consequences of their positions, and the polarisation gets worse.

Critical Thinking

1. What are some examples of Americans' views on issues of public importance changing fairly quickly?

2. What are some of the "large bundle of important cases" that the U.S. Supreme Court has decided in the last ten years?

3. Present evidence that the Supreme Court typically does not adopt positions contrary to what the majority of Americans think about an issue.

Internet References

The Supreme Court of the United States
 http://www.supremecourt.gov
The University of Chicago Press: The Hollow Hope
 http://www.press.uchicago.edu/ucp/books/book/chicago/H/bo5828816.html

---

** As suggested, the Court seldom gets out too far in front of public opinion, sometimes declining to hear cases that involve controversial issues until public opinion and the views of members of the other two branches have begun to coalesce.

Article   Prepared by: Bruce Stinebrickner, *DePauw University*

How the Sausage Is Made

Supreme Court decisions aren't just dashed off, even when the justices know how they'll vote. It takes time—a lot of it.

Margot Sanger-Katz

Learning Outcomes

After reading this article, you will be able to:

- Assess whether it would be preferable—and possible—for the U.S. Supreme Court to function less as "nine separate law firms" and more as a single entity.

- Consider the amount of "hard work" done at the Supreme Court after oral arguments on a particular case occur and whether the process should be streamlined.

Two days after the marathon health care arguments ended at the Supreme Court in March, the nine justices met alone in a room and cast their votes in the historic case*. It would be easy to think that all the hard work was done—the justices had read the briefs, questioned the lawyers, and made up their minds about the case. Which might explain why Washington was abuzz about a rumor that the Court would issue its judgment before Memorial Day.

It didn't. And it probably won't issue one until the term ends in late June.

For the justices, everything is in the writing, and judicial writing takes time. Policy wonks care about the bottom line, but the Court cares about the future. Choosing one line of legal reasoning instead of another can influence a spate of future cases. And the case challenging the Affordable Care Act contains three core issues that, depending on the decision, could have big effects beyond health care. "The justices are attuned to the

fact that these decisions will be quoted for years to come, if not decades to come," said Steven Engel, a partner at the Dechert law firm and a former law clerk for Justice Anthony Kennedy.

In the post-argument conference, justices are assigned to write the majority and dissenting opinions. But even a justice who chooses her words carefully must win over four colleagues if she wants her written opinion to carry the day. The Court's traditional deadline for the circulation of first drafts is June 1, which means that the justices may just be reading the first version of the majority opinion in the case this week. If they don't like what they read, they'll make their views known, also in writing. Draft opinions and memoranda are still circulated on paper, hand delivered in manila envelopes. The memos are typically addressed to the justices using their first names, except for the chief justice, who is called Chief, former clerks say.

In cases where most members of the Court agree, this process can be fairly streamlined. But close cases often require more back and forth. Because there's little wiggle room in the event of a five-justice coalition, each justice's comments will require detailed attention, lest they stray from the majority position. (It's not clear whether all or part of the decision in the health care case will turn out to be 5–4 splits, but many legal analysts believe that Kennedy's vote will be critical in determining key issues.) It also means the opinion must be carefully constructed to please the least convinced party in the coalition, which can be tricky. In *Miranda v. Arizona*, the 1966 case that forced police to read criminal suspects their rights, Justice William Brennan submitted 21 pages of revisions to Chief Justice Earl Warren's

---

*Note that this article is written in the context of the *first* momentous case on Obamacare heard by the Supreme Court. The Court's ruling was announced in late June 2012, a short while after this article was first published. The article's discussion of the process by which the Supreme Court reaches decisions and issues opinions applies generally to how the Court operates.

original majority draft. "This will be one of the most important opinions of our time, and I know that you will want the fullest expression of my views," he wrote, according to *Storm Center,* a book on the workings of the Court by University of Virginia political scientist David O'Brien. Brennan's changes were incorporated.

Tom Goldstein, a lawyer who frequently argues before the Court and who publishes the Supreme Court news site *SCOTUSblog,* said that it's helpful to think of the justices as nine separate law firms, each with its own staff and process. "They have the right to review everything and make their own comments," he said.

Decisions in high-profile cases like this one can frequently contain dissents written for posterity. Justices are more likely to write in dissent, use rhetorical flourishes, or provide a detailed parade of horribles that will result from the majority's view. (Sometimes, such dissents are written with an eye to attracting an uncertain justice to switch sides.) Dissent writing typically doesn't begin until the majority draft has circulated, but the majority author may want to address key points in the dissents through additional revisions. Rinse, repeat. "It's an iterative process," said Kevin Walsh, an associate professor at the University of Richmond School of Law who clerked for Justice Antonin Scalia. "The bigger the case, the harder the issues, the more iterations."

The health care case is more complicated than even the typical blockbuster. The justices asked to consider more questions than they normally do; more lower courts than usual have weighed in; and the briefing pile (thanks to the litigants, outside lawyers hired by the Court, and a record number of friend-of-the-Court submissions) is enormous. Law clerks working on the case may have to read thousands of pages before they're up to speed—far more than in a typical case. Meanwhile, the justices and their clerks are also managing the Court's other cases; more than 15 decisions are expected before the end of the term, according to *SCOTUSblog.*

And even when the sides seem settled, sometimes they're not. About once per term, according to former clerks, a justice changes his mind during the process of writing, reading, and revising. That's what happened in *Planned Parenthood v. Casey,* the 1992 abortion decision for which Justice Anthony Kennedy switched sides midstream, ultimately writing to preserve key parts of *Roe v. Wade.* Sometimes, a justice in the majority will be moved by a persuasive dissent. Other times, the justice writing the majority opinion will realize, once she sits down, that an argument that sounded superficially appealing just doesn't hold together, said Carrie Severino, who clerked for Justice Clarence Thomas and is now the chief counsel and policy director of Judicial Crisis Network.

All of which is to say: These things take time. The health care case is likely to stretch into the very last week of the Court's term. If the justices' current schedule holds, smart gamblers would bet on a June 25 decision.

Critical Thinking

1. Why does Supreme Court opinion-writing take so much time after the justices have met and cast their votes after hearing oral arguments on a case?

2. Why can it be helpful to think of the justices as "nine separate law firms" instead of a single court?

3. About how often per term does a justice change his or her mind after casting his or her vote on a case "in conference"? What are some of the explanations for why such a change of mind occurs?

Internet References

United States Supreme Court
www.supremecourt.gov

Scotusblog
www.scotusblog.com

Article   Prepared by: Bruce Stinebrickner, *DePauw University*

Rare Scrutiny for a Court Used to Secrecy

PETER WALLSTEN, CAROL D. LEONNIG, AND ALICE CRITES

Learning Outcomes

After reading this article, you will be able to:

- Consider and appraise the role and functioning of the FISA court.
- Critically assess the way FISA court judges are selected.
- Reflect on the origins of the FISA court.

Wedged into a secure, windowless basement room deep below the Capitol Visitors Center, U.S. District Court Judge John Bates appeared before dozens of senators earlier this month for a highly unusual, top-secret briefing.

The lawmakers pressed Bates, according to people familiar with the session, to discuss the inner workings of the United States' clandestine terrorism surveillance tribunal, which Bates oversaw from 2006 until earlier this year.

Bates had rarely spoken of his sensitive work. He reluctantly agreed to appear at the behest of Senate Intelligence Committee Chairman Dianne Feinstein (D-Calif.), who arranged the session after new disclosures that the court had granted the government broad access to millions of Americans' telephone and Internet communications.

The two-hour meeting on June 13 featuring Bates and two top spy agency officials—prompted by reports days earlier by *The Washington Post* and Britain's *Guardian* newspaper about the vast reach of the programs—reflects a new and uncomfortable reality for the Foreign Intelligence Surveillance Court and its previously obscure members. Within the past month, lawmakers have begun to ask who the court's judges are, what they do, why they have almost never declined a government surveillance request and why their work is so secretive.

The public is getting a peek into the little-known workings of a powerful and mostly invisible government entity. And it is seeing a court whose secret rulings have in effect created a body of law separate from the one on the books—one that gives U.S. spy agencies the authority to collect bulk information about Americans' medical care, firearms purchases, credit card usage and other interactions with business and commerce, according to Sen. Ron Wyden (D-Ore.).

"The government can get virtually anything," said Wyden, who as a member of the Senate Intelligence Committee is allowed to read many of the court's classified rulings. "Health, guns, credit cards—my reading is not what has been done, it's what can be done."

Members of Congress from both parties are pursuing legislation to force the court's orders into the open and have stepped up demands that the Obama administration release at least summaries of the court's opinions.

Critics, including some with knowledge of the court's internal operations, say the court has undergone a disturbing shift. It was created in 1978 to handle routine surveillance warrants, but these critics say it is now issuing complex, classified, Supreme Court-style rulings that are quietly expanding the government's reach into the private lives of unwitting Americans.

Surveillance court judges are selected from the pool of sitting federal judges by the chief justice of the United States, as is required by the law that established the panel. There is no additional confirmation process. Members serve staggered terms of up to seven years.

Typical federal courts are presided over by judges nominated by presidents and confirmed by the Senate. Cases are argued by two opposing sides; judges issue orders and opinions that can be read, analyzed and appealed; and appellate opinions set precedents that shape American jurisprudence.

The surveillance court is a different world of secret case law, non-adversarial proceedings, and rulings written by individual judges who rarely meet as a panel.

Judges generally confer only with government lawyers, and out of public view. Yet the judges have the power to interpret the Constitution and set long-lasting and far-reaching precedent on matters involving Americans' rights to privacy and due process under the Fourth Amendment. And this fast-growing body of law is almost entirely out of view of legal scholars and the public. Most Americans do not have access to the judiciary's full interpretation of the Constitution on matters of surveillance, search and seizure when it comes to snooping for terrorist plots—and are limited in their ability to challenge it.

All 11 of the current members were tapped by Chief Justice John G. Roberts Jr. Ten were originally appointed to the federal bench by Republican presidents. Six are former prosecutors.

"The judges that are assigned to this court are judges that are not likely to rock the boat," said Nancy Gertner, a former federal judge from Massachusetts who teaches at Harvard Law School. Gertner, a former defense and civil rights lawyer named to the bench by Democrat Bill Clinton, added: "All of the structural pressures that keep a judge independent are missing there. It's one-sided, secret, and the judges are chosen in a selection process by one man."

Steven Aftergood, director of the government secrecy program at the Federation of American Scientists, called the court "an astonishing departure from what we thought we knew about the judiciary."

Defending the Court

Several current and former members of the court, as well as government officials, reject the criticism. They say internal checks are built into the system to ensure Americans' rights are not violated.

The court's current chief, D.C. District Court Judge Reggie B. Walton, was so perturbed about recent critiques of the court that he issued a rare public statement in the wake of newspaper reports about the court's approval of the phone and Internet surveillance programs.

"The perception that the court is a rubber stamp is absolutely false," Walton said. "There is a rigorous review process of applications submitted by the executive branch, spearheaded initially by five judicial branch lawyers who are national security experts and then by the judges, to ensure that the court's authorizations comport with what the applicable statutes authorize."

Administration officials echoed those sentiments last week during a public hearing before the House Intelligence Committee, telling lawmakers that the process of seeking approval for a new warrant takes extensive time and effort. The judges "push back a lot," said Deputy Attorney General James Cole. "These are very thick applications that have a lot in them. And when they see anything that raises an issue, they will push back and say, 'We need more information.'"

Roberts and an aide vet judges as candidates for the secret court. The contenders, who have undergone Senate confirmation for their original judicial posts, are screened again using an unusually exhaustive FBI background check that examines their lives "going back to birth," according to a person with knowledge of the process. Candidates are told to withdraw if anything in their lives could prove embarrassing—the chief justice reads each FBI report. He has rejected candidates for traits such as excessive alcohol use, the person said.

The court was expanded from seven judges after the attacks of Sept. 11, 2001. At least three of the judges must live in the Washington area to ensure that a judge is always personally reachable by government officials in case of emergencies.

Court members also continue to manage their regular dockets as district judges.

One of the most recent appointees, Judge Michael W. Mosman of Oregon, drew attention in 2008 when, in his position as a district court judge, he temporarily blocked a new state law allowing gay people to obtain domestic-partnership status.

Days after U.S. District Judge Rosemary M. Collyer's March appointment to the secret court, her decision in a high-profile case involving government secrecy was overturned. She had ruled that the CIA could keep secret its list of drone targets, but a higher court overruled her.

Another member is Susan Webber Wright, the Arkansas judge who presided over the Paula Jones sexual-harassment suit against Clinton and famously held the president in contempt.

Walton is a former prosecutor who sentenced former Richard B. Cheney adviser I. Lewis "Scooter" Libby to more than two years in prison for his role in the Valerie Plame leak case. President George W. Bush later commuted Libby's sentence.

Court officials reject suggestions that the judges reflect any partisan or ideological bent. They note that two former presiding judges—Joyce Hens Green and Colleen Kollar-Kotelly— were appointed to the federal bench by Democratic presidents. Neither is currently on the surveillance court.

Judges say they take the roles seriously.

"There's no question that every judge who has ever served on this court has thought it was the most significant thing they've ever done as a judge," U.S. District Judge Royce C. Lamberth said in a rare public interview on the subject posted on a federal court Web site in 2002. "When I did the hearings on the embassy bombings in Africa, we started the hearings in my living room at 3:00 in the morning. And some of the taps I did that night turned out to be very significant and were used in the New York trials of the people indicted for the bombings."

Tensions have bubbled to the surface in recent days, with some of the court's judges privately expressing frustration that it has become the center of attention and an object of criticism. They note that Congress helped pass the laws allowing the government's broad spying powers and that the administration instructs the court to keep its inner workings secret.

Walton, who took over as chief earlier this year, issued an order last month demanding that the Obama administration respond to a request from a civil liberties group, the Electronic Frontier Foundation, for the release of a classified ruling in which the court found that the government had engaged in unconstitutional surveillance of Americans. The court has even taken the rare step over the past two weeks of creating a public docket Web page featuring the Electronic Frontier Foundation case as well as a separate, new motion brought by the American Civil Liberties Union seeking records of the phone surveillance program.

Bates's June 13 appearance before lawmakers came after Feinstein, a staunch defender of the program, called Roberts to request that he dispatch Bates to the briefing. The session was open to all senators; 47 attended, according to someone familiar with the meeting.

Bates, a former prosecutor and Bush-appointed judge in the D.C. district court, rebuffed several questions about the court's orders, telling senators they should address their questions to executive branch officials, according to people briefed on the session. He stressed that the government's collection and surveillance programs were classified as top-secret by the Obama administration, not by the judiciary.

Still, the government almost always gets much of what it wants from the court.

In 2012, the court received 1,789 requests for electronic surveillance, according to the annual report it files with the Senate. One was withdrawn. The rest were approved, sometimes after back-and-forth interactions in which judges required the government to tweak or scale back its plans. Significant opinions in recent years have been sent to congressional intelligence committee members but remain classified.

'Expansive' Rulings

Now, outside critics, lawmakers and some with internal knowledge of the court are starting to push for an overhaul.

Wyden said the surveillance court has issued "pretty stunning rulings, rulings that I think are about as expansive as anything you can imagine."

Wyden pointed to court orders authorizing collection of bulk phone data, which *The Post* reported had dated to 2006, as indicators of the court's broad view of government powers. At issue is a provision of the Patriot Act, passed by Congress after the Sept. 11 attacks, which permitted the FBI to compel the production of "business records" deemed relevant to terrorism and espionage investigations and to share those with intelligence officials.

Those orders followed a turbulent time for the secret court. Some judges were outraged that they had not been aware of the Bush administration's warrantless wiretapping operation, which was first reported by the *New York Times* in late 2005. One member of the panel, U.S. District Judge James Robertson, resigned in protest, confiding to colleagues that he was concerned the program may have been illegal and could have tainted the court's work.

One person close to the court, speaking on the condition of anonymity to discuss the secretive body, said the newly revealed orders indicate a shift in which the court blesses the bulk collection of Americans' communications data to make investigations easier rather than weighing the merits of violating the privacy of one person on a case-by-case basis. Before this change, the person said, "it was one warrant at a time."

The court's under-the-radar approach proved a particular challenge this spring to the Electronic Frontier Foundation when it sought to file its motion seeking release of the prior finding of the unlawful government surveillance. It turned out that the mere act of finding the court proved a steep hurdle.

Repeated calls to the court clerk from the foundation went unreturned, said David Sobel, an attorney for the group. The group wound up submitting the motion through a staffer at the Justice Department, whose officials were actively opposing the group's efforts.

"We never had any direct contact with the court," Sobel said, "and the other party in the proceeding was the gatekeeper."

Chief Justice Roberts himself signaled some discomfort with the system during his 2005 confirmation hearings.

"I'll be very candid," he told senators. "When I first learned about the FISA court, I was surprised. It's not what we usually think of when we think of a court. We think of a place where we can go, we can watch, the lawyers argue, and it's subject to the glare of publicity. And the judges explain their decision to the public and they can examine them. That's what we think of as a court."

Critical Thinking

1. When was the FISA court established and how has its role in American government changed in the post-9/11 world?

2. Who selects FISA court judges and how many of the current eleven FISA court judges were originally nominated to their federal judgeships by Republican presidents?

3. What distinguishes the operations of the FISA court from the usual operations of other courts in the American political system?

Create Central

www.mhhe.com/createcentral

Internet References

U.S. Supreme Court
www.supremecourt.gov

Scotusblog
www.scotusblog.com

U.S. Foreign Intelligence Surveillance Court Public Filings
www.uscourts.gov/uscourts/courts/fisc/index.html

Federal Judicial Center: History of the Federal Judiciary— Foreign Intelligence Surveillance Court
www.fjc.gov/history/home.nsf/page/courts_special_fisc.html

Article   Prepared by: Bruce Stinebrickner, *DePauw University*

Legislation Is Just the Start

The new financial reform law is a good reminder of how much takes place in Washington after a bill gets signed. In the nation's capital, says former Congressman Lee Hamilton, "legislation is just the start."

LEE HAMILTON

Learning Outcomes

After reading this article, you will be able to:

- Weigh the consequences of bureaucrats' significant roles in implementing policy such as the major financial reform law passed in 2010.

- Consider whether—and, if so, why—you are troubled by a major law that requires 350 rules, 47 studies, and 74 reports to be completed after its passage.

Y ou might imagine, now that President Obama has signed the massive financial reform package into law, that the issue is behind us. Hardly. In a way, the President's signature was just the starter's pistol.

This is because, despite its length—over 2000 pages—and the many months of negotiations that went into crafting it, the financial overhaul measure leaves countless issues to be resolved later by federal regulators and the lobbyists who will try to influence their decisions. It is a textbook example of the limits inherent in a legislative product, and of the manner in which Congress relies on a mix of concrete action and ambiguous ball-punting to cobble together a majority.

The law undoubtedly changes the nation's financial landscape. It creates a new Bureau of Financial Consumer Protection; strengthens regulation of financial holding companies; regulates derivatives; places new limits—the so-called "Volcker Rule"—on the amount of money a bank can invest in hedge funds and private equity funds; buttresses the Securities and Exchange Commission; and tries to discourage excessive risk-taking.

It is also filled with the sorts of compromises the legislative process demands. The "Volcker Rule" was written off, watered down, and then somewhat re-strengthened on its way to passage. The consumer protection agency was initially to be a standalone regulator, but then was placed within the Federal Reserve in order to calm some concerns. The language on derivatives went through a complex series of balance-seeking negotiations between those who wanted highly restrictive regulation and those who opposed it.

The result is a grand and sweeping law that nonetheless leaves many issues unresolved and much room for interpretation in the future. When you have such ambiguities in new statutes—as is frequently the case—it amounts to an invitation to further struggle on the part of the bureaucrats who must give shape and form to the ideas contained in the measure, and the lobbyists whose clients have much at stake in the results.

According to an analysis by the U.S. Chamber of Commerce, the measure calls for 350 rules to be formulated, 47 studies to be conducted—which is Congress' way of signaling action on an issue without actually making any decisions—and 74 reports. The creation of new entities—the consumer protection agency, a board of regulators to assess risk in the financial system—also will engender much executive-branch maneuvering and back-and-forth with Congress as they're set up and staffed.

Moreover, lobbyists don't stop work when a law is passed; in some ways, that's when their work truly begins, as they strive to build relationships with the regulators who will oversee their industry and try to influence the regulations that will soon enough begin to flow from various executive-branch agencies.

The difference, of course, is that for all its faults, Congress is a relatively transparent and accountable institution. What takes place in regulators' offices is far less visible. As the activity surrounding financial reform now passes beyond public view, political considerations will become less important but the stakes will grow higher. Out of the public's eye, the special interests' influence will grow, and arguments about how to interpret the language contained in the law will blossom—and, inevitably, spill over into the courts. For years to come, there will be enormous demand for lawyers capable either of making sense out of ambiguous legislative language, or of making the strongest possible arguments in favor of interpretations that just happen to favor their clients.

Yet in the end, it's the executive branch that benefits most from what Congress has done. The entire measure is a significant gift of power to federal agencies and financial regulators, who now have to make decisions about how they intend to wield their power. You can already see how significant their role will be in the early maneuvering over who might head the new Bureau of Consumer Financial Protection: each possible appointee, who must be approved by the Senate, would approach the job differently, and in the weeks following the bill's passage the nuances of their approaches were probably the hottest single topic of debate over breakfast, lunch and dinner tables in Washington.

It is important to remember, in the end, that the authority to act is not the same as acting. That is why, while Congress made some important decisions in the process of crafting its bill, the true import of the financial reform package will only reveal itself gradually. There is an old saying in Washington that "nothing is ever decided for good there." For legislation, that's certainly true.

Critical Thinking

1. How does the 2010 financial reform law signed by President Obama promise to change the nation's financial landscape?

2. What were some of the compromises contained in the financial reform legislation?

3. What are some of the government actions necessary in the aftermath of the financial reform act? Who is responsible for doing most of these tasks?

4. How many rules, studies, and reports are said to be mandated by the law?

Create Central

www.mhhe.com/createcentral

Internet References

U.S. Consumer Financial Protection Bureau
www.consumerfinance.gov

Huffington Post: All About the Consumer Financial Protection Bureau
www.huffingtonpost.com/dedrick-muhammad/consumer-financial-protection-bureau_b_3670926.html

Center for Congress at Indiana: Lee Hamilton Commentaries
http://congress.indiana.edu/lee-hamilton-commentaries

LEE HAMILTON is Director of the Center on Congress at Indiana University. He was a member of the U.S. House of Representatives for 34 years.

Hamilton, Lee. From *Center on Congress at Indiana University*, August 9, 2010. Copyright © 2010 by The Center on Congress. Reprinted by permission. Lee Hamilton is Director of the Center on Congress at Indiana University. He was a member of the U.S. House of Representatives for 34 years.

Article

Prepared by: Bruce Stinebrickner, *DePauw University*

Can Government Play Moneyball?

PETER ORSZAG AND JOHN BRIDGELAND

Learning Outcomes

After reading this article, you will be able to:

- Address the relevance of performance-based evaluation to national government programs.

- Understand the importance of ways to prevent those with vested interests in current government programs from obstructing performance-based evaluations.

Based on our rough calculations, less than $1 out of every $100 of government spending is backed by even the most basic evidence that the money is being spent wisely. As former officials in the administrations of Barack Obama (Peter Orszag) and George W. Bush (John Bridgeland), we were flabbergasted by how blindly the federal government spends. In other types of American enterprise, spending decisions are usually quite sophisticated, and are rapidly becoming more so: baseball's transformation into "moneyball" is one example. But the federal government—where spending decisions are largely based on good intentions, inertia, hunches, partisan politics, and personal relationships—has missed this wave.

Allow us to share some behind-the-scenes illustrations of what our crazy system of budgeting looks like—and to propose how the lessons of moneyball could make our government better.

When one of us (Peter) began his tenure as the director of the Congressional Budget Office in 2007, he took a Willie Sutton approach to the nation's huge and growing fiscal mess: he went after health care, which makes up roughly a quarter of the federal government's spending, because that's where the money is.

The moneyball formula in baseball—replacing scouts' traditional beliefs and biases about players with data-intensive studies of what skills actually contribute most to winning—is just as applicable to the battle against out-of-control healthcare costs. According to the Institute of Medicine, more than half of treatments provided to patients lack clear evidence that they're effective. If we could stop ineffective treatments, and swap out expensive treatments for ones that are less expensive but just as effective, we would achieve better outcomes for patients and save money.

Both parties should find much to like in such an approach. It would offer Republicans a way to constrain the growth of government spending and take pressure off private businesses weighed down with health expenses. And it would offer Democrats a means of preserving the integrity of Medicare and Medicaid and thereby restoring faith in a core government function.

And yet getting funding for the research needed to assess and compare medical treatments has been like pulling teeth. As a rule, legislators seem to lack a natural affinity for economists and budget analysts (alas, they are hardly alone). But Peter made himself exceptionally unpopular with some Democrats and many Republicans by insisting on such funding in the 2009 stimulus bill, and then working to expand it in the 2010 "Obamacare" legislation. Despite these modest successes, less than $1 out of every $1,000 that the government spends on health care this year will go toward evaluating whether the other $999-plus actually works.

Getting the right information is less than half the battle. Acting on it, once it's in hand, is harder still. As one small example, some evidence suggests that moving toward "bundled" payments for all services needed by a patient during a course of medical treatment could produce better value than paying piecemeal for each service and procedure, because the piecemeal approach creates an incentive for more care rather than better care. During one meeting with members of Congress in 2008 to discuss how to expand bundling and include a performance incentive in kidney dialysis, Shelley Berkley, a Democratic congresswoman from Nevada, accused Peter, as he remembers it, of trying to destroy the dialysis industry. "You and your staff may have your Ph.D.s, but you have no clue," he recalls her saying. "We don't need any of your fancy analysis." (Berkley says she does not remember the meeting, or those comments.) Berkley had received campaign contributions from several dialysis companies and organizations, and her husband owned a dialysis business. Whether these factors may have influenced her thinking is a question we will leave for the reader.

It is indisputable, however, that a move toward payments based on performance would harm some business interests. If most of your profits come from, say, a medical device or procedure that is covered by Medicare but doesn't work all that well, you're likely to resist anyone sorting through what works and what doesn't, never mind changing payment accordingly.

Healthcare interests are wise to invest millions of dollars in campaign contributions and lobbying to protect billions of dollars in profits.

Your other author (John) received his own lessons on why moneyball doesn't play in Washington a few years earlier, when he joined the administration of George W. Bush. Bush, of course, was not only a former baseball-team owner but also the first president to hold an M.B.A. In every domestic-policy briefing John led in the first term of the Bush administration, the president would ask some version of the following questions: How do we know this program will achieve the results as advertised? Who will run this program, and is that person an effective manager? How will that person and the program be held accountable for producing results?

Year after year, with the help of the Program Assessment Rating Tool (PART) introduced by Bush's Office of Management and Budget in 2002, the administration identified federally funded and administered programs that were not working as advertised, and tried to get them to improve or be discontinued. And yet these efforts rarely gained traction on Capitol Hill with either party.

The Bush administration initially had high hopes for this project. The goal was to build on a Clinton-era law called the Government Performance and Results Act, which aimed "to provide for the establishment of strategic planning and performance measurement in the Federal Government," but did not attempt to tie performance directly to continued financing.

By the end of Bush's second term, PART had assessed about 1,000 programs. Of them, 19 percent were rated "effective," 32 percent "moderately effective," 29 "adequate," 3 percent "ineffective," and 17 percent "results not demonstrated" (meaning that the programs couldn't be assessed, because of insufficient data). This information was used to develop the president's budget proposals to Congress, but PART was not developed in cooperation with Congress, and Congress gave its assessments little heed.

The White House Task Force for Disadvantaged Youth, which John co-chaired, highlights the extreme disconnect between effectiveness ratings and appropriation decisions. For the first time ever, in 2003, the task force tallied and studied all 339 federally funded programs addressing disadvantaged youth—a confusing and costly tangle—to find ways to improve the system. With help from 10 federal departments and from experts inside and outside of government, the task force found that the federal government was spending $223.5 billion every year on programs with aims ranging from promoting health and nutrition to preventing teen pregnancy, high-school dropouts, and youth violence. Despite this wide range, overlap among the programs was common. The task force's final report documented 67 different youth programs that promoted "character education," 89 that purported to build "self-sufficiency skills," and 97 that sought to "prevent substance abuse"—with little or no coordination or knowledge-sharing among programs with similar goals.

More troubling, the vast majority of the programs could not provide any meaningful information indicating how well they served young people. Some reported basic operational data, but few had undergone rigorous evaluations looking at how the programs affected participants. At the time of the White House Task Force report, fewer than 10 percent of the programs had been assessed by PART, and more than half had not been evaluated at all in the previous five years.

With so little performance data, it's impossible to say how many of the programs were effective. But you don't have to be a Tea Party organizer to harbor skepticism. Since 1990, the federal government has put 11 large social programs, collectively costing taxpayers more than $10 billion a year, through randomized controlled trials, the gold standard of evaluation. Ten out of the 11—including Upward Bound and Job Corps—showed "weak or no positive effects" on their participants. This is not to say that all 10 programs deserve to be eliminated. But at a minimum, collecting rigorous evidence could help spur programs to improve overtime.

One of the programs studied by the Task Force for Disadvantaged Youth that *did* collect meaningful performance data and was rated by a PART assessment was the Even Start Family Literacy Program, a Department of Education project aimed at improving the literacy of low-income parents and their children. Unfortunately, the data showed that "children and parents . . . did not gain more than children and parents in the control group." PART rated the program "ineffective."

In 2003, John and officials at the Office of Management and Budget began trying to redirect funding from Even Start to better-performing programs. But Even Start was founded in 1989 by Bill Goodling, a well-liked Republican congressman who had been the chairman of the House Education and the Workforce Committee, and had previously served as a teacher, principal, and school superintendent in Pennsylvania. So Congress continued to fund this ineffective, if well-meaning, program to the tune of more than $1 billion over the life of the Bush administration.

Even Start is no different from most federal programs. Evidence of success is barely considered when legislation is proposed and discussed in committee and on the floor of Congress. There is no systematic way in which members of Congress or other key decision makers are informed about that evidence, or lack thereof. They instead tend to rely on ad hoc assessments provided by lobbyists and interest groups. And once legislation is passed and a program is up and running, there is no mechanism for automatically tracking its effectiveness, beyond counting the number of people served by a program, no matter the impact it has on their lives.

The consequences of failing to measure the impact of so many of our government programs—and of sometimes ignoring the data even when we do measure them—go well beyond wasting scarce tax dollars. Every time a young person participates in a program that doesn't work but could have participated in one that does, that represents a human cost. And failing to do any good is by no means the worst sin possible: some state and federal programs actually harm the people who participate in them.

You've surely heard of Scared Straight, a program started in a New Jersey prison in the 1970s that brings at-risk youth to meet with hardened inmates who tell them about the harsh realities of life behind bars. The program has gotten an extra dose of attention lately because of the A&E reality TV show *Beyond Scared Straight,* which takes viewers inside similar (and generally more harrowing) prison programs for young people in different states, blue and red, across the country.

It turns out that Scared Straight-style programs are actually pretty effective—at *increasing* criminal behavior. Rigorous research conducted by Anthony Petrosino and researchers at the Campbell Collaboration shows that instead of scaring kids and turning them away from risky, criminal behavior, the programs do just the opposite: they make the kids about 12 percent more likely to commit a crime.

Fortunately, the Department of Justice is acting on these findings and warning state governments to stop funding Scared Straight and similar programs. But Scared Straight is not the only government program that's been shown to cause harm. The federal government's long-running after-school program, 21st Century Community Learning Centers, has shown no effect on academic outcomes on elementary-school students—and significant *increases* in school suspensions and incidents requiring other forms of discipline. The Bush administration attempted to reduce funding for the program. But following impassioned testimony on behalf of the program by Arnold Schwarzenegger, then a potential candidate for governor of California, congressional appropriators agreed to restore all funding. Today the program still gets more than $1 billion a year in federal funds.

What can we do to promote moneyball in government? The first (and easiest) step is simply collecting more information on what works and what doesn't. The Obama administration has already pushed federal agencies to bolster their analytic capabilities and to show how their funding priorities are evidence-based, particularly in their budget submissions. As a result, the administration's 2014 budget proposal had an unprecedented focus on evidence and results.

A nonprofit organization that advocates for evidence-based decision making, called Results for America, has proposed a number of measures that would expand on these efforts. It is calling for reserving 1 percent of program spending for evaluation: for every $99 we spend on a program to improve education, reduce crime, or bolster health, we would spend $1 making sure the program actually works.

The Harvard economist Jeffrey Liebman has written that, based on his simple but convincing calculations, "spending a few hundred million dollars more a year on evaluations could save tens of billions of dollars by teaching us which programs work and generating lessons to improve programs that don't." Who wouldn't want a 100-fold return on investment?

The more evidence we have, the stronger it is; and the more systematically it is presented, the harder it will be for lawmakers to ignore. Still, linking evaluation to program funding will be tough, as both of us have seen in practice, again and again.

One thing that is essential to a more results-driven government is holding politicians accountable for their support of failing programs. Interest groups regularly rate politicians on their adherence to a particular perspective. What if we had a Moneyball Index, easily accessible to voters and the media, that rated each member of Congress on their votes to fund programs that have been shown not to work?

Even absent such public shaming, the government is taking steps in the right direction. The Department of Education's Investing in Innovation (i3) program for improving student achievement and educator effectiveness, for instance, gives priority to projects backed by rigorous evidence of success, while still allocating a portion of its funds for promising programs willing to build evidence over time. The program originated in the rush and jumble of the Recovery Act, so it bypassed some typical congressional hurdles. But the performance mandate now built into i3's design provides a model for how the federal government can make decisions about programs based on impact. Liebman has put forward some good ideas about how to expand upon that model. He suggests that, to start, 5 percent of the dedicated funding that's delivered each year by the federal government to state and local governments—which includes major programs like the Community Development Block Grant and the Community Mental Health Services Block Grant—be reserved for programs that have demonstrated their worth. That share could rise over time as the evidence base expands.

New York City Mayor Michael Bloomberg is taking another promising approach, essentially creating probationary programs that must prove themselves to become permanent. The city's Center for Economic Opportunity seeks out new, innovative programs with potential to combat the poverty cycle, and then oversees rigorous evaluations "to determine their effectiveness in reducing poverty, encouraging savings, and empowering low-income workers to advance in their careers." The programs that produce the strongest results become eligible for further city funding; if a program isn't having the intended effect, dollars are shifted to those things that work. This approach has now spread to seven other urban areas, with the help of the Obama administration's performance-based Social Innovation Fund.

How can we steer dollars away from well-established programs that aren't working? The U.S. Department of Health and Human Services has shown one nuanced approach. In 2011, the Obama administration built on the Bush administration's attempt to examine how children were faring in individual Head Start programs across the country, and began a crackdown on providers failing the kids they were supposed to serve. Instead of threatening to scrap Head Start altogether, the agency refused to renew funding for the bottom 10 percent of local programs—132 in all. These centers were told that they had failed to meet quality standards. To requalify for Head Start funding, they would have to make substantive improvements and then compete for funds against other providers in their area. Autopilot funding for lousy centers came to an end.

Another encouraging data point: two years ago, when fiscal pressures really began to mount at the federal level, Congress finally pulled the funding for the ineffective Even Start literacy program. Over time, the data won out. "Under the gun, Congress can do the right thing," says Robert Gordon, who worked in the Office of Management and Budget under President Obama. "Now there's no money to waste, so interest-group politics and bogus arguments don't carry as much weight as they used to. There's reason for optimism."

W e're optimistic too, even though the obstacles to moneyball in government are daunting. Absent major changes in campaign finance, special interests that profit from blind budgeting will still have a powerful means of thwarting reform. Agencies' staff will roll their eyes at the next round of "budget reforms," wait out the incumbent, and then continue business as usual. And members of Congress will stay wedded to their legacy programs.

But we believe the federal budget crunch will force change. Already, many cities have had to choose between fewer cops and fewer teachers; between slower ambulance response and less-frequent garbage removal. The federal government is now beginning to face similarly stark choices. Do we really want to furlough hundreds of FBI agents at a time of heightened threats? Or lay off air-traffic controllers? Do we really want big cuts at the National Institutes of Health or to early-childhood-education investments, both of which are engines of economic growth? Do we really want to eat our seed corn?

Both parties have signed up to reduce nondefense discretionary spending—that is, the money for everything from the Food and Drug Administration to the NIH to the Veterans Administration—to levels that will be at least $350 billion lower through 2022 than they were in 2012. That would bring discretionary spending as a share of the economy to its lowest level on record (data go back to 1962). We should not do this blindly.

Moneyball doesn't happen overnight. Many of the "saber-metrics" practices that transformed baseball a decade ago can actually be traced back to the Brooklyn Dodgers general manager Branch Rickey, who is universally known for breaking the color barrier in baseball but mostly unacknowledged for being the first GM to hire a professional statistician. Rickey's approach got little traction for nearly half a century, until the

pivotal 2002 season, when the Oakland Athletics' general manager, Billy Beane, built his club on analysts' data rather than scouts' beliefs.

What prompted Beane's gutsy decision to revive the data-centered approach? With $40 million to spend on players in 2002, the A's had to compete on a comically uneven playing field with big-market teams like the Yankees, which spent $125 million on its roster that same year. In other words, scarcity drove Beane's break from established tradition. We hope and expect it will have the same effect on Washington in the years to come.

Critical Thinking

1. What is the essence of the "Moneyball" approach to baseball (and other enterprises)?
2. What seemed to motivate Congresswoman Shelley Berkley and her apparent views about some elements in the way government reimburses for healthcare costs?
3. What are some noteworthy examples of performance-based evalution of government programs that the authors report?

Create Central

www.mhhe.com/createcentral

Internet References

Results for America
   www.americaachieves.org/about-us

U.S. Government Accountability Office
   www.gao.gov

Baltimore City Public School System: Performance-Based Evaluation Handbook
   www.nctq.org/evaluation_handbook/34-07.pdf

PETER ORSZAG is a former director of both the Office of Management and Budget and the Congressional Budget Office. **JOHN BRIDGELAND** was the director of the White House Domestic Policy Council under President George W. Bush.

Article

Prepared by: Bruce Stinebrickner, *DePauw University*

Do You Want Shrapnel with That Airbag?

Culpable carmakers and captive regulators make a deadly combo.

Terry J. Allen

Learning Outcomes

After reading this article, you will be able to:

- Consider the problem of "captive agencies" in American national government and how the problem(s) might be avoided or at least lessened.

- Consider what incentives the auto industry might have to respond slowly to a situation such as the airbag safety issues described in this article.

Airbags save lives, but they are useless when they fail to deploy and ballistic weapons when they explode with shrapnel.

How's this for a job-creation program: Let's dig a yawning new circle of hell for corporate and bureaucratic decision makers who allowed the sale of flawed, fatal airbag systems. But their eternal lodgings aside, why aren't the culprits in prison for homicide?

In 2004, when an airbag exploded and shot metal shards into the driver of a Honda, neither the carmaker nor the airbag manufacturer, Takata, sounded an alert, issued a recall or sought the involvement of federal safety regulators, the *New York Times* reported.

Five years later, in 2009, Ashley Parham, an Oklahoma teen, died after the airbag in her Honda Accord exploded and speared her chest with metal fragments. Although Honda had issued a very limited recall of the airbags in 2008, the carmaker, along with Takata, denied fault and settled with Parham's family for

$5,000. The companies' decision not to sound the alarm, and to cover up the problem, left other carmakers using Takata airbags unaware of possible defects for years. And it left drivers playing Russian roulette with a device armed with the same explosive Timothy McVeigh used to blow up the Federal Building in Oklahoma City.

If the auto industry's reaction to the danger had the slow-motion lethargy of a nightmare, that of the National Highway Traffic Safety Administration (NHTSA) was nearly comatose. The federal agency responsible for vehicle safety had received complaints about exploding airbags as early as 2000, but didn't open its first investigation until 2009. Then, in "a timetable so swift that it appears to have taken even Takata by surprise," it closed the inquiry after six months, according to the *Times*. NHTSA concluded, "there are no additional vehicles to be investigated."

By 2014, an undeniable trail of bloody dots led back to Takata and the 11 U.S., German and Japanese firms that had equipped 37.8 million vehicles with dangerous airbag inflators and propellants. Finally, this year, under mounting congressional, public and media pressure, NHTSA opened a second investigation, and "urged" a nationwide recall. On December 2, testifying before a House committee, Takata refused. A week later, Honda announced an expanded "investigative" recall that would include 19 million Takata airbag-equipped cars around the world.

NHTSA's response to Takata's refusal to implement its own recall was "disappointment." With that level of regulatory zeal, it is no wonder NHTSA didn't challenge Takata's claim that the errors causing the explosions were fixable and not systemic. It was left to the media to reveal the fact that, starting in 2001,

Takata had switched to a cheaper propellant—ammonium nitrate—which deteriorates and is impaired by moisture and changes in temperature.

The propellant's explosive potential and instability also raise the serious, and seriously under-reported, issue of the U.S. market in used airbags. Recyclers, aka junkyards, "retrieve never-deployed airbags from scrapped autos and sell them as replacement parts to collision repair shops," notes Edmunds.com, an online auto resource. "It's perfectly legal—and, critics say, very dangerous." If these undeployed airbags were exposed to rain after an accident or sat in a junkyard car with a blown-out windshield, they may be useless or hazardous. And with no laws governing how used airbags must be stored, tested or installed, consumers are left ignorant of the risk.

The onus is also on consumers when it comes to spotting extremely dangerous counterfeit airbags—authentic-looking down to the logos—that are illegally imported from China.

NHTSA cavalierly "urges vehicle owners and repair professionals to use only certified, original equipment replacement parts." Its website also notes that the agency "is aware" of counterfeits for 21 automakers and more than 100 models and estimates that tens of thousands of fake bags are on the road. These can fail to deploy or, like legitimate but defective Takata bags, explode and produce "a fireball and forcefully expel metal shrapnel," a Homeland Security agent testified in court.

Unsafe at Any Speed

A similar pattern of industry cover-up and regulatory negligence marks another rash of death-by-airbag failures: Since 2001, GM has been aware that defective ignition switches shut down moving vehicles, rendering them hard to control and deactivating their airbags.

"Despite 4,800 consumer complaints and more than 30,000 warranty repairs, GM waited until 2014 to disclose this defect," a lawsuit by Arizona's attorney general charged. The recall GM initiated this February affects 2.6 million cars. But it does not include the 5,000 defective switches sold to dealers and parts shops that remain in circulation. And it's perfectly legal for those businesses not to inform customers about the recall notices.

Since airbags fail for various reasons, establishing causality is essential to finding a fix. Between 2003 and 2012, a total of 303 people died in non-rear impact crashes in which the airbag did not deploy. So far, faulty ignition switches in GM vehicles have been linked to 32 of those deaths, and the toll is rising.

Gene Mikale Erickson, who died in 2004 while riding in a Saturn Ion that veered head-on into a tree. The driver—his girlfriend, Candice Anderson, 21—survived to become another poignant and uncounted victim of GM's greed. She was convicted of criminal negligent homicide, fined and sentenced to 260 hours of community service. She was also sentenced to a decade of guilt and the condemnation of Erickson's family, until a *New York Times* investigation forced NHTSA to reveal—in an email to Erickson's mother—that the faulty switch was the real cause of the crash.

Even two years after Erickson's death, NHTSA was still sloughing off consumers who reported sudden shutdowns. It wrote a complaining GM car owner that "a review of its database . . . revealed insufficient evidence to warrant opening a safety defect investigation" into the ignition switches.

In March, excoriating the agency for its delay in launching recalls and investigations, Clarence Ditlow, head of the consumer watchdog group Center for Auto Safety, wrote NHTSA chief David Friedman charging that the only way the agency could have failed to see the non-deploying airbags as a defect trend was "if it closed its eyes."

There are other explanations for the agency's poor oversight. One is its paltry budget. But more significantly, NHTSA is a captured agency. In 2010 the *Washington Post* "found 33 former NHTSA officials now playing leading roles in helping carmakers handle federal investigations of auto defects. Many of the former NHTSA employees also work as attorneys and lobbyists for the auto industry."

An especially unsubtle case is that of David Strickland, Friedman's predecessor. When Strickland resigned as NHTSA head in December 2013, the CEO of the auto industry trade group Alliance of Automobile Manufacturers lauded him as "an administrator who always kept his door open."

That door turned out to revolve between the auto industry and the institutions and agencies tasked with regulating it. On the very day in January 2014 that Strickland left NHTSA, the agency announced it would not demand the recall of the 2.7 million Jeep Liberty and Grand Cherokee models whose gas tanks were prone to rupture in rear-end collisions. Instead the agency allowed Chrysler to "fix" just 1.5 million of the SUVs by adding a trailer hitch—a cheap, partial repair that was unproven and, some experts charged, increased the danger. Chrysler spokesperson Eric Mayne emailed *In These Times* that the "vehicles are not defective, as supported by our data." He acknowledged that at least 56 people have died in the fiery crashes; other estimates put the fatalities from ruptured gas tanks at more than 150 victims. As of December 10, Chrysler had "fixed" only 158,266 vehicles.

One month after leaving NHTSA and approving that trailer-hitch deal, Strickland took a new job—at Venable LLC, a law firm that represents various auto industry trade associations and, Consumer Affairs noted, "billed $1.1 million for its services to Chrysler over the last five years."

Another aficionado of revolving doors is the lawyer representing Takata in the airbag investigations, Ken Weinstein, a former senior NHTSA official.

Airbags save lives, but they are useless when they fail to deploy and ballistic weapons when they explode with shrapnel. If regulators and manufacturers ignore or hide the problem, whether from negligence or greed, they are as culpable in the injuries and deaths that follow as a gunman spraying bullets into a crowd.

In September 2013, Hai Ming Xu, 47, died in the crash of his 2002 Honda Acura. It was only after an autopsy that the Los Angeles county coroner determined he was killed by "a metallic portion" of the airbag inflator that "hit the deceased on the face as it deployed."

When police first arrived on the crash scene, because of the nature of Xu's injuries, they had treated his death as a homicide. It was a good call.

Critical Thinking

1. What does "NHTSA" stand for and what is the relevant entity's responsibilities?

2. What are a "captive agency" and "revolving doors" in the context of government regulation?

3. What is "industry cover-up" and how does this phenomenon apply to recent airbag safety headlines?

Internet References

National Highway Traffic and Safety Administration
   http://www.nhtsa.gov

New York Times
   http://www.nytimes.com/2015/10/22/business/takata-and-honda-kept
   -quiet-on-study-that-questioned-airbag-propellant.html?src=me&_r=0

Unit 3

UNIT

Prepared by: Bruce Stinebrickner, *DePauw University*

Process of American Politics

What distinguishes more democratic political systems from less democratic ones is the amount of control that citizens exercise over their governments. The 75 to 100 or so democratic political systems in the world differ from one another both in the extent of popular control of government *and* in relevant institutions, processes, and linkages between people and government. This unit focuses on the institutions, groups, processes, and procedures that are supposed to "link" Americans to their government and thus make the political system democratic.

Selections in this unit address parties, elections, nominations, voters, interest groups, political movements, media, and the role of money in campaigns, elections, and governing. Recent changes that may affect American politics for years to come are a major focus.

One noteworthy development in the past few decades has been growing polarization between the two major parties. Republican and Democratic members of Congress have become significantly more likely to vote with their own party in opposition to the other party, and party-line voting has become the norm on Capitol Hill. Some decry this increase in partisanship, while others think that sharper and more consistent policy differences between Democratic and Republican officeholders will make American elections more consequential.

Incumbents' advantages in winning re-election to both the Senate and especially the House of Representatives have grown in recent years. Incumbency advantages—including the way House districts are drawn, name recognition, and easier access to campaign contributions—are likely to remain a concern for those who would like to reform the democratic process in the United States.

Besides built-in advantages for incumbents, the American electoral system suffers from all sorts of other shortcomings. Many of these problems became apparent during the Florida centered controversy in the 2000 presidential election, after which reform measures were enacted in both Congress and many states. Despite some apparent improvements in the way elections are conducted in the American political system,

many peculiarities in the electoral system remain, and they are addressed in various selections in this unit.

Campaign financing became a widespread concern after the 1972 presidential election. Major campaign finance reform laws enacted in 1974 and 2002 (the latter is known as the McCain-Feingold Act) were designed to regulate the influence of campaign contributions in elections and governing, but they have met, at best, with only partial success. The history of campaign finance laws is intertwined with a handful of Supreme Court decisions that have ruled key components of the laws unconstitutional. In its controversial 5-4 ruling in *Citizens United v. Federal Election Commission* in January 2010, the Supreme Court voided a central element in the McCain-Feingold Act that restricted corporate and labor union spending in connection with election campaigns. As a consequence, the 2010 mid-term congressional elections and the 2012 presidential and congressional elections were held under a new set of ground rules. An estimated total of $6 billion dollars was spent in 2012 American election campaigns.

The fundamental challenge of reconciling free speech, freedom of individuals to spend money as they wish, and the fairness of elections remains. In the summer of 2007, Barack Obama publicly pledged to accept public financing—which is accompanied by the requirement that a candidate use only the funds provided by the government—if he or she became his or her party's presidential nominee. A year later, Obama changed his mind and became the first presidential candidate to decline public financing for his general election campaign because such funding first became available in 1976. Obama made this decision after campaign aides told him that he could raise more than three times as much money from supporters as the sum provided through public financing. Consistent with his aides' prediction, Democratic candidate Obama raised and spent more than three times as much money as his 2008 general election opponent, Republican John McCain, who accepted public financing *and* the accompanying spending limit. A noteworthy irony was that Democrats have generally been stronger proponents of campaign finance regulation and public financing than Republicans, notwithstanding McCain's longstanding leadership in reform efforts.

During the 2012 election cycle, Obama supporters were initially reported to be reluctant to take advantage of *Citizens United*'s lessened restrictions on some kinds of election-related spending. But that reported self-restraint disappeared in the presidential campaign's competitive home-stretch. Once again, individuals and organizations supporting Obama—not to mention Obama himself, who has been a critic of the ways that American election campaigns are financed—might be said to have chosen expediency over principle and helped their preferred candidate to win. In 2012, the Obama and Romney presidential campaigns each raised and spent about $1 billion.

A number of selections in this unit address how media—old and new—shape political communication and political behavior in the American political system. Television, radio, Internet sources, and newspapers are not merely passive transmitters of information. They inevitably shape—or distort—what they report to their audiences and greatly affect the behavior of people and organizations in politics.

In 2008, Barack Obama's campaign organization worked to perfect some of the Internet fundraising techniques pioneered in 2004 by Howard Dean's ultimately unsuccessful campaign for the Democratic presidential nomination. Obama's remarkable run for the presidency included his outspending and beating Democratic rival Hillary Clinton, who herself raised and spent more money on her nomination campaign than any other candidate up to that point—*except* Obama. Obama's record-setting performance that year stemmed mostly from unprecedentedly successful online fundraising, which relied, of course, on a medium that was essentially unknown to the general public a quarter-century earlier.

The Internet and social media played increasingly important roles in election campaigns in 2012 and 2014. Online fundraising, "viral" communications among interested activists, sophisticated efforts to get out the vote on Election Day, "micro-targeting" of campaign appeals, and the like were all made possible by technology that was virtually unthinkable a few decades ago.

Article   Prepared by: Bruce Stinebrickner, *DePauw University*

Parallel Universes

As demographics have tilted the presidency to Democrats, geography has tightened the GOP's grip on the House.

DAVID WASSERMAN

Learning Outcomes

After reading this article, you will be able to:

- Understand how demography, geography, and the electoral systems used to select presidents, senators, and members of the House of Representatives combine to create the "parallel universes" that the author addresses.

- Put into perspective the continuing likelihood that Democrats will, on average, fare well in presidential elections while Republicans will generally be the favorites to maintain majority control of the House of Representatives.

Three days after the election, an e-mail arrived in my inbox from a veteran Democratic media consultant who cut many an ad for the more conservative elements of his party. Like other armchair pundits, he marveled at the ease of President Obama's reelection and Democrats' against-the-odds pickups in the Senate but couldn't fathom how they could have simultaneously "blown it" in the House. In particular, he took issue with the assertion that House Democrats and party strategists deserved credit, not condemnation, for "beating the point spread" by picking up eight House seats, even though they fell 17 seats short of a majority.

"A friendly disagreement" about the Democratic Congressional Campaign Committee, he wrote. "After record losses two years ago, we entered this campaign with the smallest caucus of a generation. With the [Senate Democrats] and Obama bucking headwinds and succeeding, the DCCC simply failed. The Blue Dogs have gone from once 45 to about a dozen. . . . And the DCCC spinning success unfortunately proves their vision of success will mire my party in minority status for a long time."

The Republicans, of course, viewed the outcome in even more merciless terms. The following week, when Democratic Leader Nancy Pelosi announced she would stay in her post despite Democrats' continued minority status, the National Republican Congressional Committee crowed to reporters in an e-mail release, "There is no better person to preside over the most liberal House Democratic Caucus in history than the woman who is solely responsible for relegating it to a prolonged minority status."

But in blaming the DCCC or Pelosi for Democrats' predicament in the House, both the Democratic ad man and the GOP spin machine demonstrated classic historical nearsightedness. To cast House Democrats as suddenly feeble, incompetent, insular Bad News Bears is to overlook a tectonic shift in the structure of the electorate that was decades in the making and culminated in 2012's emphatically indecisive "split mandate."

Democrats' coalition may now occupy the inside track to the White House, but the GOP seems to have a hammerlock on the House for years to come. It's a remarkable inversion. Between 1968 and 2008, Republicans controlled the White House for 28 of 40 years, and Democrats controlled the House for 28 of 40 years.

The South accounted for much of the "old" divide. Dixie started voting markedly more Republican at the presidential level in 1968, and the only two Democrats to crack the GOP's grip on the White House over the next 40 years were Southerners. But the shift took much longer in the House, where Democrats hung onto a majority of Southern seats until 1994.

In 2008, the election of the first non-Southern Democrat to the White House since John F. Kennedy in 1960 signaled a new generation of political leadership. However, something more subtle and just as consequential has also taken place. A perfect synthesis of demography and geography—a long time coming but hastened by the rise of Obama's coalition—has helped turn the old "default" party advantages upside down.

Welcome, then, to the new normal. A growing coalition of young, nonwhite, and college-educated voters is now sufficiently large to allow Democrats to win statewide elections, and, conveniently for their party, America votes for both the White House and the Senate on a statewide basis.

But, just as conveniently for Republicans, this same coalition is way too clustered in too few congressional districts to allow Democrats to win the House in the absence of a huge anti-GOP wave, the likes of which we saw in 2006 and 2008 when voters took out their anger on an unpopular Republican president.

Staggeringly, Obama won reelection with 62 percent of Electoral College votes by winning just 22 percent of the 3,100-plus counties nationwide. Without his huge margins generated from minority and young voters in just three counties—Broward Country, Fla., Cuyahoga County, Ohio, and Philadelphia County, Pa.—Obama would have actually lost those three states and, with them, the Electoral College. Partly as a consequence of this urban concentration, House Democrats were left stranded with just 31 percent of seats in these states, even as Obama walked away with 100 percent of their electoral votes.

The Blue and the Gray

In their 2002 book *The Emerging Democratic Majority,* political scientists John Judis and Ruy Teixeira shined a spotlight on Democrats' burgeoning edge in "ideolopolises," postindustrial metropolitan regions, typically anchored by large research universities and surging high-tech sectors, that had become magnets for a young, diverse, and well-educated professional class with bohemian values.

Describing these centers as the "breeding ground" for a new Democratic majority, Judis and Teixeira predicted, "Democrats could enjoy by 2008 a state-by-state advantage of 332 electoral votes, well more than they need for a majority." The prediction, celebrated when Obama won 365 electoral votes in 2008 but questioned when Republicans wrested control of the House in 2010, saw vindication when the very coalition the authors envisioned propelled Obama to reelection with exactly 332 electoral votes in November.

This demographic realignment has been taking shape for a long time. In 1980, Ronald Reagan won 56 percent of white voters on his way to defeating Democratic incumbent Jimmy Carter by 10 percentage points, 51 percent to 41 percent. In 2012, GOP nominee Mitt Romney took 59 percent of white voters, yet lost by 4 points, 47 percent to 51 percent. It's obvious what changed: In 1980, white voters were 88 percent of the electorate; by 2012, they had fallen to just 72 percent of the electorate.

	Landslide county voters	Non-landslide county voters
'92	38.6%	61.4%
'96	42.3	57.7
'00	45.3	54.7
'04	48.3	51.7
'08	48.4	51.6
'12	50.1	49.9

Pulling Apart
A slim majority of voters now live in counties that gave either presidential nominee at least 60 percent of the vote, an 11 percentage point rise over the last 20 years.

Simply put, the Democrats' coalition is still in the midst of a growth spurt, while the Republicans' alliance continues to atrophy. In 1992, national exit polls showed that African-Americans were 8 percent of all voters and gave Democratic nominee Bill Clinton 83 percent of their votes; Latinos were just 2 percent of all voters and gave Clinton 61 percent of their support. In 2012, African-Americans were 13 percent of the electorate and gave Obama 93 percent of their vote, while Latinos ballooned to 10 percent of all voters and gave Obama 71 percent.

The yawning holes in the GOP's future aren't just race-related; huge age and educational gaps may be even more worrisome. Unlike Clinton's consistent performance across the electorate in 1992, Obama's support among different age groups in 2012 was a sliding scale. He won 18-to-29-year-old voters by 60 percent to 37 percent and 30-to-39-year-olds by 55 percent to 42 percent, but he lost 40-to-49-year-olds by 2 percentage points, 50-to-64-year-olds by 5 points, and 65-plus voters by 12 points. In contrast to Clinton, Obama performed 6 points better among the surging share of college-educated whites than he did with the shrinking ranks of whites without college degrees.

Just as menacing to the GOP as the obvious pitfalls of relying on an electoral base in the twilight of life, data show that political attachments formed early in life are quite durable. A 2006 Pew Research Center study found that the two strongest Republican age cohorts were voters who had entered the electorate during the presidencies of Dwight Eisenhower and Reagan. As these voters exit the electorate over the next 40 years, the impact of a "lost generation" for the GOP, consisting of highly educated voters who came of age during the unpopular George W. Bush presidency and the rise of Obama, poses obvious and daunting long-term challenges for the party's efforts to win a national election.

Sorting It Out

In 2008, observing an increasingly transient and politically polarized society, Texas journalist Bill Bishop wrote in *The Big Sort* that "the country may be more diverse than ever from coast to coast" but is "filled with people who live alike, think alike, and vote alike. . . . Pockets of like-minded citizens have become so ideologically inbred that we don't know, can't understand, and can barely conceive of 'those people' who live just a few miles away." Bishop adds, "As some 10 million Americans moved each year from one county to another, counties clearly were growing less competitive and more politically segregated."

How the changing America votes may showcase stark divides, but *where* it votes is even more striking and proves Bishop prophetic. At the same time that surges of African-Americans, Latinos, twentysomethings, and college-educated whites in urban "ideopolises" have propelled Democrats to victory in consecutive elections in formerly Republican bastions such as Colorado, Florida, and Virginia, there's another side of the coin: Democrats have never been so demoralized in older, whiter rural America, and the Democratic base has never been so concentrated in its predominantly urban strongholds.

Consider that in 1988, losing Democratic nominee Michael Dukakis carried 819 of the more than 3,100 U.S. counties. He won 75 percent of the vote in the ancestrally Scots-Irish coalfields of Knott County, Ky.; 62 percent in the West Texas Panhandle's cotton fields of Dickens County; and 56 percent in the traditionally Cajun oil and gas fields of tiny Cameron Parish, La. He also won just 31 percent of the vote in central Florida's swampy Osceola County; 34 percent in suburban Atlanta's Clayton County; and 49 percent in flinty Washington County, encompassing Vermont's capital of Montpelier.

Fast-forward to 2012, and winning Democratic nominee Barack Obama carried just 690 counties, 129 fewer than Dukakis. He won only 26 percent of the vote in Knott County, 21 percent in Dickens County, and a startling 11 percent in Cameron Parish. But thanks to a booming Puerto Rican population fueled by Orlando's hospitality sector, Obama won Osceola County with 62 percent of the vote. A rapid migration of affluent African-Americans into Atlanta's southern suburbs helped Obama to 85 percent in Clayton County and he carried Washington County, home to the main ice-cream factory of prototypical liberal New York emigrants Ben Cohen and Jerry Greenfield, with 72 percent.

The urbanization and geopolitical polarization of the country has been gradual yet astonishing. In 1988, about 35 percent of all voters lived in the 819 counties that Dukakis carried; in 2012, about 57 percent of all voters lived in the 690 counties that Obama won. In 1992, while Clinton captured the White House by more than 5 points, only 39 percent of voters lived in "landslide counties"—places that gave either nominee more than 60 percent of the two-party vote. In 2012, for the first time since the nationwide Reagan landslide of 1984, a slim majority of voters lived in landslide counties, even though Obama won reelection by less than 4 percentage points.

Democrats' increasing focus and reliance at the top of the ticket on tight clusters of minority, young, and college-educated voters has created an unprecedented down-ballot conundrum. To begin with, Democrats are so much more concentrated on the map than Republicans that they are "wasting" votes in safe, minority-majority congressional districts, many of which are mandated by the Voting Rights Act. But their magnetic cultural attraction to overwhelmingly liberal enclaves such as Austin, Texas, and Madison, Wis., has led them into a trap: They've become easier to pack into safe seats, while surrounding areas shed Democratic voters.

In 2010, when the Democratic "surge vote" vanished and Republicans swept elections at every level, the GOP earned the right to draw congressional boundaries following the 2010 census in four times as many districts as the Democrats controlled. As a result, in 2012, when many surge voters reentered the fold, House Democrats won about 1.5 million more votes nationwide than Republicans, yet captured only 201 of 435 seats. Republicans

won a higher share of districts than their share of the vote in 32 of 50 states: Notably, they won only 49 percent of the total House vote in both North Carolina and Pennsylvania, yet won nine of 13 seats in North Carolina and 13 of 18 in Pennsylvania. Nationally, Romney carried a slim majority of congressional districts.

By purging Democrats and minorities from their own districts and into Democratic quarantine zones, Republicans may have drawn themselves into a durable House majority. But they have also drawn themselves into an alternate universe of voters that little resembles the growing diversity of the country. When the next Congress commences in January, 88 percent of House Republicans will be white males (versus just 47 percent of House Democrats), and very few will have been elected from competitive districts where there is any incentive to reach across the aisle.

In fact, an entrenched GOP House may indefinitely reinforce the image problems plaguing the party in statewide elections for the White House and the Senate. In "governing from the minority" and refusing to cooperate, Republicans risk further alienating voters—a potentially self-perpetuating cycle.

Boom and Bust

The two parties' polar-opposite profiles don't just manifest themselves in the divides between urban and rural, and between the Capitol and 1600 Pennsylvania Avenue. They also play out on the electoral calendar. We may be entering a boom-and-bust period where Democrats' coalition of younger and minority voters who are newer to the electoral process is much more likely to turn out in force in presidential elections. The GOP's more reliable, time-tested coalition of older and whiter voters tends, on the other hand, to surge as a share of the electorate in midterm years. These alternating electorates, rather than changing minds, portend continued volatility in the years to come.

Will this pattern be ironclad over the next 40 years? Of course not. Voter fatigue after eight years of Obama may allow Republicans to win the White House in 2016, and a strong backlash against a Republican president on the part of independent voters may allow Democrats to win the lower chamber sooner or later.

But in the new electoral normal, split control, dizzying partisan swings, and gridlocked negotiations between Democratic presidents and GOP House speakers may be the rule rather than the exception. Demography and geography, more so than policy and personality, may be destiny.

Critical Thinking

1. Why are Democrat candidates advantaged in presidential and state-wide elections at the same time that Republicans

have an advantage with respect to the U.S. House of Representatives?

2. What explains the following percentages? In 2012 Obama won 62% of the Electoral College votes and only 22% of the more than 3,100 counties in the country.

3. How could Democrats win 50.5% of votes for House candidates in 2012 and yet win only 46.2% of House seats?

Create Central

www.mhhe.com/createcentral

Internet References

United States Elections Project
www.elections.gmu.edu

Real Clear Politics
www.realclearpolitics.com

FiveThirtyEight
http://fivethirtyeight.blogs.nytimes.com

Article Prepared by: Bruce Stinebrickner, *DePauw University*

How Politics Breaks Our Brains, and How We Can Put Them Back Together

We're partisans by nature, and once we pick a side we see the world in red or blue.

BRIAN RESNICK

Learning Outcomes

After reading this article, you will be able to:

- Understand from an evolutionary perspective why partisanship is so prevalent in politics.

- Consider the role of "dehumanization" in interactions among people and, by extension, nation-states.

I'm lying in the metal coffin of an MRI machine, listening to what sounds like jackhammers and smelling my own breath go stale. My head is secured in place. I have a panic button. I won't press it, but I do grip it tightly. Above me, faces flash on a screen.

Some are human, others are dolls, and some are digitally blended to be something in between. It's my job to figure out which are which. And as I do, researchers at New York University's brain-imaging center are tracking what goes on in my head.

I'm not sick, and we're not here to test my calm in the face of claustrophobia. Instead, I'm a subject for research on a bigger question: Is the human political brain broken?

The NYU team is trying to show that our brains are hardwired for partisanship and how that skews our perceptions in public life. Research at NYU and elsewhere is underscoring just how blind the "us-versus-them" mind-set can make people when they try to process new political information. Once this partisanship mentality kicks in, the brain almost automatically pre-filters facts—even noncontroversial ones—that offend our political sensibilities.

"Once you trip this wire, this trigger, this cue, that you are a part of 'us-versus-them,' it's almost like the whole brain becomes re-coordinated in how it views people," says Jay Van Bavel, the leader of NYU's Social Perception and Evaluation Lab.

Our tendency toward partisanship is likely the result of evolution—forming groups is how prehistoric humans survived. That's helpful when trying to master an unforgiving environment with Stone Age technology. It's less so when trying to foster a functional democracy.

Understanding the other side's point of view, even if one disagrees with it, is central to compromise, policymaking, and any hope for civility in civic life. So if our brains are blinding us to information that challenges our partisan predisposition, how can we hope ever to find common ground? It's a challenge that is stumping both the electorate and the elected officials who represent them. Congressional hearings are hearings in name only—opportunities for politicians to grandstand rather than talk with each other. And the political discussion, even among those well versed in the issues, largely exists in parallel red and blue universes, mental spheres with few or no common facts to serve as starting points.

But rather than despair, many political-psychology researchers see their results as reason for hope, and they raise a tantalizing prospect: With enough understanding of what exactly makes us so vulnerable to partisanship, can we reshape our political environment to access the better angels of our neurological nature?

What does any of this have to do with photos of dolls? The researchers are testing one of partisanship's more frightening features: It allows us, even pushes us, to dehumanize those we categorize as "them."

I'm tasked with distinguishing humans from nonhumans, and it's not as easy as it sounds. While some of the faces appear to be normal photographs of men and women, others are warped into something that would have scared me as a child—faces that look like masks. They have no creases in their plasticky skin, and their big, anime-style eyes shine death stares. They are distinctly nonhuman. It's the ones in between that pose the problem, however. A face that's 90 percent human and 10 percent doll is plainly seen as human. But when the face is 50 percent doll and 50 percent human, that's where partisan perspective takes over.

For the first trial I am just shown a set of faces, but for the next run, Van Bavel introduces a twist: The faces are divided into two groups. Before I see the first group, the American flag flashes, and I'm told I'm looking at my countrymen. Before the second, a Russian flag appears. These are faces of Russians.

As I try to assess which faces have a soul behind them, a dark facet of partisan psychology surfaces. If the face belongs to a team member—in my case, an American—I'm more likely to assign them humanity. I'm less inclined to do the same for Russians.

It's not entirely my fault—or, at least, not the fault of any conscious decisions. Instead, it's just my brain process following a well-worn pattern. When Van Bavel looks at the brain scans of people in his dollhouse experiment, he finds that the brain regions used to empathize with others aren't as active when a person is evaluating faces he or she has been told belong to the other team.

Humans' willingness to dehumanize is often mentioned alongside some of the darkest chapters of history—the Holocaust, genocide in Rwanda, the Khmer Rouge—when regimes went to great lengths to build anger against "the other." In my case, the experiment relies on a national identity reinforced since birth.

But to create the base "us and them" structure, none of that is needed. The brain is so hardwired to build such groups that Van Bavel says he can turn anyone on the street into a partisan. "I can do it in five minutes with a random stranger," he says. All it takes is a coin flip.

"Somebody comes into your lab and you tell them, 'You're part of the blue team,'" he explains. "The next person who comes in, you flip a coin, let's say it comes up the other way. And you say, 'You're on the red team.'"

That's it. The teammates never have to meet. Or interact. There doesn't need to be anything at stake. But within minutes, these insta-partisans like their teammates better than they like the other guys. And it shows when Van Bavel puts his subjects through his MRI dollhouse.

Red-team members are more likely to see humans when they're told they're looking at fellow red-team faces. Blue-team members respond the same way. Other tests reveal that red-team members remember red-team faces more accurately, and if Van Bavel asks subjects to allocate money, red-team members will pay out more to their own. Team members also have less sympathy for those on the other side, and even experience pleasure while reading about their pain.

I'm not just inside the MRI to be stumped by Russian dolls. The researchers are also checking to see if my brain has a conservative or liberal shape.

In 2011, a team of British scientists published a paper that found that brain structures correlated with political orientation. Specifically, conservatives tended to have larger amygdala areas—brain matter that plays a role in fear conditioning—than liberals. The results added to a body of research that finds conservatives and liberals have different physiological responses to the environment, and even perceive the world differently.

At NYU, they're testing that conclusion, and the magnets around me are measuring the volume of my amygdala. Before my MRI, I took a test aimed at giving me a score on the researchers' "system-justification scale," a measure that correlates with one component of where a person falls on the liberal-to-conservative spectrum. People who score high on system justification tend to be patriotic and defenders of the status quo. Those who score low tend to be the rebels. So far, with 100 participants, Van Bavel's group is finding meaningful differences between the brains of high system-justifiers and low system-justifiers.

(Colleagues joked that I might want to keep my test results to myself if I wanted to continue working as a nonpartisan journalist in Washington. But—for the record—I'm a lab-certified moderate: "Yeah, you were right in the heart of the distribution, not only in the terms of your system-justification tendencies but also your amygdala volume is very healthy," Van Bavel tells me the day after, laughing.)

But when it comes to American politics, how troubled should we be by any of these findings? America's partisan divide is as old as America's democracy. And it's neither feasible nor desirable to hope for a national consensus on every issue. Even if we all worked from the same set of facts, and even if we all understood those facts perfectly, differences of opinion would—and should—remain. Those opinions are not the problem. The trouble is when we're so blinded by our partisanship that it overrides reason—and research suggests that is happening all the time.

With just a hint of partisan priming, an Arizona State University researcher was able to instantly blind Democrats to a noncontroversial fact, leading them immediately to fail to solve the easiest of math problems. In the 2010 experiment, political scientist Mark Ramirez asked subjects two similar questions. The control group saw this question: "Would you say that compared to 2008, the level of unemployment in this country has gotten better, stayed the same, or gotten worse?" A separate group saw this one: "Would you say that the level of unemployment in this country has gotten better, stayed the same, or gotten worse since Barack Obama was elected President?"

The key difference between the two: the first mentions the time period for assessing unemployment, while the second frames the issue around President Obama. When asked the first question, Democrats and Republicans responded similarly, with most saying unemployment had remained about the same. But among subjects who got the second question, opinions shifted along partisan lines: Around 60 percent of Democrats said unemployment had gotten better or somewhat better, and about 75 percent of Republicans said the opposite.

In fact, the unemployment rate increased between Obama's election and Ramirez's study. One can argue about whether this is a fair frame for evaluating this or any president's economic record, but from a raw-numbers perspective, the rise in the unemployment rate between 2008 and 2010 is indisputable.

But even giving Democrats that information did not increase the accuracy of their responses. Ramirez's study asked some participants the following question: "The U.S. Bureau of Labor Statistics shows unemployment has increased by 4.6 percent since 2008. Would you say that the level of unemployment in this country has gotten better, stayed the same, or gotten worse since Barack Obama was elected President?"

Clearly, the answer is in the sentence that immediately precedes the question. But the mention of Obama launched a partisan mental process that led many astray: Nearly 60 percent of Democrats said unemployment had lessened since Obama's election.

Essentially, once Democrats focused on Obama, most of them largely ignored the facts. (About 80 percent of Republicans got the answer right when it was spoon-fed to them, but Republicans tempted to cry victory should be cautioned that researchers have found them to be similarly off base in assessing the economy when one of their own is in the Oval Office.)

Ramirez's experiment also reveals that our biases don't completely blind us to information, however. When he gave Democrats the correct unemployment statistics, it did not change their answers, but it did make them less confident in those responses, as reported in a post-test questionnaire. "It tells me that people might actually be processing the information in an unbiased way," Ramirez says.

The question, then, is how to amplify that unbiased processing to overcome the partisan blindness.

Brendan Nyhan knows just how hard it is to move that mental needle.

"I had the dream of, if we give people the right information, it'll make a difference," says Nyhan, a political scientist at Dartmouth and contributor to *The New York Times's* The Upshot.

But after 15 years of throwing facts in people's faces, Nyhan has found the matter to be much more complicated. In the early 2000s, he cofounded the fact-checking website *Spinsanity* to combat the "he said, she said" coverage he saw in the media. "I'm very proud of the work we did, but it did illustrate how hard it was to change people's minds, even among the select group of people who were willing to take the time to read a nonpartisan fact-checking website," Nyhan said.

More recently, Nyhan attempted to debunk an argument that is growing in popularity but utterly lacking in scientific support: that parents shouldn't have their children vaccinated.

Nyhan and his collaborators wanted to convince parents who were against vaccinations that their opposition was unfounded. Working with a large sample of 1,759 parents, the team sent them a variety of material, including pamphlets that explained the lack of evidence linking vaccinations with autism, explanations of the dangers of measles, photos of sick children whose diseases could have been prevented, and a story about an infant who almost died from infection. Some were appeals to pure reason; some were appeals to pure emotion.

Nothing worked. One of the interventions—the pamphlet explaining the lack of evidence—actually made anti-vaccination parents even less inclined to vaccinate. "Some of the conclusions of that research people find pretty depressing," Nyhan says. "Myself included."

In another study, Nyhan wanted to see if he could find a real-world way to press actual politicians to be better handlers of the facts. In the months leading up to the 2012 election, Nyhan and coauthor Jason Reifler performed an experiment on 1,169 unwitting state legislators. They wanted to see if fact checks could motivate the politicians to be more truthful. A third of the legislators received a letter that contained a veiled threat. It read: "Politicians who lie put their reputations and careers at risk, but only when those lies are exposed." The letter then reminded the politicians that PolitiFact, a fact-checking group, operated in their state. The letter clearly implied, "PolitiFact will be watching you." Another third of the lawmakers received a letter that excluded references to fact checking. The last third received no letter.

Throughout the election cycle, Nyhan and Reifler logged the politicians' PolitiFact ratings (from "true" to "pants on fire"). They also had a research assistant comb through the media coverage of each legislator, searching for critical stories. The results, pending publication in the *American Journal of Political Science,* were limited but promising. Overall, only a very few legislators—27 out of 1,169—were called out on lies. But of those 27, only five had received the threatening letter—less than a third. That's reason enough to research the idea further. "This study was a first step," Nyhan says.

One way to help people look past their innate partisanship? Pay them to do it.

"Human psychology isn't going to change," he says. "The factors that make people vulnerable to misinformation aren't going to change. But the incentives facing elites can change, and we can design institutions that function better or worse under polarization and that do a better or worse job at providing incentives to make accurate statements."

There's an easier way to help people look past their innate partisanship: Pay them to do it.

A 2013 study out of Princeton found that monetary incentives attenuate the partisan gap in answers to questions about the economy. The researchers designed an experiment similar to Ramirez's unemployment study but with a modification: Some participants were plainly informed, "We will pay you for answering correctly." All it took was $1 or $2 to dramatically improve the chances of a right answer, cutting the partisan gap between Republicans and Democrats in half—half!

Of course, a mass "pay Americans to pay more attention to facts" campaign isn't happening. So the question, then, is how do we get people to be more objective, without throwing money at them?

Jimmy Carter discovered one answer during the 1978 peace negotiations between Egyptian President Anwar Sadat and Israeli Prime Minister Menachem Begin. The talks were on the brink of collapsing in their final hours, and the prime minister was prepared to walk. That's when Carter directed his secretary to find out all the names of Begin's grandchildren. Carter autographed photos for them and personally gave them to the Israeli leader. "He had taken a blood oath that he would never dismantle an Israeli settlement," Carter later recalled in an interview. "He looked at those eight photographs and tears began to run down his cheeks—and mine—as he read the names."

A few minutes later, Begin was back at the negotiating table. By appealing to a nonpolitical idea Begin cared about—his family—Carter was able to bring him to a place where he could bend.

The technique works even when world peace isn't on the line. Kevin Binning, a University of Pittsburgh psychologist, used it to reshape the way partisans reacted to a 2008 presidential debate.

Just two days before the election, Binning assembled 110 self-identified Republicans and Democrats—60 Rs and 50

Ds—to watch a recording of a recent debate between Obama and Republican nominee John McCain. Before they viewed the debate, however, one group of participants was given a list of nonpolitical values such as "social skills" and "creativity," and then asked to write briefly about an instance when their own behavior had embodied one of those values. (The other group also wrote about nonpolitical values, but they were asked to write about how those might be important to other people, not about their personal experiences.)

By having one group write about nonpolitical experiences, Binning wanted to get participants thinking of themselves as individuals rather than partisans. The idea was that affirming the human identity would make people feel more receptive to ideas that didn't align with their worldview.

It worked. When Binning asked the participants to judge the candidates' performances, members of that group were more likely than those in the other to give a favorable rating to the opposition candidate.

"It's not like all of a sudden I say, 'Well, yeah, McCain actually won the debate,'" he explains, "but we might say, 'Well, yeah, Obama, I think he did have some good points, but McCain may have had some other good points as well. I don't need to just blindly embrace Obama.'"

Which seems like the ideal way to converse about politics, right? And it wasn't a one-time effect. Ten days after the election, Binning asked the Republicans in the group what type of president they thought Obama would be. Those who had been part of the group that wrote personally about nonpolitical values before watching the debate were significantly more optimistic about the Obama presidency.

So how might we persuade people to set aside their blind partisanship in other contexts? Let's start with a forum in which the stakes are infinitely lower than at the Middle East peace talks but where the partisan vitriol runs every bit as high: Internet comment sections.

Comment sections bring out the worst in partisan thinking: ad hominem attacks, people who clearly will not be convinced of the other side, and stubborn arguments where users talk past one another, not with each other. But maybe the structure of comment sections, rather than the people doing the commenting, has turned them into such intellectual sewers—and maybe a tweak or two at the margins could clean them up.

"You can think of comment sections as mini-institutions," Nyhan says. "It's a context in which debate is happening, and if we can help people be more civil toward each other, that might be a positive step."

Talia Stroud is trying to take that step. As the director of the Engaging News project at the University of Texas (Austin), she leads a research group with the goal of making the Internet more civil for politics. "It's unbelievably difficult," she says.

One way to start, her research suggests, is to reevaluate the "like" button, a common feature on comment threads. In the context of a political-news article, "liking" a comment or a post could activate us-versus-them thinking. "Liking" something means you associate with it. It reminds people of their partisanship. "So we did a study where we manipulated whether it was a 'like' button or a 'respect' button," Stroud says. She found that people were more willing to express "respect" for arguments that ran counter to their own.

It's "not 'I like what you're saying' but 'I respect it' even though I might not agree with you," she says. "That showed some of the power of really small things and changes that could be easily implemented."

A Month of speaking to scientists about the political brain produced no shortage of depressing conclusions. Their research reveals our brains to be frustratingly inept at rational, objective political discourse. And those revelations come at a time when elected officials have strong incentives to stay the partisan course, and when the people who elect those officials are increasingly getting their political news through sources pre-tailored to reinforce their opinions.

But the research is more than just another explanation for our current partisan morass. On balance, it offers a better case for optimism—about Congress, about voters, about your outspoken extremist uncle at Thanksgiving, and about the power of reason in democracy. Because the research is also revealing that our brains, while imperfect, are surprisingly flexible, and that they can be nudged in a better direction. Yes, we wall ourselves off from unappealing truths. But when motivated—by money, by the right environment, by an affirmed sense of self, by institutions that value truth and civility—those walls come down.

Outside of the laboratory, people are putting that research into practice, developing civic forums with our mental shortcomings in mind.

After a dispute over a coal plant divided Tallahassee, Florida, into furiously partisan camps, Allan Katz, then a city commissioner, decided he had enough. "It was very nasty, it was very contentious, it was very personal," Katz recalls of the 2006 debates. "Facts didn't matter."

Katz, who is also a former U.S. ambassador to Portugal, joined with other community members to create the Village Square, which hosts events where the public is invited to discuss ongoing issues with experts and activists. Incivility and non-truths are not tolerated. During debates, the Village Square employs fact checkers to keep people in line. "So people couldn't make s—t up," Katz says. There's also a civility bell: If people start yelling, the bell is rung to remind them of their better nature.

For the first meeting, 175 people showed up. Now the Village Square is running 20 programs a year in Tallahassee, and it has expanded into St. Petersburg, Kansas City, and Sacramento.

In Tallahassee, city officials ask the Village Square to host public forums on divisive issues.

When people consider themselves to be part of the same team, they do a much better job of dropping their combative stance and processing the world through a less partisan lens.

"You're not trying to turn liberals into conservatives or vice versa," Katz says. "But the only way to get people to see the other point of view, even if they don't agree with it, is to do it in person."

Katz and his fellow organizers are relying on people finding a common humanity, and in so doing, he is playing to one of the brain's great strengths: The same tribal cognitive processes that make it easy to turn people against one another can also be harnessed to bring them together.

When people consider themselves to be part of the same team, be it as Village Square participants, as fellow Americans, or even—one might dream—as fellow members of Congress, they do a much better job of dropping their combative stance and processing the world through a less partisan lens.

And we make those identity jumps all the time, as our brains are wired to let us do.

Sometimes, in the middle of his red team/blue team exercise, Van Bavel will switch a participant from one group to the other. "We say, 'Listen, there's been a mistake, you're actually on the other team,'" he says. "And the moment we do, we completely reverse their empathy. Suddenly, they care about everybody who is in their new in-group."

Suddenly, they see the other side.

Critical Thinking

1. What does it mean to say that human brains are "hardwired for partisanship"?

2. Describe two experiments that show the hard-wired partisanship in human brains.

3. Suggest some experiments in which researchers attempted to counteract or overcome the strong inclination toward partisanship in human beings.

Internet References

Rawzen.org
http://www.rawzen.org/?p=110

Science: How Stuff Works
http://science.howstuffworks.com/life/inside-the-mind/human-brain/brain8.htm

Article
Prepared by: Bruce Stinebrickner, *DePauw University*

Six Myths about Campaign Money

The Supreme Court's ruling in *Citizens United* has spawned arguments that oversimplify money's real role in politics.

ELIZA NEWLIN CARNEY

Learning Outcomes

After reading this article, you will be able to:

- Understand why various myths about campaign financing contain seeds of truth but are nevertheless misleading.

- Assess whether the *Citizens United* ruling by the United States Supreme Court was as significant as many observers seem to believe.

W hen the Supreme Court decided in January to toss out the decades-old ban on direct corporate and union campaign spending, U.S. politics changed overnight. In *Citizens United v. Federal Election Commission,* the high court ruled 5–4 that unions and corporations could spend money from their vast treasuries on campaigns. The decision applies to for-profit and nonprofit corporations alike, scrambling the deck for political players of all stripes.

The ruling also intensified the never-ending political money wars: Democrats have fought in vain to push through a broad new disclosure bill, and Republicans have renewed their systematic legal assault on the remaining campaign finance laws. The Court, in a deregulatory mood, appears eager to dismantle the rules still further. At the same time, voters are unusually engaged in the campaign finance debate.

It's a critical turning point in the world of election law, but advocates fighting over free speech versus corruption remain as polarized as ever. Both sides trot out arguments that oversimplify money's real role in politics and make it harder to identify solutions and common ground. Each of the following six myths contains a grain of truth but papers over important nuances. Inevitably, regulating democracy is messy and complicated. The solution rarely can be reduced to a sound bite; there often is no silver bullet.

Corporate Money Will Now Overwhelm Elections

President Obama has been among those sounding the alarm that corporations, in the wake of *Citizens United,* will swamp campaigns with private money.

"This ruling opens the floodgates for an unlimited amount of special-interest money into our democracy," Obama declared in his weekly radio address shortly after the ruling. "It gives the special-interest lobbyists new leverage to spend millions on advertising to persuade elected officials to vote their way, or to punish those who don't."

Reform advocates toss around big numbers and dire warnings. They point to ExxonMobil's $85 billion in profits in 2008 and note that if the company spent just 10 percent of that on politics, the outlay would be $8.5 billion. That's three times more than the combined spending of the Obama and McCain presidential campaigns and every single House and Senate candidate in that election.

So far, however, no such corporate spending tsunami has materialized. If anything, labor unions have jumped in more quickly to exploit the new rules, dumping millions of dollars into Arkansas's Democratic Senate primary and other high-profile races this year. One reason may be that, unlike corporate executives, union leaders don't risk offending shareholders and customers if they openly bankroll candidates.

Actually, neither unions nor corporations will shift vast new resources into campaigns, some political scientists argue. The reason? These players could spend any of their money on politics, through issue advertising, even before the *Citizens United* ruling. Their one constraint was that they had to avoid explicit campaign messages, such as "vote for" or "vote against." The high court's ruling will make such issue advocacy less common because corporate and labor leaders are free to pay for unvarnished campaign endorsements and attacks.

"I don't think you're suddenly going to find 1 percent of corporate gross expenditures moving into politics, largely because there were so many ways to spend that money before," says Michael J. Malbin, executive director of the nonpartisan Campaign Finance Institute. Even before the ruling, about half of the states permitted direct corporate and union campaign expenditures—yet that money didn't appear to overwhelm state races.

To be sure, corporate campaign spending often flies below the radar, in both state and federal elections. Corporations tend to funnel their money through trade associations and front groups, making it hard to trace. New business- and GOP-friendly groups have cropped up, pledging to spend tens of millions of dollars in the coming election. Moreover, it's still early: Most big spending doesn't surface until the last two months before Election Day. And the post-*Citizens United* landscape is so uncertain that its real impact may not be felt until 2012, some experts predict.

Still, ominous talk of exponential campaign spending hikes is starting to look overstated. In the short term, at least, the ruling may do more to change the nature of political spending than its volume.

The *Citizens United* Ruling Won't Change Much

In the absence of an obvious corporate money surge, some analysts have downplayed the *Citizens United* ruling's importance, arguing that it does little to alter the political playing field.

"In a lot of ways, this decision is more marginal than cataclysmic in terms of what it will do to the campaign finance system," election lawyer Joseph Sandler, the former Democratic National Committee counsel and a member of Sandler Reiff & Young, maintained in a conference call the day the Court ruled. The decision's fans have tended to pooh-pooh the public reaction as so much hysteria and hyperbole.

But, in fact, the ruling has sweeping, long-term ramifications, election-law experts and even some conservatives say. Although spikes in corporate and union spending have yet to materialize, the decision signals a turnabout on the Supreme Court and a seismic shift in constitutional and campaign finance law.

That's because the Court's action sets legal precedents that threaten other long-standing pillars of the campaign finance regime, from disclosure rules to party spending curbs, the foreign-money ban, and even contribution limits. *Citizens United* is but one of dozens of campaign finance challenges that conservatives have brought and continue to bring before the high court, emboldened by its deregulatory tilt under Chief Justice John Roberts.

Some of these challenges have fallen short. In *Doe v. Reed,* the Court in June tossed out a suit brought by conservative activist James Bopp Jr. challenging state disclosure rules for voters who sign ballot petitions. Also in June, the Court turned back a Bopp-led challenge to the federal ban on soft (unregulated) money. In *Republican National Committee v. Federal Election Commission,* Bopp had argued that the RNC should be free to collect soft money for independent spending that's not coordinated with candidates.

Still, the high court all but invited further challenges that may succeed down the road. It concluded, for example, that if Bopp could show that petition signers had been harassed, the disclosure rules may, in fact, violate the Constitution. *RNC v. FEC* may also be back. That case was an "as-applied challenge," limited to specific circumstances. But the Court left the door open to a broader, facial attack on the soft-money rules.

"I have little doubt that if a facial challenge is brought to the soft-money provisions, the justices will be ready to hear it," says Richard L. Hasen, a professor at Loyola Law School in Los Angeles.

Most important, the high court's *Citizens United* opinion articulates a new, unusually narrow view of what constitutes corruption. The majority abandoned the position, upheld in previous Supreme Court cases, that campaign finance limits may be justified on the grounds that big money gives its donors "undue influence" or "access."

"The fact that speakers may have influence over or access to elected officials does not mean that these officials are corrupt," the majority opinion states, explaining that only quid pro quo corruption may be regulated. If access and ingratiation are not corruption, Hasen notes that places contribution limits, among other regulations, in serious jeopardy.

"It's a very narrow definition of corruption that is going to have, I predict, a range of very negative consequences across the campaign finance spectrum," he says. The upshot: After several decades of straddling the fence on political money but largely upholding regulations, the high court has shifted sharply in favor of free speech. Over time, disclosure and public financing may be the only regulations that this Court finds constitutional.

Congress Is More Corrupt Than Ever

Given the public's disgust with government these days, it should come as no surprise that most voters think that Washington lawmakers are in the pocket of special interests.

In one poll, nearly 80 percent of respondents told a bipartisan team of researchers earlier this year that members of Congress are controlled by the groups that help fund their political campaigns. By contrast, fewer than 20 percent said that lawmakers "listen more to the voters." Such attitudes cut across the political spectrum, according to pollsters at Greenberg Quinlan Rosner Research (D) and McKinnon Media (R), which conducted the survey.

Yet leading political scientists have found the exact opposite; they've hunted in vain for proof of a correlation between money and votes over a period of decades. In study after study, "the evidence is scant to nonexistent" that political action committee contributions affect roll-call votes, says Stephen Ansolabehere, a professor of government at Harvard University.

Ansolabehere says he began his academic career convinced that campaign contributions "are an important leverage point for corporations and interest groups." But after reviewing some 80 political science analyses spanning several decades, from the 1970s through about 2005, he admits that he was forced to reconsider. The vast majority of studies, he says, conclude that "the probability of success of a bill was unaffected by total contributions."

What really sways lawmakers, the studies suggest, are constituents and party affiliation. "Constituent need trumps all," Ansolabehere says. "And party is also very important. So once you factor in parties and constituents, there is just not much room there for contributors and interest groups to have much influence."

True, reform advocates—and many lawmakers—say that such ivory-tower analyses don't square with real life inside the

Beltway. Direct PAC contributions, which these academic studies target, represent only a small slice of the political money pie. Independent campaign expenditures and largely unregulated issue ads play a growing role, as do "bundled" contributions that lobbyists round up to curry favor with candidates.

Policy-making, of course, goes way beyond simple roll-call votes. Millions in corporate profits can ride on whether a bill is postponed, amended, or even scuttled—decisions that take place at the margins and behind closed doors, and leave no trace.

One political scientist who thinks that these academics are "out of their minds" is Rep. Mike Quigley, D-Ill., elected on the heels of the scandal that ousted Gov. Rod Blagojevich, D-Ill., now awaiting a verdict in his corruption trial. Quigley has a master's degree in public policy from the University of Chicago, but he takes issue with his fellow academics.

"I don't need that degree to help me understand the connection between money and policy decisions," he says. "It's very hard to prove an actual quid pro quo. Although some [politicians] are stupid and go over the top, most are careful." Quigley adds that he has heard his House colleagues wonder aloud how their votes will affect PAC contributions: "Members think about their constituencies, of course. But they're also thinking about the PACs."

Even so, reflexive public cynicism overlooks new rules and attitudes since the Watergate era, when donors carried around briefcases stuffed with cash. Lawmakers now face contribution limits and reporting rules; the soft-money ban enacted in 2002; and the stricter ethics and lobbying rules imposed in 2007 after the Jack Abramoff lobbying scandal.

The atmosphere has changed, too. Ethics-compliance teams and seminars are de rigueur at lobby shops and on Capitol Hill, and the Internet has made it easier for follow-the-money watchdog groups, reporters, bloggers, tweeters, and even average citizens to connect the dots.

"I think the people up on the Hill are bending over backwards to make sure they don't even approach the lines that have been set by the Honest Leadership and Open Government Act and the Senate ethics rules," said William J. McGinley, a partner at Patton Boggs who specializes in political law. "And I think the culture has changed quite a bit."

There is no shortage of controversies, of course—witness the recent Office of Congressional Ethics investigation into more than half a dozen lawmakers who collected donations from Wall Street donors within 48 hours of the House vote on financial services legislation. Still, popular caricatures of a widely corrupt Congress tar all lawmakers with the same brush even as politicians arguably face more-exacting rules, expectations, and public scrutiny than ever.

Money Equals Speech

If money were really speech, as conservatives like to argue, then virtually all election laws would be unconstitutional.

That is not the case—at least not yet.

Certainly, the First Amendment exhorts that "Congress shall make no law . . . abridging the freedom of speech, or of the press." In their systematic legal challenge to virtually the entire campaign finance regime, free-speech champions invariably quote this mandate. In its *Citizens United* ruling, the Supreme Court acknowledges that political speech "is central to the meaning and purpose of the First Amendment."

But even this deregulatory high court has not gone so far as to conclude that all election rules violate the Constitution. Contribution limits, for one, are a constitutional means "to ensure against the reality or appearance of corruption," the *Citizens United* majority found. The Court also left other key rules, including the soft-money ban and the disclosure laws, firmly in place.

In equating money with speech, conservatives cast political contributions in a rosy light. More campaign spending is invariably better, they insist, because donations underwrite ads and communications that enrich the public dialogue. Given how much corporations spend on commercial products such as potato chips, foes of regulation argue, U.S. elections actually cost remarkably little.

"This case will lead to more spending in political elections," enthused former FEC Chairman Bradley Smith, a professor at Capital University Law School and the chairman of the Center for Competitive Politics, shortly after the *Citizens United* ruling. "We expect to see more speech. We think that's a good thing."

But even if blatant corruption is not rampant on Capitol Hill, as many voters presume, private money potentially distorts policy-making—if for no other reason than that lawmakers must devote so much time to begging for it. American democracy, after all, is not fast-food advertising.

"If large concentrations of wealth can move easily and freely, and increasingly without transparency, through the political system, it's bound to have some influence on the nature of those decisions," says Thomas Mann, a senior fellow in governance studies at the Brookings Institution. "It doesn't have to be a quid pro quo to harm the political system."

Over time, the Supreme Court's logic in *Citizens United* may, in fact, lead it to dismantle all but a few core regulations, as some scholars predict. But we're not there yet. In the meantime, limiting campaign cash remains constitutional, and unfettered private money cannot be genuinely equated with freedom of speech.

Disclosure Is the Silver Bullet

In throwing out the longtime corporate and union spending bans, Associate Justice Anthony Kennedy assured that disclosure laws would safeguard against abuses.

"With the advent of the Internet, prompt disclosure of expenditures can provide shareholders and citizens with the information needed to hold corporations and elected officials accountable for their positions and supporters," Kennedy wrote for the majority in *Citizens United*.

Yet Kennedy's idealized vision of transparency is at odds with the real world of politics, many scholars argue. For one thing, no law requires corporations to tell shareholders whether they're spending treasury money on elections, points out Monica Youn, counsel to the democracy program at New York University School of Law's Brennan Center for Justice.

"Justice Kennedy's decision assumed a background of disclosure laws that simply didn't exist," she says. "When corporate spending does occur, it tends to be covert and to be very hard to track."

Indeed, disclosure rules are particularly spotty when it comes to independent campaign expenditures. Unlike PACs that donate directly to politicians, which must exhaustively report every penny that comes in and goes out of their coffers, groups that spend money independently of candidates need not tell much about their funding sources.

Such independent spenders must report only the money explicitly *earmarked* for an ad. That means that overhead costs paid for by a corporation or a union might never see the light of day. Money transfers between committees also routinely obscure funding sources. For their part, nonprofit advocacy groups, which are increasingly a magnet for political money, face virtually no reporting requirements.

These loopholes prompted Sen. Charles Schumer, D-N.Y., and Rep. Chris Van Hollen, D-Md., to write a broad disclosure bill in response to *Citizens United.* The measure would block big spenders from hiding behind shadowy groups with patriotic names, the lawmakers said, by forcing those running campaign ads to report their top donors and appear in on-air disclaimers.

But the bill died by filibuster in the Senate last month after winning approval in the House. Controversial provisions involving government contractors and foreign-owned corporations hurt the so-called Disclose Act—Democracy Is Strengthened by Casting Light on Spending in Elections. Republicans assailed it as pro-union, and critics blasted a last-minute exemption for the National Rifle Association and other big national groups.

The Disclose Act's real problem, however, was that it imposed elaborate reporting rules not only on unions and corporations but also on all incorporated groups—including advocacy and nonprofit organizations on the Left and Right. It's one thing, it turns out, to require politicians and political parties to publicly report their activities; it's another to ask grassroots groups to do the same.

This helps explain why Republicans, having argued for decades that disclosure is the solution to regulating political money, have reversed course. If anything, conservatives are pushing for less transparency, not more, in a series of legal and regulatory challenges. Disclosure is under fire, says Richard Briffault, a Columbia University law professor, in part because it is taking center stage as one of the few remaining campaign finance restrictions that this Supreme Court appears likely to uphold.

"Disclosure has many values," Briffault says. "But we are becoming more aware of the down sides of disclosure, and we may need to focus more carefully on what we need to know."

It would be nice if disclosure could offer up a clean, popular solution to the campaign finance mess. But like so many facets of election law, disclosure is turning out to be incomplete, complex, and controversial.

Public Financing Will Never Happen

It's true that public financing fixes in their current form will probably not win approval in this Congress, or even the next. But the mantra that public financing will *never* pass overlooks some important recent developments.

- An innovative model for public financing that would provide multiple matching funds to reward candidates for collecting small, low-dollar donations has the potential to resuscitate the debate and bridge partisan divides.

- Advocates are better funded and organized than ever. A pair of good-government groups has pledged to spend $5 million this year and as much as $15 million over the next 18 months on a high-profile lobbying and advertising campaign to promote the Fair Elections Now Act to publicly fund congressional candidates. The House version of this bill has 159 co-sponsors, and 30 more will soon sign on, its backers say.

- Voters are unusually angry about political money. Anti-Washington sentiment; the *Citizens United* ruling; and high-profile lobbying wars over health care, Wall Street, and climate-change legislation have all thrust special-interest money into the public eye. Voters overwhelmingly object to the *Citizens United* decision, and a majority of them support the Fair Elections Now Act, recent polls show.

Outside the Beltway, "people seem much unhappier with the system than I can recall," observes former FEC Chairman Trevor Potter, president of the nonpartisan Campaign Legal Center. "And I think that inevitably pushes public funding, and new forms of the match, to the forefront."

Public financing faces big hurdles, of course. A Republican takeover of one or both chambers on Capitol Hill this fall will kick the can farther down the road. Recession and unemployment may make it harder to convince voters that lawmakers deserve what critics call taxpayer-financed campaigns.

Half a dozen states offer public financing to statewide and legislative candidates, but even these efforts are under fire. Recent lawsuits, including one heading for the Supreme Court, challenge state rescue funds that give more money to publicly financed candidates who face deep-pocketed opponents. If these suits prevail, fewer candidates may want to participate in the system.

The Achilles' heel of both the presidential and the state public financing models is that they impose spending caps on candidates who opt into the system. That makes the money unappealing and explains why presidential candidates, including Obama, have abandoned public financing.

This problem, however, is easy to fix: Simply drop the spending caps. Leading political scientists argue that it's time to adopt a "floors-not-ceilings" approach that matches small donations without limiting spending. Such a model appeals to some conservatives and may move to the fore if the high court continues to roll back existing rules.

"There's donor fatigue, there's candidate fatigue, and there's lobbyist fatigue," says ex-Rep. Bob Edgar, D-Pa., the president of Common Cause, which has teamed with Public Campaign to push for public financing. The two groups just launched their first wave of TV ads. It may be a quixotic quest, but slowly, over time, public financing may gain traction.

Critical Thinking

1. Why is a large increase in corporate spending on elections not likely to occur in the aftermath of the *Citizens United* ruling?
2. What consequences will the Supreme Court's narrow definition of corruption in the *Citizens United* case have on campaign financing?
3. What do academic analyses conclude about the effect of PAC contributions on Congressional votes? What do those who disagree with these studies argue about?

4. Why is disclosure not an effective response to the anticipated increase in corporate influence on elections following the *Citizens United* decision?
5. What three reasons, according to Eliza Carney, suggest that public financing of elections is still a possibility?

Create Central

www.mhhe.com/createcentral

Internet References

Federal Election Commission
www.fec.gov
OpenSecrets.org: Center for Responsive Politics
www.opensecrets.org

Article

Prepared by: Bruce Stinebrickner, *DePauw University*

Who Wants to Buy a Politician?

After Citizen United, it turns out that surprisingly few people and corporations do—at least though campaign spending.

BINYAMIN APPELBAUM

Learning Outcomes

After reading this article, you will be able to:

- Consider whether a democratic political system would be well-served by government, rather than private donors (be they individuals or corporations), funding election campaigns.

- Ponder how, in a democratic and "free" society, wealthy people and groups can be prevented from having disproportionate influence over government and whether such influence, if and when it occurs, is a 'bad' thing.

Don Blankenship, the recently indicted former chief executive of Massey Energy, has a history of donating a lot of money to West Virginia politicians. In 2004, for instance, Blankenship spent $3 million to support the election of a lawyer named Brent Benjamin to the state's Supreme Court of Appeals. It was, notably, more than three times the amount spent by Benjamin's own campaign. But for Blankenship, it appeared to be a beneficial investment. Once seated, Benjamin cast the deciding vote to overturn a $50 million jury verdict against Massey.

Spending on election campaigns has long been considered a pretty good way for people and companies, who have money, to influence politicians, who need it. That's why the government spent the better part of a century imposing various restrictions on such spending. But in recent years, federal courts have knocked down many of these barriers: A series of decisions, most notably the Supreme Court's 2010 ruling in the Citizens United case, now effectively allow people and companies to spend as much as they like. Soon after the Citizens ruling, experts forecast that a flood of money would follow. And in some elections, it has. In last month's midterms, competitive United States Senate races in North Carolina and Colorado each drew more than $100 million in estimated spending, the first time any congressional races have crossed that line.

Such extravagance, however, is proving to be the exception. Even the 2012 presidential election, which recorded $2.6 billion in campaign spending, underperformed many forecasts. And spending has declined in each of the last two congressional elections. Candidates and other interested parties spent $3.7 billion on this year's midterms, down from an inflation-adjusted total of $3.8 billion in 2012, which was less than the $4 billion spent in 2010, according to the nonprofit Center for Responsive Politics. (These figures do not include a few hundred million dollars in unreported spending on issue ads.) In fact, spending has dropped as the economy has grown and despite a series of contests in which at least one house of Congress was plausibly at stake. "Dire warnings rang out that the decision would herald a new era in politics," wrote Adam Bonica, a Stanford University political scientist, in a 2013 paper about the effects of Citizens United. "Three years on, there is little evidence that these predictions have come to pass." Over the past year, Americans spent more on almonds than on selecting their representatives in Congress.

Stephen Ansolabehere, a professor of government at Harvard University, says that the facts are surprising only if we subscribe to an incorrect view. In a 2003 paper, "Why Is There So Little Money in U.S. Politics?" he argued that people and corporations actually view giving money as an ineffective way to influence politicians. Donations, Ansolabehere says, are best understood as a form of consumption, akin to making a charitable contribution. Donors are supporting a cause they believe in, and they take pleasure in doing so. "We basically think that giving money makes you feel good," Ansolabehere told me.

Most campaign money, after all, comes in smaller chunks from individual donors. People who gave $3 to Barack Obama's presidential campaign in 2008 could not have reasonably expected that their small contributions would influence the future president. Even those who give larger sums rarely contribute the maximum allowed by law, as might be expected of someone trying to buy influence. Instead, individual contributions have increased over time merely in proportion to personal income. Excepting lower-income families, who rarely give to campaigns, Americans from the upper-middle class on up give approximately the same percentage of their income, about 0.04 percent, according to Ansolabehere's research, to politicians and political groups. Corporations also spend relatively little, and their spending has not increased substantially in recent years. "If companies thought they could just buy politicians," said Timothy Groseclose, an economics professor at George Mason University, "we should see much more money being spent there."

In reality, examples like the Massey Energy case are rare. And in 2009, the Supreme Court ordered the West Virginia courts to reconsider its verdict. That year, Blankenship told Adam Liptak of *The Times,* "I've been around West Virginia long enough to know that politicians don't stay bought." Justice Anthony Kennedy noted in his Citizens United opinion that 100,000 pages of briefs had not included a single clear example of a quid pro quo purchase of a lawmaker's vote.

One reason is that buying elections is economically inefficient. Most voters, like most consumers, have defined preferences that are difficult for advertisers to shift. Chevron spent roughly $3 million during a recent campaign backing certain City Council candidates in Richmond, Calif., where it operates a major refinery. Voters instead chose a slate of candidates who want to raise taxes. "Campaign spending has an extremely small impact on election outcomes, regardless of who does the spending," the University of Chicago economist Steven Levitt concluded in a 1994 paper. He found that spending an extra $100,000 in a House race might be expected to increase a candidate's vote total by about 0.33 percentage points. Investors appear to agree that companies can't make money by investing in political campaigns. A 2004 study found that changes in campaign-finance laws had no discernible impact on the share prices of companies that made donations.

The low level of campaign spending, however, may obscure the real power of wealthy individuals and corporations. Michael Munger, a professor of political science at Duke University, told me that companies are mostly satisfied with the status quo, so they behave more like firefighters than like police officers. Instead of getting involved in each campaign, in other words, they sit back

and wait for an alarm to ring. "Incumbents and large corporations can basically spend as much as it would take to defeat some change that would harm them," he said. "And most of the time that is zero. But the potential is basically infinite." They spend around 10 times as much on lobbying, suggesting that it's less effective to influence the selection of policy makers than to influence the policy-making process itself. "If you can give a key piece of information to a politician," Groseclose told me, "that seems to be more valuable than a campaign contribution."

There may also be limits on how much money congressional campaigns can truly spend. House elections would presumably be more expensive if seats in Congress were directly available for sale. Campaign spending, however, is focused on influencing voters, and the prices for most of the necessary materials—people, paper, advertising time—are set in a broader marketplace, which keeps prices under control. During the midterms, television stations in several contested markets reported that they had sold all of their available slots. One station in New Hampshire actually issued refunds after selling more ads than it could air.

Moreover, carefully drawn district maps limit the number of competitive House races, and control of available resources has shifted from candidates to national groups that focus on those races. Americans may be spending more on almonds than on elections, in other words, because in a growing number of races there is effectively nothing to buy.

Critical Thinking

1. Summarize recent trends in campaign spending.
2. Explain why giving money to political campaigns might be judged to be "ineffective."
3. What does it mean to say that most companies behave like firefighters and not police officers when it comes to campaign contributions?

Internet References

Campaign Money.com
   http://www.campaignmoney.com
Center for Responsive Politics
   http://www.opensecrets.org
Federal Election Commission
   www.fec.gov

BINYAMIN APPELBAUM is an economics reporter at *The Times.*

Article   Prepared by: Bruce Stinebrickner, *DePauw University*

Identity Politics

What happens when faith is put to a vote?

ROBERT DAVID SULLIVAN

Learning Outcomes

After reading this article, you will be able to:

- Assess why Catholics now vote so much like non-Catholic Americans and why that pattern differs from how Catholics voted a half-century ago.

- Consider whether religion-based analyses of the sort reported in this selection should be welcome in a democratic political system.

- Discuss whether the American political system would be better served if such analyses were not available?

- Consider the fault line in voting behavior between frequent church-goers and less frequent ones. Is it surprising? Do you think it's a problem? Discuss why or why not.

Fifty years ago this fall, the Democrats won their highest percentage ever in a presidential election, and Catholics formed the party's bedrock constituency. Still reeling from the assassination of John F. Kennedy, Catholics voted for his successor, Lyndon Johnson, by a margin of three to one (76 percent to 24 percent, according to Gallup). This was not quite as high as Kennedy's margin, but Catholics became more powerful than ever in the Democratic Party, since the almost universally Protestant "Solid South" was in the process of breaking away from a party it once dominated. With big majorities in Congress as well as the presidency, a Democratic Party that united racial and religious minorities (African-Americans and Jews as well as Catholics) had an opportunity to reshape American life.

The United States did change quite a bit over the next decade, but the Democratic coalition fell apart with the very next presidential election, and the Catholic bloc eventually fractured

for good. In 2012, Gallup estimated the Catholic vote at 49 to 48 Democratic, and most other polls showed Catholics giving Barack Obama a margin no bigger than his four-point lead nationwide. In 1965, according to "Vital Statistics on Congress," a joint effort from the Brookings Institution and the American Enterprise Institute, 93 of the 108 Catholic members of Congress were Democratic. In 2013, the caucus was much larger, but more divided. This time, 93 (yes, the same number) of 163 Catholic members were Democratic.

It is still tempting to generalize about American Catholics, who make up about one-quarter of the national population. This past May, *The New York Times* ran an article on the rarity of women governors in the Northeast that included this explanation: "Beyond the region's political culture, the states' demography has also traditionally worked against women. 'They are older, with a blue-collar electorate in an industrial economy and a heavy Catholic population,' said Celinda Lake, a Democratic pollster."

This was a cheap shot, since the article included no evidence that Catholics are less likely to vote for women. More often, there are stories like the one in *Politico* that ran after Mitt Romney selected Paul Ryan, a Catholic, as his running mate in 2012. The choice "all but guarantees a fierce election-year fight for the affections of Catholic voters," wrote James Hohmann. But his story actually illustrated a split among Catholic voters (some emphasizing "social" issues, others talking about "social justice") that would persist whatever the two major candidates did.

Indeed, most polls show Catholics are now close to the national average in their voting habits and in their views on major issues. "The Catholic vote tends to mirror the national vote, uncannily so," wrote Gerald F. Seib, of *The Wall Street Journal,* in a March story on a meeting between President Obama and Pope Francis. Perhaps "uncannily" implies an unwarranted surprise at that fact. "Catholics are remarkably—and I mean *really remarkably*—average across major demographic categories," wrote Frank Newport, editor-in-chief of Gallup, in a blog post in 2013 citing data on age, educational attainment, family income and party identification (30 percent Democratic, 25 percent Republican and 36 percent independent). The one exception was that 29 percent of Catholics claimed Hispanic heritage, compared with 13 percent of all Americans.

Losing Catholics

Polling data suggests that the political fault line in 2014 is not between Protestants and Catholics, but between frequent churchgoers and less committed adherents of all religions. A survey in August by Marquette University of the Wisconsin electorate (who will decide whether to re-elect Gov. Scott Walker, a Republican, this fall) found no significant difference between Catholic and Protestant respondents on most matters: 39 percent of Catholics and 38 percent of Protestants approved of President Obama's job performance, while 33 percent of Catholics and 36 percent of Protestants had a favorable view of the Tea Party. Forty-nine percent of Catholics and 53 percent of Protestants favored raising the minimum wage, and the Affordable Care Act won the support of 34 percent of Catholics and 35 percent of Protestants.

But weekly churchgoers were significantly more likely to favor Republican candidates and positions. There was majority support for raising the minimum wage only among voters who attend church less than once a week, and support for the Affordable Care Act was highest among those who "never" attend services. The poll is consistent with other studies indicating that Catholics who say they attend Mass weekly have more traditional views and are less supportive of government activism than those who say they attend Mass less frequently or not at all.

How did the Democratic Party lose their sizable advantage with Catholic voters? Its position on abortion—specifically the 1973 *Roe v. Wade* Supreme Court decision—is surely a factor. Jimmy Carter was the last Democratic nominee to express support for tighter restrictions on abortion, and his 57 percent of the Catholic vote (according to Gallup) has not been matched since. Pro-life Catholics have found themselves in alliance with Southern evangelical Protestants, and it is the Republican Party that has welcomed them.

A broader issue is respect for religion itself. The Democratic Party has gained a reputation as being uncomfortable with spiritual language and values. The Republicans, in contrast, have highlighted the piety of its presidential candidates and promised a greater role for religion in civic life, from sanctioning prayer in school to giving religious groups more responsibility in providing services to the poor.

The Republican Party has also been stoutly in defense of the Pledge of Allegiance (including the added phrase "under God") and a constitutional amendment banning the desecration of the American flag. The conflation of religious values with patriotism has long been a characteristic of the Republican Party— "Our form of government has no sense unless it is founded in a deeply felt religious faith, and I don't care what it is," said Dwight Eisenhower shortly after being elected president, putting both the secularist and the Communist outside the bounds of acceptability—but it was Ronald Reagan who made it synonymous with the G.O.P.

The Great Communicator is the primary subject of Rick Perlstein's sprawling book *The Invisible Bridge: The Fall of Nixon and the Rise of Reagan,* which covers much of the period when the Catholic vote became untethered from the Democratic Party. Perlstein's thesis is that the Vietnam War and the Watergate scandal, in addition to rising crime rates and an energy crisis, posed some tough questions about the future of the United States, but we decided to learn nothing from these traumatic events and instead turned to Reagan, the enemy of nuance and champion of American exceptionalism.

Voters' Block

After the Kennedy presidency, Americans from nearly all religious groups became concerned with the apparent unraveling of civil society. The former Nixon advisor Patrick Buchanan, in an interview this summer with *America,* said that the Democratic Party's response to social upheaval and its nomination of "amnesty and abortion" candidate George McGovern alienated what had been a loyal bloc: "I think many Catholics of that generation—conservative, traditionalist Catholic union folks— were much closer to Richard Nixon than they were to the elites demonstrating on the campuses or the rioters . . . . Cultural, moral and social issues brought postwar Catholics into the Nixon new majority."

Writing about *The Invisible Bridge,* Kevin Drum of *Mother Jones* suggests that it could have benefited from more of an attempt to understand this point of view: "I wish Perlstein had gone a little lighter on his obvious contempt for Reagan and spent a little more time owning up—perhaps uncomfortably— to just what it was about the liberalism of the 70s that finally drove so many voters crazy."

Jimmy Carter—a deeply religious but ecumenical Baptist— temporarily got many of these voters back in 1976, but Reagan was more than adept in appealing to the Catholic vote during the 1980s.

Perlstein notes that one of Reagan's favorite quotations to drop into his speeches came from Pope Pius XII: "The American people have a genius for great and unselfish deeds. Into the hands of America God has placed the destiny of an afflicted mankind." Reagan may have interpreted the statement as more of a blank check of approval than it really was, but citing the pope as an authority was a shrewd way of easing religious doubts about a my-country-right-or-wrong nationalism. Running for the 1976 Republican nomination, Reagan also told an Illinois audience, "I happen to believe there was a divine plan in the settling of this land between the oceans."

After the Reagan administration, the Democratic Party continued to facilitate a divorce from Catholic voters. In his 1990 book *Under God: Religion and American Politics,* Garry Wills expressed astonishment at the tone-deafness of its 1988 presidential nominee: "[Michael] Dukakis was the first truly secular candidate we have ever had for the presidency. Not a 'secularist' as Pat Robertson would define that term, not a militant against religion, but someone entirely free from religion." That Dukakis was the first non-Protestant nominee since Kennedy earned him little headway with Catholic voters, who gave him only about half their vote after delivering strong majorities for Protestants Hubert Humphrey and Jimmy Carter.

Since then, the so-called Catholic vote has been divided pretty much down the middle, reflecting the nation as a whole— still significantly more Democratic than white Protestants, but not as reliably Democratic as African-Americans or voters who do not identify with a specific Christian church. The changing identities and priorities of the two major parties undoubtedly drove some Catholic voters away from the Democrats, but changing economic circumstances must also be considered.

"It's got to do with class," the political scientist Nelson Polsby told *America* in 2004 ("Catholics and Candidates" 5/17/04). "Lots of Catholics do what Protestants do. When they make more money, they are likely to be Republican."

John Kenneth White, a professor of politics at The Catholic University of America, agreed: "In the 1960s, '70s and '80s, Catholics had become part of the haves . . . . They've got their green eyeshades on and they're looking at their tax bills."

Selective Catholicism

Catholic identity has not become invisible in American politics. It is a constant theme in coverage of Paul Ryan, the Catholic member of Congress from Wisconsin and the 2012 Republican vice-presidential nominee. Mr. Ryan has been making a case for smaller government and more market-based solutions to poverty, but he frequently has to battle accusations that his worldview comes more from atheist perspectives and Ayn Rand, the author of *Atlas Shrugged*, than from his church. "If somebody is going to try to paste a person's view on epistemology to me, then give me Thomas Aquinas," Paul Ryan fretted to Robert Costa, of *The National Review,* in 2012. "Don't give me Ayn Rand."

Mr. Ryan would not get the support of a group called Nuns on the Bus, which is organizing a voter drive across the country this fall. In covering their kick-off event with Joe Biden (the first Catholic vice president), Jennifer Jacobs, of *The Des Moines Register*, wrote, "They draw attention to the 'wealth gap,' health care for all, immigrants' rights, nonviolent solutions to conflict, a 'living wage,' housing policy, and not forcing Americans to spend down to zero before they qualify for food stamps, Medicaid or other social services." But she also noted, "They leave issues such as abortion and gay rights to other groups." It seems that the price of admission to the big leagues of national politics is to be carefully selective about Catholic doctrine.

Abortion is a support beam of our newly polarized two-party system, with nearly all elected Democrats on the "pro-choice" side and nearly all elected Republicans (including Paul Ryan) in favor of anti-abortion legislation. As long as this is the case, it is hard to envision a more unified Catholic vote than what currently exists.

The polarized two-party system may be one reason for the rising number of voters who call themselves independent. "Some voters who identify as independents are partisans who don't wish to identify that way for a specific and logical reason," the political scientist Julia Azari, of Marquette University, writes on the Mischiefs of Faction blog. "They might be Democrats who lean with the party in a doveish direction, but break with it on abortion."

So if religious beliefs can influence partisan identification, can partisanship, in turn, influence religious identification? In a 2010 Forum on Religion & Public Life, held by the Pew Research Center, professor David Campbell, of Notre Dame (co-author of *American Grace: How Religion Divides and Unites Us*), noted, "For many Americans, Republican equals religion." As a result, he speculated, "when asked today, are you of a particular religion, [many Americans] think, well, wait a second, religion—that equals a particular brand of politics. That's not my politics . . . . Ergo, they report, I don't have a religion."

Because the Catholic vote tracks so closely with national election results, it is tempting to speak of Catholics as a powerful swing group, but slack and elastic may be better adjectives. If you limit the Catholic vote to those who attend Mass weekly, you would get one result, and if you expand it to include Catholics uncomfortable with the "religion equals Republican" perception, you might get something quite different.

"I believe in an America," John F. Kennedy said in his famous 1960 address to the Greater Houston Ministerial Association, "where there is no Catholic vote, no anti-Catholic vote, no bloc voting of any kind."

Kennedy, in fact, owed his election to an almost-unanimous Catholic bloc, but his vision has since come true.

Critical Thinking

1. Summarize how today's Catholics compare to other Americans in their voting patterns and views on major issues.

2. Compare your answer to question 1 with Catholics' voting patterns in the past.

3. Identity the religion-related "fault line" that today is far more significant in voting patterns than the differences between Catholics and Protestants.

Internet References

United States Conference of Catholic Bishops
  http://usccb.org

Washington Post—Chart: The United States of Catholics and Protestants
  http://www.washingtonpost.com/news/wonkblog/wp/2015/03/04/chart-the-united-states-of-catholics-and-protestants

ROBERT DAVID SULLIVAN, a freelance writer and editor living in the Boston area, is the author of America's "(Un)Conventional Wisdom" blog.

Article

Prepared by: Bruce Stinebrickner, *DePauw University*

America Observed

Why foreign election observers would rate the United States near the bottom.

Robert A. Pastor

Learning Outcomes

After reading this article, you will be able to:

- Summarize the ways in which government's running of U.S. elections falls short of the way elections are run in most other western democracies.

- Consider why fundamental electoral reforms have not occurred even after the embarrassing spectacle of the 2000 presidential election.

Few noticed, but in the year 2000, Mexico and the United States traded places. After nearly two centuries of election fraud, Mexico's presidential election was praised universally by its political parties and international observers as free, fair, and professional. Four months later, after two centuries as a model democracy, the U.S. election was panned as an embarrassing fiasco, reeking with pregnant chads, purged registration lists, butterfly ballots, and a Supreme Court that preempted a recount.

Ashamed, the U.S. Congress in 2002 passed the Help America Vote Act (HAVA), our first federal legislation on election administration. But two years later, on November 2, more than 200,000 voters from all 50 states phoned the advocacy organization Common Cause with a plethora of complaints. The 2004 election was not as close as 2000, but it was no better—and, in some ways, worse. This was partly because the only two elements of HAVA implemented for 2004 were provisional ballots and ID requirements, and both created more problems than they solved. HAVA focused more on eliminating punch-card machines than on the central cause of the electoral problem, dysfunctional decentralization. Instead of a single election for president, 13,000 counties and municipalities conduct elections with different ballots, standards, and machines. This accounts for most of the problems.

On the eve of November's election, only one-third of the electorate, according to a *New York Times* poll, said that they had a lot of confidence that their votes would be counted properly, and 29 percent said they were very or somewhat concerned that they would encounter problems at the polls. This explains why 13 members of Congress asked the United Nations to send election observers. The deep suspicion that each party's operatives had of the other's motives reminded me of Nicaragua's polarized election in 1990, and of other poor nations holding their first free elections.

Ranking America's Elections

The pro-democracy group Freedom House counts 117 electoral democracies in the world as of 2004. Many are new and fragile. The U.S. government has poured more money into helping other countries become democracies than it has into its own election system. At least we've gotten our money's worth. By and large, elections are conducted better abroad than at home. Several teams of international observers—including one that I led—watched this U.S. election. Here is a summary of how the United States did in 10 different categories, and what we should do to raise our ranking.

1. Who's in Charge? Stalin is reported to have said that the secret to a successful election is not the voter but the vote counter. There are three models for administering elections. Canada, Spain, Afghanistan, and most emerging democracies have nonpartisan national election commissions. A second model is to have the political parties "share" responsibility. We use that model to supervise campaign finance (the Federal Election Commission), but that tends to lead either to stalemates or to collusions against the public's interest. The third, most primitive model is when the incumbent government puts itself in charge. Only 18 percent of the democracies do it this way, including the United States, which usually grants responsibility to a highly partisan secretary of state, like Katherine Harris (formerly) in Florida or Kenneth Blackwell in Ohio.

2. Registration and Identification of Voters. The United States registers about 55 percent of its eligible voters, as compared with more than 95 percent in Canada and Mexico. To ensure the accuracy of its list, Mexico conducted 36 audits between 1994 and 2000. In contrast, the United States has thousands of separate lists, many of which are wildly inaccurate. Provisional ballots were needed only because the lists are so bad. Under HAVA, all states by 2006 must create computer-based, interactive statewide lists—a major step forward that will work only if everyone agrees not to move out of state. That is why most democracies, including most of Europe, have nationwide lists and ask voters to identify themselves. Oddly, few U.S. states require proof of *citizenship*—which is, after all, what the election is supposed to be about. If ID cards threaten democracy, why does almost every democracy except us require them, and why are their elections conducted better than ours?

3. Poll Workers and Sites. Dedicated people work at our polling stations often for 14 hours on election day. Polling sites are always overcrowded at the start of the day. McDonald's hires more workers for its lunchtime shifts, but a similar idea has not yet occurred to our election officials. Poll workers are exhausted by the time they begin the delicate task of counting the votes and making sure the total corresponds to the number who signed in, and, as a result, there are discrepancies. When I asked about the qualifications for selecting a poll worker, one county official told me, "We'll take anyone with a pulse." Mexico views the job as a civic responsibility like jury duty, and citizens are chosen randomly and trained. This encourages all citizens to learn and participate in the process.

4. Voting Technologies. Like any computers, electronic machines break down, and they lose votes. Canada does not have this problem because it uses paper ballots, still the most reliable technology. Brazil's electronic system has many safeguards and has gained the trust of its voters. If we use electronic machines, they need paper-verifiable ballots.

5. Uniform Standards for Ballots, Voting, Disputes. The Supreme Court called for equal protection of voters' rights, but to achieve this, standards need to be uniform. In America, each jurisdiction does it differently. Most countries don't have this problem because they have a single election commission and law to decide the validity of ballots.

6. Uncompetitive Districts. In 2004, only three incumbent members of Congress—outside of House Majority Leader Tom DeLay's gerrymandered state of Texas—were defeated. Even the Communist Party of China has difficulty winning as many elections. This is because state legislatures, using advanced computer technologies, can now draw district boundaries in a way that virtually guarantees safe seats. Canada has a nonpartisan system for drawing districts. This still favors incumbents, as 83 percent won in 2004, but that compares with 99 percent in the United States. Proportional representation systems are even more competitive.

7. Campaign Finance and Access to the Media. The United States spent little to conduct elections last November, but almost $4 billion to promote and defeat candidates. More than $1.6 billion was spent on TV ads in 2004. The Institute for Democracy and Electoral Assistance in Stockholm reported that 63 percent of democracies provided free access to the media, thus eliminating one of the major reasons for raising money. Most limit campaign contributions, as the United States does, but one-fourth also limit campaign expenditures, which the Supreme Court feared would undermine our democracy. In fact, the opposite is closer to the truth: Political equality *requires* building barriers between money and the ballot box.

8. Civic Education. During the 1990s, the federal government spent $232 million on civic education abroad and none at home. As a result, 97 percent of South Africans said they had been affected by voter education. Only 6 percent of Americans, according to a Gallup Poll in 2000, knew the name of the speaker of the House, while 66 percent could identify the host of *Who Wants to Be a Millionaire?* Almost every country in the world does a better job educating citizens on how to vote.

9. The Franchise. The Electoral College was a progressive innovation in the 18th century; today, it's mainly dictatorships like communist China that use an indirect system to choose their highest leader.

10. International Observers. We demand that all new democracies grant unhindered access to polling sites for international observers, but only one of our 50 states (Missouri) does that. The Organization for Security and Cooperation in Europe, a 55-state organization of which the United States is a member, was invited by Secretary of State Colin Powell to observe the U.S. elections, yet its representatives were permitted to visit only a few "designated sites." Any developing country that restricted observers to a few Potemkin polling sites as the United States did would be roundly condemned by the State Department and the world.

On all 10 dimensions of election administration, the United States scores near the bottom of electoral democracies. There are three reasons for this. First, we have been sloppy and have not insisted that our voting machines be as free from error as our washing machines. We lack a simple procedure most democracies have: a log book at each precinct to register every problem encountered during the day and to allow observers to witness and verify complaints.

McDonald's hires extra workers at lunchtime, but this has not yet occurred to our election officials. Poll workers are exhausted by the time they start counting votes.

Second, we lack uniform standards, and that is because we have devolved authority to the lowest, poorest level of government. It's time for states to retrieve their authority from the counties, and it's time for Congress to insist on national standards.

Third, we have stopped asking what we can learn from our democratic friends, and we have not accepted the rules we impose on others. This has communicated arrogance abroad and left our institutions weak.

The results can be seen most clearly in our bizarre approach to Iraq's election. Washington, you may recall, tried to export the Iowa-caucus model though it violates the first principle of free elections, a secret ballot. An Iraqi ayatollah rejected that and also insisted on the importance of direct elections (meaning no Electoral College). Should we be surprised that the Iraqi Election Commission chose to visit Mexico instead of the United States to learn how to conduct elections?

Critical Thinking

1. What is the central cause of the multiple shortcomings in the way that U.S. elections are conducted?

2. What are the three models used for administering elections in a democracy? What are the drawbacks of the model used by the United States?

3. What are the advantages of a nationally administered election system?

4. What three reasons does Robert Pastor give for the poor U.S. performance in conducting elections?

Create Central

www.mhhe.com/createcentral

Internet References

Federal Election Commission
www.fec.gov
Fair Vote: The Center for Voting and Democracy
www.fairvote.org

ROBERT A. PASTOR is director of the Center for Democracy and Election Management and a professor at American University. At the Carter Center from 1986–2000, he organized election-observation missions to about 30 countries, including the United States.

Pastor, Robert A. From *The American Prospect*, vol. 16, No. 1, January 4, 2005, pp. A2–A3. Copyright © 2005. Reprinted with permission from Robert A. Pastor and The American Prospect, Washington, DC. All rights reserved. www.prospect.org.

Article   Prepared by: Bruce Stinebrickner, *DePauw University*

Contemporary American Democracy in Operation: The Electoral Process in 2012

BRUCE STINEBRICKNER

Learning Outcomes

After reading this article, you will be able to:

- Identify and critique peculiar features of the electoral system used to select presidents and members of Congress.

- Consider why Americans do not, in general, seem unduly concerned about the many peculiarities and even shortcomings in how American national government election are run.

The 2012 American national government elections are over. President Obama and Vice President Joe Biden were re-elected, and 435 seats in the U.S. House of Representatives and 33 seats in the U.S. Senate were filled. An estimated six-billion dollars were spent, and an estimated one-million TV ads were aired, along with innumerable Internet, radio, and newspaper ads. Journalists, political scientists, and other observers have endlessly chronicled, dissected, and critiqued candidates' campaigns and the election results.

This article will focus on four significant features of the contemporary U. S. electoral system as it operated during the 2012 election cycle: (1) the *staggered* schedule of national elections, (2) the *narrowing* of presidential election campaigns stemming from the Electoral College system, (3) the *lag time* between Election Day in November and when successful candidates take office, and (4) controversial voter ID laws, voter turnout, and state governments' roles in running national government elections. A consideration of these features in the context of the 2012 elections is a consideration of essential elements of contemporary American democracy itself.

> *The Separation of Powers, "Divided Government,"*
> *and the Staggered Schedule of Elections for Top*
> *National Government Officials*

Built into the structure of American national government are the familiar notions of three branches and the so-called separation of powers. As political scientist Richard Neustadt

perceptively observed in the mid-twentieth century, the structure of government established by the U.S. Constitution provides not for a "separation of powers," but for a system of "separated institutions sharing powers." Prominent examples of such "sharing" provisions are easy to identify. Enacting legislation involves both legislative and executive branches; in the sphere of military operations, the legislative branch has the power to declare war and the head of the executive branch, the president, serves as commander-in-chief of U.S. armed forces; the president nominates Cabinet officers, Supreme Court justices, and other high-ranking government officials, but one house of Congress, the Senate, has the power to approve or reject the president's nominations; the president proposes treaties to the Senate, but a two-thirds majority vote is necessary to approve them.

In the contemporary American political system, a total of 537 national government officials are elected: president and vice president in the executive branch, and, in the legislative branch, 435 members of the House of Representatives and 100 senators. Given that the executive and legislative branches *share* so many important powers, it is noteworthy that candidates of one major party frequently occupy the presidency and vice-presidency while candidates of the other major party occupy the majority of seats in one or both houses of Congress.

"Divided government" (hereafter DivGovt), the term that political scientists use for this state of affairs, has been the most common outcome of national government elections since World War II. For about 60% of the time, neither party has controlled all three elected entities in the national government. In this historical context, the DivGovt outcome of the 2012 elections is hardly unusual: in 2013–14, Democrats will occupy the presidency and vice presidency as well as the majority of seats in the U.S. Senate, while Republicans will have majority control of the House of Representatives. Contributing to the 60% incidence of DivGovt is the constitutionally-prescribed scheduling of elections wherein American voters never get to choose all elective national government leaders (that is, president and vice president and *all* the members of the House of Representatives and of the Senate) at one time. *Never.*

Table 1 Constitutionally Mandated Staggering of National Government Elections in Presidential and Mid-term Election Years—2000–2016

Year	President/Vice President	House of Representatives	Senate
2000 (presidential election year)	Yes	All 435 members	About 1/3 of members
2002 (mid-term election year)	No	All 435 members	About 1/3 of members
2004 (presidential election year)	Yes	All 435 members	About 1/3 of members
2006 (mid-term election year)	No	All 435 members	About 1/3 of members
2008 (presidential election year)	Yes	All 435 members	About 1/3 of members
2010 (mid-term election year)	No	All 435 members	About 1/3 of members
2012 (presidential election year)	Yes	All 435 members	About 1/3 of members
2014 (mid-term election year)	No	All 435 members	About 1/3 of members
2016 (presidential election year)	Yes	All 435 members	About 1/3 of members

Biennial American national government elections can be conveniently divided into presidential election years and mid-term (short for "mid-presidential term") election years. Table 1 illustrates the constitutionally prescribed staggering of national government elections for 2000–2016: presidential/vice-presidential elections occur every four years simultaneously with elections for the entire 435-member House of Representatives, but for only about one-third of the 100-member Senate. In the intervening even-numbered years, the entire House and a different one-third of Senate seats are filled in mid-term elections. Underlying this staggered schedule of elections are terms of different lengths for presidents/vice presidents, House members, and senators: four, two, and six years, respectively. **(1)**

As already noted, DivGovt has prevailed about 60% of the time since 1946. But mid-term elections have been more likely to result in DivGovt than presidential year elections have been: 12 of 17 (71%) mid-term elections have resulted in DivGovt since World War II, while 8 of 17 (47%) of presidential year elections have. In the twenty-first century, two (2006 and 2010) of three mid-term elections have resulted in DivGovt; in contrast, only one (2012) of four presidential year elections has. Three of four presidential year elections—all but 2012—have been followed by what political scientists call "unified government" (hereafter UniGovt), wherein one party controls all three elected entities in American national government. But only seven national government elections have been held in this century, and the 2000 elections resulted in UniGovt for only about five months before 19 months of DivGovt followed. **(2)** Thus, it is unclear whether these twenty-first century results reflect mere happenstance or a development worthy of note.

Why are presidential election years more likely to result in UniGovt? For one thing, while presidential election years do not provide voters with the opportunity to fill all 537 elective positions in the executive and legislative branches at one time (because only one-third of Senate seats are up for election), presidential years give voters the opportunity to fill more of the 537 elective positions than mid-term election years do. In presidential years, two of the three elected entities in American national government are up for election, as is one-third of the remaining entity, the Senate. Combined with this scheduling

fact is the "presidential coat-tail effect," wherein House and Senate candidates of the same party as the winning presidential candidate tend to get more votes than they otherwise would, thus sometimes riding to electoral success on their presidential candidate's "coat-tails," so to speak. Moreover, American voters have a well-documented tendency to vote against the party of the president in mid-term elections. Taken together, these factors help explain why presidential elections since World War II have more frequently resulted in UniGovt than mid-term elections have.

The five most recent national government elections (2004, 2006, 2008, 2010, and 2012) can illustrate how the staggered schedule of elections seems to increase the likelihood of DivGovt. In the presidential election year of 2004, American voters generally favored Republican candidates. The national elections that year were followed by UniGovt in which Republicans occupied the White House (President George W. Bush), the majority of House seats, and the majority of Senate seats. By November 2006, Americans were disenchanted with the Bush presidency and Republicans' UniGovt performance, and Democratic candidates won a clear majority of seats in the House of Representatives and won enough of the 33 Senate seats up for election to control a bare majority of the 100 seats in the Senate. But, as Table 1 shows, the presidency and vice-presidency were not contested that year. Republican President George W. Bush and Vice President Dick Cheney remained in office, and DivGovt prevailed from January 2007 until January 2009, during which time voter dissatisfaction with Republicans continued. The presidential year elections of 2008 brought UniGovt, this time with Democratic party control of the presidency (Obama), vice-presidency (Biden), the House, and the Senate.

In many other democratic political systems with a two-party system, the strong voter support for candidates of one major party (Democrats) and widespread negative sentiments toward the other major party (Republicans) reflected in the 2006 elections would have resulted in the functional equivalent of UniGovt under the favored party's control. In the American political system, however, the three-branch structure and staggered schedule of elections enabled Republicans to keep control of the presidency and vice-presidency after the 2006 elections. Those two top executive branch offices were not up for election that year, and Republicans George W. Bush and Dick Cheney continued in office for the remaining two years of the four-year terms to which they had been elected in 2004. **(3)**

By 2010, two years after Democratic President Barack Obama and his fellow Democrats had begun a period of UniGovt as a result of the presidential year elections of 2008, the shoe was on the other party's foot, so to speak. Americans, apparently displeased with the Obama presidency and the consequences of Democrats controlling both the executive and legislative branches since January, 2009, voted so as to give Republicans majority control of the House of Representatives. But even strong support for Republican candidates for the 37 Senate seats up for election in 2010 was not enough for Republicans to gain a majority in the Senate, and, consistent with Table 1, President Obama and Vice President Biden were not up for election. Just as occurred after the mid-term elections four years earlier, DivGovt followed the 2010 mid-term elections.

In both 2006 and 2010, a majority of American voters favored candidates of one major party—and presumably, to at least some extent, the policies with which those candidates were identified—over candidates of the other major party. Yet the staggered schedule of elections prevented voters' strong support for one party—and opposition to the other—from resulting in the preferred party having control of both executive and legislative branches. In turn, the party favored by the majority of voters did not have a clear opportunity to lead the government in directions that that party's candidates had supported while running for office. One such Republican policy direction after the 2010 election would have likely been the repeal of the Affordable Care Act, the historic health care reform legislation that came to be known as Obamacare. Passed early in 2010 during Democratic UniGovt, Obamacare was scheduled to take full effect in 2014. Public opinion polls in fall 2010 consistently showed that a clear majority of Americans supported repeal of Obamacare. In the context of the staggered schedule of American national government elections and DivGovt, however, Republicans' mid-term success could not bring about that legislative result.

In the 2012 elections, Americans voted so as to keep a Democratic president and vice president in office, a Republican majority in the House of Representatives, and a Democratic majority in the Senate. This was the first presidential election year in the twenty-first century that has resulted in DivGovt. As already noted, since 1946 mid-term elections have been more likely to produce DivGovt than presidential year elections, which, of course, is not to say that presidential year elections *never* result in DivGovt.

For over two decades, political scientists have been systematically researching what difference, if any, DivGovt and UniGovt make. In his 1991 book *Divided We Govern,* Professor David Mayhew presented painstakingly gathered evidence from the 1946–1990 period supporting the counter-intuitive conclusion that DivGovt and UniGovt affected neither the number of major laws enacted nor the number of major investigations

of the executive branch launched by Congress. Subsequent research by other political scientists—and some follow-up research on the 1991–2002 period by Mayhew himself—has suggested that, while variation between DivGovt and UniGovt may not lead to *as* important or *as* extensive differences as might be expected, some important differences may result.

The enactment of the landmark Obamacare legislation in March 2010 occurred during Democratic UniGovt in the second year of the Obama presidency. In the American political system of the early twenty-first century, it seems almost impossible to imagine any such far-reaching health care reform legislation being passed under DivGovt. Notwithstanding Mayhew's important findings about UniGovt/DivGovt, it seems plausible that UniGovt is today a necessary condition for reform legislation of the historic proportions of Obamacare. **(4)**

What I am about to say may surprise some introductory students of American national government: *the three-branch "separated institutions sharing powers" structure of American national government that the Constitution establishes is not the only way to structure government in a democratic political system.* Nor is it necessarily the best way. Parceling out shares of power to three co-equal branches may prevent government from getting things done and/or give the impression of endless and unproductive squabbling between political parties and among branches of government. In *Federalist 51*, James Madison, the architect of America's three-branch structure of government, wrote that "ambition must be made to counteract ambition" in order to keep (even democratic) government from getting out of control. Today, of course, many observers of the contemporary American political system see "gridlock" and "stalemate" where Madison might well see appropriate and useful conflict and balancing among the branches.

When DivGovt occurs, incumbent candidates and parties can more plausibly blame the other party for government shortcomings while they have been in office. In the 2012 presidential election campaign, for example, we heard President Obama say that he would have accomplished more in the last two years of his first term in office if only Republicans, especially House of Representatives Republicans, had not blocked what he wanted to do. One example cited was his proposal of an American Jobs Act in fall 2011, an attempt, he said, to address continuing high unemployment in the country by enacting an additional economic stimulus measure. But, according to Obama's narrative, DivGovt—personified by majority Republican control of the House of Representatives resulting from the 2010 mid-term elections—prevented him from helping jobless Americans. As we have seen, the staggered schedule of elections makes DivGovt more likely. Also made more likely—and probably more credible—in election campaigns is what is sometimes called the "blame game," wherein opposing candidates deny responsibility for government shortcomings by blaming the other party for obstructing desirable policies in periods of DivGovt.

Writ Large in 2012: The Electoral College's Narrowing of the Presidential General Election Campaign

The Electoral College's 538 members elect the president and vice president as the second stage of a two-stage process in which American voters choose members of the Electoral College who, in turn, vote for president and vice president. In all but a handful of the fifty-seven presidential elections held since 1788, the Electoral College winner also received the most votes from the American public. In 2012, President Obama won both the popular vote (with about 51% of the vote) and the Electoral College (with about 62%, that is, 332 of 538 votes). Even in the four or five presidential elections in which the Electoral College has "misfired"—that is, selected a president who did not receive the most popular votes—the Electoral College outcome has been shaped by state-by-state popular voting totals. **(5)** An Electoral College "misfiring" occurred most recently in 2000, when George W. Bush became president even though he received fewer popular votes than his opponent, Al Gore.

Besides Electoral College "misfiring" and how it fits with democratic ideals, another consequence of the Electoral College system today assumed what seemed to be unprecedented prominence in 2012. Even casual observers of the 2012 contest between Obama and Romney could hardly have missed the disproportionate attention paid to "battleground states," the ten or so states that each of the two presidential tickets seemed to have a reasonable chance of winning and that were expected to decide the overall Electoral College outcome. Objective observers and the candidates themselves regarded the remaining 40 states as certain or at least fairly certain to support one candidate over the other; according to the "winner-take-all" (or "unit rule") procedures operating in forty-eight states and the District of Columbia, each of these states would then deliver its entire slate of Electors to the preferred candidate. In 2012, the Electoral College system narrowed the presidential general election campaigns from *national* campaigns to campaigns focused on the ten battleground states in which fewer than one-quarter of all Americans lived.

The concentration of attention and resources—in particular, television advertising, candidate time, and organizational efforts—on the "battleground states" is not new. What *is* new is that, as of 2012, "the battleground has grown almost comically small." **(6)** Increasingly, like-minded Americans of the same socio-economic classes are tending to cluster in where they reside, fewer states are competitive in presidential elections, and the presidential campaign "battleground" shrinks.

In the very close 1960 presidential election campaign pitting John Kennedy against Richard Nixon, Kennedy visited 49 states and Nixon visited all 50. By contrast, in 2012, candidates Obama and Romney each campaigned in only ten states after their respective party conventions. Campaign advertising reflects the same trend. In 2008, TV presidential campaign ads appeared in about 100 of 210 media markets; in 2012, the number 100 had shrunk by "one-third to one-half." **(7)**

The 2012 Obama campaign understandably concentrated its early—and late, for that matter—TV advertising in battleground states, and especially in its early advertising sought to "define" Romney in negative terms. Many election observers have concluded that the Obama campaign's early and effective advertising in battleground states was a crucial factor in the president's re-election. The Romney campaign and Romney supporters also concentrated their TV advertising in the battleground states, much of it, of course, criticizing President

Obama's first four years in office. I myself watched television in four states during the last three months of the election campaign, and the differences were stark. In New York (safe for Obama), Indiana (safe for Romney), and Georgia (safe for Romney), I saw virtually no TV ads about the presidential campaign. In Ohio, the airwaves were saturated with them, most of them negative.

In the course of the 2012 presidential campaigns, citizens living in the most competitive states may well have developed more polarized attitudes about the two candidates than did citizens in non-competitive states that were not subjected to massive amounts of negative TV advertising. This would seem an anomalous, even perverse, result, and one that would be attributable to the workings of the contemporary Electoral College system and the shrinking of the "battleground" on which presidential election campaigns are waged.

The most populous battleground state in the twenty-first century has consistently been Florida. Its pivotal importance in close presidential elections was highlighted in 2000 when George W. Bush's controversial and exceedingly narrow margin over Al Gore in the state gave Bush the presidency. In subsequent presidential elections in 2004, 2008, and 2012, presidential candidates have continued to pay great attention to Florida.

Disproportionate numbers of senior citizens and Cuban-Americans live in Florida, and we can wonder whether presidents or aspiring presidents' policies on Medicare, Social Security, and relations with Cuba are unduly affected by Floridians' views. In a roughly analogous situation, observers have long asserted that if Iowa did not play such a prominent role in the presidential nominating process, national government subsidies for ethanol production, which aid Iowa farmers, would be less than they currently are, if they existed at all. Candidates for their parties' presidential nominations seem inclined to support ethanol subsidies rather than offend voters in the often pivotal state of Iowa. Turning our attention back to Florida and presidential general elections, we can consider anew the possibility of Floridians' undue influence on Medicare, Social Security, and Cuba policies. The Social Security and Medicare entitlement crises facing the American political system certainly do not stem entirely—or even predominantly—from Florida's twenty-first century status as the most populous battleground state. Yet presidents' willingness to consider revising entitlements for senior citizens or revamping American-Cuban relations may well be affected—at least at the margins—by the electoral importance of Florida in the Electoral College system.

Lag time between the November Elections and when Successful Candidates Take Office

I am writing this article in early December 2012, about a month after Election Day. By the time you read it, the lag time between Election Day and when the winning candidates take office in January 2013 will be over. But that does not make the issue of lag time any less potentially significant for the contemporary American political system.

On November 6, 2012, Americans chose a president and vice president, 435 members of the House of Representatives, and 33 senators. On January 3, 2013, the successful 468 House and Senate candidates will take office; on January 20, 2013, President Obama and Vice President Biden will begin their second four-year terms. More than eight weeks will elapse between Election Day and when new members of the 113th Congress will take office, and nearly eleven weeks will pass before President Obama and Vice President Biden begin their second terms. During the intervening period, the "old" 112th Congress and President Obama, completing his first four-year term, will be responsible for crucial taxing and spending decisions and other pressing matters as well, including the volatile relationship between Israelis and Palestinians that erupted into violence in November and the rebellion against the dictatorial Assad regime in Syria that has led to a civil war with a death toll in the tens of thousands.

Just as with staggered elections and the Electoral College, Americans take for granted the lag time between Election Day in early November and the dates on which successful candidates take office in January. Until the addition of the Twentieth Amendment to the U. S. Constitution in 1933, the gap between Election Day and the dates when the new—or newly re-elected—president, vice president, and members of Congress took office was even longer, stretching over four months from early November to early March.

Unless the "old" Congress and the "old" president act in the "lame duck" period between Election Day, 2012, and January 1, 2013, American national government will go over a so-called fiscal cliff, the result of several pieces of legislation that set the date when Bush era tax cuts expire and when mostly across-the-board national government spending cuts (called "sequestration") automatically take effect. Most economists, not to mention the authoritative Congressional Budget Office, have said that if these automatic changes go into effect at the start of 2013, the country's fragile economic recovery from the Great Recession of 2008–2009 will be jeopardized. In their view, raising taxes and decreasing national government spending across-the-board would combine to *de*-stimulate the economy and reverse the country's slow recovery from the Great Recession. The two-month gap between Election Day and the dates when those elected—or re-elected—to the executive and legislative branches take office means that lame-duck officials are responsible for deciding what, if anything, to do to avoid the "cliff."

Taxing and spending issues played a prominent role in 2012 election campaigns, and appropriately so, given that government fiscal problems and the health of the American economy are related. It should be neither surprising nor particularly blameworthy that the 112th Congress and President Obama "kicked the can down the road" until after the November 6 election. In other words, they postponed the likely-to-be-tough negotiations that would almost inevitably precede the challenging decisions to be made. That such negotiations and decision-making would be challenging and inevitable, and that Congress and the president had earlier and repeatedly "kicked the can down the road" seems to stem, at least partly, from divided government. And, of course, divided government itself is partly a consequence of the American political system's staggered schedule of elections, as already noted earlier in this piece.

Deferring decision-making on whether and how to avoid the "fiscal cliff" until after the November 2012 elections meant that that decision-making would be left to the lame-duck 112th Congress and to a president holding office as a consequence of his having been elected in November 2008.

As I write these words in early December, 2012, how the "fiscal cliff" negotiations among congressional leaders and President Obama will play out and what decisions will be made are unknown. What *is* known is that the elected national government office-holders responsible for the decision-making in November and December of 2012 do *not* hold their government offices as the result of the most recent national elections held on November 6. The lag time built into the American political system means that the officeholders responsible for running the executive and legislative branches of American national government until January, 2013, include one group of officials elected somewhat more than six years earlier (about one-third of senators), another group elected somewhat more than four years earlier (another one-third of senators as well as the president and vice president), and a third group elected somewhat more than two years earlier (almost all House members and the remaining one-third of senators).

As it happened, the 2012 elections resulted in continuity of top government leaders between 2012 and 2013/14 and reduced, it would seem, the potential for lame-duck indecisiveness or inaction stemming from the lag time built into the American political system. In 2013/14, President Obama and Vice President Biden will continue in the two top executive branch positions; Republican John Boehner, Speaker of the House during the 112th Congress, will continue in that position in the 113th Congress because Republicans kept their majority control of the House of Representatives; and Senators Harry Reid, a Democrat, and Mitch McConnell, a Republican, will continue as majority and minority leaders, respectively, of the Senate because Democrats retained their majority status in the Senate.

Now imagine a different set of outcomes from the 2012 elections. Suppose Mitt Romney and Paul Ryan were president-elect and vice president-elect, respectively, during the eleven weeks before their inaugurations on January 20, 2013. Also imagine that Republicans had won enough Senate seats to have transformed Republican Mitch McConnell into majority leader at the start of the 113th Congress in early January. Given these scenarios, consider the legitimacy—in a purportedly democratic system whose citizens had just spoken in national elections—of decisions about the looming fiscal cliff and other pressing matters that involved President Barack Obama and Senate Majority Leader Harry Reid, both of whom would have been leaving their leadership positions in January.

We can only guess at what the short-term and long-term outcomes of the counter-factuals posed in the preceding paragraph would have been, but two of the most infamous lame-duck periods in U.S. history can give us pause for thought. Between the election of Abraham Lincoln in November 1860 and his becoming president in March 1861, seven Southern states seceded from the Union, setting the stage for the bloody Civil War that did not commence until after Lincoln was inaugurated. In

November 1932, the United States and the world were enduring the Great Depression. Democratic presidential candidate
Franklin D. Roosevelt defeated incumbent Republican President Herbert Hoover, and Democratic majorities won control
of both the House of Representatives and the Senate. Roosevelt
and the new Congress waited four long months before taking
the reins of government and beginning to enact the set of programs and policies that came to be known as "The New Deal."

In November 2012, the United States faced a very fragile
economy in the aftermath of the Great Recession of 2008–09,
the biggest economic downturn since the Great Depression. The
country did not have to wait four months for the newly elected
officeholders to take office (as had been the case in 1932–33),
and, as already noted, the "new" set of national government
leaders just (re-)elected remained essentially unchanged from
the "old" group of leaders. Despite these 2012 circumstances,
the lag time between Election Day and office-taking remains
a distinctive and potentially problematic feature of American
democracy.

How does lag time in the American political system compare
with corresponding intervals in other democracies? In many parliamentary systems, a newly elected prime minister usually takes
office within a week or two after the elections. *Within a week!*
This sort of timetable applies to Great Britain, where parliamentary government was born; to the U. S.'s northern neighbor, Canada; and to India, the world's most populous democracy. Voters
go to the polls, the votes are counted, the winners are declared,
and prime ministers take office, usually all within a week or
two. Why, in an industrialized twenty-first century democracy
with communications devices and information systems of which
people could only dream a few decades ago, wait two or more
months for newly elected officials to take office? **(8)**

*Voter ID Laws, Voter Turnout, and State Govern-
ments' Responsibility for Running National Government Elections*

Since 2011, laws requiring photo IDs in order to vote were
introduced in more than 30 states and more than a half-dozen
such laws were enacted. **(9)** Critics expressed concern that such
requirements suppress voter turnout and, in particular, minority and lower-income voter turnout. Court cases ensued, and
different rulings were handed down with respect to different
states. Indiana's strict photo ID law (passed in 2006 and requiring that voters show government-issued photo identification)
was upheld by the U. S. Supreme Court in 2008. Viewing all
these happenings in the context of the larger issue of voter turnout rates in American national government elections can be
instructive.

In the 2012 presidential election, an estimated 59% of the
voting-eligible population turned out to vote. **(10)** That is about
three percentage points lower than 2008, about one percentage
point lower than 2004, and five percentage points higher than
2000. It is also higher than the average turnout rate of about
55% for the last seven presidential elections in the twentieth
century (1972–1996). In presidential elections in the 1950s and
1960s, before the minimum legal voting age was lowered to
eighteen, voter turnout rates ranged between 60 and 65%.

Among the world's democratic political systems, American
national election turnout rates are among the lowest, with most
other industrialized democracies having turnout rates between
70% and 85% in comparable national government elections.
Two countries with compulsory voting laws, Australia and Belgium, average in the vicinity of 85% to 90%.

Political scientists know a considerable amount about the
effect of many procedural variables on voter turnout rates in
the American political system and they are continuing to conduct systematic research that will likely produce even greater
understanding. Much, but not all, of what they have found fits
comfortably with common sense. Allowing voter registration
on Election Day ("Election Day Registration")—or not requiring registration at all, as in North Dakota—seems to increase
voter turnout rates by significant amounts. **(11)** Lengthening
the hours during which polling places are open on Election
Day also tends to increase voter turnout rates. Absentee voting
procedures, literacy tests, poll taxes, eligibility of incarcerated
individuals and of felons who have completed their sentences,
and the like are other variables known to decrease or increase
voting turnout. Holding elections on weekends (when fewer
people work) or having Election Day a mandated public holi-
day would seem likely to increase voter turnout rates, if the
experience of some European democracies is a reliable guide.

Interestingly, strict voter ID laws that require voters to show
a government-issued photo ID have not yet been conclusively
shown to affect voter turnout rates systematically. **(12)** But these
laws have been enacted relatively recently and the 2008 presidential election, which featured an African-American, Barack
Obama, as the Democratic candidate, may not have produced
typical turnout patterns. Additional research on the effects of
such photo ID laws may well show the results that many observers and activists expect and fear: the disproportionate reduction
of voter turnout among those who are lower-income, less well-
educated, and racial minorities.

The growing availability of "early voting" (that is, allowing
any registered voter to cast his or her ballot before Election Day
without claiming absence or unavailability on Election Day)
in more than two-thirds of the states has not been matched by
irrefutable evidence of increased voter turnout. Indeed, some
have argued that the opposite may even be true—"early voting"
could conceivably work to reduce overall voter turnout. Some
research suggests that almost all early voters were highly likely
to vote anyway, and one unanticipated consequence of "early
voting" is that those individuals who do not vote early feel less
social and political pressure to vote on Election Day when it
finally arrives, thus working to reduce overall voter turnout. **(13)**

When Americans wring their hands about relatively low
voter turnout rates, they should realize that there are relatively
easy and reliable ways to increase (or decrease) those rates.
Allowing voters to register on the same day that they vote (or,
as North Dakota does, not requiring registration at all) and pro-
active efforts by governments to register citizens to vote ahead
of time and to inform and mobilize citizens to vote are among
the ways to increase voter turnout. But a fundamental question underlies discussion of procedural steps that increase or
decrease voter turnout rates: in a democratic political system, to

what extent should voting participation be facilitated, encouraged, and made easy?

The American public and government officials differ among themselves about this fundamental question. Disagreements about specific measures that increase or decrease voter turnout rates seem to stem from the issue of how easy—or hard—citizens' participation in national government elections should be. Related to—or underlying—responses to this question are considerations of partisan advantage or disadvantage that result in different views about voter ID laws and other regulations that would seem likely to inhibit or encourage voting. Procedural obstacles are thought to be more likely to discourage lower-income, less well-educated, and minority citizens from voting, and all these groups are more likely to identify with the Democratic party.

The key role of state governments in conducting national government elections must not be overlooked in a discussion of voter turnout rates. Illustrating state governments' roles are the newly restrictive voter ID laws enacted before the 2012 elections in some states but not others. Other significant procedural variations among the states include whether all voters receive and cast their ballots by mail (Oregon), by when voter registration must be completed in order for a citizen to be allowed to vote (Minnesota, Maine, and about a half-dozen other states allow "Election Day Registration" and generally report higher voter turnout rates than other states), the length of time during which the polls are open on Election Day, and, more generally, the extent to which governments are pro-active in working to mobilize the electorate to vote (TV advertising, education in the schools, pro-active or "easy" voter registration, etc.).

That American national government elections are not administered by American national government officials is noteworthy *and* peculiar. Think about it: national government elections are, for the most part, run by the fifty state governments under loose national government regulations and requirements, and some states even delegate considerable discretion to counties and cities. Until American national government elections are run by the national government, *state-by-state* variations that work to increase or decrease voter turnout rates in *national* government elections will continue and be potentially problematic. The controversies in 2012 about voter ID laws should be viewed as addressing one tip of an iceberg created by the noteworthy and peculiar role of state governments in national government elections.

Concluding Discussion

Americans are urged, encouraged, or at least nudged to vote by a variety of sources—teachers, parents, schools, pastors, friends, newspapers, TV ads, candidates for office, and the like. A majority of them do, at least in presidential election years. This article has addressed four features in the American national government electoral process against the backdrop of recent elections: (1) the constitutionally-mandated *staggered* election schedule for filling positions in the national government's legislative and executive branches, (2) the *narrowing* effect of the Electoral College system on presidential election

campaigns, (3) the long *lag time* between Election Day and when the winning candidates for president, vice president, and Congress take office, and (4) voter turnout rates and photo ID laws in the context of the central roles of state governments in running national government elections.

Americans who were interested in the national government elections of 2012 typically focused their attention on who was going to win (the so-called "horse race" perspective) and/or who *should* win and why (policies, personal characteristics, party affiliation, etc.). As a voter wanting the best possible election outcomes—victories by candidates whom I favored and whose polices, I thought, would be best for the country (and for the world)—so did I. Socialization and news media reports worked to reinforce Americans' preoccupations with who is winning and for whom to vote.

I have certainly not addressed all the significant, interesting, and, yes, debatable features of the American electoral process in this article. Omitted from consideration have been a number of significant features related to the way Americans choose their top national government leaders, including (i) the unique nominating process by which major party presidential candidates are chosen, (ii) the constitutionally mandated malapportionment of the U.S. Senate, wherein the least populous state, Wyoming (population: roughly 570,000), and the most populous state, California (population: roughly 38,000,000) each get the same number of senators, (iii) the partisan and presumably self-interested re-districting process for the House of Representatives that is centered, for the most part, in state legislatures and that produces "safe seats" for members of both parties in the vast majority of the 435 House constituencies, and (iv) the ways that, particularly in the wake of the Supreme Court's *Citizens United* ruling in 2010, American national government elections campaigns are financed.

Each of the features identified in the preceding paragraph is consequential or potentially consequential. The idiosyncratic contours of the presidential nomination process often significantly affect the sorts of major party candidates from whom American voters choose their president. The two-senators-per-state principle and the elimination of effective two-party competition in all but about two- to three-dozen of the 435 House seats both contribute to how the contemporary U.S. Congress functions (or malfunctions). Finally, while some critics' worst fears about the financing of the 2012 elections were not realized, the ways in which American election campaigns are financed remain a matter for serious concern.

Elections have consequences. *So do processes and procedures relating to the electoral system.* The phenomena addressed in this article can and do affect the outcomes of elections and the functioning of American national government. Those interested in American national government elections and the complexities of the American political system are well-advised to shift their gaze beyond particular candidates, particular campaigns, and particular election outcomes—interesting and significant as they might be—and pay more attention to electoral processes and procedures of the sort addressed here.

Notes

I want to thank Maryann Gallagher, Kelsey Kauffman, Kyle Kerrigan, Deepa Prakash, Avery Robinson, and Jonathan Rosario for their helpful comments on earlier drafts of this article. Maryann, a departmental colleague who teaches and writes about American politics—as I do—offered a number of particularly helpful suggestions and criticisms, most of which have been incorporated in one way or another. Thanks a second time to Jonathan Rosario, a senior Political Science major at DePauw University, for providing a list of relevant bibliographic sources relating to voter ID laws and the like that he prepared while working on his senior seminar paper. Last but certainly not least, thanks to David Mayhew, my PhD dissertation advisor many years ago, who, over a long lunch in November 2012 and in a few emails before and after that lunch, shared relevant particulars and insights from his vast store of knowledge about American politics and political science research.

I also want to thank Professor Ben Scafidi and the Department of Political Science at Georgia College and State University at Milledgeville for inviting me to deliver a lecture on their campus on Constitution Day, September 17, 2012. The seeds of this article were planted as I prepared that lecture.

1. The three sets of elected national government officeholders are also elected, for the most part, from different constituencies. Presidents/vice presidents are elected in what is, in effect, a national election mediated by the state-by-state Electoral College system; almost all House members (excluding the seven from the least populous states, each of which has only a single House member who is elected "at-large" from the entire state) are elected from congressional districts into which forty-three of the states are divided, with districts averaging about 700,000 residents; and senators are elected in state-wide elections in each of the fifty states.

2. A short-lived period of UniGovt under Republican control occurred after the inauguration of President George W. Bush and Vice President Dick Cheney (both Republicans) in late January 2001. The November 2000 elections resulted in a Republican majority in the House of Representatives, a Senate that was evenly divided between Republicans and Democrats, and Republicans occupying the presidency and vice presidency. After Cheney became vice president of the United States as well as president of the Senate (that is, the presiding officer of the Senate) on January 20, 2001, he cast his tie-breaking vote in favor of Republicans, giving the party majority control of the Senate. In early June of that year, however, Senator James Jeffords of Vermont renounced his Republican party affiliation and began caucusing with Senate Democrats, thus beginning approximately nineteen months of DivGovt during which Republicans controlled the presidency/vice-presidency and House of Representatives, but Democrats controlled the Senate. *www.senate.gov/pagelayout/history/one_item_and_teasers/ partydiv.htm*. Accessed November 25, 2012.

3. In parliamentary systems of government, executive and legislative officeholders are not separately elected, as they are in the American political system, and, in turn, the functional equivalent of DivGovt is unusual or even impossible. I suppose that coalition governments in multi-party parliamentary systems, wherein no single party has enough parliamentary seats to "form

a government" by itself, might be said to resemble, in some respects, what is known as DivGovt in the U.S.

4. Mayhew's 1991 book triggered a great deal of political science research on the consequences of divided and unified government. David R. Mayhew, *Divided We Govern: Party Control, Lawmaking, and Investigations, 1946-2002*, second edition (New Haven, CT: Yale University Press, 2005) includes both Mayhew's original 1991 book addressing 1946-1990 and an epilogue treating 1991-2002. Frank R. Baumgartner *et al.* report that UniGovt tends to produce more important legislation than DivGovt in "Divided Government, Legislative Productivity, and Policy Change in the US and France," manuscript submitted to *British Journal of Political Science*, March 12, 2012. www.unc.edu/~fbaum/papers/ Divided_Government_BJPS.pdf. Accessed November 25, 2012.

5. The unclear case occurred in 1960, when the Electoral College selected John Kennedy to be president. Whether Kennedy or his opponent Richard Nixon won a plurality of the very close national popular vote that year depends on interpretation of the popular vote in Alabama, where the voting public elected a slate of eleven Electoral College members that included six anti-Kennedy conservative Democrats.

6. This quote comes from Adam Liptak, "The Vanishing Battleground," November 4, 2012 *New York Times—Sunday Review*, pp. 1ff. Much of the commentary in the rest of this paragraph and the two succeeding paragraphs also comes from Liptak. Political scientists Alan Abramowitz and Kyle L. Saunders have provided data that confirm Liptak's observation about the decreasing number of competitive states in presidential elections. The numbers of states in which the winning candidate's margin of victory was 5% or less in the presidential elections of 1960, 1976, 2000, and 2004 were 24, 24, 15, and 12, respectively. "'Why Can't We All Just Get Along?' The Reality of a Polarized America," *The Forum* 3(2) (2005), p. 13.

7. Liptak attributes these figures to Elizabeth Wilner of Kantar Media's Campaign Media Analysis Group.

8. One possible response is that, in the British, Canadian, and Indian parliamentary systems, a newly elected prime minister who defeats an incumbent prime minister would have, before a national parliamentary election, almost always have served as "Leader of the Opposition," the "shadow" prime minister whose everyday leadership responsibilities with respect to his or her Opposition party are highly relevant preparation for serving as prime minister. Moreover, the Opposition "front bench" that flanks the Leader of the Opposition consists of a number of "shadow ministers" who generally immerse themselves in the workings of various ministries or departments for which they are likely to assume governing responsibility alongside the new prime minister in an incoming Cabinet. In turn, if the incumbent prime minister and the incumbent governing party(ies) are to be replaced by the Leader of the Opposition and the opposition party(ies) after an election, the identities of the new leadership team are mostly determined ahead of time and the new ministers are usually relatively well-prepared to take over the reins of government quickly.

In the American political system with its "separated institutions sharing powers" structure of government, presidential candidates who defeat an incumbent president (such as Mitt Romney would have been had he beaten Barack Obama in 2012) no doubt give some thought during their campaigns to the identities of their prospective top aides and Cabinet members. Moreover, if non-incumbent presidential candidates were going to assume office within a week or two after winning the presidency, they would doubtless think more about such matters during their campaigns and perhaps even publicly name the top echelons of their prospective administrations before Election Day.

9. For details, see website of the Brennan Center for Justice at NYU Law School. [www.brennancenter.org/content/resource/voting_law_changes_in_2012/ Accessed December 2, 2012], website of the National Conference of State Legislatures [www.ncsl.org/legislatures-elections/elections/voter-id.aspx. Accessed December 2, 2012], and "Counting Voters, Counting Votes," *The Economist*, October 27th, 2012, p. 34.

10. The 59% estimate is calculated from estimated vote totals in a November 22, 2012, email to me from Professor Michael McDonald of George Mason University. Professor McDonald is known to be an expert on voter turnout in American elections, and the authoritative website for his United States Election Project is the source of the other voter turnout data used in the rest of this paragraph. http://elections.gmu.edu/bio.html. Accessed November 25, 2012.

11. Barry C. Burden *et al.*, "Election Laws, Mobilization, and Turnout: The Unanticipated Consequences of Election Reform," January 5, 2012, unpublished paper. https://docs.google.com/a/depauw.edu/viewer? a=v&q=cache:UI8Dkg-W8OxsJ:electionadmin.wisc.edu/bcmm12.pdf+&hl =en&-gl=us&pid=bl&srcid=ADGEESi dal5arwDmt_zh8qySEg-OkDK5HOY4ikmzyKagNNCp4Fl3p-BASU-dD5RUqrKy9YOu-bSqUVl6BD4fFZGbdoB0QXqsO_YpuYdXgyVVnKAq0KI58-FhhSIxoZpxWFclTHCmZeGc8kS& sig=AHIEtbRG3Wq9_913-VQ4bN1ELv20Rql0OUw. Accessed November 25, 2012.

12. See Jason D. Mycoff *et al.*, "The Empirical Effects of Voter-ID Laws: Present or Absent?" *PS: Political Science and Politics* 42 (2009), 121–126. Even though Mycoff et al.'s research points to the absence of empirical effects from voter ID laws at the time of their research, other research has shown that low-income, less well-educated, and minority citizens are less likely to possess suitable government-issued photo IDs than other citizens. The website for the Brennan Center for Justice presents a wealth of information about voting procedures, photo ID laws, and related topics, and strongly suggests that photo ID laws make voting by minorities and low-income citizens more difficult. The website also lists dozens of relevant scholarly pieces. Brennancenter.org. Accessed December 2, 2012.

13. Burden *et al.*

Critical Thinking

1. What does it mean to say that the American political system has a "staggered" schedule of national elections? What has been one major consequence of such "staggering" for American national government since World War II?

2. In what way(s) did the Electoral College system "narrow" the 2012 presidential general election campaign? In your view, was that good or bad for American democracy? Why?

3. What is the lag time that occurs after national government elections are held in early November? Do you agree that this "lag time" is problematic or potentially problematic for the American political system? Why or why not? How does lag time in the American political system compare with the corresponding period of time in parliamentary democracies?

4. How are voter turnout, photo ID laws, and state governments' responsibilities in running national government elections related to one another? Do you think that state governments' major role in national government elections is appropriate? Why or why not?

5. Identify additional features of the American national government's electoral system that are briefly raised near the conclusion of the article. Assess the significance of each of them, and consider whether they seem to be as consequential for the American political system as the four features to which the bulk of the article is devoted.

6. Do you agree that electoral processes and procedures have consequences and that Americans should pay more attention to the features of the American electoral system addressed in this selection? Why or why not?

Create Central

www.mhhe.com/createcentral

Internet References

Fair Vote: The Center for Voting and Democracy
www.fairvote.org
United States Election Project
www.elections.gmu.edu

Article   Prepared by: Bruce Stinebrickner, *DePauw University*

Modern Pollster

The profession must adapt to cell phones and the Internet.

JOHN J. MILLER

Learning Outcomes

After reading this article, you will be able to:

- Consider the place of political polling in the American political system and assess whether, all in all, political polling contributes to or undermines American democracy.

- Ponder what role, if any, American national government should play in regulating, supporting, and perhaps even "doing" political polling.

- Think about the political effects, besides undermining the accuracy of political polling, of cell phones and the Internet on the American political system.

A few days before Eric Cantor lost his Virginia congressional district's GOP nomination last year, his campaign touted the finding of an internal poll. It showed Cantor, the majority leader of the House, beating his challenger, Dave Brat, 62 percent to 28 percent. As good as this 34-point lead looked, its release signaled that Cantor sensed trouble. He was right to fret: On June 10, voters favored Brat by eleven points.

Cantor's defeat marked one of the most startling upsets in recent political history, and official Washington, worried whenever an incumbent falls, wondered what went wrong. Had Cantor neglected his constituents? Had he irritated conservatives over immigration? Had late-deciding voters broken for Brat in the final hours? Whatever the factors, just about everybody agreed on one thing: The pundits didn't see it coming.

"It was an aberration," says John Mc-Laughlin, the pollster who worked for Cantor. He blames the surprise on sabotage—i.e.,

Democrats who took advantage of Virginia's open-primary laws to cast protest votes against a GOP heavyweight.

Whatever the causes of the blindsiding, the plain fact is that polling is getting harder, especially at the local level, and the supposed aberrations could become routine. Pollsters are scrambling to keep up with changes in technology and behavior that have rendered traditional survey methods obsolete. "We're facing serious challenges," says Scott Keeter of the Pew Research Center. Steve Mitchell, a longtime pollster in Michigan, is more dramatic: "I'm not sure I'll be able to do this for more than two or three more election cycles," he says. "We could be watching the death of polling."

The birth of polling came in the 19th century, as newspapers tried to gauge popular sentiment by sending reporters into the streets, armed with questionnaires and tasked with collecting opinions. By the 1930s, George Gallup, Elmo Roper, and others had improved upon these primitive practices. They pioneered new approaches that relied on sampling and probability. Even so, they suffered a few remarkable failures—none more notorious than the one represented in the iconic photo of a grinning President Truman in 1948, when he held up a copy of the *Chicago Tribune* with its erroneous banner headline, "Dewey Defeats Truman." As the historian Philip White points out in *Whistle Stop,* his recent book on the election, Gallup and Roper separately made a series of methodological mistakes. They also had become so convinced of Thomas E. Dewey's inevitable victory that they stopped polling before the race was really over.

Yet they were smart enough to learn from their failures, and also to take advantage of the rise of the telephone, which made it possible for researchers to call just about anybody and produce almost completely random samples of the population. Their work began to look scientific, and polling entered a kind of golden era in the 1970s that mixed relatively low costs with reliable conclusions. Ever since, most political polls have gotten the right result not just most of the time, but the vast majority of the time.

Recent elections, however, have presented new challenges. In 2012, GOP presidential nominee Mitt Romney was certain that he would win. Anybody who doubts the sincerity of his conviction need only watch the opening scene of *Mitt*, the Netflix documentary on his campaign. "Does someone have a number for the president?" said Romney on Election Night, recognizing for the first time that he would have to concede. "Hadn't thought about that." The reason he hadn't thought about it was that his pollsters had fed him lousy data—information that Romney and many of his supporters chose to believe, even as it contradicted other surveys that showed the race tipping to President Obama.

The polls of 2014 saw nothing quite so spectacular, and they did a fairly good job of picking winners and losers. Yet they commonly underestimated the strength of GOP candidates—a flaw on display perhaps most prominently in Virginia's Senate race, in which Republican Ed Gillespie nearly ousted Mark Warner, the Democratic incumbent. Most polls had predicted a double-digit win for Warner, who in the end prevailed by less than a percentage point. Many Republicans wondered whether more-accurate polling would have boosted GOP turnout and generated a different outcome.

So what's going on? Several factors have conspired in recent years to disrupt longstanding practices in public-opinion research, making it more difficult and expensive to arrive at reliable results. They can be summed up in two words: contact and cooperation.

The rise of cell phones has made it easier than ever to reach people, but it also has had the paradoxical effect of complicating the work of pollsters. That's because close to half of all households have dropped their landlines, driving a wedge between phone numbers and places of residence. Pollsters no longer can look at area codes and make safe assumptions about where people live. It's even harder among particular demographic groups, such as the young, the poor, and minorities, whose cell-phone use is even higher than average. Call-screening technologies and voicemail compound the problem by encouraging people to turn down callers they don't know. Finally, a federal law prevents pollsters from auto-dialing cell phones—a consumer-protection measure that dates from when airtime was calculated in dollars per minute but is still on the books today. So reaching people on cell phones takes more effort, raising the costs of polling.

Even when pollsters connect with potential survey respondents, they face a new dilemma: a growing reluctance to cooperate. In 1997, according to the Pew Research Center, pollsters could count on initial conversations to turn into successful interviews more than one-third of the time. By 2012, this rate had dropped to less than 10 percent. So it takes many more calls—and deeper pockets—to yield the same results. "I used to do 300 interviews in races for the state legislature," says Bill McInturff of Public Opinion Strategies. "Last year I was down to 250."

A final complication for political polls involves timeliness. When pollsters conduct market research on brands and products, they can go into the field for weeks at a time, ask people what they think about Chevy and Ford or Coke and Pepsi, and emerge with trustworthy results. In politics, however, pollsters are often chasing the news and trying to spot daily trends. Clients want numbers overnight, whether they're candidates trying to craft messages or media companies seeking a snapshot of a race following a major event. It's even tougher when they have to burrow down to the level of legislative districts. "Pollsters are still pretty good at big public questions, such as the presidential approval rating," says Karlyn Bowman of the American Enterprise Institute. "Local elections are getting a lot harder."

Many pollsters are turning to the Web. The ordinary online poll, of course, is grossly unrepresentative, allowing anybody who stumbles on it to join in. Re-search firms, however, are striving to form large panels of survey participants whose information, when crunched the right way, provides true reflections of public opinion. "There's a lot of trepidation because nobody knows the rules," says Michael Link of the Nielsen Company. "The old style of polling developed over decades. Right now, we're in the middle of a paradigm shift that's only a few years old. We're facing a steep learning curve."

One experiment has shown promising results. SurveyMonkey, which helps companies, schools, and communities conduct polls of targeted audiences, regularly invites people who have finished one of its polls to take another. Using this piggybacking technique last fall, Survey-Monkey completed 135,000 interviews in the 45 states with contested races for the governorship or the U.S. Senate, keeping the results secret until after the election. Jon Cohen, a former pollster for the *Washington Post*, managed the project. As the results poured in, he saw something different from what the public polls were showing. "I spent October pulling out my hair, wondering why we had a Republican bias," he says, referring to the fact that GOP candidates tended to do better in SurveyMonkey's polls than in the polls reported by the press. Following the elections, SurveyMonkey released its results: Its polls had picked the winner in 69 of 72 races, missing only the contests for governor in Connecticut, Florida, and Maryland. Even more impressive, its predicted margins of victory were closer to the mark than those of just about everyone else, even though nobody had used a telephone.

Online polls enjoy other advantages. Over a landline, pollsters can ask people whether they think the United States is on the "right track" or the "wrong track." On smartphones and computers, however, they can also test television advertisements, bumper stickers, campaign logos, and anything else that involves an image. John McLaughlin may have gotten burned in Eric Cantor's primary last year, but he also helped Nathan Deal, the Republican governor of Georgia, win reelection. "We polled on the Web, so we were able to test nine ads with a panel of voters, who ranked them in order of preference," says McLaughlin. "This helped us see what worked and what didn't work, and to tailor messages to specific groups." His method combined the breadth of a poll with the detail of a focus group, all in the service of winning votes.

Candidates who appear to trail their opponents have a favorite cliché: The only poll that matters is the one on Election Day. Good candidates always have known that this is at best a half-truth—and perhaps with the rise of new forms of polling, the rest will come to appreciate it as well.

Critical Thinking

1. Summarize the history of political polling in the United States.

2. Identify three factors that complicate accurate political polling today.

3. Explain why "ordinary on-line polling" is unreliable, and how SurveyMonkey is attempting to overcome the problems.

Internet References

Gallup Polls
www.fec.gov

Real Clear Politics
http://realclearpolitics.com

Article   Prepared by: Bruce Stinebrickner, *DePauw University*

Who Gave Us Obamacare?

The medical industry provided crucial support.

KEVIN GLASS

Learning Outcomes

After reading this article, you will be able to:

- Understand the role of major interest groups in the enactment of Obamacare legislation.

- Assess the goals and self-interest of interest groups who helped shape Obamacare legislation.

"We can no longer afford to put health-care reform on hold."

It was on February 24, 2009, a little over a month after he assumed office, that President Obama spoke these words to a joint session of Congress. What happened next—behind the curtain, in the effort to pass Obamacare—is not pretty.

Negotiations started almost immediately. In his speech, the president had promised to bring together "businesses and workers, doctors and health-care providers" in order to shape the massive legislation. Bill and Hillary Clinton's attempt to remake the health-care sector was thought to have failed because of industry hostility to their efforts. The Obama administration, therefore, would welcome health-industry lobbyists to the White House with open arms.

"After promising to conduct the health-care negotiations on C-SPAN," a House Energy and Commerce Committee staffer tells NATIONAL REVIEW, "President Obama worked behind closed doors to cut deals with the various special-interest groups." The health-care industry, for its part, was no longer focused on resisting a government intrusion into the private economy. It knew that an alliance between big business and big government could bear big fruits, so it loaded up with policy experts and lobbyists who would help it shape the legislation to its advantage. The American Hospital Association (AHA), the American Medical Association (AMA), and the Pharmaceutical Research and Manufacturers of America (PhRMA) have their fingerprints all over Obamacare.

On May 15, 2009, the AHA, the AMA, and PhRMA teamed up—along with the labor union SEIU, the insurance group AHIP,

and the medical-device manufacturers' association AdvaMed—to release a joint statement in support of the developing plan. "Health-care reform will not be sustainable," it said, "unless the nation brings down the rate of growth of health-care spending. . . . To be successful, we must take action in a public-private partnership. We look forward to offering cost-savings recommendations in the weeks ahead." What the public didn't see was the furious wheeling and dealing between the industry and the Obama administration over these "cost-savings" recommendations. It was a "public-private partnership" that allowed both sides to get much of what they wanted from Congress.

Earlier this year, the House Energy and Commerce Committee concluded an investigation that revealed a startling degree of coordination between the White House and health-industry groups in these efforts. Representative Marsha Blackburn (R., Tenn.), vice chairman of the Subcommittee on Oversight and Investigations, did a lot of the legwork on that investigation. She tells NATIONAL REVIEW that "throughout 2009 and early 2010, the White House did engage in these closed-door negotiations."

The key White House players were Nancy-Ann DeParle and Jim Messina. DeParle was head of the Office of Health Reform (which was created by President Obama) and was colloquially known as the "health-care czar." Messina, a White House deputy chief of staff, acted as a liaison between health-industry groups and the president. DeParle and Messina were at the beck and call of lobbyists, working behind the scenes to secure the goodies that the groups wanted in exchange for their support.

The White House held a series of meetings with the major groups in April and May 2009, trying to discern which concessions would win them over. While every group was opposed to the idea of a government-run insurance plan (a "public option"), they were all cautiously hopeful that they'd somehow be able to protect their interests. Cultivating this attitude was an important goal for the White House: If President Obama could convince people that health-care reform was inevitable, he would be able to peel off opposition groups by offering specific provisions they desired. The industry was being given a choice: Join the team and try to get something out of the legislation or stay on the sidelines and lose.

The American Hospital Association was among the first to take the deal. In negotiations in late June and early July, the White House sought a $155 billion reduction in subsidies and payments to hospitals for Medicare, Medicaid, and uncompensated-care programs. The AHA agreed, but the sides soon began sniping at each other, and the AHA started separate negotiations on the same issues with the Senate Finance Committee. This caused Nancy-Ann DeParle to complain to Linda Fishman, one of the AHA's top lobbyists. DeParle wrote: "We are taking all sorts of incoming from press about specific things you have sought in the [Senate Finance Committee] deal. . . . We are saying that we are not party to such an agreement—we agreed to a number, $155 billion. I know you understand that you are much more likely to end up where you want to be if you don't box us in." This veiled threat worked: The AHA suddenly insisted to the press that it wasn't pushing for anything outside of the White House agreement and would continue to support the administration.

What the AHA wanted most was to preserve the flow of government money to its member hospitals, especially through Medicare and Medicaid. In exchange, the AHA agreed to the $155 billion in payment cuts, spent incredible sums of money on lobbying, and steered most of its campaign donations toward Democrats. Despite supporting the White House through the legislative process, the AHA never issued an official endorsement of the final Obamacare legislation, but two weeks after President Obama signed the bill, it unrolled an unusual million-dollar ad campaign in the districts of 16 Democratic House members, most of them in vulnerable seats in red states, thanking them for their "yes" votes.

The American Medical Association also walked a tightrope. Like the other groups, it was steadfastly against a public option, but otherwise it tried to cast itself as a partner of the administration. And there was a laundry list of items it wanted in the bill. As outlined in a memo from Richard Deem, its head lobbyist, to DeParle, its priorities included medical-liability reform and the so-called doc fix, a permanent repeal of the payment structure under which doctors are underpaid for services to Medicare and Medicaid patients.

The AMA was more trusting than other industry groups in the Obama administration's willingness and ability to deliver what it promised. "It was a bit of naïvete on the part of the AMA," Dr. Marcy Zwelling, an AMA member and former president of the Los Angeles County Medical Association, tells NATIONAL REVIEW. "They did not understand the politics. They did not understand that they were being used. And they *were* used."

Negotiations got off to a rocky start. In early May 2009, AMA representatives met with Senate Finance Committee chairman Max Baucus but found him unhelpful. "[I] don't think it went well from a health-sector-community perspective," Deem wrote to DeParle. He also observed that "we are taking grief from our members because the perception is we are serving them up for payment cuts. . . . It seems like the goal posts are being moved."

AMA members were becoming uncomfortable with the direction their board of trustees was taking. The AMA's position on Obamacare "was not representative of the AMA as a whole," Dr. Zwelling says. Doctors were worried that their organization was being politicized in the White House's push for health-care reform.

After its abortive talks with Baucus, the AMA turned to the White House. On July 7, they struck an informal deal, but secrecy was of the utmost importance. "There is some chatter in the health-policy world about a possible physician agreement [a deal under which the AMA would support Obamacare]," Deem wrote to DeParle. "We [are] treating our discussions with you as highly confidential. If asked by reporters we are providing low-key generic responses." The way the AMA subsequently went about campaigning for Obamacare, however, was anything but low-key. In the following weeks and months, it funded ads explicitly backing President Obama. When the reform approached passage in October, the AMA helped the White House identify which senators were persuadable and deployed its lobbyists and members to influence them.

But it also became clear in October that the AMA had been cheated on the doc fix. In order for Obamacare to receive a good score from the Congressional Budget Office, the fix—which would have added more than $200 billion to the deficit over the next ten years—would have to be removed. Privately, Democratic leaders were assuring the AMA that separate doc-fix legislation would still be passed and the AMA took them at their word. But the Senate passed a provision that created the Independent Payment Advisory Board, an selected commission that would have power over physician-payment rates for Medicare. IPAB would be empowered to cut doctors' payments, and as the legislation was written, IPAB would be tasked with cutting them drastically.

The AMA had a chance to stand up for its doctors as, after the IPAB provision was included in the Senate's bill, it went back to the House for approval. In January 2010, however, Richard Deem wrote to DeParle, "We expected and are getting a lot of flak from individual physicians," but "we do not totally reject the concept of an advisory board." Publicly, the AMA was against the IPAB provision of Obamacare as written, but the organization was refusing to throw its weight behind the doctors' opposition. AMA support for Obamacare would move forward.

On March 19, 2010, two days before the final vote in Congress, the AMA reiterated its endorsement of the bill. James Rohack, the association's president, expressed reservations about IPAB and hoped that a permanent doc fix could be agreed upon, but claimed that "this bill will help patients and physicians." For its trouble, the AMA got a *six-month* doc fix in a separate piece of legislation. Another short-term fix was passed before the end of 2010, but it will expire this year. AMA lobbyists are still pushing for a permanent solution.

Perhaps the biggest health-care prize for the White House was the support of the drug industry. PhRMA spends tens of millions of dollars on lobbying every year, and the administration knew that its support would be hugely influential.

In the spring of 2009, the White House's courtship of PhRMA began. After a meeting in May between Joel Johnson, a lobbyist who represents drug companies, and White House chief of staff Rahm Emanuel, Johnson established the terms of their relationship in an e-mail: PhRMA needed "a direct line of communication, separate and apart from any other coalition." The drug companies promised to work with the White House to control drug-price inflation, and in exchange they would have a seat at the table to help craft the legislation.

It was a rocky road, but the White House would eventually deliver for PhRMA as it had not for the AMA. On June 22, 2009 President Obama announced that the White House had reached an agreement in which the drug industry would concede $80 billion in projected future revenues on drugs sold to the government (mostly for Medicare). What the president did not announce were the provisions that PhRMA demanded as a condition of its agreement.

The drug lobby had two main policy goals: It wanted to make sure that price controls and a "public option" were not forced onto Medicare Part D, and it wanted to make sure the bill didn't include a provision allowing drug reimportation. Reimportation would allow health-care providers and consumers in the United States to bring in American pharmaceutical products from other countries—such as Canada—in which drugs are sold at lower prices. This would force pharmaceutical companies selling in the United States to compete with lower-priced versions of both foreign drugs and their own products. This was something that PhRMA obviously wanted to avoid.

The fight over the public option was long and difficult. Liberal Democrats in the House worked tenaciously to get one into the bill, but lobbying by the AMA, PhRMA, and other health-care groups, combined with the White House's hands-off approach, prevented them from succeeding. On reimportation though, the Obama administration strongly backed the drug companies. DeParle wrote to PhRMA lobbyists that Obama's policy would be, "based on how constructive you guys have been, to oppose importation on the bill." The administration also supported PhRMA on price controls on Medicare Part D.

In the weeks after the June 22 deal was announced, however, it seemed likely to fall apart. Henry Waxman, chairman of the House Energy and Commerce Committee, balked at the deal and claimed that the House's developing version of the health-care legislation needn't be bound by it. Waxman wanted more than the $80 billion in concessions that the drug industry had already made. He considered both drug reimportation and price controls to be on the table. And he claimed the White House didn't feel particularly beholden to the deal either.

Bryant Hall, one of PhRMA's lead lobbyists, leapt into action and worked with Jim Messina to get the White House and PhRMA on the same page. Multiple media outlets had confirmed that President Obama had backed off of the previous PhRMA deal, but within hours the storyline changed again. Hall convinced Messina to tell both *Politico* and the *New York Times* that the White House was standing behind the deal and didn't support Waxman's attempt to push for more. It was an incredible display of PhRMA's political clout, and even Hall's colleagues were stunned after he bragged, "I pushed Jim Messina to do it."

Just when it seemed everything had been smoothed over, the Obama team muddied the waters. On July 21, 2009, President Obama read a speech off a teleprompter that implied that drug companies were part of a cabal of "special interests" working to delay or kill reform efforts. Messina, according to the congressional investigation, asked the president why he was suddenly hostile to PhRMA again, and Obama replied, "I was wondering the same." It turned out that someone on the speech-writing team hadn't gotten the memo that the White House and the drug companies were on the same side.

"I guess we didn't give enough in contributions and media ads," read an internal e-mail from a drug-industry lobbyist at the time. "Perhaps no amount would suffice." Messina and Emanuel reassured Hall that the president's newest attack on drugmakers was merely a teleprompter mistake. Yet at the end of July, President Obama gave a speech implying that drug makers had gotten a sweetheart deal and that they might be asked to make additional concessions. Hall complained that the president "beat the piss out of us again" and worried that White House senior adviser David Axelrod was pushing a new, tougher line against the drug companies.

His fears were confirmed as, in the first week in August, Bloomberg reported that Axelrod had told Democrats there was no deal between the White House and PhRMA. Afterward, a furious Hall had to be talked down by Messina once again. They then conducted a joint PR campaign, outflanking Axelrod.

Messina told a *New York Times* reporter to reiterate that the White House was standing behind the original deal, and Hall had a PhRMA spokesperson persuade CBS News not to run a story reporting that the White House wasn't sticking by its end of the deal and drug reimportation would be back on the table. These efforts finally sealed the deal: While reimportation and the public option would continue to be mentioned occasionally, by the fall the White House had gotten PhRMA behind Obamacare.

Now they just had to sell the thing to the American people.

With the White House's blessing, a 501(c)(4) organization was set up to run a pro-health-care-reform ad campaign in April 2009. Explicit in PhRMA's deal with the White House was PhRMA's promise to donate significant amounts of money to this organization, known as Healthy Economy Now. It received over $10 million from PhRMA, alongside smaller donations from the AMA, the Federation of American Hospitals, the AARP, and Blue Cross/Blue Shield. Throughout the spring and summer of 2009, Healthy Economy Now spent tens of millions on ads in states whose congressional representatives were thought to be persuadable.

Another group, Americans for Stable Quality Care, was set up in a joint effort by health-industry groups and received and spent even more money than Healthy Economy Now had. PhRMA poured almost $60 million into it. Because the legislation had started to come together in its specifics, this group was even more explicit in its advocacy of particular measures in Obamacare, including the individual mandate, the Medicare expansion, and the requirement that insurers cover individuals with preexisting conditions.

Part of PhRMA's deal with the White House was that it would team up with Families USA, an SEIU-connected 501(c)(4) group, to bring back "Harry and Louise," a series of advertisements run against the 1993–94 Clinton health-care plan. This time Harry and Louise would be staunchly pro-reform, and they would be supported by PhRMA and Families USA to the tune of $4 million.

The American Medical Association, increasingly concerned that its doc fix wouldn't make it into the final legislation, took to the airwaves with some major ad buys separate from the campaigns it helped run with Healthy Economy Now and Americans for Stable Quality Care. The AMA ran two multimillion-dollar campaigns, in October 2009 and January 2010, upping the pressure on Congress for the permanent doc fix. With no pressure from the White House, however, the campaigns failed, and the AMA was denied one of its key policy goals.

President Obama signed his health-care legislation on March 23, 2010, 13 months after his address on the subject to the joint session of Congress. The process had been messy, but he had succeeded where President Clinton had failed, because he had learned the lessons of the 1990s reform fight. He bought off big business, he played the media, he demanded that the health-care industry pony up millions of dollars to support his message—and he won. But he has not owned up to his backroom tactics. "The administration essentially told the American people that how the law was written was none of their business," a congressional staffer tells NATIONAL REVIEW. Representative Blackburn notes that "everybody but the White House has cooperated" with her investigation.

Industry groups paid up big time, got some things they wanted, and failed to get others. Big business has long tried to steer government policy, but in this instance the stakes were greater than usual. The AMA, the AHA, and PhRMA—all of which declined interview requests for this piece—saw a future with an expanded government role in the health-care industry, and they worked to shape that future with an eye to their own interests. Their efforts helped bring about a new system in which the government has more power than ever before over the health-care industry, from macro issues to the smallest minutiae. They must accordingly bear a large portion of the blame for this massive and unprecedented intrusion of government into private life.

Critical Thinking

1. Why would hospitals, health insurance companies, organizations of medical professionals, and the like be so interested in health-care reform legislation?

2. Compare the merits of open, transparent formulation of policy proposals such as Obamacare and "behind the scenes," closed-door processes.

3. What is the so-called public option, and why did it not, despite considerable support from interested parties, wind up in the final Obamacare legislation? Would you have favored a public option? Why or why not?

4. Do you think that the policy formulation process for Obamacare described by Kevin Glass is typical of the way major legislation is handled in American national government? Why or why not?

Create Central

www.mhhe.com/createcentral

Internet References

American Medical Association
www.ama-assn.org/ama
American Hospital Association
www.aha.org
Pharmaceutical Research and Manufacturers of America
www.phrma.org

KEVIN GLASS is the managing editor of Townhall.com.

Article   Prepared by: Bruce Stinebrickner, *DePauw University*

The Long Game

Americans for Prosperity is just getting started.

ALEX ROARTY

Learning Outcomes

After reading this article, you will be able to:

- Assess the likely impact that Americans for Prosperity will have on the American political system.

- Weigh whether free-spending organizations such as Americans for Prosperity are desirable features of the American political system.

Democrats entered the fall of 2013 looking like a slight favorite to retain the Senate. They left the winter of 2014 looking like an undisputed underdog. What happened? The botched rollout of the Affordable Care Act hurt Democrats badly. But the damage from that debacle would have been a lot less potent if not for the efforts of one conservative group in particular. Since October, Americans for Prosperity has spent the kind of money on TV that nobody has ever seen before in the early months of a midterm election—more than $40 million. Just about all of it has targeted a handful of vulnerable Senate Democrats. And just about all of it has ticked off a list of arguments for why Obamacare has ruined health care.

Most of the political world knows the basics about AFP: It's funded in part by billionaire industrialists (and favorite Democratic villains) Charles and David Koch. Unlike a lot of conservative outside groups, it doesn't go out of its way to annoy the Republican Party's powers that be. D.C. insiders have also probably heard of the group's president, Tim Phillips, a longtime GOP hand who once worked for former Virginia Gov. Bob McDonnell. And they probably remember that the group spent gobs of money—unsuccessfully—in the last presidential election trying to put Mitt Romney in the White House.

But for such an important organization, that's an awfully bare cupboard of facts. "Opaque" is the word many people reach for to describe AFP—and that's when they talk about it at all. A few political consultants I contacted, the types normally keen to opine on anything, declined an interview. The implicit message: Americans for Prosperity doesn't like its inner workings exposed to the world.

Recently, however, Phillips agreed to speak to me about the organization's long-term thinking and goals. After an initial phone conversation, we met in a coffee shop downstairs from the group's national headquarters in Arlington, Va. His overriding message during our conversation was simple: AFP is not just interested in this year's Senate elections. It has much bigger ambitions.

"It's a little frustrating when someone says, 'Oh, this is a political effort about the U.S. Senate,' " said Phillips, who at 49, with thinning brown hair, looks the part of an upper-level manager. "They don't look at the totality of what Americans for Prosperity is doing."

The group has chapters in 34 states and claims millions of volunteers. In many ways, it's akin to a third party, albeit one that doesn't run its own candidates. Every gear in the machine churns toward one objective: remaking the country in a fiscally conservative image—at the local, state, and federal levels. Its vision is a country with fewer taxes, less regulation, and the nearly unfettered right of individuals to do what they want without interference from a meddlesome government—essentially, the kind of place Ayn Rand would have wanted to make a home in.

For the moment at least, these goals align perfectly with the GOP's agenda of reclaiming the Senate in 2014. But are there potential costs for the Republican Party when a group like AFP acquires so much power and influence?

State-Level Success

Of course, AFP's leaders don't see themselves as a political juggernaut capable of overwhelming their foes. Like a lot of groups with power, they consider themselves a mere counterbalance to opposition forces—in this case, the network of liberal activist organizations and unions that constitute the institutional heft of the progressive movement.

Americans for Prosperity was formed in 2004 as a spin-off from a free-market group called Citizens for a Sound Economy. (FreedomWorks was also a spin-off from the organization.) AFP had only four state chapters then, according to Phillips (who has been president since the start). Some state chapters had the humblest of beginnings. Take the group's Wisconsin branch: Phillips recalls that the grassroots activists at its 2005 launch event numbered a paltry 14.

> **"It's been frustrating in Washington. We've lost some tough battles, But at the state level, I would argue, it's been a once-in-a-generation moment of free-market policy victories."**
>
> —Tim Phillis

But it didn't take long for AFP to become a force in the Badger State, which by 2011 had become arguably the country's foremost battleground for conservatives and progressives. AFP spent heavily to help Scott Walker withstand an attempted recall, and thereby preserve his victories against public-sector unions.

It wasn't just Wisconsin. In Michigan, AFP helped to successfully push for right-to-work legislation. And in Florida, it helped to defeat Republican Gov. Rick Scott's attempt to expand Medicaid this year.

Indeed, Americans for Prosperity has had a lot more success influencing state government than influencing the federal government. "It's been frustrating in Washington. We've lost some tough battles," Phillips says. "But at the state level, I would argue, it's been a once-in-a-generation moment of free-market policy victories."

Good for the GOP?

The group's most ambitious goal is to repeal Obamacare. As Phillips tells it, the current spending spree on Senate elections is just one step in a long-term plan to get rid of the law. Next year, he hopes that a Republican Senate and House will force Obama to veto their efforts to repeal the least popular parts of the legislation, such as the individual mandate. "If he has to veto those, it keeps it in front of the public and it shows him as unwilling to take some reasonable common-sense reforms," Phillips says. "It keeps the issue very much front and center."

That would undoubtedly be satisfying to AFP and to conservative activists. But whether it would be good politics for the Republican Party remains to be seen. Many GOP strategists and leaders have gingerly begun acknowledging that the health care law, as much as they might dislike it, is getting close to impossible to repeal. Moreover, at a moment when the party is trying to expand its coalition and generally soften its image, throwing people off their health insurance by repealing Obamacare entails obvious political risk.

AFP, of course, doesn't see it this way. For one thing, the group disputes the premise that people would be kicked off insurance with the repeal of Obamacare. "Just speaking purely hypothetically, who says people would have to lose their insurance?" says Levi Russell, AFP's national spokesman. In addition, while Phillips is aware of the GOP's challenges, he doesn't think that Republicans are courting disaster with their current coalition. "I think that the public-policy arena is incredibly volatile," he says. "You look at the last 150 years—just when one side or the other thinks they have a permanent governing coalition, they're proven dramatically wrong."

Already during Obama's presidency, Phillips argues, there has been a pendulum swing against big government. He cites the example of climate change. "We've gone from both nominees in 2008 not just broadly supportive of reforms in the name of global warming but actually backing cap-and-trade, which was the most aggressive, intrusive policy put forward in a serious fashion on the energy issue," he says. "We've gone from that to the policy being deader than a doornail. It's not even brought up in polite company anymore."

As for Romney's defeat: It wasn't because of his small-government agenda but because he simply wasn't a good salesman. "Governor Romney struggled with explaining his own success with the business world and how it's helped people, not hurt people," Phillips says.

Not surprisingly, that explanation raises hackles on the Democratic side. "I would put that same assessment in the same category as the Republicans who thought they were going to win the election the week before the election," says Joel Benenson, the Obama campaign's chief pollster in 2012. "That couldn't be further from the truth. The campaign was fought, day in and day out, over a contrast in economic vision and economic values."

Whatever the explanation for 2012, Americans for Prosperity is hoping for better results in 2014—and in the years ahead. If its overwhelming spending so far this year is any indication, AFP is going to be a power center in American politics for a long time. "We're genuinely a long-term effort," Phillips says. "We're not about some election cycle."

Critical Thinking

1. What is the central long-term objective of Americans for Prosperity?

2. When was Americans for Prosperity founded and who are its most noteworthy financial supporters?

Create Central

www.mhhe.com/createcentral

Internet References

Americans for Prosperity
 http://americansforprosperity.org/
Fact Check.org: Americans for Prosperity
 http://www.factcheck.org/2014/02/americans-for-prosperity-3/

Article   Prepared by: Bruce Stinebrickner, *DePauw University*

Movements Making Noise

The early 21st century will be remembered as an era of tumult and protest in the United States and abroad.

FRANCES FOX PIVEN

Learning Outcomes

After reading this article, you will be able to:

- Understand the important role of popular movements in American history.

- Consider which popular movements of today will be viewed in years to come as having successfully achieved their goals.

American political history is usually told as the story of what political elites say and do. The twists and turns, advances and setbacks, wars, disasters and recoveries, are said to be the work of the founders, or of the presidents, or of the courts, or of the influence of a handful of great people who somehow emerge from the mass.

But this history can also be told as the story of the great protest movements that periodically well up from the bottom of American society and the impact these movements have on American institutions. There would be no founders to memorialize without the Revolutionary-era mobs who provided the foot soldiers to fight the British; no films about the quandaries of Abe Lincoln during the Civil War without the abolitionists and the thousands of runaway slaves; no Labor Day to celebrate without the sit-down strikers; no Martin Luther King to beatify without a movement of poor blacks who defied the Southern terror system.

When historians look back at the decades of the transition to the twenty-first century, I think they will see a distinctive era of tumult and protest, in the United States and across the globe. The perspective gained by the passage of time will show the broad similarities of these protests—both in their scale and in the societal upheavals they reflect and foretell—to the popular insurgencies of the nineteenth century that accompanied the spread of capitalist industrialization. In both periods, dramatic changes in the economy meant new hardships, broken compacts, and the uprooting of peoples from familiar places and accustomed ways of life. In the nineteenth century, some named the new system driving these developments "capitalism"

or "industrialism." Now we name the monster machine propelling diverse local disasters "neoliberal globalization."

It is not easy to fix the exact moment that this era of popular protest against neoliberalism began. Maybe it was with the rise of the indigenous Zapatista movement in the early 1990s. Peasants from the Lacandon jungle armed themselves with wooden rifles (as well as real guns) and proclaimed neoliberal globalization as the target of their protests. Remarkably, they found an eager worldwide audience, and their uprising helped to give energy and élan to the emerging global justice movement. Soon after, in the wake of the imposition of austerity policies by the IMF and international finance, popular insurgencies spread across Latin America, toppling governments and challenging American domination of the hemisphere, with consequences that are still unfolding. Other uprisings spread across North Africa, from Tunisia and Egypt to Libya and Syria. Meanwhile, youthful insurgents mounted protests against austerity policies across Europe. In England, groups like UK Uncut targeted austerity policies, which were also the backdrop for the huge street riots in 2011; in Spain, there were the Indignados; in France, the riots by young people from the *banlieues;* in Greece, anarchist youths mounted continuous street protests against the austerity measures imposed by the Greek government and European financial overlords; and students in Canada, the UK, Chile and elsewhere mobilized campaigns against higher fees and mounting student debts. In Quebec, a large and tenacious student movement even won its main demands.

This worldwide upheaval is also unfolding in the United States. True, there was an interregnum after the Battle of Seattle in 1999, when not much seemed to be happening, even as inequality soared, wages stagnated, and public programs were slashed. Then, in the face of growing anti-immigrant fervor, the immigrants' rights protests erupted, followed by the activism of immigrant youths over the Dream Act. New attacks on public-sector worker rights in states where Republicans made gains in 2010 led to huge and sustained protest rallies in Madison and elsewhere, and in Ohio the attack was beaten back. In Chicago, the teachers union took on Mayor Rahm Emanuel and together with mobilized parents won a contract fight that highlighted not only job security but educational quality. And in recent weeks, small-scale actions by Walmart warehouse and retail workers associated with OUR Walmart have raised hopes for a union breakthrough at the world's retail giant. And of course there is Occupy, the chameleon-like movement that is the master of the spectacle and the message.

In fact, it is spectacles and messages, parades and banners and exultant crowds, that usually come to mind when we think of movements. Those images do indeed convey part of what movements do: they use the drama of the street spectacle to raise issues that political elites paper over and to recruit new adherents to the movement. Sometimes movement drama and spectacle even succeed in dispelling some of the rhetorical fog and complexity that obscure what is actually happening in government.

But the great movements that changed the course of our history accomplished more than spectacle and communication: they actually exercised power. They forced elites to inaugurate reforms that they otherwise would have avoided, as when the writers of the Constitution bent to popular enthusiasm for direct democracy and ceded to voters the right to elect representatives to the lower house, or when the Thirteenth Amendment was passed during the Civil War ending chattel slavery. Or, later in the nineteenth century, when Congress responded to widespread agitation among farmers and workers with legislation to curb monopolies. Or in the 1930s, when the national government finally granted workers the right to organize and inaugurated the first government income-support programs. Or when the Southern apartheid system was struck down in response to the civil rights movement. Or when the antiwar movement helped to force the withdrawal of American forces from Southeast Asia.

None of these reforms were as far-reaching or complete as movement activists had hoped, but neither would any of them have occurred without those movements. So just what *is* it that movements do that sometimes gives them power, at least so long as the movement is surging?

Movements are powerful when they threaten to disrupt major institutions. Think of society as a complex tangle of cooperative relations that we call "institutions." Capitalists invest in plants and machinery, workers run these machines, warehouse workers distribute the products, salespeople contract to sell them, and so on. All of these activities must go forward for the economy to work. Similarly, for cities to work, people have to walk the streets, or drive their autos or ride the subways, and for these systems to function, people also have to cooperate, to obey the rules and fulfill their appointed roles.

Most of the time, all of the contributors to these institutions do what they're supposed to do. But this cooperation does not eliminate the conflict between those who boss and those who (usually) obey, those who get more and those who get less—maybe much less. When institutionalized and cooperative activities become contentious, the basic relationship of cooperation

can become the locus of conflict. People can and do withdraw cooperation, or in the formulation of Gene Sharp, they refuse. They refuse, that is, to perform their normal rule-bound roles in institutional life. They strike—against the factories, or the schools, or the traffic system, or the warehouse contractors, or Walmart. It is the actuality or threat of this mass refusal and the disorder it threatens that constitutes the distinctive power of protest movements.

Occupy seems to be reaching for this kind of power with the idea for a campaign it calls Strike Debt. At its core, the idea is simple, and it is very much a strike. Occupy thinks that just as bosses are dependent on workers, so are lenders dependent on borrowers. If workers walk out, the enterprise stops. If borrowers refuse to pay their debts, the lenders could be in real trouble. Each side depends on the other. The millions of underwater mortgage holders, of student debtors and credit card holders, need the bank loans—but so do the banks need those borrowers, and they especially need them to cooperate by paying their monthly charges. Otherwise, the capital that the banks list on their books begins to drain away.

The scale of the disruption contemplated by Strike Debt explains why the simple idea has such frightening implications. Just because mass default on debts would cause chaos in the powerful financial sector and beyond, there are multiple barriers in place that would have to be overcome or circumvented, from the shame our culture heaps on debtors, to the reprisals available in bad credit ratings and wage garnishments, to the full weight of the forces of law and order that can be deployed against those who organize the action.

So there are large risks to the idea, and without strategies to circumvent or lower those risks, the Strike Debt campaign may not happen. Still, the great movements that succeeded in changing history also confronted the threat of reprisals, the more so when their refusals targeted powerful antagonists. The sit-down strikers of the 1930s are a pre-eminent example. They not only defied fundamental laws governing property relations, but the factories they occupied were owned by the most powerful corporations in America. The sit-downers won—not everything the workers wanted, but more than could otherwise have been imagined.

One more observation about the protest movements of our time. Most of the movements of the past seem to have been fueled by simple grievances, or at least the participants were quieted by responses to such grievances—by wage increases, for example, or protection of the right to vote. Maybe all great movements also have a strong utopian streak, but the utopian—and anarchistic—themes in contemporary movements stand out. Occupy doesn't issue demands because it doesn't want to dicker, because it doesn't believe in dickering for half a loaf. It sees itself as a movement creating a new society. And we hear echoes of this hope again and again in many other contemporary movements.

If we step back and contemplate the quandaries in which we find ourselves, this utopianism may be something we should treasure. After all, the climate change scientists make clear that the world really is at risk of going to hell. To save ourselves, we need more than jobs or higher wages or more progressive taxes. We need to reimagine our collective life so that it doesn't depend on producing more and more stuff for more and more people, which is what most of our ideas of progress have usually been about. I don't know whether it is possible to expunge our obsession with economic growth, but if it is, I suspect that only a cultural transformation fueled by the utopianism of contemporary movements can do it.

Critical Thinking

1. In what way were the American Revolution, the Civil War, and the Civil Rights Movement attributable to popular movements and protests and not to the likes of Washington, Lincoln, and Martin Luther King?

2. Do popular movements engage only in communication and spectacle? Why or why not?

Create Central

www.mhhe.com/createcentral

Internet References

Occupy Wall Street
http://occupywallst.org

OUR Walmart
http://forrespect.org

Strike Debt
http://strikedebt.org

FRANCES FOX PIVEN a faculty member of the CUNY Graduate Center, has written many books and articles about protest movements, most recently *Challenging Authority: How Ordinary People Change America.*

Piven, Frances Fox. Reprinted by permission from the February 18, 2013, pp. 11, 12, 14 issue of *The Nation*. Copyright © 2013 by The Nation. For subscription information, call 1-800-333-8536. Portions of each week's Nation magazine can be accessed at www.thenation.com.

Article   Prepared by: Bruce Stinebrickner, *DePauw University*

Balancing Act

Is the media today hopelessly biased? Where can you go to find the unvarnished truth?

Frederick Allen

Learning Outcomes

After reading this article, you will be able to:

- Recognize different sources or types of news media bias and evaluate them.

- Understand why news media bias can never be completely eliminated.

A few days before the 2012 presidential election, Joe Scarborough, the conservative host of *Morning Joe* on liberal MSNBC, proclaimed, "Anybody that thinks this race is anything but a tossup right now is such an ideologue . . . they're jokes." He felt reports that put Obama ahead were biased, and he had one particular culprit in mind, Nate Silver, a presumably liberal polling expert who calculated that President Obama had a 79 percent chance of beating Romney.

There was just one problem. It turned out to be Scarborough himself whose judgment was clouded by bias—as Silver recognized when he offered to bet the anchorman $1,000 on the outcome of the election, a wager Scarborough wouldn't take. Silver turned out to be amazingly accurate in how he called the race.

That's the problem with media bias. We all know it's there, and we all know we need to see it, detect it, and overcome it if we're ever going to know the truth, but we also all see it in different places. All too often, we think whoever we agree with is unbiased. It's the other guy, the one we disagree with, who holds the biased opinion. How, then, are we ever to get at the truth, the truth we need, not only just to know what's going on, but to be responsible citizens in a democracy?

It's a very old problem, and it's not about to go away, though there are definitely things we can do to try to smoke out biased reporting and see the facts more clearly. We'll get to that later, but first, a little history. Bias in the media wasn't always considered a negative. In fact, until about 100 years ago, it hardly ever occurred to anyone that media should be unbiased. Everyone

agreed that an informed electorate was the basis of a free society, but they didn't take that to mean that the news should be delivered without a point of view. They did agree, however, that in the U.S. the freedom of the press was sacred. That was a founding principle of our nation, and one of the great things that set us apart from every government that had come before.

The idea of a truly free press was born in 1735, when a New York newspaperman named John Peter Zenger was put on trial for libel for defaming the royal governor. Zenger's lawyer insisted that he was innocent because what he had printed was the truth. No law at the time protected a journalist who told truth that hurt a public official, but the jury set Zenger free anyway—and established the notion of a press unafraid to speak truth to power as a cornerstone of liberty.

What makes the jury's decision all the more intriguing is that it was quite well known that Zenger's paper had been founded expressly to attack the royal governor. Freedom of the press was considered to be quite a separate matter from bias, as indeed it should be. By the time of the American Revolution, the colonies were awash in partisan newspapers and pamphlets. One of the British outrages that led to the Revolution was the Stamp Act—which put a tax on newspapers. In Europe the press had always been controlled by the ruling aristocracy and bent to serve its purposes; in the colonies, it became the weapon of the people, and publications like Thomas Paine's pamphlet *Common Sense* fired the people to revolt against their overseas overlords. The only kind of media bias anyone really worried about was bias imposed from above, by the king and his men.

And so, when the Constitution was written its very first amendment stated "Congress shall make no law respecting an establishment of religion, or prohibiting the free exercise thereof; or abridging the freedom of speech, or of the press . . ."

With those words, a free press was enshrined along with freedom of speech and religion as one of our most crucial liberties. The government went well beyond mere words in supporting it, too. Where other nations heavily taxed their newspapers, the young United States did the opposite. It subsidized them.

The Postal Act of 1792, which established the nation's mail service, gave newspapers discounted postage rates, and legislators often provided funding for papers in their districts.

With that help the American press flourished so much that by 1835 the U.S. had five times as many daily papers as the British Isles. However, high officials often hated and distrusted what the papers printed. In 1798 President John Adams went so far as to push through the notorious Sedition Act, which made it a crime to publish "false, scandalous, and malicious" writings about the president or Congress. The law would backfire badly, turning its victims into free speech martyrs. Thomas Jefferson got rid of the Sedition Act soon after he was elected president.

Not all bias is political bias. In the 1830s James Gordon Bennett used sensationalism and colorful embroidering of the truth to build his *New York Herald* into the biggest newspaper in the world. As but one lurid example, his paper described the corpse of a murdered prostitute in 1836 as follows: "The perfect figure, the exquisite limbs, the fine face, the full arms, the beautiful bust, all, all surpassed in every respect the Venus de Medici."

Newspapers were, after all, businesses first, and the primary concern was selling papers. By 1871 a British observer would describe the typical American newspaper as "a print published by a literary Barnum, whose type, paper, talents, morality, and taste are all equally wretched and inferior; who is certain to give us flippancy for wit, personality for principle, bombast for eloquence, malignity without satire, and news without truth or reliability."

How biased was the press in the 19th century? In 1860 Bennett's *Herald* reported that Abraham Lincoln was "a fourth-rate lecturer who cannot speak good grammar."

By the end of that century, the United States was a nation of mass-readership newspapers. Joseph Pulitzer's *New York World* led the way, with signs in its city room that read, "Accuracy, Accuracy, Accuracy! Who? What? Where? When? How? The Facts—The Color—The Facts!"

Despite the noble motto, in the *World* and in its archrival, William Randolph Hearst's *Journal*, "there was a lot of willful omission and lying," as Brooke Gladstone, media historian and host of the NPR show *On the Media*, points out in her book, *The Influencing Machine*. Hearst himself is best remembered for his (possibly apocryphal) 1897 telegram to the artist Frederic Remington, who told him there was no fighting in Cuba to report on: "Please remain. You furnish the pictures, and I'll furnish the war."

The tide began to turn with the century. Adolph Ochs bought *The New York Times* in 1896 and announced that it would henceforth "give the news . . . impartially, without fear or favor, regardless of party, sect, or interest involved." Lack of bias became a new ideal in the Progressive Era of the early 1900s. In 1904 Joseph Pulitzer endowed one of the first journalism schools, at Columbia University, to "raise journalism to the rank of a learned profession," and others soon followed. In 1922 editors founded their first professional association, the American Society of Newspaper Editors, and drafted a code of ethics that declared, "News reports should be free from opinion or bias of any kind."

Impartiality became such a widely accepted ideal through the middle of the 20th century that even as there got to be more and more sources for news, with the rise of broadcast radio and television, people assumed that news, wherever it came from, was always as accurate and unbiased as possible. That's why in the 1960s Walter Cronkite, the friendly uncle of all America, could close his nightly *CBS Evening News* broadcast by declaring, "And that's the way it is."

Of course, that wasn't really quite the way it was. Cronkite's show was less than half an hour of quick reports on one news team's choice of important events. Throughout the midcentury of the conformist press, a lot didn't get reported, or at least fully examined. In what is possibly the most extreme example of bias by omission, when the atomic bombs dropped on Hiroshima and Nagasaki, the government controlled all the reporting on the subject, and the official word was that no deadly radiation was released. Americans had little idea of the horror in those cities until a year later, when John Hersey, writing in *The New Yorker* magazine, uncovered the story no newspaper had gotten, with descriptions like the following: "hundreds and hundreds. . . were fleeing. . . . The eyebrows of some were burned off and skin hung from their faces and hands. . . . Some were vomiting as they walked. Many were naked or in shreds of clothing."

This is but one example of the many ways news can be biased even when reporters try their damnedest not to insert opinion into a story. Gladstone identifies the types of non-political bias that she looks for:

- Commercial bias. The preference for new, exciting stories over less dramatic news.
- Bad news bias. Bad news sells more papers because we are drawn to stories that scare us.
- Status quo bias. The underlying assumption that the system works and things are mostly okay.
- Access bias. Reporters don't want to alienate their sources, so they tend to tread lightly around issues that would be sensitive to them.
- Visual bias. The preference for stories with good pictures.
- Narrative bias. The preference for stories with a clear beginning, middle, and end.
- Fairness bias. Giving all sides of an issue equal weight even when some points of view may be just stupid or even crazy.

The mainstream media began to fracture in the 1960s, and some trace this to the day Walter Cronkite, "the most trusted man in America," came out against the Vietnam War. Was it a newsman's place to take sides? His stand helped bring an end to Lyndon Johnson's presidency. Shorty thereafter, impartial newsgathering was joined by outright newsmaking when the staid *Washington Post* did the fearless investigative reporting that broke through the Watergate cover-up and ultimately brought down Richard Nixon.

But those changes were minor compared to the impact of the technological developments that followed. First there was the rise of cable TV, multiplying the number of outlets for news.

Then there came the cultural earthquake of the Internet. In the past 15 years, as the Internet has become something almost every American relies on every day, newspapers have fallen into a struggle to survive, losing to the Web both the advertising dollars that are their life blood and the readers they exist to serve. They have had to lay off so many reporters that most of them simply can't cover the news the way they used to. At the same time, the Web has become a democracy of instant news-gathering and reporting by absolutely anybody with access to a smartphone. There are now fewer trained professional journalists but far more amateur ones. In this blizzard of reporting, it's become exponentially more difficult for the reader to separate what is accurate from what is whim, conjecture, or nonsense.

The sheer numbers of amateur journalists—nowadays anyone in the presence of a newsworthy event is likely to tweet and share on Facebook what they see and hear—ensures that ordinary people will break a lot of news. Sometimes the news is real. An early example of this came in 2002, when Senator Trent Lott praised the era of segregation at a birthday party for his colleague Strom Thurmond. No one in the traditional press noticed; but a bunch of bloggers, including Joshua Micah Marshall of Talking Points Memo and Andrew Sullivan of *The Dish,* did. Their reporting of the incident ultimately led Lott to resign as Senate minority leader. Similarly the video of Mitt Romney making remarks about the "47 percent" during the 2012 presidential campaign was first uncovered by a pro-Obama opposition researcher who simply trawled the Internet for video that could embarrass Romney, and then news organization *Mother Jones* published it online. And it was a blogging website that revealed that the girlfriend of college football star Manti Te'o didn't really exist, after the entire mainstream media had missed that story.

But the web is full of rumors and fabrications, too, now that anybody can write and publish anything there. The myth of Barack Obama's having been born in a foreign country and given a fabricated birth certificate was drummed up and kept alive by countless online conspiracy theorists in defiance of fully established truth, taking on a kind of zombie life long after it had been discredited. In 2012 much of the mainstream media reported that Google was buying a Wi-Fi provider named ICOA for $400 million; that turned out to be a complete online fabrication.

It can all get so confusing that even the government of the world's biggest country can be fooled: On its website last year, the satirical newspaper *The Onion* reported North Korean leader Kim Jong Un had been voted the sexiest man on earth, and China's *People's Daily Online,* an organ of the ruling Communist party, earnestly passed along the news. In the words of Gladstone, "The reality that anyone with a cell phone can now presume to make, break, or fabricate the news has shaken our citadels of culture and journalism to the core."

So today it can be harder than ever to know what to believe, who is telling it straight, and what is the product of terrible reporting, extreme bias, or even outright dishonesty. But just as everyone today can act as a journalist, everyone can act as a fact-checker, too, and the Web swarms just as thickly with people exposing bias and falsehood as it does with people creating it. Sites like politifact.com and factcheck.org and snopes.com exist solely to sniff out rumors and reveal the truth. If you're a careful, critical reader, you can often find the truth very easily once your suspicions are aroused.

Our nation has always relied on a press that is free, considering it nothing less than a foundation of our democracy. But we have always paid the price for that freedom, allowing voices that are reckless or bigoted or plain wrong to be heard too. Finding the news you can trust has always been every citizen's job. It has just gotten more complicated. And above all, remember that media is biased because people are biased. Every one of us is biased; we all see the world through the lenses of our personal beliefs and predispositions, and we all like to hear news in a way that supports our own preexisting views, reinforcing our own biases that we may not even know exist. As Gladstone puts it, "News consumers say they want objectivity, but they choose news outlets that reflect their views." That's just human nature.

Critical Thinking

1. What does the episode involving the host of "Morning Joe"—Joe Scarborough—and Nate Silver, elections forecaster who had said that President Obama was likely to be re-elected, tell us about media bias?

2. How did nineteenth century American newspapers differ from their counterparts in the twentieth century?

3. What are seven different kinds of news media bias that Brooke Gladstone has identified? Do you think that each is objectionable? If so, do you think that each is equally objectionable?

Create Central

www.mhhe.com/createcentral

Internet References

Factcheck
www.factcheck.org
Accuracy in Media
www.aim.org

FREDERICK ALLEN wrote "Learning to Love Our Lobbyist Friends" in the March/April issue.

Article   Prepared by: Bruce Stinebrickner, *DePauw University*

Campaign Coverage
in the Time *of* Twitter

How technology has transformed reporting on presidential politics.

Jodi Enda

Learning Outcomes

After reading this article, you will be able to:

- Assess changes in recent years in professional journalists' coverage of election campaigns.

- Ponder what additional changes in coverage are likely to occur in the near future.

The late, legendary R.W. Apple Jr. covered 10 presidential elections for the New York Times, the last in 2004. Once dubbed "America's most powerful political reporter," Apple was notorious for his ambition, his appetite and his ability. He lived large, ate large, spent large and, above all, wrote large. Everything about the man was outsize. His Rolodex was especially grand: He knew everyone, from county chairmen to presidents, and they knew him. For decades, it was so.

Yet less than five years after his death, the iconic political reporter better known as "Johnny" would barely recognize the beat he dominated for so long. He wouldn't know many of the young new reporters on the campaign trail, of course, but neither would he know a number of the media outlets that employ them. More significant, Apple wouldn't recognize the way reporters of today do the very job that he defined—interview by interview, word by carefully chosen word—through all those election cycles.

No longer do reporters slog elbow to elbow with presidential contenders vying for votes in Iowa and New Hampshire. No longer do they get to know the candidates in a way that voters do not—up close and personal, with their feet up, their guard down and, perhaps, a drink at the ready. No longer do they have the luxury of weeks or days or even hours to gather string and dig deep and analyze before they write a story. Heck, many reporters scarcely have time to write what Apple would have considered stories, so busy are they thumbing 140-character tweets, tapping out blog posts and shooting or appearing in video.

Johnny Apple might have ruled the road by virtue of his overbearing personality, abundant eccentricities, audacious expense accounts and sheer chutzpah. Writing in The New Yorker in 2003, Calvin Trillin noted that "Apple stories constitute a subgenre of the journalistic anecdote." But it was his exquisite skill that made him a staple of the Times' front page and allowed him to frame issue upon issue. His reporting was deep, his access to sources vast, his writing both good and fast. On stories long and short, he provided insight that was unique, analysis that was apt, historical details that put the news in perspective. He wrote with the authority acquired not only by spending years on a beat, but by researching excessively and reporting tirelessly. He was a master at what we used to call shoe-leather reporting.

I can't imagine him tweeting.

Or being a captive of a social network culture that measures scoops in seconds and requires journalists to stop reporting in order to tweet or blog or post video in incremental, bare-boned tidbits.

To be sure, Apple valued scoops and had more than his share of them. Then again, he had all day, if not longer, to chase them, confirm them, put flesh on them and make them worth reading. It's a luxury few of his journalistic successors enjoy.

"There truly isn't a news cycle," says Jeff Zeleny, who, as the current national political correspondent for the Times, is Apple's rightful heir.

Although Zeleny still has more opportunities to develop his stories than many of his competitors, he, too, is caught up by the demands of *social media*. This year, he tells me, he started tweeting. He also blogs and appears in video posted on the paper's Web site. In the early morning hours of Sunday, May 22, I spotted Zeleny sitting alone in the corner of a trendy Washington restaurant during a pulsating party peopled by journalists, lobbyists and political operatives. It didn't take long to discover that he and some others in the room were tweeting the news that Indiana Gov. Mitch Daniels had decided not to seek the Republican presidential nomination. While Zeleny was hunched over his BlackBerry tapping out a quick story for the Times' blog (which he tells me he expanded when he got home), I heard two party-goers from competing news outlets acknowledge, only slightly begrudgingly, that his tweet beat theirs by some number of seconds.

"As a guy who remembers covering campaigns before cell-phones, the whole thing seems stuck on fast forward to me, because we're all essentially on deadline every hour as opposed to a couple times a day," says Howard Kurtz, who for many years wrote about the media for the Washington Post and now serves as Washington bureau chief for the newly conjoined Newsweek and Daily Beast. "The fact that we can post stories or tweet items instantaneously is a terrific development but also threatens to overwhelm us with the ephemeral."

> **As a guy who remembers covering campaigns before cellphones, the whole thing seems stuck on fast forward to me, because we're all essentially on deadline every hour as opposed to a couple times a day.**
>
> —Howard Kurtz

Competition for scoops, always robust, has intensified not only because of the 24/7 news cycle brought on by cable news and the Internet but because of the upsurge in Web sites, including The Daily Beast, that provide original reporting. During the last presidential election, most sites that were not part of larger news organizations—primarily the old-school kind such as newspapers, magazines and television networks—simply aggregated or regurgitated campaign news that was first reported elsewhere. (Politico, which was created in the Web era and made a splash covering the 2008 race, has a print product.)

That was then. Now, as newspapers and magazines continue to pare both their staffs and their campaign budgets, many old-time journalists are migrating to Web sites with newly minted Washington bureaus and hotel reservations in early caucus and primary states. Well-known Washington fixtures—among them Kurtz, Howard Fineman, Tucker Carlson, Carl Cannon—left traditional media outlets to play leading roles at Web publications. Some of the sites, such as The Daily Caller, were founded after the last presidential race. Some, like Yahoo!, are dispatching campaign reporters for the first time. Others, including Talking Points Memo, Real Clear Politics and The Huffington Post (now a part of AOL), have beefed up their political staffs appreciably.

Despite hiring in some quarters, it is quite possible that the majority of people tracking the candidates this year don't fit the traditional definition of journalist at all. They include full- and part-time bloggers, paid and un-, people with other careers who report on the side, people who attend campaign events and blog or tweet their impressions, supporters and opponents of candidates, even people called "trackers" who are paid by partisan organizations to follow candidates with an eye toward

contradictions or gotcha moments that could take them down a notch or altogether. In 2008, HuffPost broke new ground with a citizen-based reporting project called Off The Bus, which showcased stories by no fewer than 12,000 unpaid bloggers. It is planning an even bigger reprise in 2012.

"Use of social media and electronic media obviously means that anybody with a laptop, anybody with a PDA, is a journalist," says Roger Simon, Politico's chief political columnist and another newcomer to news-by-tweet.

The crucial questions, of course, are whether these changes are good for political journalism and whether they are beneficial to readers and viewers, particularly those who vote. As with so many things, the answers are nuanced and full of he said-she said/on one hand-on the other hand vacillation. Even practitioners of the latest forms of political reporting are torn about their effectiveness. Almost to a person, they bemoan the loss of time to engage in in-depth reporting, to go beyond the story of the day to unearth the insightful gems that really tell us something instructive, something fundamentally important, about the men and women who would be president.

"We're much more likely this cycle to have covered in detail the medication [Republican presidential candidate] Michele Bachmann takes for her headaches than the policy ideas that are coming out of her mouth," says Susan Page, Washington bureau chief for USA Today. "One is easy to understand, interesting, likely to get a lot of hits. Policy issues are harder, difficult to make sexy. It requires a different kind of commitment."

At the same time, though, political reporters extol the technology that allows them to know everything a candidate says and does (publicly, at least), that gives them easy access to anything that journalists, bloggers and even regular Joes who attend campaign events write or tweet or post, and that might—just might—help journalism, if not newspapers, survive. As to my query about the impact on the electorate and, therefore, on democracy itself, my rather large sampling of political reporters (many of whom I befriended—not friended—while covering earlier campaigns myself) was generally positive. Voters have access to more information than ever before, these journalists say, though they might not have the time or inclination to look for it.

"I think the pluses of technology are obvious. What it allows you to do is layer the coverage in a way that allows voters to drill down and see what they want to," says Kathy Kiely, managing editor of politics at National Journal. She is pleased that news outlets can link to documents and audio and video of candidates. "I'm a big believer in the power of words, but there's nothing like actually hearing the voice of a candidate, the timbre, how they're saying something.

"The downside—and this is what we really have to be cautious about—is becoming so enamored of the here and now that we forget to put things in perspective. We love to chase the fire bell. One of the things that I worry about is that with Twitter and any of the instant communications tools that, to quote T.S. Eliot, we end up measuring out our lives in coffee spoons. We are obsessed with beating the competition by one or two seconds," Kiely says. "The balancing act is trying to take advantage of the new technology to engage readers, to get the word out about a story but, at the same time, examining your conscience and saying, 'Am I really providing enough perspective, context, or am I just tweeting the election away?'"

Carl Cannon is a veteran newspaper, magazine and Web writer known for lengthy, heavily reported discourses tinged with historical reference. Named in February the Washington editor of RealClearPolitics, a Web site that started as an aggregator and now produces original reporting, Cannon worries that journalists are losing sight of the big picture.

"Everybody wants the latest-latest," he says. "This is the good news and the bad news of Internet journalism. You have something new, people click on it. That's good because we worried for a time that the only thing left would be opinion journalism. But people care about the news. The bad news is it's trivial and/or incremental—the latest lint."

Journalists (however defined) aren't the only ones who have changed the way they do things. It was not so long ago that presidential wannabes actually talked to reporters, schmoozing with them on the campaign plane or in the back of the bus, currying favor with the scribes they sometimes loathed and feared—but always needed. In 2000, I was among a large group of reporters with whom Al Gore danced and joked (off the record) during a birthday party he threw for his wife, Tipper, atop a riverboat that was slowly making its way down the Mississippi. That same year, many of us spent days crammed into the rear of a campaign bus with John McCain, who answered as many questions as we could ask while crisscrossing South Carolina.

In campaigns of yesteryear, a candidate would wander back to the press section of his chartered plane from time to time so that he (it was always a "he" then) could get to know reporters and reporters could get to know him. They might talk movies or sports or, possibly, issues. Often, these sessions were off the record. That doesn't happen anymore, not in an era when the traveling press records a candidate's every utterance on smartphones.

"The mores of the plane have changed," says Howard Fineman, editorial director for the AOL Huffington Post Media Group and a 30-year veteran of Newsweek. "The old days where the candidates used to play cards and drink bourbon with the reporters are gone with the teletype machines."

Politico's Simon recalls how his access to candidates has declined, bit by bit, during the course of covering 10 presidential races, for several news outlets, starting in 1976. That year, he says, Ronald Reagan routinely invited reporters to sit with him at a table in the rear of his campaign bus. In those years, Simon and other reporters had plenty of time to talk to candidates one on one or in small groups. "Nowadays," he says, "a reporter considers herself or himself lucky if the press secretary returns the call."

While the distance between candidate and reporter is partly a function of the size of the traveling press corps (I've been at events in Iowa and New Hampshire where journalists outnumbered potential voters), it was exacerbated by the Internet and social media.

"The candidates are more afraid of us because of the echo chamber effect that the electronic media feed into," Simon

says. "Everything is written, tweeted, retweeted, goes on TV, in print, blogged. The smallest slip can destroy a candidacy."

Adds Kiely: "The ubiquitous YouTubization of campaigns means that everyone is a lot more guarded than they used to be."

No politician wants to be the next George Allen, the Republican senator from Virginia who in 2006 upended his own reelection campaign when he called a Democratic volunteer—armed with a video camera at an Allen event—"macaca," a term widely considered to be a racial slur. The young Democrat posted the video online, where it went viral, effectively ending Allen's campaign.

These days, candidates prefer to talk directly to voters, skipping the middle men—the old media that Apple knew so well—and utilizing Facebook, Twitter, YouTube and other new-media tools. To sell themselves, they create their own video, carefully scripted and edited, with nothing left to chance. To make announcements, they go straight to Twitter, often not bothering to alert the press first. They live-stream their events so that voters can watch them as they occur, unfiltered by the evening news. They ask supporters to "Like" or "Friend" them on Facebook, endorsements that, cumulatively, could prove at least as influential as those bestowed by editorial boards.

These days, candidates prefer to talk directly to voters, skipping the middle men and utilizing Facebook, Twitter, YouTube and other new-media tools.

Republican candidates this summer even debated via Twitter, taking questions from, well, people who tweet. President Barack Obama responded to tweeters' questions during a July town hall meeting.

New-media tools allow candidates to engage in conversation directly, in a way they never could before, with citizens who don't live in early voting states like Iowa, New Hampshire and South Carolina. And they give campaigns inordinate control over their messages.

Consider the launch of Tim Pawlenty's campaign for the Republican presidential nomination. Pawlenty's press secretary, Alex Conant, boasted that the former Minnesota governor announced his exploratory committee in a video first posted on Facebook and then on YouTube. The night before he officially joined the race, Pawlenty's campaign posted a "teaser video" online. (It wasn't much of a tease, since Pawlenty's candidacy was never really in doubt.) Video on campaign Web sites or YouTube serves a dual purpose: It gets the message out without the expense of advertising, and it frequently generates free publicity from the press and blogs. (Pawlenty dropped out of the race in August after a disappointing third-place finish in the Iowa Straw Poll.)

Candidates also utilize new-media tools as a means to defend themselves. With the help of electronic alerts, they have near-immediate access to almost everything that is written about their campaigns. This allows aides to lobby writers to quickly change what they don't like.

"During the '08 campaign, I posted an item at one event, and by the time I got to the next event, they were questioning something in it," recalls Mark Z. Barabak, national political correspondent for the Los Angeles Times. Today, that would be considered glacial. "Now," Barabak says, "you hear from them minutes later."

By way of example, he notes that he didn't even know the paper had posted his story one night this July until he received an e-mail from an aide to Texas Gov. Rick Perry, who was displeased with something Barabak had written and wanted it changed. Following a rapid exchange of messages, the two agreed to disagree.

The campaign of Republican Jon Huntsman has set up an entire operation—which it calls the "Reality Room"—to respond to tweets and other postings that contain inaccurate information about the former Utah governor and ambassador to China.

"That really allows us to rapidly respond in a literal sense," says Press Secretary Tim Miller. "Rapid response has always been part of a campaign. But we're trying to do rapid response in real time."

Not only does the Reality Room react to journalists but also to voters who are tweeting or blogging about Huntsman, Miller says. Eventually, he says, the campaign will have a way to determine which tweets are most influential so it can focus its energy there.

Miller, who worked on John McCain's primary campaign in 2008, says candidates' communications shops have to be more nimble now because reporters and non-reporters are writing and tweeting about things that in the past would have been considered too trivial.

"The day-to-day campaign minutiae is being followed by everybody. Last time it was just Politico and a handful of people that were really looking at the nitty-gritty of the campaign," he says. Now, Miller points out that even the most esteemed newspapers have set up blogs both to break news around the clock and to provide a home for information that might not be significant enough to make the print product. The New York Times has The Caucus; the Washington Post has The Fix and The Fast Fix; the Wall Street Journal has Washington Wire; NBC News has First Read. ABC News, which began The Note as an internal e-mail, now posts it as a blog. And Politico has Mike Allen's influential Playbook. On top of that, several organizations, including Politico, the Wall Street Journal, the New York Times and the Washington Post, issue "news alerts"—e-mails to lists of subscribers—notifying them of breaking news stories, significant and not.

Miller has joined the fray in his own way by writing The Morning Hunt, described as "a daily-ish primer of everything in Huntsworld and the random musings of our comms team." Unlike reporters' musings, those of Miller and his colleagues are distributed by e-mail to a select group of people and are on background.

If you ask a bunch of political journalists to identify the biggest change in political reporting this election cycle, the answer comes in a short burst: "Twitter!"

The microblogging service was founded in 2006 but played little if any role in the 2008 campaign. Now, however, it has become an indispensable tool for campaigns and the people who cover them.

"We all follow the candidates on Twitter," USA Today's Page says. "Twitter for me has replaced watching the wires. It's a faster way to find out what's happening. . . . On Twitter, I see what [GOP frontrunner] Mitt Romney just said but I also see what Herman Cain [a second-tier candidate] just said. You see if the New York Times has posted a story but also if The Daily Caller has posted a story. It's 360 degrees. No one is filtering the news for you. It's not just what the AP thought the lead was."

National political reporters tell me they use Twitter to follow each other as well as to keep track of what local reporters in key political states are writing. It puts them in touch with bloggers from around the country. It lets them know when the campaigns are releasing information.

The proliferation of social media means that reporters have to know how to do a lot more, technologically speaking, than ever before. "Nobody's just a reporter anymore," says Mark Edgar, deputy managing editor of the Dallas Morning News. "Everybody is a blogger, a videographer, a photographer, a writer, a tweeter." Readers, too. Gone are the days when reporters would open the mail to find handwritten notes from readers, sometimes around the edges of a clipped newspaper article. Instead, reader comments are public, posted at the bottom of stories.

"It's definitely a two-way conversation," says David Kurtz, managing editor and Washington bureau chief of Talking Points Memo. Readers send links, tips, insights, he says. "That helps inform our coverage."

Political reporters say technological innovations, far from detracting from their journalism, give them new avenues with which to reach readers.

Lynn Sweet, Washington bureau chief for the Chicago Sun-Times, says the trick is to figure out the best way to deliver each facet of information. Consider: In July, Sweet participated in a conference call with Obama adviser David Plouffe, who was opining on the contentious debt ceiling debate. One vivid quote—in which Plouffe likened House Speaker John Boehner's proposal to the Loch Ness monster—grabbed her attention, so she tweeted it before hanging up the phone. After the call, she lengthened her report in a blog post. She retools stories for the print version of the paper and often posts what she writes on her Facebook page. To complete the circle, all of her work snakes its way onto her blog and into tweets.

"I have it set up so that my blog headlines automatically go to my Twitter feed. It's just another way of letting people know what I file," Sweet says. "Because I have various outlets, I can decide where information goes."

The plane was once the place to be. Winging across the country, making three, four, five stops a day, chewing the fat with candidates, staffers and other journalists and moving from event to event to event was a treasured opportunity for political reporters. The plane provided journalists with valuable access to candidates and to the people who were running their campaigns, honing their images, crafting their policies and framing their speeches. It gave reporters an inside peek at a campaign. And it was the best way to keep tabs on a candidate.

Not anymore. With Twitter, Facebook, YouTube, live streaming and other innovations, it's no longer necessary to be with a candidate to know what he or she is doing. In fact, several veteran reporters tell me it can be a disadvantage to be stuck "in the bubble."

It's also outrageously expensive. Traveling with campaigns can cost many thousands of dollars a week, money that news organizations can't afford to spend the way they did in the past. As a result, regional newspapers that previously placed reporters on campaign planes, papers like the Boston Globe, the Houston Chronicle and the Dallas Morning News, either have stopped altogether or pulled back significantly. Television networks, meanwhile, stopped assigning their big-name talent to travel with candidates and instead created the so-called "embed" system, in which young producers are on "body" coverage.

"There are fewer people observing these candidates up close and more people writing about them from afar. There are a lot more people opining, Hogging, tweeting, but not out there looking at candidates face to face," says Zeleny of the New York Times, one of the papers that still assigns reporters to trail candidates. "That's not a great trend."

Some outlets are trying to continue to travel, in creative ways. For instance, National Journal and CBS are teaming up to embed young journalists bearing video recorders with each candidate, Kiely says. CBS will edit video and National Journal will provide text to be used on both of their websites.

Most news organizations are going to more of a zone coverage. They'll send reporters to Iowa and New Hampshire—to the first caucus and primary, respectively. After that, they'll travel when they see a good reason to.

"Even if we had unlimited resources, I don't think spending every day trapped in the bubble is the smart way to go," says Howard Kurtz, of Newsweek and The Daily Beast. "I think you learn more when you dip in and out and have more perspective on the race. With so many news organizations covering this campaign, we have no desire to duplicate what the AP does. We are going to concentrate on breaking stories, painting a fuller portrait of the candidates and doing smart analysis of the dynamics of the race."

Kurtz, who continues to critique the media in a blog and on "Reliable Sources," a show he hosts on CNN, voices comments that are similar to many I hear from people at news outlets old and new. Editors at print publications are particularly concerned with saving money, but their counterparts at Web sites are focused on doing things differently. Sure, they say, they'll write about the candidates' activities. But that's just one piece of the campaign puzzle.

"Our task is to find new and interesting stories and not duplicate what perfectly good reporters are doing," says Tucker Carlson, editor in chief of The Daily Caller. Carlson, a print and broadcast journalist known for his conservative punditry, says

We are going to concentrate on breaking stories, painting a fuller portrait of the candidates and doing smart analysis.

—Howard Kurtz

the one-and-a-half-year-old outlet has 31 reporters and editors, who also write. They are looking for innovative ways to cover the campaign and the candidates. In July, The Daily Caller broke the story that Michele Bachmann suffered from migraine headaches.

Talking Points Memo's David Kurtz (who is not related to Howard Kurtz) says he will use his reporters to write stories not presented elsewhere. "We want to bring a more robust, textured coverage that includes traditional ways of reporting, but that also takes stories that are bubbling up from the state and local level and elevates them to the national level," he says. "We want to cover the horse race, but we also want to go deeper. Horse race coverage is insular and incestuous. We're very conscious of not getting caught up in that."

He says TPM will assign reporters who are experts on such issues as health care and debt reform to take a close look at candidates' positions and track records.

Chris Lehmann, managing editor of the Yahoo! News blog network, says his staff will use crowdsourcing—by asking questions of its readers—as one way to learn what voters are thinking. "We understand that our readers are a big asset," he says. "We're a new-media company, and that's how we think. It's the largest readership on the Web. We would be foolish not to get them involved." Lehmann reports that the group of five blogs received more than 1 billion hits in its first year, which ended in July.

The behemoth that is AOL and The Huffington Post will be covering the campaign in a number of new ways this time around, Fineman tells me. First, he says, HuffPost has tripled its Washington staff to 30. Then, he says, it is dispatching a bunch of video people, which it calls "preditors" (for "producer-editors") to the campaign trail to augment staff-written stories and produce some of their own. What's more, it will boost its coverage exponentially through its Patch network of more than 850 hyperlocal news sites in 22 states. Fineman says the company is hiring 33 professional journalists to run 11 Patch sites in Iowa, New Hampshire and South Carolina, three of the states where the first voters will weigh in next year. Journalists and nonjournalists blog on the sites.

Patch sites in Minnesota informed HuffPost's coverage of the government shutdown there this summer, and Fineman says a similar partnership will go a long way toward enhancing its coverage of the presidential race.

"We have national reporters to chase after Rick Perry," Fineman says of the Texas governor. "What we want Patch editors to do is tell us what the local selectman is saying. What are they saying at the megachurch? What are they saying at the coffee shop?" Because of Patch's extensive reach, he says, "Nobody else will have that capability, nobody."

OffTheBus, HuffPost's citizen-based reporting project, drew fire in 2008 for its reliance on unpaid bloggers. One of them, Mayhill Fowler, who spent her own money trailing candidates across the country, gained national attention when she quoted Barack Obama telling contributors—herself included—that it wasn't surprising that voters in downtrodden small towns become "bitter" and "cling to guns or religion or antipathy to people who aren't like them . . . as a way to explain their frustrations." (See The Beat, October/November 2008.)

HuffPost is inviting citizen journalists to come aboard—but stay off the bus—again.

And what of the plane?

"At the appropriate time, we'll have people on board, of course," says Fineman, an old hand at campaign travel. "We can afford it. But most of the people are standing around on the tarmac twittering the whole time or sending e-mails . . . When you're on the plane, you're in the worst place because you're not on the ground and you're not in the blogosphere, unless the plane has Wi-Fi."

Reporters might be choosy about which campaign events they attend, but a new breed of players called "trackers" most certainly are not. These people almost always show up, says Miller, Huntsman's press secretary. Trackers are not journalists. They are partisans, and they follow candidates they hope will lose. So far in this campaign, with only a Republican primary, the trackers are Democrats.

Armed with video cameras, the youthful brigade aims to hit just about every Republican town hall meeting, speech, meet-and-greet and press conference.

What does this have to do with journalism? Everything. Rodell Mollineau, president of the new Democratic organization American Bridge 21st Century, oversees 15 trackers and expects to hire more. He has dispatched them to each early primary or caucus state to track nearly every appearance by a Republican candidate. He also has 22 researchers doing what traditionally has been a behind-the-scenes job called opposition (or "oppo") research. The purpose is not only to look for gotcha moments, Mollineau says, though he wouldn't mind if one occurs. It also is to look for contradictions. And to bring them to the attention of reporters.

"There's a very strong press corps out there," says Mollineau, who was previously a spokesman for Senate Majority Leader Harry Reid (D-Nev.). "You can't cover everything. Sometimes our trackers and our research will help uncover story lines that a reporter didn't see or, frankly, didn't have time to cover, because they had to cover the story of the day."

As an example, he mentions a small to-do in May, when Pawlenty repeatedly referred to "Iran" and "Iranians" although he was clearly talking about the American military involvement in Iraq. The reporters on hand largely ignored the mistake. That's where American Bridge stepped in. Mollineau made the video available, and it wound up in many a blog post written by traditional journalists and others. Politico's Ben Smith credited American Bridge for tipping him off.

"Is it game changing?" Mollineau asks. "No. But did it create a little bit of a buzz? Yes."

Next year, after Republicans have selected a nominee, Mollineau anticipates American Bridge's role will be more significant. "I think we all know that candidates on the Republican side tend to run to the right in primaries and then become centrist in the general election," he says. "Voters have a right to know which candidate it is: Is it a radical right candidate or a centrist candidate? It also is something that journalists will want to look at."

American Bridge is not the only group working to fill in journalistic gaps. Bill Burton, until last year a deputy press secretary in the Obama White House, runs Priorities USA and Priorities USA Action. The former is a nonprofit that fights on behalf of the middle class. The latter is a superPAC—a political action committee that can raise and spend unlimited amounts of money—that fights on behalf of Obama and against potent Republican superPACs that are trying to unseat him.

Because reporters are tweeting and blogging and shooting video and filing all day long, they have little time to dig into candidates' backgrounds and their positions on issues, Burton says. He says his group will "do what we can to raise awareness of some of the issues that are overlooked as a result of reporters doing less in-depth reporting."

When Johnny Apple died in October 2006, his Times colleague Todd Purdum wrote an eloquent obituary that quoted Apple in an old interview with Lear's magazine: "Newspaper people love impossible dreams. . . . I suppose we're reckless sentimentalists. If we didn't love impossible dreams, we would not still be working in an industry whose basic technology was developed in the 16th and 17th centuries."

That technology changed mightily before Apple died, and changes still.

The impossible dreams did not.

As in Apple's life, political reporting is very much about ferreting out information that is important to the functioning and the future of our democracy. Maybe it's the resilience of that dream—rather than the tweets, the blog posts, the circle of friends or number of clicks—that still defines what or who a journalist is. Maybe it's the curiosity, or the tenacity. Maybe it's the willingness—indeed, resolve—to get to the bottom of a story, to root out the truth, that will determine the future of political reporting, whether it is delivered in a 140-character tweet, a 240-word blog post, a 10- or 20- or 50-inch story or a two-minute video.

Or whether it is tossed onto doorsteps each morning or whisked across the globe in a matter of seconds.

Critical Thinking

1. What are the ways that social media have changed how professional journalists cover election campaigns today? Do you think that the contemporary ways of covering campaigns is superior or inferior to how they were covered two or three decades ago?

2. How have technology advances changed who can—and does—cover election campaigns? Is this change a good thing? Why?

3. How and why have candidates behaved differently because of the existence of social media and reporters' use of them?

4. What are "trackers" and what is "American Bridge 21st Century"? What do they do and how significant are they in contemporary campaign coverage?

5. Some might argue that journalism and campaign coverage is fundamentally different since the coming of social media; others might hold that the core elements remain the same: ferreting out and reporting information that is important in the functioning of the American political system. Which view do you support? Why?

Create Central

www.mhhe.com/createcentral

Internet References

Poynter Online
www.poynter

Tech President
www.techpresident.com

Senior contributing writer **JODI ENDA** (jaenda@gmail.com) has written about Bloomberg News and coverage of foreign news and federal departments and agencies in recent issues of AJR. She covered the White House, presidential campaigns and Congress for Knight Ridder.

Enda, Jodi. From *American Journalism Review*, Fall 2011, pp. 15–21. Copyright © 2011 by the Philip Merrill College of Journalism at the University of Maryland, College Park, MD 20742-7111. Reprinted with permission.

Article   Prepared by: Bruce Stinebrickner, *DePauw University*

The Varnished Truth

Getting the news from Comedy Central

JAMES T. KEANE

Learning Outcomes

After reading this article, you will be able to:

- Understand the appeal of getting political news through TV comedy shows.

- Weigh the assertion that it is naïve to think that any source of news is without bias, from mainstream network evening news shows to *The New York Times*.

One day last fall, an explosion of texts and tweets about police brutality began to appear on the Internet concerning an incident at the Occupy Cal protests on the steps of Sproul Hall at the University of California, Berkeley. Because most college students have camera phones, many captured on video footage of officers beating students, dragging a professor across the lawn by her hair and kneeling on the neck of a student being handcuffed. I saw the footage myself for the first time that night on "The Colbert Report," where Stephen Colbert quoted from an Associated Press story that described the violence as "pulling people from the steps and nudging others with batons."

"Yes, 'nudging,'" Colbert noted in his deadpan delivery as the footage rolled, "just like the Rodney King nudging. Or when Bull Connor set up that slip-'n'-slide in Birmingham."

The studio audience howled and so did viewers, judging by the frequency with which Colbert was quoted afterward. Note that there's a lot going on between the delivery and the viewer in moments like that. First, Colbert is presuming a fairly high level of cultural literacy on the part of his viewers (Bull Connor is not a household name anymore); second, the joke implies that both Colbert and his audience share a reflexive distrust of the way a venerable news organization like the Associated Press delivers content; and third, much of Colbert's audience (including me) was getting their news from what is explicitly a comedy show.

With Quips and Cynicism

"The Daily Show With Jon Stewart" (where Colbert got his start) has a similar modus operandi. It delivers news wrapped in comedy, pop-culture references and often an ironic distance from momentous historical events. When President Obama announced an impromptu televised press conference last May to deliver news that would capture world headlines (the death of Osama bin Laden), Jon Stewart quipped, "As Hollywood has taught us, when a black president interrupts your show, a meteor is headed for the earth." There's that combination again—humor, cynicism about the entertainment element of the news cycle and a pop-culture reference that the audience can take satisfaction in recognizing. (It has been 14 years, after all, since Morgan Freeman announced the earth's impending destruction in "Deep Impact.")

Despite a brief jump last year in viewers of the Big Three evening national news broadcasts, Nielsen Media Research has shown a steady decline in the audience for these television programs since 2001. Some of this is due to the growth of the Internet and the transformation of the news cycle into a 24/7 enterprise. Gone are the days when a company could issue bad news on a Friday afternoon and hope that by Monday someone else's gaffes would occupy the attention of reporters. But much of the decline is also attributable to a sea change in the way Americans receive information and interact with public figures. Ask your friends and family where they get their news; if you're talking to someone under a certain age, they will likely say Stewart or Colbert.

Why Comedy?

But Stewart and Colbert are comedians, not news anchors. Colbert's entire *shtick* originated as a mockery of Bill O'Reilly's punditry from the right on "The O'Reilly Factor." Why do jokesters bring many of us so much of our news? Are we shallower than our parents? Do we need sugar with our medicine?

Are we more cynical than previous generations, refusing to accept information without ironic distance? The answer is complicated.

First, there has been an erosion of trust in "the news" as anything approaching the truth. This is a positive development in many ways. It is naïve to assume that Walter Cronkite could be trusted to deliver unvarnished truth, or that *The New York Times* delivers "all the news that's fit to print." We all have biases and blind spots and cut some intellectual corners. That has been apparent ever since a sitting president assembled an "enemies list" that put journalists among his nemeses. The media have their own agenda, and so does everyone they report on. So does the audience. If you watch the commercials between news segments on NBC, ABC or CBS (ads for medical care, defenses against crime and "how to protect your assets" are ubiquitous) you'll see that the content follows certain motifs, like the fear of change. Mainstream news programs routinely report on the ways in which "our way of life" is being threatened or destroyed and seldom acknowledge that such ways of life are unsustainable or contrary to the public good. *Écrasez l'infâme* to all that.

Second, we have seen a cultural shift in the relative importance of personality as it relates to content. This is as true of Colbert and Stewart as it is of O'Reilly and Rush Limbaugh. Can you remember the particular personality characteristics of Tom Brokaw, Peter Jennings or Dan Rather? Or do they blend together? Those anchors of the 1980s and '90s were deliberately bland to reflect an Everyman persona. But with hams like Stewart and Colbert, much of their viewer appeal is tied up in their personality, regardless of the content. In fact, we're usually waiting for the laugh more than for the news they riff on. The flip side of this focus on personality is delight in the failure of such persons to live up to the standards their cultic status places on them. One can see again Limbaugh's public scandals here, or the endless speculation among Catholic media about Colbert's background. (Is he a catechist? Does he have 11 children? Does he go to Mass every week? Does he really hate liturgical dance?) As much as we want the person to exemplify the content, we place a surprising amount of weight on that public personality's private affairs.

Third, these shows have become news sources because of the ever-increasing compartmentalization of information in U.S. culture. The worldwide revolution in communications has put much more information at our fingertips, but it has not changed our ability to process it. We tend to compartmentalize where we receive our input, and we want it from people who look and act like us.

A dangerous result is that one is confirmed repeatedly in one's narrow worldview without having to listen to opposing perspectives. Of course, opposing views were not regularly offered by the "mainstream news" either. A hegemonic information culture has been replaced by a completely fractious one, not necessarily to the good.

Why is it that Colbert and Stewart, the darlings of liberal sophisticates and urban hipsters, convey their product through comedy, while O'Reilly, Limbaugh, Ann Coulter and Glenn Beck convey theirs through personas of perpetual outrage? It has to do with the ways in which we put each other down. The great weapon of the social conservative is to suggest that his or her ideological opponents have no values and no moral center. The great weapon of the social progressive is to suggest that his or her opponents are unsophisticated rubes, not in on the joke. The anger and professional outrage one hears from conservative pundits is paralleled by the mocking, ironic tone of comedians on the left. Both sides play to particular audiences. It really is just entertainment.

One last question: if the news is becoming entertainment, and entertainment is delivering the news, will the generations that get their news from such shows be able to process world events and social trends in nuanced and thoughtful ways? If our sources of information are filtered through the comic instincts of teams of writers with particular interests and biases, won't we be increasingly polarized around political and social issues? The writer Joe Keohane presented evidence to support that view in an essay in *The Boston Globe* last year: when we Americans are confronted with information contrary to our strongly held views, we tend to become even more deeply convinced of what we already believed. Worse, Keohane found that the more "politically sophisticated" you think you are, the less likely you are to accept facts contrary to your worldview.

There is something troubling about a culture of information that relies on laughs at the foibles of ideological strangers. While these shows are not going away, it might be a valuable corrective to recover some sense of the comic axiom that the most fruitful target of humor is ourselves.

Critical Thinking

1. Why do many (especially young) Americans get their news from TV comedy shows?
2. What is the relationship between "political sophistication" and the likelihood that one accepts facts contrary to his or her worldview? Why do you think such a relationship exists?

Create Central

www.mhhe.com/createcentral

Internet References

The Daily Show with Jon Stewart
    www.thedailyshow.com
Comedy Central
    www.comedycentral.com

JAMES T. KEANE, S.J., *is a student at the Jesuit School of Theology of Santa Clara University in Berkeley, Calif. He is a former associate editor of* America.

Unit 4

UNIT

Prepared by: Bruce Stinebrickner, *DePauw University*

Products of American Politics

"**P**roducts" refer to government policies that the American political system produces. The first three units of this book pave the way for this fourth and concluding unit because the products of American politics are very much the consequences of the rest of the political system.

The economy and the government's taxing and spending policies are often prominent policy issues in the American political system. One of the most remarkable consequences of 12 years (1981–1993) under President Ronald Reagan and the first President Bush was enormous growth in budget deficits and the national debt. During the Clinton presidency (1993–2001), the United States experienced the longest period of continuous economic growth in its history, accompanied by low unemployment and low inflation rates. Continuing economic growth and increased tax revenues led to budget surpluses in the last three years of the Clinton presidency, amid predictions that the entire national debt would be eliminated within a decade or so. In the last months of the Clinton administration, however, signs of an economic slowdown appeared. President George W. Bush pushed tax cuts through Congress early in his presidency (2001–2009), the country entered a recession in the second half of Bush's first year in office (2001), and the 9/11 terrorist attacks seemed to accelerate the economic downturn and an increase in budget deficits. By 2007, with the costs of the wars in Iraq and Afghanistan continuing to mount and the retirement of the baby boomer generation drawing ever nearer, sizable annual budget deficits and mounting national debt had returned, and the country's fiscal policies once again caused growing concern.

In 2008, home mortgage and other financial market problems shook the foundations of the nation's credit and banking systems, bringing Wall Street woes and what came to be called the Great Recession. Meanwhile, the national government's budget deficits soared. By late 2008, it was unclear whether the Big Three automakers, traditional mainstays of American industry, would avoid bankruptcy as two of them publicly sought a bailout from Washington in order to survive. Economic problems in the United States reverberated around the globe, and many observers correctly predicted that the economic downturn was going to be the worst since the Great Depression of the 1930s.

In its first months in office, the Obama administration concentrated on the country's economic woes. The remaining half of the $700 billion in the Troubled Asset Relief Program (TARP), enacted in the last months of the Bush administration, was used to prop up failing financial institutions as well as General Motors and Chrysler. Moreover, President Obama pushed Congress for a stimulus package to try to get the economy growing again, and the result was the $787 billion Recovery Act of February 2009.

By late 2009, economic growth had returned amid continuing high unemployment rates that threatened "a jobless recovery." TARP and stimulus spending, combined with the costs of wars in Iraq and Afghanistan and other costs associated with the recession, made national government budget deficits reach the highest levels since the end of World War II. While Obama's supporters claimed that his actions had saved the country from another Great Depression, Obama's critics expressed concern about the huge budget deficits, the mounting national debt, and when prosperity and economic stability would return to the United States. By the late summer of 2010, the recovery continued to be weak, with high unemployment figures, an extremely slow housing market, minimal economic growth, and growing fears of a so-called double-dip recession. In this context, it was unsurprising that President Obama's public approval ratings declined to below 50 percent. Republicans fared well in the November 2010 congressional elections, regaining majority control of the House of Representatives and gaining six seats in the Senate.

The beginning of a new period of "divided government" in January 2011 seemed to bring heightened policy tensions in Washington. A debt ceiling crisis occurred during the summer of 2011, with an uneasy agreement reached just before the U.S. government was to default. That "uneasy agreement" included automatic, mostly across-the-board, spending cuts beginning on January 1, 2013, the same date on which the Bush era tax cuts were due to expire, *unless* subsequent legislative action amending the cuts and/or tax revenues occurred.

As the economy's slow and fragile recovery continued during President Obama's fourth year in office, economists warned of an impending "fiscal cliff." Given the economic realities in 2012, they said, the combination of across-the-board cuts in government spending and the expiration of the Bush era tax cuts would likely result in another recession. But President Obama and the 112th Congress "kicked the can down the road," postponing until after Election Day serious efforts to avoid the "fiscal cliff" that loomed ahead.

More "uneasy agreements" were reached by March 2013, but the terms of those agreements on taxing, spending, and the debt ceiling made it almost inevitable that another crisis would arrive the following fall. And it did, leading to a sixteen-day government shutdown beginning on October 1, 2013, the second-longest government shutdown of any consequence in U.S. history. A temporary "truce" led to reopening the government in mid-October and, surprisingly, a budget deal was worked out by December 2013, which in turn led to suspending the debt ceiling in February 2014 to avoid a U.S. default. Economists of all stripes breathed a sigh of relief because of the widespread belief that a U.S. default might well be catastrophic for both the United States and world economies.

Given the foregoing account of U.S. fiscal and economic woes over the past three decades or so, it should come as no surprise that several selections in this unit treat fiscal and economic issues. As such, they complement selections in Unit 1 that address economic growth, unemployment, income inequality and economic mobility, national government deficits and debt, taxation, and the like.

Other selections in Unit 4 address U.S. national and homeland security and make efforts to put American foreign and defense policy into larger perspective.

Barack Obama made his early opposition to the Iraq war a cornerstone of his 2008 presidential candidacy and promised to remove U.S. troops from Iraq in a timely manner if he became president. By late 2008, the Iraqi government declared that U.S. troops should be removed from Iraq within three years. During the transition period between his November 2008 election and his inauguration on January 20, 2009, Obama announced that he would keep President Bush's Secretary of Defense, Robert Gates, whose responsibilities would include overseeing the safe withdrawal of U.S. troops from Iraq. This move suggested that, at long last, American policymakers and the American public were moving toward a bipartisan consensus about ending U.S. military involvement in Iraq. In the second month of his presidency, Obama announced his plan to withdraw U.S. combat troops by August 2010, and the planned withdrawal occurred on schedule 18 months later.

Even as his Iraq withdrawal plan was being met with approval by most Americans, in the fall of 2009 President Obama found himself wrestling with various military options in Afghanistan, which ranged, according to some observers, from "bad" to "worse." U.S. military forces in Afghanistan faced a growing Taliban insurgency, and the corrupt Afghanistan government led many Americans to wonder whether mounting U.S. casualties in Afghanistan were justified. In December 2009 the commander-in-chief announced a new plan that would increase the number of U.S. troops in Afghanistan (a so-called surge) and change

tactics used to fight the Taliban. By the end of American combat troop withdrawals from Iraq in August 2010, additional U.S. troops were in place in Afghanistan, and the nation and the world waited to see whether the new strategy would be successful.

In another foreign policy arena, Syria was in the midst of a civil war whose outcome could not be predicted. American accusations that the Syrian government used chemical weapons to kill more than 1,000 people in late August 2013 led to an interesting sequence of events. President Obama almost immediately began planning a cruise missile attack on selected Syrian targets, and then surprised everyone at the last minute by seeking Congressional support for his planned attack. Congressional support for the president's plan seemed very much in doubt, and he then suddenly changed course and accepted a proposal from Russian President Vladimir Putin to get Syria to identify its chemical weapons holdings and surrender them to international authorities over a period of months. By the fall of 2014, the chemical weapons disposal arrangements seemed to be working reasonably well, but another Syria-related crisis had arisen, this one centered around an extremist Islamic organization known as ISIS (Islamic State in Iraq and Syria).

In August and September 2014, Syria-based ISIS made the gruesome beheadings of two Americans available on the Internet for all the world to see. Similar beheadings of two British citizens quickly followed. In response, President Obama publicly discussed a military campaign against the Islamic extremist organization, which already controlled a great deal of northeastern Syria and which had been taking over Iraqi territory in the face of little to no resistance from Iraqi troops. In September, President Obama told the nation and the world in a televised address that he planned to order the commencement of U.S. airstrikes on ISIS locations in Syria. Such bombing had already occurred in Iraq. Moreover, he said, the United States would train and equip moderate Syrian rebels who, along with ISIS, had been fighting the Syrian regime of Bashar el-Assad for several years and get other nations to join a united front against ISIS by providing military and other assistance. At the same time, Obama promised that there would be no U.S. combat "boots on the ground." But a few days later the Chairman of the Joint Chiefs of Staff's seemingly contradictory statement to a congressional committee cast doubt on the president's words.

At this writing in late October 2015, a year of U.S. bombing of ISIS targets in Syria has not vanquished the Islamic extremist group. A handful of other nations have joined in the airstrikes, and U.S. military "advisors" seem to have been gradually drawn into combat roles, with one mission resulting in the death of an American soldier. Russian President Putin's decision to provide military support to besieged Syrian President Assad has further complicated U.S. efforts in the region.

Meanwhile, other contentious problems remained, particularly those involving Russia-Ukraine relations and other arenas in the Middle East. The Russia-Ukraine crisis touched off by Russia's March 2014 annexation of Crimea, a part of Ukraine, continued for months, although by fall 2014 some tentative progress in reducing tensions seemed to have been made. In September 2013, newly elected Iranian President Rouhani made several statements that included overtures to the United States and resulted in the first conversation—a 15-minute phone call—between a U.S. president and Iranian leader since 1979. Hopes rose that Iran would agree to refrain from building nuclear weapons and that, in turn, economic sanctions against Iran could end. In the summer of 2015, the U.S., Iran, and five other nations announced a deal aimed at halting Iran's development of nuclear weapons, while Its opponents in the U.S. Congress suggested that it would do no such thing. Finally, violent outbreaks occurring in the latter half of 2015 seemed to make a lasting settlement between Israel and Palestinians living under Palestinian Authority jurisdiction as distant a possibility as ever.

A daunting list of policy challenges and policy questions faced American national government as the end of President Obama's seventh year in office approached. These included the state of the American economy, the increasingly unequal distribution of wealth and income in the United States, the continuing implementation of core elements in Obamacare, long-deferred problems stemming from the presence of millions of "undocumented aliens" in the United States, the urgent need to mitigate the adverse consequences of climate change, and global instability and national security threats stemming from a number of sources around the world.

Selections on the *products* of American national government and selections on the *foundations, structures,* and *process* of the American political system in this book all provide bases for understanding contemporary American national government at work.

Article　　　　　　　　　　　　　Prepared by: Bruce Stinebrickner, *DePauw University*

America the Undertaxed

U.S. Fiscal Policy in Perspective.

ANDREA LOUISE CAMPBELL

Learning Outcomes

After reading this article, you will be able to:

- Understand how overall U.S. tax revenues as a percentage of GDP compare with those of other countries and consider the pros and cons of low and high taxation rates.

- Decide whether it is likely that Americans and their government will, in the next generation or two, significantly raise (or lower) the percentage of GDP that tax revenues constitute.

T he most important debates in U.S. politics today center on the cost and the role of government. Cutting taxes, limiting expenditures, and reducing debt have become the chief concerns of Republicans, whereas Democrats generally seek to preserve or even expand government spending and are willing to raise taxes to do so. The looming expiration of the George W. Bush tax cuts at the end of 2012 and the economy's weak recovery give these debates special urgency, as decisions made in the next few months are likely to shape the nation's economic, social, and political trajectory for years to come.

Behind each party's position lies not only a particular collection of interest groups but also a story about what the government's role in the U.S. economy is and what it should be. Democrats think Washington can and should play a more active part, using taxation, regulation, and spending to keep the economy growing while protecting vulnerable citizens from the ravages of volatile markets. Republicans, in contrast, think Washington already does too much; they want to scale government back to liberate markets and spur economic dynamism.

When mulling these stories, it can be useful to put U.S. fiscal policy in perspective. Compared with other developed countries, the United States has very low taxes, little redistribution of income, and an extraordinarily complex tax code. These three aspects of American exceptionalism deserve more attention than they typically receive.

Extremely Low and Incredibly Consistent

The first striking feature of the fiscal state of the United States, when compared with those of other developed countries, is its small size. As of 2009, among the 34 members of the Organization for Economic Cooperation and Development (OECD), a collection of the world's most economically advanced democracies, the United States had the third-lowest ratio of taxes to GDP (see chart). But it is important to look at pre-recession data, which better reflect long-term trends. In 2006, before the financial crisis struck, OECD tax statistics showed that total taxes in the United States—at all levels of government: federal, state, and local—were 27.9 percent of GDP, three-quarters the percentages in Germany and the United Kingdom and about half of those in Denmark and Sweden. Among the rich democracies in 2006, only South Korea had lower taxes.

The reason for this discrepancy is not that the United States has lower personal income tax revenues than its OECD counterparts. In fact, in 2006, personal income taxes at the federal, state, and local levels in the United States came to 10.1 percent of GDP, just above the OECD average of 9.2 percent. Instead, the disparity results from the low effective rates—or nonexistence—of other forms of taxation. To take one example, in 2006, the U.S. corporate income tax at all levels of government collected 3.4 percent of GDP, compared with an average of 3.8 percent across the OECD. During that same year, according to the OECD, U.S. social insurance taxes brought in

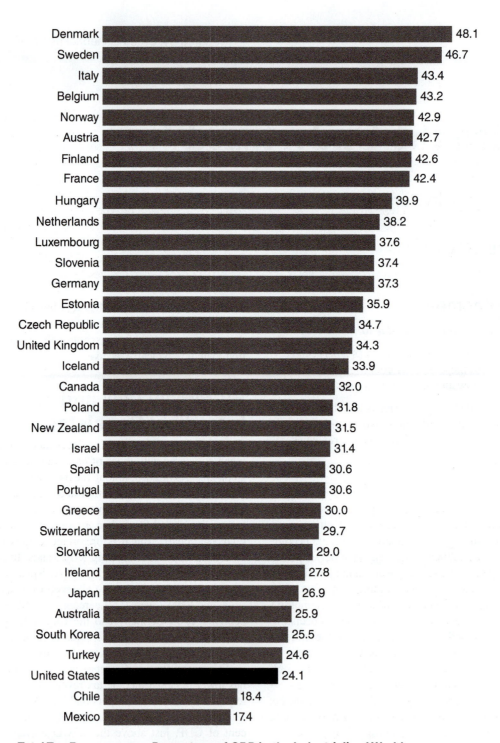

Total Tax Revenues as a Percentage of GDP in the Industrialized World

Source: Organization for Economic Cooperation and Development, 2009.

6.6 percent of GDP, compared with an average of 9.2 percent among the OECD nations. Yet the biggest difference between the United States and other OECD countries is in consumption tax revenue. Most U.S. states have sales taxes, and the federal government maintains excise taxes (taxes on such goods as alcohol, cigarettes, and fuel) and customs duties (taxes on imported goods). Yet none of those taxes currently collects the same amount of revenue as a value-added tax (VAT) would (a VAT is a consumption tax that collects revenue from the value added by each business at each stage in the chain of production of a given product).OECD statistics show that VATS bring in an average of 6.7 percent of GDP among the OECD nations, accounting for the majority of the difference in total tax revenues between the United States, which does not have a VAT, and the rest of the OECD.

U.S. tax revenue is not only low but also consistently low, having equaled roughly the same share of the economy for 60 years. Since the tremendous growth of the federal government during World War II, federal tax revenues have hovered around 18 percent of GDP. This stability has also proved to be true of state and local tax levels, which have fluctuated between eight and ten percent of GDP over the same period. Over that time, taxes in the other OECD countries have grown more than in the United States. In 1965, total tax revenues stood at about 25 percent of GDP in the United States and across the rest of the OECD. But by 2000, tax revenue represented 30 percent of GDP in the United States and 37 percent in the rest of the OECD. The enacting of VATS throughout the OECD during the 1960s and 1970s accounts for much of the difference. It also accounts for the steadiness of European tax revenues through the global financial crisis. By 2009, total tax revenues had dropped to 24 percent of GDP in the United States, but they had fallen just two points, to an average of 35 percent of GDP, in the other OECD countries.

Although tax receipts have composed approximately the same share of GDP for decades in the United States, their composition has changed. In particular, the corporate tax has plunged as a source of federal revenues, from 30 percent in the 1950s to ten percent today. As Republicans are quick to point out, the United States does have one of the highest statutory corporate tax rates in the developed world. Combining the federal and state levels, the top rate of these taxes is 39 percent, compared with an average of 36 percent across the G-7 and 31 percent across the OECD. Yet as with the individual income tax, the United States applies these statutory rates to a narrower base of taxpayers than other advanced countries do, due to various corporate tax credits and breaks, such as the accelerated depreciation of machinery and equipment and the deferral of taxes on income earned abroad. As a result, according to a report issued by the U.S. Treasury Department, between 2000 and 2005, on average, U.S. businesses paid an effective tax rate of only 13 percent, nearly three percent below the OECD average and the lowest rate among the G-7 countries.

The United States currently taxes top earners at some of the lowest effective rates in the country's history.

Whereas corporate tax revenues have fallen, revenues from payroll taxes for programs such as Social Security and Medicare have grown. The Urban-Brookings Tax Policy Center found that these taxes rose from 23 percent of federal revenue in 1970 to 40 percent in 2010. In fact, the majority of Americans pay more in payroll taxes than in federal income taxes. This is the case in part because the United States imposes payroll taxes on all wages without the exemptions and deductions so common to individual and corporate income taxes and in part because the Earned Income Tax Credit, which helps offset the federal income and payroll taxes of low-wage workers, reduces or eliminates income taxes for many with low earnings.

Even as payroll tax revenues have risen, the individual income tax, which in 2010 accounted for 42 percent of national revenue, has remained the main source of federal income. According to the Urban-Brookings Tax Policy Center, for decades prior to the Bush tax cuts of 2001-3, despite many alterations to tax bases and rates, the individual income tax provided a steady and large percentage of federal revenue. That is because the government tended to compensate for changes in rates by expanding or shrinking the tax base when necessary. During the 1970s, the tax code featured 25 income brackets and a top rate of 70 percent. Legislation passed during Ronald Reagan's presidency reduced the number of brackets to just two, dropped the top rate to 28 percent, ended a number of tax breaks, and pegged the brackets to inflation, ending so-called bracket creep, in which inflation forced taxpayers into higher tax brackets even though their real incomes stayed flat. President George H. W. Bush brought the top rate back up to 35 percent, and President Bill Clinton further raised it to 39.6 percent, but each administration added a number of new tax breaks, from an expansion of the Earned Income Tax Credit to a credit for a child's tuition. The Bush tax cuts reduced taxes on capital gains and dividends and on estates and cut the top tax rate yet again, to 35 percent.

The largest tax reductions from these changes went to high-income households. In fact, the United States currently taxes top earners at some of the lowest effective rates in the country's history. Data from the Internal Revenue Service (IRS) show that the top one percent of taxpayers paid an average federal income tax rate of 23 percent in 2008, about one-third less than they paid in 1980, despite the fact that their incomes are now much higher in both real and relative terms. Although the rich enjoyed by far the largest tax cuts, the middle class is also paying lower taxes. In 2011, the effective federal income tax rate for a family of four with a median income was just 5.6 percent, compared with 12 percent in 1980. And because of the Earned Income Tax Credit, about 40 percent of low-income U.S. households do not pay any federal income tax.

Altogether, the adoption and continuation of the Bush tax cuts has slashed federal revenues by about three percent of

GDP, to levels not seen since shortly after World War II. As a result, the individual income tax now constitutes a smaller share of the economy than it did 30 years ago, falling from 10.4 percent of GDP in 1981 to 8.8 percent in 2005. By permitting extensive loopholes, failing to create effective consumption taxes, and cutting individual income taxes, the United States has created a tax system that collects far less revenue relative to GDP than many of its OECD counterparts.

Unequal Spread

On the surface, U.S. tax policies seem quite progressive. The individual income tax, for example, is scaled to match relative earnings, so that those who take in less income pay less in taxes and those who earn more income pay more in taxes. And as mentioned above, the United States has not implemented a VAT, which is considered regressive because lower-income households tend to spend everything they earn, meaning that the VAT takes a greater share of their earnings than it does for high-income households, which spend only part of their incomes and save the rest. But appearances can be deceiving unless fiscal policy and government spending are considered together. In Europe, regressive taxes are matched with highly redistributive states. In the United States, mildly progressive taxes are matched with a not very redistributive state. As a result, the United States experiences greater inequality than most other advanced nations, with the tax-and-transfer system doing little to alleviate it.

The Occupy Wall Street movement has cast into sharp relief the vast and growing income inequality in the United States. Analyzing IRS data, the economists Thomas Piketty and Emmanuel Saez have found that the share of total income going to the top one percent of earners—those with annual incomes of $400,000 or more—increased from nine percent in 1970 to 23.5 percent in 2007. The 2007 amount represented the highest level in the United States since 1928 and exceeded those for Europe and Japan that year, where the share going to the top one percent of earners was 11 percent in Germany, 9 percent in Japan, 8.7 percent in France, and 5 percent in the Netherlands. Although the 2008 financial crisis reduced the incomes of the top one percent in the United States by a fifth, by 2010 their earnings had largely recovered. And wealth is even more concentrated than income. According to the economist Edward Wolff, in 2007, the top one percent in the country earned just over 20 percent of all income but held more than 30 percent of all wealth.

As the top has risen, the bottom and the middle have faltered. Congressional Budget Office data show that between 1979 and 2007, before-tax incomes increased by 240 percent for the top one percent but by just 20 percent for the middle fifth of earners and by ten percent for the bottom fifth. Although the bottom 90 percent lost less income than the top

one percent as a result of the financial crisis, their earnings have not recovered as much as those of the top earners. In fact, according to Saez, average income in the bottom 90 percent remains at the lowest level since 1983. This dearth of earnings exists in large part thanks to the prevalence of low-wage work in the United States compared with other advanced countries. The Center on Budget and Policy Priorities, a research and policy institute on fiscal matters, has found that almost one-third of Americans have "low incomes," meaning ones below 200 percent of the poverty line. By analyzing OECD data, the economist Timothy Smeeding discovered that the proportion of full-time workers earning less than 65 percent of the median wage in the United States—around 25 percent—is twice as high as in France and Germany and five times as high as in Finland and Sweden.

To be sure, other advanced democracies also suffer from high market-generated inequality. The economists Smeeding and Katherin Ross Phillips have shown that rates of market-income poverty—the proportion of people living in households with incomes that are below 40 percent of the median disposable income—are quite high across the advanced democracies. In fact, according to Smeeding and Ross Phillips, the United States' market-income poverty rate of 17.2 percent for working-age adults is only slightly higher than Germany's (14.9 percent) and Sweden's (15.8 percent) and even lower than Canada's (18.4 percent) and the United Kingdom's (25 percent). Yet unlike the United States, these countries reduce such market-generated poverty through redistribution—less through their tax systems than through their social welfare programs. Although each of these countries imposes generally progressive personal income taxes, they earn much of their revenue from regressive VATs. But these nations steer income from their VATs to wide-ranging social safety nets, thereby redistributing income more evenly across their societies. Smeeding and Ross Phillips found that after the implementation of universal transfer and social assistance programs, poverty among those aged 25 to 64 fell: to 6.9 percent in Canada, 5.9 percent in the United Kingdom, 3.5 percent in Germany, and 1.8 percent in Sweden. Meanwhile, in the United States, it remains at 10.9 percent. Working-age populations in most advanced countries pay higher taxes but receive extensive benefits from social welfare systems, meaning reduced poverty and inequality.

The United States, on the other hand, appears at first glance to have a more progressive tax system than many other OECD members—one that, by shifting tax burdens from the poor to the rich, would theoretically alleviate poverty along the same lines as redistributive programs. Yet the overall U.S. tax system is only mildly progressive. In part, that is because the United States carries out much of its redistributive effort not through social programs but through tax expenditures, that is, forgone revenue in the form of tax credits, deductions, and exemptions. By introducing such measures, the government aims to subsidize certain economic activities. For example, the interest deduction for individuals with home mortgages supports homeownership, and the tax credit for research and experimentation subsidizes corporate innovation. Such expenditures now amount to $1.1 trillion in forgone revenue per year, more than the sum raised by the individual income tax.

The problem is that such expenditures do not reallocate income and resources effectively. True, the Earned Income Tax Credit assists the working poor, and other tax breaks, such as the Child Tax Credit (a reduction in taxes of up to $1,000 for each dependent child under the age of 17, which phases out at higher incomes), benefit many middle-income households. But the majority of the largest tax expenditures help the affluent the most. The Urban-Brookings Tax Policy Center estimates that in 2011, households with incomes in the top fifth of the income distribution received two-thirds of the benefits from tax expenditures, with the top one percent receiving a quarter of them. Much of this disparity has to do with the fact that only 30 percent of tax expenditures are credits, in which the size of the break is the same regardless of income. The other 70 percent of tax expenditures are deductions from taxable income, the value of which rise at higher incomes. For example, a family paying $5,000 in home mortgage interest would receive a $1,750 tax break if it belonged to the 35 percent tax bracket but only a $500 break if it belonged to the ten percent bracket.

In addition to containing tax breaks that favor the rich, the U.S. tax code includes many regressive and flat taxes, which tend to exact more from the poor. These include the Social Security and Medicare payroll taxes, income and sales taxes in many states, and many others. When such taxes are combined with the reduction of progressive taxes for high-income households, the overall tax system—federal, state, and local—becomes only slightly progressive. This means that the share of taxes paid by each income group essentially resembles the share of income that it receives, which would not be the case in a more progressive system. According to the Institute on Taxation and Economic Policy, a fiscal think tank, in 2011, the lowest fifth of earners received 3.4 percent of total income and paid 2.1 percent of total taxes, the middle fifth received 11.4 percent of income and paid 10.3 percent of taxes, and the top one percent received 21 percent of income and paid 21.6 percent of taxes.

The United States achieves comparatively little redistribution through social programs as well, devoting less than many other advanced countries to such services. Although Social Security and Medicare reduce poverty among the elderly, working-age people receive fewer universal benefits than those in other countries, from national health insurance to paid leave for new parents. Outside of Medicaid and food stamps, programs that have grown in recent years, most social assistance initiatives meant to aid the poor remain small and have fallen in real value over time. That is why, despite having nearly the highest per capita GDP in the world, the United States has the highest poverty rate among rich nations.

A Taxing Code

The United States' fiscal state is not only small and minimally redistributive compared with those of other advanced nations; its tax code is also far more complicated. This complexity makes it much more difficult and costly for households and businesses to comply with the rules. And it undermines public trust in the system, with taxpayers fearing that those with better knowledge of how to navigate the system of loopholes, particularly the rich, get away with not paying their fair share.

To get a sense of the immense complexity of the U.S. system, consider that the Internal Revenue Code is almost 12 times as long as the New Testament. The 2012 instruction booklet for the 1040 individual tax form and the accompanying schedules is 188 pages long; the one for the "EZ" form is 43 pages. A 2003 IRS report estimated that individual taxpayers pay $18.8 billion, spending 25 hours and $149 per taxpayer, on compliance each year, mainly through payments made to accountants and agencies to help them sort out their taxes. Corporate taxes are even denser. According to the U.S. Treasury Department, large corporations spend over $40 billion annually on compliance.

The tax expenditure system is one major reason for this intricacy. Each exclusion, deduction, and credit adds another layer of complexity to the code and increases the time needed to prepare one's taxes. Taxing families rather than individuals complicates the system even more, since this method makes it difficult to calculate the proper tax withholding for each partner. Another culprit is the Alternative Minimum Tax (AMT), which is meant to prevent high-income taxpayers from using exclusions and deductions to avoid paying the federal income tax. This system requires some taxpayers to calculate their tax liability twice, once under the regular income tax and then again under the AMT, and pay whichever is higher. Although meant for those in the highest tax brackets, the AMT now affects more ordinary taxpayers because the government did not peg its parameters to inflation, and some very high earners have tax rates outside the parameters of the AMT, allowing them to pay the regular tax instead.

As the economists Joel Slemrod and Jon Bakija have noted, many peers of the United States have put in place far less complex tax systems, making compliance much easier. Several dozen countries utilize a return-free system for most taxpayers. They can do this because they tax individuals rather than families and withhold taxes from both income in the form of wages and income in the form of interest. These two features allow countries to precisely calibrate withholdings to actual tax liabilities. It is also much easier to implement such a system when governments hand out tax breaks either as credits that are equal for all taxpayers or as deductions that are set at a flat rate. In the United Kingdom, for example, the equivalent of the U.S. home mortgage interest deduction is a flat 15 percent reduction on the interest paid on the mortgage applied directly by the bank. Meanwhile, several countries, such as Australia, the Netherlands, and the United Kingdom, require any changes in tax rules to include estimates of the costs of compliance.

To get another sense of the difference between the United States and other developed countries, consider the subsidization of the cost of raising children. Many advanced-country governments calculate and send allowances to families with children. In the United States, however, households with children must navigate and administer a complex system of tax breaks themselves, such the Child Tax Credit and the Earned Income Tax Credit. And if they file their returns incorrectly, the IRS may fine them. That is why even many low-income families rely on tax-preparation firms, which have lobbied against periodic attempts to simplify the tax-paying process, such as having the IRS mail out draft returns for households in straightforward situations. Perhaps it comes as no surprise that when a 2003 survey by National Public Radio, the Henry J. Kaiser Family Foundation, and Harvard University asked Americans what bothers them most about taxes, respondents were more than twice as likely to cite the complexity of the system as the amount they pay.

How to Pay the Price

The Central debate in U.S. politics is whether to keep taxes, particularly federal taxes, at their current levels in the long term or emulate other advanced nations and raise them. In making this choice, Americans will undoubtedly have to prioritize some values and programs over others. But the polarized conversation about this issue thus far has clouded understanding of the actual likely consequences of each course.

If the government fails to raise more revenue, it will no longer be able to afford programs that many Americans say they want, from Social Security to Medicare. A 2008 survey of the American National Election Studies, a biennial study of national election outcomes, showed that a majority of Americans supported increased spending in such areas as financial aid for college, support for the poor, and improved public education. Yet without greater financial flexibility, the U.S. government cannot meet those demands. The consequences of the current system are thus known: the need to slash many of the social safety programs that Americans have come to depend on.

Congressman Paul Ryan (R-Wis.) has spearheaded a movement of budget hawks proposing to address this budget crisis by reducing federal spending to 16 percent of GDP by 2050 (it was 24 percent in 2011). This would represent the lowest level of spending since World War II, before Congress introduced Medicare, Medicaid, the interstate highway system, and most federal aid for education. Although Ryan's cuts might alleviate the revenue problem, low earners would bear the brunt. According to the Center on Budget and Policy Priorities, 62 percent of the spending reductions would affect low-income households, which would also face higher federal taxes due to a reduction in the Earned Income Tax Credit. Meanwhile, Ryan's plan would give those with incomes over $1 million a tax cut of $265,000, and that is on top of the Bush tax cuts already in place.

President Barack Obama, by contrast, has suggested boosting tax revenues, proposing to raise the rates of the top two tax brackets. Another way to add revenue would be to introduce new tax brackets. This would allow the government to differentiate among extremely high levels of income better than it can with the current system, which sets the top bracket at $388,350 and does not distinguish between the merely affluent and the superrich. In 2007, the top one percent paid an average federal income tax rate of 22.4 percent. As the economists Peter Diamond and Saez have noted, increasing that rate to 29.4 percent would raise one percent of GDP in additional revenue; increasing it to 43.5 percent would raise three percent of GDP and still leave the share of after-tax income for these top earners at a level that is more than twice as high as in 1970.

What, then, are the consequences of changing the tax system? The first question is whether higher taxes would harm the economy. Taxation affects economic growth in complex ways. To be sure, at very high rates, taxes can drag down the economy, and government activity and investment, fueled by tax revenues, can drive it. But the connection between relative rates of taxation and economic prosperity may not be as strong as both supporters and opponents of tax hikes think. Slemrod and Bakija found little correlation across the OECD countries between taxes as a percentage of the economy and the size of the economy itself, as measured by per capita GDP. Nor, according to their research, is there a high correlation between taxes as a percentage of GDP and the annual rate of economic growth. There is some evidence of a similar lack of correlations across time in the United States. The U.S. economy grew at a faster pace before the Bush tax cuts rather than after, and it grew more in the 1950s and 1960s than it has recently, even though taxes as a percentage of the economy were the same then as they are today. Raising taxes moderately—perhaps by a few percentage points of GDP—would certainly provide the government with much-needed revenue. And it might not have a detrimental impact on the U.S. economy, perhaps even spurring it.

Similarly, many worry that higher taxes would cause people to work less productively or spend less money. Yet there is little evidence that tax rates affect the participation of either middle- or high-income individuals in the work force. And despite higher taxes, higher earners ultimately did not spend much less during the 1990s, since the total income of the top one percent during that decade rose. Somewhat higher taxes would likely alter behavior to some extent. But with the earnings of the top one percent mostly back to their pre-recession levels, past experience suggests that a tax hike today would not severely damage the economy, and productivity might even rise with the security and investments that government spending can provide.

In proposing all these options, from reducing spending to raising revenue, policymakers are confronting the reality of U.S. fiscal policy: compared with its counterparts among the advanced nations, the United States' tax system collects little revenue, poorly redistributes that money across the population, and is mind-bogglingly complex. The decision of whether to change that system is a political one; whether and how to undertake tax reform is ultimately a referendum on the direction in which Americans would like to take their country.

Critical Thinking

1. Contrast what are said to be Republicans' and Democrats' positions with respect to the role of government in the economy. Of which party's general orientation are you more supportive? Why?
2. Do you think that most Americans know how the U.S. compares with other industrialized nations with respect to level of taxes, redistribution of income, and complexity of tax code? Did you before reading this article? Given how the U.S. compares with other countries, do you support the U.S.'s level of taxation, amount of redistribution of income, and complex tax code? Why or why not?
3. Do you think raising taxes would harm the economy? Why or why not?
4. Do you agree that whether to modify U.S. fiscal policy and especially tax policy is a fundamental choice about the direction in which the United States should move? Why or why not?

Create Central

www.mhhe.com/createcentral

Internet References

Tax Foundation
www.taxfoundation.org
Paul Krugman
http://krugman.blogs.nytimes.com
Americans for Tax Reform
www.atr.org
New York Times, "Why Taxes Aren't as High as They Seem"
www.nytimes.com/2012/01/20/us/politics/why-americans-think-the-tax-rate-is-high-and-why-theyre-wrong.html?_r=0
Wall Street Journal, "Millionaires Support Warren Buffet's Tax on the Rich"
http://blogs.wsj.com/wealth/2011/10/27/most-millionaires-support-warren-buffetts-tax-on-the-rich

ANDREA LOUISE CAMPBELL is Professor of Political Science at the Massachusetts Institute of Technology.

Article

Prepared by: Bruce Stinebrickner, *DePauw University*

The Great Regression

The decline of the progressive income tax and the rise of inequality.

SAM PIZZIGATI AND CHUCK COLLINS

Learning Outcomes

After reading this article, you will be able to:

- Know and appraise the variations in maximum income tax rates in the United State since 1913.

- Understand the different views of Presidents Eisenhower, Kennedy, and Reagan on income tax rates for Americans who earn the highest incomes.

W hatever happened to the "progressive" income tax, the notion that taxpayers who make more money should pay taxes at a higher rate? Tax progressivity today has virtually disappeared. We have, in effect, a flat tax for our most financially favored. A taxpayer who pockets $45 million a year—or $450 million—pays federal income taxes at the same top rate as someone making $450,000. That's not quite what our progressive forebears had in mind 100 years ago this month when they cheered ratification of the Sixteenth Amendment, finally giving Congress the power to impose a federal income tax. Progressives back then hoped the income tax would deal a body blow to plutocracy. But the first tax schedule, enacted soon after the amendment's ratification in 1913, set the top rate at a mere 7 percent, not the 68 percent progressives in Congress had sought.

World war would soon shift the tax terrain. In 1916, a Congress hungry for war "preparedness" revenue pushed the top rate to 15 percent. With that hike, one prominent House Democrat pronounced, tax rates had reached their "very highest notch." Not for progressives: in 1917, social reformers ranging from newspaper publisher E.W. Scripps to labor leader Sidney Hillman redefined the tax debate with a national campaign that advocated "a conscription of wealth"—a 100 percent tax on income over $100,000. By war's end, income tax rates would stretch all the way up to 77 percent.

The post–World War I right-wing resurgence then turned the tax tables. Top rates would fall throughout the Roaring Twenties, down to 25 percent. Treasury Secretary Andrew Mellon, the Pittsburgh iron and steel tycoon, even engineered a $1.27 billion tax rebate for himself and his fellow deep pockets.

The Great Depression and World War II would, in turn, reverse the Mellon tax cuts. First in 1932, and then repeatedly over the next decade, progressives defeated conservative attempts to raise needed revenues via a regressive national sales tax—and kept up the pressure for "soak the rich" rates. By 1942, President Franklin Roosevelt himself was calling for a 100 percent tax rate on income over $25,000 (about $350,000 today). Tax rates would top off at 94 percent during World War II and hover around 90 percent for the next two decades.

High tax rates on high incomes, back in that early postwar era, struck even eminently respectable Americans as absolutely necessary to social stability and progress. Stiff tax rates served "to counteract undue concentration of wealth," as Wall Street tax lawyer Randolph Paul, FDR's point man on taxes during World War II, explained in 1947. "If the nation's wealth flows into the hands of too few rather than into the hands of the many, the resulting amount of saving will be greater than can be absorbed. Our economy can take only so much of this sort of thing before it has a violent convulsion." Republican President Dwight Eisenhower saw high taxes on high incomes as an antidote to the "opulence" that inexorably leads a nation to "depravity and ultimate destruction." In the 1950s, under Ike, income over $400,000 faced a 91 percent federal rate. The Eisenhower-era rich, even after loopholes, felt a real tax bite. In 1955, the IRS took 51.2 percent of America's top 400 incomes.

And today, after thirty years of rising income inequality and shrinking tax progressivity? In 2007, America's top 400 had an average tax bill, after loopholes, of just 16.6 percent. These 400 reported incomes averaged an astounding $345 million, more than twenty-five times (after adjusting for inflation) the $13 million that the top 400 took home in 1955.

What went so terribly wrong? How could our tax progressivity have deteriorated so astonishingly? The conventional story line blames Ronald Reagan. But the dismantling of tax progressivity began about two decades earlier, under John Kennedy. "As they say on my own Cape Cod," JFK famously assured America, "a rising tide lifts all the boats." And nothing would cause the tide to rise faster, he contended in 1963, than tax cuts for everybody, the rich included. Steep tax rates, his economists told him, had become a "heavy drag" on growth, so his administration proposed reducing the top rate from 91 to 65 percent.

Conservatives soon enough took Kennedy's tax-cut case to the next logical level: If tax cuts could create the magical outcomes JFK promised, why stop at the 70 percent top rate Congress OK'd in 1964? Why, indeed? In the 1980s, Ronald Reagan cut the top rate first to 50 percent, then 28 percent, clearing the way for America's plutocratic restoration.

Where does all this leave us on income taxation's 100th anniversary? Should progressives today simply recommit ourselves to restoring Ike-era tax rates? The reality we face suggests otherwise. Steeply graduated rates, as traditionally structured, haven't been sustainable anywhere for more than a few decades. The super-rich have always been able to make them crumble. One reason: the 99 percent have never been able to rouse a passion on behalf of high top rates that matches the passion of the 1 percent—and the 0.1 percent—against them. The super-rich essentially take steeply graduated tax rates much more personally than the 99 percent.

Given this historic dynamic, should we focus our tax attention elsewhere? Attractive options certainly do beckon. Instead of trying to raise top rates, we could concentrate on ending tax preferences for capital gains and dividends. We could go after overseas tax havens. We could press for financial transaction, wealth and carbon taxes. All of these options could make significant contributions to the struggle against inequality. All deserve pursuing.

But we need not give up on steeply graduated tax rates; we need, instead, to find an approach that gives the 99 percent a greater incentive to defend them. Suppose, for instance, we set the entry threshold for a new 91 percent maximum rate as a multiple of our nation's minimum wage—say, twenty-five times? That was the ratio between CEO and typical worker pay for much of the mid–twentieth century, before recent decades left top corporate pay averaging over 300 times workers' take-home.

The federal hourly minimum sits today at $7.25. A married couple working at minimum-wage jobs now annually earns just over $30,000. If we pegged entry into the top bracket at twenty-five times that, taxpayers making over $750,000 would face the 91 percent top rate. But if the minimum wage rose to $10 an hour, the top bracket wouldn't kick in until just over $1 million.

In today's plutocratic America, the rich get richer by exploiting the poor. In an America that tied maximum tax rates to minimum wages, the rich would regularly "get richer"—that is, pay less in taxes—only if low-wage workers were taking home bigger paychecks.

Happy 100th birthday, progressive income tax! There may be some life in you yet.

Critical Thinking

1. What did the Sixteenth Amendment empower Congress to do and when was it added to the Constitution?

2. What was the highest income tax rate in American history, at what time was it imposed, and what is the highest rate today? What is your view of the decline in maximum income tax rates, especially since 1960?

3. Why would linking the entry threshold for the maximum income tax rate to a multiple of the minimum wage be likely to engage miiddle- and lower-class Americans? Do you think that such a proposal is a good idea?

Create Central

www.mhhe.com/createcentral

Internet References

Internal Revenue Service
www.comedycentral.com

CNN—Money: Top Income Rate: How U.S. Really Compares
http://money.cnn.com/2013/04/01/pf/taxes/top-income-tax/index.html

SAM PIZZIGATI, an Institute for Policy Studies associate fellow, is the author of the just-published *The Rich Don't Always Win: The Forgotten Triumph Over Plutocracy That Created the American Middle Class, 1900–1970* (Seven Stories Press). **CHUCK COLLINS,** the author of *99 to 1: How Wealth Inequality Is Wrecking the World and What We Can Do About It* (Berrett-Koehler), directs the institute's program on inequality and the common good. The two edit Inequality.Org.

Article   Prepared by: Bruce Stinebrickner, *DePauw University*

10 Practical Steps to Reverse Growing Inequality

This diabolical trend is threatening the foundations of our society.

ROBERT B. REICH

Learning Outcomes

After reading this article, you will be able to:

- Assess whether and, if so, how much, of a threat growing inequality poses to the U.S. economy, Americans' ideal of equal opportunity, and American democracy.

- Weigh whether the fact that the two top years of income inequality in the past century were 1928 and 2007 has any significance for relevant policy making.

- Assess the likely usefulness and feasibility of the 10 steps that Robert Reich proposes to reverse widening income inequality in the United States.

S ome inequality of income and wealth is inevitable, if not necessary. If an economy is to function well, people need incentives to work hard and innovate. The pertinent question is not whether income and wealth inequality is good or bad. It is at what point do these inequalities become so great as to pose a serious threat to our economy, our ideal of equal opportunity and our democracy.

We are near or have already reached that tipping point. It is incumbent on us to dedicate ourselves to reversing this diabolical trend. It will not happen automatically, because the dysfunctions of our economy and politics are not self-correcting when it comes to inequality. In order to reform the system, we need a political movement for shared prosperity. Herewith, a short summary of what has happened, why it has happened, how it threatens the foundations of our society, and what we must do to reverse it.

The data on widening inequality are remarkably and disturbingly clear. The Congressional Budget Office has found that between 1979 and 2007, the onset of the Great Recession, the gap in income—after federal taxes and transfer payments—more than tripled between the top 1 percent of the population and everyone else. The after-tax, after-transfer income of the top 1 percent increased by 275 percent, while it increased less than 40 percent for the middle three quintiles of the population and only 18 percent for the bottom quintile.

The gap has continued to widen in the recovery. According to the Census Bureau, median family and median household incomes have been falling, adjusted for inflation; while according to the data gathered by my colleague Emmanuel Saez, the income of the wealthiest 1 percent has soared by 31 percent. In fact, Saez has calculated that 95 percent of all economic gains since the recovery began have gone to the top 1 percent.

Wealth has become even more concentrated than income. An April 2013 Pew Research Center report found that from 2009 to 2011, "the mean net worth of households in the upper 7 percent of wealth distribution rose by an estimated 28 percent, while the mean net worth of households in the lower 93 percent dropped by 4 percent."

T his trend is now threatening the three foundation stones of our society: our economy, our ideal of equal opportunity and our democracy.

In the United States, consumer spending accounts for approximately 70 percent of economic activity. If consumers don't have adequate purchasing power, businesses have no incentive to expand or hire additional workers. Because the rich spend a smaller proportion of their incomes than the middle class and the poor, it stands to reason that as a larger and larger share of the nation's total income goes to the top, consumer demand is dampened. If the middle class is forced to borrow in order to maintain its standard of living, that dampening may come suddenly—when debt bubbles burst.

Consider that the two peak years of inequality over the past century—when the top 1 percent garnered more than 23 percent of total income—were 1928 and 2007. Each of these periods was preceded by substantial increases in borrowing, which ended notoriously in the Great Crash of 1929 and the near-meltdown of 2008.

The anemic recovery we are now experiencing is directly related to the decline in median household incomes after 2009, coupled with the inability or unwillingness of consumers to take on additional debt and of banks to finance that debt—wisely, given the damage wrought by the bursting debt bubble. We cannot have a growing economy without a growing and buoyant middle class. We cannot have a growing middle class if almost all of the economic gains go to the top 1 percent.

Widening inequality also challenges the nation's core ideal of equal opportunity, because it hampers upward mobility. High inequality correlates with low upward mobility. Studies are not conclusive because the speed of upward mobility is difficult to measure. But even under the unrealistic assumption that its velocity is no different today than it was 30 years ago—that someone born into a poor or lower-middle-class family today can move upward at the same rate as three decades ago—widening inequality still hampers upward mobility. That's simply because the ladder is far longer now. The distance between its bottom and top rungs, and between every rung along the way, is far greater. Anyone ascending it at the same speed as before will necessarily make less progress upward.

In addition, when the middle class is in decline and median household incomes are dropping, there are fewer possibilities for upward mobility. A stressed middle class is also less willing to share the ladder of opportunity with those below it. For this reason, the issue of widening inequality cannot be separated from the problems of poverty and diminishing opportunities for those near the bottom. They are one and the same.

The connection between widening inequality and the undermining of democracy has long been understood. As former Supreme Court Justice Louis Brandeis is famously alleged to have said in the early years of the last century, an era when robber barons dumped sacks of money on legislators' desks, "We may have a democracy, or we may have great wealth concentrated in the hands of a few, but we cannot have both."

As income and wealth flow upward, political power follows. Money flowing to political campaigns, lobbyists, think tanks, "expert" witnesses and media campaigns buys disproportionate influence. With all that money, no legislative bulwark can be high enough or strong enough to protect the democratic process.

The threat to our democracy also comes from the polarization that accompanies high levels of inequality. Partisanship—measured by some political scientists as the distance between median Republican and Democratic roll-call votes on key economic issues—almost directly tracks with the level of inequality. It reached high levels in the first decades of the twentieth century when inequality soared, and has reached similar levels in recent years.

When large numbers of Americans are working harder than ever but getting nowhere, and see most of the economic gains going to a small group at the top, they suspect the game is rigged. Some of these people can be persuaded that the culprit is big government; others, that the blame falls on the wealthy and big corporations. The result is fierce partisanship, fueled by anti-establishment populism on both the right and the left of the political spectrum.

Between the end of World War II and the early 1970s, the median wage grew in tandem with productivity. Both roughly doubled in those years, adjusted for inflation. But after the 1970s, productivity continued to rise at roughly the same pace as before, while wages began to flatten. In part, this was due to the twin forces of globalization and labor-replacing technologies that began to hit the American workforce like strong winds—accelerating into massive storms in the 1980s and 1990s, and hurricanes since then.

Containers, satellite communication technologies, and cargo ships and planes radically reduced the cost of producing goods anywhere around the globe, thereby eliminating many manufacturing jobs or putting downward pressure on other wages. Automation, followed by computers, software, robotics, computer-controlled machine tools, and widespread digitization, further eroded jobs and wages. These forces simultaneously undermined organized labor. Unionized companies faced increasing competitive pressures to outsource, automate or move to nonunion states.

These forces didn't erode all incomes, however. In fact, they added to the value of complex work done by those who were well educated, well connected and fortunate enough to have chosen the right professions. Those lucky few who were perceived to be the most valuable saw their pay skyrocket.

But that's only part of the story. Instead of responding to these gale-force winds with policies designed to upgrade the skills of Americans, modernize our infrastructure, strengthen our safety net, and adapt the workforce—and pay for much of this with higher taxes on the wealthy—we did the reverse. We began disinvesting in education, job training, and infrastructure. We began shredding our safety net. We made it harder for many Americans to join unions. (The decline in unionization directly correlates with the decline of the portion of income going to the middle class.) And we reduced taxes on the wealthy.

We also deregulated. Financial deregulation in particular made finance the most lucrative industry in America, as it had been in the 1920s. Here again, the parallels between the 1920s and recent years are striking, reflecting the same pattern of inequality.

The parallels between the 1920s and recent years are striking, reflecting the same pattern of inequality.

Other advanced economies have faced the same gale-force winds but have not suffered the same inequalities as we have because they have helped their workforces adapt to the new economic realities—leaving the United States the most unequal of all advanced nations by far.

What We Must Do

There is no single solution for reversing widening inequality. French economist Thomas Piketty has shown that rich nations are moving back toward the large wealth disparities that characterized the late nineteenth century, as the return on capital exceeds the rate of economic growth. His monumental book *Capital in the Twenty-First Century* paints a troubling picture of societies dominated by a comparative few, whose cumulative wealth and unearned income overshadow the majority who rely on jobs and earned income. But our future is not set in stone, and Piketty's description of past and current trends need not determine our path in the future. Here are 10 initiatives that could reverse the trends described above:

1. **Make work pay.** The fastest-growing categories of work are retail, restaurant (including fast food), hospital (especially orderlies and staff), hotel, childcare, and eldercare. But these jobs tend to pay very little. A first step toward making work pay is to raise the federal minimum wage to $15 an hour, pegging it to inflation; abolish the tipped minimum wage; and expand the Earned Income Tax Credit. No American who works full time should be in poverty.

2. **Unionize low-wage workers.** The rise and fall of the American middle class correlates almost exactly with the rise and fall of private-sector unions, because unions gave the middle class the bargaining power it needed to secure a fair share of the gains from economic growth. We need to reinvigorate unions, beginning with low-wage service occupations that are sheltered from global competition and from labor-replacing technologies. Lower-wage Americans deserve more bargaining power.

3. **Invest in education.** This investment should extend from early childhood through world-class primary and secondary schools, affordable public higher education, good technical education, and lifelong learning. Education should not be thought of as a private investment; it is a public good that helps both individuals and the economy. Yet for too many Americans, high-quality education is unaffordable and unattainable. Every American should have an equal opportunity to make the most of herself or himself. High-quality education should be freely available to all, starting at the age of 3 and extending through four years of university or technical education.

4. **Invest in infrastructure.** Many working Americans—especially those on the lower rungs of the income ladder—are hobbled by an obsolete infrastructure that generates long commutes to work, excessively high home and rental prices, inadequate Internet access, insufficient power and water sources, and unnecessary environmental degradation. Every American should have access to an infrastructure suitable to the richest nation in the world.

5. **Pay for these investments with higher taxes on the wealthy.** Between the end of World War II and 1981 (when the wealthiest were getting paid a far lower share of total national income), the highest marginal federal income tax rate never fell below 70 percent, and the effective rate (including tax deductions and credits) hovered around 50 percent. But with Ronald Reagan's tax cut of 1981, followed by George W. Bush's tax cuts of 2001 and 2003, the taxes on top incomes were slashed, and tax loopholes favoring the wealthy were widened. The implicit promise—sometimes made explicit—was that the benefits from such cuts would trickle down to the broad middle class and even to the poor. As I've shown, however, nothing trickled down. At a time in American history when the after-tax incomes of the wealthy continue to soar, while median household incomes are falling, and when we must invest far more in education and infrastructure, it seems appropriate to raise the top marginal tax rate and close tax loopholes that disproportionately favor the wealthy.

6. **Make the payroll tax progressive.** Payroll taxes account for 40 percent of government revenues, yet they are not nearly as progressive as income taxes. One way to make the payroll tax more progressive would be to exempt the first $15,000 of wages and make up the difference by removing the cap on the portion of income subject to Social Security payroll taxes.

7. **Raise the estate tax and eliminate the "stepped-up basis" for determining capital gains at death.** As Piketty warns, the United States, like other rich nations, could be moving toward an oligarchy of inherited wealth and away from a meritocracy based on labor income. The most

direct way to reduce the dominance of inherited wealth is to raise the estate tax by triggering it at $1 million of wealth per person rather than its current $5.34 million (and thereafter peg those levels to inflation). We should also eliminate the "stepped-up basis" rule that lets heirs avoid capital gains taxes on the appreciation of assets that occurred before the death of their benefactors.

8. **Constrain Wall Street.** The financial sector has added to the burdens of the middle class and the poor through excesses that were the proximate cause of an economic crisis in 2008, similar to the crisis of 1929. Even though capital requirements have been tightened and oversight strengthened, the biggest banks are still too big to fail, jail or curtail—and therefore capable of generating another crisis. The Glass-Steagall Act, which separated commercial- and investment-banking functions, should be resurrected in full, and the size of the nation's biggest banks should be capped.

9. **Give all Americans a share in future economic gains.** The richest 10 percent of Americans own roughly 80 percent of the value of the nation's capital stock; the richest 1 percent own about 35 percent. As the returns to capital continue to outpace the returns to labor, this allocation of ownership further aggravates inequality. Ownership should be broadened through a plan that would give every newborn American an "opportunity share" worth, say, $5,000 in a diversified index of stocks and bonds—which, compounded over time, would be worth considerably more. The share could be cashed in gradually starting at the age of 18.

10. **Get big money out of politics.** Last, but certainly not least, we must limit the political influence of the great accumulations of wealth that are threatening our democracy and drowning out the voices of average Americans. The Supreme Court's 2010 *Citizens United* decision must be reversed—either by the Court itself, or by constitutional amendment. In the meantime, we must move toward the public financing of elections—for example, with the federal government giving presidential candidates, as well as House and Senate candidates in general elections, $2 for every $1 raised from small donors.

It's doubtful that these and other measures designed to reverse widening inequality will be enacted anytime soon. Having served in Washington, I know how difficult it is to get anything done unless the broad public understands what's at stake and actively pushes for reform.

That's why we need a movement for shared prosperity—a movement on a scale similar to the Progressive movement at the turn of the last century, which fueled the first progressive income tax and antitrust laws; the suffrage movement, which won women the vote; the labor movement, which helped animate the New Deal and fueled the great prosperity of the first three decades after World War II; the civil rights movement, which achieved the landmark Civil Rights and Voting Rights acts; and the environmental movement, which spawned the National Environmental Policy Act and other critical legislation.

> **We need a movement for shared prosperity—one on a scale similar to the Progressive movement at the turn of the last century.**

Time and again, when the situation demands it, America has saved capitalism from its own excesses. We put ideology aside and do what's necessary. No other nation is as fundamentally pragmatic. We will reverse the trend toward widening inequality eventually. We have no choice. But we must organize and mobilize in order that it be done.

Critical Thinking

1. How has the distribution of income in the United States changed between 1979 and 2007?

2. According to Robert Reich, what three foundation stones of our society are being threatened by growing income inequality?

3. What are some of the important steps recommended by Robert Reich to reverse widening inequality in the United States?

Create Central

www.mhhe.com/createcentral

Internet References

Pew Research Center: Income Inequality
    http://www.pewresearch.org/topics/income-inequality
Robert Reich.org
    http://robertreich.org

ROBERT B. REICH, Chancellor's Professor of Public Policy at the University of California, Berkeley, was secretary of labor in the Clinton administration. His award-winning film, Inequality for All, is available on Netflix and other video-streaming services as well as on DVD.

Article

Prepared by: Bruce Stinebrickner, *DePauw University*

Global Warming Left Out in the Cold

How the fossil-fuel boom killed the political will for congressional action on climate change.

AMY HARDER

Learning Outcomes

After reading this article, you will be able to:

- Assess the relative importance of the economy, national security, and the environment as reasons for supporting conservation efforts and renewable energy today.

- Explain how the United States domestic energy boom has led environmental groups and sympathetic policy makers to shift focus and emphases in their efforts to combat climate change.

W hen then-presidential candidates Barack Obama and John McCain were duking it out for the White House in 2008, they disagreed on many things, but the coming of the green revolution wasn't one of them.

If elected, Obama said in Cedar Rapids, Iowa, that summer, "I'll invest in renewable energies like wind power, solar power, and the next generation of homegrown biofuels. That's how America is going to free itself from our dependence on foreign oil—not through short-term gimmicks, but through a real, long-term commitment to transform our energy sector."

McCain sounded a similar note in Houston.

"To make the great turn away from carbon-emitting fuels, we will need all the inventive genius of which America is capable," he said that June. "We will need an economy strong enough to support our nation's great shift toward clean energy."

A convergence of concerns—about the economy, national security, the environment—had created a broad, politically diverse constituency for renewable energy—and, by extension, the first really formidable alliance in Washington positioned to address global warming. The moment looked ripe for Congress to pass comprehensive legislation aimed at cutting carbon emissions.

But the extraordinary political coalition that seemed poised to confront the challenge of climate change has since been fractured, in large part by an old nemesis: fossil fuels. Fracking has produced a glut of oil and natural gas that has made some of the top concerns of the 2008 campaign less pressing—or at least appear that way—and has sapped the will on the Hill to even discuss an issue that not long ago was at the top of the agenda.

The Rise of the Coalition

During the 2008 campaign, the United States was importing nearly 60 percent of its oil from foreign countries—not all of them especially stable or friendly. Gasoline cost more than $4 a gallon at the pump. The nation's dependence on fossil fuels was increasingly viewed as an economic liability and a national security concern in addition to an environmental problem. And the environmental implications were themselves of growing concern to Americans, with 66 percent of respondents telling Gallup back then that they worried "a great deal" or "a fair amount" about global warming—a number that had been rising steadily over the past few years.

The "green economy," meanwhile, offered the prospect of millions of new jobs, energy independence, and, eventually, cheap power. Talk of "clean coal" was raising hopes in the increasingly desperate company towns of West Virginia and Kentucky.

Suddenly, working to combat climate change wasn't just for tree-huggers anymore.

"You found this coalition of energy-security folks and environmental folks who were banding together. I think it was a forceful coalition," says Frank Verrastro, a senior vice president at the Center for Strategic and International Studies.

So forceful that even Sarah Palin—not yet McCain's "drill, baby, drill"-chanting running mate—treated the move toward renewable energy as inevitable. In a press release issued in August 2008, the Alaska governor responded to Obama's energy plan by praising his call to lease more of the National Petroleum Reserve and to finish building the Alaska natural-gas pipeline, saying, "This is a tool that must be on the table to buy us time until our long-term energy plans can be put into place."

Recalls Verrastro: "The thinking then was, if you use this moment in time to be transformative, we could reduce our oil imports, get a new economy, use green technology to be the next wave of the dot-coms, and at the same time improve the environment; that's a win-win-win all around."

The solution to Al Gore's "inconvenient truth" was starting to look pretty politically convenient.

From Bust to Boom

Then, amid a recession that followed an epic financial meltdown that left widespread unemployment and foreclosures in its wake, the United States improbably found itself in the middle of a domestic energy boom. And two of the three legs of the political coalition for climate-change action— national security and economic necessity—snapped off?

> "Had it not been for the extraordinary increase in U.S. oil production since 2008, everything else being equal, we'd be talking about an oil crisis right now."
>
> —Daniel Yergin, vice chairman, IHS

This boom was born largely of technology, the one-two punch of horizontal drilling and fracking that enabled producers to tap into hard-rock shale formations that had, until then, trapped vast oil and natural-gas reserves.

Today the United States is producing more oil than it has since 1995 and more natural gas than at any other time in the nation's history. It is on track this year to become the biggest natural-gas producer in the world, and to import just 28 percent of its oil. By 2015, the United States is expected to take over the top oil-producing spot from Saudi Arabia.

The impact has been felt both at home and abroad. U.S. drivers paid on average $3.49 per gallon of regular unleaded gasoline last year, the lowest prices since 2010, according to AAA. Although prices at the pump in the United States are not directly tied to the nation's energy production, experts say America's oil boom has helped stabilize domestic costs by helping to keep global oil prices in check—and has perhaps even helped avert disaster.

"Had it not been for the extraordinary increase in U.S. oil production since 2008, everything else being equal, we'd be talking

about an oil crisis right now," says Daniel Yergin, vice chairman of consulting firm IHS and author of *The Quest: Energy, Security and the Remaking of the Modern World.* He says the American oil boom has helped make up for the lack of production in other places such as Libya, which have been rocked by political unrest. Yergin adds that the surge in fuel production also enabled Obama to coordinate oil sanctions on Iran. "We have added 2.7 billion barrels a day of oil since 2008. The Iranian sanctions wouldn't have worked without that oil," he says.

Electricity prices are also at their lowest levels since 2009, almost entirely due to cheap natural-gas. And Yergin's firm recently released a report finding that the supply chain for the shale-oil and natural-gas boom is supporting 2.1 million U.S. jobs. There's even something for environmentalists to like: Natural gas emits 50 percent less carbon than coal, and tapping the nation's vast reserves has helped lower U.S. emissions to levels not seen in decades.

Yet all this good news has been terrible news for political unity—and potential action—on climate change.

"In arguments many people have made—" 'You may care about carbon, but I care about dollars for terrorists or U.S. exposure to oil price shocks'—the latter two members of the coalition are gone," says Douglas Holtz-Eakin, who advised McCain on policy issues during his presidential campaign. "Given the domestic energy production, the money is coming here and not going to terrorists, and exposure to oil price shocks are less."

Verrastro, who recently cowrote a book looking at these issues with Kevin Book, managing director at ClearView Energy Partners, concurs. "All of a sudden we have all this low-priced natural gas that was creating jobs—more so than the green stimulus," Verrastro says. "Then we found all this oil. The pressure came off. There was no reason to stick together on economic security and environmental grounds, as they were now heading in opposite directions."

Shifting Political Winds

All of this has led to a point where President Obama, perhaps the green economy's top champion, now touts the nation's fossil-fuel boom. "When I travel, what's striking to me is people around the world think we've got a really good hand," he said in November to *The Wall Street Journal* CEO Council. "They say America is poised to change our geopolitics entirely because of the advances we've made in oil production and natural-gas production. It means manufacturing here is much more attractive than it used to be. That's a huge competitive advantage."

And John McCain, who sponsored climate bills in 2003 and 2005, doesn't talk about climate change anymore. In fact, hardly any congressional Republicans talk about climate change, and many who do express doubt that human activity is responsible for it, or even that it is happening at all. The few Democrats who discuss it regularly—led by Sen. Sheldon Whitehouse of Rhode Island and House Energy and Commerce Committee ranking member Henry Waxman of California, who is retiring at the end of this session—are mostly preaching to the choir.

"I see the Congress so caught up in budget reconciliation, sequestration, debt limits, continuing resolutions, it's just simply not on the radar," McCain said in an interview. He noted that both the nation's move toward energy independence and the poor economy have helped cut Capitol Hill's appetite for addressing global warming.

A reduced dependence on foreign oil "probably has something to do with it," McCain added. "I also think we hit an economic downturn, and that shifted a lot of priorities, and it gave a much higher importance to the cost of energy and the cost of developing alternative energy."

Environmental groups have also played a role in turning the conversation on the Hill. Organizations that once focused almost entirely on pressing for a shift from fossil fuels to renewable energy now maintain that renewables are growing at record speed and that efforts to undo state renewable-energy standards have failed, and they have turned their attention to fighting to ensure that fracking is done safely. "Environmentalists may be more concerned now about fracking and shutting down coal," said Eileen Claussen, president of the Center for Climate and Energy.

All of these factors have helped moved renewables from the main stage to the side stage—and climate change offstage entirely.

"What has happened more recently is there is not such the urgency on the climate-change side. And there is this euphoria—justifiable euphoria—in our ability to produce more oil and gas," says former Sen. Byron Dorgan, D-N.D., whose home state is at the forefront of America's booming oil industry. "It persuades some people to believe, 'OK, we're producing more and using less, our imports are down, so game, set, match, it's over.' "

"I worry a little bit that there is this notion, 'Boy, we're just awash in oil and gas, so that's it. We don't need to do anything more.' That's exactly the wrong thing," adds Dorgan, who now cochairs the Bipartisan Policy Center's Energy Project.

"I worry a little bit that there is this notion, 'Boy, we're just awash in oil and gas, so that's it. We don't need to do anything more.' That's exactly the wrong thing."

—Former Sen. Byron Dorgan, D-N.D., whose home state is at the forefront of America's booming oil industry.

Risky Business?

Dorgan isn't the only one who's worried.

"Unfortunately, our country—the American population and policymakers—have been raised on a steady diet of 'we need to end our dependence on foreign oil' since the Nixon administration," says Robbie Diamond, founder and president of Securing America's Future Energy, an energy-security think tank devoted to weaning the U.S. off oil, no matter where it comes from. "The production we've seen is fabulous. It's important for the country. It's great from a jobs perspective and balance of payments. But does it solve our national security and economic security risks? The answer there is, absolutely not."

Diamond and other experts note that the oil market is still global and that U.S. domestic production can only affect it so much. It's just a matter of time until Mideast conflict or something else causes a major disruption that sends oil prices skyrocketing, he says. He notes that global spare capacity was near a record low of 1.5 million barrels this summer. "You're one Libya away from $115 [a barrel] oil," Diamond says. "Believe me, that's when they will start talking: 'Hmm, I thought we were producing all that oil, and doesn't it make a difference?' That's the lost story, and that's the counterintuitive story."

Those who work daily in the national security world say oil prices are the least of their fears.

"The security threats stemming from climate change are massive," says Mike Breen, executive director of the Truman National Security Project and a former Army captain who served in Iraq and Afghanistan. Breen recalls the U.S. military's top officer in the Pacific region, which includes North Korea, saying last March that the biggest threat to the region was climate change, because rising sea levels and extreme weather such as heat waves are likely to exacerbate tensions in already unstable areas. He says not enough lawmakers are talking about the problem.

"The security community knows it's happening, and the political dialog hasn't caught up," Breen says.

Indeed, if anything, the political dialog on climate change has regressed. Today's voters—and the lawmakers who represent them in Washington—are focused on the benefits of the oil and gas boom, and on local environmental concerns, not on the effects of global warming, which often seem intangible, buried in scientific reports most people don't read, or far away, like islands of the South Pacific. To be sure, Superstorm Sandy and other extreme-weather events in the United States have at times refocused the public's attention, but those moments have been fleeting, and so far they haven't moved the needle toward action on Capitol Hill.

"Now, what [the public] sees are cheaper energy prices, and it just swings it against anything on the climate front," Holtz-Eakin says. "They don't have a sense that there is a climate issue. It's just something people babble about in *The New York Times*."

Back to the Future?

In the wake of the coalition's unraveling, Obama has been stepping up—but in a political environment that is now openly hostile to his efforts.

He is moving forward unilaterally to regulate carbon emissions from the nation's power plants—a decision that isn't making any side especially happy. Republicans and coal-state Democrats are blasting him for supposedly killing the coal industry and the jobs that go along with it, while the loudest remaining voices on global warming warn that the president's proposed rules won't do nearly enough.

"President Obama's Climate Action Plan is an important step toward curbing carbon emissions," Whitehouse said in a statement to *National Journal*. But "Congress must act and pass a carbon fee that places the cost of climate change where it belongs—on large carbon polluters. Pricing carbon pollution will make the market more efficient and generate revenue to return to the American people."

But what exactly would it take to get Congress to act?

Former Rep. Bob Inglis, R-S.C., said the realization that we're not shielded from oil-price spikes combined with a stronger economy will help revive the topic politically.

"We're going to be very disappointed with what [the energy boom] means for us at the pump. It's going to mean nothing," says Inglis, who is now executive director of the Energy and Enterprise Initiative. "The second long-term trend is, as the Great Recession gives way to a great recovery, then the ability to think in time horizons longer than this month's mortgage payment and this month's paycheck will give us the ability to focus on things like climate change."

The second part of that equation may already be falling into place: A Gallup Poll last April suggested that Americans' concerns about global warming were increasing again, after hitting 10-year lows in 2010 and 2011.

Would McCain ever lead again on the issue?

"Sure, any time—I would," McCain says. "We've got to show people that it makes sense fiscally. In other words, don't increase taxes, and you'd find the most efficient way to address the issue without raising people's cost of energy."

If McCain does, says Holtz-Eakin, he's going to need . . . a coalition.

"There will be no successful up-or-down vote on climate policy in the U.S. Congress," he says. "We've seen people try this, and it just doesn't happen. That means carbon policy must be tied in with something else."

Critical Thinking

1. What three concerns had created a broad constituency for renewable energy in the United States in 2008?

2. What developments lessened two of these concerns to such an extent that the push for renewable energy weakened significantly?

Create Central

www.mhhe.com/createcentral

Internet References

Environmental Protection Agency (EPA)
www.epa.gov
National Geographic: Global Warming
http://environment.nationalgeographic.com/environment/global-warming
Natural Resources Defense Council: Global Warming
http://www.nrdc.org/globalwarming

Article   Prepared by: Bruce Stinebrickner, *DePauw University*

Lethal Responsibility

Reframing gun control as a public safety issue.

GEORGE B. WILSON

Learning Outcomes

After reading this article, you will be able to:

- Distinguish between approaching gun control as an issue of criminality and approaching it as an issue of public safety.

- Weigh the pros and cons of focusing on much-publicized mass shootings such as in Newtown, CT, and concentrating on gun fatalities that occur in Americans' home on a day-by-day basis.

- Evaluate the three steps that George B. Wilson proposes.

T he question of guns in society is often framed as an issue about "protecting good guys from bad guys." The bad guys include not only criminals but also people with a tendency to deal with emotional problems by acting violently against their fellow citizens. Once you name the issue that way, all responses to the issue will be geared to forestalling criminal behavior.

In the conversation occurring across the country, this way of structuring the question appears to be winning. All the options under consideration seem to be aimed at preventing tragedies like the shooting in Newtown, Conn. It is a laudable objective, to be sure, but to adopt it as the only one, or even the primary one, would be a serious mistake.

Why focus on situations that, however ghastly, occur quite rarely, when the number of gun injuries and fatalities occurring in the home—whether through sudden bursts of anger, domestic conflicts or children just playing around with their parents' firearms—far outnumber those resulting from mass murders?

If we really want to diminish the number of deaths by firearms, we need to be clear that gun deaths are often not a matter of bad guys versus good guys; they are more frequently a matter of careful gun owners as contrasted with careless ones. Both have the right to possess guns. Most gun owners are responsible in exercising that right. But many are not, with fatal consequences—and they are neither criminals nor people with mental problems.

Instead of focusing on criminal behavior (which many believe will have little effect, simply because criminals can always beat the system), we need to institute policies that define responsible gun behavior and attach serious consequences for those "good guys" who are not criminals but who behave without any sense that their behavior diminishes the well-being of the rest of society. The dominant issue is not one of criminality but of public safety. The overarching goal is to diminish the number of deaths due to irresponsible behavior.

How might that be accomplished? I propose a three-pronged strategy.

1) A single registry of all gun owners. The aim of this registry is not to constrain lawful citizens unfairly but rather to supply public officials with the information they need if they are to fulfill their responsibility for safeguarding the citizenry.

For this discussion, the trajectory of our country's response to automobiles is an illustrative one. Ninety years ago anyone could buy a car and drive it. No license was required. A driver was simply expected to use the car in a responsible way. The invention was so new that people did not yet know, experientially, how hazardous it could be. But the occurrence of serious accidents soon showed the wisdom of requiring some form of driver identification. Then gradually we learned that even with clearer expectations people did not take the trouble to learn how to drive responsibly. That led to the requirement of drivers' education programs. We became aware of physical impediments, like impaired vision, and developed strategies for recognizing them. Today a vision test is mandatory. We also instituted quality controls in the manufacturing of the vehicle itself.

For any of these improvements to occur, evidence-based data were needed. The same thing is true with data on gun ownership. In the absence of a national database, no policy decisions can be evaluated.

Over a reasonable period of time, all gun owners should be required to register their firearms with a government agency. After that period anyone possessing an unregistered gun would be subject to penalty. Obviously not all guns would be registered in that first period, but we should not let the perfect be the enemy of the good. Over time the expectation would be taken for granted—like other forms of certification—as part of responsible citizenship.

2) Mandatory training before a permit is issued. Experience has proven that many owners simply do not appreciate what it takes to use a firearm safely. A loaded firearm is an inherently hazardous object. Its potential toxicity respects no difference in psychological status; it simply is dangerous. (An interesting byproduct of mandatory training would be the emergence of a new industry: officially certified training programs, which would also generate new jobs.)

Since experience shows that as we age our competences diminish, there would be provision for periodic recertification (just as your eyes are tested each time you renew your driver's license).

3) Penalties for abdication of responsibility. This is the necessary linchpin. A citizen might be able to show evidence of recent completion of training and have the required license, but accidents still happen. People—many people, according to statistics—die from guns in the hands of the "good guys" who happen to act irresponsibly and carelessly.

A father leaves for work; his 6-year-old son gets into the closet, plays with the gun and kills his sister. A licensed owner gives his gun to a friend who has a fight with his wife; the fight escalates; he grabs the gun and she dies. An owner needs money and sells his gun without leaving any record; it passes through many hands until it lands in the hands of a criminal.

Our traditional response to such deaths is, "How sad! What a tragedy." Instead, our law should say to the original owner, "When you bought that hazardous object, you became an agent of society, responsible to your fellow citizens for its proper custody and use. You were trained to fulfill that responsibility. You have failed to live up to it and society exacts a penalty for that abdication. As long as you remain the licensed owner you retain responsibility for what happens. Accidents' are no excuse."

What might we expect from the implementation of such a strategy? Responsible gun owners should applaud it. It adds extra protection for them and their families, while affirming the contribution they make to society by taking their responsibility seriously.

As implementation begins, we should anticipate a slow learning curve: "Are they really serious?" But as new cases result in convictions, the public at large will begin to be more aware that ownership brings with it serious consequences. (It is assumed that a dramatic educational effort would accompany the implementation.) Each potential new buyer would be compelled to weigh the slight risk of a criminal break-in against the far greater risk of becoming responsible for an "accidental" tragedy. Some present owners might even find it more attractive to eliminate that personal risk by participating in a gun buy-back program.

Careful or careless? It is not simply a personal choice; it is a social responsibility—even for the good guys.

Critical Thinking

1. What is the author's argument in favor of conceiving of gun control as a matter of public safety and not criminality? Do you find it persuasive?

2. What are the three steps the author proposes to reduce gun deaths caused by irresponsible behavior?

Create Central

www.mhhe.com/createcentral

Internet References

National Rifle Association
nra.org

Policymic: Nine Things You Didn't Know about the Second Amendment
www.policymic.com/articles/24557/9-things-you-didn-t-know-about-the-second-amendment

The Atlantic: The Death of Gun Control
www.theatlantic.com/politics/archive/2013/09/the-death-of-gun-control/279638

GEORGE B. WILSON, S.J., is a retired human systems practitioner in Cincinnati, Ohio.

Article   Prepared by: Bruce Stinebrickner, *DePauw University*

The Tyranny of Metaphor

Three historical myths have been leading American presidents into folly for nearly a century. Is Obama wise enough to avoid the same fate?

ROBERT DALLEK

Learning Outcomes

After reading this article, you will be able to:

- Understand the three "historical myths" that Robert Dallek presents and assess his conclusion that they negatively affect American leaders' approach to foreign and military policies.

- Determine the extent to which Dallek's three "myths" have any useful ideas or perspectives to offer for American foreign and military policies.

I n 1952, British historian Denis William Brogan published a brilliantly perceptive article on "The Illusion of American Omnipotence." In the midst of the Korean War, Brogan was not only commenting on Americans' frustration with their inability to prevail decisively against supposedly inferior Chinese and North Korean forces, but also cautioning against other misadventures in which the United States falsely assumed its superpower status assured a military victory in any conflict it chose to fight. Brogan could just as easily have titled his essay "The Omnipotence of American Illusion" in an echo of Friedrich Nietzsche's critique of true believers. "Convictions," the great German philosopher wrote, "are more dangerous enemies of truth than lies."

Brogan and Nietzsche might well have been talking about the last 100 years of American thinking about foreign policy and the convictions—or call them illusions—that have shaped it along the way, across administrations led by men as diverse in outlook and background as Woodrow Wilson, Dwight Eisenhower, and George W. Bush.

There is certainly much about America's world dealings in the 20th century that deserves praise: victory in World War II, the Truman Doctrine, the Marshall Plan, JFK's diplomacy during the Cuban missile crisis, the Camp David peace accords, the Panama Canal treaty, Richard Nixon's opening to China, and détente with the Soviet Union, to mention the most obvious. But a more rounded view would have to include its many stumbles. Three enduring illusions—a misguided faith in universalism, or America's power to transform the world from a community of hostile, lawless nations into enlightened states devoted to peaceful cooperation; a need to shun appeasement of all adversaries or to condemn suggestions of conciliatory talks with them as misguided weakness; and a belief in the surefire effectiveness of military strength in containing opponents, whatever their ability to threaten the United States—have made it nearly impossible for Americans to think afresh about more productive ways to address their foreign problems. Call it the tyranny of metaphor: For all their pretensions to shaping history, U.S. presidents are more often its prisoners.

Universalism: The misguided faith in America's power to transform the world.

Even Barack Obama, who rode his opposition to the Iraq war into the White House and has kept his campaign promise to withdraw U.S. combat troops, is not immune from history's illusions. How could he be? Domestic politics are as much a part of foreign policy as assessments of conditions abroad. But Obama might yet succeed in fending off such pressures. The president is keenly interested in making the wisest possible use of history, as was evident to me from two dinners 10 other historians and I had with him at the White House over the past two years. For despite the many countercurrents confronting him, Obama was eager to learn from us how previous presidents transcended their circumstances to achieve transformational administrations.

Such lessons must weigh heavily as Obama faces his next momentous decision on what to do in Afghanistan while praying that Gen. David Petraeus, the hero of the Iraq surge, can duplicate the feat before the public's patience runs out. So far, the president has avoided either fully embracing the Afghan war or calling for outright withdrawal. His commitment of 30,000 additional troops was meant to reassure America's national security hawks that he is as determined as they are to defend the country's safety from future attacks. At the same time, his promise to begin withdrawing U.S. forces in July 2011 suggests his understanding that Afghanistan could be another Vietnam— a costly, unwinnable conflict that could tie the United States down in Asia for the indefinite future. It might also be, of course, that Obama has serious doubts about the value of sending American soldiers to die in a far-off, impoverished land of little strategic value, but understands that simply to walk away from the conflict carries unacceptable political risks, undermining his ability to enact a bold domestic agenda that is central to his administration and his chances for a second term.

Just as President Harry Truman could not ignore the political pressure from the China Lobby to back Chiang Kaishek's failing regime against Mao Zedong's Communists in the middle of the last century, so Obama is mindful of the political risks of appearing irresolute. Already, his predecessor's U.N. ambassador, John Bolton, has blamed Obama's Afghan withdrawal timeline for sending "a signal of weakness that our adversaries interpret to our detriment." Former Vice President Dick Cheney has referred to the president as someone who "travels around the world apologizing." Bush himself previewed a similar line of attack in a 2008 speech in Israel, in which he criticized Obama and others then calling for engagement with Iran. "We have heard this foolish delusion before," Bush said. "As Nazi tanks crossed into Poland in 1939, an American senator declared: 'Lord, if I could only have talked to Hitler, all of this might have been avoided.' We have an obligation to call this what it is—the false comfort of appeasement, which has been repeatedly discredited by history."

Can Obama escape this trap? To do so, he'll need to study his predecessors' mistakes and learn from those few U.S. presidents who managed to avoid being tyrannized by metaphor. And he'll need to understand how we got here.

America's love affair with universalism, the first of the three illusions, began in January 1918 with President Woodrow Wilson's peace program, his Fourteen Points: the seductive rationalizations for U.S. participation in a "war to end all wars" and make the Western world "safe for democracy." Such high-minded ends appealed to Americans as validations of the superiority of their institutions. They were enough to convince an isolationist America to sacrifice more than 50,000 lives in the last 19 months of Europe's Great War. The 20 postwar years, which saw the rise of communism, fascism, Nazism, and Japanese militarism leading to World War II, gave the lie to Wilson's dreams of universal peace and self-governance, driving Americans back into their isolationist shell until the attack on Pearl Harbor demonstrated that the "free security" provided by vast oceans and weak neighbors no longer guaranteed their country's safety.

Yet Wilson's idealistic hopes for a better world did not disappear on the beaches of Normandy or in the caves of Iwo Jima. If anything, World War II reinforced Americans' unrealistic expectations that they could reduce—if not end—human conflict. Wilsonianism found continuing life in the birth of the United Nations and the triumph of democracy in Germany, Japan, Spain, South Korea, Taiwan, and parts of Latin America. But Wilson's vision was again elevated to a sacred doctrine that repeatedly played America false. Eager to believe that World War II would largely cure countries of their affinity for bloodshed, Americans persisted in seeing the Allies—Britain, China, the Soviet Union, and the United States—as permanent friends acting in concert to keep the postwar peace.

The onset of the Cold War brought an abrupt end to these dreams. But convictions about the irresistible attraction of U.S. institutions encouraged the hope that inside every foreigner was an American waiting to emerge, an outlook that shaped American thinking not only during the years of anti-communist struggle, but all the way up to Bush's rationale for fighting in Iraq. Today, Bush's prediction that the destruction of Saddam Hussein's military dictatorship would transform the Middle East into a flourishing center of traditional American freedoms is proving to be as elusive as Wilson's original grandiose vision. The imperfect U.S.-sponsored regimes in Baghdad—and Kabul too, for that matter—are a far cry from the robust democracies Bush hoped would become the envy of the region. "The survival of liberty in our land increasingly depends on the success of liberty in other lands. The best hope for peace in our world is the expansion of freedom in all the world," Bush said in his very Wilsonian second inaugural address, though U.S. military chiefs in Iraq and Afghanistan have since managed to move the goal posts, promising to establish reasonably pro-American governments that can handle their own security.

Most of the evidence, however, points to an unpredictable future for both countries, where political instability, anti-Americanism, and military coups seem unlikely to disappear. It may be that 10 or 20 or 30 years of U.S. stewardship will bring freedom and prosperity to Iraq and Afghanistan, but Americans have limited patience with nation-building that costs them unacceptable amounts of blood and treasure—and often have a better collective sense of what American power can realistically achieve than the government's best and brightest. They have not forgotten the Vietnam War, even if, at times, their leaders seem to have.

Indeed, Vietnam is always there as a trap for the American leader, a trap set by the deadly and persistent second illusion— that a failure to combat every act of international aggression is tantamount to appeasement, a return to the failed passivity of the 1930s. This illusion has time and again led the United States into unwise and costly military adventures. While Winston Churchill was marvelously right in saying that Britain had a choice between war and dishonor at Munich in 1938 and that Neville Chamberlain's appeasement of Adolf Hitler would produce both, Munich was never the perfect analogy for dealing with subsequent conflicts, as Churchill himself acknowledged. As he put it in 1950, "The word 'appeasement' is not popular, but appeasement has its place in all policy. Make sure you put it in the right place. Appease the weak. Defy the strong." But for hawks, it is always Munich 1938—no matter whether the aggressor is Saddam Hussein, Slobodan Milosevic, or "Baby Doc" Duvalier—and presidents from Truman to Bush have been led by the appeasement metaphor into misjudgments that have harmed the United States and undermined their presidencies.

Truman, for example, justified his decision to enter the Korean War in 1950 as a way to deter the Soviet Union, which he saw as the architect of the conflict, from future acts of aggression that could touch off a World War III. Truman had reason enough to combat Pyongyang's aggression: South Korea's collapse would have undermined confidence in America's determination to defend Japan and Western European allies. Comparisons between Stalin and Hitler and predictions that Korea was the start of a worldwide communist offensive like the Nazi reach for global control, however, were decidedly overdrawn. But the power of the anti-appeasement proposition was so great in 1950 that one can search in vain for dissenting voices.

Had Truman aimed simply to restore South Korea's independence, his decision to enter the Korean fighting would look much different today. Instead, he chose to follow Gen. Douglas MacArthur's advice to destroy North Korea's communist regime by crossing the 38th parallel. It was a blunder based on two false assumptions: that the Chinese would not enter the conflict and that if they did, they would be roundly defeated, with the likely collapse of their communist regime. Instead, China's direct entry into the war produced a military and political stalemate, delayed a possible rapprochement with Beijing for years, and destroyed Truman's presidency. With his approval rating falling to 24 percent, he could neither enact his Fair Deal nor maintain public backing for the war.

President Lyndon B. Johnson, of course, was another casualty of the Munich analogy. Recalling the political consequences for his party from the 1949 "loss" of China that right-wing Republicans like Joseph McCarthy used to label Democrats as appeasers of Chamberlain scale, he committed the United States to a war in Southeast Asia even more politically destructive to his administration and the country than any act of passivity might have produced. Johnson came to lament Vietnam's cost to him and his administration, complaining about the "bitch" of a war that distracted him from his true love—building the Great Society.

The failure in Vietnam produced a new metaphor: Fighting a Third World country on hostile terrain was to be avoided at all costs. When George H.W. Bush convinced Congress and the country to oust Iraq from Kuwait in 1991, it was an uphill struggle to persuade Americans that he was not involving them in another Vietnam. Yet he succeeded by invoking that appeasement metaphor yet again: "If history teaches us anything, it is that we must resist aggression or it will destroy our freedoms," Bush explained in making his case for the war. "Appeasement does not work. As was the case in the 1930s, we see in Saddam Hussein an aggressive dictator threatening his neighbors." Such overblown warnings were enough to sell the Persian Gulf offensive, but postwar arguments that America had now kicked the Vietnam syndrome were premature—and may have sown the seeds of his son's disastrous 2003 invasion of Iraq.

The third illusion U.S. presidents often hold is that militarized containment—the belief that containing or preventing enemy aggression depends on a military threat to their survival—is the right way to avoid the traps set by the first two.

The core conviction here has been that America won the Cold War because it understood that the Soviet Union was intent on world domination and that the best way to counter its ambitions short of all-out war was to contain its reach for control by a combination of economic, political, and military initiatives that would discourage Moscow from aggression and strain its limited resources to the breaking point, forcing communism's collapse.

From the start, however, containment was a contested doctrine. In his famous "Long Telegram" of February 1946 and "X" article in *Foreign Affairs* the next year, George F. Kennan, who headed the State Department's new policy planning staff, counseled the White House to contain Soviet Russia's "expansionist," "messianic" drive for world control. Kennan later regretted having stated his views in such evangelistic language; it encouraged anti-communists to take his advice as a call for military as well as political and diplomatic action.

In fact, Kennan never believed that Moscow intended a military offensive against Western Europe. In his judgment, Soviet acts of aggression would take the form of political subversion, calculated steps to bring pro-Soviet governments to power wherever possible as Moscow drove to win what it saw as the inevitable competition between communism and capitalism. Kennan's formula for victory was economic aid fostering political stability in countries potentially vulnerable to communism's siren song. He wisely described Soviet communism as a system of state management and controls that would eventually collapse when its inability to meet consumer demands for the sort of material well-being and freedoms enjoyed in the West became evident. Accordingly, he vigorously opposed hawkish Cold War initiatives such as the establishment of the North Atlantic Treaty Organization, armed intervention in Vietnam, and the development of the hydrogen bomb as needless escalations that would only ensure a harsh Soviet response.

Appeasement: The misguided fear that conciliatory talks are a dangerous weakness.

Kennan was a prophet without a following—at least within the U.S. government. Secretary of State Dean Acheson told him to take his Quaker views to a more hospitable setting than he could possibly find in Washington. Kennan found a home in Princeton, N.J., at the Institute for Advanced Study, but vindication would not become fully evident until the close of the Cold War. As his life ended in 2005 at the age of 101, he was convinced more than ever that the tyranny of military containment had done little, if anything, to assure America's victory in that struggle. He saw the invasion of Iraq as another example of misplaced faith in a military solution to a political problem. In a September 2002 interview, a 98-year-old Kennan described Bush's talk of a pre-emptive war against Iraq as "a great mistake."

No postwar U.S. presidents were more mindful of the need to rely on diplomatic and political initiatives in fighting the

Cold War than Dwight D. Eisenhower and John F. Kennedy. They understood that Truman's greatest foreign-policy successes were the Truman Doctrine, which committed U.S. financial aid to shoring up Greece and Turkey against communist subversion, and the Marshall Plan, which consisted of multi-billion-dollar grants to support European economies as a bar to communist political gains in Britain, France, the Netherlands, Belgium, Italy, and Scandinavia.

True, Eisenhower and Kennedy were not averse to using subversion to undermine unfriendly regimes in the Middle East and Latin America, as the historical record demonstrates in U.S. dealings with Iran, Nicaragua, and Cuba during the 1950s and 1960s. Nor were they consistently wise in sanctioning clandestine operations that did not necessarily serve long-term U.S. interests. Both presidents, however, saw the reliance on direct military action to defeat the communists as a step too far. For all the rhetoric in the 1952 campaign about rollback and liberation (Adlai Stevenson has "a PhD from Dean Acheson's cowardly college of communist containment," Richard Nixon taunted), Ike would not unleash America's military power to oust Kim Il Sung's communist regime from Pyongyang, as South Korea's Syngman Rhee and conservative Republicans in the United States urged. Nor would he support Hungary's attempt to throw off Soviet control in 1956 with armed intervention or rely on more than rhetorical threats to deter the Chinese from attacking Quemoy and Matsu, the islands between the Chinese mainland and Taiwan. And he resisted French pressure to intervene with air power to prevent defeat at Dien Bien Phu and the loss of Vietnam, which struck Eisenhower as an effort to involve the United States in a war Paris had already lost and America would not assuredly win.

Kennedy was as cautious as Eisenhower about relying on armed intervention to serve the national interest. Despite intense pressure from U.S. military chiefs in 1961 to rescue the Cuban insurgents at the Bay of Pigs by using American air power against Fidel Castro's forces, Kennedy rejected a direct U.S. part in the fighting. True, the invaders were U.S. surrogates armed and financed by the CIA, but Kennedy wisely concluded that the price of open U.S. intervention would be greater—a barrage of anti-American propaganda in the Third World—than the embarrassment from a defeat. During the 1962 Cuban missile crisis, the demands on Kennedy from his generals to bomb Soviet missile installations and invade the island to topple Castro were intense. But Kennedy insisted on a "quarantine" and diplomatic solution that, as we know now, saved the world from a devastating nuclear war.

Containment: The misguided belief in the surefire effectiveness of military strength.

Kennedy was also a reluctant supporter of expanded U.S. military action in Vietnam. At the same time he increased the number of U.S. military advisors in Saigon from roughly 700 to more than 16,000, he saw a commitment of U.S. ground troops to South Vietnam's defense as a potential trap that could shift the burden of the war to the United States and turn the conflict into another Korea. In the months before he was assassinated in November 1963, he directed Defense Secretary Robert McNamara to lay plans for the withdrawal of the advisors. (He also signed on to a coup by South Vietnamese generals against Ngo Dinh Diem's government, aiming to create a more stable political rule that would reduce the need for U.S. military intervention.) We will never know exactly what Kennedy would have done about Vietnam in a second term, but it seems unlikely that he would have followed Johnson's path. As Kennedy told *New York Times* columnist Arthur Krock, "United States troops should not be involved on the Asian mainland." He warned Arthur Schlesinger, the historian and presidential advisor, that sending combat troops to Vietnam would place far greater demands on U.S. commitments than the public would tolerate and would not allow him to sustain public backing for other initiatives his administration might hope to take. The history of LBJ's presidency fully vindicates Kennedy's doubts.

Eisenhower and Kennedy have much to teach Obama and anyone else who becomes president; American leaders invariably confront such demands to use military force. The two men could resist that pressure because they were military heroes who could convince the public that they understood the use of armed strength better than domestic hawks urging action. Presidents without military records—like Obama—are at a disadvantage that they need to counter through vigorous rhetoric, a technique deployed with great success by the likes of leaders as Franklin D. Roosevelt and Ronald Reagan.

Counter it they must, for the metaphors that have dominated American thinking about foreign affairs over the last hundred years are not simply objects of historical curiosity. As Obama understands, they remain powerful engines of influence on decision-making about vital questions of war and peace. In trying to forge sensible responses to the challenges posed by Afghanistan, Iran, North Korea, and the persistent Israeli-Palestinian conflict, Obama knows that the shadows of past failures hang over him, whether the misguided belief in turning authoritarian adversaries into Jeffersonian democrats or the false choice of favoring militant containment over anything that even remotely resembles appeasement. His room to maneuver is therefore limited—at least if he hopes to act with the sort of public support required to put across his domestic agenda while also moving boldly to tame international dangers.

Obama seems keenly aware of the main lesson of Vietnam: Don't let the appeasement metaphor, cliché, conviction, call it what you will, lock you into an unwinnable war that destroys your presidency. He appreciates that a grand design or strategy in foreign affairs does not readily translate from one crisis to another. Appeasement was a terrible idea in dealing with Hitler, but avoiding it was never the right argument for crossing the 38th parallel in Korea or embroiling the United States in Vietnam. (After all, a stalemate in the first war and a defeat in the second did not deter the United States from winning the larger Cold War.) Nor is Obama persuaded by grand Wilsonian visions of bringing democracy to Iraq and Afghanistan; he has made clear that he does not see military solutions to the problems America faces in those two countries. He has openly described the invasion of Iraq as a "mistake" and seems determined to de-escalate U.S. involvement in Afghanistan as soon as possible.

But no matter how conscious Obama is of the perils of history's traps, he faces no small challenge in convincing political opponents to relinquish the outworn foreign-policy clichés that have been of such questionable service to America's well-being. As Germany's Otto von Bismarck is said to have observed more than 100 years ago, great statesmen have the ability to hear, before anyone else, the distant hoofbeats of the horse of history. More often than not, however, it is the accepted wisdoms—or the wrong lessons of history altogether—that govern the thinking of publics and the behavior of their leaders.

Critical Thinking

1. What are the three historical myths that have, according to Robert Dallek, led American presidents astray in foreign and national security policy for the past century or so?

2. What are examples of each historical myth leading to unfavorable consequences for the U.S. in the world?

3. What experience did Presidents Eisenhower and Kennedy share that advantaged them—in the national security sphere—over presidents such as Barack Obama and George W. Bush?

Create Central

www.mhhe.com/createcentral

Internet References

Council on Foreign Relations
   www.cfr.org
American Diplomacy
   www.unc.edu/depts/diplomat
Beyond Intractability: "Nation Building"
   www.beyondintractability.org/essay/nation-building

Presidential historian **ROBERT DALLEK** is author, most recently, of *The Lost Peace; Leadership in a Time of Horror and Hope, 1945–1953*.

Dallek, Robert. Reprinted in entirety by McGraw-Hill Education with permission from *Foreign Policy*, November 2010, pp. 78–85. www.foreignpolicy.com. © 2010 Washingtonpost. Newsweek Interactive, LLC.

Article　　　　　　　　　　　Prepared by: Bruce Stinebrickner, *DePauw University*

Worth Fighting—or Not

In judging which of its dozen major wars America should have fought, *unintended consequences* **often outweigh the intended ones.**

BURT SOLOMON

Learning Outcomes

After reading this article, you will be able to:

• Better judge what wars (if any?) are worth fighting and which (if any?) are not.

• Assess whether recent (and current) wars in which the United States has participated were (are) worth fighting.

W ar is hell, but it can also be useful as hell. Even if that isn't always obvious at the time. Ponder, for a moment, the War of 1812. When the fledgling United States of America repulsed the British—again—in 1815, the war "felt like a loss or a tie," according to Allan Millett, a military historian at the University of New Orleans. The torch had been put to the Capitol and the White House, and the Battle of Baltimore produced the lyrics of a National Anthem that generations of Americans would struggle to sing. The Americans hadn't won; the British had lost.

Only as the years passed did it become clear that the war had truly served the United States as a Second War of Independence. It forced Britain to respect its former colony's sovereignty; helped to nudge the Spanish out of Florida; persuaded the European colonial powers to accept the Louisiana Purchase and to stop aiding the Indians, thereby opening the way to Western expansion; and prepared the geopolitical groundwork for the Monroe Doctrine. Not for another 186 years, until September 11, 2001, would the continental United States suffer a foreign attack.

"In the long run," Millett judged, "it worked out."

Unintended consequences can also work in the other direction, of course. Consider the following zigzag of events. The humiliating American defeat in the Vietnam War may have encouraged the Soviet Union's adventurism, notably its invasion of Afghanistan in 1979, four years after North Vietnamese troops seized control of South Vietnam. The Afghan mujahedeen eventually drove the Soviets out, with the covert support of the United States, as dramatized in the 2007 movie *Charlie Wilson's War.*

Bunker Hill to Baghdad

Revolutionary War
War of 1812
Mexican War
Civil War
Spanish-American
WWI
WWII
Korean War
Vietnam War
Persian Gulf War
War in Afghanistan
War in Iraq

• All wars, in a sense, are **wars of choice.**
• The smaller wars the U.S. has fought often turned out pretty well: **low cost with high impact.**
• Vietnam is the war from which the **fewest benefits** seem to have flowed, historians say.

The playboy member of Congress, a Texas Democrat, prevailed upon Israel, Egypt, Saudi Arabia, Pakistan, and the U.S. Congress to cough up billions of dollars and untraceable weaponry.

But recall the movie's penultimate scene, when Wilson fails to persuade his fellow House appropriators to spend a pittance to rebuild Afghan schools, in hopes of reconstructing a land left broken by war and occupation. The resulting power vacuum allowed the Taliban to emerge as the mountainous nation's militantly Islamic rulers, offering sanctuary and succor to Al Qaeda as it prepared its terrorist attacks on New York City and Arlington, Va., on 9/11. Surely, the best and brightest who botched the Vietnam War hadn't given the slightest thought to backward Afghanistan or to the World Trade Center's twin towers, which were dedicated just six days after the last U.S. troops withdrew from Vietnam in 1973.

Sometimes, the desirability of a particular war will rise and fall over time. When Chou En-lai, the Chinese premier, was asked to assess the French Revolution fought nearly two centuries before, he famously replied: "It is too early to say." Consider the oscillating historical verdicts on the Mexican War. President Polk and Mexican dictator Santa Anna "were as combustible a combo as [Bush] 43 and Saddam," said Philip Zelikow, a historian at the University of Virginia who was a foreign-policy adviser for both Presidents Bush. When the war ended in 1848, it was counted as a clear-cut American success, assuring that Texas would remain part of the United States and adding territories that became the states of Arizona, California, and New Mexico. But after 1850, this territorial expansion reignited the political battles over slavery that the war's opponents (including a one-term member of Congress named Abraham Lincoln) had feared, thereby accelerating the descent into civil war. But that was then. Now, with the Civil War long past, it is hard to imagine the United States without the former chunks of Mexico. At least it was—until Texas Gov. Rick Perry, a Republican, raised the possibility recently that his state might want to secede from the U.S.

With occasional exceptions, the minor wars that the United States has waged from time to time have worked out pretty much as hoped. From the Barbary pirates to Grenada to Bosnia and Kosovo, clear objectives and a sufficiency of military force led to success at a low cost. But in America's 12 major wars during its 233 years of independence, things have rarely played out as expected, in the aftermath of the conflicts if not during them.

Historians, probably wisely, are wary of balancing the costs and benefits of America's past wars and delivering a bottom-line judgment. But if pressed, they'll divide them into a few "good" wars, especially the American Revolution, the Civil War, and World War II; several muddled wars; and a real stinker, Vietnam, the only one that America has lost outright.

Which brings us, of course, to the two wars that the United States is fighting now. There are reasons for hope and reasons for skepticism about the likely outcome of both. The war in Afghanistan, which President Obama has escalated, threatens to become the first war of necessity that the United States loses, especially if the nation next door, nuclear-armed Pakistan, devolves into chaos. In Iraq, the prospect of a reasonably stable, tolerably democratic regime has grown. But even in the unlikelier event that Iraq becomes a beacon of democracy for a mostly despotic Middle East, because of the high costs—including the encouragement of a nuclear-armed Iran and an ebb in American influence—some foreign-policy experts doubt that history will ever judge the Iraq war as worth the fight.

Apples and Oranges

How to judge a war? Let us count the ways.

Thucydides, the historian of ancient Greece who chronicled the Peloponnesian War, categorized wars by the aggressor's motivation for starting them—namely, fear, honor, and interests. In judging the importance of the national interest, "most people put it first, and they're mostly wrong," said Donald Kagan, a professor of classics and history at Yale University. "It's way down the list." Alarm at foreigners' intentions and,

especially, feelings of dishonor are more often the main reasons that nations go to war, he says.

Another way of judging the usefulness of a war is by assessing the need for it. In *War of Necessity, War of Choice: A Memoir of Two Iraq Wars,* published in May, Richard Haass distinguishes between a necessary Persian Gulf war, in 1991, when he served on the staff of President George H.W. Bush's National Security Council, and an unnecessary invasion of Iraq begun in 2003, while he directed the State Department's policy planning. A war of necessity, in his thinking, is one that involves a vital national interest and in which military force is the only option that might succeed—judgments that entail "elements of subjectivity," Haass, who is now president of the Council on Foreign Relations, noted in an interview. Rare, after all, is the war that its proponents don't try to sell to the public as essential, even when it isn't. Zelikow, who served as the executive director of the bipartisan commission that examined 9/11, is skeptical of the distinction. "It takes a post facto argument and makes it sound like objective history," he said. "The only war we did not choose is the one that was brought to New York City on 9/11."

Maybe the purest way of judging a war is to contemplate whether it is just or unjust to fight, an exercise most usefully pursued before the shooting starts. Michael Walzer, a political philosopher and professor emeritus at the Institute for Advanced Study in Princeton, N.J., is the author of *Just and Unjust Wars,* published in 1977 in the wake of Vietnam. The factors in figuring a war's justice are a mix of morality and fact, taking into account whether a nation was attacked or is (credibly) about to be attacked; its efforts to find peaceful solutions; the international or legal legitimacy of its military response; its likelihood of success; and, once a war has begun, the conduct of the fighting.

But these judgments, too, are "different," Walzer acknowledged in an interview, from the practical considerations—measured in lives, treasure, territory, security, and power—that determine whether a nation benefits, on balance, from starting or entering a war. Indeed, neither the justice nor the necessity of a war bears more than an incidental correlation to whether, in hindsight, it was worth fighting. Walzer regards the Mexican War, for instance, as an "unjust war that worked out well," for the United States at least. In Haass's mind, the American Revolution probably ought to be counted as a war of choice, though a "warranted" one that should have been fought. Even a war of choice can be worth fighting—it's just that "the standards are higher," he said—if its benefits sufficiently exceed its costs, measured both in the short and longer term.

"Each had benefits," said Mackubin Owens, a professor of strategy and force planning at the U.S. Naval War College, referring to the major wars that the United States has fought. The problem for decision makers, of course, is that neither costs nor benefits can be known with any certainty—or even good guesswork—in advance. A war's consequences, more often than not, are unfathomable. Even afterward, as any fair-minded historian will attest, it is no easy task to judge. Start with the impossibility of placing a value on the lives lost and disrupted; take into account the improbability of divining the

U.S. Wars: Worth Fighting?

Historians, if pressed, will divide America's wars into a few "good" wars—especially the American Revolution, the Civil War, and World War II; several muddled wars; and a real stinker, Vietnam.

	Revolutionary War (1775–83)	War of 1812 (1812–15)	Mexican War (1846–48)	Civil War (1861–65)	Spanish-American War (1898–99)	World War I (1917–18*)	World War II (1941–45*)	Korean War (1950–53)	Vietnam War (1964–73)	Persian Gulf War (1990–91)	War in Afghanistan (2001–)	War in Iraq (2003–)
Strategic Benefits	Won independence	Gained recognition of Louisiana Purchase, lessened Indian threat, laid groundwork for Monroe Doctrine	Assured Texas as a state, seized New Mexico, Arizona, California	Preserved the Union, ended slavery	Incorporated Puerto Rico and Hawaii, assured U.S. predominance in Americas	Emerged as world power	Defeated Nazi Germany and Japan	Discouraged Communist aggression, kept Japan and South Korea as U.S. allies	None	Blocked Saddam Hussein from threatening Saudi oil	Ousted Al Qaeda from camps	Created U.S. ally in Arab Middle East
Strategic Cost	Tories punished, Indians harmed	Failed to gain control of Canada	Inflamed debate over slavery	Devastation	Annexation of the Philippines brought conflict with Japan	Diplomatic aftermath led to World War II	Enabled Soviet hegemony in Eastern Europe, Cold War	Led to two decades of antipathy with mainland China	First U.S. defeat, reduced diplomatic influence, caused domestic discord	Left Saddam in power	Destabilized Pakistan	Diminished American influence, emboldened Iran
American Deaths (total serving)	25,324 (290,000)	2,260 (286,730)	13,283 (78,718)	498,332 (3,713,363)	2,446 (306,760)	116,516 (4,734,991)	405,399 (16,112,566)	36,574 (1,789,000**)	58,209 (3,403,000**)	382 (694,550**)	685† (More than 1.9 million troops have served in these wars since 9/11)	4,294†
Financial Cost (in billions of constant 2008 dollars)	$1.8	$1.2	$1.8	$60.4	$6.8	$253	$4,114	$320	$686	$96	$189††	$642††

* Duration of U.S. involvement.
** In war zone only.
† As of May 30, 2009.
†† Does not include $75.5 billion in supplemental war funding requested in April 2009.
Sources: Oxford Companion to American Military History; Defense Department; Congressional Research Service.

future; and imagine the necessarily speculative character of the counterfactuals—what would have happened had the war not broken out. This is far beyond the reach of any mathematical or actuarial formulation.

Worse, weighing the costs and benefits of a war is an exercise in comparing apples and oranges. Consider the war in Korea, which lasted from 1950 to '53. The U.S.-led combat to repel Communist North Korea's invasion of anti-communist (though autocratic) South Korea proved popular with the American public at first. But that support soured, especially when an armistice settled on virtually the same boundary between the two Koreas that existed when the war began, at the cost of 36,574 American lives. Nonetheless, as the Cold War went on, it became clear that in this first test of resolve after World War II, the U.S. willingness to stand up to Communist aggressiveness cooled Soviet strongman Joseph Stalin's geopolitical ambitions and kept South Korea—and Japan—allied with the West. "I thought it was a just war at the time," Walzer recounted, and "I think it probably helped in the eventual victory over communism."

Andrew Bacevich, a professor of international relations at Boston University, agrees—up to a point. "The initial U.S. response to Korea was a war that we needed to fight," he said. But a crucial mistake was made in conducting it: President Truman's decision to acquiesce in Gen. Douglas MacArthur's desire to invade the North drew Communist China into the war and ultimately produced a stalemate. The consequences, Bacevich said, went beyond the estimated 30,000 additional American Millet to include two decades of enmity between the United States and China—until President Nixon opened the door in 1972—and a failure to exploit the Sino-Soviet schism in a manner that might have weakened the Soviet Union and bolstered the West. "It sent us down a path," he pointed out, "that cast the decision to go in in a different light." Bacevich cautioned against trying to arrive at "concise judgments" about the desirability of the Korean—or any—War.

The "Good" Wars

The nation's first war, for its independence, was probably its most essential—and successful. King George III had committed "a long Train of Abuses and Usurpations," as Thomas Jefferson detailed in the Declaration of Independence, even as the Founding Draftsman glossed over perhaps the most threatening of the British monarchy's tyrannical acts. Yale's Kagan cited Britain's efforts, from 1763 on, to impose taxes and restrictions that suppressed the commercial ambitions of an entrepreneurial people. Hence the impulse for independence.

Still, only a third of the colonists, historians estimate, supported a rebellion against their British masters; a third remained loyal to the Crown and the rest were ambivalent or indifferent. Many of the Tories paid a price for their loyalty, Bacevich noted, in having to knuckle under or flee. The continent's aboriginal inhabitants likewise did not fare well. Conceivably, the colonists might have acted like their neighbors to the north—Canada waited until 1867 to obtain self-government

from Britain without shedding blood—although it is daunting to find anyone who would make that case today.

The Civil War, pitting brother against brother, produced a more vehement diversity of opinion, at the time and ever since. The war was probably unavoidable, most historians say, given the conflicts between the North and the South in their economies—with or without slavery—and their cultures. Had the conflict not broken out in 1861, they suppose, it would have happened later. And by the time the Civil War ended, it accomplished more than its participants had imagined. Early on, President Lincoln declared that he was willing to keep slavery or to end it, in whole or in part, as long as the Union was preserved; the Emancipation Proclamation referred to abolition in the rebellious states as a matter of "military necessity."

Had the South successfully seceded, historians debate whether slavery would have faded out on its own as the soil in the cotton fields was depleted, or, rather, would have spread to states farther west and into Latin America. A popular theme in counterfactual histories posits that the Confederacy and the Union would have reunited eventually. In any event, slavery would presumably have ended sometime (Brazil became the last country in the Western Hemisphere to abolish it, in 1888), although maybe not quickly enough for a slow-changing electorate to choose an African-American president in 2008. But was an earlier end of slavery "worth 600,000 deaths? It's hard to say," concluded Max Boot, a senior fellow at the Council on Foreign Relations. "There wasn't a lot of whooping for joy in 1865. Wars look better when the human costs have faded into history."

> "There wasn't a lot of *whooping for joy* in 1865. Wars look better when the human costs have faded into history."
>
> —Max Boot

The classic "good" war, fought by the Greatest Generation, was good ol' Double-U-Double-U-Two. The United States had to be dragged into the Second World War—until the Japanese bombed Pearl Harbor—over the isolationists' objections that the fighting in Europe and Asia was, for a nation protected by oceans, a war of choice. Before it ended, the human costs were staggering, estimated at more than 72 million deaths worldwide, including 405,399 Americans. But the benefits, historians say, were mightier still: the defeat of Hitler's Germany, with its ambitions to control Europe and beyond, and the end of Japan's brutal imperialism across the Far East.

Nonetheless, World War II can be blamed for an unintended consequence—and it was a biggie. The defeat of Nazi Germany left a power vacuum, especially in Eastern Europe, that for nearly a half-century allowed the Soviet Union to its way. A strong Germany, BU's Bacevich said, would have restrained Soviet aggression, but America's entry ensured Germany's defeat. The United States was drawn into the Cold War, featuring an Iron Curtain, a nuclear arms race, the Berlin air-lift, hot wars in Korea and Vietnam, the Cuban missile crisis, and decades of living on the brink of World War III. So which would have better served U.S. interests after World War II: victory by a hegemonic Stalin, or by a genocidal Hitler? Pick your poison.

Wars of Confusion

Something else troubles historians in recounting World War II: It might have been avoided. Winston Churchill, Britain's wartime prime minister and a historian in his own right, described it as a necessary war that shouldn't have been fought.

But it was, and historians blame the sloppy diplomacy that marked the end of World War I. The United States, had it accepted the Treaty of Versailles, would have joined with Britain and France in policing the European peace, presumably to block Hitler from remilitarizing the Rhineland in 1936. That would have prompted the German generals to fire him as chancellor, Kagan said, and "Hitler would never have risen to power." An intransigent President Wilson, unwilling to accept Senate skeptics' reservations about the treaty, is usually accorded the bulk of the blame.

For historians with a taste for slapstick, World War I is the classic case of diplomatic bungling that leads to an unnecessary war. In Lenin's view, both sides were engaged in an imperialist war, trying to carve up spheres of influence. For the European powers, the war proved pointlessly destructive.

But not necessarily for the United States. "The U.S. might have limited the damage of World War I if it had credibly prepared to intervene in 1916 and used that threat to mediate negotiations that leaders on both sides wanted," according to Zelikow. It didn't. But by entering the war in 1917, almost three years after it started in Europe, American troops ended the military stalemate, defeating Kaiser Wilhelm's aggressiveness and bringing the conflict to a triumphal conclusion.

Historians disagree over what might have happened had Germany prevailed. Years later, a German historian found archival evidence that the kaiser's ambitions for a "Greater Germany" extended into Russia and France. The power of a militarily mighty, scientifically advanced, boldly affluent Germany might have blocked—or at least complicated—the emergence of America as a world power. But Walter McDougall, a professor of history and international relations at the University of Pennsylvania, contends that it also would have meant "no Bolshevism, no Holocaust, perhaps no World War II, atomic weapons, or Cold War."

As it happened, WWI fell laughably short of Wilson's idealistic hopes for a war that would end all wars and would make the world safe for democracy. Yet America benefited greatly. Its 19 months at war "gave the U.S. more diplomatic leverage than it probably deserved," military historian Millett said. The war's devastation in Europe held an extra benefit for the United States: It ensured an economic superiority over Germany and Britain, the strongmen of the prewar world, that America has never relinquished.

America's emergence onto the international scene had begun during its previous war. As with World War I, the Spanish-American War of 1898 has given historians fits. Driven by domestic politics in the United States as well as in Spain, it was set off by the typically American blur between idealism and naked self-interest. The Spanish brutalities in Cuba spurred William Randolph Hearst to sell his newspapers by inspiring American intervention in a situation on its doorstep. On a Friday afternoon, after his boss had knocked off for the weekend, the imperialist-minded assistant Navy secretary—Theodore Roosevelt, by name—ordered some battleships moved closer to the Philippines. The result was a quick and relatively bloodless conflict that was "clearly a war of expansion," said Edward (Mac) Coffman, a retired military historian at the University of Wisconsin. It freed Cuba from Spanish rule and, according to Owens at the Naval War College, "basically made it clear that we're the dominant power in the Western Hemisphere. Now we had a seagoing Navy capable of projecting power and an ability to defend the Monroe Doctrine."

The war against Spain probably benefited, on balance, the inhabitants of Puerto Rico and Hawaii by bringing them under U.S. control. But some historians discern a downside in America's trophy of the war. "The annexation of the Philippines created a 'hostage' that the Japanese could attack at will," Millett said. "Long-term, it was a political and strategic disaster," one that put the United States "crosswise" with Japan, fueling an antipathy that exploded on December 7, 1941. The Bataan Death March, in 1942, was another unintended consequence.

Julian Zelizer, a historian at Princeton University, posits a longer-term cost of the Spanish-American War. It was a turning point for the United States, he said, in establishing an "expansionist model" for wielding its influence overseas. He sees in it the roots of another, sadder war seven decades later in Vietnam.

> "The annexation of the Philippines created a 'hostage' that the Japanese could attack at will. Long-term, it was a *political and strategic disaster.*"
>
> —Allan Millett, on the Spanish-American War

The Ugliest War

The widely ridiculed "domino effect," so often invoked by Lyndon Johnson in making his case for the Vietnam War, wasn't in itself a stupid idea. "A number of dominoes fell," Graham Allison, a professor of government at Harvard University and former Pentagon adviser, pointed out. Communism's advance in Vietnam ushered in a Communist regime in Laos (which remains in power, as it does in Vietnam) and another, far more virulent version in Cambodia.

Yeah, so? Even if the United States had won in Vietnam, historians say, the benefits wouldn't have been worth the costs. A pro-Western regime in South Vietnam wouldn't have mattered. Thailand and Indonesia would be just about the same. "I lost 58,000 colleagues," said Owens, a Marine veteran of Vietnam who was wounded twice. Tallying up the economic costs and the turmoil in the streets at home, he now concludes that the war probably wasn't worth fighting. ("Though who could say that [the turmoil] wouldn't have happened anyway?") Internationally, the defeat in Vietnam contributed to the image of the United States, which had never lost a war, as a paper tiger.

The miscalculations made in conducting the war are legendary, starting with the "ludicrous" assumption (as Allison put it) among U.S. decision makers that North Vietnam was acting as an agent for China, its enemy of many centuries' standing. A tour of the Hanoi Hilton that showcases John McCain's Navy uniform at the end begins with a guillotine dating from the 19th-century days of French colonial rule. The Americans who decided on the war failed to understand the enemy, a mistake they would make again in Iraq.

"The threat was not real, the death toll was so big, and it affected the U.S. role in the world," Princeton's Zelizer said. "A pretty big catastrophe."

Who was to blame? President Eisenhower comes in for the greatest share from historians. By backing the French as they were being driven out of Vietnam and committing Washington to support a corrupt and unpopular government in Saigon, Yale's Kagan said, Eisenhower made it politically dangerous for Presidents Kennedy and Johnson to back away from Vietnam without seeming soft on communism. In private (though taped) conversations with Sen. Richard Russell, D-Ga., who was a friend, Johnson sounded far more ambivalent about a war that ultimately ruined his presidency and drove him from the White House.

Two Iraq Wars

After the moral morass of Vietnam came the clarity of the Persian Gulf War. When Iraqi troops invaded Kuwait in 1990 and British Prime Minister Margaret Thatcher prevailed on Bush 41 not to go "wobbly," the carefully planned and well-executed war fulfilled Bush's vow: "This will not stand." Kuwait regained its freedom, and Saddam Hussein's forces were forced back across the border into Iraq. With only 382 Americans killed, the United States accomplished a lot at a relatively low cost.

"It would have been a disaster if Saddam Hussein had kept Kuwait," because it would have furthered his progress toward development of a nuclear bomb and destabilized the Middle East, according to Boot of the Council on Foreign Relations. For the United States, something even more vital was at stake. "It was about oil," said Harvard's Allison, citing the fear that the Iraqi dictator would march his troops beyond Kuwait and into Saudi Arabia, in hopes of manipulating the world's—and America's—oil supply. The invasion did not stand. Threat undone.

Yet Bush's famed prudence, reflected in his decision not to chase the Iraqi army back to Baghdad or to oust Saddam from power, took on a different cast during his son's presidency a dozen years later. With a half-million U.S. troops already on the scene, the elder Bush might have had an easier time changing the Baghdad regime than George W. Bush did. The unfinished business of the first Iraq war led, as events (and perhaps a father-and-son psychodrama) unfolded, to the second, harder war.

The two military ventures showed that the political appeal of a war bears little relationship to its utility. "Iraq I passed the Senate by only five votes and was absolutely right," Zelikow said. "Iraq II passed the Senate by 50 votes and was iffy."

The younger Bush might have tried other, less costly ways to alter Iraqi behavior. An assassination or a coup could have sufficed to change the leadership. Or, Haass wrote, "the United States could well have accomplished a change in regime behavior and a change in regime threat without regime change." The costs of the six-year-long war have exceeded 4,300 American military deaths, a price tag of nearly $1 trillion or beyond—and something less tangible but perhaps more consequential. "Iraq contributed to the emergence of a world in which power is more widely distributed than ever before," Haass maintained, "and U.S. ability to shape this world much diminished."

So, will the potential benefits of the second Iraq war ever be judged worth the price? On that, the jury is out. It could take 10 or 20 or 30 years, foreign-policy experts say, to determine whether the Iraqi government functions as a democracy that is able to bring stability, without a dictator's iron hand, to a nation of sectarian hatreds. Proponents say that the odds of a tolerably good outcome are about even.

But *how* good an outcome is still possible seems harder to gauge. The neoconservative enthusiasts for the Iraq war (along with the likes of *New York Times* columnist Thomas Friedman) envisioned a shining democracy in a reborn nation that would inspire the undoing of Islamic autocracies across the Middle East. Haass believes that such a goal has become "unreachable." Whether anything less would produce enough benefits to make the war ultimately worth fighting will depend, at least in part, on the price. Haass said he sees no plausible scenario by which the direct and indirect costs of the war wouldn't outweigh its benefits. U.S. mistreatment of Iraqi insurgents at Abu Ghraib prison and the indefinite detention of accused enemy combatants at Guantanamo Bay sullied America's good-guy image across the Muslim world (and elsewhere) and surely led to the recruitment of additional terrorists.

Potentially, the most perilous of these costs extend beyond Iraq's borders. The chaos of war and the rise to power of Iraq's Shiite majority have emboldened the imperial ambitions of Shiite-dominated Iran. Moises Naim, the editor of *Foreign Policy,* fears that the Iraq war has encouraged Iran to develop nuclear weaponry, which in turn could inspire Egypt, Saudi Arabia, and possibly Arab Gulf states to do the same. "Is a shining, democratic Iraq," he asked, "worth a neighborhood full of nuclear bombs?"

War(s) of Necessity

Another cost of the Iraq war has been the distractions it has caused, not only in Iran and North Korea, which is pursuing a nuclear program of its own, but also Afghanistan. Barack Obama repeatedly leveled such a charge about the neglect of America's other ongoing war during his 2008 campaign. As president, he has announced the deployment of an additional

17,000 troops to Afghanistan, ousted his top general on the scene, and—in next year's budget, for the first time—has proposed to spend more Defense Department money in Afghanistan than in Iraq. Invading Afghanistan after 9/11 was widely considered necessary, not only to clean out Al Qaeda's camps but also to ensure a stable government that wouldn't give terrorists safe haven again.

"We had to do it, no matter what," Boot said. "Even if it doesn't work, no one will fault Bush [for invading], though maybe for how he fought it." Experts on all sides say that the war is "losable," as Kagan put it, but they're hopeful that it isn't too late to change tactics and win. This was evidently the Obama administration's motivation in recently replacing the cautious American commander in the field with an advocate of counterinsurgency.

Haass, for one, no longer regards the war in Afghanistan as essential to U.S. national security. As long as the American military continues to strike at terrorist-related targets, the United States could accept a "messy outcome" in Afghanistan, he said, one that allows the Taliban to make some political inroads in a civil war. Afghanistan has evolved from a war of necessity, Haass said, into "Mr. Obama's war of choice."

But there is plenty of reason to worry about the deteriorating situation just beyond Afghanistan's borders. In the muddled Afghan war, "what's at stake is Pakistan anyway," military historian Millett said. The nuclear-armed nation, with its shaky democratic government, is facing the Taliban on the doorstep of Islamabad, the Pakistani capital. Should Pakistan's government collapse or if any of its nuclear weapons fall into the wrong hands, the United States could well find itself in yet another war of necessity, one that would prove treacherous to lose.

Critical Thinking

1. What has been the most common result of the small wars the U.S. has fought? What has been the predominant outcome of the large wars it has fought?

2. Why is calculating the potential and actual costs and benefits of a war so difficult? How do "unintended consequences" often overshadow intentions?

3. What wars are widely considered to be "good wars" in U.S. history? What characterizes these wars?

4. What are some of the potential long-term costs and benefits of the current U.S. war in Iraq?

5. What is a "war of necessity" compared with a "war of choice?"

Create Central

www.mhhe.com/createcentral

Internet References

Council on Foreign Relations
www.cfr.org
American Diplomacy
www.unc.edu/depts/diplomats
United States Department of Defense
www.defense.gov

bsolomon@nationaljournal.com.

Article   Prepared by: Bruce Stinebrickner, *DePauw University*

Back to Normalcy

Is America really in decline?

PAUL KENNEDY

Learning Outcomes

After reading this article, you will be able to:

- Summarize and evaluate Paul Kennedy's argument that the pre-eminent role of the United States in world affairs will almost inevitably decline in coming decades.

- Summarize the three "legs" on which the influence of the United States in world affairs are said to rest, and evaluate the strength of each of the "legs" today.

W here on earth is the United States headed? Has it lost its way? Is the Obama effect, which initially promised to halt the souring of its global image, over? More seriously, is it in some sort of terminal decline? Has it joined the long historical list of number one powers that rose to the top, and then, as Rudyard Kipling outlined it, just slowly fell downhill: "Lo, all our pomp of yesterday/At one with Nineveh and Tyre"? Has it met its match in Afghanistan? And has its obsession with the ill-defined war on terrorism obscured attention to the steady, and really much more serious, rise of China to the center of the world's stage? Will the dollar fall and fall, like the pound sterling from the 1940s to the 1970s?

It is easy to say "yes" to all those questions, and there are many in Latin America, Europe, the Middle East, Asia, and in the United States itself, who do so. But there is another way to think about America's current position in today's mightily complicated world, and it goes like this: All that is happening, really, is that the United States is slowly and naturally losing its abnormal status in the international system and returning to being one of the most prominent players in the small club of great powers. Things are not going badly wrong, and it is not as if America as becoming a flawed and impotent giant. Instead, things are just coming back to normal.

H ow would this more reassuring argument go? Well, we might start with a historical comparison. In about 1850, as the historian Eric Hobsbawm points out in his great work *Industry and Empire,* the small island-state of Britain produced perhaps two-thirds of the world's coal, half its iron, five-sevenths of its steel, and half of its commercial cotton cloth.

This extraordinary position was indeed abnormal; that is, it could not last forever. And as soon as countries with bigger populations and resources (Germany, the United States, Russia, Japan) organized themselves along British lines, it was natural that they would produce a larger share of world product and take a larger share of world power and thus cut Britain's share back down to a more normal condition. This is a story which economic and political historians take for granted. It is about the tides of history and the shifts of power that occur when productive strength moves from one part of the world to another. It's actually a sensible way of thinking about history over the long term.

So why should we not look at America, and America's present and future condition, in the same calm way? It is of course a much broader and more populous country than Britain was and is, and possesses far more natural resources, but the long-term trajectory is roughly the same. After 1890, the United States had slowly overtaken the British Empire as the world's number one by borrowing critical technologies (the steam engine, the railway, the textile factory), and then adding on its own contributions in chemical and electrical industries, and blazing the way in automobile and aircraft and computer hardware/software production. It was assisted by the good fortune of its geographic distance from any other great power (as Britain was by its insularity), and by the damage done elsewhere by World Wars I and II (as Britain was by the damage done elsewhere by the Revolutionary and Napoleonic wars). By 1945, therefore, America possessed around half of the world's GNP, an amazing share, but no less than Britain's a century earlier when it held most of the world's steam engines. But it was a special historical moment in both cases. When other countries began to play catch-up, these high shares of world power would decline.

I n the American case, we might tease out this argument by returning to a point made almost 20 years ago by the Harvard scholar Joseph Nye, that America's strength and influence in world affairs was like a sturdy three-legged stool; that is, the nation's unchallenged place rested upon the mutually reinforcing legs of soft power, economic power, and military power. In all three dimensions, Nye suggested, the United States was comfortably ahead of any other competitor. Global shares of relative strength were being diffused, perhaps, but in no way enough to shake America's dominant role.

How does this assessment look today? Of the three legs to Nye's stool, soft power—the capacity to persuade other nations to do what America would like—looks the shakiest. This is not a measure of strength that can be computed statistically, like steel output or defense spending, so subjective impressions enter into the debate. Nevertheless, would anyone dispute the contention that America's ability to influence other states (such as Brazil, Russia, China, India) has declined during the past two decades? When Nye wrote, he pointed to the significance of popular culture (Hollywood, blue jeans), the dominance of the English language, the increasing standardization of U.S. business (from chain hotels to accounting rules), and the spread of democracy, all as signs of America's influence.

Those were interesting thoughts, but we have since seen that radical students from Ankara to Amsterdam can still wear blue jeans but demonstrate against the United States, and that it is quite possible that a totally free voting system in (say) Egypt, Saudi Arabia, and China would lead to parliamentary majorities highly critical of Washington's policies. The Pew Foundation's regular poll of global opinion suggests diminishing approval of America, despite a short-term upward blip in favor of Obama. Soft power comes and goes very fast.

As to the weakening of the second leg of the stool, America's relative economic and foreign-currency heft, well, a person would have had to have been blind and deaf not to observe its obvious deterioration in recent years. If anything surprises me, it is how fast and how large the relative weakening has been: A truly competitive great power should not have its trade deficits widening so fast, nor its federal, state, and municipal deficits ballooning at such a pace, literally, into the trillions of dollars. It is unsustainable, although that fact has been obscured by the thousands of American economists and investment advisers who emit positive noises to their clients and who themselves simply cannot think strategically. The collective folly of portfolio advisers is compounded by the current congressional baying for China's currency to get stronger and stronger and stronger. Is that what the United States really wants—to get relatively weaker? At a certain stage in the past 500-year history of currencies and power, the Dutch guilder hustled the Spanish escudo off the scene; then the pound sterling hustled the guilder (and franc and mark) off the scene; then the dollar hustled the pound off the scene. What is Washington risking as it presses for a stronger Chinese currency? My apprehension is that it risks a much stronger Chinese political influence in the world.

America's military strengths are, by contrast, still remarkable; at least this one leg of the stool is sturdy. But how sturdy? Well, almost half of the world's current defense expenditures come from the United States, so it is not surprising that it possesses a gigantic aircraft carrier Navy, a substantial Army and Marine Corps that can be deployed all over the globe, an ultra high-tech Air Force, and logistical and intelligence-gathering facilities that have no equal. This is the strongest leg of the three. But it is not going unchallenged, and in several regards.

The first is in the rise of irregular or "asymmetrical" warfare by non-state actors. Anyone who has seen the recent award-winning movie *The Hurt Locker*, about the U.S. Army's uncomfortable and bloody experiences in Iraq, will know what this means. It means that the narrow streets of Fallujah, or, even more, the high passes of the Helmand mountains, equalize the struggle; high-tech doesn't quite work against a suicide bomber or a cunningly placed road mine. General Patton's style of warfare just doesn't succeed when you are no longer running your tanks through Lorraine but creeping, damaged and wincing, through the Khyber Pass. Sophisticated drones are, actually, stupid. They help avoid making the commitment to winning on the ground, and they will eventually lose.

Secondly, there is the emergence, along the historical pattern of the rise and fall of the great powers, of new challenger nations that are pushing into America's post-1945 geopolitical space. Putin's Russia is clawing back its historic zones of control and, frankly, there seems little that Washington can do if Belarus or a kicking-and-screaming Latvia is reabsorbed by the Kremlin. India is intent on making the term "Indian Ocean" not just a geographic expression; in ten or 20 years' time, if its plans are fulfilled, it will be in control. Which is rather comforting, because it will thwart China's purposeful though clumsy efforts to acquire much-needed African mineral supplies. But China, in its turn, and through its very new and sophisticated weapons systems (disruptive electronic warfare, silent submarines, sea-skimming missiles), may soon possess the capacity to push the U.S. Navy away from China's shores. Like it or not, America is going to be squeezed out of Asia.

Overall, and provided the gradual reduction of America's extensive footprint across Asia can occur through mutual agreements and uninterrupted economic links, that may not be a bad thing. Few, if any, Asian governments want the United States to pull out now, or abruptly, but most assume it will cease to be such a prominent player in the decades to come. Why not start that discussion now, or begin a rethink? American hopes of reshaping Asia sometimes look curiously like former British hopes of reshaping the Middle East. Don't go there.

Finally, and most serious of all, there is America's dangerous and growing reliance upon other governments to fund its own national deficits. Military strength cannot rest upon pillars of sand; it cannot be reliant, not forever, upon foreign lenders. The president, in his increasingly lonely White House, and the increasingly ineffective Congress, seem unable to get a harsh but decent fiscal package together. And now, the Tea Party nutcases are demanding a tax-cut-and-spend policy that would make the famous Mad Hatter's tea party itself look rather rational.

This is not a way to run a country, and especially not the American nation that, despite its flaws, is the world's mainstay. This is worrying for its neighbors, its many friends and allies; it is worrying for even those states, like India and Brazil, that are going to assume a larger role in world affairs in the years to come. We should all be careful to wish away a reasonably benign American hegemony; we might regret its going.

But the ebb and tides of history will take away that hegemony, as surely as autumn replaces the high summer months with fruit rather than flower. America's global position is at present strong, serious, and very large. But it is still, frankly, abnormal. It will come down a ratchet or two more.

It will return from being an oversized world power to being a big nation, but one which needs to be listened to, and one which, for the next stretch, is the only country that can supply powerful heft to places in trouble. It will still be really important, but less so than it was. That isn't a bad thing. It will be more normal.

Critical Thinking

1. What are the key parallels between Britain's place in world affairs in the mid-19th century and that of the United States today?

2. What are the three legs of the "three-legged stool" on which a nation-state's status in world affairs is said to rest? How is the contemporary U.S. faring with respect to each leg?

3. What does it mean to say that the standing and role of the U.S. in world affairs has been "abnormal" for the past half-century or more? What is the title of the piece, "Back to Normalcy," meant to convey?

Create Central

www.mhhe.com/createcentral

Internet References

Council on Foreign Relations
www.cfr.org
American Diplomacy
www.unc.edu/depts/diplomat
Tribune Content Agency: Paul Kennedy
www.tmsfeatures.com/columns/political/international/paul-kennedy

PAUL KENNEDY is a professor of history and director of international security studies at Yale University. He is the author of *The Rise and Fall of the Great Powers.*

Article   Prepared by: Bruce Stinebrickner, *DePauw University*

Don't Tread on Me

With the troops coming home and budget cuts in effect, the military is about to lose its blank check—but not if the Pentagon and its allies get their way. A field manual for the epic battle over defense spending.

DAVE GILSON

Learning Outcomes

After reading this article, you will be able to:

• Assess how reasonable the overall cost and size of the U.S. military is.

• Identify one area of military spending that seems too much or too little and explain why.

To hear the Pentagon brass and their allies describe it, the nation is facing a grave new security threat: sequestration. Under the automatic budget cuts that kicked in last March, the Pentagon must trim nearly $1 trillion over the next decade—cuts originally intended to be so unpalatable as to force Congress to make a lasting budget deal. That didn't work out, but now congressional hawks, defense officials, and weapons contractors are warning that if the cuts aren't eliminated, America's military superiority will be.

But before you plan a bake sale to help the Pentagon pay its bills (or draw up your wish list for spending that new peace dividend), consider this: Even after the sequester, the Pentagon's base budget is set to remain well above pre-9/11 levels for the next decade, and the military is taking a far smaller haircut than it did after Vietnam and the Cold War wound down. "These 'terrible' cuts would return us to historically high levels of spending," snaps Winslow Wheeler of the Project on Government Oversight. Even if the sequester were to be scrapped, the Pentagon could reduce its budget by $100 billion a year without undermining its readiness, according to Lawrence J. Korb, a senior fellow at the Center for American Progress.

Facing $37 billion in cuts in 2013, the Pentagon furloughed contractors, delayed contracts, and grounded planes. But sequestration doesn't touch overseas operations—that is wars—soldiers' pay or benefits, veterans' benefits, or the nuclear arsenal. With another $52 billion set to be sliced, reversing those cuts has become the centerpiece of talk of a "grand bargain" to end the cycle of budget crises and fiscal hostage-taking.

Republicans have proposed increasing defense spending and taking more money from Obamacare and other social programs, while Democrats have said they'd scale back the defense cuts in exchange for additional tax revenue.

Both ideas are likely nonstarters, which means that after the next rounds of budget theater are over, sequestration may remain as the blunt, imperfect tool that forces the military to shed some of the bulk it acquired while fighting two of the

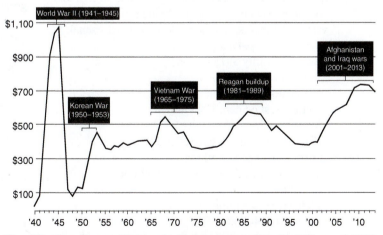

The Missing Peace Dividend   Defense spending (in billions of 2013 dollars) dropped sharply after earlier conflicts. But perhaps not this time.

For credits, sources, and more charts and maps, visit motherjones.com/pentagon longest and most expensive wars in our history. Deprived of its blank check, the Pentagon might heed the hawkish Capitol Hill insider who once called for the "bloated" defense establishment to "be pared down" and retooled for the 21st century. That insider? Vietnam vet and retired Republican senator from Nebraska Chuck Hagel, before he became secretary of defense.

1. **Our military is mind-bogglingly big.**

    The Pentagon employs **3 million people,** 800,000 more than Walmart.

    The Pentagon's 2012 budget was **47 percent bigger** than Walmart's.

    Serving **9.6 million people,** the Pentagon and Veterans Administration together constitute the nation's largest health care provider.

    70 percent of the value of the federal government's $1.8 trillion in property, land, and equipment belongs to the Pentagon.

    Los Angeles could fit into the land managed by the Pentagon **93 times.** The Army uses **more than twice** as much building space as all the offices in New York City.

    The Pentagon holds **more than 80 percent** of the federal government's inventories, including **$6.8 billion** of excess, obsolete, or unserviceable stuff.

    The Pentagon operates **more than 170 golf courses** worldwide.

2. **One out of every five tax dollars is spent on defense**

    The $3.7 trillion federal budget breaks down into mandatory spending—benefits guaranteed the American people, such as Social Security and Medicare—and discretionary spending—programs that, at least in theory, can be cut. In 2013, more than half of all discretionary spending (and one-fifth of total spending) went to defense, including the Pentagon, veterans' benefits, and the nuclear weapons arsenal.

    Mandatory Spending
    Social Security $813 billion
    Medicare $504 billion
    Medicaid $267 billion
    Net interest on debt $223 billion
    TANF and income security $392 billion
    SNAP and food assistance $105 billion
    Farm subsidies $22 billion
    Children's health insurance $10 billion
    Discretionary Spending
    Defense $652 billion
    Veterans $140 billion*
    Homeland security $55 billion
    Education $74 billion
    Natural resources and environment $35 billion
    Science, technology, and space $31 billion

International aid $26 billion
Community and regional development $27 billion
Housing assistance $44 billion
Transportation $91 billion
Energy $10 billion
Classified
CIA, NSA, and "black budget" $53 billion
*Includes mandatory and discretionary spending

3. **We're the world's 800-pound gorilla.**

    When it comes to defense spending, no country can compete directly with the United States, which spends more than the next 10 countries combined—including potential rivals Russia and China, as well as allies such as England, Japan, and France. Altogether, the Pentagon accounts for nearly 40 percent of global military spending. In 2012, 4.4 percent of our GDP went to defense. That's in line with how much Russia spends; China spends 2 percent of its GDP on its military.

The Last Superpower
International military spending (in billions of 2013 dollars)

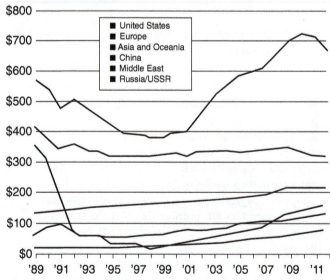

Asia and Oceania excluding China; Europe excluding Russia.

4. **We paid for two wars with credit.**

    As the Pentagon scrambles to find a trillion dollars in cuts, here's a quick reality check: The wars in Iraq and Afghanistan cost $1.5 trillion, about twice the cost of the Vietnam War in inflation-adjusted dollars. And that's just the "supplemental" military spending passed by Congress for the wars—the regular Pentagon budget also grew nearly 45 percent between 2001 and 2010. The main budget proposals in Washington would only bring the Pentagon's base (nonwar) budget down to around 2008 levels.

Back to the Future
The Pentagon's base budget (in billions of 2013 dollars) is set to go back to mid-2000s levels.

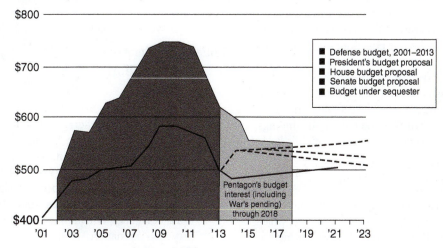

Legend:
- Defense budget, 2001–2013
- President's budget proposal
- House budget proposal
- Senate budget proposal
- Budget under sequester

Pentagon's budget interest (including War's pending) through 2018

The funds to fight in Iraq and Afghanistan came entirely from borrowing, contributing nearly 20 percent to the national debt accrued between 2001 and 2012. And there's more to come: Between paying down those obligations and caring for vets, economists Joseph Stiglitz and Linda Bilmes estimate that the wars' overall costs will top $4 trillion.

5. The wartime wage gap

About three-quarters of the Pentagon's budget goes to hardware, contractors, and operations, with the rest spent on the troops. But while the number of Americans in uniform increased 3 percent during the past decade, the annual cost per person doubled, to around $115,000. Congress approved multiple raises during the Iraq and Afghanistan wars, but a look at base pay rates (what soldiers earn before add-ons like housing allowances and combat pay) shows that the wartime wages didn't trickle down the chain of command. Some of that can be explained by "brass creep"—the swelling ranks of generals and admirals who earn high salaries and retire with cushy pensions.—AJ Vicens

Change in average base pay, 2001–2013

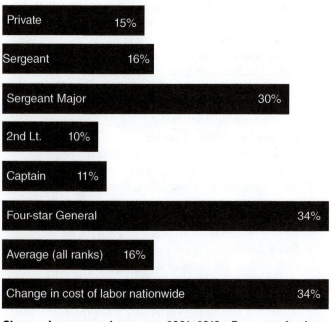

Private	15%
Sergeant	16%
Sergeant Major	30%
2nd Lt.	10%
Captain	11%
Four-star General	34%
Average (all ranks)	16%
Change in cost of labor nationwide	34%

Change in average base pay, 2001–2013 Base pay for Army ranks and their equivalents in other services, measured in real dollars.

6. Where does the Pentagon's money go?

The exact answer is a mystery. That's because the Pentagon's books are a complete mess. They're so bad that they can't even be officially inspected, despite a 1997 requirement that federal agencies submit to annual audits—just like every other business or organization.

The Defense Department is one of just two agencies (Homeland Security is the other) that are keeping the bean counters waiting: As the Government Accountability Office dryly notes, the Pentagon has "serious financial management problems" that make its financial statements "inauditable." Pentagon financial operations occupy one-fifth of the GAO's list of federal programs with a high risk of waste, fraud, or inefficiency.

Critics also contend that the Pentagon cooks its books by using unorthodox accounting methods that make its budgetary needs seem more urgent. The agency insists it will "achieve audit readiness" by 2017.

First time Pentagon was required to be audited	1997	When the Pentagon says it will be ready for an audit	2017

7. **Military overruns and rip-offs have a long (and expensive) history**

   1778: General George Washington decries the suppliers overcharging his army: "It is enough to make one curse their own Species, for possessing so little virtue and patriotism."

   1794: The Navy's first order for frigates faces shipyard delays, and its cost shoots up to more than $1.1 million.

   1861: A House committee exposes fraud, favoritism, and profiteering in Civil War contracting. Its findings, writes the *New York Times*, "produce a feeling of public indignation which would justify the most summary measures against the knaves whose villainy is here dragged into daylight."

   1941: Sen. Harry Truman kicks off a dogged investigation of wasteful war production. The Truman Committee, which runs into World War II, is credited with saving as much as $15 billion (more than $230 billion in today's dollars).

   1975: Wisconsin Sen. William Proxmire calls out the Pentagon for maintaining 300 golf courses around the world. (Today it has at least 170.)

   1983: President Ronald Reagan announces the Strategic Defense Initiative, a.k.a. "Star Wars," a system of ground- and space-based lasers that will stop incoming nuclear missiles. Still unrealized, the program has cost more than $209 billion.

   1985: Pentagon profligacy makes headlines with reports of $640 toilet seats, $660 ashtrays, $7,600 coffeemakers, and $74,000 ladders. "Our attack on waste and fraud in procurement—like discovering that $436 hammer—is going to continue," Reagan says, "but we must have adequate military appropriations."

   2001: No-bid Pentagon contracts explode after 9/11, jumping from $50 billion in 2001 to $140 billion in 2010.

   2001: Halliburton subsidiary KBR takes over a contract to feed soldiers in Iraq. It raises the price of a meal from $3 to $5 while subcontracting the services back to the previous contractor.

   2009: After safety problems and cost overruns, the Pentagon cancels the F-22 Raptor fighter jet (estimated price tag: $412 million per plane) and puts the money toward buying F-35S.

   2010: The Government Accountability Office (GAO) finds that the Defense Logistics Agency is sitting on $7.1 billion worth of excess spare parts.

   2010: An anonymous congressional earmark sets aside $2.5 billion for 10 C-17 aircraft the Air Force says it does not need.

   2011: Boeing charges the Army $1,678 apiece for rubber cargo-loading rollers that actually cost $7 each.

   2012: One-quarter of the $1.6 trillion being spent on major weapons systems comes from unexpected cost overruns.

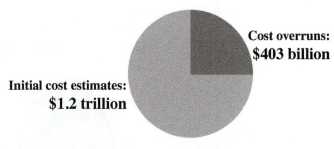

Cost overruns: **$403 billion**

Initial cost estimates: **$1.2 trillion**

   2012: The Air Force scraps a new logistics management system that has shown "negligible" results—after spending $1 billion on it.

   2012: Sen. Tom Cobum (R-Okla.) slams $68 billion in frivolous Pentagon spending: "Using defense dollars to run microbreweries, study Twitter slang, create beef jerky, or examine *Star Trek* does nothing to defend our nation."

   2012: The House oversight committee finds that the Swiss contractor that fed troops in Afghanistan was overpaid by $757 million. The company claims it's still owed $1 billion.

   2013: The military and VA are found to have spent $1.3 billion on a failed health records system for vets. That's after the Pentagon already spent $2 billion on an unsuccessful upgrade of its electronic medical records system.

   2013: The Army announces plans to replace its camouflage pattern, which was introduced in 2004 and cost $5 billion to develop. The new one will cost $4 billion.

   2013: Sen. John McCain (R-Ariz.) decries the F-35 Joint Strike Fighter as "one of the great national scandals that we have ever had, as far as the expenditure of taxpayers' dollars are concerned.")

   2013: The Pentagon plans to scrap more than 85,000 tons of equipment in Afghanistan, part of $7 billion worth of gear being left behind as the troops come home.—*Eric Wuestewald*

8. **Anatomy of a budget buster**

   In the early 2000s, the Pentagon began developing a new generation of stealthy, high-tech fighter jets that were supposed to do everything from landing on aircraft carriers and taking off vertically to dogfighting and dropping bombs. The result is the F-35 Joint Strike Fighter, whose three models (one each for the Navy, Air Force, and Marines) are years behind schedule, hugely over budget, and plagued with problems that have earned them a reputation as the biggest defense boondoggle in history.

   Rolling out the F-35 originally was expected to cost $233 billion, but now it's expected to cost nearly **$400 billion.** The time needed to develop the plane has gone from 10 years to 18.

Estimated F-35 Costs, 2001–2012

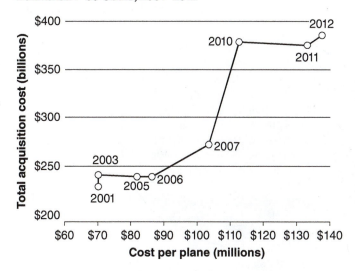

Lockheed says the final cost per plane will be about $75 million. However, according to the Government Accountability Office, the actual cost has **jumped to $137 million.**

It was initially estimated that it could cost another **$1 trillion or more** to keep the new F-35S flying for 30 years. Pentagon officials called this "unaffordable"—and now say it will cost only $857 million. "This is no longer the trillion-dollar [aircraft]," boasts a Lockheed Martin executive.

Planes started rolling off the assembly line before development and testing were finished, which could result in **$8 billion worth of retrofits.**

A 2013 report by the Pentagon inspector general identified **719 problems** with the F-35 program. Some of the issues with the first batch of planes delivered to the Marines:

- Pilots are not allowed to fly these test planes at night, within 25 miles of lightning, faster than the speed of sound, or with real or simulated weapons.
- Pilots say cockpit visibility is worse than in existing fighters.
- Special high-tech helmets have "frequent problems" and are "badly performing."
- Takeoffs may be postponed when the temperature is below 6o8 F.

The F-35 program has 1,400 suppliers in **46 states.** Lockheed Martin gave money to **425 members** of Congress in 2012 and has spent **$159 million** on lobbying since 2000.

9. **Ways to save a few billion...**

There are savings to be had within the Pentagon's massive budget—if politicians can weather the storm that kicks up whenever a pet project is targeted. Here are 10 ideas for major cuts from an array of defense wonks, from the libertarian Cato Institute and the liberal Center for American Progress to the conservative American Enterprise Institute. For a complete list of ideas and their backers, go to *motherjones.com/pentagon*

PROPOSAL	ESTIMATED SAVINGS
Get rid of all ICBMS and nuclear bombers (but keep nuclear-armed subs).	$20 billion/year
Retire 2 of the Navy's 11 aircraft carrier groups.	$50 billion through 2020
Cut the size of the Army and Marines to preg-interests.	At least $80 billion over
Slow down or cancel the pricey F-35 fighter jet program.	At least $4 billion/year
Downsize military headquarters that extend interior	$8 billion/year
Cancel the troubled V-22 Osprey tiltrotor and use helicopters instead.	At least $1.2 billion
Modify supplemental Medicare benefits for veterans.	$40 billion over 10 years
Scale back purchases of littoral combat ships.	$2 billion in 2013
Cap spending on military contractors below 2012 levels.	$2.9 billion/year
Retire the Cold War-era B-1 bomber.	$3.7 billion over 5 years

10. . . . if Congress can make a deal.
    Familiar battle lines are being drawn as the fight over the defense budget heats up, making chances of a compromise unlikely.

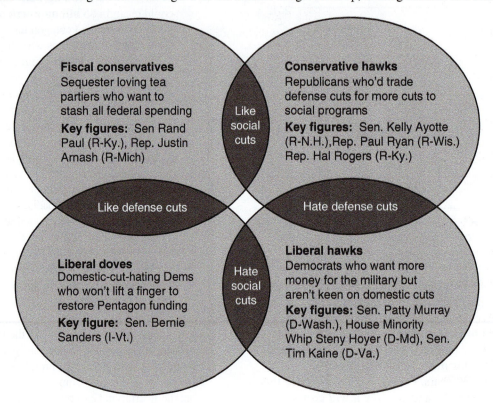

Fiscal conservatives
Sequester loving tea partiers who want to stash all federal spending
Key figures: Sen Rand Paul (R-Ky.), Rep. Justin Arnash (R-Mich)

Conservative hawks
Republicans who'd trade defense cuts for more cuts to social programs
Key figures: Sen. Kelly Ayotte (R-N.H.),Rep. Paul Ryan (R-Wis.) Rep. Hal Rogers (R-Ky.)

Like social cuts

Like defense cuts

Hate defense cuts

Liberal doves
Domestic-cut-hating Dems who won't lift a finger to restore Pentagon funding
Key figure: Sen. Bernie Sanders (I-Vt.)

Hate social cuts

Liberal hawks
Democrats who want more money for the military but aren't keen on domestic cuts
Key figures: Sen. Patty Murray (D-Wash.), House Minority Whip Steny Hoyer (D-Md), Sen. Tim Kaine (D-Va.)

Charge!

The Pentagon handed $361 billion to contractors in 2012. Some items on its shopping list:

Planes and helicopters **$32.6 BILLION**	Nuclear reactors **$2.5 BILLION**	Small-arms ammunition **$978 MILLION**
Petroleum and oil **$21.6 BILLION**	Drugs and pharmaceuticals **$2.5 BILLION**	Destroyers **$977 MILLION**
Guided missiles **$10.4 BILLION**	Combat ships and landing vessels **$2.2 BILLION**	Night-vision equipment **$834 MILLION**
Combat/assault vehicles **$5.2 BILLION**	Unmanned aircraft and drones **$2.2 BILLION**	Fruit and vegetables **$783 MILLION**
Dairy and eggs **$4 BILLION**	Aircraft carriers **$1.5 BILLION**	Bakery and cereal products **$738 MILLION**
Amphibious assault ships **$3.9 BILLION**	Meat, poultry, and fish **$1.2 BILLION**	Nonalcoholic beverages **$554 MILLION**
Space vehicles **$3.6 BILLION**	Bombs **$1 BILLION**	Land mines **$547 MILLION**
Submarines **$3.4 BILLION**		Small arms **$413 MILLION**

Sugar, confectionery,
and nuts
$294 MILLION

Composite food
packages (MRES)
$260 MILLION

Soap, toothpaste, and
shaving preparations
$226 MILLION

Footwear
$152 MILLION

Bulk explosives
$103 MILLION

Live animals (not for food)
$102 MILLION

Bolts and screws
$86 MILLION

Soups and bouillons
$85 MILLION

Tobacco products
$85 MILLION

Coffee, tea, and cocoa
$73 MILLION

Grenades
$26 MILLION

Underwear and nightwear
$18 MILLION

Badges and insignia
$16 MILLION

Blood and blood products
$1 MILLION

Critical Thinking

1. How do proposed cuts in defense spending after the winding down of wars in Iraq and Afghanistan compare with the size of cuts after the Vietnam War and the end of the Cold War?

2. What are the size and cost of the U.S. military? How does U.S. defense spending compare with defense spending in other countries?

3. For what sorts of things does the U.S. military spend its money? In what proportions?

Create Central

www.mhhe.com/createcentral

Internet References

Global Issues: World Military Spending
http://www.globalissues.org/article/75/world-military-spending#InContext USMilitarySpendingVersusRestoftheWorld

United States Department of Defense
http://www.defense.gov

Article   Prepared by: Bruce Stinebrickner, *DePauw University*

The Killing Machines

MARK BOWDEN

Learning Outcomes

After reading this article, you will be able to:

- Assess the moral and legal dimensions of U.S. drone use to kill suspected terrorists in foreign countries.

- Weigh whether the tactical advantages of using drones against terrorists or suspected terrorists outweigh possible moral and political considerations.

I. Unfairness

Consider David. The shepherd lad steps up to face in single combat the Philistine giant Goliath. Armed with only a slender staff and a slingshot, he confronts a fearsome warrior clad in a brass helmet and chain mail, wielding a spear with a head as heavy as a sledge and a staff "like a weaver's beam." Goliath scorns the approaching youth: "Am I a dog, that thou comest to me with staves?" (1 Samuel 17)

David then famously slays the boastful giant with a single smooth stone from his slingshot.

A story to gladden the hearts of underdogs everywhere, its biblical moral is: *Best to have God on your side*. But subtract the theological context and what you have is a parable about technology. The slingshot, a small, lightweight weapon that employs simple physics to launch a missile with lethal force from a distance, was an innovation that rendered all the giant's advantages moot. It ignored the spirit of the contest. David's weapon was, like all significant advances in warfare, essentially unfair.

As anyone who has ever been in combat will tell you, the last thing you want is a fair fight. Technology has been tilting the balance of battles since Goliath fell. I was born into the age of push-button warfare. Ivy Mike, the first thermonuclear bomb, capable of vaporizing an entire modern metropolis, of killing millions of people at once, was detonated over the Pacific before my second birthday. Growing up, the concept of global annihilation wasn't just science fiction. We held civil-defense drills to practice for it.

Within my lifetime, that evolution has taken a surprising turn. Today we find ourselves tangled in legal and moral knots over the drone, a weapon that can find and strike a single target, often a single individual, via remote control.

Unlike nuclear weapons, the drone did not emerge from some multibillion-dollar program on the cutting edge of science. It isn't even completely new. The first Predator drone consisted of a snowmobile engine mounted on a radio-controlled glider. When linked via satellite to a distant control center, drones exploit telecommunications methods perfected years ago by TV networks—in fact, the Air Force has gone to ESPN for advice. But when you pull together this disparate technology, what you have is a weapon capable of finding and killing someone just about anywhere in the world.

Drone strikes are a far cry from the atomic vaporizing of whole cities, but the horror of war doesn't seem to diminish when it is reduced in scale. If anything, the act of willfully pinpointing a human being and summarily executing him from afar distills war to a single ghastly act.

One day this past January, a small patrol of marines in southern Afghanistan was working its way at dusk down a dirt road not far from Kandahar, staying to either side to avoid planted bombs, when it unexpectedly came under fire. The men scattered for cover. A battered pickup truck was closing in on them and popping off rounds from what sounded like a big gun.

Continents away, in a different time zone, a slender 19-year-old American soldier sat at a desk before a large color monitor, watching this action unfold in startlingly high definition. He had never been near a battlefield. He had graduated from basic training straight out of high school, and was one of a select few invited to fly Predators. This was his first time at the controls, essentially a joystick and the monitor. The drone he was flying was roughly 15,000 feet above the besieged patrol, each member marked clearly in monochrome on his monitor by an infrared uniform patch. He had been instructed to watch over the patrol, and to "stay frosty," meaning: *Whatever happens, don't panic*. No one had expected anything to happen. Now something was happening.

The young pilot zoomed in tight on the approaching truck. He saw in its bed a .50-caliber machine gun, a weapon that could do more damage to an army than a platoon of Goliaths.

A colonel, watching over his shoulder, said, "They're pinned down pretty good. They're gonna be screwed if you don't do something."

The colonel told the pilot to fix on the truck. A button on the joystick pulled up a computer-generated reticle, a grid displaying exact ground coordinates, distance, direction, range, and so on. Once the computer locked on the pickup, it stayed zeroed in on the moving target.

"Are you ready to help?" the colonel asked.

An overlay on the grid showed the anticipated blast radius of an AGM-114 Hellfire missile—the drone carried two. Communicating via a digital audio link, the colonel instructed the men on the ground to back away, then gave them a few seconds to do so.

The pilot scrutinized the vehicle. Those who have seen unclassified clips of aerial attacks have only a dim appreciation of the optics available to the military and the CIA.

"I could see exactly what kind of gun it was in back," the pilot told me later. "I could see two men in the front; their faces were covered. One was in the passenger seat and one was in the driver's seat, and then one was on the gun, and I think there was another sitting in the bed of the truck, but he was kind of obscured from my angle."

On the radio, they could hear the marines on the ground shouting for help.

"Fire one," said the colonel.

The Hellfire is a 100-pound antitank missile, designed to destroy an armored vehicle. When the blast of smoke cleared, there was only a smoking crater on the dirt road.

"I was kind of freaked out," the pilot said. "My whole body was shaking. It was something that was completely different. The first time doing it, it feels bad almost. It's not easy to take another person's life. It's tough to think about. A lot of guys were congratulating me, telling me, 'You protected them; you did your job. That's what you are trained to do, supposed to do,' so that was good reinforcement. But it's still tough."

One of the things that nagged at him, and that was still bugging him months later, was that he had delivered this deathblow without having been in any danger himself. The men he killed, and the marines on the ground, were at war. They were risking their hides. Whereas he was working his scheduled shift in a comfortable office building, on a sprawling base, in a peaceful country. It seemed unfair. He had been inspired to enlist by his grandfather's manly stories of battle in the Korean War. He had wanted to prove something to himself and to his family, to make them as proud of him as they had been of his Pop-Pop.

"But this was a weird feeling," he said. "You feel bad. You don't feel worthy. I'm sitting there safe and sound, and those guys down there are in the thick of it, and I can have more impact than they can. It's almost like I don't feel like I deserve to be safe."

After slaying Goliath, David was made commander of the Israelite armies and given the hand of King Saul's daughter. When the Pentagon announced earlier this year that it would award a new medal to drone pilots and cyber warriors, it provoked such outrage from veterans that production of the new decoration was halted and the secretary of defense sentenced the medal to a review and then killed it. Members of Congress introduced legislation to ensure that any such award would be ranked beneath the Purple Heart, the medal given to every wounded soldier. How can someone who has never physically been in combat receive a combat decoration?

The question hints at something more important than war medals, getting at the core of our uneasiness about the drone. Like the slingshot, the drone fundamentally alters the nature of combat. While the young Predator pilot has overcome his unease—his was a clearly justifiable kill shot fired in conventional combat, and the marines on the ground conveyed their sincere gratitude—the sense of unfairness lingers.

If the soldier who pulls the trigger in safety feels this, consider the emotions of those on the receiving end, left to pick up the body parts of their husbands, fathers, brothers, and friends. Where do they direct their anger? When the wrong person is targeted, or an innocent bystander is killed, imagine the sense of impotence and rage. How do those who remain strike back? No army is arrayed against them, no airfield is nearby to be attacked. If they manage to shoot down a drone, what have they done but disable a small machine? No matter how justified a strike seems to us, no matter how carefully weighed and skillfully applied, to those on the receiving end it is profoundly arrogant, the act of an enemy so distant and superior that he is untouchable.

"The political message [of drone strikes] emphasizes the disparity in power between the parties and reinforces popular support for the terrorists, who are seen as David fighting Goliath," Gabriella Blum and Philip B. Heymann, both law professors at Harvard, wrote in their 2010 book, *Laws, Outlaws, and Terrorists: Lessons From the War on Terror.* "Moreover, by resorting to military force rather than to law enforcement, targeted killings might strengthen the sense of legitimacy of terrorist operations, which are sometimes viewed as the only viable option for the weak to fight against a powerful empire."

Is it any wonder that the enemy seizes upon targets of opportunity—a crowded café, a passenger jet, the finish line of a marathon? There is no moral justification for deliberately targeting civilians, but one can understand why it is done. Arguably the strongest force driving lone-wolf terror attacks in recent months throughout the Western world has been anger over drone strikes.

The drone is effective. Its extraordinary precision makes it an advance in humanitarian warfare. In theory, when used with principled restraint, it is the perfect counterterrorism weapon. It targets indiscriminate killers with exquisite discrimination. But because its aim can never be perfect, can only be as good as the intelligence that guides it, sometimes it kills the wrong people—and even when it doesn't, its cold efficiency is literally inhuman.

So how should we feel about drones?

II. Gorgon Stare

The Defense Department has a secret state-of-the-art control center in Dubai with an IMAX-size screen at the front of the main room that can project video feed from dozens of drones at once. The Air Force has been directed to maintain capability for 65 simultaneous Combat Air Patrols. Each of these involves multiple drones, and maintains a persistent eye over a potential target. The Dubai center, according to someone who has seen it, resembles a control center at NASA, with hundreds of pilots and analysts arrayed in rows before monitors.

This is a long way from the first known drone strike, on November 4, 2002, when a Hellfire missile launched from a Predator over Yemen blew up a car carrying Abu Ali al-Harithi, one of the al-Qaeda leaders responsible for the 2000 bombing of the USS *Cole*. Killed along with him in the car were five others, including an American citizen, Kamal Derwish, who was suspected of leading a terrorist cell based near Buffalo, New York. The drone used that day had only recently been reconfigured as a weapon. During testing, its designers had worried that the missile's backblast would shatter the lightweight craft. It didn't. Since that day, drones have killed thousands of people.

John Yoo, the law professor who got caught up in tremendous controversy as a legal counselor to President George W. Bush over harsh interrogation practices, was surprised that drone strikes have provoked so little hand-wringing.

"I would think if you are a civil libertarian, you ought to be much more upset about the drone than Guantánamo and interrogations," he told me when I interviewed him recently. "Because I think the ultimate deprivation of liberty would be the government taking away someone's life. But with drone killings, you do not see anything, not as a member of the public. You read reports perhaps of people who are killed by drones, but it happens 3,000 miles away and there are no pictures, there are no remains, there is no debris that anyone in the United States ever sees. It's kind of antiseptic. So it is like a video game; it's like Call of Duty."

The least remarkable thing about the system is the drone itself. The Air Force bristles at the very word—*drones* conjures autonomous flying robots, reinforcing the notion that human beings are not piloting them. The Air Force prefers that they be called Remotely Piloted Aircraft. But this linguistic battle has already been lost: my *New Oxford American Dictionary* now defines *drone* as—in addition to a male bee and monotonous speech—"a remote-controlled pilotless aircraft or missile." Even though drones now range in size from a handheld Raven, thrown into the air by infantry units so they can see over the next hill, to the Global Hawk, which is about the same size as a Boeing 737, the craft itself is just an airplane. Most drones are propeller-driven and slow-moving—early-20th-century technology.

In December 2012, when Iran cobbled together a rehabilitated version of a ScanEagle that had crashed there, the catapult-launched weaponless Navy drone was presented on Iranian national television as a major intelligence coup.

"They could have gone to RadioShack and captured the same 'secret' technology," Vice Admiral Mark I. Fox, the Navy's deputy chief for operations, plans, and strategy, told *The New York Times*. The vehicle had less computing power than a smartphone.

Even when, the year before, Iran managed to recover a downed RQ-170 Sentinel, a stealthy, weaponless, unmanned vehicle flown primarily by the CIA, one of the most sophisticated drones in the fleet, it had little more than a nifty flying model. Anything sensitive inside had been remotely destroyed before the Sentinel was seized.

James Poss, a retired Air Force major general who helped oversee the Predator's development, says he has grown so weary of fascination with the vehicle itself that he's adopted the slogan "It's about the datalink, stupid." The craft is essentially a conduit, an eye in the sky. Cut off from its back end, from its satellite links and its data processors, its intelligence analysts and its controller, the drone is as useless as an eyeball disconnected from the brain. What makes the system remarkable is everything downrange—what the Air Force, in its defiantly tin-eared way, calls PED (Processing, Exploitation, and Dissemination). Despite all the focus on missiles, what gives a drone its singular value is its ability to provide perpetual, relatively low-cost surveillance, watching a target continuously for hours, days, weeks, even months. Missiles were mounted on Predators only because too much time was lost when a fire mission had to be handed off to more-conventional weapons platforms—a manned aircraft or ground- or ship-based missile launcher. That delay reduced or erased the key advantage now afforded by the drone. With steady, real-time surveillance, a controller can strike with the target in his sights. He can, for instance, choose a moment when his victim is isolated, or traveling in a car, reducing the chance of harming anyone else.

I recently spoke with an Air Force pilot who asked to be identified only as Major Dan. He has logged 600 combat hours in the B-1 bomber and, in the past six years, well over 2,000 hours flying Reapers—larger, more heavily armed versions of the Predator. He describes the Reaper as a significantly better war-fighting tool for this mission than the B-1 in every measure. The only thing you lose when you go from a B-1 to a Reaper, he says, is the thrill of "lighting four afterburners" on a runway.

From a pilot's perspective, drones have several key advantages. First, mission duration can be vastly extended, with rotating crews. No more trying to stay awake for long missions, nor enduring the physical and mental stresses of flying. ("After you've been sitting in an ejection seat for 20 hours, you are very tired and sore," Dan says.)

In addition, drones provide far greater awareness of what's happening on the ground. They routinely watch targets for prolonged periods—sometimes for months—before a decision is made to launch a missile. Once a B-1 is in flight, the capacity for ground observation is more limited than what is available to a drone pilot at a ground station. From his control station at the Pentagon, Dan is not only watching the target in real time; he has immediate access to every source of information about it, including a chat line with soldiers on the ground.

Dan was so enthusiastic about these and other advantages of drones that, until I prodded him, he didn't say anything about the benefit of getting to be home with his family and sleep in his own bed. Dan is 38 years old, married, with two small children. In the years since he graduated from the Air Force Academy, he has deployed several times to far-off bases for months-long stretches. Now he is regularly home for dinner.

The dazzling clarity of the drone's optics does have a downside. As a B-1 pilot, Dan wouldn't learn details about the effects of his weapons until a post-mission briefing. But flying a drone, he sees the carnage close-up, in real time—the blood and severed body parts, the arrival of emergency responders, the anguish of friends and family. Often he's been watching the people he kills for a long time before pulling the trigger. Drone pilots become familiar with their victims. They see them in the ordinary rhythms of their lives—with their wives and friends, with their children. War by remote control turns out to be intimate and disturbing. Pilots are sometimes shaken.

"There is a very visceral connection to operations on the ground," Dan says. "When you see combat, when you hear the guy you are supporting who is under fire, you hear the stress in his voice, you hear the emotions being passed over the radio, you see the tracers and rounds being fired, and when you are called upon to either fire a missile or drop a bomb, you witness the effects of that firepower." He witnesses it in a far more immediate way than in the past, and he disdains the notion that he and his fellow drone pilots are like video gamers, detached from the reality of their actions. If anything, they are far more attached. At the same time, he dismisses the notion that the carnage he now sees up close is emotionally crippling.

"In my mind, the understanding of what I did, I wouldn't say that one was significantly different from the other," he says.

Drones collect three primary packages of data: straight visual; infrared (via a heat-sensing camera that can see through darkness and clouds) ; and what is called SIGINT (Signals Intelligence), gathered via electronic eavesdropping devices and other sensors. One such device is known as LIDAR (a combination of the words *light* and *radar*), which can map large areas in 3-D. The optical sensors are so good, and the pixel array so dense, that the device can zoom in clearly on objects only inches wide from well over 15,000 feet above. With computer enhancement to eliminate distortion and counteract motion, facial-recognition software is very close to being able to pick individuals out of crowds. Operators do not even have to know exactly where to look.

"We put in the theatre [in 2011] a system called Gorgon Stare," Lieutenant General Larry James, the Air Force's deputy chief of staff for intelligence, surveillance, and reconnaissance, told me. "Instead of one soda-straw-size view of the world with the camera, we put essentially 10 cameras ganged together, and it gives you a very wide area of view of about four kilometers by four kilometers—about the size of the city of Fairfax, [Virginia]—that you can watch continuously. Not as much fidelity in terms of what the camera can see, but I can see movement of cars and people—those sorts of things. Now, instead of staring at a small space, which may be, like, a villa or compound, I can look at a whole city continuously for as long as I am flying that particular system."

Surveillance technology allows for more than just looking: computers store these moving images so that analysts can dial back to a particular time and place and zero in, or mark certain individuals and vehicles and instruct the machines to track them over time. A suspected terrorist-cell leader or bomb maker, say, can be watched for months. The computer can then instantly draw maps showing patterns of movement: where the target went, when there were visitors or deliveries to his home. If you were watched in this way over a period of time, the data could not just draw a portrait of your daily routine, but identify everyone with whom you associate. Add to this cell phone, text, and e-mail intercepts, and you begin to see how special-ops units in Iraq and Afghanistan can, after a single nighttime arrest, round up entire networks before dawn.

All of this requires the collection and manipulation of huge amounts of data, which, James says, is the most difficult technical challenge involved.

"Take video, for example," he says. "ESPN has all kinds of tools where they can go back and find Eli Manning in every video that was shot over the last year, and they can probably do it in 20 minutes. So how do we bring those types of tools [to intelligence work]? *Okay, I want to find this red 1976 Chevy pickup truck in every piece of video that I have shot in this area for the last three months.* We have a pretty hard push to really work with the Air Force Research Lab, and the commercial community, to understand what tools I can bring in to help make sense of all this data."

To be used effectively, a drone must be able to hover over a potential target for long periods. A typical Predator can stay aloft for about 20 hours; the drones are flown in relays to maintain a continuous Combat Air Patrol. Surveillance satellites pass over a given spot only once during each orbit of the Earth. The longest the U-2, the most successful spy plane in history, can stay in the air is about 10 hours, because of the need to spell its pilot and refuel. The Predator gives military and intelligence agencies a surveillance option that is both significantly less expensive and more useful, because it flies unmanned, low, and slow.

Precisely because drones fly so low and so slow, and have such a "noisy" electronic signature, operating them anywhere but in a controlled airspace is impractical. The U.S. Air Force completely controls the sky over active war zones like Afghanistan and Iraq—and has little to fear over countries like Yemen, Somalia, and Mali. Over the rugged regions of northwestern Pakistan, where most drone strikes have taken place, the U.S. operates with the tacit approval of the Pakistani government. Without such permission, or without a robust protection capability, the drone presents an easy target. Its datalink can be disrupted, jammed, or hijacked. It's only slightly harder to shoot down than a hot-air balloon. This means there's little danger of enemy drone attacks in America anytime soon.

Drone technology has applications that go way beyond military uses, of course—everything from domestic law enforcement to archeological surveys to environmental studies. As they become smaller and cheaper, they will become commonplace. Does this mean the government might someday begin hurling thunderbolts at undesirables on city sidewalks? Unlikely. Our entire legal system would have to collapse first. If the police just wanted to shoot people on the street from a distance, they already can—they've had that capability going back to the invention of the Kentucky long rifle and, before that, the crossbow. I helped cover the one known instance of a local government dropping a bomb on its own city, in 1985, when a stubborn back-to-nature cult called Move was in an armed standoff with the Philadelphia police. Then-Mayor Wilson Goode authorized dropping a satchel packed with explosives from a hovering helicopter onto a rooftop bunker in West Philadelphia. The bomb caused a conflagration that consumed an entire city block. The incident will live long in the annals of municipal stupidity. The capability to do the same with a drone will not make choosing to do so any smarter, or any more likely. And as for Big Brother's eye in the sky, authorities have been monitoring public spaces from overhead cameras, helicopters, and planes for decades. Many people think it's a good idea.

The drone is new only in that it combines known technology in an original way—aircraft, global telecommunications links, optics, digital sensors, supercomputers, and so on. It greatly lowers the cost of persistent surveillance. When armed, it becomes a remarkable, highly specialized tool: *a weapon that employs simple physics to launch a missile with lethal force from a distance,* a first step into a world where going to war does not mean fielding an army, or putting any of your own soldiers, sailors, or pilots at risk.

III. The Kill List

It is the most exclusive list in the world, and you would not want to be on it.

The procedure may have changed, but several years back, at the height of the drone war, President Obama held weekly counterterror meetings at which he was presented with a list of potential targets—mostly al-Qaeda or Taliban figures—complete with photos and brief bios laid out like "a high school yearbook," according to a report in *The New York Times*.

The list is the product of a rigorous vetting process that the administration has kept secret. Campaigning for the White House in 2008, Obama made it clear (although few of his supporters were listening closely) that he would embrace drones to go after what he considered the appropriate post-9/11 military target—"core al-Qaeda." When he took office, he inherited a drone war that was already expanding. There were 53 known strikes inside Pakistan in 2009 (according to numbers assembled from press reports by *The Long War Journal*), up from 35 in 2008, and just five the year before that. In 2010, the annual total more than doubled, to 117. The onslaught was effective, at least by some measures: letters seized in the 2011 raid that killed Osama bin Laden show his consternation over the rain of death by drone.

John Brennan instituted weekly conclaves—in effect, death-penalty deliberations—where targets were selected for summary execution.

As U.S. intelligence analysis improved, the number of targets proliferated. Even some of the program's supporters feared it was growing out of control. The definition of a legitimate target and the methods employed to track such a target were increasingly suspect. Relying on other countries' intelligence agencies for help, the United States was sometimes manipulated into striking people who it believed were terrorist leaders but who may not have been, or implicated in practices that violate American values.

Reporters and academics at work in zones where Predator strikes had become common warned of a large backlash. Gregory Johnsen, a scholar of Near East studies at Princeton University, documented the phenomenon in a 2012 book about Yemen titled *The Last Refuge*. He showed that drone attacks in Yemen tended to have the opposite of their intended effect, particularly when people other than extremists were killed or hurt. Drones hadn't whittled al-Qaeda down, Johnsen argued; the organization had grown threefold there. "US strikes and particularly those that kill civilians—be they men or women—are sowing the seeds of future generations of terrorists," he wrote on his blog late last year.

Michael Morrell, who was the deputy director of the CIA until June, was among those in the U.S. government who argued for more restraint. During meetings with John Brennan, who was Obama's counterterrorism adviser until taking over as the CIA director last spring, Morrell said he worried that the prevailing goal seemed to be using drones as artillery, striking anyone who could be squeezed into the definition of a terrorist—an approach derisively called "Whack-A-Mole." Morrell insisted that if the purpose of the drone program was to diminish al-Qaeda and protect the United States from terror attacks, then indiscriminate strikes were counterproductive.

Brennan launched an effort to select targets more carefully. Formalizing a series of ad hoc meetings that began in the fall of 2009, Brennan in 2010 instituted weekly conclaves—in effect, death-penalty deliberations—where would-be successors to bin Laden and Khalid Sheik Mohammed were selected for execution before being presented to Obama for his approval. Brennan demanded clear definitions. There were "high-value targets," which consisted of important al-Qaeda and Taliban figures; "imminent threats," such as a load of roadside bombs bound for the Afghan border; and, most controversial, "signature strikes," which were aimed at characters engaged in suspicious activity in known enemy zones. In these principals' meetings, which Brennan chaired from the Situation Room, in the basement of White House, deliberations were divided into two parts—law and policy. The usual participants included representatives from the Pentagon, CIA, State Department, National Counterterrorism Center, and, initially, the Justice Department—although after a while the lawyers stopped coming. In the first part of the meetings, questions of legality were considered: Was the prospect a lawful target? Was he high-level? Could he rightly be considered to pose an "imminent" threat? Was arrest a viable alternative? Only when these criteria were deemed met did the discussion shift toward policy. Was it smart to kill this person? What sort of impact might the killing have on local authorities, or on relations with the governments of Pakistan or Yemen? What effect would killing him have on his own organization? Would it make things better or worse?

Brennan himself was often the toughest questioner. Two regular meeting participants described him to me as thoughtful and concerned; one said his demeanor was "almost priestly." Another routinely skeptical and cautious participant was James Steinberg, the deputy secretary of state for the first two and a half years of Obama's first term, who adhered to a strict list of acceptable legal criteria drawn up by the State Department's counsel, Harold Koh. This criteria stipulated that any drone target would have to be a "senior member" of al-Qaeda who was "externally focused"—that is, actively plotting attacks on America or on American citizens or armed forces. Koh was confident that even if his criteria did not meet all the broader concerns of human-rights activists, they would support an international-law claim of self-defense—and for that reason he thought the administration ought to make the criteria public. Throughout Obama's first term, members of the administration argued about how much of the deliberation process to reveal. During these debates, Koh's position on complete disclosure was dismissively termed "the Full Harold." He was its only advocate.

Many of the sessions were contentious. The military and the CIA pushed back hard against Koh's strict criteria. Special Forces commanders, in particular, abhorred what they saw as excessive efforts to "litigate" their war. The price of every target the White House rejected, military commanders said, was paid in American lives. Their arguments, coming from the war's front line, carried significant weight.

Cameron Munter, a veteran diplomat who was the U.S. ambassador to Pakistan from 2010 to 2012, felt that weight first-hand when he tried to push back. Munter saw American influence declining with nearly every strike. While some factions in the Pakistani military and Inter-Services Intelligence believed in the value of strikes, the Pakistani public grew increasingly outraged, and elected officials increasingly hostile. Munter's job was to contain the crisis, a task complicated by the drone program's secrecy, which prevented him from explaining and defending America's actions.

Matters came to a head in the summer of 2011 during a meeting to which Munter was linked digitally. The dynamics of such meetings—where officials turned to policy discussions after the legal determination had been made—placed a premium on unified support for policy goals. Most participants wanted to focus on the success of the battle against America's enemies, not on the corrosive foreign-policy side effects of the drone program.

At the decision meetings, it was hard for someone like Munter to say no. He would appear digitally on the screen in the Situation Room, gazing out at the vice president, the secretary of defense, and other principals, and they would present him with the targeting decision they were prepared to make. It was hard to object when so many people who titularly outranked him already seemed set.

By June of 2011, however, two events in Pakistan—first the arrest and subsequent release of the CIA contractor Raymond Davis, who had been charged with murdering two Pakistanis who accosted him on the street in Lahore, and then the Abbottabad raid that killed bin Laden—had brought the U.S.–Pakistan partnership to a new low. Concerned about balancing the short-term benefits of strikes (removing potential enemies from the battlefield) and their long-term costs (creating a lasting mistrust and resentment that undercut the policy goal of stability and peace in the region), Munter decided to test what he believed was his authority to halt a strike. As he recalled it later, the move played out as follows:

Asked whether he was on board with a particular strike, he said no.

Leon Panetta, the CIA director, said the ambassador had no veto power; these were intelligence decisions.

Munter proceeded to explain that under Title 22 of the U.S. Code of Federal Regulations, the president gives the authority to carry out U.S. policy in a foreign country to his ambassador, delegated through the secretary of state. That means no American policy should be carried out in any country without the ambassador's approval.

Taken aback, Panetta replied, "Well, I do not work for you, buddy."

"I don't work for you," Munter told him.

Then Secretary of State Hillary Clinton stepped in: "Leon, you are wrong."

Panetta said, flatly, "Hillary, *you're* wrong."

At that point, the discussion moved on. When the secretary of state and the CIA director clash, the decision gets made upstairs.

Panetta won. A week later, James Steinberg called Munter to inform him that he did not have the authority to veto a drone strike. Steinberg explained that the ambassador would be allowed to express an objection to a strike, and that a mechanism would be put in place to make sure his objection was registered—but the decision to clear or reject a strike would be made higher up the chain. It was a clear victory for the CIA.

Later that summer, General David Petraeus was named to take over the intelligence agency from Panetta. Before assuming the job, Petraeus flew from Kabul, where he was still the military commander, to Islamabad, to meet with the ambassador. At dinner that night, Petraeus poked his finger into Munter's chest.

"You know what happened in that meeting?" the general asked. (Petraeus had observed the clash via a secure link from his command post in Afghanistan.) "That's never going to happen again."

Munter's heart sank. He thought the new CIA director, whom he liked and admired, was about to threaten him. Instead, Petraeus said: "I'm never going to put you in the position where you feel compelled to veto a strike. If you have a long-term concern, if you have a contextual problem, a timing problem, an ethical problem, I want to know about it earlier. We can work together to avoid these kinds of conflicts far in advance."

Petraeus kept his word. Munter never had to challenge a drone strike in a principals' meeting again during his tenure as ambassador. He left Islamabad in the summer of 2012.

By then, Brennan's efforts to make the process more judicious had begun to show results. The number of drone strikes in Pakistan and Yemen fell to 88 last year, and they have dropped off even more dramatically since.

The decline partly reflects the toll that the drone war has taken on al-Qaeda. "There are fewer al-Qaeda leadership targets to hit," a senior White House official who is working on the administration's evolving approach to drone strikes told me. The reduction in strikes is "something that the president directed. We don't need a top-20 list. We don't need to find 20 if there are only 10. We've gotten out of the business of maintaining a number as an end in itself, so therefore that number has gone down."

Any history of how the United States destroyed Osama bin Laden's organization will feature the drone. Whatever questions it has raised, however uncomfortable it has made us feel, the drone has been an extraordinarily effective weapon for the job. The United States faced a stateless, well-funded, highly organized terrorist operation that was sophisticated enough to carry out unprecedented acts of mass murder. Today, while local al-Qaeda franchises remain a threat throughout the Middle East, the organization that planned and carried out 9/11 has been crushed. When bin Laden himself was killed, Americans danced in the streets.

"Our actions are effective," President Obama said in a speech on counterterrorism at the National Defense University in May.

Don't take my word for it. In the intelligence gathered at bin Laden's compound, we found that he wrote, 'We could lose the reserves to enemy's air strikes. We cannot fight air strikes with explosives.' Other communications from al-Qaeda operatives confirm this as well. Dozens of highly skilled al-Qaeda commanders, trainers, bomb makers, and operatives have been taken off the battlefield. Plots have been disrupted that would have targeted international aviation, U.S. transit systems, European cities, and our troops in Afghanistan. Simply put, these strikes have saved lives.

So why the steady drumbeat of complaint?

IV. Drones Don't Kill People. People Kill People

The most ardent case against drone strikes is that they kill innocents. John Brennan has argued that claims of collateral carnage are exaggerated. In June 2011, he famously declared that there had not been "a single collateral death" due to a drone strike in the previous 12 months.

Almost no one believes this. Brennan himself later amended his statement, saying that in the previous 12 months, the United States had found no "credible evidence" that any civilians had been killed in drone strikes outside Afghanistan and Iraq. (I am using the word *civilians* here to mean "non-combatants.") A fair interpretation is that drones unfailingly hit their targets, and so long as the U.S. government believes its targets are all legitimate, the collateral damage is zero. But drones are only as accurate as the intelligence that guides them. Even if the machine is perfect, it's a stretch to assume perfection in those who aim it.

For one thing, our military and intelligence agencies generously define *combatant* to include any military-age male in the strike zone. And local press accounts from many of the blast sites have reported dead women and children. Some of that may be propaganda, but not all of it is. No matter how precisely placed, when a 500-pound bomb or a Hellfire missile explodes, there are sometimes going to be unintended victims in the vicinity.

How many? Estimates of body counts range so widely and are so politicized that none of them is completely credible. At one extreme, anti-American propagandists regularly publish estimates that make the drone war sound borderline genocidal. These high numbers help drive the anti-drone narrative, which equates actions of the U.S. government with acts of terror. In two of the most recent Islamist terror attacks as of this writing—the Boston Marathon bombing and the beheading of a soldier in London—the perpetrators justified their killings as payback for the deaths of innocent Muslims. At the other extreme, there is Brennan's claim of zero civilian casualties. The true numbers are unknowable.

Ground combat almost always kills more civilians than drone strikes do. When you consider the alternatives, you are led, as Obama was, to the logic of the drone.

Secrecy is a big part of the problem. The government doesn't even acknowledge most attacks, much less release details of their aftermath. The Bureau of Investigative Journalism, a left-wing organization based in London, has made a strenuous effort, using news sources, to count bodies after CIA drone strikes. It estimates that from 2004 through the first half of 2013, 371 drone strikes in Pakistan killed between 2,564 and 3,567 people (the range covers the minimum to the maximum credible reported deaths). Of those killed, the group says, somewhere between 411 and 890—somewhere between 12 percent and 35 percent of the total—were civilians. The

disparity in these figures is telling. But if we assume the worst case, and take the largest estimates of soldier and civilian fatalities, then one-quarter of those killed in drone strikes in Pakistan have been civilians.

Everyone agrees that the amount of collateral damage has dropped steeply over the past two years. The Bureau of Investigative Journalism estimates that civilian deaths from drone strikes in Pakistan fell to 12 percent of total deaths in 2011 and to less than 3 percent in 2012.

No civilian death is acceptable, of course. Each one is tragic. But any assessment of civilian deaths from drone strikes needs to be compared with the potential damage from alternative tactics. Unless we are to forgo the pursuit of al-Qaeda terrorists entirely, U.S. forces must confront them either from the air or on the ground, in some of the remotest places on Earth. As aerial attacks go, drones are far more precise than manned bombers or missiles. That narrows the choice to drone strikes or ground assaults.

Sometimes ground assaults go smoothly. Take the one that killed Osama bin Laden. It was executed by the best-trained, most-experienced soldiers in the world. Killed were bin Laden; his adult son Khalid; his primary protectors, the brothers Abu Ahmed al-Kuwaiti and Abrar al-Kuwaiti; and Abrar's wife Bushra. Assuming Bushra qualifies as a civilian, even though she was helping to shelter the world's most notorious terrorist, civilian deaths in the raid amounted to 20 percent of the casualties. In other words, even a near-perfect special-ops raid produced only a slight improvement over the worst estimates of those counting drone casualties. Many assaults are not that clean.

In fact, ground combat almost always kills more civilians than drone strikes do. Avery Plaw, a political scientist at the University of Massachusetts, estimates that in Pakistani ground offensives against extremists in that country's tribal areas, 46 percent of those killed are civilians. Plaw says that ratios of civilian deaths from conventional military conflicts over the past 20 years range from 33 percent to more than 80 percent. "A fair-minded evaluation of the best data we have available suggests that the drone program compares favorably with similar operations and contemporary armed conflict more generally," he told *The New York Times*.

When you consider the alternatives—even, and perhaps especially, if you are deeply concerned with sparing civilians—you are led, as Obama was, to the logic of the drone.

But don't drone strikes violate the prohibition on assassination, Executive Order 12333? That order, signed by Ronald Reagan in 1981, grew out of revelations that the CIA had tried to kill Fidel Castro and other leftist-leaning political figures in the 1960s and 1970s. It was clearly aimed

Annual Editions: American Government

at halting political assassinations; in fact, the original order, signed in 1976 by Gerald Ford, refers specifically to such acts. Attempting to prevent acts of mass murder by a dangerous international organization may stretch the legal definition of armed conflict, but it is not the same as political assassination. Besides, executive orders are not statutes; they can be superseded by subsequent presidents. In the case of President Bush, after the attacks of September 11, Congress specifically authorized the use of lethal operations against al-Qaeda.

When Bush branded our effort against al-Qaeda "war," he effectively established legal protection for targeted killing. Targeted killing is a long-established practice in the context of war. According to international treaties, soldiers can be killed simply for belonging to an enemy army—whether they are actively engaged in an attack or only preparing for one, whether they are commanders or office clerks. During World War II, the United States discovered and shot down the plane carrying Admiral Isoruku Yamamoto, the commander in chief of the Japanese navy, who had been the architect of the attack on Pearl Harbor. The order to attack the plane was given by President Franklin Roosevelt.

But beyond what international treaties call "armed conflict" is "law enforcement," and here, there are problems. The 1990 United Nations Congress on the Prevention of Crime and the Treatment of Offenders laid out basic principles for the use of force in law-enforcement operations. (The rules, although nonbinding, elaborate on what is meant by Article 6 of the International Covenant on Civil and Political Rights, to which the United States has agreed.) The pertinent passage—written more than a decade before weaponized drones—reads as follows:

> Law enforcement officials shall not use firearms against persons except in self-defense or defense of others against the imminent threat of death or serious injury, to prevent the perpetration of a particularly serious crime involving grave threat to life, to arrest a person presenting such a danger and resisting their authority, or to prevent his or her escape, and only when less extreme means are insufficient to achieve these objectives. In any event, intentional lethal use of firearms may only be made when strictly unavoidable to protect life.

Once the "war" on al-Qaeda ends, the justification for targeted killing will become tenuous. Some experts on international law say it will become simply illegal. Indeed, one basis for condemning the drone war has been that the pursuit of al-Qaeda was never a real war in the first place.

Sir Christopher Greenwood, the British judge on the International Court of Justice, has written: "In the language of international law there is no basis for speaking of a war on al-Qaeda or any other terrorist group, for such a group cannot be a belligerent, it is merely a band of criminals, and to treat it as anything else risks distorting the law while giving that group a status

which to some implies a degree of legitimacy." Greenwood rightly observes that America's declaration of war against al-Qaeda bolstered the group's status worldwide. But history will not quarrel with Bush's decision, which was unavoidable, given the national mood. Democracy reflects the will of the people. Two American presidents from different parties and with vastly different ideological outlooks have, with strong congressional support, fully embraced the notion that America is at war. In his speech at the National Defense University in May, Obama reaffirmed this approach. "America's actions are legal," he said. "Under domestic law and international law, the United States is at war with al-Qaeda, the Taliban, and their associated forces." He noted that during his presidency, he has briefed congressional overseers about every drone strike. "Every strike," he said.

Bin Laden himself certainly wasn't confused about the matter; he held a press conference in Afghanistan in 1998 to declare jihad on the United States. Certainly the scale of al-Qaeda's attacks went well beyond anything previously defined as criminal. But what are the boundaries of that war? Different critics draw the lines in different places. Mary Ellen O'Connell, a law professor at the University of Notre Dame, is a determined and eloquent critic of drone strikes. She believes that while strikes in well-defined battle spaces like Iraq and Afghanistan are justified, and can limit civilian deaths, strikes in Pakistan, Yemen, Somalia, and other places amount to "extrajudicial killing," no matter who the targets are. Such killings are outside the boundary of armed conflict, she says, and hence violate international law.

Philip Alston, a former United Nations special rapporteur on extrajudicial, summary, or arbitrary executions, concedes that al-Qaeda's scope and menace transcend criminality, but nevertheless faults the U.S. drone program for lacking due process and transparency. He told *Harper's* magazine:

> [International] laws do not prohibit an intelligence agency like the CIA from carrying out targeted killings, provided it complies with the relevant international rules. Those rules require, not surprisingly when it's a matter of being able to kill someone in a foreign country, that all such killings be legally justified, that we know the justification, and that there are effective mechanisms for investigation, prosecution, and punishment if laws are violated. The CIA's response to these obligations has been very revealing. On the one hand, its spokespersons have confirmed the total secrecy and thus unaccountability of the program by insisting that they can neither confirm nor deny that it even exists. On the other hand, they have gone to great lengths to issue unattributable

assurances, widely quoted in the media, both that there is extensive domestic accountability and that civilian casualties have been minimal. In essence, it's a 'you can trust us' response, from an agency with a less than stellar track record in such matters.

President Obama has taken steps in recent months to address Alston's concerns. He has begun transferring authority for drone strikes from the CIA to the Pentagon, which will open them up to greater congressional and public scrutiny. He has sharply limited "signature strikes," those based on patterns of behavior rather than strict knowledge of who is being targeted. (Because most signature strikes have been used to protect American troops in Afghanistan, this category of drone attack is likely to further diminish once those forces are withdrawn.) In his May speech, he came close to embracing "the full Harold," publicly outlining in general terms the targeting constraints drafted by Koh. He also made clear that the war on al-Qaeda will eventually end—though he stopped short of saying when. American combat troops will be gone from Afghanistan by the end of next year, but the war effort against "core al-Qaeda" will almost certainly continue at least until Ahman al Zawahiri, the fugitive Egyptian doctor who now presides over the remnants of the organization, is captured or killed.

Then what?

"Outside of the context of armed conflict, the use of drones for targeted killing is almost never likely to be legal," Alston wrote in 2010. Mary Ellen O'Connell agrees. "Outside of a combat zone or a battlefield, the use of military force is not lawful," she told me.

Yet this is where we seem to be headed. Obama has run his last presidential campaign, and one senses that he might cherish a legacy of ending three wars on his watch.

"Our commitment to constitutional principles has weathered every war, and every war has come to an end," he said in his May speech. "We must define the nature and scope of this struggle, or else it will define us. We have to be mindful of James Madison's warning that 'no nation could preserve its freedom in the midst of continual warfare.'"

The changes outlined by the president do not mean we will suddenly stop going after al-Qaeda. If the war on terror is declared over, and the 2001 Authorization for Use of Military Force (AUMF) is withdrawn, then some other legal justification for targeting al-Qaeda terrorists with drones would be necessary, and would likely be sought.

"We believe we have a domestic and international legal basis for our current efforts," Ben Rhodes, who is Obama's deputy national-security adviser for strategic communications, told me. "If you project into the future, there are different scenarios, you know, so they are kind of hypothetical, but one is that you might have a narrower AUMF that is a more targeted

piece of legislation. A hypothetical: the Taliban is part of the AUMF now, but we could find ourselves not in hostilities with the Taliban after 2014." In that case, the military authority to attack Taliban targets, which account for many drone strikes and most signature strikes, would be gone. Another scenario Rhodes sketched out was one in which a local terrorist group "rose to the level where we thought we needed to take direct action. You might have to go back to Congress to get a separate authorization. If we need to get authority against a new terrorist group that is emerging somewhere else in the world, we should go back to Congress and get that authorization."

You can't know in advance "the circumstances of taking direct action," Rhodes said. "You may be acting to prevent an imminent attack on the United States or you may be acting in response to an attack, each of which carries its own legal basis. But you have to be accountable for whatever direct action you are taking," rather than relying on some blanket authority to strike whomever and whenever the president chooses. "You would have to specifically define, domestically and internationally, what the basis for your action is in each instance—and by each instance, I don't mean every strike, per se, but rather the terrorist group or the country where you are acting."

Seeking such authorization would help draw the debate over continued drone strikes out of the shadows. Paradoxically, as the war on terror winds down, and as the number of drone strikes falls, the controversy over them may rise.

V. Come Out with Your Hands Up!

Once the pursuit of al-Qaeda is defined as "law enforcement," ground assaults may be the only acceptable tactic under international law. A criminal must be given the opportunity to surrender, and if he refuses, efforts must be made to arrest him. Mary Ellen O'Connell believes the Abbottabad raid was an example of how things should work.

"It came as close to what we are permitted to do under international law as you can get," she said. "John Brennan came out right after the killing and said the SEALS were under orders to attempt to capture bin Laden, and if he resisted or if their own lives were endangered, then they could use the force that was necessary. They did not use a drone. They did not drop a bomb. They did not fire a missile."

Force in such operations is justified only if the suspect resists arrest—and even then, his escape is preferable to harming innocent bystanders. These are the rules that govern police, as opposed to warriors. Yet the enemies we face will not change if the war on terror ends. The worst of them—the ones we most need to stop—are determined suicidal killers and hardened fighters. Since there is no such thing as global police, any force employed would likely still come from, in most cases, American special-ops units. They are very good at what they do—but under law-enforcement rules, a lot more people, both soldiers and civilians, are likely to be killed.

It would be wise to consider how bloody such operations can be. When Obama chose the riskiest available option for getting bin Laden in Abbottabad—a special-ops raid—he did so not out of a desire to conform to international law but because that option allowed the possibility of taking bin Laden alive and, probably more important, because if bin Laden was killed in a ground assault, his death could be proved. The raid went well. But what if the SEAL raiding party had tripped Pakistan's air defenses, or if it had been confronted by police or army units on the ground? American troops and planes stood ready in Afghanistan to respond if that happened. Such a clash would likely have killed many Pakistanis and Americans, and left the countries at loggerheads, if not literally at war.

There's another example of a law-enforcement-style raid that conforms to the model that O'Connell and other drone critics prefer: the October 1993 Delta Force raid in Mogadishu, which I wrote about in the book *Black Hawk Down*. The objective, which was achieved, was to swoop in and arrest Omar Salad and Mohamed Hassan Awale, two top lieutenants of the outlaw clan leader Mohammed Farrah Aidid. As the arrests were being made, the raiding party of Delta Force operators and U.S. Army rangers came under heavy fire from local supporters of the clan leader. Two Black Hawk helicopters were shot down and crashed into the city. We were not officially at war with Somalia, but the ensuing firefight left 18 Americans dead and killed an estimated 500–1,000 Somalis—a number comparable to the total civilian deaths from all drone strikes in Pakistan from 2004 through the first half of 2013, according to the Bureau of Investigative Journalists' estimates.

The Somalia example is an extreme one. But the battle that erupted in Mogadishu strikes me as a fair reminder of what can happen to even a very skillful raiding party. Few of the terrorists we target will go quietly. Knowing they are targets, they will surely seek out terrain hostile to an American or UN force. Choosing police action over drone strikes may feel like taking the moral high ground. But if a raid is likely to provoke a firefight, then choosing a drone shot not only might pass legal muster (UN rules allow lethal force "when strictly unavoidable in order to protect life") but also might be the more moral choice.

The White House knows this, but it is unlikely to announce a formal end to the war against al-Qaeda anytime soon. Obama's evolving model for counterterrorism will surely include both raids and drone strikes—and the legality of using such strikes outside the context of war remains murky.

Ben Rhodes and others on Obama's national-security team have been thinking hard about these questions. Rhodes told me that "the threat picture" the administration is mainly concerned with has increasingly shifted from global terrorism, with al-Qaeda at its center, to "more traditional terrorism, which is localized groups with their own agendas." Such groups "may be Islamic extremists, but they are not necessarily signing on to global jihad. A local agenda may raise the threat to embassies and diplomatic facilities and things like [the BP facility that was attacked in Algeria early this year], but it diminishes the likelihood of a complex 9/11-style attack on the homeland."

If terrorism becomes more localized, Rhodes continued, "we have to have a legal basis and a counterterrorism policy that fits that model, rather than this massive post-9/11 edifice that we built." This means, he said, that post-2014 counter-terrorism will "take a more traditional form, with a law-enforcement lead. But this will be amplified by a U.S. capability to take direct action as necessary in a very narrowly defined set of circumstances." What U.S. policy will be aiming for, Rhodes said, is "traditional [law-enforcement-style] counterterrorism plus a limited deployment of our drone and special-forces capabilities when it is absolutely necessary."

To accommodate the long-term need for drone strikes, Obama is weighing a formal process for external review of the target list. This might mean appointing a military-justice panel, or a civilian review court modeled on the Foreign Intelligence Surveillance Court, which oversees requests to monitor suspected foreign spies and terrorists in the United States. But this raises thorny constitutional questions about the separation of powers—and presidents are reluctant to concede their authority to make the final call.

How should we feel about drones? Like any wartime innovation, going back to the slingshot, drones can be used badly or well. They are remarkable tools, an exceedingly clever combination of existing technologies that has vastly improved our ability to observe and to fight. They represent how America has responded to the challenge of organized, high-level, stateless terrorism—not timidly, as bin Laden famously predicted, but with courage, tenacity, and ruthless ingenuity. Improving technologies are making drones capable not just of broader and more persistent surveillance, but of greater strike precision. Mary Ellen O'Connell says, half jokingly, that there is a "sunset" on her objection to them, because drones may eventually offer more options. She said she can imagine one capable of delivering a warning—"Come out with your hands up!"—and then landing to make an arrest using handcuffs.

Obama's efforts to mitigate the use of drones have already made a big difference in reducing the number of strikes—though critics like O'Connell say the reduction has come only grudgingly, in response to "a rising level of worldwide condemnation." Still, Obama certainly deserves credit: it is good that drones are being used more judiciously. I told Ben Rhodes that if the president succeeds in establishing clear and careful guidelines for their use, he will make a lot of people happy, but a lot of other people mad.

"Well, no," Rhodes said. "It's worse than that. We will make a lot of people mad and we will not quite make people happy."

No American president will ever pay a political price for choosing national security over world opinion, but the only right way to proceed is to make targeting decisions and strike outcomes fully public, even if after the fact. In the long run, careful adherence to the law matters more than eliminating another bad actor. Greater prudence and transparency are not just morally and legally essential, they are in our long-term interest, because the strikes themselves feed the anti-drone narrative, and inspire the kind of random, small-scale terror attacks that are bin Laden's despicable legacy.

In our struggle against terrorist networks like al-Qaeda, the distinction between armed conflict and law enforcement matters a great deal. Terrorism embraces lawlessness. It seeks to disrupt. It targets civilians deliberately. So why restrain our response? Why subject ourselves to the rule of law? Because abiding by the law is the point—especially with a weapon like the drone. No act is more final than killing. Drones distill war to its essence. Abiding carefully by the law—man's law, not

God's—making judgments carefully, making them transparent and subject to review, is the only way to invest them with moral authority, and the only way to clearly define the terrorist as an enemy of civilization.

Critical Thinking

1. What is the connection between the biblical David vs. Goliath fight and the use of drones by the United States today?

2. What are key technical, tactical, moral, and legal concerns or possible concerns about U.S. use of drones?

Create Central

www.mhhe.com/createcentral

Internet References

Council on Foreign Relations: Transferring CIA Drone Strikes to the Pentagon
http://www.cfr.org/drones/transferring-cia-drone-strikes-pentagon/p30434
The Guardian: Drones
http://www.theguardian.com/world/drones

MARK BOWDEN is a national correspondent for *The Atlantic*.